Information Sciences Series

Information Retrieval On-Line

F. W. Lancaster
University of Illinois

and

E. G. Fayen
Computer Sciences Corporation

A WILEY–BECKER & HAYES SERIES BOOK

 MELVILLE PUBLISHING COMPANY
Los Angeles, California

Copyright © 1973, by John Wiley & Sons, Inc.
Published by **Melville Publishing Company**
a Division of John Wiley & Sons, Inc.

Library of Congress Cataloging in Publication Data:

Lancaster, Frederick Wilfrid, 1933–
Information retrieval on-line.

(Information sciences series)
"A Wiley Becker & Hayes series book."
Includes bibliographies.
1. Information storage and retrieval systems.
2. On-line data processing. I. Fayen, Emily Gallup, joint
author. II. Title.
Z699.L34   029.7'53   73–9697
ISBN 0–471–51235–4

Printed in the United States of America

10 9 8 7 6 5 4 3 2 1

Information Sciences Series

Information is the essential ingredient in decision making. The need for improved information systems in recent years has been made critical by the steady growth in size and complexity of organizations and data.

This series is designed to include books that are concerned with various aspects of communicating, utilizing, and storing digital and graphic information. It will embrace a broad spectrum of topics, such as information system theory and design, man-machine relationships, language data processing, artificial intelligence, mechanization of library processes, nonnumerical applications of digital computers, storage and retrieval, automatic publishing, command and control, information display, and so on.

Information science may someday be a profession in its own right. The aim of this series is to bring together the interdisciplinary core of knowledge that is apt to form its foundation. Through this consolidation, it is expected that the series will grow to become the focal point for professional education in this field.

Preface

The field of information retrieval is rapidly changing. The application of computers, little more than a decade old, has revolutionized many procedures of information handling. The more recent emergence of on-line systems offers new possibilities for developing services of improved flexibility, increased sophistication, and wider accessibility.

This book deals with on-line systems for bibliographic search and retrieval. The literature on this subject is increasing rapidly and new systems are appearing all the time. We have attempted to provide a broad survey of the characteristics, capabilities, and limitations of present systems. Our emphasis is on the design, evaluation, and use of on-line retrieval systems, primarily from the viewpoint of the planner and manager of information services. It is oriented toward the "intellectual" aspects of information retrieval rather than the hardware or programming aspects. We hope that this book may have some value for all students of library and information science.

Urbana, Illinois   *F. W. Lancaster*

Washington, D.C.   *E. G. Fayen*

Acknowledgments

We are very grateful to all the publishers and other companies who have given us permission to reproduce materials in this book. Specific acknowledgments of figures and tables are included in the text itself. We are particularly indebted to the American Library Association for permission to reproduce the quotation from Warheit in Chapter Twelve; to Lincoln Laboratory, MIT for permission to reproduce the quotation from Armenti, Hall, and Sholl in Chapter Twelve; to the AFIPS Press for permission to reproduce the quotation from Marcus, Benenfeld, and Kugel in Chapter Fifteen; to the System Development Corporation for permission to reproduce extensive quotations from SDC reports, especially in Chapters Seventeen and Eighteen; to Pergamon Press for permission to reproduce the quotation from Negus and Hall in Chapter Eighteen; and to the Computer Science Department, Queen's University of Belfast for permission to reproduce the quotation from Higgins and Smith in Chapter Eighteen.

We must also express our appreciation to four students in the Graduate School of Library Science at the University of Illinois: to Ruth Lerner, who typed the entire manuscript through numerous versions, to Lynda Molodow for completing the final typescript, and to Carol Boast and Ruthie Bishop for checking the many references and generally cleaning up the text.

Contents

Information Retrieval
On-Line

Chapter One

Some Characteristics of On-Line Retrieval Systems

Put simply, an on-line information retrieval* system is one in which a user can, via computer, directly interrogate a machine-readable data base of documents or document representations. In an on-line system there is two-way communication between the computer and the user by way of input/output devices such as a teletypewriter or cathode ray tube display connected to the computer by some communication channel, which may be a regular telephone line. Although an on-line system may be operated in a dedicated mode, it is more often implemented in a time-shared environment. The term *time-sharing* has been defined in various ways. Fundamentally, time-sharing implies the use of the computer in such a way that it shares its processing time between two or more completely independent activities. A time-shared system thus allows different users simultaneous access to the computer. An on-line, time-shared system will operate via a number of independent, concurrently usable terminals, giving each terminal user processing time when he needs it and creating the illusion (most of the time) that he is the sole user of the computer facilities. Another expression associated with on-line computing is *real-time*. Real-time operation implies that the computer receives data, processes it, and returns results quickly enough for these results to be utilized in the continuation of the task being conducted. Applied to information

---

*Throughout this book we will use the expression *information retrieval* in the way it is generally used in the literature, namely to describe a system capable of retrieving information relating to documents, usually a representation or surrogate of a document (e.g., title or abstract). Further, most of our discussion will relate to retrieval by subject rather than by author or other characteristic.

retrieval, real-time implies that the computer responds quickly enough to interact with a user's heuristic search processes. It is contrasted with *delayed-time*, which is a characteristic of batch-processing systems. To all intents and purposes, we can regard a real-time retrieval system as one capable in some way of responding so rapidly to a query that its response may be regarded as immediate or almost immediate. An on-line, real-time system permits conversational interaction between the user and the computer. Further information on the characteristics of time-shared systems in general is provided in concise form in a review paper by Pyke (1967).

Digital computers have existed for about 25 years, but their application to information retrieval is of more recent origin. Most of the large computer-based retrieval systems in this country date back only a decade. It is convenient to summarize the development of "hardware" for information retrieval as follows:

1. Before the 1940s: mostly card catalogs and printed book indexes.
2. During 1940–1949: the first application of semimechanized approaches, including edge-notched cards and the optical coincidence (peek-a-boo) principle; the first microfilm searching system (the Rapid Selector).
3. During 1950–1959: the first fairly widespread use of punched card data processing equipment; some early computer systems; further microimage searching systems.
4. During 1960–1969: more general application of digital computers to information retrieval in an off-line, batch-processing mode; some experiments with on-line, interactive systems; more advanced microimage searching systems.
5. From 1970 to the present: definite trend toward design of on-line systems and conversion of batch systems to the on-line mode.

Purely manual systems, such as printed indexes and card catalogs, have the following characteristics:

1. They are random-access devices. It is possible to go directly to the file and to consult only the portion that we need to consult.
2. They allow the conduct of interactive, browsing, heuristic searches.
3. Searches are conducted one at a time; that is, a particular searcher will normally be seeking information on a single topic. However, many individuals may be searching the file at the same time.
4. The person with a need for information (i.e., the *practitioner* in a field) can conduct his own search in the index if he so desires. He need not delegate the literature searching activity to a librarian or other information specialist (*intermediary*).
5. There is no time delay. Providing one has physical access to the index one can search it when the need for information arises.

The advent of punched card and, later, computer systems changed this entire searching picture. The first mechanized systems were designed for an off-line, batch-processing mode of operation. The major disadvantages of this mode of operation are the following:

1. There is very little possibility for browsing.
2. A search strategy cannot be developed heuristically. The searcher has essentially one chance to conduct a successful search and must therefore think in advance of all likely approaches to retrieval.
3. The search must be delegated to an information specialist. The patron of the information service is not able to conduct his own searches. Unfortunately delegation causes problems. Users sometimes have difficulty in describing what they are seeking, and search analysts may misinterpret a user's requirements. These problems exist in all delegated search systems. They were fully documented in the evaluation conducted by Lancaster (1968) on MEDLARS.
4. There is a time delay. In a batch-processing system there is an inevitable delay in obtaining search results. There is certainly no opportunity for real-time response.

The on-line search system has none of these disadvantages. Even for delegated searches conducted by trained analysts, the on-line mode has the advantages of rapid response and the capability for interactive, browsing, heuristic searches. Ultimately, however, on-line systems should be capable of being used in a nondelegated search mode. That is, the practitioners in a field should be able to undertake, productively, their own literature searches without the interposition of an information specialist. The problems of misinterpretation and miscommunication are thereby avoided.

Figure 1.1 illustrates the steps occurring in the information retrieval process in the delegated search situation from the time the user first approaches the system to the time the system delivers some response. For each step in the complete cycle the diagram indicates the most important factors affecting the success or failure of the search. Clearly, the interface between the requester and the search analyst is critical to the entire process. However excellent the vocabulary of the system and the indexing procedures followed, a search has little hope of success if the user's request statement imperfectly represents his true information needs or if the search analyst seriously misinterprets the requirements of the user.

In an on-line system, in which the user himself is interrogating the data base directly, these problems are circumvented. However, other problem areas are likely to assume greater importance in this situation. For example, the user who is not an information specialist is likely to be less familiar with system vocabulary and with indexing policies and procedures. The quality of his search strategies is likely to suffer accordingly. An on-line system

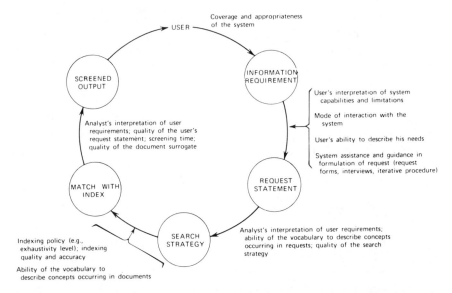

Figure 1.1.   Factors affecting performance of an information retrieval system used in a delegated search mode.

intended for direct use by the practitioner of a field poses problems of design and implementation very different from the problems posed by an off-line system intended for delegated search. In the following chapters we will discuss factors affecting performance of on-line, interactive systems, design and implementation requirements, and characteristics of existing on-line systems.

REFERENCES

Lancaster, F. W. (1968). *Evaluation of the MEDLARS Demand Search Service.* Bethesda, Md.: National Library of Medicine.

Pyke, T. N., Jr. (1967). "Time-Shared Computer Systems." *In* F. L. Alt and M. Rubinoff (eds.), *Advances in Computers,* vol. 8, New York: Academic Press, pp. 1–45.

Chapter Two

Equipment for On-Line Retrieval

Chapter One has described briefly what an on-line information retrieval system is and how it differs from its predecessors. This chapter is devoted to the physical components of on-line retrieval systems, shows the typical organization of such systems, and describes the basic hardware components involved. This chapter also includes mention of the various types of terminals available for use in on-line retrieval systems and concludes with an example of sign-on procedures for on-line networks.

As noted in Chapter One, on-line retrieval systems are usually associated with the concept of time-sharing and remote access. In general, on-line information retrieval systems may be characterized as time-shared computerized communications networks. These networks are designed to meet the information retrieval requirements of a variety of users who require on-line access to a central data base from their respective remote locations. Furthermore, response to the user is usually required to occur in something approximating real-time; that is, in a conversational mode in which response to the user occurs within a few seconds or a minute or two at most. A typical example of an on-line remote-access system that supports such user response is the reservation system in use by most major airlines today. Although these systems are not information retrieval systems according to the definition given in Chapter One, they are very similar from a systems standpoint. On-line information retrieval systems and the airlines reservation systems both provide on-line access to a central data base for a number of remote users. Both usually operate in time-shared mode, and both provide response to the user in real-time. The major difference between the airlines reservation systems and an on-line information retrieval system is in the nature of the data base and the type of retrieval performed on it.

Figure 2.1 is a schematic illustration of the basic configuration of a computer communications network such as would be required to support an on-line information retrieval system. We shall now examine each of the components of this system in more detail.

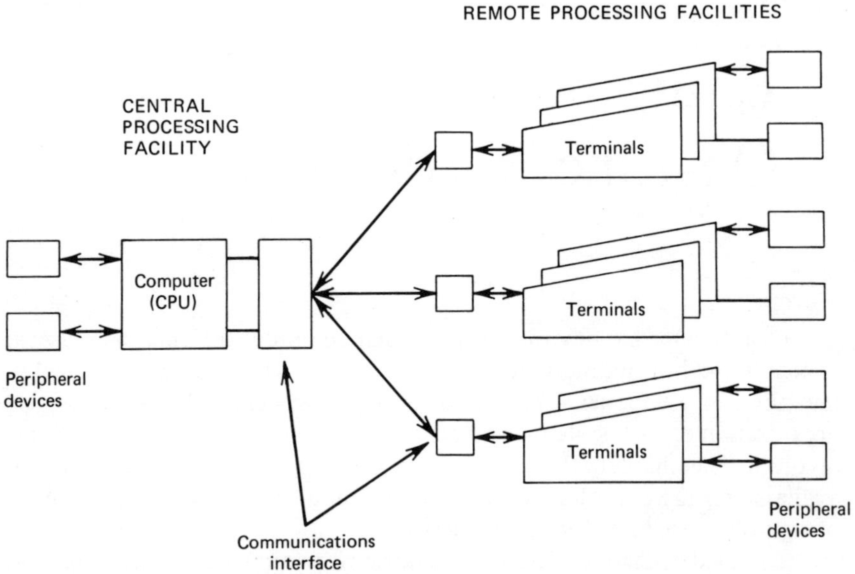

Figure 2.1.   Schematic representation of a computer communications network.

Central Processing Facility (CPF).   The CPF is the heart of the system. It supports and controls the remote operations of the various users. The CPF consists of three major parts: the computer itself, local peripheral devices, and communications interface equipment to connect the CPF with the rest of the network. Let us examine each of these components in more detail:

Computer.   The computer, or central processing unit (CPU), is the most important part of the whole system. Without it, the system could not function at all. It performs all the operations required to add information to the data base, maintains the information in its files, and performs the operations needed to retrieve information from the data base upon receipt of the proper instructions from a local or remote installation. The CPU performs all arithmetic computations and logical comparisons, and controls all the read/ write operations needed to support the system. It also allocates its resources in order to be able to serve the requirements of several on-line users simultaneously.

Peripheral Equipment.   This part of the CPF consists of all the auxiliary equipment needed to support the CPU. There is some leeway permitted in the choice of peripheral equipment, i.e., most systems have some but not all of the available devices. These include equipment such as high-speed printers, tape drives, on- and off-line storage devices (e.g., tapes, disks, drums, and data cells), COM* equipment, card reader/punches, and so forth.

Communications Equipment.   This is another important part of the whole system, as it serves to link the CPF with the rest of the network. This equipment is of several types: communications processors, multiplexing devices, and modems or acoustic couplers.

- Communications processors: These devices are used to remove the burden of communications handling from the central computer. They may also be used to translate messages from the remote facilities into a form that is acceptable to the central computer if required. Some of these devices are programmable (i.e., they may be instructed to perform some simple functions unique to the application, such as validation of a message before passing it on to the CPU), while others are not. The IBM 2703 is a good example of a widely used nonprogrammable device. Mini-computers are often used when a programmable device is required. Either programmable or non-programmable devices may be used alone or in combination, depending on the application.
- Multiplexing devices: Multiplexing is the process of dividing a transmission line into two or more channels either by splitting the frequency band transmitted by the channel into narrower bands, each of which is used to constitute a distinct channel, or by allotting this common channel to several different information channels one at a time. The first type of multiplexing is called *frequency division multiplexing*, while the second is known as *time division multiplexing*.
- Communications interface: Modems and/or acoustic couplers are used to connect the CPF to the communications lines that link the network together. Modems are modulation/demodulation devices that convert the digital signals generated by the computer equipment into an analog form compatible with the communications facilities (e.g., telephone lines) and back again into digital form. Modems are sometimes referred to as *data sets*. Those manufactured by Western Electric Co., and leased from the Bell Telephone System

---

*Computer-output-microfilm.

and other carriers, are known as *Dataphones*. If the data to be transmitted over the communications lines are in the form of audible tones, an acoustic coupler may be used. In some instances, where the computer and the remote facilities are not too distant, the modems or acoustic couplers can be eliminated altogether, and the terminals can be connected directly to the computer.

Finally, the computer communications network is linked together by some type of communications medium. Telephone lines, either dial-up or dedicated, are the most common, but coaxial cable, microwave transmission, and other techniques are also used. It is beyond the scope of this book to explore the details of communications technology, but the interested reader can find much detailed information in several excellent books by Martin (1967, 1970, 1971, 1972a, 1972b). A useful introductory paper has been written by Becker (1969) and another by Worley (1969). We should briefly mention that communications lines are characterized by *bandwidth* (the width of the frequency band that can be transmitted over the line), *speed* (measured in *bauds*, i.e., number of bits per second, or number of characters per second which may be transmitted over the line), and whether the line is *simplex*, *half duplex*, or *duplex* (a simplex line can transmit in only one direction; a half duplex line can transmit in two directions, but only in one direction at a time; and a *full duplex* line can transmit in either direction at any time). These communications lines may be connected one-to-one between each remote processing facility and the CPF or many-to-one between a group of remote processing facilities and the CPF. Obviously, it is less costly if more than one remote processing facility can share a single line. This arrangement is called a *multidrop* or *multipoint* network.

Remote Processing Facility (RPF).   The RPF includes all portions of the system that are not directly a part of the CPF. Remote is a relative term; that is, a facility qualifies as remote if it is in another room, on another floor, across the city, or across the country from the CPF. Basically, a RPF must support on-line data entry and reception, and must permit on-line interaction with the CPF. These functions may be performed using a single piece of equipment such as a cathode ray tube (CRT) terminal, but this is not a requirement. For example, data entry may be made via card reader, magnetic tape reader, paper tape reader, or other device connected to a telecommunications line. In these cases, the data entry operation is not considered to be on-line, since it must be prepared ahead of time for transmission. However, once the initial data entry has been completed, the response and further dialogue with the system may take place on-line. An example of this type of arrangement is illustrated by an information retrieval system in which the user formulates a search strategy off-line, punches up a paper tape with his search terms and logic, reads the paper tape, and transmits the search data to the CPF. The user then receives the search results on-line at a terminal at his remote location. He might then modify his search strategy on-line at the terminal and continue an interactive dialogue with the system until the desired search results are obtained.

By far the most common means of data entry in a RPF is through the use of some type of on-line terminal. These terminals generally have at least a typewriter-like keyboard that may be used to enter alphameric information. Other features such as paper tape reader, function switches, data tablets, light pens, and so forth may be included, depending on the requirements of the particular application and the sophistication of the terminal being used.

Data reception at the RPF may be supported by a line printer attached to the terminal [as with a standard Model 33 KSR (Keyboard-Send-Receive) Teletype], a CRT display, a high-speed printer, a COM device, or one of several other pieces of equipment. Additional equipment usually present at the RPF includes modems and acoustic couplers to connect it to the communications lines. A variety of peripheral devices such as Xerox copiers and microfilmers may also be available to record the information obtained by the retrieval and to aid in disseminating it to the user at the RPF.

On-Line Terminals.   Most of the components of a typical on-line information retrieval system are completely transparent to the user; that is, the user need not even know of their existence in order to operate the system effectively. The one component with which the user must be concerned is the on-line terminal. As far as the user is concerned, the terminal *is* the system, and its ease of operation and responsiveness will probably be the deciding factor in acceptance of an on-line information retrieval system by its clientele. The choice of terminal for a particular application is therefore of the utmost importance. As we shall see, there are many, many types of terminals available for use in on-line systems, and the user must somehow sort his way through them and select the ones best suited to meet his particular needs.

Basically, all terminals for use in on-line systems can be divided into two groups—those with CRT display capability and those without. Terminals that do not have an attached CRT usually rely on a typewriter-like keyboard for data entry with an attached line printer for output. One of the most widely used of these devices is the Model 33 KSR Teletype. This equipment has a four-row keyboard for data entry. It has standard uppercase alphabetic characters, numeric characters, a few special symbols (e.g., +, =, $), and some control characters for the device itself. Figure 2.2 shows this keyboard.

The Model 33 KSR Teletype has an attached line printer that produces a record of both incoming and outgoing transmissions on a continuous paper form. The Model 33 ASR (Automatic Send-Receive) Teletype combines the printing and keyboard facilities of the KSR with an attached paper tape

Figure 2.2. Keyboard of the Model 33 KSR Teletype. Reproduced by permission of Teletype Corporation.

Figure 2.3. Paper tape reader/punch from the Model 33 ASR Teletype. Reproduced by permission of Teletype Corporation.

Figure 2.4.   Model 33 ASR Teletype. Reproduced by permission of Teletype Corporation.

punch/reader. Figure 2.3 shows the paper tape punch/reader from the Model 33 ASR Teletype, and Figure 2.4 shows the entire device as it would appear at the RPF.

Other widely used terminals that do not have a CRT display are the IBM 2740 and 2741. Both terminals use an IBM Selectric typewriter with additional electronics to support on-line data entry and reception. Several options are available for the basic terminal that provide a variety of special capabilities including various types of interrupts, repeating character features on the keyboard, and a dial-up feature that permits connection to the telephone network using a Dataphone. The IBM 2741 (Figure 2.5) must

Figure 2.5.   IBM 2741 terminal. Reproduced by permission of International Business Machines Corporation.

be used in a direct point-to-central computer hookup, while the IBM 2740 (Figure 2.6) may be used in a multipoint array; that is, the 2740 may be connected to another IBM 2740 which is connected to the computer at the CPF.

Many more terminals without displays are available with a wide range of capabilities and prices. Information on these terminals is readily obtainable from the various trade journals or directly from the manufacturers.

It is when we attempt to survey the available terminals with CRT display capability that the proliferation of these devices truly becomes apparent. As on-line systems gained in popularity and widespread use, countless manufacturers recognized that new and better terminals would be needed to support them. Many computer hardware manufacturers therefore developed and marketed families of terminals which were each hailed as being bigger,

Figure 2.6. IBM 2740 terminal. Reproduced by permission of International Business Machines Corporation.

better, faster, more versatile, and cheaper than any of the others. Today, CRT terminals are available in an almost endless variety of capabilities and prices from the most inexpensive stripped-down model to the most sophisticated three-dimensional multicolored dynamic graphics display.

All CRTs have several things in common. First, a CRT terminal requires a keyboard for alphameric data entry and a CRT for output. Second, they frequently have one or more additional devices for data input such as light pens, data tablets, etc. The primary internal components of all CRT terminals are a memory and a character generator. A memory is used so that data need not be transmitted character-by-character as it is input to the CPF. The memory is usually at least large enough to hold a screenful or a *page* of data. This page of data may then be transmitted all at once to the CPF when the user enters the appropriate command. The concept of paging may also be used to allow more than one screenful of data to be stored in the terminal's memory. This feature permits a large amount of data such as a list of vocabulary terms to be stored at the terminal and displayed to the user a screenful at a time. Thus, the user may browse through the vocabulary by requesting that the desired portions of it be displayed on the CRT in response to the commands he issues. The memory can also be used to store an image of a form to be used for data entry. Because the image is stored locally at the terminal, it need not be continually refreshed from the CPF. Using the paging concept again, more than one form, or pages of a multipart form, may also be stored in the terminal's memory and displayed as desired. The terminal memory may be loaded either from the CPF or locally using the keyboard or other data input device.

The character generator accepts coded representations of characters (usually in ASCII* format) and converts them to a pattern that can be electronically displayed on the face of the CRT. Basic character generators can produce 64 uppercase alphameric characters and a few special symbols. Extended character generators are available that can produce 96 or more uppercase and lowercase characters, special symbols, and line-drawing characters. Special character generators are available to meet particular requirements. Figure 2.7 shows a typical CRT terminal (IBM 2260) with a data display.

Most CRT terminals have one or more optional data entry and editing devices available. These include function switches, cursors, the joystick, light pens, data tablets, and so forth. Some of the most common of these features are described below.

Cursor.   The cursor is a spot or other symbol on the face of the CRT that indicates the location at which the next data entry or reception operation will take place. Some cursors blink on and off, while others glow continuously. Some CRT terminals use a vertical and horizontal spacer bar to position the cursor, while others use a mouse or joystick.

Mouse.   The mouse is a small box that rests on two wheels and a ball-point support pin. It may be moved around in two dimensions to position the cursor at the desired location on the screen. The advantage of the mouse is that the cursor spot may be removed to the desired location directly rather than by moving up or down the desired number of lines and over the desired

---

*ASCII format is a standard set of bit combinations that are to be used to represent the various alphameric characters. ASCII stands for American Standard Code for Information Interchange (U.S.A. Standard X3.4—1967), and ASCII format is a coded representation for characters conforming to this standard.

Figure 2.7. IBM 2260 terminal. Reproduced by permission of International Business Machines Corporation.

number of spaces. It may also pinpoint a location that is not precisely located at the position where a character would be written on the CRT. This feature is useful for work involving graphic data.

Joystick.   The joystick is similar to the mouse, but it uses a lever in a control box to position the cursor. The lever is moved around in the box to position the cursor at the desired location on the screen. This device is also especially useful for graphic data work.

Light Pen.   The light pen looks very much like a fat ball-point pen. It emits a stream of electrons and is used to "write" directly on the CRT screen. The light pen may be used for alphameric data entry such as the selection of terms from a vocabulary listing by indicating the desired term or terms using the light pen to mark a predefined spot on the screen. The light pen may also be used to draw lines and is therefore useful in systems with graphic data input.

Function Keys.   Function keys are used to save steps in data entry. They are generally used to set up a preexisting condition so that minimal data need be entered by the user. For example, to return to the airlines reservation system mentioned earlier, function keys might be used to indicate an activity such as "make a reservation" or "cancel a reservation." The user then need only press the proper function key, and then key in the flight number, number of seats, class, and passenger name. Figures 2.8 and 2.9 show typical terminals with function keys.

In addition to these special data entry devices, most CRT terminals have format and editing features available. Format control usually refers to the use of the CRT as a form completion tool; i.e., it is used to guide the user in correctly entering data required to complete a particular input form. For example, an information systems user might use a CRT terminal to index a

Figure 2.8.   DATA 100 terminal. Reproduced by permission of DATA 100 Corporation.

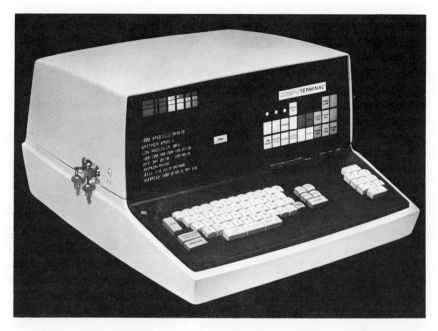

Figure 2.9. Terminal with function keys. Reproduced by permission of Wyle Computer Products, Inc.

document on-line. The format control capabilities of the CRT terminal would show the user where to enter title, author names, index terms, and other data elements. Format control also prevents the user from entering data in areas that must be protected from erroneous data entry, such as the identification number of the item being processed.

The editing features are perhaps the most valuable tools of all for the user of an on-line CRT. It is the editing capabilities that enable him to correct mistakes as he is keying the data in without rekeying large portions of the data. Typical editing functions available on CRT terminals are: erase character, erase to end of line, erase to end of message, erase to end of display, insert character in line, insert character in display, delete character in line, delete character in display, insert line, and delete line. Some terminals also have a right-justify feature that allows data to be entered in a line without the rest of the data being lost. Instead, the *overhang* data is wrapped around and appears on the next line. The remainder of the text is similarly adjusted to allow for the added data. This feature will also permit data to be removed and the space closed up. Each of these functions normally occurs at the location on the screen specified by the cursor position. Figure 2.10 shows a CRT terminal keyboard with some of the editing keys mentioned above.

Figure 2.10. CRT terminal with editing keys. Reproduced by permission of Wyle Computer
Products, Inc.

Terminals that are limited to alphameric capabilities can only accept
and display members of the character set that has been previously defined
for them. Terminals with graphics capabilities can accept nonalphameric
data, such as might be drawn on a CRT screen using a light pen, and can
display nonalphameric data such as charts or line drawings. For most
information retrieval applications, an alphameric display is all that is
required.

It is possible to have a video display using a terminal other than a CRT
terminal, and some interesting alternatives to the CRT are now emerging.
Noteworthy among these is the plasma display terminal developed at the
University of Illinois. The plasma terminal, as described by Stifle (1971),
incorporates a gas-filled glass panel, upon the face of which characters are
generated by means of gas discharges. The terminal was developed for use
with the PLATO system of computer-aided instruction, and it incorporates
a random-access slide projector, thus permitting the powerful combination
of static pictorial material (on slides) with instructional material (in digital

form). An important recent development is the *touch panel*, which is a plasma panel with an overlaid matrix of beams, permitting a user to select any data element displayed simply by touching it with his finger. Another plasma display, also allowing data selection by touch, has been demonstrated by Control Data Corporation.

Useful surveys of available displays were published by Auerbach (1971), Bryden (1971), and O'Hare (1971). These sources should be consulted for further information. The Auerbach volume covers about 150 separate displays, but even this survey is not 100% complete.

Now that we have examined the types of terminals available for use in on-line systems, the next area to be examined is how the user actually interfaces with the system, i.e., what steps must take place for the user to use the system.

The first step is for the user to log-in. Logging-in is the process by which the user identifies himself to the system and tells the CPF that he requires some service. The identifying data may consist of a number or code word to identify the RPF from which the user is addressing the CPF. The user enters this data, and the CPF responds with a message indicating that it has received the data and usually with a request for a password. This password should be closely guarded at the RPF and should be changed periodically, as it is usually the only safeguard to prevent unauthorized users from gaining access to the system. After the user has keyed-in the password and the system has verified it, the CPF will usually respond with a request for the type of operation the user wishes to perform. From this point on, the procedures become almost entirely application-dependent, and they are discussed fully in other chapters of this book. The remaining common operation is logging-off.

After the user has completed all his intended actions at the terminal, he is ready to sign off. If he has information that he wants to save for another time, he should always instruct the system to save whatever files he has created before signing off; otherwise, in most systems, all will be lost. Signing off is usually very easy. In some systems, the user keys in a "K" (for *kill*) or "OFF" or "BYE", and a carriage return. The computer system will usually respond with a reply that means essentially, "Are you sure?" If you are, usually hitting the carriage return key is sufficient, but some systems require another K or other positive action indicating that the session is over.

A typical log-in procedure using a typewriter terminal is listed below; "C" indicates messages sent by the computer, while "U" indicates entries made by the user.

U: User dials the CPF or otherwise makes it known that he wishes to use the services of the computer

C :   CPF responds with a *beep* tone
U :   CR (carriage return)
C :   PLEASE SIGN ON
U :   ID 503 (and a password which does not print)
C :   DIALCOM TIME-SHARING
C :   PLEASE IDENTIFY YOUR PROJECT
U :   4444/500 (or any other identification)
C :   ON AT 09:00   01/07/72

In a time-shared system using terminals with no CRT capability, the computer system usually prints a question mark or some other special character at the start of the line where user data is expected. When a CRT display is available, the CPF usually sets the cursor at the location where the user entry should be made.

In some systems, the remote terminals at the RPF are signed on by the CPF at the beginning of the day or whenever remote operation is scheduled to start. In these systems, all the user need do is turn on the terminal. The system will then respond with a message showing that it is ready for use, and the user may proceed.

REFERENCES

Auerbach Publishers (1971). *Auerbach on Alphanumeric Displays*. Princeton, N.J.: Auerbach.

Becker, J. (1969). "Telecommunications Primer." *Jour. Library Automat.* **2**(3), 145–156.

Bryden, J. E. (1971). "Visual Displays for Computers." *Computer Design* **10**(10), 55–77.

Martin, J. T. (1967). *Design of Real-Time Computer Systems*. Englewood Cliffs, N.J.: Prentice-Hall.

Martin, J. T. (1970). *Teleprocessing Network Organization*. Englewood Cliffs, N.J.: Prentice-Hall.

Martin, J. T. (1971). *Future Developments in Telecommunications*. Englewood Cliffs, N.J.: Prentice-Hall.

Martin, J. T. (1972a). *Introduction to Teleprocessing*. Englewood Cliffs, N.J.: Prentice-Hall.

Martin, J. T. (1972b). *Systems Analysis for Data Transmission*. Englewood Cliffs, N.J.: Prentice-Hall.

O'Hare, R. A. (1971). "Interactive CRT Terminals. Part 2. Alphanumeric CRT Terminals and Systems." *Mod. Data* **4**(7), 62–75 (July).

Stifle, J. (1971). *A Plasma Display Terminal*. Urbana, Ill.: University of Illinois, Computer-based Education Research Laboratory.

Worley, A. R. (1969). "Practical Aspects of Data Communications." *Datamation* **15**(10), 60–66.

Chapter Three

Searching the On-Line Data Base

This chapter will describe typical procedures that can be used to interrogate a bibliographic data base through the use of on-line terminals. We will assume, for the time being, an indexed data base; i.e., one in which the document record consists of full bibliographic citation plus assigned index terms or descriptors. Some special procedures relevant to the searching of nonindexed data bases (i.e., *free text* or *natural language*) will be discussed later. For convenience, we will concentrate on the description of procedures used in one particular system, namely ORBIT,* a product of System Development Corporation (Seiden, 1971), but will draw additional examples and variant procedures from other systems.

Typically, any on-line retrieval system will operate via three major modes: start-up (logging-in and identifying the file to be interrogated), search, and browsing and printing. Given the desire to find documents on a particular topic, the searcher, once he has logged-in and obtained access to the data base, will normally enter one or more descriptors. Let us say that he enters the descriptor KORSAKOFF'S SYNDROME (Figure 3.1). In most systems the program will first respond by displaying the number of documents indexed under the descriptor chosen. Such numbers are usually referred to as *postings* or *tallies*. In the example of Figure 3.1, the number of postings for KORSAKOFF'S SYNDROME is shown to be 14. In other words, should the user decide to have all citations bearing this term shown at the terminal, there would be a total of fourteen printed or displayed.

---

*See Chapter Five for discussions of the various systems mentioned in this chapter.

S.S.1
  USER: KORSAKOFF'S SYNDROME
  PROG: PSTG (14)
S.S.2
  USER: 1 OR WERNICKE'S ENCEPHALOPATHY
  PROG: PSTG (27)
S.S.3
  USER: IMMUNOELECTROPHORESIS OR IMMUNOASSAY OR
         FLUORESCENT ANTIBODY TECHNIC OR
         BRAIN CHEMISTRY
  PROG: PSTG (2556)
S.S.4
  USER: 3 AND SCHIZOPHRENIA
  PROG: PSTG (35)
S.S.5
  USER: 4 AND NOT CHILD
  PROG: PSTG (28)

Figure 3.1. Sample user inputs and system responses in an on-line search.

In the Intrex search system (see Chapter Five), tallies for a string of terms entered by a searcher will be displayed, as well as the tallies for combinations of those terms. Suppose, for example, the searcher enters the string "titanium compound resistivity." This will generate a display which appears as follows:

titanium	199	199
compound	382	17
resistivity	945	6

This display shows the number of occurrences of each word in the corpus (left-hand column) and the number of occurrences of each combination (right-hand column). Thus, in this example, "titanium" occurs 199 times in the document collection, "titanium" and "compound" co-occur 17 times, and these two words co-occur with "resistivity" 6 times. A similar feature is present in the STAIRS system of IBM.

In ORBIT, and in several other on-line systems, any conventional boolean algebraic strategy (AND, OR, NOT) can be entered immediately by the searcher, who also has the possibility of combining various search statements.* For example, if he is interested in either Korsakoff's Syndrome or Wernicke's Encephalopathy, his initial search statement could have been

---

*For a fuller discussion of the use of boolean algebraic search strategies consult *The Principles of MEDLARS* (National Library of Medicine, 1970).

KORSAKOFF'S SYNDROME OR WERNICKE'S ENCEPHALOPATHY*

Alternatively, if he had previously entered the first descriptor alone, he could incorporate this into a second search statement. In Figure 3.1, for example, his second search statement (S.S.2) asks for either his first descriptor (S.S.1) or WERNICKE'S ENCEPHALOPATHY. The program responds by indicating that 27 documents bear one or the other (or both) of these descriptors. There is essentially no limit to the number of descriptors that may be requested in an *or* relationship. Search statement S.S.3 (Figure 3.1) asks for any one of four terms, and one could increase such a list considerably in a situation in which many nearly synonymous terms exist.

Obviously, the more terms we ask for as logical alternatives (i.e., in an OR relationship), the more documents will match the requirement. We can *restrict* the scope of the search in one of several ways. First, we can demand the co-occurrence of two or more terms (i.e., place them in an AND relationship), as

KORSAKOFF'S SYNDROME AND CIRCADIAN RHYTHM AND HUMAN

Here we are specifying that we are interested only in documents that have been indexed under all three terms. Again the program responds by indicating how many documents match this logical requirement. If there is no match, the system response will be "NONE." Search statements can be combined in most on-line systems. In Figure 3.1, for example, the fourth statement combines a previous list of terms in an OR relationship with the additional term SCHIZOPHRENIA. Note how the ANDing of descriptors rapidly reduces the set of matching documents. There were 2556 documents matching the ORed set of S.S.3, but when it was ANDed with the single term SCHIZO-PHRENIA, the matching set dropped dramatically to 35.

In the ORBIT† implementation of MEDLINE (Medical Literature Analysis and Retrieval System On-Line), another way of narrowing the scope of a search is by combining a main term with a *subheading* (i.e., a general modifier) as in

SCHIZOPHRENIA/IMMUNOLOGY OR SCHIZOPHRENIA/METABOLISM

---

*In certain systems, however, including NASA's RECON and Lockheed's DIALOG, as originally designed, it was not possible to enter strings of terms in direct boolean expressions in this way. Terms could only be entered one at a time, or selected from a display presented by the system. At a later time in the dialogue, terms previously selected could be combined in various ways.

†The System Development Corporation (SDC) ORBIT system has been through a series of developments, and it has been known variously as ORBIT, ORBIT II, and ORBIT III. We will refer to it throughout merely as ORBIT.

In this strategy we are specifying interest in items indexed under SCHIZO-PHRENIA only if one of two particular subheadings has been used with it.

A third common way of restricting the scope of a search is by the use of negation (logical NOT), as in

SCHIZOPHRENIA AND NOT CHILD

which specifies interest in any items indexed under SCHIZOPHRENIA as long as the descriptor CHILD has not also been used in indexing. Negative statements can be combined with other statements, as in S.S.5 of Figure 3.1.

It is possible in many systems to construct a single search statement incorporating all types of logical operators (AND, OR, NOT), but different systems will have different conventions for achieving this. Consider, as an example, the statement

A *and* B *or* C

In ORBIT, this would be interpreted as (A *and* B) *or* C, whereas in the Data Central system of Mead Corporation (Giering, 1972), the same statement would be interpreted as A *and* (B *or* C). In Data Central, use of the ampersand (&) differs from use of AND, as in

A AND (B OR C)
(A & B) OR C

Clearly, we must be fully familiar with the conventions of a particular system before we can use it effectively.

Different conventions also exist for representing boolean operators in search strategies. In the CIRCOL intelligence retrieval system (U.S. Air Force, 1970), for example, the entry

nephritis, nephrosis, uremia

is read as nephritis *or* nephrosis *or* uremia. The logical AND in this system is expressed by the ampersand (&) as

metal & diffusion

In Data Central, the logical negation is introduced by AND NEQ. In RECON, symbols are used to combine terms—the plus (+) for the *or* relation, the asterisk (*) for the *and* relation, and the minus (−) for a negation.

These are conventions that the searcher must learn and live with. Although the conventions of one system may appear simpler than those of another, these conventions will have no direct effect on the performance of the system. That is, we can generally expect to be able to input the same logical search requirement in system A as we can in system B, even if the search conventions in the two systems are quite different. The proliferation of different searching procedures is not particularly desirable, however, and may present problems in information centers where a number of systems are in use. As more and more bibliographic systems become available, the need for greater conformity increases. One interim approach, allowed in some systems, is a RENAME command which allows selected commands of one system to be translated into command names that the user is more familiar with, perhaps because he uses them in another system.

Vocabulary Display

So far we have considered only the simple querying of a data base by the use of straightforward boolean strategies. Other types of querying are possible in many systems, and various aids to the searcher are frequently provided. If we are searching a system based on a controlled vocabulary, the vocabulary itself will be stored as a machine-readable file in the system and facilities for viewing this vocabulary selectively must be provided. For example, in ORBIT, the command "NEIGHBOR" will cause the display of a term along with others alphabetically adjacent to it in the vocabulary. Thus, "NEIGHBOR LEUKEMIA" will generate this display:

> LEUCOSARCOMA (MH)
> LEUCUTIA T (AU)
> LEUKEMIA (MH)
> LEUKEMIA L1210 (MH)
> LEUKEMIA, EXPERIMENTAL (MH)

The neighbor display also shows the number of times terms have been used in indexing (postings or tallies). Such an alphabetical display assists the searcher by suggesting terms that may bear some useful relationship to the original term entered (insofar as alphabetical proximity is likely to bring some conceptually related terms together). In this particular case, the searcher might be led to recognize that LEUKEMIA, EXPERIMENTAL is really the descriptor that most closely represents his current interests. The maximum number of neighbor terms that the ORBIT system will display is ten at one time. However, the seacher has the option of continuing up or down the alphabetic display by use of a further command. If the term entered by the searcher, after the NEIGHBOR command, is not contained in the data base (e.g., it may be misspelled), the set of terms alphabetically close to it is still displayed by the system. This is a very valuable feature in that it allows a certain amount of compensation for human error. It is perhaps particularly useful for searching names of authors where the user is unsure of the correct spelling. In MEDLINE, unless otherwise specified by the searcher, subject terms (MH, for "main heading" in the above example) are interfiled with author entries (AU) in the display. This is a disadvantage, since one would never be interested in finding an author whose name was alphabetically adjacent to a subject term, or vice versa, and a plethora of author entries might very well prevent a number of related descriptors from appearing together in the display.

In RECON (National Aeronautics and Space Administration, 1966, 1970) also, an alphabetical display of terms surrounding any descriptor may be generated by depressing the EXPAND key on the RECON keyboard.

	EXPAND ST/AIR POLUTION DETECTION	REF		DESCRIPTOR	TP	ACC	TS
REF	DESCRIPTOR	TP	ACC TS	E10	ST/AIR SPEED------------O	60	0
E01	ST/AIR MASS-------------O		38 0	E11	ST/AIR TO AIR----------O	64	0
E02	ST/AIR MASSES-----------N		217 6	E12	ST/AIR TO AIR MISSILE---O	36	0
E03	ST/AIR NAVIGATION-------B		725 34	E13	ST/AIR TO AIR MISSILES--N	196	13
E04	ST/AIR PIRACY-----------N		13 4	E14	ST/AIR TO AIR REFUELING-B	22	2
E05	ST/AIR POLLUTION--------B		1150 36	E15	ST/AIR TO AIR ROCKETS---U	0	1
E06	-ST/AIR POLUTION DETECTIO			E16	ST/AIR TO SURFACE-------O	108	0
E07	ST/AIR PURIFICATION-----B		168 9	E17	ST/AIR TO SURFACE		
E08	ST/AIR SAMPLING---------B		342 6		MISSILE-------------O	44	0
E09	ST/AIR SICKNESS---------U		0 1				
ENTER:						-MORE-	

Figure 3.2. Example of term expansion on RECON. Reproduced by permission of the National Aeronautics and Space Administration.

Figure 3.2 shows a display generated by RECON in response to the entry of the term AIR POLLUTION DETECTION. Note the following on this display:

1. For all recognized indexing terms (i.e., terms that are legitimate descriptors in the controlled vocabulary of the system), the number of postings is presented (in the column headed ACC, for "accessions"). From this display you can see that AIR POLLUTION has been used 1150 times in indexing and AIR SAMPLING has been used 342 times.

2. Although the original search term is not a recognized descriptor in the vocabulary (this is shown by the fact that no postings appear in the ACC column), it nevertheless generates an alphabetical display and appears in its correct place in this display. The ORBIT system, as we have stated earlier, includes a similar facility.

3. Each descriptor on the display is given a unique reference number (REF). This reference number can be used by the searcher to select

a term from the display and to incorporate this term into a search strategy.

4. For each descriptor displayed, the number of terms to which it is related (hierarchically or otherwise) in the vocabulary of the system is shown. In the column TS (for "thesaurus structure"), AIR MASSES is shown to be connected to 6 other terms in the vocabulary, while AIR NAVIGATION is connected to 34 other terms. It is possible, for any descriptor in the vocabulary, to request a display of those terms to which it is connected in the thesaurus structure.

The RECON system was designed for NASA by Lockheed Missiles & Space Co., based on a system previously developed by the Lockheed Information Sciences Laboratory. This system, known as DIALOG, is available from Lockheed. DIALOG, as described by Summit (1968), operates through the following major commands:

EXPAND. This will cause a display of all terms alphabetically close to the terms entered (see Figure 3.3). Each descriptor appears with a temporary identification number by which it may be referenced, a count of the number

EXPAND IT = MATHEMATICS			
REF DESCRIPTOR	TP	CIT	RT
E15 IT = MATHEMATICS			
PLACEMENT EXAMINATION/	1		
E16 IT = MATHEMATICS PROGRAM	1		
E17 IT = MATHEMATICS TEACHERS	68	11	
E18 IT = MATHEMATICS	4		
E19 IT = MATHEMATICS			
INSTRUCTION	1		
E20 IT = MATRICES	1		
E21 IT = MATRICES	2		
E22 IT = MATRICULATION/			1
E23 IT = MATRIX ALGEBRA	1		
E24 IT = MATRIX GANE/	1		
E25 IT = MATRIX GANET	1		
E26 IT = MATRIX TASKS	1		
E27 IT = MATRIX SETS	1		
E29 IT = MATSUMOTO	1		
E30 IT = MATTER	12	8	
E31 IT = MATTHEW ARNOLD	1		
ENTER			

Figure 3.3. Example of term expansion on DIALOG. Reproduced from *DIALOG Terminal Users Reference Manual* by permission of Lockheed Palo Alto Research Laboratory.

of times it has been used in indexing, and a count of the number of terms
that are shown to be related in the vocabulary. A display of the related terms
may be obtained by depressing the EXPAND key and entering the descriptor
identification number. Figure 3.4 shows such a display of terms related to
MATHEMATICS EDUCATION.

```
EXPAND IT = MATHEMATICS EDUCATION
REF   DESCRIPTOR                    TP   CIT   RT
R01   IT = MATHEMATICS EDUCATION    323   5
R02   IT = EDUCATION            3    553   61
R03   IT = COLLEGE MATHEMATICS  4    102   6
R04   IT = ELEMENTARY SCHOOL
         MATHEMATICS            4    426   6
R05   IT = MATHEMATICS          4    761   33
R06   IT = SECONDARY SCHOOL
         MATHEMATICS            4    338   5
ENTER
```

Figure 3.4. Another example of term expansion on DIALOG. Reproduced from *DIALOG
Terminal Users Reference Manual* by permission of Lockheed Palo Alto Research Laboratory.

SELECT. This command, when used with a descriptor identification
number from the display, causes all citations bearing the selected descriptor
to be collected for further processing. Each selected descriptor is assigned an
identification number and is typed on the console printer together with a
figure representing the number of citations to which it has been assigned.

COMBINE. This command is used to combine terms or groups of terms
already selected. Any boolean expression is possible:

> COMBINE A + B (logical *sum*; either A or B or both)
> COMBINE A * B (logical *product*; A *and* B)
> COMBINE A − B (negation; A *but not* B)

The COMBINE command results in a display of a figure indicating the total
number of citations satisfying the search logic.

DISPLAY. This command causes bibliographic records to be displayed
on the CRT.

KEEP. This command allows the user to save selected citations for later
printout on-line or off-line.

TYPE. This command causes a selected citation to be printed on-line at the
console printer.

PRINT.   This command causes a selected citation or set of citations to be printed on the off-line printer.

These commands are also the major commands used in RECON. RECON and DIALOG differ somewhat from ORBIT and CIRCOL in that they were designed for indirect search. A string of descriptors, in a boolean logical expression, could not be entered directly in these systems as originally designed. Instead, the user was required to select descriptors one at a time (although, once a display was generated, several could be selected from this display by identifying number) and later combine his selections using the AND, OR, and NOT operators. While this indirect approach may give more help to the inexperienced searcher, it may be somewhat tedious and frustrating to the sophisticated searcher who would like to enter a strategy directly. Modifications have since been made to these systems to make more direct search possible.

Given a controlled vocabulary that has some hierarchical structure, either through a classified (genus–species) term organization or by means of the BT–NT* relations of a conventional thesaurus, the on-line system should be capable of displaying any hierarchy or portion of a hierarchy. In MEDLINE, the searcher can request a hierarchical display by means of the "TREE" command. Thus, "TREE LEUKEMIA" will generate

> NEOPLASMS
>   LEUKEMIA
>   LEUCOSARCOMA
>   LEUKEMIA, EXPERIMENTAL
>   LEUKEMIA, LYMPHOCYTIC
>   LEUKEMIA, MONOCYTIC
>   LEUKEMIA, MYELOCYTIC
>   LEUKEMIA, PLASMACYTIC
>   LEUKEMIA, SUBLEUKEMIC
>   SEE ALSO RELATED
>   LEUKEMOID REACTION

Such classified display will bring a whole group of generically related terms together and is therefore likely to be much more valuable to the searcher than the alphabetical display. The MEDLINE search program, as shown in the above example, will display, for any descriptor requested, the term immediately above it and the terms immediately below it in the hierarchy. Terms shown, in the controlled vocabulary of the system, to be related to the term entered in ways other than the true genus–species relation are also displayed.

---

*Broader term–narrower term.

In the experimental BOLD system, as described by Burnaugh (1967), the entry of a term followed by a question mark caused the program to communicate back other entries having similar spelling or recorded as being synonymous or superordinate terms in the vocabulary. Thus,

.HEAT?
The following may be similar to heat
heat
thermodynamics
enthalpy
heat exchangers
heat of formation
heat of fusion
heat of sublimation
heat production
heat resistant alloys
heat resistant polymers
heat transfer
heat treatment
heaters
heating
*end

In conducting a search, we may wish to coordinate (AND) a complete hierarchy of terms with one or more other terms. For example, we may be interested in the subject of leukemia in pregnancy. In other words, we want to retrieve any document indexed under the term PREGNANCY and also under any term from the leukemia hierarchy. We should not need to list all the leukemia terms. The on-line system should give us the ability to refer to a complete hierarchy and to incorporate the entire hierarchy into a search strategy. This can be done in MEDLINE as long as we know the category number of a particular term (we can get this by another on-line command or by consulting a printed tool). The category (tree) number for LEUKEMIA in MEDLINE is C2.10, and the strategy EXPLODE C2.10 will cause the system to display the total number of citations for all terms in this tree (i.e., provide a combined count of the postings for all leukemia terms). We can then combine the entire category with the other aspect of the search in the form

PREGNANCY AND EXPLODE C2.10

This strategy will reveal the number of documents that have been indexed under the term PREGNANCY and also under any term from the leukemia hierarchy of C2.10. We can, if we wish, combine two or more complete hierarchies into a strategy. Thus,

EXPLODE C2.10 AND EXPLODE A11.30.32

will retrieve any documents indexed under any leukemia term (C2.10) and also under any chromosome term (A11.30.32).

Other Searching Aids

One of the problems encountered in on-line systems used by people who are not information specialists is that of training the searcher to construct valid boolean strategies. Hall, et al. (1972) have experimented with the use of a matrix displayed on a CRT device. The matrix is arranged in the form of a logical expression into which the searcher merely types the terms he wishes to incorporate. A simplified representation of such a display is

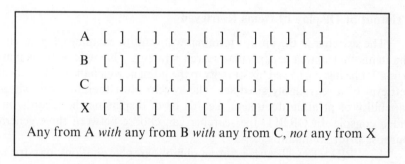

With this display the searcher merely enters his search terms into the appropriate boxes. All terms entered into a particular field (A, B, C, X) are interpreted as being in an OR relationship. The fields A, B, and C are in an AND relationship one to another, and the field X is in an AND NOT relationship with respect to the other fields.

In the bibliographic access system that is part of the SUNY (State University of New York) Biomedical Communication Network, it is possible to modify descriptors (index terms) by words in titles of documents (Pizer, 1969). Suppose, for example, we are looking for papers on "acute frontal sinusitis." The most specific index term available in the system is SINUSITIS. However, we can modify this by stating that a document should only be retrieved if it is indexed under SINUSITIS and at the same time contains the phrase "acute frontal" in its title. This type of strategy will, of course, be likely to retrieve only the most highly relevant items. ORBIT also has a title search capability, and it will in fact rank documents in order of the degree of match between document title and request statement.

An interesting feature of SUPARS [Syracuse University Psychological Abstracts Retrieval Service (SUPARS, 1971)] is the inclusion of *stored searches*. In response to the entry of any keyword, it is possible to obtain a listing of all previous search strategies that have incorporated this keyword. Two types of output can be requested. LIST SEARCHES requests a printout of each search strategy as originally submitted to the system, along with an indication of the number of documents retrieved and printed in each search. LIST WORDS requests a printout of all unique words found in the retrieved strategies, along with the number of searches in the data base containing these unique words. By drawing upon searches made in the past by users with similar interests, the searcher may obtain useful ideas for additional search approaches and specific applicable terms. The feature also has possible value in contributing to the development of a form of controlled vocabulary (see Chapter Eleven).

Printout or Display of Items Retrieved

The searcher at the on-line terminal will want to examine some or all of the items that match a particular search strategy. This will be particularly true after he has narrowed his strategy to the point at which the tallies indicate retrieval of a reasonably sized set. The system must therefore provide the capability of printing document records or of displaying the records on a video console. In ORBIT, the searcher can choose between three general-purpose print commands:

1. "PRINT" will cause printout of bibliographic citations for retrieved items only.
2. "PRINT FULL" will cause printout of citation plus a list of all the index terms assigned to the document.
3. "PRINT TRIAL" will cause printout of title plus index terms only.

In addition, the system permits sampling in the records of retrieved citations. Most systems offer options as to what portions of the records are to be displayed and how these are to be sequenced and formatted. Figure 3.5 shows a typical display of bibliographic records as they would appear in the RECON system. Records that are unusually lengthy would require display on the screen in a series of stages (*pages*). On-line systems employing video display are likely to have a supplementary teleprinter (e.g., xerographic) to allow the generation of hard copy of any record displayed on the CRT. Figure 3.6 illustrates such a printout from EARS (Epilepsy Abstracts Retrieval System), an application of the Data Central system. This is a printout of the exact record displayed on the CRT. Note that this system contains the full abstract of each item. Given a color CRT, it is possible with the Data Central system to have the words which cause the item to be retrieved appear on the screen

```
                    TYPE 68A81393/2
A68-81393   67/10/00  8 PAGES    UNCLASSI
FIED DOCUMENT
   GAS CHROMATOGRAPHIC DETERMINATION OF L
EAD TETRAETHYL IN THE ATMOSPHERE  LA DET
ERMINAZIONE GAS CROMATOGRAFICA DEL PIOMB
O TVTRAETILE NELL'ATMOSFERA.
   (DETERMINATION OF TETRAETHYL LEAD IN A
TMOSPHERE BY GAS CHROMATOGRAPHY)
   A/PERIN, G.   (AA/PADUA, U., IST. D'IG
IENE, ITALY/.)
      IN MEDICINA DEL LAVORO, VOL. 58, OCT.
   1967, P. 624-631.   IN ITALIAN.
      /*DETECTION/*GAS CHROMATOGRAPHY/*LEAD
COMPOUNDS/ AIR POLLUTION/ AIR SAMPLING/
CONCENTRATION (COMPOSITION)/ DOSAGE/ GA
S ANALYSIS
                    TYPE 67A11037/2
A67-11037   ISSUE 1    PAGE 50    CATEGORY
   11   66/10/00  8 PAGES    UNCLASSIFIED D
OCUMENT
   HOW AIR POLLUTION CONTROL INSTRUMENTAT
ION DEVELOPED FOR THE AEROSPACE INDUSTRY
CO5LD BENEFIT THE URBAN SOCIETY.
   (AIR MONITORING INSTRUMENTS USED IN DE
TECTION AND CONTROL OF AIR POLLUTION)
   A/MCKELVEY, J. W.   (AA/MARTIN MARIETT
A CORP., MARTIN CO., DENVER, COLD./.)
MEMBERS, $0.75, NONMEMBERS, $1.00.
      I STRUMENT SOCIETY OF AMERICA, ANNU
AL CONFERENCE AND EXHIBIT, 21ST, NEW YOR
K, N.Y., OCT. 24-27, 1966, PREPRINT.   8
P.
      /*AIR POLLUTION/*CONTROL SYSTEM/*INST
RUMENTATION/*MONITOR/ AIR/ CONFERENCE/ C
ONTROL/ DVTECTION/ EVALUATION/ INSTRUMEN
T/ OPERATION/ POLLUTION/ SYSTEM
```

Figure 3.5. Sample display of citations on RECON. Reproduced by permission of the National Aeronautics and Space Administration.

in a color different from that of all other words displayed. Various other methods of "highlighting" the text words matching the search strategy have been tried by Data Central. These include, for black-and-white terminals, blinking the characters, dropping the words a little below the level of the others on the line, varying the intensity, or simply "flagging" the words with some symbol such as an arrow or asterisk. Figure 3.7 is an illustration of a printout from another system, AIM–TWX. For a search retrieving a relatively small number of documents, the searcher is likely to have all document records printed at the terminal. If the search will retrieve a large number of documents, on the other hand, he is more likely to view a selection on-line only (to make sure that the search is retrieving the type of document he expected) and to request that the complete search results be printed off-line and mailed to him.

CLASSIFICATION
7.1

ENGLISH TITLE
ABNORMAL CEREBRAL POTENTIALS ACTIVATED
BY AUTOELECTROGENESIS UNDER
PHOTOSTIMULATION

ORIGINAL LANGUAGE
SPANISH

TITLE IN ORIGINAL LANGUAGE
POTENCIALES CEREBRALES ANORMALES
ACTIVADOS POR LA PROPIA ELECTROGENESIS
CEREBRAL BAJO FOTOESTIMULACION

AUTHOR
CHIRINOS E.

AUTHOR'S AFFILIATION
CAT. DE PSICOFISIOL., ESC. DE PSICOL.,
UNIV. CENT. DE VENEZUELA, CARACAS

SOURCE JOURNAL
ACTA CIENT. VENEZ.

CODEN CODE
ACVEA

ABSTRACT
REPORT PRESENTED AT THE ANNUAL MEETING
OF THE VENEZUELAN ASSOCIATION FOR THE
ADVANCEMENT OF SCIENCE. EEG TRACINGS
ARE SHOWN FROM PATIENTS EXPOSED TO
INTERMITTENT LIGHT STIMULATION BY
MEANS OF A FLASHING LAMP CONNECTED TO
THE EEG APPARATUS AND ACTIVATED BY THE
CEREBRAL POTENTIALS. VARIOUS
PATHOLOGIC FEATURES IN EEGS MADE BY
THIS TECHNIC WERE POINTED OUT AND
THEIR NEUROPHYSIOLOGIC IMPLICATIONS
WERE DISCUSSED.

PRIMARY INDEX OF TERMS
EEG* EEG ACTIVATION* PHOTIC
STIMULATION

Figure 3.6. Full printout of record from EARS.

USER: QUADRIPLEGIA/COMPLICATIONS

PROG: PSTG---NUMBER POSTINGS---THE NUMBER OF UNIT RECORDS
MATCHING THIS SEARCH STATEMENT IS (19)

SS 3 /C?---SEARCH STATEMENT 3 OR COMMAND?--
ENTER EACH STATEMENT NUMBER 3 OR ANY COMMAND.

USER: "PRINT FULL 1"

AU - WHARTON GW
AU - MORGAN TH
TI - ANKYLOSIS IN THE PARALYZED PATIENT.
SO - J BONE JOINT SURG (AMER) 52 105–12 JAN 70
LA - ENGLISH
AN - 4571321
PY - 1970
ED - 700305
MH - ADULT
MH - ANKYLOSIS/ETIOLOGY
MH - ANKYLOSIS/RADIOGRAPHY
MH - ELBOW JOINT
MH - FEMALE
MH - HAND
MH - *HIP/RADIOGRAPHY
MH - HIP JOINT
MH - HUMAN
MH - KNEE JOINT
MH - MALE
MH - MIDDLE AGE
MH - OSSIFICATION, PATHOLOGIC/ETIOLOGY
MH - OSSIFICATION, PATHOLOGIC/RADIOGRAPHY
MH - *PARAPLEGIA/COMPLICATIONS
MH - QUADRIPLEGIA/COMPLICATIONS
MH - SHOULDER JOINT
MH - SPINE
JC - HJR

HOW MANY MORE ON-LINE?

USER: NONE

Figure 3.7. Sample citation printout from AIM–TWX.

Interactive Search

If the user of the on-line terminal is given the facility to view document representations at various stages of his search, it is obvious that the search can be *interactive*. That is, the searcher can try various term combinations, view records of documents matching these strategies, examine the indexing terms assigned to these, select pertinent terms, and incorporate these into new strategies. Searching in the on-line system is a heuristic process. It involves selection of terms, using vocabulary displays provided by the system; combining terms into various logical statements; seeing how many items satisfy these logical statements; viewing a selection of these items at the terminal; modifying the strategy, where necessary, after examining selected items; and eventually printing out a complete list of items satisfying the strategy or strategies finally decided on.

In the experimental SMART system of Salton (Ide, 1969; Ide and Salton, 1969; Lesk and Salton, 1969; Salton, 1968, 1971), search strategies may be modified automatically on the basis of feedback provided by the searcher at the on-line terminal. Automatic query reformulation procedures merely require the user to select relevant titles from a display (*relevance feedback*). The automatic feedback procedures essentially upweight the values of query terms associated with documents known to be relevant or add new terms to the query from these documents (*positive feedback*), and in some approaches they may downweight terms associated with nonrelevant documents (*negative feedback*). Positive feedback moves a query toward other documents like those known to be relevant, while negative feedback (especially useful where no relevant documents are uncovered by a first search) moves the query *away* from documents known not to be relevant. For most users, this process is more successful than nonautomatic feedback. However, for more sophisticated and patient users, improved results are possible if the users rephrase their queries themselves, using displays of titles, abstracts, and dictionaries of terms.

Terse and Verbose Forms

Most on-line systems allow the user to decide whether he wants the system to communicate with him in terse or verbose form. Three levels of communication are available in ORBIT. In Figure 3.1 the system responses are given in symbolic version. The full version of "PSTG (14)" is

The number of unit records matching this search statement is (14)

while the intermediate version is

Number postings (14)

The neophyte user would normally select the expanded versions. When he gains greater familiarity with the system, he will graduate to a briefer, more symbolic method of communication.

Natural Language Searching

It is extremely difficult to operate nonmechanized systems without the use of a controlled vocabulary in both indexing and searching. However, a computer system can operate successfully on natural language (*free text*). Natural language data bases are particularly attractive in on-line systems, because these systems allow exploratory strategies, viewing of selected portions of text, and rapid modification of the strategy on the basis of this browsing process. A number of natural language systems, designed for on-line implementation, exist; some are experimental, others are commercially available. Perhaps the best-known commercially available system is Data Central (Giering, 1972). This system is in use in many applications, including a large legal retrieval system of the Ohio Bar Association and EARS of the National Institute of Neurological Diseases and Stroke (Porter, et al., 1970). Data Central will work on the full text of documents or on document abstracts. Inverted files are created for all words in a corpus that are not on a stop list (this list would include nonsubstantive words such as articles, prepositions, and conjunctions), and all of these words, and combinations of them, are searchable in the system.

Systems such as Data Central are designed to operate on boolean search expressions. However, somewhat modified procedures may be used in searching free text. In a free text system we need the capability of using word distance to restrict the scope of a search. For example, we may be interested in term A in relation to term Q, but only when A and Q appear in the same paragraph, in the same sentence, within x words of each other, or in immediate physical juxtaposition in a text. In CIRCOL, the strategy

hydrostatic & extrusion (+1)

will only retrieve documents in which the word "hydrostatic" is adjacent to the word "extrusion," indicated by the requirement (+1); in other words, it will only retrieve documents bearing the term "hydrostatic extrusion." Similarly, a & b (−1) means that b must immediately precede a, while a & b (not +1) means that a and b must appear in the same document, but b must not immediately follow a. In Data Central, the strategy

AMYLOIDOSIS (W5) KIDNEY

specifies that, for a document to be retrieved, it must contain the word "amyloidosis" and the word "kidney" and that these words must not be more than five words apart (not counting stop words). This system allows a search to be made for a particular word occurring within x words of any search word in either direction.

Natural language systems also commonly allow searches to be conducted on word truncations. For example, we can use a strategy CONVUL #, where # indicates that the searcher does not care which letters follow. This would retrieve any document containing the word "convulsion" or "convulsions" or "convulsing" or "convulsed." This facility is extended further in the TIP system at Massachusetts Institute of Technology (MIT), where it is possible to search on truncations or on character-strings within a larger string (Mathews, 1967). For example, the command "find title magnet" will cause a search for any title containing the string "magnet" at the beginning of a word (magnet, magnetic, magnetism, and so on), whereas "find title + magnet" will cause a search for the string wherever it appears, including such constructions as "paramagnetic" and "ferromagnetism." In some systems, left truncation is allowed, as well as right truncation. This can be a very powerful device. For example, . . . MYCIN is likely to retrieve most references to antibiotics, and left truncations such as . . . OTOMY, . . . ECTOMY, and . . . PLASTY are likely to retrieve a wide range of surgical procedures. Left truncation is common in batch systems designed for text searching, but it is expensive to implement in the inverted file organization that is common in most on-line searching systems (see Chapter Four).

A somewhat similar device is the "universal character," used to indicate that any character may appear in a particular position. For example, SM #TH indicates that any letter may appear between the M and the T. The universal character device is useful in cases in which we are unsure of the correct spelling of a word, as perhaps a proper name.

The TIP system searches on words occurring in titles of papers contained within its data base, and a searcher may specify any boolean combination of words. For example,

Find title x-ray and title diffraction

specifies that a paper will be retrieved if its title contains both the word "x-ray" and the word "diffraction."

In Data Central, plural or possessive forms of words containing five or more letters in the singular, and regularly formed, are automatically retrieved when the singular form is entered. Thus, PICTURE will also retrieve items containing PICTURES, PICTURE'S, and PICTURES'.

English Sentence Input

A number of natural language systems are designed to accept requests in English sentence form rather than as boolean algebraic expressions.

Examples are Salton's SMART system (Ide, 1969; Ide and Salton, 1969; Lesk and Salton, 1969; Salton, 1968) and the BROWSER system (Browsing On-Line with Selective Retrieval) of Williams (1969; Williams and Perriens, 1968). The BROWSER system searches on abstracts. From a corpus of abstracts, after common (syntactic) words are deleted, a dictionary of word roots (*rootwords*) is created. Abstract numbers are posted to the rootwords in a normal inverted file arrangement. The dictionary carries statistics on the number of occurrences of each rootword in the corpus. Each rootword is also given on *information value* (*I-value*), which is inversely proportional to the number of occurrences of the rootword in the corpus (i.e., the rarer words are most discriminating and therefore they are presumed to be most potent for retrieval purposes). The words used by a searcher, in a natural language request statement, are checked against the search term dictionary. Those recognized are arranged in descending order of I-value and searched in the inverted file. Document abstracts in the corpus are given a numerical value in relation to the request, this value being the sum of the I-values of all terms matching between the request and the document. Document abstracts are displayed to the searcher in descending order of I-value, which should equate approximately with descending order of relevance to the request.

SMART (Ide, 1969; Ide and Salton, 1969; Lesk and Salton, 1969; Salton, 1968, 1971), although not designed originally as an on-line system, has interactive and iterative features that make it highly suitable for implementation in the on-line mode. The system operates on free text (usually abstracts) and will accept queries in English sentence form. At input, a text is reduced to word roots by a *stem-suffix cutoff* procedure. Each word stem is given a weight in relation to the document based on frequency of occurrence and other criteria. The word stem is assigned one or more *concept numbers* from a *synonym dictionary*, which is usually a human-prepared, machine-stored thesaurus, although recent work has been conducted on machine-generated thesauri and *word discrimination lists. Statistical phrases* (based simply on co-occurrence of thesaurus concepts in a text) and *syntactic phrases* (based on co-occurrence in a specified syntactic relationship) may also be assigned automatically. In entering a natural language request, the searcher has the option of specifying any of several levels of search sophistication from simple word stem match to the use of thesaurus groups or the syntactic phrases. Each document in the file is given a *correlation coefficient* to express its degree of match with the request statement. The entire collection is ranked on the basis of these correlation coefficients, and those items with the highest value (and, hopefully, most likely to be relevant) are displayed first or appear at the head of a printout.

SMART is designed for use with *iterative searches*. The searcher will receive preliminary results from one search option, will evaluate these, and will indicate which of the retrieved items are relevant and which are not.

When these relevance decisions are fed back into the system, the search programs automatically modify the weights of terms in the request statement so as to bring the statement closer to the profiles of the relevant documents in the collection and thus improve the quality of the second search.

Another system designed to accept requests in English language form has been described by Curtice and Jones (1969). This system, IRMA (Internal Report Management Aid), will accept queries in sentence form, subject them to an automatic indexing routine, and report back to the display scope those words or word pairs recognized in the vocabulary. The user thus builds up a list of terms describing his interests. "All necessity for specifying logical combinations of terms is removed from the requestor: the search strategy is under automatic control. The search program automatically weights the query terms, looks up the records in which they occur, and sorts the records prior to presentation on the display. The retrieved records are shown to the user in decreasing order of a calculated weight based on the sum of the weights of the terms in the query which the record contains" (p. 4).

The operations of IRMA can be illustrated by means of a simple example. Suppose the requestor asks for "anything related to medical electronics." The system responds by listing the terms it recognizes in this query (i.e., the terms existing in its inverted search files) as follows:

> 01 ELECTRONICS
> 02 MEDICAL
> 03 MEDICAL ELECTRONICS

The requestor may then ask for an expansion on this list of search terms by means of the command AUTOSEARCH. This command causes the search programs to look for other terms that are statistically associated with these original search terms. As a result of the *associative query expander*, seven additional candidate terms are added to the query term list:

> 04 CARE
> 05 DEVELOPMENT WORK
> 06 THERMAL
> 07 ASW SYSTEMS
> 08 MEDICAL PRODUCT
> 09 HEALTH CARE
> 10 THERMAL ANALYSIS

The searcher decides that terms 4, 6, 7, and 10 are probably irrelevant and therefore deletes them with the simple command "IGNORE 4/6/7/10." At the same time he decides to add a new term CLINICAL LABORATORIES. This term, while not itself recognized, generates the candidate search terms LABORATORIES, LABORATORY, and CLINICAL. The final list of search terms is now

ELECTRONICS	LABORATORIES
MEDICAL ELECTRONICS	LABORATORY
DEVELOPMENT WORK	CLINICAL
MEDICAL PRODUCT	
HEALTH CARE	

The searcher then requests a display of records matching this list of query terms, using the command DISPLAY. Each of the terms is given a weight based on its frequency of usage in the collection, the terms with lowest usage being assigned the highest weight. The document records bearing the highest weights (the document weight is based on the number of its terms matching the query terms and the combined weights of these matching terms) are then displayed, one at a time in descending order of rank, on the screen, until the searcher has seen sufficient items and no longer requests additional items to be displayed.

LEADER, a system developed and operated at Lehigh University, is also based on natural language input and will accept queries in English sentence form. It is described in Chapter Five.

Searching by Other Characteristics

An on-line retrieval system should have the capability of providing access to documents by characteristics other than true subject characteristics. For example, approaches by author, language, name of journal, date, and possibly place of publication, should all be allowed. Some of these (e.g., date, language) might never be used alone, but only in conjunction with other requirements (e.g., LEUKEMIA *and* 1970 *and* SPANISH).

Most systems will allow use of arithmetic as well as boolean operators. The Data Central system, for example, recognizes all the following:

AEQ	Arithmetically equal to
ANEQ	Arithmetically not equal to
LSS	Less than
NLS	Not less than
GTR	Greater than
NGT	Not greater than

In information retrieval systems, such operators are mostly used to effect date restrictions. By using *greater than* and *less than*, for example, we can specify that only documents published within a particular time period should be retrieved.

An important feature of TIP (Mathews, 1967) is the ability to conduct various types of searches on bibliographic citations. The TIP unit record is somewhat unique in that it includes a full bibliographic citation, including institutional affiliation of the authors, and a list of all papers cited by the paper recorded. This allows the conduct of searches by the principle of bibliographic coupling (Kessler, 1963a, b). Two papers are considered to be coupled if they share one or more common references. The strength of the couple increases with the number of shared references. Thus, if paper A has five references in common with paper B, the two papers are bibliographically coupled with a strength of five.

The hypothesis upon which bibliographic coupling is founded is that if two papers share common references, there is a reasonable expectation that they deal with the same subject matter. Moreover, the higher the strength of the couple, the more likely it is that the papers are directly related. If we come to TIP already knowing one or more relevant papers within the data base, or if we use the conventional keyword approach to identify some relevant papers, we can then request that the system should find other papers bibliographically coupled to those we already know to be relevant. The user command

Find share citations with phys rev

v 137, p 1

specifies that any articles should be retrieved that are shown to be coupled bibliographically to the article appearing on the first page of volume 137 of the *Physical Review*.

A search can also be conducted in TIP by a more conventional method called citation tracing. That is, if we know a particular paper to be highly relevant to the subject of our search, we can request retrieval of all papers contained in the TIP data base that cite this earlier paper. The use of citation searching and bibliographic coupling in TIP has been discussed by Alt and Kirsch (1968). Citation searching is also possible in REQUEST, an experimental on-line system developed at the University of Illinois (Carroll, et al., 1968).

Search Languages

In the above discussion we have mentioned several possible approaches to the implementation of an on-line searching system, namely:

1.   Indexed data base using a controlled vocabulary. Searching conducted on controlled terms in formal boolean statements. Example: MEDLINE (ORBIT).

2. Free text data base. Searching conducted by means of formal boolean statements on any natural language terms. Example: Data Central.
3. Indexed data base. Searching conducted by means of queries in English sentence form.
4. Free text data base. Searching conducted by means of queries in English sentence form. Examples: SMART, BROWSER.

Smith and Shoffner (1969) refer to the type of language in which the searcher must use an artificial language, governed by careful rules, as "phrase-structure" languages. "These languages are not 'English-like' and the user must learn new rules in order to use the system. These rules can be kept simple, straightforward and reasonably mnemonic, however, and this minimizes difficulties in learning the system. Languages constructed in this manner, despite their simplicity, are rich enough to incorporate the full range of retrieval capabilities" (p. [1]).

We will discuss the desirable properties of search languages, and the advantages and disadvantages of both controlled vocabularies and natural language, in later chapters.

REFERENCES

Alt, F. L., and R. A. Kirsch (1968). "Citation Searching and Bibliographic Coupling with Remote On-Line Computer Access." *Jour. Res. Nat. Bur. Stand. Sect. B, Math. Sci.* **72B**(1), 61–78.

Burnaugh, H. P. (1967). "The BOLD (Bibliographic On-Line Display) System." *In* G. Schechter (ed.), *Information Retrieval: A Critical Review*. Washington, D.C.: Thompson, pp 53–66.

Carroll, D. E., R. T. Chien, K. C. Kelly, F. P. Preparata, P. Reynolds, S. R. Ray, and F. A. Stahl (1968). *An Interactive Document Retrieval System*. Urbana, Ill.: University of Illinois, Coordinated Science Laboratory, R-398.

Curtice, R. M., and P. E. Jones (1969). *An Operational Interactive Retrieval System*. Cambridge, Mass.: Arthur D. Little.

Giering, R. H. (1972). *This Is Data Central* (*1972 Technical Specifications*). Dayton, Ohio: Data Corporation, DTN-72-2.

Hall, J. L., A. E. Negus, and D. J. Dancy (1972). "On-Line Information Retrieval: A Method of Query Formulation Using a Video Terminal." *Program* **6**(3), 175–186.

Ide, E. (1969). "Relevance Feedback in an Automatic Document Retrieval System." *In* Cornell University, Department of Computer Science, *Information Storage and Retrieval: Scientific Report no. ISR-15 to the National Science Foundation.* (Gerard Salton, Project Director), Ithaca, N.Y.

Ide, E., and G. Salton (1969). "User-Controlled File Organization and Search Strategies." *Proc. Amer. Soc. Information Sci.* **6**, 183–191.

Kessler, M. M. (1963a), "Bibliographic Coupling between Scientific Papers." *Amer. Documentation* **14**(1), 10–25.

Kessler, M. M. (1963b). "Bibliographic Coupling Extended in Time." *Information Storage and Retrieval* **1**(4), 169–187.

Lesk, M. E., and G. Salton (1969). "Interactive Search and Retrieval Methods Using Automatic Information Displays." *AFIPS Conf. Proc. Spring Joint Computer Conf.* **34**, 435–446.

Mathews, W. D. (1967). "The TIP Retrieval System at MIT." *In* G. Schechter (ed.), *Information Retrieval: A Critical Review*. Washington, D.C.: Thompson, pp. 95–108.

National Aeronautics and Space Administration (1966). *NASA/RECON User's Manual*. Washington, D.C.: NASA.

National Aeronautics and Space Administration (1970). *What NASA/RECON Can Do for You*. Washington, D.C.: NASA.

National Library of Medicine (1970). *The Principles of MEDLARS*. Bethesda, Md.: National Library of Medicine.

Pizer, I. H. (1969) "A Regional Medical Library Network." *Bull. Med. Library Assoc.* **57**(2), 101–115.

Porter, R. J., J. K. Penry, and J. F. Caponio (1970). "Epilepsy Abstracts Retrieval System (EARS): A New Concept for Medical Literature Storage and Retrieval." *Proc. Amer. Soc. Information Sci.* **7**, 171–172.

Salton, G. (1968). *Automatic Information Organization and Retrieval*. New York: McGraw-Hill.

Salton, G., ed. (1971). *The SMART Retrieval System: Experiments in Automatic Document Processing*. Englewood Cliffs, N.J.: Prentice-Hall.

Seiden, H. R. (1971). *ORBIT System Information*. Santa Monica, Ca.: System Development Corporation.

Smith, S. F., and R. M. Shoffner (1969). *A Comparative Study of Mechanized Search Languages*. Berkeley. Ca.: University of California, Institute of Library Research.

Summit, R. K. (1968). *Remote Information Retrieval Facility*. Palo Alto, Ca.: Lockheed Missiles & Space Co., NASA CR-1318.

SUPARS (1971). *SUPARS Users Manual*. Syracuse, N.Y.: Syracuse University, School of Library Science.

U.S. Air Force (1970). *CIRCOL User's Guide*. Wright-Patterson Air Force Base, Ohio: U.S. Air Force, Foreign Technology Division, FTD-MP-22-09-70.

Williams, J. H., Jr. (1969). *BROWSER: An Automatic Indexing On-Line Text Retrieval System*. Annual progress report. Gaithersburg, Md.: IBM Federal Systems Division, AD 693 143.

Williams, J. H., Jr., and M. P. Perriens (1968). *Automatic Full Text Indexing and Searching System*. Gaithersburg, Md.: IBM Federal Systems Division.

Chapter Four

File Design
for On-Line Systems

If one were to attempt to give a single characteristic which would distinguish the information storage and retrieval systems that are products of the 1970s from those of the 1960s, it would most likely be the need for quick response. Almost as soon as people started to make widespread use of the information storage and retrieval systems available to them, they made it clear that their need for information was also a need for quick answers—a need for response in real-time. This requirement was undoubtedly a primary motivation behind the evolution of the information storage and retrieval systems of the 1960s into the on-line systems that we have today. Historically, information storage and retrieval systems have always stretched the capabilities of the available computer systems. The huge amounts of data, retrieval requirements, and publication requirements that grew out of efforts to disseminate the stored information to as wide an audience as possible, all have at one time or another forced computer scientists into extending the state-of-the-art of computer technology to meet the demands of the new systems. The movement to on-line information storage and retrieval systems has presented a special challenge. New storage devices, advances in computer communications technology, and new techniques of data base design all had to happen before on-line systems could become a reality. Furthermore, all the new techniques had to be fitted together to result in a smoothly operating system.

The development of any computer system involves three major tasks as a first step:

- The choice of computer and input/output (I/O) capabilities to meet the system requirements.

- Consideration of the physical characteristics and capabilities of the storage media available.
- Design of an effective data base for the system.

The process of accomplishing these three tasks is known as systems design and, for the most part, it is beyond the scope of this book. *Design of Real-Time Computer Systems* by Martin (1967) is an excellent source for the reader who is interested in the techniques of designing on-line computer systems. The operational details of the hardware used for the storage devices and computer communications equipment is also beyond our scope. Another work by Martin (1969), entitled *Telecommunications and the Computer*, is suggested for the reader who is interested in these aspects of computer systems. Because the characteristics of the various storage devices are essentially machine-dependent (e.g., IBM disk storage bears only some similarity to Honeywell disk storage), the manuals published by the manufacturers and the various trade journals are the best sources in this area. Furthermore, storage device technology is advancing so rapidly that an exhaustive discussion of storage device characteristics would be out of date almost before it could be written. The one remaining area, that of data base design for on-line information storage and retrieval systems, is the subject of this chapter. We have attempted, in the following pages, to describe at some length the basic concepts of file and data base design and to illustrate how these techniques are applied in the design of on-line information storage and retrieval systems.

Basics

There are three major factors that must be considered in designing the data base for any computerized on-line retrieval system:

- The types and amount of data to be stored and retrieved.
- The logical arrangement of the data elements with respect to themselves, to the user, and to the system.
- The techniques by which the data are to be stored and retrieved.

It will be helpful at this point to define a few terms. We shall use the term *data base* to mean a collection of information that is organized in a meaningful manner. *Data base structure*, then, is the organization of the information in the data collection to show the established logical relationships among the various types of data. The complete specification of the data base for a system involves precise definition of the kinds of information to be stored in the system, the relationships of the various types of data to each other and to the system, and the physical organization of the information within the computer system. The technique of providing this specification for a particular application is known as *data base design*.

As has been noted above, the data to be stored and retrieved by the computer system contribute significantly to the design of the system. For example, there are a number of items of information (data) associated with each document that is to be referenced in the system. There may also be data associated with the vocabulary required to support subject indexing, searching, and so forth. There will undoubtedly be data elements that are needed only by the computer system itself in order to perform as required. These items all taken together form the total data collection. It is obvious that for a large system this collection of data is much too large and unwieldy to be handled all together, and therefore, as a first step, the total data collection must be broken up into manageable chunks of information. The usual designation for such a chunk of information is the *record*. A *record* is defined as a collection of related data elements, items, or codes that are logically treated as a unit. For a typical document storage and retrieval system, then, one type of record that would exist is a record for the document. This record would be a collection of all the information about a document that is required by the system, e.g., its title, authors, date of publication, cataloging information, subject terms, and any other information that is required to support the system. Meadow (1967) is a good source for more detailed information in this area.

Usually, one record is established for each document to be referenced in the system. In some systems, the records may actually consist of the entire text of the document, as for example, an abstract, newspaper article, telegram, diplomatic communique, or other brief item. Note, however, that the *one record–one document* premise does not necessarily mean that there would be a single record for each distinct physical item in the collection. For example, there could be only one record for a book-in-part or monographic series, even though there might be several distinct items involved. Furthermore, there could be individual records for each article in a journal issue or for each report in a series. In any case, it is obvious that one of the first tasks facing the data base designer is to determine the various classes of items for which records are to be established in the system. Remember also that in addition to the records for the various kinds of documents, most systems will require records for vocabulary terms, cross-references, hierarchical listings, and any other authoritative items required by the system.

Record Structures

For each type of record identified as being required by the system, a *record structure* must be devised to hold all the information that is to be contained in each record. For example, records for documents would contain title information, author names, cataloging data, subject terms, and similar data, while records for vocabulary terms would contain the name of the term, any use restrictions, cross-reference information, and so on. The individual pieces of information that make up the records are variously called *data elements*, *fields*, or *subfields*. We shall use the term *field* throughout this chapter to mean a logically complete unit of information such as an author's name, a title, subject terms, or other data in the record. These fields have several properties which should be examined in more detail.

Length.   Fields may be *fixed* or *variable* in length; e.g., a field for "date of publication" would be fixed if the date information were always represented as a series of six digits for month, day, and year (e.g., 060572) or variable if the field permitted values such as "Summer–Fall 1972" or "March 15, 1970." A few systems permit only fields of fixed length. In such a case, a field length is chosen which is the maximum likely to occur. When the data occupies less space, the remainder of the field is usually padded with blanks.

Occurrence.   Fields may be *singly occurring* or *multiply occurring*. For example, a document is likely to have only one date of publication, so the date field would be singly occurring. However, a document might have more than one author, so the author field would be multiply occurring. Some data base systems do not permit multiply occurring fields, and for these some other technique must be used. For example, several separate author fields, Author-1, Author-2, Author-3, can be used to enter as many names as are required for the document.

Presence in the Record.   Some fields must be present in the record for every occurrence of a record in the system, i.e., they are *required* fields. Others may or may not be present, depending on the document. An example of a required field might be the accession number or other unique identifier for the document. An example of a nonrequired field might be "supplementary title"; i.e., there will be many documents in the system that will have no supplementary title information and thus there will be no data to enter in this field. Some systems allocate space in the storage medium for all fields in a record structure and require that a maximum size be established for them, whether all fields actually contain data or not. Others only allocate space as needed.

The term *subfield* will be used in this chapter to designate the smallest logical element of information in a record that can be retrieved, modified, or otherwise accessed. Note that this is not meant to exclude retrieval via a string processor in which one or more characters or other bits of information smaller than a subfield can be retrieved. Subfields may be used when the system requires information that is normally considered a logical unit, such as an author's name, to be still further subdivided. In most systems, for example, the author names are entered in multiply occurring fields. The names appear exactly as they will be used for retrieval, printing in a publication or on catalog cards, or any other system output. But some systems specify that the author name shall be further divided into parts, i.e., patronymic, Christian or given, honorifics, and so forth. Thus, a name like "Sir Winston Churchill" might be stored as one field; e.g., CHURCHILL, WINSTON, SIR, all in one author field, or it might be stored in three fields; e.g., CHURCHILL | WINSTON | SIR.* The point of all this is that the data base designer must not only identify all the pieces of information which must be a part of each record, but must also decide how it is to be arranged within the record structure to meet the retrieval, publication, and any other requirements imposed by the system.

As with fields, records may be fixed or variable in length. If all the records for a particular application (e.g., all document records) have the same number of fields, the fields occur the same number of times, and the data stored in the fields is always less than or equal to some maximum previously determined length, then the records will have fixed length. Records will be of variable length if any of the following are true:

- Some fields may occur more times in one record than another.
- Some fields may be absent from a record.
- The data in the fields have no maximum length established (except possibly a physical limitation such as the amount of data that will fit on one track of a disk).

Once a record structure has been devised which meets both the user and system requirements, the next step is to organize the records into collections that the system can handle. Records are generally grouped into collections of similar records, such as all the records for journal articles or all the records for vocabulary terms. These collections of similar records are called *files*. Some typical files that might be used in an on-line storage and retrieval system are

- Various document files
- User profiles
- Vocabulary terms
- Vocabulary cross-references
- Vocabulary hierarchical structure
- Search strategies

There are many, many ways in which the records can be organized within such files, and the remainder of this chapter is devoted to this topic.

---

*Note that this raises another problem: Should the punctuation which will be needed in printing be stored in the fields or generated at publication time?

File Organization

There are several operations involving files that the computer system must be able to perform regardless of the data contained in the file:

- Specification of the file; e.g., how big it is, how big the records are, where the file is to be stored, how the records are to be stored in the file, and how the records are to be accessed.
- Addition of records to the file.
- Modification or retrieval of records within the file.
- Deletion of records from the file.
- Deletion of the file from the system.

Some systems also permit the file specification to be modified; that is, fields may be added to the record structure, fields may be deleted from the record structure, or the record structure may be otherwise modified. Other systems require that the old file be deleted from the system and a new file having the desired properties be created. Because of the complexity of these operations and because most users have similar sets of file-handling requirements, the computer manufacturers very often provide the software needed to perform these basic file-handling operations. Usually each manufacturer permits several different types of file organization for a particular piece of hardware such as an IBM 360/50 or a CDC 6400. The different file organizations permitted are basically distinguished by the way the records are physically stored in the system and the way in which the records may be retrieved.

At this point, let us define a few more terms that will be useful in the discussions which follow. Let us distinguish between *storage media* and *storage devices*: The storage media are the physical materials on which the information is actually stored, e.g., magnetic tapes, punched paper tapes, punched cards, disk packs, film strips, etc. The storage devices are the hardware units that physically control the reading and writing of data on the storage media. Some typical storage devices are magnetic tape drives, disk drives, magnetic drums, and data cells. The storage devices and storage media together permit two basic techniques of accessing the information that is stored. These are *sequential access* and *direct access*. Sequential access means that the storage device is capable only of processing records in sequential fashion; that is, records must be read from the file or written on the file in sequential order. This is the only type of access possible when magnetic or punched paper tapes are used as the storage medium. Direct access means that a single record can be read from the file or written on the file without affecting any other records. Some examples of storage media which permit direct access of the data are disk packs, magnetic core storage, and drum storage devices. These storage devices are engineered so that they can be instructed to locate the starting point of the data that is to be stored or read from the storage medium. The user supplies the location of the data, i.e., the direct address of the data, and the hardware device then locates that point and processes the data. Note that the characteristics of the storage media and hardware devices control, to a certain extent, the types of file organizations that can be supported in a particular system.

Now that we have examined the physical means of storing and accessing files, we turn our attention to some software, or logical, aspects of file organization. On-line information storage and retrieval systems generally require on-line access to the data base for retrieval purposes at the very least. Some systems require that on-line update of the data base also be supported, but this requirement creates special problems which are really beyond the scope of this book. We shall limit the file design considerations presented in this chapter to those systems with a requirement for on-line retrieval, and with a data base stored on disk or some other direct-access storage device.

Retrieval is generally accomplished using one or more *keys* which may be logically manipulated. Flores (1970) defines a key as a field or a set of fields which identifies a record. The key serves two purposes: It determines the order in which the records are entered in the file, and it is used to find a record in the file that has a prescribed identifier. The key is composed of information that is contained in the records themselves. Flores points out that in many applications the key that is used to determine the order in which the records are entered in the file (e.g., accession number) and the key that is used to search the file are identical. As indicated above, the accession number, or some other unique identifying number assigned to each document as it is processed, is very often used to determine the order in which the records are logically arranged in the file, and it may also be used as a unique identifier for retrieving a particular record from the file. Other keys that could be used are subject terms, author names, date of publication, language, and so forth. Note, however, that the identifying number key has a special place in the system. This is because of its uniqueness; that is, there is a one-to-one correspondence between the list of numbers and the collection of document records. This means that the record for any document in the system can be retrieved by specifying only its unique identifying number. As we shall see, this feature is important to the timely and efficient retrieval of document records in an on-line system.

It is necessary at this point to note the difference between the *name* of a field (e.g., author, subject index terms) and the *value* of the field (e.g., Irving, Clifford; drug therapy). The records in the system which contain the same value in a particular field form a subset of the entire data base, or a *partition*. Lefkovitz (1969), for example, defines a key as a single file partition or *list*. Thus, every record in the file that contains a particular value for a field is a member of the file partition characterized by that key. One such partition, for instance, might be formed by all the documents in the system that were indexed using the term HEART; another such list is formed by all the documents indexed using the term DRUG THERAPY, and so forth.

Traditionally, two logical file organization techniques have been used in information storage and retrieval systems applications. These are the *linear*, or *sequential*, and *inverted* file organizations. They are still probably the most widely used of all the file structures in information systems applications, although several others are being used to meet special requirements in some systems.

Linear Files

A linear or sequential file is organized such that each record in the file is logically adjacent to the preceding record in the file. For example, if the records are to be entered in the file in order by accession number, the record for accession number 9743 would logically fall between the records for accession number 9742 and accession number 9744. If the linear file is also a *sequential file*, this implies that the records are physically arranged in the storage media in the same order as their logical sequence, as shown here:

$$\vdots$$

#9742
Document
Record

#9743
Document
Record

#9744
Document
Record

#9745
Document
Record

$$\vdots$$

In this example, the accession number has been chosen as the key for ordering the file. Records may also be stored sequentially without the use of any key at all. For example, in a system that handles telegrams and other diplomatic communiques, the records might simply be entered sequentially in the file in the order of their arrival. In either case, the important thing is that in a *sequentially ordered file,* the logical order of the records and the physical order of the records in the file are the same.

The major advantage of a sequentially organized file is that it is easy and quick to retrieve a number of records in sequence. Furthermore, it is relatively easy to determine if a particular record is present in the system by performing a binary search of the file using the key.

The disadvantages of sequentially organized files are associated with maintenance of the files and searches for particular values in fields other than the key. Let us consider the file maintenance problems first. Because the records are stored physically adjacent to each other in the storage medium, if a record must be inserted between two existing records, they must be "pushed apart" to make room for the new record. This requires recopying the entire file in order to make room for the new record. By the same token, when records are to be deleted from the file, the remaining records must be pushed together so that there are no gaps between records. This operation also requires that the file be recopied. Furthermore, if any changes are to be made to an individual record that will result in a new record that is longer or shorter than the old record, the file will have to be copied in order to allow for the change. Several techniques have been devised to overcome these problems; one method is to add new records to the end of the file as they are encountered and maintain a list of records that are to be deleted and any other changes to the file. Then all the necessary changes are made during a batch update of the file, requiring only one recopying operation to accommodate all the changes.

The major disadvantage of searching sequential files lies in the fact that each and every record in the file must be examined if the search involves a field which is not the key for the file. As can be imagined, this is a very time-consuming operation if the files are large. Batch-mode operating systems are sometimes able to use sequential files efficiently for searching, anyway, because a large number of searches are collected and processed all at one time. Under this mode of operation, each record is examined to see if it satisfies any one of the requirements of any of the search strategies that are being processed. This technique results in acceptable processing time for the batch of searches, although it would be exorbitant for a single search. Of course, such a technique is not at all suited to on-line use unless the files are small enough so that the search can be performed in a relatively short time. For example, there are some systems, such as SHOEBOX, developed by the Mitre Corporation, that search the text files on-line in a sequential fashion; but these systems do not try to search a very large collection of information at once.

One way to circumvent the large amount of time required to search a sequential file is to create other sequential files in the system that are ordered on other keys or fields that might be useful for retrieval. But this technique requires that if n sequentially ordered files are created for a basic set of records, the system now requires n times as much storage. Furthermore, the file maintenance problem is made more complex because, with this scheme, if a file or record is to be modified, all the other files in which the record occurs must also be maintained.

List Organization

To avoid some of these difficulties, linear files can also be produced using a *list organization*. The list organization technique permits the logical arrangement of records (such as those in a linear file) and the physical arrangement of those records to be entirely independent. This is possible because the list organization allows the location of the next record in the logical sequence to be indicated by a pointer which is kept with the preceding record in the sequence. This pointer may be any indicator which shows the location of the next record and which will allow the accessing mechanism to retrieve it directly. For example, the following is a list of four terms from a hypothetical vocabulary:

HEART

HEART DISEASE

HEART SURGERY

HEART THERAPY

The logical order of the terms in this list is alphabetical, and let us assume that the linear file in which the records for these terms are to be stored is to be in alphabetical order as well. The four term records then are stored in locations 1, 50, 27, and 100. Location 1 has been chosen quite arbitrarily in this example, and any other would do just as well. The list organization of these records requires that the records contain a pointer to the location of the next record as well as all the information that would normally appear in the record for the term. The four term records and their associated pointers are:

Loc	Record	Pointer
1	HEART	50
50	HEART DISEASE	27
27	HEART SURGERY	100
100	HEART THERAPY	0

Note that the pointer value is zero for the last record in the file.

It is obvious that there are many keys associated with records for documents that could be used to produce a logically ordered listing of the document collection; that is, ordered lists could be produced on such fields as author name, accession number, report number, and so forth. List organizations permit a record to be a member of as many lists as desired. Therefore, all the probable search fields could be selected as keys for creating various lists of documents in the collection. The records could be sequenced logically using each of these keys. The advantage of list structures over sequential organization of the files now becomes obvious, because only one copy of the records is required using a list structuring technique to support all the various ordered lists. Let us return to the example of the four vocabulary terms. Suppose the terms have postings as follows:

HEART	5000
HEART DISEASE	3500
HEART SURGERY	2500
HEART THERAPY	4000

Suppose that in addition to the alphabetical listing of the terms we also want to list them in order by the number of postings, with the highest number first. We then have two lists as shown below:

List 1		List 2	
HEART	50	5000	100
HEART DISEASE	27	4000	50
HEART SURGERY	100	3500	27
HEART THERAPY	0	2500	0

Note that the information for all the lists can be carried with the term records by adding as many sets of pointers as are required.

This leads to a second advantage of list structures over sequential files; because there is now only one copy of each record in the system, if a record is to be updated, there is only one copy of the record to change.

Addition and deletion of records in a list organization is easy, too. Records are inserted in the list by (*a*) changing the pointer of the record preceding the record to be added to show the location of the new record, and (*b*) carrying the pointer to the next succeeding record in the pointer area of the new record. For example, suppose the term HEART ATTACK, located at 75, is to be added to our list of four terms. The new list then appears as shown below:

Old List		New List	
HEART	50	HEART	75
HEART DISEASE	27	HEART ATTACK	50
HEART SURGERY	100	HEART DISEASE	27
HEART THERAPY	0	HEART SURGERY	100
		HEART THERAPY	0

Deletion involves replacing the pointers to the record deleted with the pointer to the next succeeding record. For example, if HEART SURGERY is to be removed, the following list will result:

HEART	75
HEART ATTACK	50
HEART DISEASE	100
HEART THERAPY	0

Deletion and addition of records are more complicated when the records are members of more than one list, because all the pointers must be modified. Deletion, in particular, requires that all the preceding records be located and their pointers changed. To aid in this process, some systems carry pointers both to the next succeeding and last preceding records for each record in the file.

Inverted Files

As was noted earlier in this chapter, the files in the system may be partitioned by grouping together all those records that have in common a particular value in a specific field. This partitioning capability is the basis for the *inverted file* or *inverted list* organization. The partitioning results in the file being broken up into collections of records, all of which have some common value; e.g., HEART TRANSPLANT used as a subject index term. This is called a *subfile*. An inverted file is created by establishing a collection of subfiles consisting of all the file partitions that are generated by grouping records that have some field value in common. Usually, one inverted file is established for each field which is desired as a major retrieval element in the system. Candidates might be subject index terms, author names, language, date of publication, and so forth.

Some of the early versions of inverted files used the *values* of the various fields that were being used to build the subfiles as *indexes* to the files. The inverted file for subject index terms, for example, used the various vocabulary terms as the index and stored the accession numbers or some other unique identifier for the document records with the vocabulary terms, as shown below:

HEART   #1045, #1047, #3026, #3085, . . .
HEART DISEASE   #3026, #4427, #6035, . . .

We see that this organization has two very important advantages.

1. Since all the terms in the records also appear in the index or list, they can then be deleted from the records, resulting in a saving of storage space.

2. Since the accession numbers to all the documents are stored with the index, boolean search logic can be evaluated using these numbers before any records are actually retrieved from the storage media.

Dodd (1969) points out that a totally inverted list organization, i.e., one in which there is an inverted list built for each data element in the system, makes every data item available for retrieval. But this organization does require a *dictionary* or *directory* containing all the data values in the system and the addresses of all locations where those values occur. The resulting dictionary may be as large as or larger than the data itself. The major advantage of this type of organization is that it allows access to all the data in the system with equal ease. However, there is a penalty for all this ease of retrieval, namely, storing and maintenance of the data is more cumbersome than with other organizations because the large dictionaries must be maintained as well. Dodd suggests that a file organization which provides the advantage of list organization without the disadvantages of a totally inverted file structure can be produced by combining a list organization with a random or sequential file organization. Then inverted lists or files can be created for the fields which are most frequently searched, and the sequential or random files of the records themselves can be searched if data from other fields are needed. In actuality, instead of a pure random or sequential file organization, an *indexed sequential organization* is often used. Indexed sequential files have the property that the records may be accessed either by the use of an index or in a sequential mode. For example, the document records could be sequenced by accession number and the list of numbers then used as an index to the sequential file in which the records are stored. This technique has an advantage over random file organization in that it permits records of variable length to be stored adjacent to one another. This results in a considerable saving in space over the usual random file organization which requires fixed-length records. It has advantages over pure sequential organization, because records can be accessed without involving other records and because it simplifies many of the update and maintenance problems that are characteristic of sequential files.

Let us turn now to an example. Assume that we have a document collection of 10,000 items and that we want to provide, as a minimum, subject retrieval for that collection. The first step would be to establish a record for each of the 10,000 items and then to structure these records into a data base that will provide the desired retrieval capabilities. At the very least, then, we would want to establish an inverted file on subject index terms. There would then be a dictionary or directory which has an entry for each subject index term that appears in at least one record for a document. Associated with these entries are pointers to the records in which the term is used. If the document records are stored in an indexed sequential file, this pointer might be the accession number of the document. This value then is used in a subsequent dictionary lookup operation to get the actual address of the desired record. The following is a representation of the inverted file for our example:

HEART
575
1034
6045
9374

HEART DISEASE
1034
5043
7799
9374

HEART SURGERY
575
5043
6565

Note that all the evaluations of a search expression involving subject index terms for this data base can now be performed using just the dictionary entries; that is, no access to the storage devices need be made until after a count of the total number of documents satisfying the query has been derived. This count can then be displayed on-line to the user. He may next request that some of the records be displayed, or he may decide that the search strategy he used was too narrow or too broad and revise it. If he decides that he wants to see some of the records, only then are the records retrieved from the storage device.

To summarize the foregoing, let us briefly examine the computer actions that would take place when a retrieval operation such as "find all the documents about heart transplants written by Christian Barnard" is to be performed. If the document record file is linear, the entire document file must be read into core one at a time to see if any document record contains "Christian Barnard" in the author field and "HEART TRANSPLANT" in one of the subject index term fields. The author field is examined first to see if the desired value is present. If it is, the subject term fields are examined one at a time to see if "HEART TRANSPLANT" is present. If neither condition is met or if one condition is met, but not both, the record is passed over and the next record is read into core for processing. If the desired qualifications are met, the record is declared a *hit* and is written out, either to tape or disk for subsequent display, or it is immediately displayed at the user's terminal as it is found. Note that the entire file must be passed in order to generate a total *hit count* and in order to retrieve all the records. If a *list structure* is used, the list for author may be examined to determine those records (if any) which were authored by Christian Barnard. If any are found, those records and only those records need be retrieved for further examination. These then may either be read in from the sequential file (if a linear organization is used) or selected from the random file (if a random storage device is used) and only these records are checked for the presence of the term "HEART TRANSPLANT." As above, hits are declared as they are found, but no total hit count can be derived until all the candidate records are processed. If the document records are arranged using an inverted file, the inverted file for author and subject term must be checked. The entry (or entries) under "Christian Barnard" in the author file will be compared with the entries under "HEART TRANSPLANT" in the subject term file. If any agree, they are declared hits. Note that with this organization, the total hit count can be found at once, because when all the entries under "Christian Barnard" and "HEART TRANSPLANT" have been compared, the process is complete. If a pure inverted file organization has been used, i.e., the records themselves appear with the appropriate entries in the inverted file, they are immediately available for display to the user. If an *inverted list organization* has been used, the address of the records that are hits must still be found either using the accession number directory or a dictionary lookup for the accession number so that the records can be retrieved for display to the user. Note that retrieval using multidirectories, as is the case with a fully inverted list structured file, is exactly the same as for an inverted file, except that the actual records are not available at the time the search logic is evaluated. The records themselves are retrieved as the last step of the query process.

Flores (1970) has compared the efficiency of the various file organizations for searching in terms of the number of *looks* the system must make in order to find a particular item in the system. To return to our example, assume that our document collection of 10,000 items (D) has been indexed using an average of eight terms per document (T). Then there are 80,000 items of subject information in the data base ($n = D \times T$). Assume that the subject term directory contains P terms with an average of Q entries per term. Note that $P \times Q = n$. On the average, a linear search would require that we look halfway through a sequential file of the document records to find the one indexed using the terms HEART DISEASE and HEART THERAPY. Thus, on the average, the number of looks to find the right record is $D/2 \times T/2$, or $n/4$, looks. On the average, a search of a random file of the document records would require the same number of looks.

A directory search over a fully inverted file structure yields the following figures: On the average we must look halfway through the directory to find each of the desired items HEART DISEASE or HEART THERAPY, or

P/2. Then we must look, on the average, halfway through each list of directory entries to find a document record that is indexed using both terms, or Q/2. Thus, the total number of looks is $(P/2 + P/2) + (Q/2 + Q/2)$ or $P + Q$ looks. Let us put some numbers in. Assume that there are 1000 subject index terms, or $P = 1000$, and that the average utilization per term is 80, or $Q = 80$. We conclude that, for our example, a linear or random search would require n/4, or 20,000, looks on the average. The directory search would require $P + Q$, or 1080, looks. Flores has shown that when P and Q, i.e., the number of entries in the directory and the number of postings for each entry, are equal to $\sqrt{n}$, the number of looks is minimized. For example, our document collection of 10,000 items with eight postings should have about 280 index terms with an average of 280 postings per term in order to optimize the searching. Note that this result of Flores has implications for the size of vocabularies used in retrieval systems. He has shown that the number of postings per term and the number of terms should be about equal for maximum efficiency in searching. Unfortunately, the great majority of retrieval systems have very different characteristics, with many terms and few postings to any one term.

Recall that the discussion of inverted files suggested that there could be inverted files not only for subject terms, but also for any other frequently searched fields such as author, language, date of publication, and so forth. In a system using directories or inverted files on more than one field, the number of looks required to isolate the desired record can be further reduced. Flores has also shown that the number of looks is minimized when the number of directories, the number of entries in the directories, and the number of postings under each entry in the directories are all about equal in size. It is rarely possible to achieve this in practice, but it is a useful figure for the system designer to keep in mind when structuring the data base for a new system.

Clustered File Organization

Salton (1972) has mentioned another alternative to the inverted file structure. Salton calls his technique a *clustered* file organization. This results in documents and records which have similar sets of subject terms being grouped together into clusters. Each *cluster* is identified by a representative cluster profile. This profile is a set of weighted terms representative of the document records included in the corresponding cluster. The file then consists of a number of cluster profiles, or *profile vectors*, and subject terms for the documents that are members of each cluster. Salton reports that a search in such a clustered file is carried out first by comparing each query with the file of profile vectors. For profiles which exhibit a sufficiently high similarity with the query, the individual document vectors (subject indexing terms) are examined next and the document citations are ranked for output purposes in decreasing query–document similarity order. Then the clusters of documents are retrieved in a single access per cluster from the storage medium.

Salton concludes that the clustered file organization is more economical of storage and permits more flexibility in searching than the inverted file organization. Further, it permits gradual restructuring of the file to reflect changes in user interest and provides a method for gradually transferring infrequently used document records out of the most active portion of the file into some auxiliary area which may be accessed if necessary but would not normally be searched. Salton is very critical of inverted files, because such structures do not readily permit the implementation of systems that allow partial matches between documents and queries and thus allow the ranking of search output.

In summary, this chapter has attempted to present an introduction to some of the many aspects of file and data base design. It has shown how the data in a system is organized into logical and physical chunks that the computer can process. The data, in order of increasing amount, can be referenced by bit, byte, alphameric character, word, field, record, block, file, and data base. We have discussed some of the fundamental techniques of organizing these data and designing the data base for the system, and we have reviewed some commonly used file organization techniques.

One of the difficult aspects of data base design and file design is that the whole area is extremely application-dependent, and a requirement which is engraved in stone in one system or for one application may be utterly immaterial in another. The data base designer must try to gather all the information available about the requirements to be imposed on the system and then must try to derive an optimal file and data base structure to support them. For further information on current trends in data base design, the reader is referred to McLaughlin (1972), Patterson (1972), and Schubert (1972).

REFERENCES

Dodd, G. G. (1969). "Elements of Data Management Systems." *Computing Surveys* 1 (2), 117–133.

Flores, I. (1970). *Data Structure and Management.* Englewood Cliffs, N.J.: Prentice-Hall.

Lefkovitz, D. (1969). *File Structures for On-Line Systems.* New York: Spartan.

McLaughlin, R. A. (1972). "Building a Data Base." *Datamation* 18 (7), 51–57.

Martin, J. T. (1967). *Design of Real-Time Computer Systems.* Englewood Cliffs, N.J.: Prentice-Hall.

Martin, J. T. (1969). *Telecommunications and the Computer*. Englewood Cliffs, N.J.: Prentice-Hall.

Meadow, C. T. (1967). *The Analysis of Information Systems*. New York: Wiley.

Patterson, A. C. (1972). "Data Base Hazards." *Datamation* **18** (7), 48–50.

Salton, G. (1972). "Dynamic Document Processing." *Commun. ACM* (July), 658–668.

Schubert, R. F. (1972). "Basic Concepts of Data Base Management Systems." *Datamation* **18** (7), 42–47.

Chapter Five

Some Notes on Existing On-Line Systems

Cuadra (1971) has estimated that there are at least 150 on-line systems that are capable of bibliographic search and retrieval. Most of these are general-purpose data management systems, but there are many designed specifically for retrieval of bibliographic data. We will describe some of the more important or interesting of these systems here. Some are fully operational in the sense that they already provide a service to a group of real users, while others are purely experimental at the present time. One or two are no longer in operation, but have been included because of various interesting features. Some commercially available services are included, as well as systems designed and operated by individual institutions. The purpose of this chapter is to provide a guide to major on-line retrieval systems, and retrieval experiments, existing in 1973. Brief details only are presented but, whenever possible, references to sources of further information are provided. Some of the systems are referred to, for illustrative purposes, throughout this book.

A survey of five on-line systems was produced by Welch (1968). The most comprehensive survey of on-line systems for bibliographic retrieval was prepared by Seiden (1970) of the System Development Corporation for the National Library of Medicine. Seiden's report includes tables summarizing the technical features, search capabilities, and on-line operating characteristics of eleven bibliographic retrieval systems. A further review of eight document processing systems including five that are on-line was prepared by Fong (1971) for the National Bureau of Standards. In 1972, the National Science Foundation awarded a grant to the Institute for Communication

Research, Stanford University, to undertake a comparison of the features and capabilities of the major systems existing for on-line, interactive bibliographic search.

New developments in on-line systems are occurring very rapidly. Portions of this book will become outdated rather quickly. This is particularly true of the system descriptions in this chapter. However, no guide to a large number of such systems now exists, and we feel that this broad survey will be of some value.

AIM–TWX

AIM–TWX (*Abridged Index Medicus* by Teletypewriter Exchange Network) was initiated by the National Library of Medicine (NLM) in 1970. The original data base comprised all MEDLARS citations for articles from 100 key journals in clinical medicine (i.e., those journals indexed in *Abridged Index Medicus*), but was later expanded to cover 122 journals. The collection covers material back to 1965 and is updated on a monthly basis. This data base, which comprised about 180,000 items early in 1972, was loaded on an IBM 360/67 computer at the System Development Corporation (SDC) offices in Santa Monica, Ca., and could be accessed through the TWX network or via the telephone network, using any of several possible terminals. In April 1972, the file was loaded on an IBM 370/155 and became accessible through the TYMSHARE network. Access by TWX was discontinued.

The searching system by which the AIM–TWX service was implemented was a version of ORBIT (which see) to which SDC added certain further capabilities to meet special requirements of MEDLARS searching. This modified version of ORBIT was named ELHILL (after the Lister Hill National Center for Biomedical Communications).

The AIM–TWX service has been used experimentally by many medical centers in the United States since 1970 and has been received with considerable enthusiasm. As of January 1972 there were about 61 institutions making regular use of the service, including hospitals as well as medical schools. In 1971, the ELHILL (ORBIT) system was adopted for the full on-line implementation of MEDLARS (MEDLINE). The system has been described by Katter and McCarn (1971).

Operating experience has been presented by Moll (1971) and by Stiller (1970), and an evaluation of a sample of searches has been presented by Lancaster (1972). This experience will be summarized in Chapter Nine. The system has been applied in the support of information services directed explicitly at problems of patient care. For example, Blase and Stock (1972) have described the use of AIM–TWX in an experimental cancer information service.

BASIS-70

BASIS (Battelle Automated Search Information System) was developed at the Columbus Laboratories of Battelle Memorial Institute for use with a CDC 6400 computer. The system is capable of supporting up to sixty users simultaneously. It allows searching of free text or of indexed data bases and will accept search strategies in conventional boolean form. For free text searching, word proximity indicators may be used. The system can be queried remotely, via telephone lines, using teletype or CRT terminals at speeds from 10 to 400 characters per second.

As of December 1971, approximately thirty files were currently being used on BASIS-70, including a 5000 item file on copper technology operated by the Copper Data Center on behalf of the Copper Development Association and a defense metals file operated for the Metals and Ceramics Information Center. One of the newest and most challenging applications is for the U.S. Price Commission, where various types of information and data are made available to the commission's personnel to assist them in their day-to-day work. Daily updates to the Price Commission's files are made due to the commission's pressing need for the most current information.

Some much larger data bases were added to the system later. These included, in 1973, the data base of the National Technical Information Service (NTIS) and the Chemical Abstracts *Condensates* (CHEMCON) data base of the Chemical Abstracts Service. These files can be accessed through the Tymshare* network.

Like RECON (which see) in its original form, BASIS-70 does not allow direct entry of term strings with boolean connectives. Terms can only be entered one at a time so that they can be individually accepted. Later, a logical statement, in which line numbers representing the desired terms are combined using boolean operators, may be constructed. Figure 5.1 illustrates a simple search sequence based on a file of abstracts from the Cold Climatic Information Center (CCIC) which deals with the ecology of Alaska. This sequence was photographed from a Control Data Corporation (CDC) 214 high-speed terminal screen. A BASIS-70 user guide is available (Battelle Memorial Institute, 1971). The system has been described by Fried (1971).

---

*Tymshare Inc., a California corporation, offers a data communication network, based on leased telephone lines, to support remote-access, interactive, time-sharing computer services.

```
        B A S I S    7 0
  (PHASE I)
IS ON LINE
DO YOU DESIRE OPERATING INSTRUCTIONS
TYPE YES OR NO/                                        ▲
NO▲                                                    ▲
PLEASE ENTER YOUR LAST NAME. /                         ▲
PENNIMAN▲                                              ▲
ENTER THE NAME OF DATA BASE TO BE SEARCHED.
  /                                                    ▲
CCIC▲                                                  ▲
ENTER YOUR SEARCH ONE TERM AT A TIME.
  1/                                                   ▲
FISH▲                                                  ▲
    135 ITEMS
  2/                                                   ▲
AQUATIC LIFE▲                                          ▲
    144 ITEMS
  3/                                                   ▲
█-------------------------------------------------
```

(*a*)

```
                                                       ▲
GULF OF ALASKA▲
    35 ITEMS                                           ▲
  4/                                                   ▲
(LIST ALL)▲
  ITEMS-NO.-LINE---
*** 135    1/FISH
*** 144    2/AQUATIC LIFE
*** 35     3/GULF OF ALASKA
ENTER YOUR REQUEST
  4/                                                   ▲
(1 OR 2 AND 3)▲                                        ▲
    17 ITEMS
ENTER YOUR REQUEST
  5/                                                   ▲
█-------------------------------------------------
```

(*b*)

Figure 5.1. Illustration of a search sequence on BASIS-70. The connect time in this sample search is very great in relation to central processing time and peripheral processing time, because of the delay necessitated in photographing the images. Under normal circumstances this search would require a connect time of only 5–10 minutes. Reproduced by permission of Battelle Memorial Institute.

```
(DISPLAY 4)
THE DATA ELEMENTS FOR THE CCIC DATA BASE ARE
 1-ACCESSION NUMBER,
 2-AUTHOR(S),
 3-TITLE,
 4-BIBLIOGRAPHIC DATA,
 5-INDEX TERMS,
 6-ABSTRACT.
   WHAT FIELDS DO YOU WANT TO SEE⩾
ENTER FIELD NUMBERS SEPARATED BY COMMAS OR ALL
 /
 3,2,4,6
THIS PRINTOUT COULD BE LENGTHY.
HOW MANY DO YOU WANT TO SEE FIRST⩾
 /
 1_____
```

(c)

```
                -
ITEMS FROM THE CCIC DATA BASE ARE .....
                -
ITEM   1 -
   ACCESSION NUMBER IS: 4425 -
   TITLE IS:  MIDWATER TRAWLING STUDIES IN T-
   HE NORTH PACIFIC.    -
   AUTHOR(S):  WILLIAM ARON         -
   BIBLIOGRAPHIC DATA: LIMNOLOGY AND OCEANO-
     GRAPHY, VOL. 4/4, PP 409-418, 1959, ILLU-
     S., MAPS, TABS., 11 REFS.      -
   ABSTRACT :       A MODIFIED VERSION OF THE-
     ISAACS-KIDD MIDWATER TRAWL WAS USED FOR-
     149 EXPLORATORY HAULS IN THE NORTHWASTE-
     RN PACIFIC AT DEPTHS RANG ING FROM 20 TO-
     250 METERS.  CATCHES ARE DISCUSSED IN T-
     ERMS OF SUCH FACTORS AS DIURNAL MIGRATIO-
     N, SEASONAL VARIATION, PATCHINESS, AND G-
     EOGRAPHIC VARIATION.  THERE WAS WIDE DIF
   _____
```

(d)

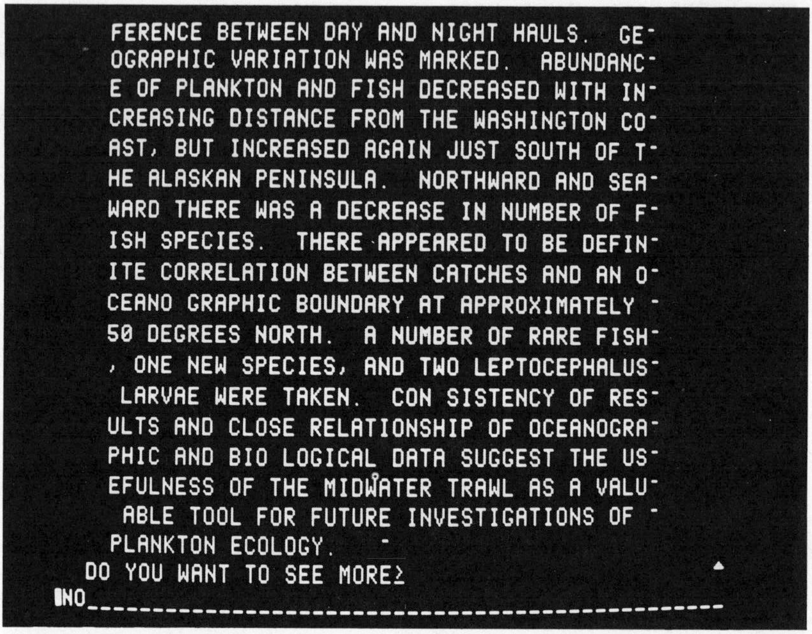
FERENCE BETWEEN DAY AND NIGHT HAULS. GE-
OGRAPHIC VARIATION WAS MARKED. ABUNDANC-
E OF PLANKTON AND FISH DECREASED WITH IN-
CREASING DISTANCE FROM THE WASHINGTON CO-
AST, BUT INCREASED AGAIN JUST SOUTH OF T-
HE ALASKAN PENINSULA. NORTHWARD AND SEA-
WARD THERE WAS A DECREASE IN NUMBER OF F-
ISH SPECIES. THERE APPEARED TO BE DEFIN-
ITE CORRELATION BETWEEN CATCHES AND AN O-
CEANO GRAPHIC BOUNDARY AT APPROXIMATELY -
50 DEGREES NORTH. A NUMBER OF RARE FISH-
, ONE NEW SPECIES, AND TWO LEPTOCEPHALUS-
LARVAE WERE TAKEN. CON SISTENCY OF RES-
ULTS AND CLOSE RELATIONSHIP OF OCEANOGRA-
PHIC AND BIO LOGICAL DATA SUGGEST THE US-
EFULNESS OF THE MIDWATER TRAWL AS A VALU-
ABLE TOOL FOR FUTURE INVESTIGATIONS OF -
PLANKTON ECOLOGY. -
DO YOU WANT TO SEE MORE≥
NO

(*e*)

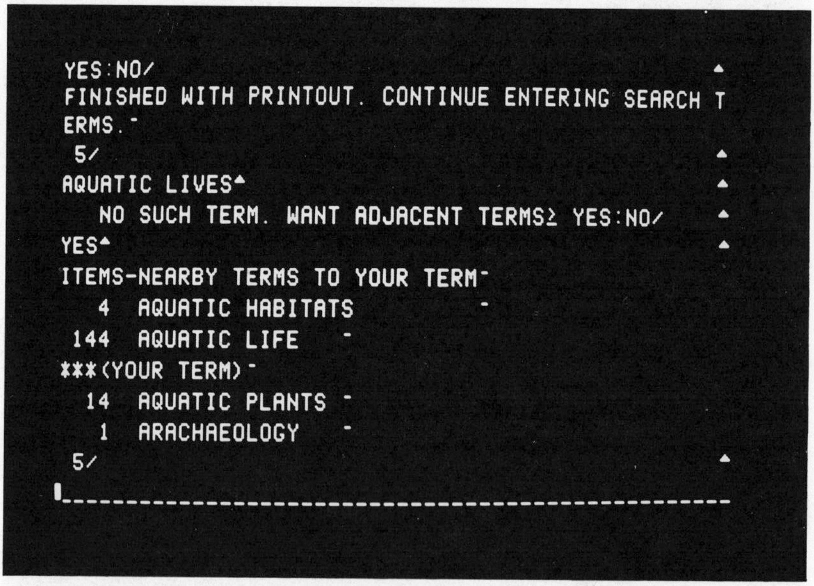
YES:NO/
FINISHED WITH PRINTOUT. CONTINUE ENTERING SEARCH T
ERMS.-
5/
AQUATIC LIVES
NO SUCH TERM. WANT ADJACENT TERMS≥ YES:NO/
YES
ITEMS-NEARBY TERMS TO YOUR TERM-
4 AQUATIC HABITATS -
144 AQUATIC LIFE -
***(YOUR TERM)-
14 AQUATIC PLANTS -
1 ARACHAEOLOGY -
5/

(*f*)

Figure 5.1. *Continued.*

```
AQUA*
 HITS-TERMS CONTAINING THIS STEM
 128  AQUATIC ANIMALS
   2  AQUATIC ENVIRONMENTS
   4  AQUATIC HABITATS
 144  AQUATIC LIFE
  14  AQUATIC PLANTS
END OF TERMS CONTAINING THIS STEM
ENTER REQUEST.
 5/
(QUIT)
    B A S I S   7 0   HAS
ENJOYED SERVING YOU.
DO YOU HAVE ANY COMMENTS⌐
YES:NO/
NO
(DONT FORGET TO ≡LOGOUT.≡ BEFORE DISCONNECTING.)
GOODBYE.............
```

(*g*)

```
 13.38.06.END     BASIS
COMMAND-
LOGOUT.
CP TIME    1.244
PP TIME    30.500
CONNECT TIME    0 HRS. 31 MIN.
 01/11/72  LOGGED OUT AT 13.39.50.<
```

(*h*)

BASIS-70 has been integrated with a random-access microfiche retrieval unit developed by Dynamic Information Systems, Inc.

BOLD

BOLD (Bibliographic On-Line Display) was an experimental system developed by System Development Corporation (Borko, 1968; Borko and Burnaugh, 1966; Burnaugh, 1966a, b, 1967). BOLD was designed to use teletypes, CRT display consoles, and light pens connected to the SDC time-sharing system for the IBM Q-32V computer.

Most of the BOLD experimentation was conducted on a data base of abstracts from the U.S. Defense Documentation Center. Any type of boolean search statement could be entered by the user, who could also obtain a display of terms related to any search term by being synonymous, super-ordinate, or similar in spelling. When the user specified the *search mode*, a display was generated to show which items in the file were indexed by which descriptor or descriptors used in the search statement. An example is shown in Figure 5.2. The search terms appear at the top of the display, and each is given an identifying number. Columns are assigned to these terms on the CRT. To the left of the display appears a list of document numbers in descending order of match with the search terms. Thus, AD 284 259 contains five of the search terms, AD 272 572 contains three, and so on. Display or printout of any of these abstracts could be requested by the searcher.

An alternative to the search mode was the *browse mode*, which generated a display indicating the divisions or major subject categories into which the document collection was organized (Figure 5.3). The searcher could use a light pen to select one of these divisions. This led to a more detailed display of the subdivisions of the major division, including statistics on the number of items contained in each subdivision. The searcher could then choose to browse among the individual items in one of these subject categories.

BROWSER

BROWSER (Browsing On-Line with Selective Retrieval) is a system developed by Williams of the IBM Federal Systems Division. It was described by Williams and Perriens (1968) and by Williams (1969). As with Salton's SMART system (which see), BROWSER operates on the natural language of documents or document abstracts. Incoming documents are processed by the deletion of common (syntactic) words and matching the remainder against a dictionary of word roots (Williams calls them *rootwords*), which has been humanly prepared. (In one application, a dictionary of about 3000 rootwords was derived from a file of approximately 17,000 patent abstracts.)

32 ENTRIES   1 DØCUMENTATIØN
ALL SEARCHED   2 INFØRMATIØN RETRIEVAL
                   3 LIBRARY SCIENCE
                   4 INDEXES
                   5 CLASSIFICATIØN
                   6 VØCABULARY

	1	2	3	4	5	6
AD - 284 259	×	×	×	×	×	
AD - 272 572	×		×	×		
AD - 278 141		×			×	×
AD - 283 335	×	×				
AD - 275 814		×		×		
AD - 274 816		×				×
AD - 271 926	×					
AD - 276 533	×					
AD - 286 511	×					
AD - 285 510	×					
AD - 271 600	×					
AD - 274 358	×					
AD - 281 909			×			
AD - 275 826				×		
AD - 275 964				×		
AD - 276 142				×		
AD - 271 124				×		
AD - 272 068				×		
AD - 278 130				×		
AD - 275 528				×		
AD - 274 026				×		
AD - 286 816				×		
AD - 274 775					×	
AD - 276 376					×	
AD - 274 260					×	
AD - 286 637					×	
AD - 266 508					×	
AD - 272 133					×	
AD - 274 774					×	
AD - 272 401						×
AD - 277 520						×
AD - 276 066						×

Figure 5.2. Search mode display from BOLD. Reproduced from Burnaugh (1966a) by permission of System Development Corporation.

THE FØLLØWING CATEGØRIES ARE AVAILABLE.

DIV 1 AERØNAUTICS
DIV 2 ASTRØNØMY. GEØPHYSICS. GEØGRAPHY
DIV 3 CHEMICAL WARFARE
DIV 4 CHEMISTRY
DIV 5 CØMMUNICATIØNS
DIV 6 DETECTIØN
DIV 7 ELECTRICAL EQUIPMENT
DIV 8 ELECTRØNICS
DIV 9 FLUID MECHANICS
DIV 10 FUELS AND CØMBUSTIØN
DIV 11 GRØUND TRANSPØRTATIØN EQUIPMENT
DIV 12 GUIDED MISSILES
DIV 13 CØNSTRUCTIØN
DIV 14 MATERIALS (NØN METALLIC)
DIV 15 MATHEMATICS
DIV 16 MEDICAL SCIENCES
DIV 17 METALLURGY
DIV 18 MILITARY SCIENCES
DIV 19 NAVIGATIØN
DIV 20 PHYSICS. CHEMISTRY (NUCLEAR)
DIV 21 PRØPULSIØN (NUCLEAR)
DIV 22 ØRDNANCE
DIV 23 PERSØNNEL
DIV 24 PHØTØGRAPHY
DIV 25 PHYSICS
DIV 26 PRØDUCTIØN. MANAGEMENT
DIV 27 PRØPULSIØN SYSTEMS
DIV 28 PSYCHØLØGY
DIV 29 QUARTERMASTER
DIV 30 RESEARCH
DIV 31 SHIPS. MARINE EQUIPMENT
DIV 32 ARTS. SCIENCES (MISC)

Figure 5.3. Browse mode display from BOLD. Reproduced from Burnaugh (1966a) by permission of System Development Corporation.

When a root is recognized, the document number is posted to this root in the normal inverted file arrangement. The rootword dictionary carries statistics on the total number of occurrences of each rootword in the corpus. It also carries an *information value* (*I-value*) for each rootword, which is inversely proportional to the number of occurrences of the rootword in the corpus. The I-value is a weighting in negative powers of 2. A value of 1.0 indicates a term that occurs in one-half of the abstracts, a value of 2.0 a term that occurs in one-quarter of the abstracts, and so on. Thus, a rare word will receive a high I-value, while a common word will receive a low one. This weighting scheme corresponds to C. E. Shannon's information theoretic notion of the lowest probability event containing the greatest amount of information. A high I-value is presumed to equate with *potency* for retrieval. No other processing of the abstract is conducted.

The user of BROWSER, rather than expressing his problem in the form of a boolean statement, simply writes a paragraph of unrestricted natural English. Alternatively, an abstract of another document known to be relevant may be used as a search statement. The terms in this statement, or rather their roots, are matched against the rootword dictionary, and those recognized become the search terms and are arranged in descending order of I-value. Each document abstract in the corpus can be given a value in relation to the search statement, this value being the sum of the I-values of the terms that match between abstract and search statement (most items in the file will, of course, have a zero value in relation to any particular request).

The system is designed for on-line, interactive use. It has been implemented on an IBM 360 with 2260 display terminals. Several browsing features are incorporated. For example, when a search statement is input and matched against the rootword dictionary, the system will display the resulting list of matching rootwords with their frequencies of occurrence and their information values (see Figure 5.4). The searcher may then add or delete words in his query based on the information displayed. Upon completion of his modifications, the search is conducted and all combinations of search words occurring in abstracts are displayed. Figure 5.5 shows such a display, which has been generated as a result of the searcher selecting certain words as his initial set of browsing terms. Numbers of the twenty-five abstracts that score highest on the match with these search terms are displayed at the top of the screen. In this display, the search terms are abbreviated to their initial letter. Thus, abstract 1 contains the roots AUTOMAT, CLASSIF, DOCU-MENT, FACTOR, and LATENT. When the searcher sees a combination of terms likely to indicate a relevant document he requests that the full abstract be displayed or printed. Further modifications to the search statement can be made as a result of viewing abstracts and identifying additional useful search words used in those judged to be relevant. The process of selecting browsing terms and viewing displays generated from them can continue until the searcher has exhausted all useful possibilities or until he has found enough relevant documents to satisfy his need. A complete example of the iterative browsing technique was presented by Williams (1971a).

The prototype BROWSER was used experimentally with data bases of 25,000 German patent abstracts, 9000 English patent abstracts, 8000 U.S.

I am interested in the automatic classification of documents into subject categories, groups, clusters, or clumps, using discriminant or latent factors. Other statistical indexing techniques include association matrices or correlation coefficients based on word occurrences.

Term			Term			Term		
ASSOC	440	4.2	AUTOMAT	479	4.1	CATEGOR	123	6.0
CLASSIF	216	5.2	CLUMP	7	10.2	CLUSTER	28	8.2
COEFF	328	4.6	CORRELAT	308	4.7	DISCRIM	77	6.7
DOCUMENT	263	4.9	FACTOR	503	4.0	GROUP	336	4.6
INDEX	268	4.9	INCLU	1376	2.6	INTEREST	336	4.6
LATENT	11	9.5	MATRI	219	5.2	OCCUR	149	5.8
STATIST	316	4.7	SUBJECT	484	4.1	TECHNIC	359	4.5
WORD	171	5.6						

Figure 5.4. Search term display from BROWSER. Reproduced from Williams (1969) by permission of International Business Machines Corporation.

	1	2	3	4	5	6	7	8	9	10	11	12	13	14	15	16	17	18	19	20	21	22	23	24	25
AUTOMAT	A			A		A	A	A			A	A		A			A	A	A				A		
CLASSIF		C	C			C	C	C			C	C			C	C	C							C	
DOCUMENT	D	D						D	D	D	D	D	D												
DISCRIM						D								D				D						D	
STATIST				S	S			S	S		S		S	S						S		S		S	S
FACTOR			F	F					F							F								F	
LATENT		L																							
WORD			W					W	W		W		W	W	W	W	W							W	W

Figure 5.5. Response index display from BROWSER. Reproduced from Williams (1969) by permission of International Business Machines Corporation.

Defence Documentation Center abstracts, and 1600 abstracts from the Navy Automated Research and Development Information System (NARDIS) (Williams, 1971b). Since January 1970, the system has been used operationally in the Patent Department of IBM Germany at Sindelfingen. This collection now approaches 100,000 patent abstracts in English and German. The BROWSER experience in Germany has been summarized by Schürfeld, et al. (1971).

CIRCOL

CIRCOL stands for CIRC-On-Line and CIRC is the Central Information Reference and Control System (U.S. Air Force, 1970). It is an intelligence retrieval system operated, via an IBM 360/65 and remote terminals, by the Foreign Technology Division, Air Force Systems Command, Wright-Patterson Air Force Base, Ohio. File management and exploitation is effected through the use of the IBM Document Processing System (DPS). Searching options include use of descriptors (from the *CIRC Thesaurus*), authors, countries, and free text searching of abstract or extract of the parent document. The size of the data base was about half a million items in 1972. The two basic types of terminals used are the IBM 2741 and model 33 or 35 teletypewriters. As of 1970, there were approximately thirty terminals in use in various parts of the country, and the system was operational for about 4 hours each day.

CIRCOL consists of two modules: the DPS (also known as DOC-PROC) and a teleprocessing system. The DPS, a program package for the processing of unformatted textual data, was designed for batch processing. The Foreign Technology Division developed the teleprocessing module to facilitate on-line interactive search. File maintenance is conducted in a batch mode.

A predecessor of CIRCOL was known as COLEX (CIRC On-Line Experimentation) and was designed by the System Development Corporation. COLEX was also the forerunner of ORBIT.

CIRCOL is being used, or has been used, at the headquarters and divisions of Air Force Systems Command, Harry Diamond Laboratories, Rome Air Development Center, Redstone Arsenal, Defense Intelligence Agency, National Library of Medicine, and the Oceanographer of the Navy.

Data Central

Data Central (Giering, 1972) is a commercially available on-line system developed and marketed by Mead Data Central Inc., a subsidiary of the

Mead Corporation.* It is designed as a multipurpose system with text-handling (search and retrieval) capabilities. Inverted search files are created for every word occurring in an input document, except for syntactic and other nonsubstantive words, which are eliminated by a stop list. All boolean searching is possible, and positional indicators (word distances) may be used. Word truncation is also possible. A keyword-in-context (KWIC) display capability allows display of a specified number of text words on either side of a search word. The system is said to be device-independent and capable of being modified to fit any hardware configuration. The system, which has been implemented on IBM 360 and 370 comuters, can be used with tele-typewriters, IBM 1050 terminals, and a number of CRT displays. Hard-copy printers may be utilized in association with the CRT terminals. A special teleprocessing package, known as TTAM (Time-Shared Teleprocessing Access Method), has been developed for use with the system.

Data Central has been used in the implementation of several important retrieval systems, including the substantial legal data base of the Ohio State Bar Association (OBAR) (Harrington, 1970; Ohio State Bar Association, 1970; Troy, 1969) and the Epilepsy Abstracts Retrieval System (EARS) of the National Institute of Neurological Diseases and Stroke (Porter, et al., 1970). The OBAR (Ohio Bar Automated Research) files include Supreme Court Decisions, Appellate Court Decisions, and a *hot file* of the most recent decisions of all courts. Files in excess of 600 million characters are currently being searched in the OBAR application of the Data Central system. Mead Data Central has also signed contracts for legal retrieval services with the Internal Revenue Service and the New York State Bar Association. Another important application is PADAT (Psychological Abstracts Direct Access Terminal), a service of the American Psychological Association, which makes available the text of *Psychological Abstracts* back to 1967. A large data base, containing technical and management data, is operated for the Environmental Protection Agency.

DDC Remote On-Line Retrieval System

This system, at the U.S. Defense Documentation Center (DDC), is designed to provide rapid, direct access to Department of Defense research reports and related documents. A Univac 1108 is used. The data base includes about 800,000 items and is growing at the rate of about 40,000 a year. The system uses typewriter terminals for input purposes and CRT devices for

---

*In 1972, the marketing of the legal applications of the system was handled by Mead Data Central and the nonlegal applications by another subsidiary, the Data Corporation. In October 1972, the Data Corporation was renamed Mead Technology Laboratories.

searching operations, but a move to CRT terminals for both functions was planned in 1972. About thirty terminals were supported in 1972: ten typewriter terminals at DDC, six at the National Technical Information Service (NTIS), and the remaining terminals (CRT) located within DDC and around the country at various military laboratories. The system provides for both secure and unclassified access. An expansion to over 100 terminals, at various remote sites, is planned. A thesaurus (not on-line) is used in the system, and a searcher can request a generic search on any descriptor in the vocabulary (i.e., a search on this descriptor and all terms subordinate to it in the hierarchy). Term truncation is possible, as well as a limited form of term weighting in searching. The system has been described by Bennertz (1971), Powers (1973), and Wolfe (1970).

According to Bennertz, the system will, in the future, operate in an interactive, conversational mode; incorporate procedures for machine-aided indexing; and provide various lexicographic files on-line. Plans for future development of the system include experiments in the use of holographic technology for full text storage and readout, and the use of facsimile transmission techniques for transfer of full text.

DIALOG

DIALOG (Summit, 1967, 1968, 1971) is a proprietary system developed by the Lockheed Palo Alto Research Laboratory. It has been implemented with a NASA collection of 300,000 citations. The system was operational in 1966, and a revised version, DIALOG II, was completed in 1969. DIALOG is still being developed as a major tool within the Lockheed Information Retrieval Laboratory. The operating environment in 1967 comprised an IBM 360/30 (with 32,000 bytes of core), two IBM 2311 disk packs (7.5 million bytes each) for programs and intermediate storage, an IBM 2321 Data Cell (415 million bytes) for data base storage, an IBM 1443 off-line printer, and an IBM 2260 display/1053 printer input/output terminal. Later implementation was on an IBM 360/40 with a Computer Communications Inc. video console. Figure 5.6 shows this display terminal, and Figure 5.7 shows the keyboard of the DIALOG system. The DIALOG keyboard has dedicated keys for the various commands.

DIALOG operates through the following major commands:

EXPAND term X. This will cause a display of all terms alphabetically close to term X in the system. Each term appears with a temporary identification number by which it may be referenced, a count of the number of times it has been used in indexing, and a count of the number of terms that are shown to be related in the vocabulary. A display of the related terms may be

Figure 5.6. DIALOG video display with associated printer. Reproduced by permission of Lockheed Palo Alto Research Laboratory.

obtained by depressing the EXPAND key and entering the descriptor identification number.

SELECT. This command, when used with a descriptor identification number from the display, causes all citations bearing the selected descriptor to be collected for further processing. Each selected descriptor is assigned an identification number and is typed on the console printer together with a figure representing the number of citations to which it has been assigned. The command can also be used to select a range of descriptors displayed at the terminal.

COMBINE. This command is used to combine terms or groups of terms already selected. Any boolean expression is possible:

> COMBINE A + B (logical *sum*; either A or B or both)
> COMBINE A * B (logical *product*; A *and* B)
> COMBINE A − B (negation; A *but not* B)

The COMBINE command results in a display of a figure indicating the total number of citations satisfying the search logic.

DISPLAY. This command causes bibliographic records to be displayed on the CRT.

KEEP. This command allows the user to save selected citations for later printout on-line or off-line.

Figure 5.7. Detailed view of the DIALOG keyboard. Reproduced by permission of Lockheed Palo Alto Research Laboratory.

TYPE. This command causes a selected citation to be printed off-line at the console printer.

PRINT. This command causes a selected citation or set of citations to be printed on the off-line, high-speed printer.

Notice that these commands are the same as those used in the NASA/RECON system as illustrated in Chapter Three. This results from the fact that Lockheed was the NASA contractor for the development of RECON, and the DIALOG language was incorporated into the RECON system. (A brief instruction manual for system users is included as Appendix B.) A predecessor of DIALOG at Lockheed was known as CONVERSE (Drew, et al., 1966). This is not to be confused with a question-answering system also known as CONVERSE, which was developed by the System Development Corporation (Kellogg, 1968).

In addition to its NASA application, DIALOG has been applied to the complete data base of the Educational Resources Information Center (ERIC) of the U.S. Office of Education (Lockheed Missiles & Space Co., 1971), to the *Nuclear Science Abstracts* data base of the U.S. Atomic Energy Commission, to the unclassified portion of the data base of the U.S. Defense Documentation Center, to the U.S. Government Research and Development Reports data base of the National Technical Information Service, and to the PANDEX file compiled by CCM Information Services. In 1973, the ERIC (115,000 citations), NTIS (150,000), and PANDEX (400,000) data bases were all available to Lockheed subscribers through the Tymshare network. DIALOG is also the system used by the European Space Research Organization (ESRO), and it has been used in various data analysis applications. For example, it has been used in the San Mateo County, Ca., Department of Public Health and Welfare for the analysis of health data contained in resident death certificates for the county (Hunter and Mazer, 1971). According to Lockheed, the present DIALOG configuration can handle files of up to 2 billion characters and can operate on full text as well as controlled vocabularies.

EARS

EARS (Epilepsy Abstracts Retrieval System) is a system of the National Institute of Neurological Diseases and Stroke (NINDS). The data base consists (in 1971) of about 8000 abstracts in the field of epilepsy and related areas, drawn from the monthly publication *Epilepsy Abstracts*, which is prepared for NINDS by the Excerpta Medica Foundation (Caponio, et al., 1970). The data base is loaded on the Data Central on-line system (which see) and the full text of the abstracts, as well as words in titles and index terms assigned by Excerpta Medica indexers, may be searched upon. EARS has all the searching capabilities of the present Data Central system, including conventional boolean search expressions, word truncation, and the ability to specify word distance in text. EARS is a free text (natural language) searching system; the searcher may use any substantive word occurring in the corpus and does not use any form of controlled vocabulary. The system has been described by Porter, et al. (1970), and an evaluation of its use was made by Lancaster, et al. (1972). Some results of this study will be presented in Chapter Nine.

ELHILL

This is essentially the ORBIT system (which see) of the System Development Corporation, modified to meet the needs of MEDLARS (Medical Literature Analysis and Retrieval System) at the National Library of Medicine (NLM). It derives its name from the Lister Hill National Center for Biomedical Communications, which is named after Senator Lister Hill. The center, part of the NLM, has been instrumental in the conversion of MEDLARS to an on-line operation. The ELHILL programs were used in the AIM–TWX experiments (which see) and have been adopted for MEDLINE (which see), the on-line version of MEDLARS. Early experiments with ORBIT applied to NLM data bases were restricted to a small collection in the field of neurology. This early version of the system was described by Scroggins, et al. (1968).

ENDS

ENDS (European Nuclear Documentation System) is a storage and retrieval system developed at the Centre for Information and Documentation of the European Communities (previously Euratom). The data base exceeds a million items, goes back to 1947, and is currently selected from fifty abstracting journals, the most important being *Nuclear Science Abstracts*. An experimental on-line system was begun in 1971 with 200,000 references from *Nuclear Science Abstracts* accessible from two CRT terminals (IBM 2265) located in Brussels and Luxembourg. The on-line program runs in a dedicated 100 K partition of the European Communities IBM 360/50 in Luxembourg. Microfiche images of abstracts of all items in ENDS are available at each terminal location. Some retrieval experiences with ENDS have been described by Vernimb (1972).

GESCAN (the Rapid Search Machine)

The Rapid Search Machine (RSM) (General Electric Co., 1969) is a product of General Electric Co., Daytona Beach, Fla. The RSM is a special-purpose information-handling system designed to perform high-speed search

Figure 5.8. The Rapid Search Machine. Reproduced by permission of General Electric Co.

Figure 5.9. Operator's console for the Rapid Search Machine. Reproduced by permission of General Electric Co.

and retrieval from magnetic tape files. It is designed particularly for very rapid searching of unstructured natural language text. Searches may be conducted in natural language words or phrases connected by boolean operators.

The RSM (see Figure 5.8) is not really an on-line system, nor is it really a computer in the conventional sense. However, it has certain features that make it resemble an on-line computer retrieval system. It has three major units: operator's console (Figure 5.9), tape transport unit, and equipment unit. The operator's console consists of a desk-mounted CRT display, a printer, and the operator control panels required for efficient operation and control of the RSM. The technical characteristics of the equipment are presented in Table 5.1.

TABLE 5.1.   Technical Characteristics of the Rapid Search Machine

Item	Description
Operator's console	Size: 60 inches wide, 34.5 inches deep, 45 inches high
	Weight: 400 pounds
Line printer	Speed: 400 characters per second
	Input code: ASCII (7 bit)
	Line length: 80 characters
	Character repertoire: 63 alphameric
	Output: Hard copy, reproducible
	Paper roll: 500 feet, 8.5 inches wide, current sensitive
	Type size: 10 point
CRT display	CRT size: 7 × 9.5 inches viewing area
	Character set: 64 alphameric symbols
	Character generation: Stroke
	Code set: 7 bit ASCII
	Characters per line: 52 maximum
	Number of lines: 40 maximum
Tape transport	Size: 68.5 inches high, 26.5 inches wide, 27 inches deep
	Weight: 500 pounds
	Tape speed: 150 inches per second
	Rewind time: 130 seconds for 2400 foot reel
	Packing density: 800 bits per inch
	Reel size: 0.5 inch × 2400 foot reel
	Number of channels: 8 plus parity
Equipment and logic rack	Size: 67 inches high, 27 inches wide, 26 inches deep
	Weight: 1100 pounds
RSM equipment	Power input: 25 amperes, 120 VAC, 60 CPS, single-phase

SOURCE: General Electric Co.

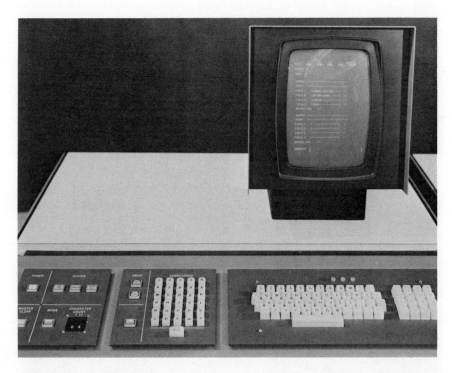

Figure 5.10. Rapid Search Machine: keyboard and CRT display. Reproduced by permission of General Electric Co.

A search strategy is entered as a string of words or phrases at the CRT device, using a special keyboard (Figure 5.10). The CRT itself carries a special formatted display (Figure 5.11) to assist the user in preparing his strategy. All words entered on a single line (*field*) of this display, separated by commas, are considered as being in a logical AND relationship unless otherwise specified. There are four boolean operators:

⟩   AND
]   OR
⟨   AND NOT
[OR NOT

These may be used to combine terms and/or to combine fields. A single field will accommodate twenty alphameric characters or punctuation marks, and the upper limit for a search is eighty characters (all four fields combined). Word truncation is possible (indeed it is usually necessary because of the limited space available on the formatted display), and a *universal character*

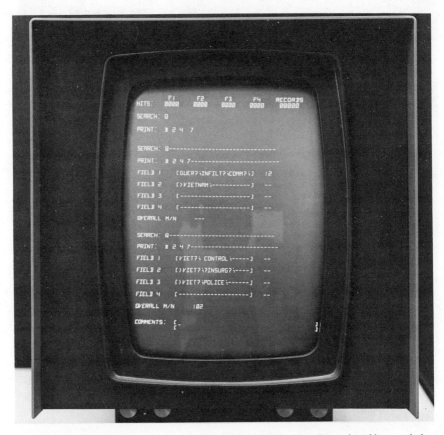

Figure 5.11. CRT formatted display on the Rapid Search Machine. Reproduced by permission of General Electric Co.

is accepted. As the search strategy is entered at the keyboard it appears on the CRT display and may be corrected, added to, or deleted, as required. Data input and alteration are very simple. When the operator is satisfied with the strategy displayed, a request is sent to the equipment unit. Control signals from this unit cause the strategy to be matched against the magnetic tape file (which has to be hand-mounted on the equipment unit). When the search strategy matches a record on the file, the *hit* registers on the CRT. That is, as the search progresses at very rapid speed, the number of hits is recorded continuously at the CRT. The RSM can in fact be used solely for counting hits and is thus useful in various statistical or management reporting applications.

More usually, however, it will be used as a retrieval device rather than a mere counting device. In this case, by activating a particular control at the console, the operator will request that all records that satisfy the search requirements be printed out on the RSM printer.

The RSM is a brute-force text-searching device, with comparatively little sophistication but great speed. Speed of searching is essentially the speed of tape transport (150 inches per second with a packing density of 800 bits per inch). However, the equipment contains no facilities for recording hits for later printing. When the data to be printed exceeds the capacity of the print buffer, the search will stop until the printer has emptied the buffer. This slows the overall search considerably. Thus, a search with few hits will go extremely fast, while one with many hits will be much slower. Only one search at a time can be conducted on the RSM. However, the CRT is so designed that it will accept two separate search strategies. While one search is being run, a second strategy can be composed at the console.

The RSM is a very efficient machine for searching relatively small files of natural language text. For very large files, occupying several reels of tape, it is less satisfactory because of the inconvenience of mounting and dismounting the tape reels. However, up to six tape drives may be added to the RSM if it is necessary to have a large file mounted and immediately accessible.

In a controlled test of the use of the RSM with a single tape containing 5360 natural language documents (approximately 2000 alphameric characters per document), the following times were recorded:

Tape running speed	3.2 minutes
Average printing speed	15 seconds per document (range 8–24 seconds)
Average search time (tape scan plus printing of hits)	9 minutes, 24 seconds
Average time to input search strategy at CRT	1 minute, 23 seconds

The RSM tape drive searches at a speed of 120,000 bits per second, while the associated Motorola electrostatic printer operates at a speed of 400 characters per second. It is possible to raise the performance of the RSM by adding a tape drive that operates with tapes of higher density. For example, one commercially available drive operates at only 48 inches per second. However, the tape packing density is much greater (5000 bits per inch) than the packing density on the regular RSM tape. So this drive allows the machine to search at a speed of 240,000 bits per second. The purchase price of an RSM was approximately $189,500 in 1971.

A more advanced version of this piece of equipment, known as the Re-Search Information System, has been described (General Electric Co., 1972). Re-Search (*Remote Search*) is capable of providing remote, simultaneous access to a central data base. Cost is approximately $260,000, but this varies with capability and configuration required. The system is described in some detail here because of its novel features and because it is little-known.

INTREX

Project Intrex (Information Transfer Experiments) is a program of research and experiments conducted at Massachusetts Institute of Technology (MIT) by means of a prototype on-line library system. The overall configuration, shown in Figure 5.12, includes a machine-stored catalog of approximately 20,000 journal articles in selected fields of materials science and engineering, as well as the full text of most of these documents in microfiche form. Intrex operates within the general time-sharing environment of MIT. The catalog can be accessed through any of the following terminals:

1. A typewriter terminal such as the IBM 2741 or the Datel 30.
2. A CRT display terminal developed for Project MAC and known as the Advanced Remote Display Station (ARDS).
3. A display designed specifically for Intrex and having the following features: (*a*) a character set of 192 different characters; (*b*) a display format of 56 × 31 characters per page; (*c*) a screen refresh rate of 60 cycles per second, providing good brightness without flicker; (*d*) subscript and superscript capabilities; (*e*) a paging capability that allows many display pages per console to be stored locally and recalled instantly; (*f*) a data communications rate, between computer and console, of 120 characters per second, with provisions for higher data rates.

This special Intrex display has been named BRISC (Buffered Remote Interactive Search Console). It is illustrated in Figure 5.13. The Intrex display facilities have been described by Haring (1968) and by Haring and Roberge (1969). Both ARDS and BRISC were developed at the Electronic Systems

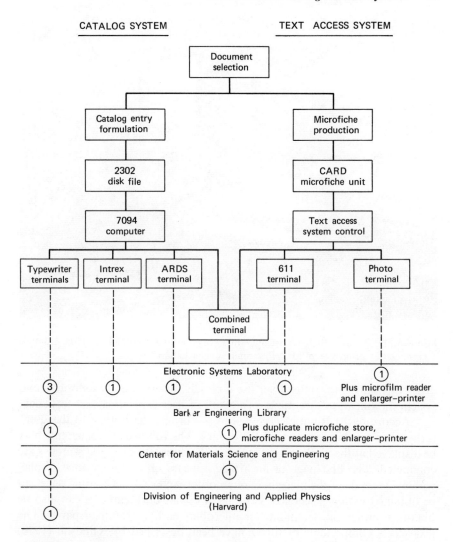

Figure 5.12. Schematic diagram of Intrex system and terminals. Reproduced by permission of MIT, Electronic Systems Laboratory.

Laboratory of MIT. It has been found that BRISC is the preferred terminal because of its large-size characters, bright display and the page storage capability of the terminal (Massachusetts Institute of Technology, 1972).

Intrex is viewed as an experimental on-line library established in order to gain insights into the design characteristics of large-scale, operational systems of a similar kind. The system is made available to a selected group

Figure 5.13. BRISC (Buffered Remote Interactive Search Console) of Project Intrex. Reproduced by permission of MIT, Electronic Systems Laboratory.

of scientists and librarians; their use is closely observed and monitored, and system modifications are made as a result of user experience and feedback.

According to Reintjes (1969), Intrex "brings the library to the user" rather than forcing him to visit the library. The full text of documents may be displayed at the work station at which the interactive catalog searches are conducted. The first page of an article appears on a storage-tube display within 7 seconds of the placement of an order, and each succeeding page can be obtained within 3 seconds. Permanent copies of documents can also be obtained, either on 35 millimeter microfilm or $8\frac{1}{2} \times 11$ inch paper. The text access components of Intrex have been described by Knudson (1970) and by Knudson and Teicher (1969). They are discussed in greater detail in Chapter Sixteen.

The Intrex *augmented catalog*, as described by Marcus et al. (1969), has been developed in great depth; no less than fifty information fields exist in a catalog entry, although not all of these fields will be relevant to any one entry. The subject indexing of the collection is achieved by the use of fairly lengthy natural language expressions chosen by an indexer and selected from the text of the document itself. No controlled vocabulary is employed in indexing. The searching system will accept abbreviated commands and is relatively insensitive to common errors of punctuation and spacing. A complete record, which will include an abstract or excerpt as well as the set of indexing expressions, is illustrated in Figure 5.14.

Intrex research has been supported by grants from the Council on Library Resources, Inc., the National Science Foundation, and the Carnegie Corporation. For an overall description of the project see a report by Overhage (1972). In 1973, the Intrex system was changing from an experimental to an operational status and was being reprogrammed for an IBM 370/165 computer.

LEADER

LEADER (Lehigh Automatic Device for Efficient Retrieval) was a prototype information system in operation at the Center for the Information Sciences, Lehigh University. The system, as described by Hillman and Kasarda (1969), accepted requests in English sentence form, processed these requests in the same way that documents were processed into the system, and looked for documents that matched the request above some preestablished threshold. In this respect LEADER was somewhat similar to Salton's SMART system (which see). Output could be made in the form of document references or of complete textual passages. The request statement could be modified via man/machine dialogue in which "LEADER instructs and interrogates the user, attempting to acquaint him with the nature of its stored information so that each inquiry can be negotiated through successive modifications of the user's stated interests. The dialogue itself is carried out on a CRT scope" (Hillman and Kasarda, 1969, p. 447). LEADER was implemented in 1968 on an IBM 1800 process control computer. Communication with the system was achieved through the use of a typewriter terminal or an IBM 2260 video display unit.

An important feature of LEADER was the inclusion of sophisticated procedures for the automatic reduction of text to surrogate form. For input to the system the full text of a document was put into machine-readable form. Thereafter, a series of programs reduced each text sentence to a string of syntactic categories (partly by table lookup and partly by supplementary automatic syntactic analysis methods), resolved each category-string into its set of canonical substrings, identified potential document *characteristics* within these canonical substrings, and assigned a weight to each characteristic relative to its importance in the parent document. A characteristic was a string selected as best representing a particular aspect of the subject matter of the document. In LEADER, a characteristic was always a noun phrase occurring as an argument of some relation expressed by a canonical component of a sentence. As a result of these various procedures a document was

DOCUMENT 9343; Elevated temperature compressive creep behavior of tungsten carbide-cobalt alloys; Smith, J.T. (TA); Wood, J.D. (JA); Lehigh University, ⟩Bethlehem⟨, ⟩Pa.⟨ (BT); AMETA. v.16,no.10,100068. pp.1219 1226.

CHOSEN   (FIELD 2)
 High temperature metallurgy (Professor Grant); Graduate student

CATALOGER   (FIELD 3)
 1502

ONLINE   (FIELD 4)
 08/22/69

MAIN   (FIELD 20)
 Personal author

AFFILIATION   (FIELD 22)
 Lehigh University, ⟩Bethlehem⟨, ⟩Pa.⟨ Dept. of Metallurgy and Materials
  Science/Battelle Memorial Institute, ⟩Columbus⟨, ⟩Ohio⟨. Powder
  Materials Application Div.;
 Lehigh University, ⟩Bethlehem⟨, ⟩Pa.⟨ Dept of Metallurgy and Materials
  Science

MEDIUM   (FIELD 30)
 Conventional

FORMAT   (FIELD 31)
 Professional journal article

ILLUSTRATIONS   (FIELD 33)
 illus.

LANGUAGE   (FIELD 36)
 English

ABLANG   (FIELD 37)
 efg

CONTRACT   (FIELD 40)
 National Science Foundation (⟩U.S.⟨) #G24000

THESIS   (FIELD 43)
 1,. Ph.D.

RECEIPT   (FIELD 46)
 12/07/67

PURPOSE   (FIELD 65)
 Theoretical and experimental

APPROACH   (FIELD 66)
 Professional

TABLE   (FIELD 67)
      I. Introduction (p.1219)
 A. Creep models (p.1220)
 B. Dislocation looping (p.1220)
 C. Dislocation climb (p.1220)
 D. Particle movement in the matrix
   (p.1220)
 II. Experimental procedure (p.1221)
 III. Results (p.1221)
 A. Quantitative metallography (p.1221)
 B. Creep deformation (p.1221)
 IV. Discussion (p.1222)
 A. WC-12 *percent* alloys (p.1222)
 B. WC-15 *percent* alloys (p.1225)
 V. Conclusions (p.1226)

Figure 5.14. Complete bibliographic record from Intrex augmented catalog. Reproduced by permission of MIT, Electronic Systems Laboratory.

BIBLIOGRAPHY   (FIELD 69)
   1e(15)
ABSTRACT   (FIELD 71)

The compressive creep deformation of two-phase tungsten carbide-cobalt
alloys with 12 and 15 *percent* Co has been investigated at
temperatures of 800, 900, and 1000 *deg*C for stresses of 10,000 to
110,000 psi. At each temperature studied, the WC-Co alloys showed a
decreasing steady-state creep rate with increasing WC particle size for
low creep-stress levels. At high stress levels, the steady-state creep
rate was observed to increase with increased WC particle size. These
observations, with additional considerations of the creep behavior,
indicated that two mechanisms were rate determining during deformation
of WC-Co alloys. To ascertain the rate-determining mechanisms during
deformation, existing creep models were extended to include the high
volume loading of dispersed WC particles present in these alloys. At
high stresses, the mechanism postulated to describe steady-state creep
deformation was the looping of dislocations in the Co matrix between WC
particles and the climb of pinched-off loops. The diffusion of Co in
the matrix around WC particles has been suggested as the rate
controlling steady-state creep mechanism at low stresses. (author)

SUBJECTS   (FIELD 73)
   elevated temperature compressive creep behavior of tungsten carbide
      cobalt alloys (1);
   effect of tungsten carbide particle size on creep in tungsten carbide
      cobalt alloys (2);
   creep models extended to include the high volume loading of dispersed WC
      particles present in WC-Co alloys (2);
   rate determining and deformation mechanism for WC-Co alloys at low
      stresses(2);
   rate determining and deformation mechanisms associated with the
      compressive creep behavior of WC-Co alloys at high stress and elevated
      temperature (2);
   dislocation looping, dislocation climb, particle movement in the matrix
      in the two-phase alloy system tungsten carbide dispersed in a cobalt
      matrix (2);
   micro-optical pyrometer (4);
   strain measurements in WC-Co alloys made by a photographic technique
      (4);
   WC-Co alloy specimens characterized by quantitative metallographic
      techniques and deformed in compression creep at 800, 900, and 1000
      *deg*C (4);
   influence of temperature, stress, WC particle size and mean free distance
      between WC particles on the creep behavior of the WC-Co alloys (2);
   creep mechanisms developed for dispersion strengthened alloys applied to
      WC-Co alloys containing 75–85 volume *percent* dispersed phase (2);

FICHE   (FIELD 5)
        Fiche No.   First Frame   Last Frame
           825   a1   a8

Figure 5.14. *Continued.*

reduced to a searchable surrogate consisting of weighted source-derived noun phrases.

In searching LEADER, the user entered a preliminary search description, via the 2260 terminal, in the form of a set of declarative English sentences. These sentences were syntactically analyzed and reduced to noun phrases which were in turn reduced to nontrivial component words. The system then presented to the user the noun phrases, derived from the document collection and stored in a noun phrase dictionary, that appeared to most closely match the significant words of his initial search description. The user could accept or reject these phrases. If he rejected them, an alternative set was generated and displayed. If he accepted any, he could choose to view any of the documents associated with these phrases in the data base. Alternatively, he could elaborate by asking to see other phrases that were most closely affiliated with the group of noun phrases he had already accepted. As a result of his interaction with the data base he could view citations or full text of documents at his terminal.

LEADER was later developed into an operating retrieval system known as LEADERMART (Kasarda and Hillman, 1972).

LEADERMART

As described by Kasarda and Hillman (1972), LEADERMART represents a full-scale implementation of the experimental LEADER system. LEADERMART became fully operational at the Mart Science and Engineering Library of Lehigh University in September 1971. LEADERMART provides a science-oriented information service for the eight interdisciplinary research centers on the Lehigh University campus. The system is maintained on a 65 K Control Data Corporation (CDC) 6400 computer, and almost one billion characters of on-line disk storage are used, mostly to store documents and their associated connectivity files. A telecommunications link connects LEADERMART with the University of Georgia.

In 1973, a number of data bases were maintained on-line for LEADERMART users, including COMPENDEX (Engineering Index) and the CHEMCON file of the Chemical Abstracts Service.

MEDLINE

MEDLINE (MEDLARS On-Line), the on-line version of MEDLARS (Medical Literature Analysis and Retrieval System), was initiated by the National Library of Medicine (NLM) in 1971 as an outgrowth of the AIM–TWX experiments. MEDLINE uses a modified version of the ORBIT system of System Development Corporation known as ELHILL. It operates on an

IBM 370/155 computer at NLM and can support multiple users simultaneously. The MEDLINE data base in May 1973 comprised about 425,000 citations for articles contained in 1200 leading medical journals and indexed into the system since January 1, 1970.

Each user of the service pays for his own terminal and telephone costs. The system can be used by teletype, TWX, IBM 2741, and other terminals operating at 100, 148, and 300 words per minute. User institutions can obtain appropriate terminals for as low as $65 per month. Modified TWX equipment, as used for interlibrary loans in many institutions, can also be applied. In addition to these costs, user institutions must agree to send at least one person to NLM for training in the use of the system, and, further, they must agree to provide bibliographic services to health professionals beyond their normal service responsibilities. In 1973, NLM announced its intention of charging users at the rate of $6 per hour for MEDLINE use, with an additional charge levied for off-line printing.

In late February 1971, NLM initiated an investigation of possible backbone communication networks which might offer the remote users of the NLM system an opportunity to lower their individual communications costs. Based on the experience of the AIM–TWX pilot project, there was a concern that unless the communications costs of the users could be reduced, the usage of any centralized retrieval system would be severely limited.

As a result of this investigation and a subsequent request for proposals, NLM negotiated contracts with the Western Union Corporation and Tymshare Inc. for telecommunications services to provide a backbone communications network for MEDLINE users. The NLM plans called for a two-phased approach toward implementing this network.

The phase I network which became operational in mid-December 1971 consisted mainly of Western Union Datacom† service supplemented by leased telephone lines from the American Telephone and Telegraph Company (AT&T). The initial network provided local telephone access to the NLM computer for all regional medical libraries and MEDLARS centers. For these users, a 300 Baud‡ channel was provided in each city to permit them to use their 30 character per second terminals. Other MEDLINE users with teletype-compatible terminals (i.e., 10 character per second ASCII) were able

---

†Datacom, a service of Western Union, provides point-to-point digital transmission between forty-five cities along Western Union's transcontinental microwave network.

‡*Baud*: "A unit of signalling speed equal to the number of discrete conditions or signal events per second. For example, one baud equals one-half dot cycle per second in Morse code, one bit per second in a train of binary signals, and one 3-bit value per second in a train of signals each of which can assume one of eight different states" (F. Casey, ed. (1970). *Compilation of Terms in Information Sciences Technology*. Washington, D.C.: Federal Council for Science and Technology, PB 193 346, p. 40).

to access the NLM computer by calling any one of the following cities: Albany, N.Y.; Cincinnati, Ohio; Atlanta, Ga.; Denver, Colo.; Dallas, Tex.; Sacramento, Ca.; or Bethesda, Md. TWX terminals with an alternate use arrangement were also able to access the network through the above cities. Sacramento and Cincinnati each have one 300 Baud channel available for users outside the regional medical libraries and MEDLARS centers. Users with IBM 2741-compatible terminals were required to access the NLM computer by placing a long-distance call to Bethesda.

The second phase of the MEDLINE network, which became operational in February 1972, consists primarily of a backbone network supplied by Tymshare Inc. and supplemented by Western Union Datacom and AT&T leased lines. The Western Union and AT&T segments of the phase II network are arranged to supplement the geographic coverage of the TYMSHARE network. Several of the Western Union lines in phase I were discontinued.

User access to the TYMSHARE segment of the network is possible through each of the following cities: Seattle, Wash.; Oakland, San Francisco, Los Altos, Palo Alto, Cupertino, Oxnard, Inglewood, Newport Beach, and San Diego, Ca.; Dallas and Houston, Tex.; Chicago, Ill.; Mishiwaka, Ind.; Jackson and Livonia, Mich.; Syracuse, Buffalo, Rochester, and New York, N.Y.; Boston, Mass.; Hartford and Darian, Conn.; Philadelphia, Pa.; Englewood Cliffs, N.J.; and Arlington, Va. A limited amount of local access to the TYMSHARE network is also available in Portland, Ore.; St. Louis, Mo.; Cleveland, Ohio; Sacramento, Ca.; and Milwaukee, Wis. The NLM network can serve at least 200 institutions with a maximum of 40–45 simultaneous users. Over 100 institutions were active MEDLINE users by the end of 1972.

The TYMSHARE segment of the network supports the following types of terminals: Teletype (TTY) terminals (10, 15, 30 characters per second), IBM 2741 (EBCDIC*) terminals, and any other terminal compatible with these types. One advantage of the TYMSHARE segment of the MEDLINE network is that users will be able to access other computers on the network by dialing the same telephone number as that used for MEDLINE. The communications network is illustrated in Figure 5.15.

In 1973 a number of separate but related data bases were available or planned for implementation through the MEDLINE network. One of these, SDILINE, is a current awareness data base which contains citations for *all* articles indexed by NLM from *all* MEDLARS journals (about 2400), but only for the latest month of processing. These citations are made available in the SDILINE data base before they appear in the monthly printed *Index*

EBCDIC: Extended Binary Coded Decimal Interchange Code, the principal code system used in IBM 360 series computers.

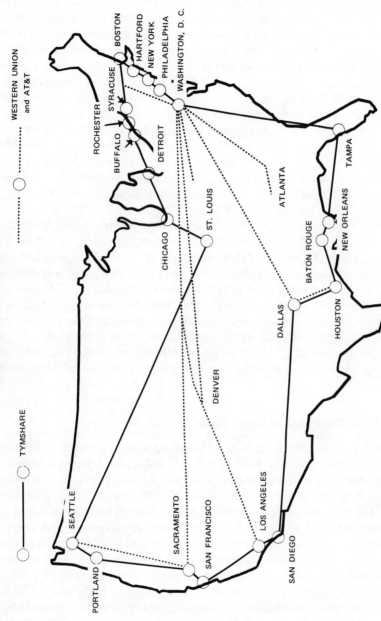

COMMUNICATIONS NETWORK

TYMSHARE

WESTERN UNION
and AT&T

Figure 5.15. MEDLINE communications network, September 1972. Reproduced by permission of the National Library of Medicine.

SEATTLE
PORTLAND
SACRAMENTO
SAN FRANCISCO
LOS ANGELES
SAN DIEGO
DENVER
DALLAS
HOUSTON
BATON ROUGE
NEW ORLEANS
TAMPA
ATLANTA
ST. LOUIS
CHICAGO
DETROIT
BUFFALO
ROCHESTER
SYRACUSE
BOSTON
HARTFORD
NEW YORK
PHILADELPHIA
WASHINGTON, D. C.

Medicus. SDILINE can be used by a health professional as a very efficient means of keeping current in his field of specialization. Once he has developed a suitable searching strategy, by trial and error, he can return to a MEDLINE terminal each month and apply this strategy to the newly added data base. Thus, he keeps continually informed of new citations (from 2400 journals) that match his current interests. CATLINE was close to implementation early in 1973. This file provides access to NLM's machine-readable book catalog. It will be searchable from several access points, including author, title, series, subject, and language. It is intended as a tool for libraries to use in acquisition, cataloging, interlibrary loan, and reference activities. SER-LINE, planned for implementation later in 1973, will provide a list of 5000–6000 biomedical serials with an indication of which of several libraries holds each title. AVLINE will be an on-line catalog of audiovisual materials; it is planned for implementation in 1974.

MEDLINE is a dynamic system, and changes are constantly being made to it. In May 1973, it was reported to be operating at a rate of 240,000 searches a year. Growth has been staggering. Between June 1972 and May 1973, use increased at a rate of about 13 % a month. That is, use was doubling in a period of 6 months. This growth rate was increasing in 1973: February use was 30 % more than in January, and March use was up a further 30 %. In March 1973, a greatly increased capacity was provided through a contract with the Computer Center of the State University of New York (SUNY). Through this contract, SUNY makes MEDLINE available to an additional 40 simultaneous users and also provides backup when the NLM computer is down.

New York Times Information Bank

This system is designed to provide direct access to abstracts of news and editorial matter from *The New York Times* and selected material from over seventy newspapers and periodicals (*National Science*, 1969). Approximately 250,000 items are added annually, about 100,000 from *The New York Times* itself. The news items themselves are converted to microfiche and stored in a microfilm retrieval device that will interface with the computer. Indexing and abstracting is conducted on-line, using video terminals (IBM 4506). The input of the indexers is scanned and corrected by senior indexers. A thesaurus is used in indexing and searching. Output consists of abstracts and full biblio-graphic data, including the address of the full clipping in the microfiche file. Within the Times building, the clipping itself may be viewed on the same CRT display (IBM 4506 with a 4275 terminal control unit); it is retrieved by the depression of a function key on the terminal and transmitted by closed-circuit television. A hard-copy print-out of any displayed item can be requested. System software was prepared by IBM Federal Systems Division to operate on an IBM 360/50. The system is designed to support up to 500 terminals on up to 120 lines. Of the 64 terminals installed in the Times building in 1972, 26 are used for indexing and 38 for searching. Full technical details on the system are included in Table 5.2.

TABLE 5.2.   Technical Fact Sheet for *The New York Times* Information Bank

Central processing unit	IBM 360/50 with a core of 524,000 bytes (which will be shared with other applications). (IBM 370/145 was under consideration in 1972.)
Mass storage devices	IBM 2314 direct access disk storage facility (200 million bytes each).
	IBM 2321 Data Cell Drive (400 million bytes each) (ultimately to be replaced by IBM 3330 disks).
Tape drives	IBM 2401 (model 4).
High-speed printer	IBM 1403 (uppercase and lowercase).
Microfiche storage and retrieval device	Foto-Mem RISAR (storage capacity of 4.95 million page images) controlled by a CENTAUR computer.[a]
In-house terminals (used for data entry, inquiry, and output)	IBM 4506 display station with 4275 terminal control unit.
Out-of-house terminals (used for inquiry and output)	Any of several compatible CRT and teletypewriter terminals.
Access method	BTAM
Operating system	DOS
Programming languages	BAL, PL/I, and COBOL.

SOURCE: *The New York Times.*
[a]This microfiche retrieval device was never fully implemented. As of March 1973, the microfiche system was based on remote display of images of fiche selected from the file by a human operator (see Chapter Sixteen).

It is intended that the information bank will be made available to outside clients as well as to staff members of *The New York Times.* Libraries or other institutions may pay a subscription fee which will enable them, via their own terminals, to access the data base remotely. The project could make available to the general public an immense data base of current information on all topics. In the words of Ivan Veit, Executive Vice President of *The New York Times,*

> We envision that the instantaneous accessibility of a gigantic store of background information on virtually every subject of human research and inquiry will

prove to be of immeasurable value not only to major reference and research libraries, general business services and other media, but also to individuals engaged in all forms of research. . . . For example, the services could be put to invaluable use by government agencies engaged in social research, scholars preparing such major documents as doctoral dissertations, general business services conducting research in specific areas for various clients, journalists marshalling material for books and articles. The list could be extended to include the news and public affairs departments of radio and television networks, advertising and public relations agencies, and the research arms of the many philanthropic foundations.

On-line indexing and abstracting operations began in December 1971, and it is expected that items from *The New York Times* itself, retroactive to January 1969, will be available on-line by the end of 1972. Indexers operate directly at the CRT, working from clippings. Indexing and abstracting is conducted as a single operation, and the bibliographic record created is very complete. Bibliographic data include journal, date, page, column, and indicators of type of item (e.g., editorial, survey, review) and of illustrations. The content of clippings is represented by descriptors denoting subjects as well as proper names. The descriptors are weighted (on a 4 point scale) to represent their relative importance to the item indexed. The abstract is also given a weight in relation to the subject sequence on an 8 point scale. For example, a particular event (e.g., an assassination attempt) may be referred to several times over several days in the press. A front page item discussing this event in full is likely to receive a top weight of 8, while later, more passing references will get lower weights.

The search system itself is very flexible and detailed (although simple and seemingly effective) instructions are built into the programs. This search system is designed for easy use by the reporters of *The New York Times*. Conventional boolean strategies are employed, and the searcher may use a number of search elements in addition to the subject descriptors. He can, for example, restrict a search by date, type of item (e.g., editorial, news analysis), illustration, source, or the weights assigned to terms or to items. The vocabulary of the system, including the cross-reference structure, can be viewed on-line. Vocabulary maintenance can also be conducted as an on-line activity.

The microform interface was designed to permit a searcher to retrieve the microfiche of any clipping, since the bibliographic records retrieved with the abstracts include unique identifying numbers for these microfiche images. For internal use within the Times building, the fiche themselves are stored in a large carousel device, which was intended to be accessed remotely and to transmit images to the viewer's screen via closed-circuit television. The microform retrieval system, built to the Times specifications by Foto-Mem Inc. (a company which has since been through bankruptcy proceedings), was not fully operational as of March 1973. At that time it was possible for a user to view the image of any selected item at his terminal, but only after a request to a human operator to extract the appropriate fiche from the central file. The searcher at the terminal has no facility for producing hard copy locally, but he may request that a paper copy be made from the file and sent to him. Users of the system away from the offices of *The New York Times* will not be able to access the microfiche file through their consoles. However, it is planned that these users will be supplied with their own microfiche files, for items from *The New York Times* only, which will permit them to view items locally on a conventional microfiche reader. As of January 1973 the U.S. State Department, the United Nations, the National Broadcasting Co., Exxon (formerly Standard Oil of New Jersey), and the Chase Manhattan Bank had all signed up to be subscribers to the information bank. Total cost to a subscriber is in the region of $25,000 a year, exclusive of communications costs.

ORBIT

ORBIT (On-Line Retrieval of Bibliographic Information Time-Shared) is a proprietary product of the System Development Corporation (Nance and Lathrop, 1968; Seiden, 1971). It developed out of the earlier COLEX (CIRC On-Line Experimentation) system designed for the Foreign Technology Division of the Air Force Systems Command (see also the section on CIRCOL). In 1971, ORBIT was in its second version (ORBIT II), and a third version (ORBIT III) was in the process of development. The system was adopted by the National Library of Medicine, where it was called ELHILL. ELHILL was first used to make available the on-line portion of the MEDLARS data base, namely those citations published in *Abridged Index Medicus*. This application was known as AIM–TWX (Abridged Index Medicus by TWX).

ORBIT has since been used to make available a very substantial portion of the MEDLARS data base for searching in the on-line mode (the on-line version of MEDLARS is now known as MEDLINE). The ORBIT system has been used by the Copper Data Center of the Battelle Memorial Institute and at the headquarters of the Copper Development Association in New York (Covington, 1969). ORBIT has also been adopted by the U.S. State Department. The CHEMCON and ERIC data bases were available on ORBIT in 1973 and could be accessed through the TYMSHARE network.

ORBIT can be implemented on an IBM 360/40 or larger computer. It can be operated via a wide variety of terminals, typewriter and video, including teletypes, IBM 2741, Execuport and CC-30 (Computer Communications Inc.).

Commercially available, ORBIT comprises two major programs: a file-generation program, which structures a data base for efficient storage and retrieval; and a retrieval program, which permits the conduct of interactive searches. ORBIT can provide a response of a few seconds in searching a file of over 100,000 records and, using a large computer configuration, can handle more than 150 users concurrently. Each unit record may contain up to 255 different categories of data (e.g., author, title). The maximum unit record size is 7100 characters, adequate for the storage of most abstracts. Up to a million records (48 million words of text) can be stored in the standard version of ORBIT II.

ORBIT is a very flexible system. It will accept direct boolean search statements, and it will permit the combination of various search statements into a complex strategy. Searches on complete hierarchies of terms can be conducted [see the explosion example in Chapter Three (p. 30)], subheadings can be searched, and the vocabulary can be viewed on-line a segment at a time. A title search capability is included in ORBIT. Many of the search examples presented in Chapter Three were drawn from ORBIT. An annotated sample printout is included as Figure 5.16.

QUOBIRD

This is an experimental retrieval system designed and operated at the Department of Computer Science, Queen's University of Belfast. In 1971 the system contained 1000 document references, with abstracts, on atomic and molecular physics drawn from the INSPEC tapes prepared by the Institution of Electrical Engineers. A growth to 10,000 references and abstracts was projected for 1972 and a growth to 100,000 references by 1973.

The system, which operates on an ICL 1907* computer, is self-instructive. The user communicates with the system in English. He begins by typing in a phrase of up to eight words. The search program eliminates nonsignificant words and then finds how many documents in the corpus contain the phrase specified by the user. This count is presented to the terminal user who may choose to:

1. Modify by the addition of a second phrase.
2. View all sentences containing the search phrase.
3. View complete abstracts containing the search phrase.
4. View the citations of documents containing the search phrase.

A sample interaction is reproduced below:

System : key?
  User : *electron excitation*
System : 173 references

---

*Produced by International Computers Ltd. (ICL).

System : R, A, P, M?

User : *M*

User : *helium*

(The choice available was
(R : References
(A : Abstracts
(P : Phrases
(M : More keys

System : New key   : 248 references
            Previous key : 173 references
            Intersection : 24 references
            Union   : 397 references
System : N, P, I, U?
  User : *I*
System : R, A, P, M?
  User : *M* ... etc.

In the Belfast work, considerable emphasis has been placed on procedures that will minimize the number of disk accesses required to complete a search, thus optimizing response time and reducing costs. This aspect of the work has been described by Higgins and Smith (1971). The general system is described by Carville, et al. (1971).

RECON

RECON (REmote CONsole) is an on-line retrieval system operated by the National Aeronautics and Space Administration (NASA) (National Aeronautics and Space Administration, 1966, 1970; Wente, 1971). Experimentation with RECON appears to go back as far as 1965, but the system has been made available to NASA personnel on a reasonably permanent basis only since 1969. The RECON data base is now located on an IBM 360/50 at the NASA Scientific and Technical Information Facility, College Park, Md. RECON stations, comprising keyboard, cathode ray display, and teleprinter, are located at NASA facilities in various parts of the country and communicate with the computer by means of leased telephone lines. There were twenty-five consoles, in several geographic locations, by 1971. The NASA IBM 360/50 has 512K of core storage, two data cells, and two 2314 disk units.

The data base consists of all citations, for technical reports and journal articles, appearing in NASA's *Scientific and Technical Aerospace Reports*, in *International Aerospace Abstracts*, and in *Aerospace Medicine and Biology*. This now represents a data base of approximately a million items. Files of NASA research resumes and contracts data, describing ongoing research and development, are also available. RECON operates on a main linear record (document) file and a set of inverted index files.

ORBIT II

SAMPLE

PRINTOUT

System Development Corporation

2500 Colorado Ave.

Santa Monica, California 90406

This folder provides a sample ORBIT II printout which illustrates the interactive exchange between the user and the system. Three major features are illustrated: search, retrieval, and tutorials. To search, the user enters a term; the program then tells him how many records, if any, contain that term. There are several commands available to assist in this process. Retrieval consists of using the PRINT command to retrieve information from records that were found during the search. Tutorials (on-line explanations) are also illustrated.

Data base contents are contained in Unit Records. The Unit Record describes the items of concern in the data base. For example, a Unit Record may consist of a bibliographic citation, a case history, a status file, etc. In this illustration, a bibliographic citation is used.

The sample printout has been reduced in size. In actual use its size would be determined by the terminal device, e.g., a teletypewriter or a 2741. The annotations have been added to help explain user-system interaction. Because of space limitations, a limited search and only a few of the more commonly used commands are shown. Also not shown are the procedures for signing in, error messages and ways to correct errors, on-line up-dates, and many of the program messages that inform or otherwise assist the user.

ANNOTATIONS

PRINTOUT

The HELLO message, available as an option, has various uses, depending upon customer needs. Here it provides status information and a security key.

HELLO FROM ORBIT II. YOUR DATA BASE WAS LAST UPDATED IN DEC 1970.
PLEASE TYPE YOUR IDENTITY CODE AND STRIKE THE CARRIAGE RETURN KEY:
USER: ordex473

The user is alerted that it is his turn by the cue word "USER:". (He is also informed about any error he makes.)

PROG:
FOR MORE INFORMATION STRIKE THE SPACE BAR AND THEN THE CARRIAGE RETURN KEY. OTHERWISE ENTER SEARCH STATEMENT 1, OR A COMMAND.

If the user so desires, the program will provide additional information about its operation.

USER: "explain unit record"

PROG:

The user enters an EXPLAIN command (used to obtain explanations of any command or program message). Commands are surrounded by quotation marks.

THE UNIT RECORD FOR EACH DOCUMENT CONTAINS THE FOLLOWING INFORMATION:

The number of elements and those which are searchable are separately determined for each data base. However; all are printable.

ABBREVI-ATION	CATEGORY NAMES	SEARCHABLE CATEGORIES
AU	AUTHORS	X
TI	TITLE	
AN	ACCESSION NUMBER	X
PD	PUBLICATION DATE	X
SH	SUBJECT HEADINGS	X
CN	CLASSIFICATION NUMBER	X
LA	LANGUAGE OF PUBLICATION	
SO	SOURCE JOURNAL	X

The user is asked to enter a search term or command. Note automatic numbering of search statements.

SS1/C?---SEARCH STATEMENT 1 OR COMMAND--
USER: air pollution

Any term of any length including numeric terms may be entered on a search term. The user enters air pollution as a search term and is informed that 423 records in the data base are indexed under that term. Had there been no postings, he would have been so advised.

PROG: PSTG---NUMBER POSTINGS (423)
SS2/C?---SEARCH STATEMENT 2 OR COMMAND--
USER: lung diseases

Figure 5.16. ORBIT sample printout. Reproduced by permission of System Development Corporation.

PROG: PSTG---NUMBER POSTINGS (1088)
SS3/C?---SEARCH STATEMENT 3 OR COMMAND--
USER: 1 and 2
PROG: PSTG---NUMBER POSTINGS (21)
SS4/C?---SEARCH STATEMENT 4 OR COMMAND--
USER: "print 2"
PROG:

AU - LEFCOE NM
AU - WONNACOTT TH
TI - THE PREVALENCE OF CHRONIC RESPIRATORY DISEASE IN MALES.
SO - CANAD MED ASS J 102 381-5 28 FEB 70

AU - LILLINGTON GA
TI - NITROGEN DIOXIDE -- THE NEW "YELLOW PERIL".
SO - JAMA 212 1368 25 MAY 70

HOW MANY MORE ON-LINE?
USER: none
SS4/C?---SEARCH STATEMENT 4 OR COMMAND--
USER: brain#
PROG: MM--MULTI MEANING (BRAIN#) (3) TERMS
SEE? (YES/NO/ALL)
USER: "?"
PROG: SEE? (YES/NO/ALL) - DO YOU WANT TO SEE THESE TERMS? ANSWER 'YES', 'NO' TO CANCEL THE REQUEST, OR 'ALL' TO RETRIEVE ON ALL OF THEM.
USER: yes
PROG:
1 BRAIN (SH)
2 BRAIN STEM (SH)
3 BRAIN RV (AU)
NUMBERS, ALL, OR NONE--SPECIFY BY LIST OF NUMBERS, ALL, OR NONE.
USER: none

1088 records are indexed under the term lung diseases.

The user now combines search statements 1 and 2. He could have started by entering air pollution and lung diseases as a single search term (all Boolean combinations including negation--not--may be used). Note that he can now refer to air pollution as 1, lung diseases as 2, the combination of them as 3, etc. There are 21 records that meet the two search criteria.

The user enters a PRINT command requesting that two records be printed. This gives him three elements--AU, TI, SO--(an arbitrary selection, modified for each data base) of the first two items that qualify. He could have specified more elements, fewer elements, or all elements.

The user is asked how many more records he wants to see on-line. However, he could have specified more in the first place or could have had other than the first two printed. He could also have had records from any previous search statement printed.

The # sign is an "any character" symbol and may be used at the end or in the middle of a term to stand for any missing character(s). This is especially useful for very long or incompletely known terms.

The user is unsure of the meaning of the last message and types in ? as a command. A brief explanation is then provided.

In this instance there are three terms that qualify, two subject headings referring to anatomical parts and an author named Brain. The user can now indicate which Brain he wants to search on. If he is still unsure, he can retrieve one or more items from each and display their titles, subject headings, and other elements.

The NEIGHBOR command retrieves the alphabetic neighbors of the search term in the index. Five are automatically displayed unless the user asks for more. This command is useful for uncertain spellings and for browsing.

The TREE command is a special command used with hierarchically structured data bases. It prints the superordinate class and all the terms in the first subordinate class. By moving up or down the tree the user can quickly determine what logically related terms may be in the index.

The user instructs the program to print the 231 records off-line. This procedure is frequently used when there are many records to print, usually after a few of them have been explored.

```
SS5/C?---SEARCH STATEMENT 5 OR COMMAND--
USER:  "neighbor durel"
PROG:
POSTINGS        TERM
  29            DURA MATER (SH)
   1            DURAND DP (AU)
   3            DURELL J (AU)
   1            DUREY D (AU)
   4            DURLACH J (AU)
       DUREL ITSELF DOES NOT EXIST IN THE INDEX
SS5/C?---SEARCH STATEMENT 5 OR COMMAND--
USER:  "tree air pollution"
PROG:
ENVIRONMENTAL HAZARDS
   AIR POLLUTION
      AIR POLLUTION, RADIOACTIVE
      AUTOMOBILE EXHAUST
      DUST
SS5/C?---SEARCH STATEMENT 5 OR COMMAND--
USER:  pregnancy and rubella or pregnancy and measles
PROG: PSTG---NUMBER POSTINGS (231)
SS6/C---SEARCH STATEMENT 6 OR COMMAND--
USER:  "print off-line"
```

Figure 5.16. *Continued.*

Search strategies must be entered in the form of boolean algebraic statements, and the searcher can only use terms appearing in the *NASA Thesaurus* or the *Subject Authority List* that was its predecessor. When a searcher enters a term in RECON, it is possible to obtain a count of the number of postings of the descriptor together with those that are alphabetically adjacent to it in the thesaurus. A further command will generate a display of descriptors that are semantically related to the original search term (i.e., those descriptors that are *related terms* in the *NASA Thesaurus*). Any search logic involving AND, OR, or NOT operations can be accepted, and limitations by date or document accession number may be placed by the searcher.

However, as RECON was originally designed, it was not possible to introduce initially a string of terms in a specified logical relationship. Instead, the searcher must build up term lists, a term at a time, and then combine terms using the AND (*), OR (+), and NOT (−) operators. Alternatively, he may select terms from a vocabulary display, in which they automatically are regarded as being in an "or" relationship, and then combine them with other terms using the AND (*) operator. Searches may also be conducted by author, corporate source, report, or contract number. Tallies, showing the number of citations satisfying a particular logical statement, are displayed on the screen. The searcher may view selected citations on this video display, may use the teleprinter to provide hard copy of anything thus displayed, or may request a full off-line printout of all citations satisfying a particular strategy.

NASA has made the RECON search programs available to industry through the Computer Software Management and Information Center (COSMIC) at the University of Georgia.

The origin and development of RECON is confusing to anyone outside the NASA organization and has not been presented clearly in the literature. RECON was actually developed in its present form for NASA by Lockheed Missiles & Space Co. and is, in fact, almost identical with a proprietary system offered by Lockheed which is known as DIALOG (which see). A source of confusion is the fact that some of the early on-line work for NASA was conducted by the Bunker-Ramo Corporation, and this organization issued some of the early RECON reports, including the first RECON user's manual. An additional cause of confusion is due to the fact that the present (1973) NASA contract for maintenance and upgrading of RECON is held by Informatics/TISCO.

RECON itself is a retrieval system only and does not handle file maintenance activities. At NASA the RECON system is used in association with STIMS (Scientific and Technical Information Modular System), a background set of programs that performs file maintenance, search, and publication functions. The combined system is known as RECON/STIMS. The Scientific and Technical Information Facility is now operated for NASA by Informatics/TISCO, which also has the responsibility for maintenance and upgrading of RECON.

The system has been adopted by a number of government agencies, including the U.S. Department of Justice and the TOXICON (which see) service of the National Library of Medicine, and the related DIALOG system by several others. The DIALOG system is also used to make the NASA date base available in Europe through the European Space Research Organization (ESRO) (Isotta, 1970; Raitt, 1970). A small RECON user group meets periodically, and a RECON news bulletin is distributed by NASA.

A major application of RECON is being made by the U.S. Atomic Energy Commission. The data base consists of approximately 200,000 items from *Nuclear Science Abstracts*, indexed by descriptors from the thesaurus of the International Nuclear Information Service (INIS). The data base is loaded on an IBM 360/75 computer at Oak Ridge National Laboratory, Oak Ridge, Tenn. The system has operated successfully for some time, with seven stations on-line to the IBM 360/75. Plans call for expansion to 100 terminals by the end of 1973 and possibly a data base of 600,000 items by that time.

In 1971–1972, new features were programmed into RECON, both by Informatics and by some of the RECON users directly, to increase the flexibility of the system. The RECON programs have been modified to permit the searching of full natural language text, including the use of word position indicators and word truncation. It is also possible, in a modification made by a RECON user, to input a complete search strategy, involving terms connected by boolean operators, rather than having to build up a strategy one element at a time.

RIOT

RIOT (Retrieval of Information by On-Line Terminal) is an experimental system at the Culham Laboratory of the United Kingdom Atomic Energy Authority. The system has been described by Negus (1971) and by Negus and Hall (1971). The early RIOT experiments were carried out on a KDF9* computer using a video terminal with linked teletypewriter; the former was for display and the latter was for printout of user–system dialogue and/or selected retrieval citations (see Figure 5.17). RIOT experiments have been conducted with small data bases in computational physics, the social sciences, and plasma physics. It is planned to implement an operating system covering 30,000 references in the field of plasma physics. The system is designed to

---

*Produced by English Electric Co.

Figure 5.17. RIOT: video terminal and linked teletypewriter. Reproduced by permission of the United Kingdom Atomic Energy Authority, Culham Laboratory.

search primarily on titles or titles augmented by additional keywords assigned by an indexer. The operational system will run on an ICL System 4/70 computer and will be largely based on the earlier RIOT work. Particular attention has been paid to ease-of-use factors as described by Hall, et al. (1972).

SMART

Although SMART was not designed originally as an on-line system, it has various interactive features that make it seem particularly suitable for implementation in the on-line mode. SMART was developed by Salton, first at Harvard and later at Cornell University. The SMART literature is extensive. The most detailed description of the system, and the theories underlying it, is contained in two books by Salton (1968, 1971), but an excellent summary of its interactive features can be found in a paper by Lesk and Salton (1969).

The SMART programs operate on the natural language of documents (usually abstracts) and of requests, and they can perform a variety of automatic text analysis, search, and retrieval operations. These text analysis procedures include synonym recognition, stem-suffix cutoff, disambiguation, phrase recognition, statistical term association, and hierarchical search expansions.

The characteristics of SMART are best illustrated by considering the processes that could be applied to a collection of abstracts on a particular topic which are available in machine-readable form. In entering these abstracts into the system, any or all of the available processing options may be used, as follows:

1. A *suffix s* process will remove the final s from plural nouns in order to treat, for example, "weld" and "welds" as identical terms.

2. A stem-suffix cutoff will reduce words to root form (e.g., "weld," "welding," "welded," and "weldability" to "weld").

3. A word root is given a weight in relation to a particular abstract, based on frequency of occurrence of the root in the abstract and the frequency of occurrence and distribution of the root over the collection as a whole (i.e., the weight is really a discrimination value).

4. Word stems are matched against a *synonym dictionary*, which is really a simple thesaurus, humanly created but machine-stored. When the root "weld" is matched against the synonym dictionary, the numerical code for the concept group in which "weld" occurs will be assigned to the document record. Presumably, this conceptual group will contain other words or roots that relate in some way to metal-joining processes.

5. The abstract may be matched against a preconstructed dictionary of *statistical phrases*, consisting mainly of word pairs. A statistical phrase from this dictionary may be assigned if the concepts represented in the phrase are found to occur in the abstract. For example, if the concept "book" and the concept "obscenity" are present in an abstract, the statistical phrase "pornographic literature" may be assigned.

6. A sentence may be syntactically analyzed and *syntactic phrases* recognized. A syntactic phrase is similar to a statistical phrase, except that each word in the phrase must hold a specified syntactic relation with the other words in the phrase. Possible ambiguities can be resolved by syntactic analysis.

7. Statistical associations between words occurring in an abstract may be used to generate further word classes that may be useful for retrieval purposes.

It must be emphasized that these are all processing options that exist. It is unlikely that all would be applied to a particular collection, except for the purpose of comparing their effectiveness.

Searches are conducted in SMART on natural language request statements. Essentially these request statements are processed in the same way that documents are processed, including reduction to word stems, assignment of conceptual group numbers and weighting of these groups. The natural language request is processed against the file of document representations, and the search program looks for abstracts that most closely match the request statement. A *correlation coefficient* is derived to show the degree of similarity between the request statement and each document, and the entire collection is ranked in decreasing order of correlation coefficient. The result is a ranked output of document representations printed in order of this degree of match. In practice, some cutoff point, or *threshold*, is usually established to avoid printing out the entire set of document representations.

SMART is a very important experimental system, because it offers many possible search options. A request can be processed against a document collection at any of several levels—simple word match, word stem match, statistical phrases, syntactic phrases, thesaurus groups, hierarchical groupings, or statistical associations. The searcher is thus given great flexibility in varying the search criteria in order to move in the direction of high recall or high precision. The system has built-in evaluation procedures whereby the results of one search option can be compared with the results of any alternative. It is intended that SMART be used with *iterative searches*. That is, the searcher will receive preliminary results from one search option, evaluate these, and indicate which of the retrieved items are relevant and which are not. When these relevance decisions are fed back into the system, the search programs automatically modify the weights of terms in the request statement so as to bring the statement closer to the profiles of the relevant documents in the collection, and thus to improve the quality of the second search. It is these iterative procedures that make SMART appear particularly suitable for use in an on-line, interactive mode, and Williamson and Williamson (1970) have in fact described a prototype on-line SMART system.

SOLER

SOLER (System for On-Line Entry and Retrieval) is an experimental interactive system operated by the Moore School of Electrical Engineering, University of Pennsylvania (Hirschfeld, 1971; Rubinoff, et al., 1968; University of Pennsylvania, 1971a, b). It operates in real-time, using teletypewriter or CRT terminals, or both. Formatted files or textual data, or combinations of these, can be accommodated. A multiplicity of data base files, which can be accessed either cooperatively or independently, can be supported. For example, the same search strategy can be applied simultaneously to multiple files, using the command RETRIEVE ANYWHERE.

SOLER will permit searching on single words and/or ordered word phrases within text, as well as on data values in formatted fields. Combinations of natural language and structured data can be handled. Because SOLER allows on-line input, it is suitable for the construction, maintenance, and exploitation of personal files. Information can be formatted by the user in any arbitrary manner. Any newly defined format can be entered and established within the system at any time, directly from the teletypewriter remote terminal or from magnetic tape or punched cards in batch mode. Individual data items within a record can be as long as 65,000 alphameric characters.

In 1971, SOLER was operational on an RCA Spectra 70/46. It is programmed entirely in COBOL and will run also on an IBM 360 series computer (360/50 or larger). The system has been used experimentally with a Toxicology Information File established by the National Library of Medicine.

SPIRES

SPIRES (Stanford Public Information Retrieval System) (Parker, 1970, 1971), a prototype system developed at Stanford University beginning in 1967, was originally restricted to the subject of physics. Now it is being expanded to other subject areas. SPIRES has been used on IBM 360/67 and 360/91 computers, and, in principle, it can handle up to 150 users at the same time, although in practice the maximum number operating the system simultaneously is about fifteen. IBM 2741 terminals are used. Costs of using the system have been estimated at about $10 per terminal hour, exclusive of storage costs.

SPIRES will permit an individual user at Stanford to construct his own personal search file, to maintain and update it, to search and retrieve from it, and to display outputs in a variety of formats. Several departments of the university have used SPIRES to build, maintain, and search files on-line.

SPIRES is integrated with the Stanford library automation system, known as BALLOTS (Bibliographic Automation of Large Library Operations Using a Time-Sharing System). This integration permits sharing of facilities, both hardware and software, and thus reduces overall costs. Shared hardware facilities include a CPU and direct-access devices. Shared software facilities include an on-line text editor, and file-handling and task-scheduling routines. The largest bibliographic data base handled is the MARC (Machine Readable Cataloging) file of the Library of Congress.

STAIRS

STAIRS (Storage and Information Retrieval System) (IBM, 1971) is an on-line text retrieval system made commercially available by IBM in 1972 and designed for operation on 360 and 370 series computers. The system can search for combinations of words in a specified boolean relationship, which occur in particular documents, paragraphs, or sentences. Word truncation is possible, and a document-ranking capability exists in the system. A SAVE function is available to allow a user to store a particular search strategy for later use. This feature allows the system to be used for purposes of selective dissemination of information (SDI). A HELP command provides tutorial assistance to the user. Multiple data bases can be accommodated by STAIRS and can be searched as though they formed a single file. The STAIRS program is based on a text searching system operational in the IBM Technical Information Retrieval Center for 3 years. In 1973, STAIRS was adopted for use in the SUNY system (see below). It was also being used with an *Engineering Index* data base.

State University of New York (SUNY) Bibliographic Retrieval System

The SUNY Biomedical Communication Network is an on-line system that has provided access to bibliographic materials in biomedicine since 1968. Twenty-one medical libraries were participating in this network in 1972, of which ten were in New York. Other participants included the National Library of Medicine, the Ohio State University Medical Center, the William H. Welch Library at Johns Hopkins University, and the University of Illinois. The software adopted by SUNY was the IBM Document Processing System (DPS), which is a module of the IBM Generalized Information System (GIS). The DPS is a batch-oriented program package designed to serve as a complete information system under the control of IBM's OS executive. Functions performed by DPS include loading and updating of files, search and retrieval, and maintenance tasks such as file compression, moving, and listing. The on-line adaptation of DPS for SUNY use has been described by Fenzl (1969). In 1973 a switch was made from DPS to the STAIRS system of IBM.

Member libraries have on-line access to a large biomedical data base via IBM 2740 communication terminals. The data base is loaded on an IBM 370/155 computer located in the offices of the SUNY central administration at Albany, N.Y. IBM 3330 direct-access storage units are used.

The SUNY data base comprised, in May 1972, the following records:
1. The MEDLARS file, back to 1964, comprising over 1.5 million journal references indexed under terms drawn from *Medical Subject Headings* (*MeSH*). Only the portion covering the period October 1969–May 1972 (about 600,000 citations) was available for on-line search.

2. Book catalog records provided by three SUNY medical libraries. This file, which goes back to 1962, contains citations to about 16,000 monographs, of which about 8000 are indexed in depth chapter-by-chapter.
3. Approximately 50,000 bibliographic records for books and serials cataloged by the National Library of Medicine and appearing in the printed *Current Catalog* of NLM. This file goes back to 1967.

Users may retrieve 3 years of data on-line; searches may be continued off-line for citations back to 1964. Off-line searches are input at a library terminal, but are processed later the same day at the computer center in Albany.

This data base is accessible to member libraries for about 38 hours during a 5 day week. The system allows conventional boolean searching on combinations of index terms from *MeSH*. In addition, it is possible to restrict an index term search by the use of words or phrases in the titles of items. For example, consider a search on the topic of "transient global amnesia." The most specific *MeSH* term available is AMNESIA. However, this can be modified by demanding that, of all items indexed under AMNESIA, only those with titles containing the phrase "transient global" should be retrieved. Some experiments in free text searching were planned by SUNY in 1972.

The Suny system has been described by Cain and Pizer (1967), Egeland (1971), and Pizer (1969, 1972). Medical library participation in the network is described by Bridegam and Meyerhoff (1970), and experience in searching the data base is described by Stiller (1970). Statistics on use of the system for the period June 1971–March 1972 are shown in Table 5.3. These figures are included merely as an indication of the user population and the extent of system use. The data relate to off-line searches (i.e., searches entered at a library terminal but processed later the same day at the computer center in Albany).

SUPARS

SUPARS (Syracuse University Psychological Abstracts Retrieval Service) is an interesting experimental on-line retrieval project based on the free text searching of a *Psychological Abstracts* data base (Cook, et al., 1971). The project has been supported by the Rome Air Development Center, Griffiss Air Force Base, N.Y., and carried out by a research team at the School of Library Science, Syracuse University, since July 1969. The data base, in October 1971, included 55,000 bibliographic citations and abstracts from *Psychological Abstracts* back to 1969. The system has used a modified version of the IBM Document Processing System (DPS), as have the CIRCOL and

TABLE 5.3. Search Statistics from the SUNY Biomedical Communication Network, June 1971–March 1972

Terminal	June	July	August	September	October	November	December	January	February	March
						Completed searches				
[a]02 Food and Drug Administration								60[d]	60[d]	28
03 Upstate Medical Center	101	70	66	130	112	94	97	140	185	170
04 Upstate Medical Center										
[a]05 Medical College of Ohio, Toledo								37	72	97
06 University of Rochester	50	62	64	54	77	59	97	85	79	77
07 Indiana University Medical Center	39	36	54	85	80	91	92	94	103	122
08 SUNY at Buffalo	102	72	113	182	227	218	207	231	260	255
09 SUNY at Buffalo										
10 SUNY at Buffalo										
11 Albany Medical College	69	33	65	79	87	76	67	103	100	75
[b]12 National Library of Medicine										
[b]13 National Library of Medicine	76[d]	6[d]	25[d]	41[d]	37[d]	139[d]	253[d]	475[d]	388[d]	75
14 Ohio State University	29	20	31	35	67	65	44	55	65	62
15 Downstate Medical Center	11	12	5	21	18	23	31	11	23	27
16 College of Medicine & Dentistry of N.J., Newark	65	40	73	56	59	126	130	110	92	144
18 Countway Library of Medicine	25	26	33	36	32	36	50	57	71	83
19 Medical College of Virginia	99	52	76	44	66	63	95	87	83	115
[c]20 New York State Library										
[c]21 SUNY at Stony Brook										
22 Cornell University Medical College	60	36	60	62	76	83	113	121	109	77
23 Johns Hopkins University	74	81	90	84	96	90	95	99	143	140
[c]24 U.S. Army Medical Research & Development										
25 Mount Sinai Hospital			18	30	32	44	65	45	43	68
26 Cornell University Life Sciences									60	79
27 University of Illinois, Chicago									25	66
Total	724	540	748	898	1029	1068	1183	1275	1513	1760

SOURCE: State University of New York.
[a]Incomplete.
[b]Terminal not used for searching.
[c]No data available.
[d]Not included in totals.

SUNY systems (which see). It has been made available, using 100 typewriter terminals located in key buildings on the Syracuse campus, to members of the university community during selected periods in 1970 and 1971. The primary operating system of SUPARS was an IBM 360/50, using approximately 64,000 bytes when operational on-line. Later, an IBM 370/155 was substituted. A special teleprocessing program was developed to enable the operating system to interface with the terminals while various on-line systems were operating concurrently.

An unobtrusive data collection program known as STATPAC was also developed and tested. STATPAC records each SUPARS search interaction and other summary statistics of frequency of use, cost of searches, CPU time expended, number of documents found, and other related data. Personal data on users is locked to prevent unauthorized access.

An interesting feature of SUPARS is a *search data base*, which permits a user to retrieve, for any word he enters, all previous search strategies that have used this word. This data base can thus be used to suggest alternative terms or search approaches.

TIP

The TIP (Technical Information Project) was one of the earliest experiments in the use of on-line computers for information retrieval activities. TIP was developed at the Massachusetts Institute of Technology (MIT) in 1962 (Kessler, 1967; Mathews, 1967). It was designed for implementation on an IBM 7094 with multiple consoles (IBM 2741) operating within the general MIT time-sharing environment. The initial data base was one in physics, consisting of over 35,000 articles from about twenty-five physics journals. This was later extended to cover about 100,000 physics items. For each physics article, the following record is stored: author, title, journal reference, institutional affiliation of authors, and a list of each journal article cited by this particular article. A typical record is illustrated in Figure 5.18. Note that journal titles are represented by code numbers: J001 V034 P0057 represents page 57 of volume 34 of the journal coded number one.

In searching the data base, the user must specify the range of records to be processed (command: *Search*), the selection criteria (*Find*), and the form of output required (*Output*). An example would be:

> Search Physical Review volumes 133 to 136
> Find title cryogenic
> Output, print title, author

This is a request for retrieval of any articles containing the word "cryogenic" in their titles, which were published in *Physical Review*, volumes 133–136.

PHYSICAL REVIEW
VOLUME 135
J001 V135 P0960
VIBRATIONAL AND CENTRIFUGAL EFFECTS ON THE MAGNETIC
SUSCEPTIBILITY AND ROTATIONAL MAGNETIC MOMENT OF THE
HYDROGEN MOLECULE
  CHAN SUNNEY I.
    PASADENA, CALIFORNIA
    CALIFORNIA INSTITUTE OF TECHNOLOGY
    GATES AND CRELLIN LABORATORIES OF CHEMISTRY
IKENBERRY DENNIS
DAS T. P.
    RIVERSIDE, CALIFORNIA
    UNIVERSITY OF CALIFORNIA
    DEPARTMENT OF PHYSICS

J001 V034 P0057	J001 V041 P0713	J001 V041 P0721
J001 V058 P0310	J001 V078 P0711	J001 V080 P0476
J001 V085 P0937	J001 V087 P1075	J001 V094 P0350
J001 V094 P0893	J001 V103 P1254	J001 V111 P0203
J001 V112 P1929	J001 V115 P0897	J001 V126 P0146
J002 V000 P0000	J002 V000 P0000	J003 V065 P0178
J012 V009 P0061	J012 V019 P1030	J012 V020 P0527
J012 V021 P2070	J012 V023 P1131	J012 V032 P0105
J012 V035 P1065	J012 V035 P1967	J012 V037 P0214
J012 V037 P1527	J012 V038 P1263	J027 V000 P0000
J027 V000 P0000	J030 V032 P0231	J030 V035 P0130
J046 V006 P0019	J055 V035 P0730	J160 V004 P0061
J311 V003 P0017	J311 V010 P0278	

Figure 5.18. Typical record from the TIP system.

The output, to be printed at the on-line terminal, is to be authors and titles of qualifying articles.

    Any boolean function can be accommodated, as in the following examples:

Find title x-ray and title diffraction
  (i.e., any titles containing both the word "x-ray" and the word
  "diffraction")
Find title x-ray or title diffraction
  (i.e., any title containing either the word "x-ray" or the word "diffraction,"
  or both)
Find title laser, author Payne
  (i.e., any article by Payne with the word "laser" in the title)
Find title magnet, citation phys rev
  (i.e., any article in *Physical Review* having "magnet" in the title)

    The TIP files are not inverted but are linearly arranged under the physics journals represented in the base. These volumes are searched in a linear manner. Mathews (1967) quotes a time of 100–150 articles per second for searching the TIP data base. The system also allows searching on the principle of bibliographic coupling, a unique feature that was discussed in Chapter Three. The range of search approaches allowed gives the user of TIP great search flexibility. He can search on authors, titles, or combinations of these, find other papers by the author of a paper known to be relevant, or find other papers *similar* to a known relevant paper in that they are coupled to it bibliographically. An example of this flexibility is presented by Brown (1966), who described the use of TIP in updating a basic handbook on plasma physics.

Since about 1966 this project has completely changed directions. Retrospective search activities are no longer emphasized. Instead, a general-purpose system for manipulation of bibliographic and other data has been developed. This system, which contains about thirty function-oriented subsystems (e.g., search, edit, format), is flexible enough to accommodate a number of different specialized applications, including the production of printed catalogs and indexes, and the control of library acquisition procedures.

TOXICON

TOXICON (TOXicology Information Conversational On-Line Network) is a retrieval system in the field of toxicology which is operated by Informatics Inc. for the Toxicology Information Program of the National Library of Medicine. In February 1973, the data base included about 180,000 abstracts and citations drawn from the Hayes File on Pesticides, the *Toxicity Bibliography*, the *Health Aspects of Pesticides Abstract Bulletin*, *Abstracts on Health Effects of Environmental Pollutants*, and *Chemical-Biological Activities* (CBAC). The RECON software is used in the system, which can be accessed remotely by telephone through a network arrangement. Access to the data base is provided on a subscription basis. The system was renamed TOXLINE in April 1973. It is available for a one-time initiation fee of $350 and a charge of $45 per hour for actual searching time.

REFERENCES

Battelle Memorial Institute (1971). *Basis-70: A User Guide*, 3rd ed. Columbus, Ohio: Battelle Memorial Institute.

Bennertz, R. K. (1971). *Development of the Defense Documentation Center Remote On-Line Retrieval System: Past, Present and Future*. Alexandria, Va.; Defense Documentation Center, AD 720 900.

Blase, N. G., and C. J. Stock (1972). "An Experimental Cancer Information Service Using AIM-TWX." *Bull. Med. Library Assoc.* **60** (1), 115–120.

Borko, H. (1968). "Interactive Document Storage and Retrieval System—Design Concepts." *In* K. Samuelson (ed.), *Mechanized Information Storage, Retrieval and Dissemination.* Amsterdam: North Holland, 591–599.

Borko, H., and H. P. Burnaugh (1966). *Interactive Displays for Document Retrieval.* Santa Monica, Ca.: System Development Corporation, SP-2557.

Bridegam, W. E., Jr., and E. Meyerhoff (1970). "Library Participation in a Biomedical Communication and Information Network." *Bull Med. Library Assoc.* **58** (2), 103–111.

Brown, S. C. (1966). "A Bibliographic Search by Computer." *Phys. Today* **19** (5), 59–64.

Burnaugh, H. P. (1966a). *The BOLD User's Manual for Retrieval.* Santa Monica, Ca.: System Development Corporation, Tech. Memo 2306/004/00.

Burnaugh, H. P. (1966b). *Data Base Generator for the BOLD System.* Santa Monica, Ca.: System Development Corporation, Tech. Memo 2306/001/02.

Burnaugh, H. P. (1967). "The BOLD (Bibliographic On-Line Display) System." *In* G. Schechter (ed.), *Information Retrieval: A Critical View.* Washington, D.C.: Thompson, pp. 53–66.

Cain, A. M., and I. J. Pizer (1967). "The SUNY Biomedical Communication Network: Implementation of an On-Line, Real-Time, User-Oriented System." *Proc. Amer. Documentation Inst.* **4**, 258–262.

Caponio, J. F., et al. (1970). "Epilepsy Abstracts: Its Role in Disseminating Scientific Information." *Bull. Med. Library Assoc.* **58** (1), 37–43.

Carville, M., L. D. Higgins, and F. J. Smith (1971). "Interactive Reference Retrieval in Large Files." *Information Storage Retrieval* **7** (5), 205–210.

Cook, K. H., et al. (1971). *Large Scale Information Processing Systems.* Final Report to the Rome Air Development Center. Syracuse, N.Y.: Syracuse University, School of Library Science, 6 vols.

Covington, M. W. (1969). "The Copper Data Center: A Worldwide Network." *In Proceedings of the Sixth Annual National Colloquium on Information Retrieval.* Philadelphia, Pa.: College of Physicians of Philadelphia, pp. 151–154.

Cuadra, C. A., (1971). "On-Line Systems: Promise and Pitfalls." *Jour. Amer. Soc. Information Sci.* **22** (2), 107–114.

Drew, D. L., R. K. Summit, R. I. Tanaka, and R. B. Whitely (1966). "An On-Line Technical Library Reference Retrieval System." *Amer. Documentation* **17** (1), 3–7.

Egeland, J. (1971). "User-Interaction in the State University of New York (SUNY) Biomedical Communication Network." *In* D. E. Walker (ed.), *Interactive Bibliographic Search: The User/Computer Interface.* Montvale, N.J.: AFIPS Press, pp. 105–120.

Fenzl, R. N. (1969). *An On-Line Adaptation of the IBM DPS Package.* A tutorial paper presented to the Chemical Literature Division, 1969 Annual Meeting of the American Chemical Society, New York City, September 11.

Fong, E. (1971). *A Survey of Selected Document Processing Systems.* Gaithersburg, Md.: National Bureau of Standards, NBS Tech. Note 599.

Fried, J. B. (1971). "Basis-70 User Interface." *In* D. E. Walker (ed.), *Interactive Bibliographic Search: The User/Computer Interface.* Montvale, N.J.: AFIPS Press, pp. 143–157.

General Electric Co. (1969). *Operator's Manual for GESCAN, the Rapid Search Machine*. Daytona Beach, Fla.: General Electric Co., Apollo and Ground Systems Space Division.

General Electric Co. (1972). *General Electric Re-Search Information System: Functional System Design Specification*. Daytona Beach, Fla.: General Electric Co., Apollo and Ground Systems Space Division.

Giering, R. H. (1972). *This Is Data Central (1972 Technical Specifications)*. Dayton, Ohio: Data Corporation, DTN-72-2.

Hall, J. L., A. E. Negus, and D. J. Dancy (1972). "On-Line Information Retrieval: A Method of Query Formulation Using a Video Terminal." *Program: News Computers Libraries* **6** (3), 175–186.

Haring, D. R. (1968). "Computer-Driven Display Facilities for an Experimental Computer-Based Library." *AFIPS Conf. Proc. Fall Joint Computer Conf.* **33**, (I), 255–265.

Haring, D. R., and J. K. Roberge (1969). "A Combined Display for Computer-Generated Data and Scanned Photographic Images." *AFIPS Conf. Proc. Spring Joint Computer Conf.* **34**, 483–490.

Harrington, W. G. (1970). "Computers and Legal Research." *Amer. Bar Assoc. Jour.* **56** (December), 1145–1148.

Higgins, L. D., and F. J. Smith (1971). "Disc Access Algorithms." *Computer Jour.* **14** (3), 249–253

Hillman, D. J. and A. J. Kasarda (1969). "The LEADER Retrieval System." *AFIPS Conf. Proc. Spring Joint Computer Conf.* **34**, 447–455.

Hirschfeld, L. J. (1971). *Design and Implementation of the Retrieval Mechanism of the SOLER Storage and Retrieval System*. Philadelphia, Pa.: University of Pennsylvania, Moore School of Electrical Engineering.

Hunter, E. D., and R. L. Mazer (1971?). *Use of an On-Line Information Retrieval System for Analysis of Health Data*. Palo Alto, Ca.: Lockheed Missiles & Space Co.

IBM (1971). *IBM System 360 and System 370 (OS) Storage and Information Retrieval System. General Information. Program Product 5734-XR3*. 1st ed. Stuttgart, Germany: IBM Germany.

Isotta, N. E. C. (1970). "Europe's First Information Retrieval Network." *ESRO/ELDO Bull* (9), 9–17.

Kasarda, A. J., and D. J. Hillman (1972). "The Leadermart System and Service." *Proc. Ann. Conf. ACM* 469–477.

Katter, R. V., and D. B. McCarn (1971). "AIM–TWX; An Experimental On-Line Bibliographic Retrieval System." *In* D. E. Walker (ed.), *Interactive Bibliographic Search: The User/Computer Interface*. Montvale, N.J.: AFIPS Press, pp. 121–141.

Kellogg, C. H. (1968). "CONVERSE—A System for the On-Line Description and Retrieval of Structural Data Using Natural Language." *In* K. Samelson (ed.), *Information Storage, Retrieval and Dissemination*. Amsterdam: North Holland, pp. 608–621.

Kessler, M. M. (1967). "The 'On-Line' Technical Information System at M.I.T. (Project TIP)." *IEEE Intern. Convention Rec.* (10), 40–43.

Knudson, D. R. (1970). "Image Storage and Transmission for Project Intrex." *In Proceedings of the Conference on Image Storage and Transmission Systems for Libraries.* Gaithersburg, Md.: National Bureau of Standards, pp. L1–L18, PB 193 692.

Knudson, D. R., and S. N. Teicher (1969). "Remote Text Access in a Computerized Library Information Retrieval System." *AFIPS Conf. Proc. Spring Joint Computer Conf.* **34**, 475–481.

Lancaster, F. W. (1972). *Evaluation of On-Line Searching in MEDLARS (AIM–TWX) by Biomedical Practitioners.* Urbana, Ill.: University of Illinois, Graduate School of Library Science, Occasional Paper No. 101.

Lancaster, F. W., R. L. Rapport, and J. K. Penry (1972). "Evaluating the Effectiveness of an On-Line, Natural Language Retrieval System." *Information Storage Retrieval* **8** (5), 223–245.

Lesk, M. E., and G. Salton (1969). "Interactive Search and Retrieval Methods Using Automatic Information Displays." *AFIPS Conf. Proc. Spring Joint Computer Conf.* **34**, 435–446.

Lockheed Missiles & Space Co. (1971). *User's Manual: ERIC/DIALOG Online Retrieval System.* rev. Palo Alto, Ca.: Lockheed Missiles & Space Co.

Marcus, R. S., P. Kugel, and R. L. Kusik (1969). "An Experimental Computer-Stored Augmented Catalog of Professional Literature." *AFIPS Conf. Proc., Spring Joint Computer Conf.* **34**, 461–473.

Massachusetts Institute of Technology (1972). *Project Intrex: Semiannual Activity Report.* Cambridge, Mass.: MIT.

Mathews, W. D. (1967). "The TIP Retrieval System at MIT." *In* G. Schechter (ed.), *Information Retrieval: A Critical View.* Washington, D.C.: Thompson, pp. 95–108.

Moll, W. (1971). "AIM–TWX Service at the University of Virginia." *Bull Medical Library Assoc.* **59** (3), 458–462.

Nance, J. W., and J. W. Lathrop (1968). *System Design Specifications: General Purpose ORBIT.* Santa Monica, Ca.: System Development Corporation, TM-DA-20/000/00.

National Aeronautics and Space Administration (1966). *NASA/RECON User's Manual.* Washington, D.C.: NASA.

National Aeronautics and Space Administration (1970). *What NASA/RECON Can Do for You.* Washington, D.C.: NASA.

National Science Research Data Processing and Information Retrieval System: Hearings before the General Subcommittee on Education of the Committee on Education and Labor, House of Representatives, 91st Congress, 1st Session, on H.R. 8809. (1969). Hearings held in Washington, D.C., April 29 and 30.

Negus, A. E. (1971). "A Real Time Interactive Reference Retrieval System." *Information Scientist* **5** (1), 29–44.

Negus, A. E., and J. L. Hall (1971). "Towards an Effective On-Line Reference Retrieval System," *Information Storage Retrieval* **7** (6), 249–270.

Ohio State Bar Association (1970). *Ohio Bar Automated Research.* Columbus, Ohio: Ohio State Bar Association.

Overhage, C. F. J. (1972). *Project Intrex: A Brief Description.* Cambridge, Mass.: MIT.

Parker, E. B. (1970). "Behavioral Research in the Development of a Computer-Based Information System." *In* C. E. Nelson and D. K. Pollock (eds.), *Communication Among Scientists and Engineers.* Lexington, Mass.: Heath, pp. 281–293.

Parker, E. B. (1971). *Requirements for SPIRES II.* Stanford, Ca.: Stanford University.

Pizer, I. H. (1969). "A Regional Medical Library Network." *Bull. Medical Library Assoc.* **57** (2), 101–115.

Pizer, I. H. (1972). "On-Line Technology in a Library Network." *In* F. W. Lancaster (ed.), *Proceedings of the 1972 Clinic on Library Applications of Data Processing.* Urbana, Ill.: University of Illinois, Graduate School of Library Science, pp. 54–68.

Porter, R. J., J. K. Penry, and J. F. Caponio (1970). "Epilepsy Abstracts Retrieval System (EARS): A new Concept for Medical Literature Storage and Retrieval." *Proc. Amer. Soc. Information Sci.* **7**, pp. 171–172.

Powers, J. M. (1973). "The Defense RDTE On-Line Systems Retrieval." *In Interactive Bibliographic Systems.* Washington, D.C.: USAEC, pp. 69–82.

Raitt, D. I. (1970). "The European Space Documentation System." *Library Assoc. Rec.* **72** (3), 97–99.

Reintjes, J. F. (1969). "System Characteristics of Intrex." *AFIPS Conf. Proc., Spring Joint Computer Conf.* **34**, 457–459.

Rubinoff, M., S. Bergman, W. Franks, and E. R. Rubinoff (1968). "Experimental Evaluation of Information Retrieval through a Teletypewriter." *Commun. Assoc. Computing Machinery* **11** (9), 598–604.

Salton, G. (1968). *Automatic Information Organization and Retrieval.* New York: McGraw-Hill.

Salton, G., ed. (1971). *The SMART Retrieval System: Experiments in Automatic Document Processing.* Englewood Cliffs, N.J.: Prentice-Hall.

Schürfeld, H., et al. (1971). *A Method for the Automatic Indexing, Storing, and Retrieving of Full-Text Documents.* Sindelfingen, Germany: IBM Germany, Patent Department, NASA Report #CO8 N71-25981.

Scroggins, J. L., J. K. Mizove, and R. D. Glass (1968). *National Library of Medicine On-Line Retrieval of Bibliographic Information Text.* Falls Church, Va.: System Development Corporation, TM-WD-731/000/00.

Seiden, H. R. (1970). *A Comparative Analysis of Interactive Storage and Retrieval Systems with Implications for BCN Design.* Santa Monica, Ca.: System Development Corporation, TM-4421.

Seiden, H. R. (1971). *ORBIT System Information.* Santa Monica, Ca.: System Development Corporation.

Stiller, J. D. (1970). "Use of On-Line Remote Access Information Retrieval Systems." *Proc. Amer. Soc. Information Sci.* **7**, 107–109.

Summit, R. K. (1967). "DIALOG: An Operational On-Line Reference Retrieval System." *Proceedings of the 22nd National Conference of the Association for Computing Machinery.* Washington, D.C.: Thompson, pp. 51–56.

Summit, R. K. (1968). *Remote Information Retrieval Facility.* Palo Alto, Ca.: Lockheed Missiles & Space Co.

Summit, R. K. (1971). "DIALOG and the User—An Evaluation of the User Interface with a Major Online Retrieval System." *In* D. E. Walker (ed.), *Interactive Bibliographic Search: The User/Computer Interface.* Montvale, N.J.: AFIPS Press, pp. 83–94.

Troy, F. J. (1969). "Ohio Bar Automated Research—A Practical System of Computerized Legal Research." *Jurimetrics Jour.* **10** (2), 62–69.

U.S. Air Force (1970). *CIRCOL User's Guide.* Wright-Patterson Air Force Base, Ohio: U.S. Air Force, Foreign Technology Division, FTD-MP-22-09-70.

University of Pennsylvania (1971a). *SOLER: System for On-Line Entry and Retrieval.* Philadelphia, Pa.: University of Pennsylvania, Moore School of Electrical Engineering.

University of Pennsylvania (1971b). *SOLER User's Manual.* Philadelphia, Pa.: University of Pennsylvania, Moore School of Electrical Engineering.

Vernimb, C. (1972). *Retrieval Experience with the European Nuclear Documentation System (ENDS).* Luxembourg: European Community.

Welch, N. O. (1968). *A Survey of Five On-Line Retrieval Systems.* Washington, D.C.: The Mitre Corporation, MTP-322.

Wente, V. A. (1971). "NASA/RECON and User Interface Considerations." *In* D. E. Walker (ed.), *Interactive Bibliographic Search: The User/Computer Interface.* Montvale, N.J.: AFIPS Press, pp. 95–104.

Williams, J. H., Jr. (1969). *BROWSER: An Automatic Indexing On-Line Text Retrieval System.* Annual progress report. Gaithersburg, Md.: IBM Federal Systems Division, AD 693 143.

Williams, J. H., Jr. (1971a). *An Iterative Browsing Technique.* Gaithersburg, Md.: IBM Federal Systems Division, AD 722 672, Contract N 00014-70-C-0297.

Williams, J. H., Jr. (1971b). "Functions of a Man-Machine Interactive Information Retrieval System." *Jour. Amer. Soc. Information Sci.* **22** (5), 311–317.

Williams, J. H., Jr., and M. P. Perriens (1968). *Automatic Full Text Indexing and Searching System.* Gaithersburg, Md.: IBM Federal Systems Division.

Williamson, D., and R. Williamson (1970). "A Prototype On-Line Document Retrieval System," *In Information Storage and Retrieval.* Section XIV. Ithaca, N.Y.: Cornell University, Department of Computer Science, Scientific Report No. ISR-18.

Wolfe, T. (1970). *An Evaluation of On-Line Information Retrieval System Techniques.* Washington, D.C.: Naval Ship Research and Development Center, AD 723 214.

Chapter Six

Performance Criteria

Before we can discuss factors affecting the performance of an on-line system, we need to consider certain criteria by which the performance of a retrieval system may be judged. In other words, we must know what requirements users have in relation to an information retrieval system. Although it is possible to generate long inventories of *user requirements*, the most important ones can be reduced to a small list, namely:

1. Coverage
2. Recall
3. Precision
4. Response time
5. User effort
6. Form of output

This list was first presented in this form by Cleverdon (1964).

Recall and Precision

All users of a retrieval system have one fundamental requirement in common—they expect the system to be able to retrieve one or more documents that contribute to the satisfaction of some information need (*relevant documents*). All users are presumed to have an information need, otherwise they would not have approached the system. Actually, this is a slight over-simplification. In some, comparatively rare situations, the user wants the system to retrieve nothing. This is the situation in which the user believes nothing exists and hopes nothing exists (e.g., certain patent searching situations). Under these circumstances (nothing existing), the system behaves perfectly if it retrieves nothing.

In most situations, however, the user wants and expects the system to retrieve some relevant documents. It is possible to express quantitatively the degree of success achieved in retrieving relevant literature from a retrieval system. The appropriate ratio is the *recall ratio*, which may be defined as

$$\frac{\text{Number of relevant documents retrieved by the system}}{\text{Total number of relevant documents contained in the system}} \times 100$$

Suppose that for a particular subject request made to some retrieval system we are able to establish that there are only ten relevant documents in the entire data base. We conduct a subject search using normal system procedures, and retrieve seven of these ten documents. The recall ratio of this search is, then, $7/10 \times 100$, or 70%.

The recall ratio is one very important measure of the success of a search. But it is not the only important measure. In fact, taken on its own it is somewhat meaningless; we can always get 100% recall for any search in any system if we are prepared to search broadly enough and thus to retrieve a sufficiently large portion of the collection. An information retrieval system is essentially a filter and, as in the case of other types of filters, it should be capable of letting through what we want and, at the same time, holding back what we do not want. The recall ratio expresses the ability of the system to let through what we want, but we also need a companion measure which will express the ability of the system to hold back what we do not want.

One such measure (there are others) is the *precision ratio*, which may be defined as

$$\frac{\text{Number of relevant documents retrieved by the system}}{\text{Total number of documents retrieved by the system}} \times 100$$

Returning to the hypothetical search mentioned above, we may find that the system retrieves a total of fifty documents (or references), seven of them relevant and forty-three not. The precision ratio for this search is $7/50$, or 14%, and we can thus say that the search has operated at 70% recall and at 14% precision. These two measures, used jointly, indicate the filtering capacity of the system. They present a reasonable picture of system effectiveness, whereas either one, on its own, is inadequate.

The precision ratio measures the efficiency with which the system is able to achieve a particular recall ratio. Clearly, achievement of 70% recall at a precision of $7/14$ (50%) indicates greater efficiency than the attainment of the same recall at $7/50$ (14%) precision or $7/100$ (7%) precision—greater filtering capacity has been brought into play. In a sense, the precision ratio may be regarded as a measure of the effort required (from the user of the system) to achieve a particular recall ratio. This effort is expended, after the search results have been delivered by the system, in the separation of the relevant items retrieved from the irrelevant items. Obviously, it takes longer to separate 7 relevant from 93 irrelevant items (7% precision) than it does to separate 7 relevant from 43 irrelevant items (14% precision), and the latter case requires more effort than the separation of 7 relevant from an equal number of irrelevant items (50% precision). Viewed in this light, the precision ratio is clearly a valid and useful measure of search efficiency.

Recall and precision tend to vary inversely in searching. That is, whatever we do to improve recall (by broadening a search), we will also tend to be reducing precision; and whatever we do to improve precision (by searching more stringently), we will tend to be reducing recall. In fact, if we conduct a search, or a whole group of searches, at varying strategy levels from very broad to very stringent, we can derive a series of performance points that will allow us to draw a performance curve resembling that of Figure 6.1.

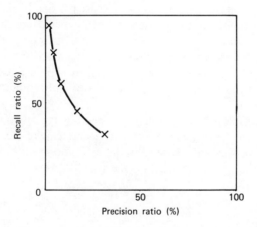

Figure 6.1. Typical plot of recall versus precision.

Different users will have different requirements regarding recall and precision. Take, for instance, the typical patron of an industrial library who comes in and asks for "some good recent articles on shielded arc welding." This man does not have a high recall requirement; i.e., he does not need or want everything on the subject.

The user who needs high recall (e.g., someone writing a book or review article or beginning a new research project) will usually tolerate a lower precision than the user who needs only "a few recent articles." The attainment of a high recall is important to him, and he will probably be willing to look through a large number of document surrogates, discarding the irrelevant ones, to assure himself that he has not missed anything of importance.

This user will probably prefer a search that achieves 90% recall but only 15% precision to one achieving 75% recall at 50% precision.

User Effort

As previously mentioned, the precision ratio is one measure of the amount of effort required to obtain a particular recall ratio. This is effort expended at the output stage—in separating relevant items retrieved from irrelevant ones. However, there are other stages at which effort can be expended by the user. For example, he can put more effort at the request stage—by a detailed discussion of his requirements with a member of the information staff or by completing a detailed search request form. Or the effort can occur at the search strategy stage—the user examines a proposed strategy and approves it, or suggests alterations, before the search is actually conducted. Finally, the effort may be made through the technique of *iterative searching*. Here a partial or preliminary search is conducted, and the user examines the output of this search, indicating which retrieved items are relevant to him and which are not. A revised search strategy is then prepared and processed against the entire data base, the strategy being designed to retrieve more documents of the type known to be relevant and less of the type known not to be. On-line systems are especially suitable for searching in an iterative way.

The more effort a user is willing to expend in exploiting an information system, the better the results are likely to be in terms of recall or precision, or possibly both. Generally speaking, the user who needs high recall will be willing to put in greater effort than the user who has less stringent recall requirements.

Response Time

Response time is obviously important to users of information retrieval systems. Almost all users will have some deadline beyond which receipt of a system response will be of no value. Nevertheless, response time is always secondary to the recall and precision requirements and is never the prime user requirement. If it were, this would imply that users would be happy with immediate access to 100% irrelevant information, which is patently absurd.

Form of System Output

Output from an information retrieval system may be in the form of document numbers, full bibliographic citations, citations plus index terms, citations plus abstracts or complete texts of documents in hard copy form or in microform. The form of output is important, because it affects the precision tolerance of the system user. A user is likely to tolerate lower precision in the product delivered by the system if this product is in a form that facilitates rapid scanning and thus allows him to discard irrelevant items fairly easily. The more information given to a user in a document representation, the easier it is for him to make accurate relevance predictions. Saracevic (1969) discovered, in an investigation of relevance prediction, that of 207 documents judged relevant from the full text, only 131 were so judged from titles and 160 from abstracts. In other words, given titles, users were able to recognize about 66% of the relevant items; given abstracts they could recognize about 80%. Similar findings have been made by other investigators.

Coverage

We have left for last a consideration of the factor of *coverage*, although in a sense it may be regarded as the most important user requirement of all—presumably, a user will not even approach a system unless he feels that its coverage is such that it will be able to contribute to satisfying his information need. However, comprehensiveness of coverage in a specific subject area is really only of concern to the user who needs high recall. In a sense, coverage is an extension of recall beyond the immediate system data base to the entire published literature. The user who needs high recall may legitimately say "You estimate you have given me about 95% of the relevant literature in your collection, but does this represent 95% of the published literature on the subject, or 50% of the published literature or only 10%?" This requester wants to find everything and is therefore legitimately concerned with the extent of system coverage (i.e., how much of the relevant literature, on the precise subject of his request, got into the system in the first place). The requester with a low recall requirement, on the other hand, is not particularly concerned about coverage. He wants a few good articles and does not really care whether these are *all* the relevant items published or only 1% of them.

Performance Criteria for the On-Line System

The various performance criteria discussed above are not peculiar to the on-line environment. Indeed, they are pertinent to all types of retrieval systems. It will now be appropriate to consider these criteria specifically in relation to on-line systems, to determine their validity in this context, and to decide on the relative importance of each.

Obviously, recall is important to the user of the on-line system. He will presumably judge the system primarily by whether or not he is able to retrieve from it items that, in some way, contribute to the satisfaction of an information need. However, high recall is likely to be less important to many users of an on-line terminal than it is to the majority of users of an off-line, batch-processing operation. Because of the comparatively long delay associated with the use of most batch systems, the majority of users tend to be seeking a comprehensive search. A typical user of off-line MEDLARS, for example, will be a scientist engaged in some relatively long-term research project. He may be writing a book or a review article. Response time is not critical, but high recall is usually quite important. In fact, the requester does not usually come to a batch system if he wants only "a few good articles." He goes to an alternative source (e.g., a printed index) where he may be able to satisfy his relatively simple need more rapidly. It is quite likely that an on-line terminal will attract a different type of user than the typical user of a batch system; or, it may attract the same user but for purposes other than those for which he would go to the batch system. That is, the on-line facility is likely to attract users who need only a few relevant references but need them right away. In an evaluation study conducted by Lancaster (1972) on AIM–TWX, it was found that the majority of users of the on-line terminal were of this type. Many searchers had not previously made use of the off-line MEDLARS facilities and, in fact, many had not been regular users of the biomedical library before the terminal was made available.

In other words, the on-line system was attracting a type of user different from the typical user of the batch system. Presumably, on-line facilities will attract users who are looking not for a comprehensive search but for a few references only. This is the type of search that would probably otherwise be conducted in published tools of one kind or another. However, the on-line system should obviously allow the conduct of highly complex searches, involving precise interrelationships between concepts, that would be difficult if not impossible to conduct by conventional manual search in a printed index.

We are not saying that on-line systems will never be used for searches in which high recall is required, or that they are inappropriate for this type of requirement, but merely that on-line systems are likely to be used for many searches in which high recall is not needed but fast response is. These are situations in which the batch system would probably not be used.

In conducting a high-recall search for a topic on which much literature exists, the on-line system will be used to test search strategies and to allow browsing in the data base. Once a seemingly satisfactory strategy is found, the full search is likely to be conducted off-line rather than at the terminal.

For those on-line searches in which the user is not looking for all relevant documents, absolute recall is somewhat meaningless. The user will stop searching when he has found enough relevant items to satisfy his needs. The efficiency of the search may then be measured in terms of the amount of effort required to find these relevant items. In this sense, effort is likely to equate with searching time. We will return to this point a little later.

A possible substitute for absolute recall in this type of situation is *relative recall*, which measures the number of relevant items retrieved as a proportion of the number the user would like to have. Thus, if a user would like five relevant items but only retrieves two, we can say that the relative recall is 2/5, or 40%. This measure, however, is very artificial, since it is hard to believe that the typical user will come to a system demanding a particular number of relevant items.

The precision ratio of a search, as we have said before, is one measure of the effort required to obtain a particular recall ratio. In a batch-processing system, it is a measure of the effort expended by the user, once the search results are delivered to him, to separate the relevant items from the irrelevant ones. The precision ratio is a somewhat less useful measure when applied to the evaluation of an on-line system. In the final output from an off-line system, irrelevant citations have no useful function and merely detract from the value of the search. A performance measure should penalize a system for retrieving irrelevant citations, and this is exactly what the precision ratio does.

The on-line system, on the other hand, is intended for heuristic, iterative searching. We try out various strategies, and examine the types of citations that are retrieved. In this situation, at certain points at least, irrelevant citations may be almost as useful as relevant ones. They may indicate defective strategies, and we can then benefit from our mistakes. Mistakes are less costly in the on-line system, because we can rectify them rapidly and easily. It is for this reason that the precision ratio is possibly a less useful measure in the on-line situation than it is in the batch-processing system.

As discussed by Marcus, et al. (1971), the Intrex investigators have discovered that "most users do not seem to want completeness and that the ability to scan selected information about many articles easily and quickly leads users to be less concerned with precision as well ... it is common to find users, who initially complain about scanning through false drops, or who initially consider 20 retrieved documents as too many to scan, changing their attitude after experiencing the ease and rapidity of scanning" (pp. 169, 170).

Unit Cost as a Performance Measure

Hopefully, as we try out various approaches at the terminal, these strategies will be improving in that they will be retrieving more relevant and less irrelevant items (i.e., precision is increasing). The fewer mistakes we make, or the faster we correct our mistakes, the faster we can discover the relevant citations and complete our search. In fact, the efficiency of the on-line search is probably best measured in terms of time; i.e., how long does it take to find x relevant items. A useful measure of search efficiency, to be used in conjunction with recall in certain cases, is the unit cost (in time) per relevant citation retrieved. Suppose searcher A spends 12 minutes at the terminal and, as a result, finds eight relevant citations. The unit cost is 12/8 minutes or 1.5 minutes per relevant citation. Searcher B, on the other hand, retrieves four relevant citations as a result of spending 20 minutes at the terminal. The unit cost of this search is 5.0 minutes per relevant citation. Clearly, search A is more efficient than search B. This does not necessarily imply that searcher A is more satisfied with the results than searcher B. Nor does the result tell us why search A was more efficient than search B. Presumably, it is for one of the following reasons:

1. Searcher A is a better or more experienced searcher than B.
2. The system gave more help to A than to B (e.g., the system vocabulary was better able to cope with A's subject than with B's).
3. The subject of B's search is inherently more difficult than that of A's.
4. Searcher A was just luckier than B in hitting upon a good strategy right away.

Be this as it may, unit cost (in time) per relevant citation retrieved can be a useful measure of search efficiency. If B undertook his search a second time and found four equally relevant citations in 5 minutes (unit cost = 1.25 minutes), we can clearly say that the second search was more efficient than the first.

The precision ratio, in an off-line system, is the only reasonable measure that we have of search efficiency in terms of the cost to the searcher of obtaining a particular recall level. It is really a measure of time—in this case, how long it takes after the search is completed to separate the relevant from the irrelevant citations. Generally speaking, in the off-line situation we have no more direct measure of search time and search efficiency. However, in the on-line search we can measure search time directly and relate this time to a particular level of achievement, namely the number of relevant documents discovered. The precision ratio appears less useful in the evaluation of on-line systems than elapsed search time and the unit cost, in time, per relevant citation retrieved.

User Effort in Relation to On-Line Systems

Unit cost, like the precision ratio, is a measure of the effort required to achieve a particular level of recall. But other aspects of user effort will affect the performance of a retrieval system, and these must be considered. For example, how much effort is required in learning to use the system? This is likely to depend largely on whether the system was designed *ab initio* as an on-line system, with the practitioners of the field in mind, or whether it is a converted batch system designed primarily to be used by information specialists. The more the system is dependent on a carefully controlled vocabulary and complex indexing protocols, the more difficult it will be to learn how to use it effectively. A natural language system is likely to be easier to learn, because it is not dependent upon indexing protocols and the language required in search strategies may be closer to the language of the practitioner than a controlled vocabulary would be. Moreover, a system that can be queried in English sentence form may require less effort from the user than one that can only be queried by precise boolean search logic.

The way in which the user is trained to operate the system is also important. Many so-called "user manuals" are badly written, lack adequate illustrations and examples, and frighten potential users by their sheer bulk. Although a complete user manual is necessary, at least for reference purposes, it should be possible to describe to the new user how to conduct relatively simple searches by a few carefully chosen words. Once he has tried the terminal a few times, he will quickly learn by experience. A *hands-on* demonstration, provided by an instructor or experienced searcher, is likely to be more effective than a printed manual. However, the search programs themselves should be instructive and should guide the user in the construction of appropriate strategies. We will return to this aspect in Chapter Fifteen.

In addition to the effort involved in learning the system, the user will be concerned with how much effort is needed to conduct an actual search. If the effort exceeds his tolerance, the user will probably abandon the system and turn to an alternative source of information. A well-designed on-line system will minimize user effort by compensating for common errors, providing simple procedures for correcting errors that do occur, requiring the minimum amount of keyboarding, and providing assistance and guidance in the creation of search strategies. This point will also be discussed in Chapter Seventeen.

Time Factors

Response time in the on-line situation takes on a somewhat different connotation than it does in other situations. Typically there may be a delay of several days between the time a user submits a request to a batch system and the time he receives a satisfactory response. At the worst, in requests made to large national information centers, the response time may run to several weeks. The only comparable delay associated with an on-line system is the possible delay that would occur while a potential user waits for a particular data base to be made available. Few, if any, on-line systems for bibliographic access are *up* constantly. Although some are available for several hours a day, five or more days a week, others may only be on-line for one designated period each week—say, 1–4 PM, Thursday. A user may thus have to wait several days to consult certain systems, although it should be possible to request that the data base be loaded at an unscheduled time if an emergency arises. When the on-line system is available, there will be no significant delay for the user, providing that he has access to a terminal and that the system is not overloaded at the time, necessitating his accessing the data base again later. However, we should also consider here the time it takes for the system to respond to a user input. This may be typically of the order of 3–10 seconds but can be degraded considerably under various conditions (e.g., searching on large groups of heavily posted terms or at times when the system is overloaded by terminal use).

According to Higgins and Smith (1971), response time will depend on several factors, including speed of the computer, amount of core storage available, operating system, number and type of users on-line at a particular time, priority given to the user by the operating system, and, finally, the efficiency of the searching programs. These authors maintain that no system response should occur more than 3–4 seconds after a command is input. In the case of a complex command, which involves a greater delay, the user should be informed that the amount of computing required will cause a delay to occur. In the QUOBIRD system at Queen's University of Belfast, as described by Carville, et al. (1971), response on a small experimental file of 1000 items is said to be almost always less than 1 second, even with other users and batch work being processed simultaneously on the ICL 1907 computer. It is claimed that this fast response is due to the considerable amount of effort that has gone into the minimization of disk accesses required. Figure 6.2 is a plot of the effect of the number of users on MEDLINE response time for both the IBM 360/50 and 370/155 computers. Note how the more powerful computer allows many more users to access the system simultaneously without severe degradation of response time. However, even with the 370/155, a marked degradation is apparent when the number of simultaneous users increases from 45 to 55. Table 6.1 presents data for the percentage of MEDLINE inputs, both queries and commands, that are responded to in various time intervals. A mathematical analysis of response time in on-line systems, for both linear and inverted file organizations, has been prepared by Cordaro and Chien (1970).

The other major time factor is the time spent at the terminal in the conduct of a search, an aspect we have already discussed in terms of unit cost per relevant item retrieved. The only further time factor of possible concern is the time elapsing between conducting an exploratory on-line search, requesting an off-line printout of the complete search results, and obtaining these off-line results from the system, probably through the mail.

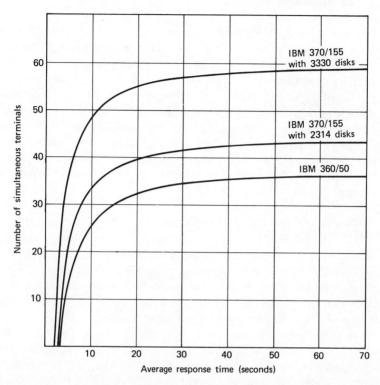

Figure 6.2. Plot showing, for MEDLINE, the effect of the number of simultaneous users on response time. Reproduced by permission of the National Library of Medicine.

TABLE 6.1. Percentage of Inputs, both Queries and Commands, to Which MEDLINE Responds in Specified Time Intervals, July 20, 1972

Time interval (seconds)	Queries	Commands	Total
0–5	86.7	91.3	87.8
6–10	9.4	6.3	8.6
11–15	2.6	1.4	2.3
16–20	0.6	0.3	0.6
Greater	0.7	0.7	0.7
	Average response = 3.44 seconds		
	Average = 18.7 simultaneous users		

SOURCE: National Library of Medicine.

Marcus, et al. (1971), reporting on findings in the Intrex experiments, point out that users both want and appreciate rapid response. "This seems to be primarily important when a user is attempting to formulate his problem in a search phase. Once documents have been identified a majority of users seem to be willing to wait as long as over-night for the full text. Nevertheless, the ability to quickly obtain text for a preliminary scan is useful in formulating strategy and for evaluating results. Rapid response permits users to change their minds as a result of what they find and to tie the computer's rather unthinking, but rapid and thorough, operation to their own intelligence. And rapid access to text is important for the user who is only looking for a fact or two" (p. 180).

Coverage of Data Base

The performance criteria of coverage and form of output are much the same for on-line and off-line systems. Presumably, the coverage of a data base is most important to the person who wants a high-recall search. Since, as we have already discussed, on-line systems are likely to be used frequently for low-recall, high-precision searches, comprehensiveness of coverage may not be an important requirement for most on-line data bases. Indeed, there may be a strong case for making available on-line only selective data bases of high-value, reasonably current material. The AIM–TWX system, for example, covers a little more than 100 English language journals selected as being of primary importance to practitioners of clinical medicine in the United States. In contrast, the entire MEDLARS data base, of which this is a subset, draws from about 2400 biomedical journals in all languages. If a selected portion of a huge data base is available on-line, it should still be possible for the searcher with a high recall requirement to develop a strategy on this subset at the terminal and then to request that this strategy be used in an off-line search on the entire data base.

Form of Output

The form in which document surrogates are presented at the on-line terminal is likely to be important to the searcher, because he will need to assess rapidly the relevance of retrieved items and to modify his strategy if it appears to be missing the mark. The more information presented to the searcher, the more accurately he will judge the potential relevance of items presented to him. Fortunately, most on-line systems provide several output options. The AIM–TWX and MEDLINE systems offer three major alternatives: PRINT, PRINT FULL, and PRINT TRIAL. The first causes a bibliographic citation to be printed, while the second causes the printing of a citation plus a complete list of index terms (*tracings*) assigned to it. The third command is a compromise which leads to the printing of a title plus index terms only (these being the key elements that a searcher will use in determining the relevance of an item). Likewise, in EARS, a searcher may specify that the output be presented in the form of bibliographic citation or of citation plus full abstract. He also has a choice between having these displayed on the CRT or printed out. In certain other on-line systems (e.g., the Rapid Search Machine), it is possible to request a printout of the entire text of a document or of certain extracts only (the portion containing the words which caused the item to be retrieved). Several on-line systems give the user the capability of specifying what portions of a record are to be displayed or printed and in what order (e.g., title, author, source, abstract, index terms), some give various sorting options, some allow a ranking of output, and a few include a highlighting feature (whereby the terms that caused an item to be retrieved are identified in some way).

The Intrex experience (Marcus, et al., 1971), with respect to the predictability of relevance from various surrogates, parallels the findings of Saracevic (1969), which were previously mentioned. Approximately 60–70 % agreement has been measured between relevance judgments made on titles and relevance judgments made on full text, while agreement in the range of 70–90 % was reached when the judgments were made on the basis of abstracts or lists of index terms instead of titles. Roughly, the *indicativity* of a record field appears to be a function of its length in English words.

Novelty

One final performance criterion is worth mentioning. This is the *novelty ratio*, which measures the proportion of retrieved relevant documents that are new to the requester (i.e., brought to his attention for the first time by the search). Thus, if a search retrieves fifteen relevant items, ten new to the requester and five not, we can say that the *novelty ratio* of the search is 66 %. When applied to retrospective search systems, the novelty ratio measures a characteristic of the user rather than a characteristic of the system. That is, it is a measure of the user's previous knowledge of the literature on his search topic. However, the novelty ratio is a useful measure of the properties of a current awareness system since, presumably, such a system is only useful if it brings relevant items to the attention of the user before he learns of them from some other source. In that an on-line system may be used on a regular basis as a current awareness tool, the *novelty ratio* is a useful and valid measure of one aspect of system efficiency—the time lag between publication of the literature and its appearance in the data base. It seems particularly important in the on-line environment that documents be entered into the data base as rapidly as possible after publication. Such a system permits very rapid access to extremely large bibliographic data bases, and it would be unfortunate if this advantage were reduced by the fact that the files were not completely up-to-date.

Summary

In evaluating the performance of an on-line search system the best overall measure would appear to be the unit cost (in time) per relevant citation retrieved. This is probably the most appropriate measure of the amount of effort involved in using the system. The measure has also been advocated by Thompson (1971). Other aspects of user effort (e.g., how long it takes to learn how to use the system) may also be important. The recall ratio will still be a valid measure for those searches in which the user requires a high, or relatively high recall. The coverage of the data base, too, will be of some importance to this type of user, while the novelty ratio of searches will be of concern to anyone using the system as a current awareness tool.

In discussing the evaluation of on-line systems, Salton (1970) agrees that measures additional to recall and precision are needed, particularly measures of human and machine effort involved in the retrieval of relevant references. He points out, however, that, in time-sharing systems, computer costs for individual tasks are hard to assess and user effort is difficult to measure.

REFERENCES

Carville, M., L. D. Higgins, and F. J. Smith (1971)."Interactive Reference Retrieval in Large Files." *Information Storage Retrieval* **7** (5), 205–210.

Cleverdon, C. W. (1964). *Evaluation of Operational Information Retrieval Systems.* Part 1: *Identification of Criteria.* Cranfield, England: College of Aeronautics.

Cordaro, J. T., Jr., and R. T. Chien (1970). *Design Considerations of On-Line Document Retrieval Systems.* Urbana, Ill.: University of Illinois, Coordinated Science Laboratory, R-456.

Higgins, L. D., and F. J. Smith (1971). *The Cost and Response of an On-Line Reference Retrieval System.* Belfast: Queen's University, Computer Science Department.

Lancaster, F. W. (1972). *Evaluation of On-Line Searching in MEDLARS (AIM–TWX) by Biomedical Practitioners.* Urbana, Ill.: University of Illinois, Graduate School of Library Science, Occasional Paper No. 101.

Marcus, R. S., A. R. Benenfeld, and P. Kugel (1971). "The User Interface for the Intrex Retrieval System." *In* D. E. Walker (ed.), *Interactive Bibliographic Search: The User/Computer Interface.* Montvale, N.J.: AFIPS Press, pp. 159–201.

Salton, G. (1970). "Evaluation Problems in Interactive Information Retrieval." *Information Storage Retrieval* **6** (1), 29–44.

Saracevic, T. (1969). "Comparative Effects of Titles, Abstracts and Full Texts on Relevance Judgments." *Proc. Amer. Soc. Information Sci.* **6**, 293–299.

Thompson, D. A. (1971). "Interface Design for an Interactive Information Retrieval System: A Literature Survey and a Research System Description." *Jour. Amer. Soc. Information Sci.* **22** (6), 361–373.

Chapter Seven

Factors Affecting the Performance of On-Line Searching Systems

The major factors contributing to the effectiveness of a search in an on-line system appear to fall into four broad groups.

1. *Systems design factors.* Some systems appear more difficult to query than others, because the language used is more complex (perhaps it is less close to natural language), the search logic is less straightforward, more steps are involved in the interrogation process, less on-line aid is given to the searcher, errors are inadequately identified or more difficult to correct, greater accuracy is required in spelling or punctuation, or for some other reason. These factors are likely to affect the tolerance of the user (if the search process is too complex or frustrating, the searcher is likely to give up in disgust) and the time it takes to conduct a search. Response time itself will be affected by disk access procedures and related factors.

2. *Hardware factors.* Video terminals generally allow faster interaction than typewriter terminals, may be more appealing to certain users, facilitate various types of display (e.g., hierarchical vocabulary display), and are much more satisfactory for scanning large amounts of text (e.g., abstracts). Keyboards that have keys dedicated to system commands may be easier to use than conventional typewriter keyboards which require the typing of a command name. The number of terminals that the system can support will affect the accessibility of the system to the user, and the number of users interrogating the system concurrently will affect response times.

140

3. *Training factors.*   The more experience a searcher has with a system, the less time he will waste at the terminal and the more effective his searches are likely to be (all other things being equal). An experienced user may search a system with a fluency that the inexperienced or casual user is not likely to achieve.

4. *Intellectual factors relating to the data base itself.*   These factors include the characteristics of the indexing, the vocabulary (index language) of the system, and the search strategies needed to interrogate the file effectively.

All these various factors will influence the effectiveness or efficiency of an on-line retrieval system, and all are referred to in various places in this book. In the long run, the intellectual factors (group 4 above) are likely to have the most significant effect on the performance of the system, and it is these factors that we will concentrate on in this chapter.

The principal intellectual factors governing the performance of any retrieval system operated in a delegated mode were depicted diagrammatically in Figure 1.1 and are presented in a somewhat different way in Table 7.1.

TABLE 7.1.   Principal Causes of Search Failure in Information Retrieval Systems

	Recall failures	Precision failures
Index language	Lack of specific terms (entry vocabulary)	Lack of specific terms (descriptors)
	Inadequate hierarchical or cross-reference structure	Defects in hierarchy
	Roles, or other relational indicators, causing *over-preciseness*	False coordinations
		Incorrect term relationships
Indexing	Lack of specificity	Exhaustive indexing
	Lack of exhaustivity	Use of inappropriate terms
	Omission of important concepts	
	Use of inappropriate terms	
Searching	Failure to cover all reasonable approaches to retrieval	Strategy not sufficiently exhaustive
	Strategy too exhaustive	Strategy not sufficiently specific
	Strategy too specific	Use of inappropriate terms or term combinations
		Defects in search logic
User/system interaction	Request more specific than actual information need	Request more general than actual information need

These factors have been discussed in more detail in an earlier book by Lancaster (1968a). Whether or not a requester approaches the system at all is dependent upon his expectations regarding coverage of the data base. Presumably, he will not approach the system unless he feels that the file is likely to contain the type of document he is seeking. Having decided to consult the system, he must make his needs known by means of a verbal request (Lancaster, 1968b). The quality of this request (i.e., the degree to which it actually matches his information requirement) is dependent upon:

1. His own ability to express himself.
2. His interpretation of system capabilities and limitations. There is a strong tendency for a user to ask for what he thinks the system can give him rather than to ask for what he is really looking for.
3. The degree of assistance given to the requester by the system. Such assistance can take various shapes: a carefully structured search request form, a formal *request interview* process, an iterative search procedure, or some type of user-training program.

The request having been made to the system, it must be translated into a formal search strategy by a member of the information staff (a search analyst). Now a new series of variables, affecting the recall and precision of the search, come into play:

1. The analysts's own interpretation of what the user really wants (which may be accurate or inaccurate).
2. The ability of the vocabulary to express the user's needs. For example, the user may specifically be seeking articles on argon arc welding (and the search analyst recognizes this), but the vocabulary may only be capable of expressing this at a higher generic level— shielded arc welding or arc welding—and thus precision failures are inevitable.
3. The ability of the search analyst to recognize and cover all possible approaches to retrieval. To take a simple example, the requester may be looking for articles on possible adverse effects of commonly consumed beverages or components thereof. The searcher uses the terms caffeine, coffee, tea, and theophylline, but forgets about the possibility of cacao and theobromine and thus misses some of the relevant documents.
4. The *level* of search strategy adopted. The searcher can choose to use a broad strategy (leading to high recall but low precision) or a tight strategy designed for high precision (but usually at the expense of a low recall) or a compromise between the two extremes.

When the search strategy is actually matched against the file of document surrogates (i.e., the search is conducted), further factors affecting performance come into play. One important performance factor is that of indexing policy, particularly policy regarding exhaustivity of indexing (which really equates with the number of index terms assigned). Perhaps the exhaustivity of indexing is inadequate to allow some of the relevant items, for a particular request, to be retrieved. Inaccuracy of indexing (omission of important terms or assignment of terms incorrectly) will also lead to recall or precision failures. The characteristics of the vocabulary affect the indexing process as much as they affect the searching process. An indexer can only adequately represent the concepts occurring in a document if there are appropriate specific terms available for him to use. Lack of specificity in the vocabulary will usually cause precision failures, but can also lead to recall failures. Further, the vocabulary must be capable, to a certain extent, of showing the syntax of the terms assigned in indexing and thereby avoiding at least some of the precision failures that would be caused by *false coordinations* or *incorrect term relationships.** The more precoordinate the vocabulary, the less the need for additional devices to show relationships between terms (e.g., links, roles, subheadings).

Finally, before the results of a search are submitted to the requester, the analyst may screen the output and eliminate items that appear to be irrelevant, with the object of improving the precision of the search to the end user. How successful this screening operation is (i.e., how much precision can be improved without having too serious an effect on recall) depends primarily upon the accuracy of the analyst's interpretation of the requester's requirements. Secondarily, the success of the screening will be affected by the quality of the document surrogate from which the analyst is working.

Of course, these various sources of failure are cumulative. For a particular search conducted in a retrieval system, some of the relevant documents may be missed by the very fact that the user's request statement is too restrictive and inadvertently excludes certain items. Others may be missed due to poor search strategy, vocabulary inadequacies, indexing policy, and indexer omissions. Finally, the analyst may eliminate some more relevant items in his screening process. With so many possible sources of loss, it is little wonder that systems do not, on the average, operate very close to 100% recall. A similar cumulative effect occurs to prevent our obtaining 100% precision.

In the above discussion we have mentioned all the factors likely to contribute in a major way to the performance of retrieval systems in general. Now we should consider which of these factors are likely to be most prevalent in the on-line system and which may be discounted or of greatly reduced

---

*A *false coordination* is the situation in which the search terms, while present in the retrieved document, are essentially unrelated. An *incorrect term relationship* is the situation in which the search terms are related in the retrieved document but not in the way that the searcher wants them related.

significance. The significance of the various factors will really depend on whether the system is used in a delegated search mode (a librarian or other information specialist conducts a search on behalf of some individual who needs information) or in a nondelegated mode (the person with the information need conducts his own search directly at the terminal), although the indexing factors will be equally significant, and will have the same effects, in either situation. Another important consideration is whether the system is a natural language system or functioning through a controlled vocabulary.

If the system is used in the delegated search mode, all the factors illustrated in Figure 1.1 will be likely to affect the performance of the system. In fact, Figure 1.1 represents any typical delegated search situation, whatever the type of system involved. The delegated on-line search is still prone to failure as a result of inadequate interaction between the requester and the system; the quality of the search is essentially predetermined by the quality of the request upon which it is based. A poor request (i.e., one that inadequately represents the information need that prompted it) will almost inevitably lead to a poor search in terms of recall or precision or both. The search strategy used by the information specialist, the adequacy of the vocabulary, indexing policy, indexing quality, and the accuracy of the screening will all substantially affect the performance of a delegated search in an on-line system. The principal difference between these factors in an on-line system and the same factors in a batch-processing system is that in the former mistakes tend to be less costly than they do in the latter. It is usually possible to interact more rapidly with the on-line system. The searcher can try alternative approaches (possibly with the requester at his elbow), obtain feedback from the requester, and thus identify defects in the original request or in the search strategies used. In other words, he conducts the search in an iterative mode and is given more than the single chance that he would normally have in searching an off-line batch system.

When the on-line system is used in a nondelegated mode, on the other hand, the situation is simplified in some respects while other factors assume increased importance. The situation is illustrated roughly in Figure 7.1. One important source of potential failure is omitted completely in this case. The search is not delegated and therefore we avoid those problems due to request statements that inadequately or inaccurately represent the information needs upon which they are based. In fact, in the nondelegated search situation, request statements as such do not really exist. There is no possibility, then, of a searcher misinterpreting a requester's requirements. On the other hand, the system user is still required to verbalize his requirement. That is, he must be able to express his need in terms that the system understands and can act upon. Usually, this will require a formal search strategy in the form of a boolean statement, although, in some systems, the user may be able to pose a query in English sentence form.

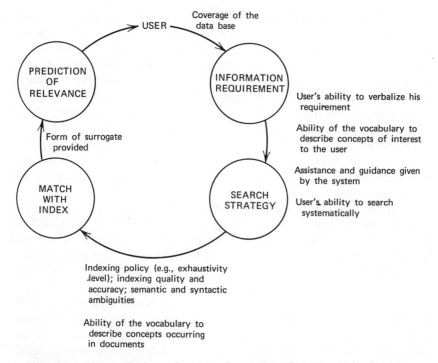

Figure 7.1.   Factors affecting performance of an on-line information retrieval system.

How successful a searcher will be at the terminal is almost entirely dependent upon (*a*) his ability to think of alternative approaches to retrieval, and (*b*) his knowledge of the vocabulary of the system. At this point, it is desirable to compare the probable effects of searching in a controlled vocabulary system versus a system capable of searching on natural language. In general, it takes a considerable amount of time to become thoroughly familiar with the terminology contained in a thesaurus or other form of controlled vocabulary. The terms in such a vocabulary have special meanings—either by definition or by usage (i.e., they may have taken on special meanings by virtue of the fact that they have been used in a particular way by system indexers, possibly over a period of several years). In other words, a controlled vocabulary system is heavily founded on indexing policies and protocols. Moreover, these policies and protocols tend to change, especially as new terms are added to the vocabulary. To use such a system effectively it may be necessary to know not only how a particular topic is indexed at the present time, but also how it was indexed in the past.

The on-line subject specialist, seeking to satisfy his own needs, is unlikely, without a considerable amount of training, to be able to use a controlled vocabulary system as effectively as an information specialist who is fully experienced in exploitation of the system and who possibly is involved in indexing, vocabulary control, and related system activities. This does not mean that the practitioner in a field *cannot* use the controlled vocabulary system. Probably, given a minimum introduction and a copy of the controlled vocabulary, he will be able to exploit it reasonably effectively. However, without an extensive training program that he may be unable or unwilling to undergo, he may never be able to search the system at a maximum level of effectiveness. Moreover, he must always translate his request into the controlled terms of the system. This will usually involve a lookup operation (on-line or in a printed tool) and is potentially a frustrating task, particularly if the searcher's terms are widely different (e.g., more specific) from the terms of the controlled vocabulary.

On the other hand, the controlled vocabulary can give the searcher a considerable amount of assistance in the formulation of his searching strategies if he has the patience and the inclination to use it fully. It can lead the searcher from the terms he originally thought of to other related terms, including synonyms, more specific terms, more generic terms, and terms semantically related in other ways.

Natural language poses a different set of problems. It is quite possible that the practitioner in the field may be able to search such a free text system more effectively than the information specialist. Here he is searching the language of the documents themselves (or at least their abstracts) rather than some metalanguage. Presumably he is more familiar with the language of his field than the information specialist. The language of the documents is likely to coincide reasonably well with his own language (i.e., the language he will use in his requests) and he should, therefore, be able to interrogate the natural language system directly. There will be no translation and therefore no lookup involved.

On the other hand, most natural language systems have no thesaurus and provide very little in the way of searching aids. The success of the search, under these conditions, is largely dependent upon the user's own ingenuity in thinking of possible ways in which a particular notion may be expressed in the literature. If he is looking for papers on levels of zarontin in the blood, a simple search on ZARONTIN *and* BLOOD LEVEL is unlikely to be effective (at least as far as recall goes). He must also recognize that zarontin may appear as *ethosuximide* and that relevant papers or abstracts may talk about *blood levels* or *serum levels*, or *concentration* in the blood or serum, or may simply talk of zarontin in the blood without ever using the terms "level" or "concentration."

The fact is that the searcher in a natural language system, on-line or off-line, needs a thesaurus just as much as a searcher in a controlled vocabulary system. In this case, the thesaurus functions as a searching aid only.

If on-line systems are to be used most effectively by the practitioner, they must provide a considerable amount of assistance to the searcher at the console. Whether the data base is in free text form or indexed using a controlled vocabulary, the searcher should be given a thesaurus (or something similar) to help him in the construction of search strategies. In the case of the controlled vocabulary system, the user should be provided with a large *entry vocabulary* of natural language terms, occurring in documents and therefore likely to occur in requests, with their equivalents in the controlled language of the system.

The searcher who is unsophisticated in information retrieval techniques will need considerable assistance at the on-line terminal. He will obviously require some instruction in how to use the system and how to formulate search statements. In some systems, including ORBIT, such instruction can be obtained through on-line printout or display at the terminal. But some users may require more than this. They may need to be led by the hand in the development of searching strategies. It is possible that the techniques of computer-assisted instruction may be applicable to this task—a point that we will return to later.

Quite apart from the intellectual factors involved in the construction of search strategies, the success or failure of a search will also be dependent upon less intellectual factors relating to ease of system use and the tolerance of the searcher. The more foolproof the system (e.g., the less sensitive it is to common errors of punctuation or spelling), the more people will be willing to persevere in its use. The searcher will rapidly lose patience with a system that repeatedly rejects search terms, especially if such rejection is for seemingly trivial reasons or if no reason for the rejection is provided by the system.

Clearly, the on-line search will be affected by characteristics of the data base, which are outside the control of the searcher. Indexing errors will prevent retrieval of relevant items or, less commonly, will cause irrelevant items to be retrieved. Precision failures will occur in a controlled vocabulary system because of lack of term specificity. Others may be caused by false coordinations or incorrect term relationships; these failures are especially prevalent in natural language searching. Further precision failures may be due to exhaustive indexing. That is, documents may be retrieved on topics for which they contain very little information. This type of failure is very likely to occur in a natural language system in which full texts or lengthy abstracts are stored. Failures of this kind may also occur, however, in controlled vocabulary systems that have adopted the policy of indexing exhaustively (i.e., using many terms). These failures are not peculiar to on-line systems and, for that reason, deserve only a passing reference here.

A final potential cause of failure in the on-line system is related to the document representation stored. Since an on-line system is intended to be used interactively and heuristically, it follows that the searcher must be given the capability of making rapid decisions on the probable relevance of retrieved items. On the basis of items displayed, he will modify his strategy in order to improve the precision and/or recall of his search. Under most conditions a document title will be an inadequate indicator of its content. The searcher should probably be given the ability to view abstracts or, in a controlled vocabulary system, the complete set of index terms assigned to an item. If the document representation (surrogate) is an inadequate indicator of content, the full interactive capabilities of the system will not be realized, and its overall effectiveness will be reduced accordingly.

REFERENCES

Lancaster, F. W. (1968a). *Information Retrieval Systems: Characteristics, Testing and Evaluation.* New York: Wiley.
Lancaster, F. W. (1968b). "Interaction Between Requesters and a Large Mechanized Retrieval System." *Information Storage Retrieval* **4** (2), 239–252.

Chapter Eight

Evaluating Effectiveness
of the System

An evaluation of a retrieval system should be conducted in such a way that it will produce answers to the following questions:
1. How well is the system functioning?
2. Can it be improved?
3. How may it best be improved?
The first question, relating to the present performance level, may be answered by *macroevaluation* (King and Bryant, 1971), which involves measuring and expressing the performance according to some type of quantitative scale, such as the various performance criteria mentioned in Chapter Six. The other two questions, on the other hand, can only be answered by a more detailed level of evaluation, namely *microevaluation*. Microevaluation involves analytical procedures whereby the major sources of system failure are identified, thus allowing corrective action to be taken to raise the performance level of the system. Microevaluation implies *diagnosis*. Evaluation is essentially a diagnostic procedure which, like other forms of diagnosis, is intended to lead to *therapeutic* action. An evaluation program, hopefully, is not conducted merely as an intellectual exercise. Thorough evaluation tends to be expensive, and we can only justify this expense if the evaluation program is likely to lead to significant improvement in the performance of the system.

Evaluation of a retrieval system can be completely subjective (i.e., nonquantitative). We can ask users to assess the value of the service provided on some broad scale, such as *major value, minor value, no value*. This type of subjective assessment is of some utility, because it at least gives us an indication of user satisfaction. However, such a sweeping evaluation is certainly not diagnostic and will not in itself lead to system improvements. It is preferable that we make our evaluation less subjective and more quantitative if possible. *Quantification* implies the use of some type of performance figure to express the degree of success of a search or other service provided. Performance figures also allow us to identify the poor searches that will be prime candidates for detailed analysis to determine causes of failure (i.e., *failure analysis*). Failure analysis, of this type, provides the diagnostic aspect of evaluation. We conduct an evaluation of an information retrieval system to obtain two types of data:

1. Performance figures for searches
2. Results of analyses of reasons for failures in searches

These data, when analyzed and interpreted, should yield recommendations from which decisions can be made on how system performance may best be improved.

To be able to quantify (i.e., derive performance figures), we must recognize criteria by which users will judge the success or failure of a search. In other words, we must know what qualities users require in an information retrieval system. In Chapter Six we discussed these user requirements and decided that, for an on-line retrieval system, the most critical are likely to be coverage, recall, and unit cost (in time) per relevant citation retrieved, although the precision ratio may also be considered to be of some importance.

We evaluate the effectiveness of an information system by determining the degree to which it meets the various user requirements. Some of this can be done by direct observation (e.g., determination of form of output) and some by relatively simple recording procedures (e.g., measurement of user time spent at the terminal). Coverage, recall, precision, and unit cost, on the other hand, can only be measured or estimated by specially devised procedures.

A complete evaluation program will comprise a number of stages, as follows:

1. Establishing the scope and purpose of the program (i.e., deciding what exactly is to be evaluated).
2. Designing the evaluation.
3. Conducting the study.
4. Analyzing and interpreting the results.
5. Making system modifications, based on the evaluation results, designed to improve the overall performance level.

The first step, defining the scope and purpose of the study, should be a task undertaken by the managers of the system to be evaluated. Presumably, they have certain specific questions they would like answered. For example, they may be particularly concerned about the system vocabulary (*index language*) and would like to know if it is sufficiently specific, across the subject areas covered, to be able to satisfy the various demands placed upon the system. Or they may want to know if the entry vocabulary is sufficiently well-developed to give the searcher maximum assistance in converting from his own language into the controlled terms of the system. An important element in an on-line evaluation may be a comparison of the effectiveness of an on-line search conducted by a scientist or other practitioner and a parallel search conducted by an information specialist. The evaluator of the system (assuming that he is not in fact also the system manager) needs to obtain from management an explicit statement of what he is to concentrate upon in his study. When he designs the evaluation program he must be sure that the data collected will, when analyzed, allow him to answer the various questions posed by management. Lancaster (1968b) has presented a sample list of some of the specific questions that might be posed in a comprehensive evaluation of a large operating retrieval system.

Note that, although an evaluation program may *concentrate* upon one particular subsystem (e.g., indexing policy and procedures), this subsystem cannot be evaluated in isolation. The various major subsystems (indexing, searching, index language, user–system interface) are closely interdependent. A change in one will have effects and repercussions elsewhere. It is not, for example, possible to evaluate indexing in any meaningful way without considering the effect of indexing policy and procedures on the searching subsystem. Likewise, a change in the vocabulary will affect both indexing and searching operations.

Performance Figures

An evaluation program must yield two types of data if it is to be useful:
1. Performance figures for a representative group of searches.
2. Examples of system failures to allow analysis of causes of failure.
The performance figures we are most interested in are recall ratios, precision ratios, and search times (to allow us to devise unit cost figures). If we can establish these performance figures for a representative set of searches conducted, we will also be able to identify examples of searches that have produced poor results (i.e., low recall, low precision, or high unit cost per relevant item retrieved). A major task of the designer of an evaluation is to establish methods that can be used to derive recall and precision figures for a number of searches. To arrive at these figures we must be able to put certain absolute values, or least estimates, into the 2×2 table illustrated in Figure 8.1. Three of these values are directly observable: the total collection size, $a + b + c + d$; the total number of items retrieved, $a + b$; and the total not retrieved, $c + d$. The other values must be established, or at least estimated, in our evaluation program. The values a and b can be established

User Relevance Judgment

		Relevant	Not relevant	Total
System Relevance Prediction	Retrieved	a hits	b noise	a + b
	Not retrieved	c misses	d correctly rejected	c + d
	Total	a + c	b + d	a + b + c + d total collection

Figure 8.1. The 2 × 2 table of search results.

relatively easily in a delegated search system. A search has been conducted for a requester and has retrieved a number of documents or document surrogates, a + b. We present these to the requester and have him tell us which items he considers relevant (a) and which he considers not relevant (b). Usually, we will want him to judge relevance on some scale (*major relevance, minor relevance, no relevance* will usually suffice). Although the topic of *relevance* has generated much literature and heated discussion, and although a great many factors influence a requester's relevance decision, when we are evaluating an operating system in its entirety we must accept that a relevant document is one that contributes to the satisfaction of the information need of the requester and an irrelevant document is one that does not. In other words, relevance assessments are value judgments placed on documents by individuals with information needs.

Once the requester has made these relevance assessments for us, we have a precision ratio, $a/(a + b)$, for the search under review. In practical application, these relevance assessments should be recorded by the requester on assessment forms or directly on a printout. We should also, if possible, ask the requester to indicate reasons for his various judgments (i.e., why is one document of major relevance, a second of no relevance, a third of minor relevance). These recorded reasons will be extremely useful in our analysis of the search performance.

We still have two values to place in the 2 × 2 table, namely c and d. These are the difficult ones to determine, but we need them in order to establish a recall ratio. There is only one way to arrive at these values absolutely (and thereby derive a *true* recall figure) and that is to have the requester examine all the nonretrieved items (c + d) and tell us which of them are relevant (c) and which are not (d). If we can get this done, we have established an absolute value for c and thus we can derive an absolute recall ratio, a/(a + c). In the evaluation of experimental or small prototype systems it is sometimes possible to do just this. However, in most operating systems, if the system functions at all effectively, c + d will be a very large portion of the entire collection and it will be quite impossible to expect the requester to examine all of these items or even a large part of them. Moreover, c + d will usually be so large that we cannot even use conventional random sampling procedures. That is, an impossibly large sample would need to be drawn from c + d to achieve any expectation of finding even one relevant document therein.

If we are evaluating a retrieval system of any size, we may just as well abandon the idea of trying to establish true recall and be satisfied with the best possible *recall estimate* we can come up with. Probably the most reasonable method of doing this is that employed by Lancaster (1968a) in his evaluation of MEDLARS. The procedure, which has been justified statistically by Shumway (1968), is illustrated in Figure 8.2.

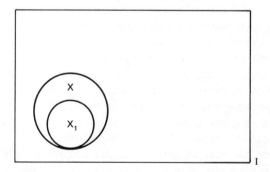

Figure 8.2.   Method of calculating recall by extrapolation from known population to unknown.

For any particular subject request posed to the collection I there will be a set of documents, X, that the requester would judge relevant if he saw them. If we knew this set X and what portion of this set was retrieved by a search in the collection, we would be able to establish absolute recall. But, as indicated above, we usually cannot establish the composition of X in a system of any significant size. However, we *can* find a portion of X, the subset

X_1, and we can base our recall estimate on the proportion of X_1 retrieved by a search in the system. The subset X_1 is a group of documents *contained in the data base of the system* and judged to be relevant by the requester but found by methods extraneous to the system being evaluated. For example, X_1 can be composed of relevant documents known to the requester at the time he first approaches the system and makes his request. Alternatively, it can be composed of documents found by the evaluator through outside sources (e.g., other information centers or published indexes), submitted to the requester for his assessment, and judged relevant by him. The subset can also be comprised partly of items from the first source and partly of items from the second. For example, a scientist comes to an information system and makes a subject request, at which time he already knows two relevant items. The evaluator does a parallel search in another source or sources and finds twelve *possibly relevant* items. Of these twelve, eight are judged relevant by the requester. We now have a group of ten documents that we know to be relevant to the request (the two the requester knew originally and the eight found subsequently). Assuming that all ten appear in the data base of the system, we have established a *recall base* of ten relevant items; i.e., the subset X_1. We now check the results of the search actually conducted by the system and find that seven of the ten items were retrieved and three were not. Our recall estimate is, then, $7/10 \times 100$, or 70%. If X_1 is a representative sample of X, we can then make the reasonable assumption that the hit rate (recall ratio) for the entire set X will approximate the hit rate for the subset X_1.

Another possible method of establishing a recall ratio is to use completely synthetic requests based upon documents known to be in the collection (i.e., *source documents*). Suppose we extract a group of 100 documents. For each, we, or preferably a group of subject specialists, make up a request for which the document is regarded as relevant (i.e., we would want this document retrieved in response to the request). The requests are composed according to certain guidelines and are made as realistic as possible. They should be of the type that might reasonably be put to the retrieval system in the normal course of events. The requests are then processed against the retrieval system, and the retrieved items are judged for relevance by the originator of the request, thus giving us a precision ratio for the search. Recall for each search can only be 1 or 0, depending upon whether or not the source document was retrieved. The technique gives us a gross recall estimate over a group of searches. If over 100 searches the source document was retrieved 77 times and missed 23 times, our recall estimate for the group of searches would be 77%.

This approach to establishing recall has been used in various retrieval tests, but is not particularly satisfactory in the evaluation of an operating system because of its artificiality. Moreover, since we know only one relevant document for each request, our recall estimate at the single search level can only be 1 or 0. Cleverdon, et al. (1966) and Lancaster have both used modified source document tests in which the source document, once used to generate a request, is discarded and the documents *cited by the source document* are assumed to be relevant and are used as the recall base for evaluating the search. Providing we can establish that the cited documents are in fact relevant to the derived request, this is a much improved procedure.

By methods described above, we can establish performance figures for a group of *test searches* and thus place all the necessary values or estimates in the 2 × 2 table of search results. Of course, we have to decide which searches we are going to treat as test searches. In a small system, we may decide to evaluate all searches conducted within a particular time period, whereas in a large system we will want to evaluate a sample only—either a purely random sample or a sample established by some stratification procedure. This question of sampling among searches is treated by King and Bryant (1971).

Failure Analysis

Having established recall ratios and precision ratios for the test searches, we must now undertake an analysis of the recall and precision failures occurring. This failure analysis is diagnostic and it is the most important part of the entire evaluation program. Take a hypothetical search for which we have determined a recall estimate of 7/10 and a precision figure of 15/40. For this search we have examples of three recall failures and twenty-five precision failures for analysis. We will probably want to analyze all the recall failures and a random sample of the precision failures.

Failure analysis involves a careful examination of the documents involved, how they were indexed, the request posed to the system, the search strategy used, and the completed assessment forms of the requester. Armed with this material, we should be able to determine the major cause of each failure. When we have conducted such a failure analysis for a significant number of searches, we should find ourselves with a large body of data which, when analyzed and interpreted, will clearly indicate the principal problem areas in the system—the areas that require attention and modification if we are to improve overall system performance.

On-Line Evaluation

The procedures discussed briefly above [a much more detailed account has been given in an earlier book (Lancaster, 1968b)] can be applied to any type of delegated search system, including the on-line system operated in the delegated mode. However, as we have stressed on several occasions, an on-line system may be most effective when operated in the nondelegated mode (i.e., by the practitioners of a field directly, without the interposition of an information specialist). Evaluation of the nondelegated on-line search presents a special set of problems and is more difficult in many ways than the evaluation of a delegated search, on-line or off-line.

The great problem is that we have very little control over the searcher at the on-line terminal, particularly when the terminal is located in or near his own office and use is not directly controlled by a librarian or other information specialist. Under these conditions, we are very heavily dependent upon the good will of the individual and his desire to cooperate with us in the evaluation of his search. However, there are certain data that we can gather directly at the terminal. Let us consider what records we need to permit a meaningful analysis of an on-line nondelegated search and what techniques we might use to collect these records.

The minimum set of records and data would appear to comprise the following:

1. Certain personal characteristics of the searcher (name, address, professional affiliation, telephone number, as a minimum).
2. A complete request statement (i.e., a full statement in the searcher's own words of what he was looking for when he first approached the on-line system).
3. The elapsed time spent by the user at the terminal.
4. A complete printout of his dialogue with the system, including a record of all the citations retrieved (i.e., printed or displayed) during the search.
5. An indication of which citations were judged relevant and which were not, preferably using some relevance scale.
6. An estimate of how many relevant citations, contained in the data base, the searcher failed to find and the identity of at least a sample of these (to derive a recall estimate and permit an analysis of reasons for recall failures).
7. The user's subjective assessment of the value to him of the search (major value, considerable value, minor value, no value, or some such scale). Preferably, we would like the user also to supply reasons to support his decisions (e.g., Why was a particular search of only minor value?).
8. (Possibly less critical.) A revised statement of information need if, after the search is completed, the user feels that his original request statement is an inadequate representation of what he was really seeking.

In addition to the above, for certain types of analyses there are other records that we may want to keep. For example, if we wish to study the effect of learning factors, we will want to know, for each search, how many times the searcher has used the on-line facilities in the past.

To gather these various data, we can use a series of evaluation forms to be completed by the searcher, we can collect data directly at the on-line terminal, or we can use a combination of these two techniques. Specially prepared forms, if properly completed, will present results in a format which makes subsequent analysis convenient. However, we are likely to be able to use forms only in a situation in which access to the console is controlled in some way. For example, if a scientist must obtain access to the terminal through a librarian or other intermediary, we could perhaps make his use of the system contingent upon his participation in the evaluation program. At the very least, the intermediary will be available to hand the necessary forms to the user and to request his cooperation. If access to the terminal is completely unrestricted (i.e., no librarian or other person controls use of the system), it may be unrealistic to expect searchers to complete evaluation forms however prominently these may be displayed at the terminal. Under these conditions, it will be preferable to gather as much data as possible at the terminal itself.

Presumably, any on-line system operating in a time-shared environment should give us the capability of monitoring all searches conducted, either by means of simultaneous monitoring on a second console or by generating a printout of an entire dialogue and examining this at leisure at a later time. However, a monitoring operation of this kind may legitimately be considered an invasion of privacy, and we should be careful to obtain the specific permission of the searcher before we oversee his search in this way.*

Personal details on the searcher can be collected at the terminal itself as part of log-in and user identification procedures. It is desirable that the searcher's full request statement also be recorded on-line and, in fact, the system can be programmed so that the user must record his request before he can operate the system in a search mode.

Elapsed time can be recorded by the system itself for each search conducted. In addition, CPU time can be recorded for each search to allow actual costs to be calculated.

A printout of the dialogue between the user and the system is essential for subsequent analysis, particularly for our evaluation of the searching

---

*In the Remote Information Query System (RIQS) at Northwestern University (see Chapter Thirteen), the user is asked by on-line message if he is willing to have his search monitored. In other systems, including SPIRES, the user is able to "turn off" the monitoring operation.

strategies used in a particular search. The printout should be complete, from log-in to log-out; should include the user's search terms and logic, system responses, and a complete list of citations retrieved (i.e., displayed at the terminal or printed out during the normal course of the search). If the search is being conducted on a typewriter terminal, we can ask the user to retain a copy of the printout and to provide this for our analysis. We could also use multiple copy paper to generate a printout for the searcher's own use and a second copy for analysis purposes. Alternatively, if the system is so designed, we can record the complete dialogue in machine-readable form, as part of overall monitoring operations, and print this out off-line for all test searches at a later time. If the searcher is using a video console, as opposed to a type-writer terminal, it is essential that we record the entire dialogue remotely (with the searcher's permission) and print it out for subsequent analysis.

The relevance assessments of the user, against individual retrieved citations, can also be recorded either on-line or on a copy of the printout. Unless the retrieval system provides abstracts, it is quite likely that the user will be unable to determine the relevance of some of the retrieved items from the details given by the system. Because we would like a true count of how many relevant documents were brought to the searcher's attention, it is probably preferable to ask the searcher to mark his relevance assessments on a copy of the printout, waiting until he has had an opportunity to see the actual documents before making his judgments. In fact, it is possible that, for purposes of the evaluation, we may need to supply copies of certain documents to the user (i.e., items that he does not have available to him locally). It is probably desirable to have the user judge the relevance of retrieved items on a 3 point scale: major value in relation to the information need that caused the search (i.e., a document that the user would not want to miss), minor value (relevant but not an essential item; he would not be too unhappy if this document were not retrieved), no value (i.e., irrelevant).

Once we have obtained these assessments of relevance, we can calculate the precision ratio of the search. Providing we have also recorded the elapsed search time, we can calculate the unit cost (in time) per relevant item retrieved.

A brief on-line questionnaire, presented to the user at the end of a search, can be used to collect various other data that we may need in the overall evaluation of a system, including the user's own subjective assessment of the value of the search. This overall judgment should also be made on some scale, as: major value, considerable value, minor value, no value. Of course, such judgments are gross and purely subjective. Nevertheless, they do give some indication of how satisfied the users of the system are—and we certainly want to know this.

Figure 8.3 shows the on-line questionnaire incorporated into the AIM–TWX system (see Chapter Five). As you can see, this questionnaire determines

PROG:
WILL YOU PLEASE ANSWER A FEW QUESTIONS? YES, NO, OR SHORT.

USER: yes

PROG:
FOR EACH QUESTION, INSERT A NUMBER AND A CARRIAGE RETURN.
WHO IS OPERATING THE TERMINAL? : 1.PHYSICIAN, 2.NURSE, 3.MEDI-
CAL STUDENT, 4.OTHER STUDENT, 5.OTHER HEALTH PROFESSIONAL,
6.INFORMATION SPECIALIST, 7.OTHER.

USER 5:

PROG:
IF OPERATOR IS HELPING OR REPRESENTING SOMEONE ELSE, WHO IS
THIS OTHER PERSON? USE CATEGORIES ABOVE, OR 0 FOR YOURSELF.

USER: 0

PROG:
INSERT APPROXIMATE NUMBER OF TIMES OPERATOR HAS PREVIOUSLY
RUN ELHILL.

USER: 1

PROG:
WHAT WAS MAIN PURPOSE IN USING ELHILL THIS TIME? : 1.DEMON-
STRATION OR TRAINING, 2.EXPERIMENTATION AND EXPLORATION
OF SYSTEM CAPABILITIES, 3.TO OBTAIN NEEDED BIBLIOGRAPHIC
CITATIONS, 4.OTHER.

USER: 3

PROG:
WHAT MAINLY PROMPTED NEED FOR THE BIBLIOGRAPHIC CITATIONS?
: 1.PATIENT CARE PROBLEM, 2.EDUCATION, 3.RESEARCH, 4.OTHER,
5.DON'T KNOW.

USER: 1,3

PROG:
WERE THE ON-LINE SEARCH RESULTS OF VALUE? : 1.MAJOR VALUE,
2.CONSIDERABLE VALUE, 3.MINOR VALUE, 4.NO VALUE, 5.DON'T KNOW.

USER: 1

PROG: **GOOD-BYE FROM ELHILL!
PGM.STOPPED
/logout
LOGGED OUT 10:13 12/04/70
TERMINAL TIME 01.77 HOURS
CPU TIME 001 MINUTES 07.1 SECONDS

Figure 8.3. On-line questionnaire as used in AIM–TWX.

what type of person is searching the system, for what purpose, how many times he has used it previously, and, if he was using the system to satisfy some information need, how valuable the search results were to him. A somewhat similar questionnaire, as used in RECON, is illustrated in Figure 8.4.

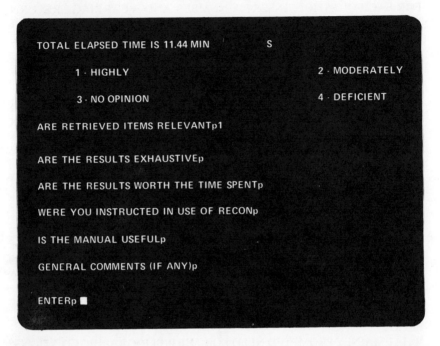

Figure 8.4. On-line questionnaire as used in RECON. Reproduced from *What NASA/RECON Can Do For You,* NASA, 1970, by permission of the National Aeronautics and Space Administration.

By methods outlined above we can obtain most of the data that we will need for the purposes of our evaluation. However, we still need to estimate recall for the searches that are part of our study. To estimate recall we can use one of the procedures mentioned earlier in this chapter—whichever one appears most appropriate and convenient to apply. To evaluate the success of a scientist (or a practitioner in some other field) using an on-line system to satisfy his own information needs, it will usually be satisfactory to estimate the scientist's recall on the basis of a second search conducted on the same topic by an information specialist more skilled in using the system. We calculate the recall ratio of the scientist's search by the equation

$$\frac{A}{A + B}$$

where A = the number of relevant documents found by the scientist and B = the number of *additional* relevant documents found by the information specialist. For the purposes of the study, the information specialist will be expected to go all out to achieve a high recall, perhaps searching in a broader way than he would under normal conditions. The assumption is that A + B = 100% of the relevant documents in the data base. This may, in fact, be a false assumption; there may be further relevant items in the data base that are retrieved in neither search. Nevertheless, for the purpose of evaluating the scientist's search, we can use this *comparative recall* figure, as long as we recognize that, in relation to *true recall*, it may be somewhat inflated. That is, the recall estimate that we obtain this way should be accepted as an upper bound on the recall of the original search. For example, if the original search retrieves three relevant items and the second search retrieves two additional ones, our recall estimate is 60% and we can be quite sure that the recall achieved by the first search was *not more than* 60%. Needless to say, any items found in the second search, but not in the first, must be submitted to the original searcher for his relevance assessments.

Although we try to obtain the best possible estimate of recall for each search studied, this value is less important than our identification of recall failures (i.e., examples of documents that were not retrieved for one reason or another in the on-line search, although the searcher subsequently judges them of relevance to his search topic). Once we have identified some recall failures and precision failures occurring in a group of searches, we can conduct an analysis to determine why these failures occurred. On the basis of such an analysis, we can decide how successfully the system is operating, what are the major factors contributing to poor search results in the system, and what steps might be taken to modify the system, or how it is used, to raise the overall performance level.

Analysis and Interpretation of Evaluation Results

In analyzing and interpreting the results of our evaluation, we will use all the pertinent data collected: performance figures, analyses of failures, and subjective indicators. We will consider how many of the users participating in the study judged the search results to be of value, and we will distinguish levels on the value scale. If possible, we would certainly like to know why a user judges a particular search to be of no value. This may be a reflection on the characteristics of the data base (i.e., it contains very little that is relevant to the subject of the search) rather than the quality of the search as such.

Recall ratios and precision ratios are indicators of which searches are most successful and which are least successful. We must be prepared to conduct detailed examinations of searches that have produced especially poor results in terms of recall or precision. Why did these failures occur, and what distinguishes these searches from those in which the results are more satisfactory? We will also want to use these figures to compare the performance of the system under various modes of operation. For example, how much evidence is there that the most experienced searchers (i.e., those who have used the system most frequently) achieve the best results on the average? Do the performance figures indicate that a particular type of user achieves better results or that there is a significant difference in performance levels in various subject areas (e.g., in a medical retrieval system, searches relating to drug therapy may produce much better results than the average for all searches conducted)?

Search times and unit cost figures will indicate which searches have been most efficient, in terms of requiring least expenditure of effort, and which have been least efficient. Again, we will want to focus attention on those searches with high unit cost per relevant citation retrieved, and to determine the precise reasons for the seeming inefficiency. Poor searching strategies may be responsible, the user may have wasted time through lack of familiarity with the commands and protocols of the system, or the system itself may have contributed to errors through idiosyncratic behavior.

An analysis of errors will be an important element in the evaluation program. We need to determine how many errors were made and to characterize these errors by type; e.g., human carelessness, mechanical failures of the computer or console, line noise. We should also try to assess the effect of these errors on searching time and, ergo, the cost per relevant citation retrieved.

The most important element in any evaluation is the diagnostic element. An analysis of reasons for recall and precision failures, if conducted on a sufficiently large sample, will tell us exactly which factors contribute most to poor search results in the particular system we are evaluating (the range of such factors was discussed in detail in Chapter Seven). Hopefully, the evaluation will also suggest ways in which the system may be improved so that fewer failures occur in the future.

This chapter is restricted to methodologies for the evaluation of on-line retrieval systems. It does not deal with evaluation results, a topic which will be discussed in Chapter Nine. In studying methodologies, however, we should spend a little time considering procedures that have already been used in the evaluation of on-line retrieval systems, although very few such evaluations have been conducted up to the present time. In the following paragraphs we will describe some studies that have been conducted in the past, concentrating upon their objectives and the procedures used. Some results from these studies will be presented in Chapter Nine.

RECON Evaluation

Perhaps the first serious attempt to evaluate an on-line system, albeit rather crude, was a study of RECON conducted by the Bunker-Ramo Corporation and reported by Meister and Sullivan (1967). The evaluation conducted was purely subjective. The acceptability of the system to NASA scientific and technical personnel was judged on the basis of (*a*) how frequently the system was used and how many of the searches conducted were judged to be successful, and (*b*) attitudes of the users toward the system.

The evaluators held informal, in-depth discussions with small groups of users. At the end of these discussions, the participants were asked to complete an *evaluative rating form*. This rating form uses seven point, semantic differential, bi-polar scales. It records a purely subjective assessment of the effectiveness and efficiency of RECON as compared with the NASA batch searching system. At a later time, a detailed questionnaire was administered to personnel who were known to have used the RECON system during the test period. There were 37 completed questionnaires in the study.

It was originally intended that more objective procedures be used in the study. A *controlled performance test* was planned to compare the performance of RECON, in terms of accuracy and speed, with the performance of a conventional off-line search. It was intended to select some searches already conducted via the off-line route and have the requester of these searches conduct his own search at the on-line terminal. The two sets of results were to be compared on the basis of number of citations retrieved and number of relevant citations retrieved. Presumably this technique would yield, for each RECON search, search time, precision ratio, and recall ratio (using as a recall base the number of relevant items discovered by the off-line search plus the number of additional relevant items discovered by the RECON search). Unfortunately, only four or five of these controlled performance tests were conducted, and the entire evaluation was therefore based on the questionnaire studies of user attitude.

As pointed out earlier, subjective studies of this type have some value as indicators of user satisfaction. However, they yield no real data on the success or failure of searches. In this study, a search was judged successful if citations were viewed by the user on the screen, regardless of whether these citations were relevant or not and regardless of how many items may have been missed by the search. In other words, a search was successful if carried to its logical conclusion (to the point at which citations are retrieved and displayed). Obviously, such a study does not allow the diagnosis of system problems and therefore provides no real data which, when interpreted, might indicate ways in which the system could be improved.

DIALOG Evaluation

Summit (1968) describes another NASA evaluation conducted in 1967 as a prelude to the eventual RECON implementation. The system studied was DIALOG, designed by Lockheed Missiles & Space Company. Remote terminals were installed at the NASA Ames Research Center and later at NASA headquarters. The NASA data base was loaded at the Lockheed Palo Alto Research Laboratory, and searches were conducted via telephone lines. Whereas the Ames searches were carried out largely by scientific and technical personnel, most of the headquarters searches were carried out by the NASA headquarters librarian.

One phase of the evaluation was conducted by collecting statistics on use of the system, including unscheduled service interruptions (and the cause of these), elapsed time per search, number of index terms and level of term coordination used, and number of items printed. Because a user would normally view an item on the screen before requesting a print, the number of items printed in this case can be assumed to be the number of relevant items retrieved by the search. User comments and reactions were solicited as part of the study, and the statistics on characteristics of usage at Ames were compared with the statistics on characteristics of system use at NASA headquarters.

Summit (1970) also describes the application of DIALOG to document files of the Educational Resources Information Center (ERIC) in 1969. A portion of the ERIC data base, about 20,000 items, was available for on-line search at the ERIC Clearinghouse on Educational Media and Technology, Stanford University, and at the regional office of the U.S. Office of Education in San Francisco. The data base was loaded at the Lockheed facility in Palo Alto and made available through remote terminals, consisting of CRT, keyboard, and console printer. In a 1-year period, some 800 searches were conducted, and over 51,000 citations and abstracts were printed. Summit reports that 90% of all the users expressed satisfaction with the search results. The Stanford experience is reported in more detail by Timbie and Coombs (1969). The study was conducted at the ERIC Clearinghouse on Educational Media and Technology to determine if educators could themselves operate the system with minimal training. The system was used by the staff of the center, and a group of *case studies* was conducted on the use of the system by researchers and practitioners in the field of education. Nine of these case studies were conducted in depth. The nine participants included a university librarian, an elementary school teacher, a physician engaged in psychiatric research, and a motivational educator in private practice. Each user had a real information need that he was seeking to satisfy when using the system.

TABLE 8.1. "Pre-DIALOG" Questionnaire Administered to DIALOG Users

*Name*_____

QUESTIONNAIRE—Part I (Pre-DIALOG Questions)

1. Please describe briefly the information you will be looking for in the ERIC file:

2. About how many documents do you expect to find in the ERIC file on this topic? (Please circle the correct answer.)

     Less than 10   10–25   26–50   51–100   More than 100

3. Have you ever used the ERIC publication, RESEARCH IN EDUCATION? (Circle your answer.)

     YES   NO   (If No, go to Question 5)

4. (If YES:) Have you searched RIE by subject?   YES   NO
             Have you searched RIE by title?   YES   NO
             Have you searched RIE by author?   YES   NO

5. Have you chosen any terms from the ERIC Thesaurus to begin your search?

     YES   NO

     (If YES:)   Please list the principal ones:

6. How familiar are you with on-line retrieval systems? (PLEASE CHECK EACH ANSWER THAT APPLIES.)
     ( ) I've heard about them.
     ( ) I've read about them.
     ( ) I've studied them in some detail.
     ( ) I've designed or cooperated in the design of an on-line system.
     ( ) None of the above.

7. How much experience with DIALOG have you had? (PLEASE CHECK EACH ANSWER THAT APPLIES.)
     ( ) I have previously used DIALOG myself, sitting at the console.
     ( ) I have watched another person use DIALOG.
     ( ) I have had no previous experience with DIALOG.

8. Have you read the DIALOG manual?   YES   NO

9. How much experience have you had with on-line retrieval systems other than DIALOG? (PLEASE CHECK THE ANSWER THAT BEST APPLIES.)
     ( ) I have used several systems, each on more than one occasion.
     ( ) I have used several systems, each on one occasion.
     ( ) I have used one system on more than one occasion.
     ( ) I have used one system on one occasion.
     ( ) I have watched others using system(s).
     ( ) I have had no previous experience with on-line systems.

SOURCE: Timbie and Coombs (1969). Reproduced by permission of ERIC Clearinghouse on Educational Media and Technology, Stanford University.

TABLE 8.2.   DIALOG Interview Guide Used After Searching Was Completed

DIALOG DEBRIEFING OUTLINE   (Questions calling for a prompt
                                         of additional information should
                                         be reprompted until the responder
                                         can't think of anything else.)

Before using the system, you said you would be searching the file for information on
_____. I realize that you haven't had a chance to
check the full texts of anything you retrieved, but do you think that you have located some
relevant information?

Were your original questions answered to your satisfaction?

What are your general feelings or comments on the system?
    (anything else?)

What would you pick out as its particularly good features?
    (anything else?)

What are its bad or awkward features?
    (something else?)

I have already asked you what questions you came in with. What, if any, new questions did you
formulate during the search?
    (any others?)

    What led you to ask those questions?

    How well did those questions get answered?

Did you run across any other material—perhaps entirely different subjects—which interests you
and which you might want to search later?

Using the printed terminal record to help you remember specific things, I'd now like you to go
back over the search explaining the strategy we used, the terms we employed, how they were
combined, what results you were getting, and what strategy changes you made and why. Sort
of a play-by-play.

Have you any other good comments on the system?
    (something else?)

Have you further bad comments?
    (anything else?)

Our interest is not only in evaluating this particular system—DIALOG—but in evaluating the
interactive features of such systems. By this I mean the searching system itself rather than the
quality of the material being searched. What difference did it make to you that you could
"keep tabs on" or "monitor" the progress of the search?
    (any other differences?)

    How did this affect the search? (if not already clear).

How do you feel about:
    the keyboard?   Was it awkward, easy to get accustomed to?

    the typed terminal record?

TABLE 8.2. *Continued*

the CRT, visual display?	What about this as compared to a single line or lines on a typewriter terminal as a means of monitoring the search?

the delays? Did they bother you?

the thesaurus?

the manual? Was it clear, useful?

Not limiting yourself to DIALOG, but to the whole ERIC system:
What good things could you see?   (anything else?)

What bad things or things that need improvement?   (anything else?)

What about the indexing?
Was it adequate?

Are the terms appropriate to the information?

Do you think that the range of information on your subject is covered as completely as it should be, or is it only adequately covered or insufficiently covered?

Have you any suggestions as to the way this could be improved?

What about microfiche as a format for the storage of information?

Have you ordered things—fiche or hardcopy—from the ERIC Document Reproduction Service in the past?

How was the service?

How useful would it be to you to get hardcopy of selected documents in two weeks at 5¢ a page? (assuming that there is no problem with finances)

How useful is hardcopy delivery in half an hour if it is 10¢ a page?

Which would you prefer? (if not already obvious)

SOURCE: Timbie and Coombs (1969). Reproduced by permission of ERIC Clearinghouse on Educational Media and Technology, Stanford University.

The session at the console was scheduled in advance and the user was sent a copy of the DIALOG user's manual to read. A set of "pre-DIALOG" questions was administered to the user (see Table 8.1), his questions about the system were answered, he was shown the terminal, and he was allowed to conduct his own search there. However, a trained ERIC searcher was available to assist with the search if needed. After the search, a *debriefing session* was used to interrogate the user on his experiences and reactions (see Table 8.2). The entire interview was tape recorded and converted to a typed transcript. Figure 8.5 illustrates an annotated dialogue of one of these case study searches. All nine are documented in the project report.

In addition to the nine case studies, nineteen other users who came to the ERIC center for information were invited to use the system, and their reactions were recorded on a special questionnaire.

SEARCH TITLE: ADULT BASIC EDUCATION PROGRAMS

The 4 column headings indicate what command was given, what set number was assigned (if a set was created),

DATE: 07/11/69

how many documents are contained in that set, and finally a description

REQUESTOR: PERSON A

of its contents.

COMMAND-OPERAND(S)	SET NO.	NO. IN SET	DESCRIPTION OF SET (+ = OR, * = AND, – = NOT)
E-IT/BASIC ADULT ED			*The index around the descriptor, BASIC ADULT EDUCATION, was expanded (E). No entries were posted to this term.*
S-E9	1	59	IT/BASIC READING *However, BASIC READING was there and was selected (S) to form set 1.*
E-E9			*BASIC READING was then expanded by its reference number, E9, in order to display its thesaurus entries. There was nothing of interest.*
E-IT/ADULT BASIC ED			*ADULT BASIC EDUCATION*
S-E5	2	126	IT/ADULT BASIC EDUCATION *was expanded and then selected to form set 2.*
E-E5			*It was expanded again by the reference number to show the thesaurus entries*
S-E12	3	57	IT/LITERACY EDUCATION *The term LITERACY EDUCATION was found there and selected.*
E-IT/REMEDIAL PROGR			*Next, REMEDIAL*
S-E3	4	63	IT/REMEDIAL INSTRUCTIONS *PROGRAMS was*
S-E4	5	4	IT/REMEDIAL MATHEMATICS *expanded, and it and a*
S-E5	6	61	IT/REMEDIAL PROGRAMS *number of alphabetically*
S-E6	7	58	IT/REMEDIAL READING *related terms were*
S-E7	8	6	IT/REMEDIAL READING CLINICS *selected (sets 4*
S-E8	9	22	IT/REMEDIAL READING PROGRAMS *through 9).*
E-E5			*REMEDIAL PROGRAMS was then expanded by reference number.*
S-E14	10	63	IT/COMPENSATORY EDUCATION *Two more terms*
S-E17	11	94	IT/EDUCATIONALLY DISADVANTAGED *(sets 10 and 11) were located in its thesaurus entries.*

Figure 8.5. Annotated case study search using DIALOG. Reproduced from Timbie and Coombs (1969) by permission of ERIC Clearinghouse on Educational Media and Technology, Stanford University.

E-E14				*COMPENSATORY*
S-E18	12	145	IT/COMPENSATORY EDUCATION PROGRAMS	*EDUCATION was then expanded by its reference number (E4) and one more relevant term was located in its thesaurus expansion (set 12).*
E-IT/ADULT EDUCATION				*The searcher now turned to*
S-E2	13	8	IT/ADULT DEVELOPMENT	*the adult aspect or concept of*
S-E5	14	231	IT/ADULT EDUCATION	*his search. Expanding ADULT*
S-E8	15	117	IT/ADULT EDUCATION PROGRAMS	*EDUCATION produced three relevant terms (sets 13, 14, 15).*
E-IT/ADULTS				*Expanding ADULTS*
S-E4	16	184	IT/ADULT VOCATIONAL EDUCATION	*produced four terms to*
S-E6	17	1	IT/ADULT VOCATIONAL EDUCATION	*be selected (sets 16*
S-E1	18	40	IT/ADULT STUDENTS	*through 19).*
S-E5	19	87	IT/ADULTS	
E-IT/BASIC SKILLS				*And finally, BASIC SKILLS, which relates*
S-E5	20	50	IT/BASIC SKILLS	*to the earlier concept, was expanded and selected.*
C-3-12/+	21	504	3+4+5+6+7+8+9+10+11+12	*Set 21 was created by the union or addition of sets 3 through 12. This set then included most of the remedial or basic education terms.*
C-1+20+21	22	595	1+20+3+4+5+6+7+8+9+10+11+12	*Set 21 was then added to sets 1 and 20 to create the basic education concept group containing everything in the ERIC files indexed by one of these terms.*
C-13-15/+	23	352	13+14+15	*Set 23 was created by adding some of the adult terms together.*
C-23+18+19	24	456	18+19+13+14+15	*This process was completed by the addition performed in set 24, which now represents the adult concept in the search.*

Note that so far set 2 has been ignored, because it precoordinates the two concepts in the search and therefore should not be included in either concept set.

Figure 8.5. *Continued*

C-22*24 25 39 $(1+20+3+4+5+6+7+8+9+10+11+12)*(18+19+13+14+15)$

*Sets 22 (the basic or remedial education concept)
and 24 (the adult education concept) were next
combined (C) to form an intersection, the AND
in boolean logic, with the resulting set 25
containing 39 items indexed by at least one term from
each concept set.*

D-25
K-25/1
K-25/2
K-25/3
K-25/4

*This set was then displayed (D) and the first
four retrieved items examined one by one on the
CRT. The relevant ones, in this case all that
were examined, were set aside using the keep (K)
command into a reference set for future attention.
This reference set is arbitrarily numbered 99.*

S-IT/ILLITERATE ADU 26 33 IT/ILLITERATE ADULTS

*In the examination of the first
four items of set 25, a new term
was turned up, ILLITERATE
ADULTS, which had not been located
earlier. This term was now selected
directly (without going through the
expansion).*

C-26*22 27 21 $(1+20+3+4+5+6+7+8+9+10+11+12)*26$

*The resulting set 26 was combined by an AND
operation with set 22 (basic education terms)
to form set 27.*

C-25+27 28 57 $((1+20+3+4+5+6+7+8+9+10+11+12)*(18+19+13+14+15))+((1+20+3+4+5+6+7+8+9+10+11+12)*26)$

*The results of this combination and the previous
one (set 25) were then added together to form
set 28. Note that the number of items in 28 is
not equal to the sum of the items in sets 25 and
27. This is so because a combination creates a
set of unique documents where no item is
repeated a second time.*

D-28
K-28/2
K-28/7
K-28/8
K-28/10
K-28/12
K-28/13
K-28/14
K-28/16
K-28/18
K-28/19
K-28/20
K-28/21
K-28/23
K-28/25
K-28/26

*Set 28 was then displayed
item by item and the relevant ones
set aside in the reference set.*

Figure 8.5. *Continued*

K-28/27
K-28/28
K-28/29

K-28/30-57   *After examining 29 references and*
                                                  keeping 18 of them, the evaluator
                                                  determined to keep all of the remaining
                                                  references and proceed further with the search.

C-2-28   29   109 $2 - (((1 + 20 + 3 + 4 + 5 + 6 + 7 + 8 + 9 + 10 + 11 + 12)*(18 + 19 + 13 + 14$
                                           $+ 15)) + ((1 + 20 + 3 + 4 + 5 + 6 + 7 + 8 + 9 + 10 + 11 + 12)*26))$
                                                  Set 29 was created by subtracting the items
                                                  already examined from set 2 the ADULT BASIC
                                                  EDUCATION set. This avoids duplicate printing
                                                  of any items.

          A second aspect of the search was begun to turn up industrial
          and job training programs which dealt with basic skills.

E-IT/INDUSTRIAL TRA   *INDUSTRIAL TRAINING*
S-E5   30   62   IT/INDUSTRIAL TRAINING   *was expanded and*
E-E5   *selected and then*
S-E13   31   56   IT/INDUSTRIAL EDUCATION *expanded to its thesaurus*
S-E14   32   14   IT/INPLANT PROGRAMS   *entry. This produced*
S-E15   33   113   IT/JOB TRAINING   *six additional relevant*
S-E16   34   10   IT/OFF THE JOB TRAINING *terms.*
S-E17   35   82   IT/ON THE JOB TRAINING
S-E19   36   240   IT/TRADE AND INDUSTRIAL
                                             EDUCATION

C-30-36/+   37   512 $30 + 31 + 32 + 33 + 34 + 35 + 36$ *The seven industrial training terms*
                                                                     were then combined by an OR
                                                                     operation to produce set 37.

C-37 + 16 + 17   38   591 $16 + 17 + 30 + 31 + 32 + 33 + 34 + 35 + 36$ *Set 37 was then added to*
                                                                                 sets 16 and 17 which also
                                                                                 relate to the same general
                                                                                 concept.

C-38*22   39   18 $(1 + 20 + 3 + 4 + 5 + 6 + 7 + 8 + 9 + 10 + 11 + 12)*(16 + 17 + 30 + 31 + 32$
                                          $+ 33 + 34 + 35 + 36)$
                                                  This sum was intersected with the basic education
                                                  concept group (set 22) to get set 39.

P-29/5   1-109   ITEMS HAVE BEEN PRINTED   *Finally two prints (P) were*
P-39/5   1-18   ITEMS HAVE BEEN PRINTED   *initiated of sets 29 and 39.*
                                                                Format 5 which contains the
                                                                indexing, cataloging, and
                                                                abstracts for each document was
                                                                chosen. After the print had
                                                                been completed off-line at
                                                                Lockheed the results were sent to
                                                                the clearinghouse for forwarding
                                                                to the evaluator.

Figure 8.5.   *Continued*

SUPARS Evaluation

Experiments with SUPARS (Cook, et al., 1971) were conducted by Syracuse University in various experimental periods during 1970–1972. The system was made available free to the 17,000 students, staff, and faculty on the university campus. SUPARS was operated for several hours each day and could be accessed by any one of 100 IBM 2741 terminals. Availability of the service was fully publicized. Use of the system was studied in the following ways:

1. A profile of user characteristics was constructed from completed user registration forms (see Figure 8.6). These forms gathered demographic-type data, use data on *Psychological Abstracts*, and data on user experience with computer terminals and retrieval systems.

2. A telephone aid service was provided to answer general questions about SUPARS and to help people experiencing difficulty in using the system. Each call was numbered and logged; user's name, social security number, and terminal identification were recorded; and a description was given in the log of the problem presented and the action taken to solve it.

3. Data were collected unobtrusively on-line by means of the STATPAC program (for further details see the section in this chapter titled "Unobtrusive Observation").

4. A sample of registrants was selected for personal interviews and these same registrants were given a semantic differential to assess their attitude to the SUPARS system. The SUPARS interview guide is illustrated in Appendix A. In the 1971–1972 phase of the study, telephone interviews were also conducted.

Intrex Evaluation

The Intrex retrieval system has been evaluated in several different ways (Marcus, et al., 1971):

1. Several dozen detailed observations of sessions involving users whose primary interest lay in obtaining information from the system. These observations involved the extensive use of interviews both before and after a session as well as monitoring during the course of the session by human observers, tape recorders and computer recording of the dialog and timing information.

2. Several hundred less detailed observations of sessions at the library station in the Barker Engineering Library at M.I.T. for which complete computer recordings of the dialog and timing information were obtained and the comments of both the advisers and users were noted.

SUPARS REGISTRATION FORM

Please fill out, fold, staple and return this preaddressed form.

1. Name _____
2. Date _____ 3. Social Security _____

4. Campus/Home Address _____
5. Campus/Home Phone _____

6. Are you primarily: Faculty _____ Undergraduate student _____ Graduate Student _____ Staff _____ Administrator _____
   Visitor _____ Other (specify) _____

7. What is your academic major or department? _____ Question does not apply _____

8. What percent of your time is engaged in: Teaching and/or learning _____ Research _____ Other _____

9. Did you register to use SUPARS last year? YES _____ NO _____

10. If YES, on the average, how often did you use SUPARS?
    a. more than once a day   c. several times a week   e. once a month   g. no time
    b. once a day   d. several times a month   f. less frequently

11. On the average, over the last 2-3 months, how frequently have you used Psychological abstracts _____ (Select one choice from 'a-g' above.

12. Estimate how frequently you see yourself using Psychological Abstracts in the next 2-3 months (assume that SUPARS computer service were NOT available)? Select ONE choice from 'a-g' above.

13. What recent interest areas are important to your use of Psychological Abstracts?
    (Most) _____
    (2nd) _____
    (3rd) _____

14. Have you used Psychological Abstracts in the last 2-3 months to help you prepare a term paper, thesis, speech, etc. _____
    (If YES, please give title or topic)

15. Do you need Psychological Abstracts in the next 2-3 months to help you find references or abstracts for a term paper, thesis, speech, etc., you are currently preparing or planning to prepare? _____
    (If YES, please give title or topic)

16. What is your specific need for Psychological Abstracts in the near future?
    To find a specific reference or abstract? _____ To keep up to date in one or two content areas? _____ To survey the literature in general? _____ To exhaustively review a specific topic or area? _____ To find several current references in an area (but not necessarily exhaustively review that area)? _____ Other (Specify) _____

17. What previous experience do you have with computer terminals? A lot? _____ ; Some? _____ ; None? _____ If you have had experience please identify type of terminal, when you used it, where used? _____

18. What previous experience do you have with computer-based retrieval systems? A lot? _____ ; Some? _____ ; None? _____ :
    If you have had experience please identify the system, and when and where you used it _____

SUPARS: Syracuse University Psychological Abstracts Retrieval Service Ext. 4220

Figure 8.6. SUPARS user registration form. Reproduced by permission of the School of Library Science, Syracuse University.

3. Observations made during training programs, demonstrations and by a few special users who were specifically asked to test the system and make comments.
4. More formal, and controlled, experiments that have focused on retrieval effectiveness and on the effectiveness of catalog information to indicate document utility (p. 162).

A considerable amount of system evaluation has been conducted of the type mentioned in item 4 above. While this work is both interesting and valuable, much of it deals with such matters as indexing policy (e.g., exhaustivity of indexing, weighting of indexing statements) and the value of various levels of document representation as indicators of subject content, which are problems not peculiar to on-line systems. More recent work has, however, investigated the special kinds of strategy and indexing best suited to on-line interaction.

AUDACIOUS Evaluation

Freeman and Atherton (1968) have reported on experiments with an on-line, interactive retrieval system known as AUDACIOUS. The data base comprised the set of references from a single issue of *Nuclear Science Abstracts*, each item having been indexed in depth using the Universal Decimal Classification (UDC). AUDACIOUS (Automatic Direct Access to Information with the On-Line UDC System) was based upon an existing retrieval system known as DATRIX. DATRIX is a system designed by the Xerox Corporation to provide access to doctoral dissertations. The investigators of AUDACIOUS were undertaking a feasibility study on the use of the UDC in an on-line, interactive environment rather than conducting a formal evaluation of the system. Nevertheless, it was possible to use a tape recorder to obtain reactions and comments of various users (physicists, engineers, students and faculty of a school of library science, information specialists, and specialists in computer-aided instruction) while operating the system.

DDC Evaluation

Use of the DDC on-line system at four sites was evaluated in 1970. System performance, system utilization, and user reaction were studied. User logs, computer logs, and user interviews were employed. A guide was developed for in-depth interviews of users. Interviews concentrated upon circumstances of use, favorable and unfavorable reactions, needed improvements, training requirements, and relevancy to the mission of the users. High-frequency users were interviewed twice, once early in the program and once quite late in the test period, in order to assess the effect of increased experience on user attitudes. Some of the results are discussed briefly by Bennertz (1971).

CIRCOL Evaluation

An evaluation was conducted on the CIRCOL system, and the results were presented by King, et al. (1972). Although conducted with an on-line system, this investigation is largely restricted to comparing results of searches using a controlled vocabulary with searches using the natural language of abstracts. The interactive capabilities of the on-line system were not exploited and, in fact, many of the results were derived by simulation. The study therefore sheds little light on the characteristics of on-line systems per se.

AIM–TWX Evaluation

The purpose of this investigation was to determine how effectively biomedical practitioners, with a minimum of introduction to the system, could conduct on-line searches to satisfy their own information needs. The searches were conducted in the *Abridged Index Medicus* data base as implemented on the on-line ELHILL system (AIM–TWX). The searches used in the study were conducted at four MEDLARS centers having the on-line search facilities available in the period November 1970–February 1971. The size of the AIM–TWX data base was approximately 100,000 citations in this period. The procedures used in the study and the evaluation results were summarized by Lancaster (1972).

Search analysts at the participating centers were asked to identify health professionals who came to the center with requests for information that might be satisfied, at least in part, by the AIM–TWX data base, and who indicated willingness to cooperate in the study. Each of these professionals was asked to complete a special search request form (Figure 8.7).

The search analyst introduced the practitioner to AIM–TWX by presenting for his examination a very brief printed description of how to use the system. This description was an outline, with text and examples, designed to give the requester just enough information to allow him to sit down at the terminal and conduct relatively simple searches. No attempt was made to describe all the ramifications and sophistications of ELHILL. The description was prepared at NLM and was standard for all users. The search analyst was allowed to answer any questions the user might have after reading the instruction summary, but was not to volunteer any additional clarification.

Having read the summary, the user was left to conduct his own search at the terminal. Logging-in to the system, a simple technical procedure, was

Name of requestor:
Title:
Organization:
Department:
Telephone:
MD, PhD, RN, other:
Major area of responsibility: Basic research
                                    Clinical research
                                    Teaching
                                    Clinical practice
                                    Other (please specify)
Number of times requester used AIM–TWX:
Subject of present search (Record below, in your own words, the subject matter for which the search is to be conducted. Be as specific as possible.)

Purpose of search: Clinical problem
                     On-going research
                     Writing a research paper
       To assist in Writing a review article or book chapter
                     Preparing lecture or other teaching function
                     Other*: Please specify:*_____

_____

Type of search:
  Are you looking for: (*a*) a few relevant papers?
                   (*b*) all possible relevant citations?

Figure 8.7. AIM–TWX search request form.

done for the user. The user had available to him: *Medical Subject Headings* (the controlled vocabulary of the system), the hierarchical structure of the vocabulary, and the full AIM–TWX user guide (for reference purposes only).

The search analyst was instructed to remain in the general vicinity of the terminal. She could answer any technical questions that arose during the search and could assist the user with *technical problems* (i.e., problems relating to the equipment and the on-line protocols, but not problems relating to MEDLARS indexing, vocabulary, or search strategies). The user was told that he was participating in an experiment and that the experimental constraints did not permit his receiving help with the intellectual aspects of the system or the search. In other words, this was a simulation of a situation in which a user is at a remote terminal and there is no trained searcher available to give advice and guidance.

A user's search was considered to be completed when either (*a*) he decided he had found enough references, or (*b*) he gave up the search after trying various approaches. The search analyst then logged-out of the system for the user.

When the search was completed, the user was asked to examine each citation that had been printed in his on-line search and to mark each with a code to indicate its relevance to his information need, on the scale:

R   Relevant
PR   Peripherally relevant
I   Irrelevant

Where necessary, copies of the actual articles were made available to allow unequivocal assessments.

A copy of the entire search dialogue was made (the user retained the original), and on this copy the analyst recorded the exact time spent by the user at the terminal (available from log-in and log-out times) and the user's subjective assessment of the value to him of the search on the scale:

MAJOR VALUE
CONSIDERABLE VALUE
MINOR VALUE
NO VALUE

The search analyst, after examining the user's results, then conducted her own search on the topic at the AIM–TWX terminal. The object was to try alternative approaches to retrieval in an effort to find additional relevant citations that the user might have missed or to find citations to articles that might be more highly relevant than those found by the user. Any new citations thus discovered were submitted to the user for relevance assessment on the same scale as that previously used.

Analysis of the user's search was conducted on the basis of his request form, the dialogue of his interaction with the system, his relevance assessments, his search time, his judgment on the value of the search, and the results of the parallel search conducted by the analyst.

In all, 48 test searches were completed. For each search the following data were collected and summarized:

1. The number of times the requester had previously used AIM–TWX.
2. Whether he wanted to find all relevant citations or only a few of them (high or low recall).
3. The precision ratio of his search. That is, the number of unique relevant citations among the total number of unique citations printed.
4. The unit cost per relevant citation retrieved.

5. The recall estimate for the user's search. The recall estimate is derived from

$$\frac{\text{Number of unique relevant citations found by user}}{\substack{\text{Number of unique relevant citations found by user and number of} \\ \text{additional unique relevant citations found by analyst}}}$$

Analyses of reasons for recall and precision failures were conducted, and the results of these will be summarized in Chapter Nine.

EARS Evaluation

In 1971, Lancaster undertook some evaluation work on EARS (Lancaster, 1972). The EARS data base comprised, at that time, about 8000 items on epilepsy and closely related topics. This collection was drawn from *Epilepsy Abstracts*, a publication prepared for the National Institute of Neurological Diseases and Stroke (NINDS) by the Excerpta Medica Foundation. The EARS file was loaded on the Data Central system and made available to a number of medical centers in the United States via telephone or TWX lines.

The complete EARS record consists of full bibliographic citation, an abstract, and a set of index terms assigned by Excerpta Medica indexers. All these elements are searchable, including all words in the abstracts with the exception of the common (syntactic) words which do not appear in the inverted search files.

The evaluation of EARS was similar in scope and purpose to the evaluation of AIM–TWX. The system was made available to six medical centers in the United States for a limited time period on an experimental basis. Neurologists and certain other health professionals at these centers were trained in the use of the system. The general objectives of the study were to determine how much use was made of the system, how successfully it was used, what problems were encountered, and what was the general user reaction. More specifically the investigation addressed itself to:

1. A detailed analysis of searching strategies and reasons for failures in searching.
2. A determination of comparative performance between (*a*) searching of the full record (citation, abstract, index terms) and (*b*) searching of the citation + index terms only.
3. A consideration of the desirability of making EARS available on a reasonably permanent basis and of expanding the data base to cover all the neurology literature.

Whereas in the AIM–TWX evaluation, access to the terminal was controlled by an information specialist (a MEDLARS search analyst), the physician users of EARS were free to operate the terminal at any time the system was available without the need to function through an information specialist. This made it much more difficult to control the study and to obtain the necessary cooperation.

In training sessions held with potential users, the importance of participating in the evaluation was emphasized, and the type of cooperation required was described. After this, the study was entirely dependent upon the willingness of the user to fill out certain forms and supply various items to the evaluator.

Before beginning a search at the terminal, a user was asked to complete a portion of an evaluation form (Figure 8.8), specifically the personal details and items 1, 2, and 3A. When the search was terminated, the user was to complete the remaining items on the form. In addition, he was to retain a copy of his dialogue with the system. Any items retrieved and printed appeared on this copy in the form either of full bibliographic citation or of abstract number only. Having checked the corresponding abstracts in the printed *Epilepsy Abstracts* (available adjacent to the terminal), the user then indicated on his printout the relevance of all items retrieved, using the scale: major relevance, minor relevance, no relevance. The evaluation form and the search printout, suitably marked, were then submitted to the evaluator. The instruction sheet given to the user is shown as Figure 8.9.

These simple procedures yielded, for each search:
1. Search topic
2. Recall requirement
3. Search strategy
4. Number of items retrieved
5. Elapsed search time
6. Precision ratio
7. Unit cost (in time) per relevant citation retrieved
8. User's subjective assessment of the value of the search

The only missing item was the recall ratio. This was estimated in a manner similar to the method used in AIM–TWX. A parallel search was conducted on each search topic by a neurologist on the staff of NINDS, who had been involved in the implementation of EARS and had several months of experience in using the system. For some of the topics, a further search was conducted by the evaluator using the index to *Epilepsy Abstracts* as a conventional manual searching tool. Additional items retrieved in these parallel searches were submitted to the original searcher for his relevance assessments, using the same scale as before.

EARS

Epilepsy Abstracts Retrieval System Search Evaluation Form

Name of searcher:_____
Title:_____
Address:_____
Telephone:_____

1. Search Topic:
   Please record below, in your own words, a full description of the subject on which you are
   seeking information from EARS:_____
   _____
   _____
   _____
   _____
   _____
   _____

2. Purpose of Search
   Are you looking for: (check one)
       A. All abstracts relevant to this topic_____ or
       B. A few relevant abstracts only_____
3. Search Time
       A. Began search at:_____
       B. Completed search at:_____

After the search is finished please answer the following questions.

4. This search was (check one)
       A. Of major value to you_____
       B. Of considerable value_____
       C. Of minor value_____
       D. Of no value_____
5. Having completed the search and examined some retrieved abstracts, do you feel that your
   original statement of search topic (item 1 above) is a reasonably adequate description of
   the information you were seeking when you sat down at the terminal?
       NO_____
       YES_____
   If NO, please record your revised statement below:_____
   _____
   _____
   _____

Thank you for your valuable assistance in our study of EARS.

Please mail this form, along with a copy of the complete teletypewriter printout (marked
with your relevance assessments) to:

> Professor F. W. Lancaster
> Graduate School of Library Science
> University of Illinois
> Urbana, Illinois 61801

Figure 8.8. EARS search request form.

To All Users of the Epilepsy Abstracts Retrieval System (EARS)

EARS is an experimental service made available to you by the National Institute of Neurological Diseases and Stroke. It is extremely important that the system be evaluated during this experimental period. We urge you to help us in this evaluation by carefully following the instructions below. Your assistance is needed to allow a meaningful evaluation and to indicate to us how the system might be improved and made more useful to you.

1. Before beginning your search please complete the top portion of the Search Evaluation Form (through item 2).

2. Record on this form the exact time that the search was begun and the exact time it was concluded at the terminal.

3. After the search is completed, carefully remove from the typewriter the entire printout of your dialogue with the system.

4. Against each abstract or abstract number on this printout (you may view the entire text of an abstract in the printed Epilepsy Abstracts) please indicate its relevance to your information need by marking with the following code:

A. Major Relevance
B. Minor Relevance
C. No Relevance

A relevant abstract should be marked as relevant even if you were already aware of the paper before conducting the search. For any paper you already knew of add a plus (+) sign to your coding. Thus, A+ indicates a major relevance paper that you were familiar with before beginning your search.

5. After evaluating the abstracts retrieved in this way, please complete the remainder of the Search Evaluation Form (items 4 and 5).

6. Mail the evaluation form plus a complete copy of the typewriter printout to Professor F. W. Lancaster as indicated on the evaluation form.

Note

If you wish to keep a copy of the printout please have your secretary make a good Xerox copy to submit to us.

At a later time we may wish to send, for your examination and assessment, some additional abstracts that may be relevant to your search topic. This, too, is part of an overall evaluation of EARS.

THANK YOU VERY MUCH FOR YOUR COOPERATION

Figure 8.9. Instructions to participants in EARS evaluation.

The recall ratio of the original search (A) was estimated as follows:

$$\text{Recall ratio of search A} = \frac{\text{Number of relevant items found by A}}{\substack{\text{Number of relevant items found by A and number} \\ \text{of additional relevant items found in parallel} \\ \text{searches}}}$$

Once all data were collected, detailed analyses were conducted on reasons for recall or precision failures, and a calculation was made on what the recall in each search would have been if the EARS record consisted only of citation plus index terms (no abstract).

Unobtrusive Observation

We have previously mentioned the possibility of using the on-line system to monitor a user's search in an unobtrusive fashion. Such monitoring can obviously play a valuable role in overall system evaluation procedures. Parker (1970) has described features of an on-line statistics gathering program.

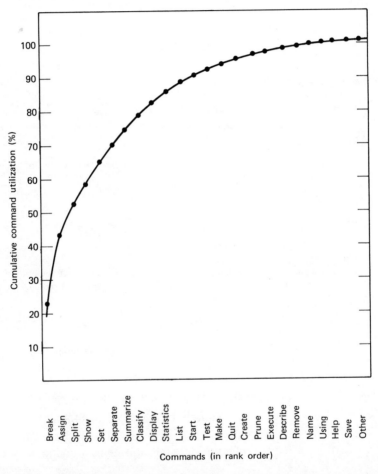

Figure 8.10. Cumulative percentage of command utilization plotted against individual commands in rank order. Reproduced from Carlisle (1972) by permission of Yale University, Department of Administrative Sciences.

The program monitors and summarizes on-line transactions. One very useful feature is a record of errors made by the searcher (e.g., invalid commands or incorrect responses). Whenever a message is received from a user that the computer cannot understand (causing, therefore, a computer prompt to be reissued or a diagnostic message sent), this message is recorded and tallied. Clearly, such information has great potential value in identifying errors or misunderstandings that occur significantly often. Such errors will suggest ways in which the system, or instructions on how to use it, may be improved. The monitoring system should also maintain statistics on how the system is used—not just how many times it is used but which files are consulted, which commands are employed, and even the frequency with which the various index terms are used.

A good example of on-line monitoring used in this way, although not in an information retrieval application, is provided by Carlisle (1972). In this application, statistics on use of the various commands are recorded automatically and these data are separated into those derived from experienced users and those derived from inexperienced users. Sample data are shown in Figure 8.10, which plots the cumulative percentage of command utilization against the individual commands in rank order, and Table 8.3, which compares command utilization by beginning and advanced users. Analyses such as this are of value in identifying commands that receive little use, and may perhaps be eliminated from the system, as well as indicating an effective training sequence (the most frequently used commands should be taught first, the next most frequently used should follow, and so on down the line). Analyses of command utilization also indicate *how* (i.e., for what purposes) the system is being used.

Another group of statistics that may be collected on-line concerns file characteristics such as: how many records are in the file, how many access points there are per record, how many authors there are per document, and average record length. According to Parker (1970), these data are already collected routinely in SPIRES, and it is intended to incorporate facilities for collecting the other types of data mentioned at a later time.

Cook (1970) and Cook, et al. (1971) have described a monitoring operation performed on SUPARS, whereby the user's dialogue with the computer is logged, compiled, and summarized. Feedback is provided in the form of a printed record of the user dialogue taking place at the consoles. The program, which is known as STATPAC, has the following features (Cook, 1970, p. 112):

> The *basic log* will record and store *for each search number*: (1) the corresponding user's social security number (a device used to gain access to the *PA* file), (2) the console ID number, (3) a complete transcript of the actual search input by the user,

TABLE 8.3. Comparison of Command Utilization by Beginners and Advanced Users

Commands	Beginners		Experienced users	
	Frequency	%	Frequency	%
1 SHOW	44	7.2	73	5.3
2 STATISTICS	24	3.9	46	3.3
3 DISPLAY	33	5.4	45	3.3
4 LIST	10	1.6	46	3.3
5 CLASSIFY	14	2.3	65	4.7
6 BREAK	131	21.5	322	23.4
7 SEPARATE	30	4.9	79	5.7
8 SET	38	6.2	74	5.4
9 ASSIGN	290	19.4	290	21.1
10 START	17	2.8	31	2.3
11 SPLIT	51	8.4	130	9.5
12 SUMMARIZE	40	6.6	60	4.4
13 TEST	10	1.6	19	1.4
14 PRUNE	1	0.2	13	0.9
15 USING			5	0.4
16 MAKE	8	1.3	18	1.3
17 EXECUTE			12	0.9
18 PRINT				
19 ERASE				
20 NAME	5	0.8	3	0.2
21 CREATE			16	1.2
22 TRUNCATE				
23 DESCRIBE	10	1.6	1	0.1
24 LINK				
25 COPY				
26 QUIT	7	1.2	11	0.8
27 HELP	2	0.3	1	0.1
28 LOOKUP				
29 CODE				
30 REMOVE			9	0.7
31 DECLARE	3	0.5		
32 SAVE	2	0.3	1	0.1
33 OTHER	10	1.6	5	0.4

SOURCE: Carlisle (1972). Reproduced by permission of Department of Administrative Sciences, Yale University.

(4) the number of documents found for the search, and (5) the abstract number and volume number of each document that was printed.

A *summary program* has been written to print out summaries of basic information in the log and additional information provided by the computer operating system. The system operator can request the summary program and have it printed out at the 2741 console by typing in a descriptive title for the summary and the inclusive dates of the time period desired.

For example, by requesting SUML: 10.1.70, 10.15.70, the operator will have printed, *for each separate day of operation*, columns giving: (1) the console identification number and the number of searches generated at that terminal, (2) the total number of terminals used, (3) the number of different social security numbers (i.e., users), (4) the number of completed searches, and (5) the elapsed CPU time, and dollar cost broken down by individual searches. For each time period requested in the summary, column totals will be printed and averages computed for selected items.

A sample STATPAC summary is shown in Table 8.4, representing a 13 day use period. The table presents a number of interesting correlations between users (represented by social security numbers), times, costs, terminals, days, documents found, and documents printed. Table 8.4 illustrates a *standard* summary, printed periodically. STATPAC includes within itself a highly flexible retrieval system which allows the system managers to specify and retrieve various combinations of data reflecting user interaction or system performance. For example, it would be possible to request a listing of the computer time used for all searches of the document data base by one-time users after a certain calendar date.

Responses from the AIM–TWX on-line questionnaire (see Table 8.5) were tabulated routinely by computer during the course of the AIM–TWX experiments. Summary tables were presented on volume of use, type of user, type of search, and user's judgment of the value of the search. Table 8.5 presents a summary of value judgments for searches conducted in April–May 1971. The user's value judgments are compared with the purposes for which searches were conducted. Average search times were also computed routinely in the AIM–TWX study.

The on-line system provides another possible mechanism for evaluation. Users should be able to record, directly on-line, any problems, suggestions, or complaints they may have. If a user of SPIRES, for example, wishes to record such a message, he merely keys in the command TO SPIRES and follows it with his message (which may be several lines long) (Parker, 1970). The messages are stored and printed out daily for inspection by the SPIRES staff. Comments can be sent by the user in the middle of a search, at exactly the moment the idea occurs to him. He can then continue with his search as if no interruption had occurred. If the message includes the user's telephone

TABLE 8.4.　Sample SUPARS STATPAC Summary for 13 Day Period

Part 1:	
Total No. of Terminals Used	44
No. of Different Soc. Sec. No.s	79
No. of Completed Searches	1371
Elapsed CPU Time	124' 34"
Elapsed Clock Time	5004' 34"
Total Cost in Dollars	$713.69
CPU/No. of Soc. Sec. No.	1' 34"
Clock/No. of Soc. Sec. No.	63' 23"
No. of Term./No. of Days	3.4
No. of Soc. Sec. No./No. of Days	6.1
No. of Searches/No. of Days	105.5
Total CPU/No. of Days	9' 34"
Total Clock Time/No. of Days	385' 11"
Total Cost/No. of Days	$54.90
Part 2:	
Cost/No. of Soc. Sec. No.	$9.03
Doc. Found/No. of Soc. Sec. No.	3724.43
Doc. Printed/No. of Soc. Sec. No.	144.35
CPU/No. of Log Nos.	5.45 min.
Clock/No. of Log Nos.	219.15 min.
Cost/No. of Log Nos.	$.52
Doc. Found/No. of Log Nos.	214.61
Doc. Printed/No. of Log Nos.	8.32
Doc. Printed/Doc. Found	.04

SOURCE: Cook, et al. (1971). Reproduced by permission of the School of Library Science, Syracuse University.

number or address, the SPIRES staff will respond to his comments or questions. It has been found that comments received in this way provide useful suggestions for system improvement or indicate ways in which instructions to users should be changed to minimize confusion. A similar feature is built into certain other on-line systems.

Katter (1970) has also emphasized the potential value of this type of ancillary recording program. Specific data to be recorded would include the frequency of occurrence of each error message and the frequency of use of the various commands. Very frequent errors can thus be identified and steps taken to modify the system in order to eliminate them. Rarely used commands can also be spotted and the need for their continued inclusion can then be

TABLE 8.5. Summary of User Evaluations for AIM–TWX Searches, as Gathered by On-Line Questionnaire, April–May 1971

Value	Purpose						
	Patient care	Education	Research	Other	Don't know	Total	%
Major	74	31	70	7	8	190	28.5
Considerable	70	39	70	5	8	192	28.8
Minor	19	6	25	1	3	54	8.1
None	11	6	17	5	7	46	6.9
Don't know	34	17	55	8	70	184	27.7
Total	208	99	237	26	96	666	100.0
%	31.2	14.9	35.6	3.9	14.4	100.0	

SOURCE: National Library of Medicine.

reviewed. Time and frequency patterns of system use can be obtained through on-line data gathering of this type.

In discussing evaluation of an experimental on-line system, Hillman (1968) proposes to maintain a record of each change in a user's request formulation as it is successively modified through interaction with the files and the text of actual documents. It is important, he feels, to document the ease or difficulty with which a user can reformulate his request as a result of system interaction. "The extent of reformulation is measured by individual differences in request terms, differences in request structures, and differences in associations." The time taken for reformulation is also recorded.

Hillman (1968) also suggests the following:

> During inquiry reformulation, users are asked to establish their own patterns of connectivity among terms by reference to their familiarity with the subject matter. User-supplied connectivities are compared with machine-derived connectivities and deviations are measured in terms of the closeness of the machine-derived set to the user-supplied set. The measure of closeness we use is topologically-derived, based either on partial distinguishability or full distinguishability, and provides us with the means for comparing the conceptual preferences of users with the conceptual structure of the stored corpus.
>
> Since one of our objectives is to bring about a rapport between the user and the system, we measure the rate at which the closeness of user-oriented concepts to machine-derived concepts can be maximized by user-machine interaction. This is done by judging (topological) closeness at each stage of the interaction. It is emphasized that every time a user modifies his inquiry on the basis of system response, he is in fact reformulating the conceptual structure of his inquiry by revising the liaisons between the topic T he is interested in and other topics with

which he believes T is associated. Each reformulation is stimulated by a display of machine-derived associations for T, which are produced at the user's request. It follows that every time the user modifies his inquiry on the basis of successive displays of connectivities, he is making an evaluative judgment. Specifically, he is comparing his own conceptual scheme with that defined for the corpus of stored data, and his aim is to bring the two conceptual schemes into the most satisfactory correspondence (p. 236).*

Treu (1971) has proposed the use of human on-line monitoring of searching activities for evaluation purposes. Using a second terminal, a skilled human observer monitors the interaction between a user and the system. Such monitoring may be more than passive; it may include "the active but inconspicuous intervention or interjection of variable messages and functions, with the intention of causing different user responses." Treu refers to this as "transparent stimulation" of the user.

Rosenberg (1973) has described another technique for monitoring user behavior. The user–system dialogue is monitored and later printed out. A time log is kept in the margin of the printout to indicate elapsed time at each stage. At the same time, the searcher makes use of a tape recorder in which he is asked to "articulate his thoughts as he goes through the computer dialogue. He verbally asks a question before putting it to the computer. He articulates his search strategy as he carries it out. He also evaluates the system's output." The taped account of the search is compared with the printout in order to recognize difficulties and problems. This technique can be used to determine, for example, lack of assistance given by the system, inadequacies in the vocabulary, and failures in search strategy. In other words, the technique is used to identify differences between what is actually searched and what the user would like to search.

On-line monitoring gives us the capability of learning more than ever before about how scientists and others use information retrieval systems, and with what degree of success. Unfortunately, this monitoring raises certain ethical and perhaps legal problems. Monitoring of a user without his direct permission might possibly be construed as a form of wiretapping, an invasion of privacy to which the United States is particularly sensitive at the present time.

The user probably should be told he is being monitored and perhaps given the option to cut off the monitoring operation. In SPIRES, for example, there is a command that will do this, although few users know of its existence. Of course, we pay the penalty for our honesty in that the user who knows he is being monitored may behave differently than he would under other circumstances.

---

*Reprinted from Hillman (1968) by permission of Microforms Marketing Corporation Inc.

The operators of a retrieval system should be able to do certain types of monitoring, without prior permission, even if this is restricted to purely statistical summaries. Such statistical data will include number of uses, number of uses per terminal, distribution of searches by connect time and CPU time, number of simultaneous users, and so on. Data of this type are actually reduced to the form of graphs, which can be displayed on a CRT, in the RIQS system (see Chapter Thirteen). Where the user is required to identify himself by category (e.g., experienced versus inexperienced), or to identify his search by type or purpose, it seems legitimate to include these variables in any data gathering activity.

In fact, it seems reasonable that the system be allowed to monitor, and collect data on, the behavior of users *in the aggregate*, as opposed to collecting data on individual, identifiable users. Such aggregate data would include statistics on how the system is used (e.g., frequency of use of terms and commands, frequency with which various sources are retrieved) and the types of problems encountered (e.g., frequency of use of various types of error message, frequency of use of the HELP command, the specific forms of help requested, and the frequency and type of use made of an EXPLAIN command).

This type of aggregate monitoring certainly seems justifiable and is of great importance to system managers in showing how the system is used and what might be done to improve its performance. The system managers are on more dangerous ground, perhaps, if they monitor the *individual* user, although the monitoring of individual search strategies could certainly be of great value in exposing system weaknesses and suggesting ways in which user training might be improved.

In this chapter we have discussed procedures specifically designed to allow the evaluation of on-line information retrieval systems. We have not attempted to discuss the problems involved in the overall evaluation of time-sharing computer systems, using such techniques as hardware monitors, bench-mark tests, analytical models, simulation techniques, and on-line data gathering programs. The evaluation of time-sharing systems in general is a subject for a book in itself. The topic has been discussed by Adams, et al. (1969), Calingaert (1967), Greco (1969), and Smith (1968), among others.

REFERENCES

Adams, R. T., W. H. G. Caldwell, and D. E. Carlton (1969). *Evaluation of Time-Sharing Systems—Benchmarks*. Atlanta, Ga.: Georgia Institute of Technology, School of Information Science, PB 189 621.

Bennertz, R. K. (1971). *Development of the Defense Documentation Center Remote On-Line Retrieval System: Past, Present and Future*. Alexandria, Va.: Defense Documentation Center, AD 720 900.

Calingaert, P. (1967). "System Performance Evaluation: Survey and Appraisal." *Commun. Assoc. Computing Machinery* **10** (1), 12–18.

Carlisle, J. H. (1972). *Interactive Man-Machine Communication: 1971 Annual Report*. New Haven, Conn.: Yale University, Department of Administrative Sciences, Tech. Report #51.

Cleverdon, C. W., J. Mills, and M. Keen (1966). *Factors Determining the Performance of Indexing Systems*. vol. 1, *Design*. Cranfield, England: College of Aeronautics.

Cook, K. H. (1970). "An Experimental On-Line System for Psychological Abstracts." *Proc. Amer. Soc. Information Sci.* **7**, 111–114.

Cook, K. H., L. H. Trump, P. Atherton, and J. Katzer (1971). *Large Scale Information Processing Systems*. Final Report to the Rome Air Development Center. Syracuse, N.Y.: Syracuse University, School of Library Science, 6 vols.

Freeman, R. R., and P. Atherton (1968). *AUDACIOUS—An Experiment with an On-Line, Interactive Reference Retrieval System Using the Universal Decimal Classification as the Index Language in the Field of Nuclear Science*. New York: American Institute of Physics, AIP/UDC 7.

Greco, R. J. (1969). *Evaluation Techniques of Real-Time Computer Systems: A Survey of Practices*. Atlanta, Ga.: Georgia Institute of Technology, School of Information Science, PB 187 860.

Hillman, D. J. (1968). "Negotiation of Inquiries in an On-Line Retrieval System." *Information Storage Retrieval* **4** (2), 219–238.

Katter, R. V. (1970). *On the On-Line User of Remote-Access Citation Retrieval Services*. Santa Monica, Ca.: System Development Corporation, TM-(L)-4494/000/00.

King, D. W., and E. C. Bryant (1971). *The Evaluation of Information Services and Products*. Washington, D.C.: Information Resources Press.

King, D. W., P. W. Neel, and B. L. Wood (1972). *Comparative Evaluation of the Retrieval Effectiveness of Descriptor and Free-Text Search Systems Using CIRCOL (Central Information Reference and Control On-Line)*. New York: Rome Air Development Center, RADC-TR-71-311. AD 738 299.

Lancaster, F. W. (1968a). *Evaluation of the MEDLARS Demand Search Service*. Bethesda, Md.: National Library of Medicine.

Lancaster, F. W. (1968b). *Information Retrieval Systems: Characteristics, Testing and Evaluation*. New York: Wiley.

Lancaster, F. W. (1972). *Evaluation of On-Line Searching in MEDLARS (AIM–TWX) by Biomedical Practitioners*. Urbana, Ill.: University of Illinois, Graduate School of Library Science, Occasional Paper No. 101.

Lancaster, F. W., R. L. Rapport, and J. K. Penry (1972). "Evaluating the Effectiveness of an On-Line Natural Language Retrieval System." *Information Storage Retrieval* **8** (5), 223–245.

Marcus, R. S., A. R. Benenfeld, and P. Kugel (1971). "The User Interface for the Intrex Retrieval System." *In* D. E. Walker (ed.), *Interactive Bibliographic Search: The User/Computer Interface*. Montvale, N.J.: AFIPS Press, pp. 159–201.

Meister, F., and D. J. Sullivan (1967). *Evaluation of User Reactions to a Prototype On-Line Information Retrieval System.* Washington, D.C.: NASA, NASA CR-918.

Parker, E. (1970). "Behavioral Research in the Development of a Computer-Based Information System." *In* C. E. Nelson, and D. K. Pollock (eds.), *Communication Among Scientists and Engineers.* Lexington, Mass.: Heath, pp. 281–293.

Rosenberg, V. (1973). "Technique for Monitoring User Behavior at the Computer Terminal Interface." *Jour. Amer. Soc. Information Sci.* **24** (1), 71.

Shumway, R. H. (1968). "Some Estimation Problems Associated with Evaluating Information Retrieval Systems." *In Evaluation of Document Retrieval Systems: Literature Perspective, Measurement, Technical Papers.* Bethesda, Md.: Westat Research Inc., pp. 78–96.

Smith, J. M. (1968). "A Review and Comparison of Certain Methods of Computer Performance Evaluation." *Computer Bull.* **12** (1), 13–18.

Summit, R. K. (1968). *Remote Information Retrieval Facility.* Palo Alto, Ca.: Lockheed Missiles & Space Co., NASA CR-1318.

Summit, R. K. (1970). *ERIC Online Retrieval System: Use of the DIALOG Online Information Retrieval System with ERIC Research in Education Files.* Palo Alto, Ca.: Lockheed Aircraft Corp., ED 040 592.

Timbie, M., and D. Coombs (1969). *An Interactive Information Retrieval System—Case Studies on the Use of DIALOG to Search the ERIC Document File.* Stanford, Ca.: ERIC Clearinghouse on Educational Media and Technology, ED 034 431.

Treu, S. (1971). "A Conceptual Framework for the Searcher-System Interface." *In* D. E. Walker (ed.), *Interactive Bibliographic Search: The User/Computer Interface.* Montvale, N.J.: AFIPS Press, pp. 53–66.

Chapter Nine

Operating Experience
and Evaluation Results

While many experiments with on-line retrieval have been conducted, we have so far accumulated comparatively little experience in the long-term use of on-line retrieval systems under actual operating conditions. The NASA system, RECON, has probably accumulated the most operating experience. Unfortunately, apart from the early and somewhat superficial study by Meister and Sullivan (1967), very little experience with RECON has been published by NASA. Caruso (1971) has stated: "Most of the literature on interactive systems is predictive or descriptive; very little use experience can be gleaned." We will however, attempt to summarize the scant operating experience that has been reported in print, including results of the few evaluations that have been conducted.

Experience with DIALOG

The evaluation of Lockheed's interactive retrieval system, DIALOG, on the NASA document collection was mentioned in Chapter Eight. Summit (1968) reports experience with the use of the system via remote terminals by engineers and scientists at the NASA Ames Research Center and by library personnel at the NASA headquarters in Washington, D.C. His report is one of the more complete accounts of operating experience published so far.

The Ames phase of the study took place during a 2 month period and occupied 44 working days or 80 terminal hours. Although some service was provided on all but two of these days, there were several service interruptions during the period and, in fact, approximately 24% of all the available terminal time was lost due to equipment, line, or software failures.

In all, 96 searches were completed at the Ames center. Some data on these searches are presented in Tables 9.1–9.4. "Number of concept groups" (Table 9.3) refers to the *exhaustivity* or *coordination level* of the search strategies used; that is, the number of terms (or groups of terms) required to co-occur; A *and* B is a two concept search, while A *and* B *and* C is a three concept search. From these data we can see that the average search time was 33 minutes (only 89 of the 96 searches were timed accurately), the average number of index terms per search was 8, the average number of concept groups was 2.7, and the average number of items printed was 22.

The average search time of 33 minutes appears rather high. However, this time includes learning and practice time. Summit (1968) reports that, after two or three searches, a user would frequently complete a relatively complex search in 8–10 minutes. Most users were apparently searching on quite specific topics and, despite the size of the data base (about 300,000 items at the time), were able to restrict the number of items retrieved (printed) quite successfully. In more than 50% of the searches the total number of items printed was less than twenty.

The figures for items printed (Table 9.4) represent items printed after having been first displayed and viewed on a CRT terminal. In other words, they were items *selected* by the searcher after having viewed representations of them (bibliographic citation plus index terms) on the screen. We can reasonably assume, therefore, that these items are in some sense *relevant* to the search topic. If we accept this assumption, and divide the average items printed into the average search time, we can arrive at a unit cost (in time) per relevant item retrieved—in this case 1.5 minutes on the average, a very respectable figure, particularly when one allows for inexperience and training time.

Seventy-five search sessions were conducted by 53 different users in the 2 month period. The number of searches per user is shown below:

Number of search sessions	Number of users
1	37
2	11
3	4
4	1

Almost a third of the participants used the system more than once, which is at least an indication that they must have been reasonably encouraged by their first attempt. The short duration of the experiment reported (2 months) reduces, however, the value of repeat usage as a gross indicator of user satisfaction.

TABLE 9.1

Elapsed search time (minutes)	Number of searches	Searches (%)
0–10	11	12.4
11–20	16	18.0
21–30	10	11.2
31–40	19	21.3
41–50	12	13.5
51–60	11	12.4
61–70	10	11.2
Average minutes per search: 33		

SOURCE: Summit (1968). Reproduced by permission of Lockheed Palo Alto Research Laboratory.

TABLE 9.2

Number of index terms per search topic	Number of searches	Searches (%)
1–5	33	34.4
6–10	39	40.6
11–15	15	15.6
16–20	4	4.2
21–25	5	5.2
Average index terms per search: 8		

SOURCE: Summit (1968). Reproduced by permission of Lockheed Palo Alto Research Laboratory.

TABLE 9.3

Number of concept groups	Number of searches	Searches (%)
1	2	2.1
2	40	41.7
3	40	41.7
4	14	14.5
Average concept groups per search topic: 2.7		

SOURCE: Summit (1968). Reproduced by permission of Lockheed Palo Alto Research Laboratory.

TABLE 9.4

Number of items printed	Number of searches	Searches (%)
0–10	37	38.6
11–20	17	17.7
21–30	15	15.6
31–40	10	10.4
41–50	6	6.3
51–60	4	4.2
61–70	2	2.1
71–80	3	3.1
81–90	1	1.0
91–100	0	0.0
> 100	1	1.0
Average items printed per search: 22		

SOURCE: Summit (1968). Reproduced by permission of Lockheed Palo Alto Research Laboratory.

User comments were solicited from the searchers on (*a*) the value of each search, (*b*) the utility of DIALOG as a search tool, (*c*) the ease of use, and (*d*) the comparative value of DIALOG versus the use of manual search tools and the off-line batch-processing NASA system. These user reactions, summarized in Table 9.5 for the 75 search sessions, were generally extremely positive, although many users failed to comment on the value of the system.

TABLE 9.5.   User Reactions to DIALOG for 75 Search Sessions

Comment	Positive	Negative	Not discussed
1. Usefulness of particular search	37	7	31
2. Desirability of having DIALOG as a search tool	36	0	39
3. Ease of learning and/or use	19	4	52
4. DIALOG versus batch or manual search	20	2	53

SOURCE: Summit (1968). Reproduced by permission of Lockheed Palo Alto Research Laboratory.

Summit (1968) reports that demand for use of the terminals was substantial in that, in the 2 month period (only 2 hours per day were available), backlogs of 1–2 weeks occurred.

In the headquarters phase of the study, occupying a 12 month period beginning in July 1967, approximately 300 searches were conducted. By this time, the files had increased to 400,000 items and 3 hours per day were available for the conduct of searches. Most of these searches were conducted by library personnel, and all of those included in Summit's analysis (174) were conducted by members of the library staff.

Approximately 300 hours of terminal time were available during the 12 month period. Compared with the Ames phase, the system was much more reliable in Washington—13% of the available time was lost, as opposed to 24% at Ames. Although equipment failures still occurred too frequently, transmission line and software failures were reduced considerably as a result of modifications made to the system.

Table 9.6 compares some of the characteristics of searches conducted at Ames with searches conducted in Washington. Unfortunately, these data are not particularly illuminating and many data that would have been interesting were not collected in the study, or at least were not included in the report. Among the interesting data that were neglected were (*a*) searching times for staff at NASA headquarters, (*b*) recall and precision estimates for the searches, (c) the requester's subjective assessment of the value of a search conducted for him by a member of the library staff, and (d) the effect of increased experience on searching times and the unit cost (in time) per relevant item retrieved.

TABLE 9.6.   Comparison of DIALOG Search Characteristics at Two Centers

	Ames	Washington
Number of terms (average)	8.0	6.5
Coordination level (average)	2.7	2.1
Number of items printed (average)	22.0	22.4

SOURCE: Summit (1968). Reproduced by permission of Lockheed Palo Alto Research Laboratory.

Timbie and Coombs (1969) have presented nine case studies on the use of DIALOG by educational practitioners at the ERIC Clearinghouse on Educational Media and Technology at Stanford University. On the whole, these users were most impressed with the speed of the system and with the way in which it "widened their horizons" by suggesting areas related to their original search topic. Most of the users found it easy to use. Four of the nine users felt that it took too long for the system to respond to a user input. Others complained that too many keys had to be used in order to enter a command. One searcher, a physician, found use of the CRT hard on the eyes after two hours of use. The favorable user comments are given in Table 9.7 and the unfavourable ones in Table 9.8. On the basis of their experience, Timbie and Coombs express their conviction that a user with no previous experience of mechanized retrieval can sit down at a terminal and, in a reasonably short time, use such a system effectively. It took about 20–30 minutes to instruct the user in how to operate the equipment, after he had read the instruction manual, and an additional $^1/_2$–1 hour to become reasonably adept in using the system. The greatest educational problem was not related to the equipment or to the commands, but to the searching principles. It was difficult to instruct people, with no previous exposure, in the principles of searching on various combinations of terms. The investigators conclude that 2 hours is enough time for the average person to become quite capable of using DIALOG, but not long enough for him to gain full familiarity with all the retrieval approaches.

Several of the participants indicated that their original search criteria were modified as a result of feedback from the system, and several also reported that, serendipitously, they discovered material of interest to them that was not directly related to the subject of their search. One user stated

TABLE 9.7.   Favorable User Comments on DIALOG

User	Statement
ABCDHI	The system has great speed, saves user's time.
CDFGI	Being able to combine sets that way is a desirable feature.
BCDH	The system opens new avenues for thought, it "widened horizons."
CHI	It is simple to use, easy to work with.
AH	It is thorough, comprehensive.
AH	It is effective.
AH	It is, in general, valuable.
BH	It exhilarates, creates interest.
EF	Having the hardcopy record to refer to is handy.
B	The system releases inhibiting mechanisms.
B	It brings us into a new level of communication and education and exploration.
B	It is challenging.
B	It provokes you to order your approach.
C	It presents good descriptions of documents.
C	It presents a variety of topics.
C	There is the attractive possibility of being able to access the system from anywhere in the country.
D	The system saves user energy.
E	The boolean logic is useful.
E	The direct sequence of going from the thesaurus to the document is nice.
E	There is a minimum amount of typing, because of the presence of the command keys.
E	The particular documents sought were identified.
E	[It is a generally attractive system]—"we'd like to have one."
E	Presented as they are on the CRT, the terms can be scanned quickly.
E	Paging was easy.
F	The expand feature was useful.

SOURCE: Timbie and Coombs (1969). Reprinted by permission of ERIC Clearinghouse on Educational Media and Technology, Stanford University.

TABLE 9.8.   Unfavorable User Comments on DIALOG

User	Statement
ABFI	There are delays when you must wait for the system.
FAIC	Considerable experience or time is needed to master the rules.
AI	Too many combinations of keys are needed to input one command.
EF	Having to build combined sets one at a time, rather than doing it with one complex statement, is inconvenient.
EF	There is a great deal of "paging" required on the CRT, because you can only look at nine terms at a time.
B	The innovative system can be frustrating for people who don't like to change.
D	The system is limited because of the original input [a reflection not on DIALOG, but on ERIC].
D	The CRT is hard on the eyes after a couple of hours.
E	Having to look back and forth from the CRT to typewriter unit is inconvenient.
E	Having to repeat pushing the button so much— for every 10 things you want printed—is inconvenient.
E	A hierarchical thesaurus display would be preferable.
E	It must be expensive.
F	It is cumbersome to use.
F	Having to use DIALOG to approach the thesaurus is inefficient [actually, of course, you don't].
F	The letters on the CRT have an unpleasant shape.
F	The CRT display is "painted on" too slowly.
G	There are weaknesses in indexing [this is not a weakness in DIALOG].
I	The hardware fails [some set numbers were not printed out during that particular session].
I	The touch of the keyboard is too different from that of most typewriters.

SOURCE: Timbie and Coombs (1969). Reprinted by permission of ERIC Clearinghouse on Educational Media and Technology, Stanford University.

that he had trouble staying on the subject of his search simply because he found so many other interesting avenues to explore.

It is interesting to note that the most sophisticated user in terms of mechanized systems (a university librarian with responsibilities for library mechanization) was most critical of the system because of the indirect search approach that is needed. DIALOG at that time required input of terms one at a time and the gradual building up of a search strategy by combining terms selected from various displays. This approach may be ideal for the relatively unsophisticated searcher but it is tedious and frustrating for searchers of greater sophistication, who would prefer to be able to enter boolean combinations of terms directly. Present versions of DIALOG allow this to some extent.

Besides the nine case studies presented by Timbie and Coombs, questionnaires were completed by eighteen other ERIC users who visited the center and tried the on-line terminal. Some reactions of these users to specific aspects of the system are recorded in Table 9.9. In this table, a scale of five gradations is used. Thus, in part *a*, twelve of the eighteen respondents cluster at the far left of the scale, indicating that the keyboard, in their judgment, was easy to use.

Experience with RECON

The RECON evaluation reported by Meister and Sullivan (1967) was conducted by means of evaluative rating forms, questionnaires, and usage logs. Over a 7 week experimental period a staggering 6133 uses were recorded at six separate NASA centers. However, the fact that citations were viewed in only 40% of these searches would tend to indicate that much of the use merely involved playing with the terminal and did not represent the conduct of real searches. In fact, only 22,545 citations were viewed over the entire group of searches (less than 4 per search).

The evaluation questionnaire was completed by 37 respondents. Each of these had conducted ten RECON searches on the average. All but five of these users felt competent in the operation of RECON, and 75% indicated that the system was easy or extremely easy to use. About 60% of the respondents found the alphabetical term display to be useful (particularly when the term first input by the searcher is not present in the data base or when the searcher spells it incorrectly) and about half the respondents found the display of cross-references to be of some value. Despite these features, however, most searchers bypassed these displays and used a direct search on terms that they felt sure would be in the system. All the users found the count of citations indexed under a particular term to be of value.

TABLE 9.9   User Reactions to Specific Features of DIALOG

(a) Keyboard						
Easy to use	6	6	4	2	0	Difficult to use
(b) Typed Terminal Record						
Easy to use	6	9	3	0	0	Difficult to use
Valuable in conducting a search	17	0	0	1	0	Not valuable
(c) CRT or Visual Display						
Easy to use	10	6	0	1	0	Difficult to use
Valuable in conducting a search	18	0	0	0	0	Not valuable
(d) Thesaurus						
Easy to use	8	2	3	0	0	Difficult to use
Valuable in conducting a search	7	4	2	0	0	Not valuable

SOURCE: Timbie and Coombs (1969). Reproduced by permission of ERIC Clearinghouse on Educational Media and Technology, Stanford University.

About one third of the respondents reported difficulty in the use of the boolean search logic, and over 80% of the users were dissatisfied with the error messages provided by the system. They were not satisfied to know that an error had occurred, but wanted to know what the error was and how it could be corrected.

Meister and Sullivan (1967) report that the most severe problem associated with the hardware aspects of RECON was the response time. Delays of several minutes after input of a message to the computer were known to occur on occasions. "Such delay times were the major factor tending to downgrade the system in users' eyes."

Nuclear Safety Information Center

Buchanan and Kidd (1969) described 2 years of experience at the Nuclear Safety Information Center (NSIC), Oak Ridge National Laboratory, with an on-line system based on an IBM 360 computer. The data base at that time consisted of 25,000 (which has since grown to over 65,000) document descriptions derived from technical reports, journal articles, and other documents relating to nuclear safety. Bibliographic data, keywords, and abstracts for new items are entered into the system via CRT consoles (IBM 2260). Retrospective searches, however, are usually conducted at typewriter-like consoles (IBM 2740) using weighted term searching. In 1971, an interactive terminal query language (NSICIRK) was added which provides direct AND, OR, and NOT logic. Figure 9.1 is a recent update of an illustration found in a report by Cottrell and Buchanan (1971), which shows the hardware configuration at the Oak Ridge Computing Technology Center (CTC) where NSIC's computer activities are conducted on a time-shared basis. A detailed description of the programs used at NSIC has been prepared by Stoutt and Yount (1970).

The most significant finding reported by Buchanan and Kidd is that, although consoles were made available, technical personnel of NSIC preferred on the whole not to undertake their own searches but to delegate to an information specialist. The reason for this, according to Buchanan and Kidd (1969), is that "the working scientist and engineer soon realizes that the most effective and efficient retrieval can be done by those who are thoroughly familiar with the way the information was input." The information specialists in this case are engineers and scientists on the staff of NSIC. It is these technical personnel who have undertaken the indexing and who are therefore presumed to be most efficient at retrieval.

A procedure was eventually arrived at whereby a telephone request is received by a technical specialist (scientist or engineer) who prepares a search strategy and inputs this to his own terminal. The output references are printed out at the terminal of the searcher and also at the terminal of the requester, allowing joint review by both parties.

AIM–TWX: Operating Experience

The AIM–TWX system (see Chapter Five) is much younger than RECON, but it has generated more operational experience in print.

Stiller (1970) has described operating experience at the National Library of Medicine in searching portions of the MEDLARS data base on-line using the SUNY and the AIM–TWX systems. She compares the capabilities of both, and contrasts these capabilities with those of MEDLARS itself

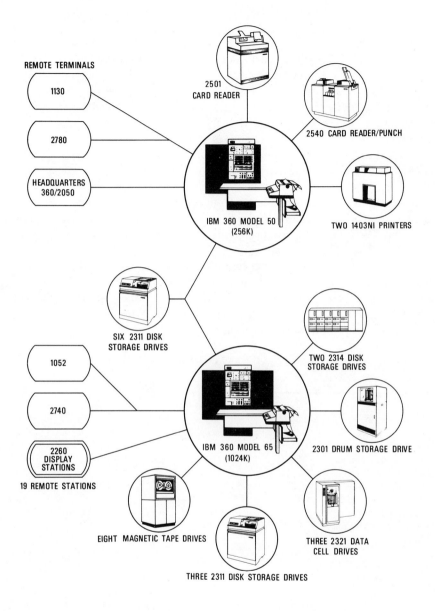

COMPUTING TECHNOLOGY CENTER PRIMARY SYSTEM

Figure 9.1. Hardware configuration at the Oak Ridge Computing Technology Center. Reproduced by permission of Oak Ridge Computing Technology Center.

when searched in the batch-processing mode. Stiller considers that the principal advantages of the partial on-line files are that they provide rapid response and allow searching strategies to be tested before being used off-line on the full MEDLARS file. The on-line searches also provide reliable estimates of the total number of citations likely to be retrieved by a full file search. In addition, the on-line systems have proved of great value in the training of MEDLARS search analysts.

However, the two systems are of limited utility in conducting comprehensive searches involving many terms drawn from the controlled vocabulary. Stiller points out, for example, that a comprehensive search on all enzymes involves more than 125 terms drawn from *Medical Subject Headings* (*MeSH*). Such a search is impossible in the SUNY system and only partly possible in AIM–TWX through the use of its *explosion* capability (see Chapter Three).

Moll (1971) reports experience in the use of AIM–TWX in the medical library at the University of Virginia. The experience covers a 19 day trial period in late 1970. During this time, the on-line terminal was available 4 hours a day. In all, 298 searches were conducted by or for 114 individual requesters, according to the distribution presented in Table 9.10.

TABLE 9.10.   Use Figures for AIM–TWX at One Medical Center, November 19–December 18, 1970

	Total requestors	Individual searches			Citations retrieved		
		Total	Successful	Unsuccessful	Total	On-line	Off-line
Virginia practitioners	50	103	83	20	2,013	381	1,632
University of Virginia medical faculty	32	84	62	22	1,655	302	1,353
University of Virginia nursing faculty	7	64	57	7	802	261	541
University of Virginia house staff and students	17	39	36	3	756	250	506
Medical Center of Virginia faculty and house staff	8	8	5	3	117	4	113
Totals	114	298	243	55	5,343	1,198	4,145

SOURCE: Moll (1971). Reproduced by permission of the Medical Library Association.

Of the 298 searches, 243 (82%) resulted in citations being retrieved and these were judged "successful." Clearly, this is a very crude measure of search success. The 55 searches that retrieved nothing can be regarded as highly successful if they truly indicate that nothing of relevance exists in the data base. The total number of citations retrieved in the 243 successful searches was 5343, an average of approximately 22 citations per search. Of these, however, only 1198 were printed on-line and, in fact, in 73 of the searches all printing was done off-line. It is obvious, therefore, that a substantial number of searches in this series were conducted in a noninteractive way; at least, the capability of viewing specimen citations was not being used.

According to Moll (1971), most of the searches were designed for high precision rather than high recall, and the majority of requesters favored this policy. He feels, although this was not tested, that the best results were achieved in searches conducted by a trained operator but with the requester at his shoulder. Under these conditions, the physicians "had an opportunity of advising the operators on means of either enlarging or narrowing the topics, or of introducing other subject terms and term combinations which would produce results."

Moll also found that on-line searchers were subject to fatigue. A continuous 4 hour stretch was too long for an operator, and a 2 hour period was found to be much better. The average number of searches per hour was 4.6, but Moll feels that this could be raised to almost 6 per hour with increased operator experience.

Cuadra (1971) has presented some further data on the characteristics of AIM–TWX searches. The average search involves the formulation and reformulation of four search statements, and an average of three terms are combined in each of these search statements. Under typical time-sharing loads, this 3 × 4 transaction can be accomplished in about 30–40 seconds of computer time. The user might spend a total of 15–20 minutes at the terminal, including the time required to obtain a printout of retrieved citations.

The value of an on-line medical retrieval system in actual problems of patient care has been demonstrated in an experimental cancer information service, supported by AIM–TWX, in the Pacific Northwest. The experiment has been described by Blase and Stock (1972).

AIM–TWX Evaluation

The formal evaluation of AIM–TWX reported by Lancaster (1972) appears to be the most detailed study of on-line searches yet conducted, although it was limited to a relatively small group based on 48 requests. The procedures used in the investigation were outlined in Chapter Eight. The principal results are summarized in Table 9.11. For each search the following data are presented:

TABLE 9.11.   Evaluation Results from 48 Searches on AIM–TWX

Search number	Number of previous uses	Recall requirement	Precision	Unit cost (minutes)	Recall estimate	Value
1	3	All	0/5 = 0		0/0 (?)	None
2	0	Few	4/10 = 40.0	2.5		
3	1	Few	6/7 = 85.7	1.8		
4	2	Few	8/10 = 80.0	1.2		
5	0	Few	7/10 = 70.0	4.3	7/7 = 100	Major
6	1	All	15/16 = 93.7	3.2	15/23 = 65.2	Considerable
7	1	Few	0/1 = 0		0/0 (?)	None
8	1	Few	0/11 = 0		0/2 = 0	None
9	4	Few	0/0		[a]	None
10	2	Few	6/6 = 100	2.0	6/8 = 75.0	Considerable
11	0	Few	11/11 = 100	2.3	11/24 = 45.8	Considerable
12	2	All	3/3 = 100	4.3	3/3 = 100	
13	0	All	12/12 = 100	2.0	12/12 = 100	Major
14	0	Few	10/13 = 76.9	2.0	10/19 = 52.6	Considerable
15	0	All	6/8 = 75.0	4.3	6/9 = 66.7	Minor
16	0	All	1/5 = 20.0	26.0	1/9 = 11.1[b]	Minor
17	1	All	0/5 = 0		0/11 = 0	None
18	3	Few	1/1 = 100	4.0	1/3 = 33.3	Major
19	0	Few	0/0		0/6 = 0	None
20	1	Few	0/7 = 0		0/1 = 0	None
21	1	All	9/19 = 47.4	5.5	9/9 = 100	Considerable
22	4	Few	29/29 = 100	1.0		Major
23	0	All	4/6 = 66.7	7.0		Minor
24	0	All	27/27 = 100	1.4	27/45 = 60.0	Considerable
25	0	All	3/7 = 42.8	10.0	3/12 = 25.0	Minor
26	2	All	2/2 = 100	12.0	2/3 = 66.7	Considerable
27	5	Few	7/7 = 100	1.4	[a]	Major
28	0	Few	12/23 = 52.2	2.2	12/13 = 92.3[b]	Major
29	1	Few	5/8 = 62.5	3.8	5/25 = 20.0	Considerable
30	20	Few	5/10 = 50.0	3.4	[a]	Major
31	7	All	16/18 = 88.9	1.2	[a]	Major
32	0	Few	21/30 = 70.0	1.0	21/33 = 63.6[b]	
33	0	Few	6/7 = 85.7	3.0	6/10 = 60.0[b]	Considerable
34	1	All	6/11 = 54.4	5.0	6/13 = 46.1	Major
35	0	All	8/8 = 100[c]	3.0	8/8 = 100[c]	
36	2	All	5/7 = 71.4	6.0	5/13 = 38.4	
37	0	All	17/19 = 89.5	3.4	17/35 = 48.5	Major
38	0	All	6/13 = 46.1	8.0	6/8 = 75.0	Major
39	1	All	0/2 = 0		0/25 = 0	None
40	0	All	23/24 = 95.8	5.2	23/45 = 51.1	Considerable
41	0	All	29/70 = 41.4	3.8	29/40 = 72.5	Minor
42	0	All	4/14 = 28.6	12.5	4/13 = 30.8	Considerable
43	2	All	10/11 = 90.9	1.5	10/11 = 90.9	Considerable
44	0	All	13/25 = 52.0	6.1	13/22 = 59.0	

TABLE 9.11. *Continued*

Search number	Number of previous uses	Recall requirement	Precision	Unit cost (minutes)	Recall estimate	Value
45	0	All	10/18 = 55.5	6.0	10/16 = 62.5	Considerable
46	0	Few	5/9 = 55.5		5/12 = 41.6	
47	0	All	39/54 = 72.2	2.4	39/40 = 97.5	Considerable
48	1	Few	115/143 = 80.4	0.25	115/226 = 50.9	Major

[a]Search analyst could think of no alternative approaches.
[b]Recall figure probably inflated.
[c]Search on author name.

1. The number of times the requester had previously used AIM–TWX.
2. Whether he wanted to find all relevant citations or only a few of them (high or low recall).
3. The precision ratio of his search. That is, the number of unique relevant citations among the total number of unique citations printed.
4. The unit cost per relevant citation retrieved. This is the total time spent at the terminal divided by the total number of unique relevant citations found. Where no relevant citations were found by the user (as in search 1) it is not possible to express a unit cost.
5. The recall estimate for the user's search. The recall estimate is derived from the equation:

$$\frac{\text{Number of unique relevant references found by user}}{\substack{\text{Number of unique relevant references found by user and number of} \\ \text{additional unique relevant references found by experienced} \\ \text{MEDLARS search analyst}}}$$

In some cases, no parallel search was conducted through error or lack of time, and blanks appear in the recall column for these searches. In other cases, the search analyst could think of no further approaches so did not undertake a parallel search; actually, we might write in 100% recall for these. Some of the recall figures are inflated; these result from searches in which the analyst printed only a selection of the citations retrieved by a strategy. Other citations, matching the strategy but not printed, are almost certainly relevant. Because they were not printed, however, and thus not assessed for relevance, these citations are not included in the recall estimates.

In other words, the recall estimates quoted in these searches should be regarded as maximum possible figures only.

The final column of the table records the user's subjective assessment of the value to him of his own search on the scale: major value, considerable value, minor value, or no value. This column has blanks for some searches in which the responsible analyst failed to obtain the user's assessment of value.

The average precision figure for the group of searches was 63.1%. In other words, on the average, over 60% of all the citations retrieved were judged to be relevant. This figure is based on 45 of the 48 searches. Two searches with zero retrieval were omitted from the precision calculation, and so was search 35, which was an author search and therefore could not reasonably be expected to score less than 100%. It is extremely noteworthy that a group of biomedical specialists with a minimum of exposure to the system (half the group had never used AIM–TWX before and most of the remainder had used it only on one or two occasions) should be able to conduct searches to satisfy their own needs, using a controlled vocabulary, and achieve a precision in excess of 60%. In terms of precision there were few really bad searches. Searches 1, 7, 8, 17, 20, and 39 achieved zero precision. That is, they retrieved some citations (the worst, search 8, retrieved 11), but none were relevant. However, in the case of two of the searches, 1 and 7, the MEDLARS analyst was unable to find any relevant citations so that for these there is a strong possibility that no relevant citations exist in the AIM–TWX data base. Nine of the searches achieved 100% precision. It is worth remembering that in the full evaluation of MEDLARS (Lancaster, 1968) the average precision for 300 off-line searches conducted by trained analysts was only 50%.

Another interesting figure is the unit cost (in time) to the user per relevant citation retrieved. This figure is obtained by dividing the total time at the terminal by the number of relevant citations retrieved. It is a valid measure of the cost to the user in finding relevant references. The unit cost is available for 39 of the searches. For 8 searches, no relevant citations were retrieved, and it is not possible to express a unit cost for these. For 1 search, terminal time was not recorded, so this too is omitted. For the 39 searches, the unit costs range from a high of 26.0 minutes (search 16 took 26 minutes and retrieved only one relevant citation) to a remarkable low of 0.25 minute (search 48 discovered 115 relevant citations in 29 minutes). The average unit cost, over the 39 searches, is 4.5 minutes per relevant citation, and the median unit cost is 3.4 minutes. For 30% of the searches, the unit cost per relevant citation was 2 minutes or less. Considering that most searches were reasonably complex, requiring coordinations between two or more aspects, these search times appear to be satisfactory and well within tolerable limits.

The most reliable average recall figure is based on a group of 36 searches. This group excludes 5 searches for which, through error, no parallel analyst searches were conducted. It also excludes 2 searches for which no relevant references were retrieved by either search, as well as 4 searches in which the recall estimate is inflated (for reasons mentioned above) and 1 search conducted on the name of an author only (where it would be very difficult to get less than 100%). The group includes, however, 4 searches in which the search analyst felt unable to improve on the user's search. These were all scored 100% recall for the user. For the group of 36 searches, the average recall was 57.6%. This estimate is almost identical to the average recall (57.7%) achieved over 300 searches in the full MEDLARS study (Lancaster, 1968). Recall estimates range from 100% for 7 searches to zero recall for 5 searches. The worst recall result occurred in search 39, where the user was unable to find any relevant citations, but the analyst found 25.

An overall average recall estimate of 57% appears to be entirely satisfactory for these searches, particularly when we consider that almost half the requesters (22 of 48) indicated that they were looking for a few citations only. To these requesters, recall is unimportant. In fact, if we take the group of 22 searches for which high recall was required, and for which we appear to have reasonably good recall estimates, the average recall is somewhat higher, 61.7%, than for the entire group of 36 searches.

Perhaps the best indication of the success of a search is the user's own subjective assessment of its value to him. Value judgments were obtained for 39 of the 48 searches, with the following results:

Major value	12	30.8%
Considerable value	14	35.9%
Minor value	5	12.8%
No value	8	20.5%

Again, this may be interpreted as indicating a satisfactory result, especially when we consider that in the case of two of the "no value" searches the result appears to reflect the absence of relevant citations in the AIM–TWX data base (both analyst and user were unable to find any relevant items) rather than defects in searching strategies. That 67% of the users judged their searches to be of considerable or major value is surely encouraging for the future of on-line searching by biomedical practitioners.

It is interesting to consider the possible effects of the learning process on the results achieved at the terminal. Dividing the searches into three groups, by number of previous uses of AIM–TWX, we arrive at the following results:

	Precision	Recall	Unit cost
System not used before (24 searches)	62.4	58.7	5.4
Used once or twice before (17 searches)	56.8	46.6	4.1
Used more than twice before (7 searches)[a]	62.7	86.6	2.2

[a]Five of these seven searches were judged of major value by the users.

No particularly clear picture emerges from these figures, except that increased experience appears to reduce the unit cost per relevant citation retrieved. This is to be expected; as experience at the terminal increases, less time is wasted in entering invalid terms or using incorrect constructions. From the above table, we can see that the most experienced group of users achieved the best results in terms of recall, precision, and unit cost. However, the group of users who had searched AIM–TWX on one or two occasions before the test search actually performed less well, in terms of recall and precision, than the group who had not previously used the system. Unfortunately, these samples are too small to indicate anything very clearly and there are too many other variables affecting the results, besides the variable of learning. One of these is the complexity of the request.

It is more revealing to compare the characteristics of a group of "worst" searches with the characteristics of a group of "best" searches. When we examine the searches with high-recall and high-precision results, we see that most have the following features:

1. They involve relatively simple relationships.
2. The terms of the request statement translate fairly directly into headings from *MeSH*, the controlled vocabulary of the system.

Some examples are:

Search 12   Cryosurgery of rectal carcinoma
             (Searched on CRYOGENIC SURGERY *and* RECTAL NEO-PLASMS)
Search 13   Histocytochemistry and electrophoresis of creatine kinase
             (Searched on CREATINE KINASE *and* HISTOCYTO-CHEMISTRY *or* ELECTROPHORESIS)
Search 27   Reviews on childhood schizophrenia
             (Searched on SCHIZOPHRENIA, CHILDHOOD, *and* REVIEW)

The poor searches, on the other hand, may be divided into two categories:

1. Requests for which nothing of more than peripheral relevance is found in the data base, but a lot of time is wasted in establishing this. Examples are searches 8 and 20, respectively, on the skin punch biopsy technique in plastic surgery and the selection of patients for rhinoplasty. In these cases, poor results are due to the fact that little relevant literature exists, at least in this data base, and we cannot really blame the searcher for this.

2. Requests that require more sophisticated search techniques, either because they involve more complex conceptual relationships or because it is by no means obvious, to the inexperienced searcher, what the appropriate *MeSH* terms should be. A good example is search 19 on hyperalimentation, in which the term HYPER-ALIMENTATION was tried but rejected (it is not a *MeSH* term). Other combinations (e.g., PARENTERAL FEEDING *and* WATER-ELECTROLYTE BALANCE) are needed for a success-ful search. The inexperienced user could hardly be expected to know this. But the system is obviously at fault. An on-line system used by health professionals needs a full entry vocabulary.* The AIM–TWX system had no built-in entry vocabulary, and *MeSH* itself is grossly lacking in specific entry terms. Terms such as "hyperalimentation," describing concepts upon which literature exists in the system, should appear in an on-line entry vocabulary, with appropriate mappings to *MeSH* terms or combinations.

An example of a more complex search, in which the user had little success, is search 39, relating to solutions used in automatic clinical blood cell counters. The user tried only BLOOD CELL COUNT *and* SOLUTIONS, whereas most of the relevant citations were retrieved by the MEDLARS analyst on ERYTHROCYTE COUNT/INSTRUMENTATION *or* BLOOD CELL COUNT/INSTRUMENTATION.

From the detailed examination of 48 searches, it is possible to make some generalizations relating to the searching of this system by biomedical practitioners who are not information specialists:

1. Searches tend to be quite effective and efficient where the conceptual relationships are not highly complex and where *MeSH* terms match request terms fairly closely.

---

*An entry vocabulary is a vocabulary of natural language expressions, occurring in documents and requests, with appropriate mappings to the controlled terms of the system. This will be discussed in detail in Chapter Eleven.

2. Lack of an entry vocabulary seriously hampers the user in cases where his request terms have no exact equivalent in *MeSH*.
3. Users are most successful in relatively simple approaches. When they try more sophisticated techniques, they often go astray.
4. A major cause of low recall is the user's failure to recognize all possible approaches to retrieval. For example, in search 46, relating to the postgastrectomy "dumping" syndrome, the user tried DUMPING SYNDROME/THERAPY, but overlooked DUMPING SYNDROME/SURGERY. Other examples are the use of the term EMBOLISM, but not EMBOLISM, FAT; the use of INFANT, but not INFANT, NEWBORN or INFANT, PREMATURE; the use of ANEURYSM, MYCOTIC, but not the related term ENDOCARDITIS, BACTERIAL; and the use of HYPER-THYROIDISM, but not the more specific GOITER, EXOPH-THALMIC.
5. The interactive capabilities of the system are comparatively little used. Frequently, the searcher remains with his original search strategy and does not allow himself to be led to alternative approaches.
6. Very few users choose the *print full* option (see Chapter Three). Those who do, however, generally find it useful to (*a*) successively narrow the scope of a search by discovering new terms in the profiles of displayed items, (*b*) expand the scope of a search by discovering new terms, (*c*) expand the scope of a search by discovering new facets of interest.

The results of the AIM–TWX study were surprisingly good. Although a few users went badly astray, the majority were able to conduct productive searches. The precision achieved in most cases was high, and the cost in time appears to be well within tolerable limits. It is not to be expected that the requester himself will perform as well as a trained analyst. He cannot master the complete vocabulary, indexing policies, and niceties of search strategy in a matter of minutes. Nevertheless, acceptable results were obtained in most cases by a simple and straightforward approach. It is noteworthy that many of these users were seeking only a few relevant references. They did not require high recall. Frequently, they were satisfied with the results of their own efforts and did not really need the additional analyst search, which was conducted in any case for the purpose of the study. For the user who would like everything in the data base the search analyst will usually be able to find some additional references, because he is able to think of alternative approaches. It is also noteworthy, however, that in several cases the searcher was not able to find any additional material and in some instances did not even try because he felt there was little possibility of improving the user's search.

Although it would be desirable to have more evidence on this point, by means of additional searches conducted with the same controls, the study seems to indicate that many biomedical practitioners of the type encountered in this experiment could exploit AIM–TWX profitably with the minimum of introduction to the system and without the necessity for having a trained MEDLARS analyst at their elbow. In other words, it would be perfectly practical to provide such a service in medical centers (where there is an indicated demand) remote from MEDLARS search facilities. However, it would always be desirable to have one or more people at this center (e.g., the librarian) more fully familiar with the system and its capabilities. In particular, someone should be knowledgeable in the purely technical aspects of logging-in, logging-out, and recognizing and dealing with technical problems as they arise. If the terminal were serviced by a computer facility, such technical matters could be handed adequately by the staff of this center. It would also be useful if a MEDLARS analyst could be available, perhaps via telephone, to help with real problems.

AIM–TWX was shown to meet a definite need. The great majority of the searches conducted as part of this experiment could not have been conducted in the printed *Index Medicus.* They involve conceptual relationships that would be virtually impossible to handle without some facility for term coordination. Moreover, in many cases, the searches made use of terms that would not necessarily be *print* terms (i.e., terms under which the citations would appear in the printed index). AIM–TWX, then, is not made redundant by either *Index Medicus* or *Abridged Index Medicus,* the printed indexes generated from this same data base. Moreover, it appears that the system is frequently used for searches that would probably not be conducted in MEDLARS by the off-line route—the type of search in which the requester seeks a few references and needs them right away. The on-line system, then, serves a function that is not fulfilled by either the full MEDLARS batch-processing service or the various printed products of MEDLARS. Further, search analysts at the participating centers have become aware that the AIM–TWX facility is attracting users who have not previously requested MEDLARS searches *and, in fact, have not been regular users of the medical library in the past.*

The principal limitation of ELHILL (ORBIT), as revealed by this study, is that it requires virtual perfection in the entering of search terms and commands. Although it is relatively easy to make corrections, the system makes little attempt to compensate for human error. Unfortunately, it is very easy to make simple mistakes, particularly if one is not used to typing or other keyboarding activities.

SUNY Experience

Stiller's comments on the use of both the SUNY and AIM–TWX systems were summarized earlier (Stiller, 1970). Bridegam and Meyerhoff (1970) have reported the experience of two participants in the SUNY Biomedical Communication Network: the Edward G. Miner Library at the University of Rochester and the Health Sciences Library at the State University of New York at Buffalo. For a 28 week period, they report a total usage of 1473 searches at Rochester (two terminals) and 2698 searches at Buffalo (three terminals), an average of 52.6 and 96.3 searches per week at the two institutions, respectively. They project these figures to a total of 1368 searches per year per terminal at Rochester and 1669 searches per terminal per year at Buffalo. Average cost per search was calculated to be $3.65 at Rochester and $3.00 at Buffalo. During the 28 week period, there were approximately 200 members of the university staff trained in the use of the terminal at each institution. Parenthetically it should be observed that the 2740 terminals were used for requesting interlibrary loans as well as for conducting bibliographic searches.

The authors report that, because of its novelty, the terminal draws curious faculty, staff, and students into the library. Some of these may not be previous users of the library. As a result, the library staff is given the opportunity to explain to the visitors other facets of the library's services and other bibliographic tools that are available. The service thus has some definite publicity value, in addition to its obvious utility in bibliographic searching and in interlibrary lending.

By 1972, the great majority of searches in the network were being conducted by trained analysts, rather than medical practitioners, using a more direct search language than that used in the search experience described by Bridegam and Meyerhoff. The direct search language was also used by Stiller.

Further experiences with the SUNY system, at the Parkinson Information Center (PIC), Columbia University, were presented by Rae (1970). According to Rae, a major obstacle to use of the system is the need to train users both in the mechanics of operating the terminal and in the logic of indexing and searching strategies. Such training activities absorbed a considerable amount of the time of a library search analyst at PIC. Rae urges that the system should guide users on-line through incorporation of computer-assisted instruction techniques. Major hardware problems reported by Rae were the noise and comparative slowness of the typewriter terminal used (IBM 2740). The noise of this terminal in the normal library environment was sufficient to distract other library users and to cause them to react negatively. At a print rate of 15 characters per second, the 2740 was tedious to use for many search printouts, which frequently took 10 minutes or longer to print (a PIC citation with descriptors frequently exceeds 1500 characters). Clinicians and medical researchers were found to become impatient while waiting for the full printout to appear. Moreover, the system does not allow communication with the computer while search results are being printed. A search thus cannot be interrupted, and it is possible to wait several minutes while the terminal is printing unwanted citations or even garbage.

Software problems were also noted by Rae. In particular, the IBM software (the Document Processing System) was found to function very slowly on the very complex strategies that were sometimes needed in PIC searches. In 1972, the software was operating much faster on an IBM 370/155 using 3330 storage units.

Egeland (1971) reports a survey of 241 SUNY users in which it was found that only 44 (18%) preferred to operate the terminal themselves and 187 (78%) preferred to have their searches processed by a trained specialist. This finding supports the experience of Buchanan and Kidd (1969) at the Nuclear Safety Information Center.

Experience with AUDACIOUS

The report on AUDACIOUS by Freeman and Atherton (1968) contains some observations on the use of the experimental system by about fifty people. Most users perceived the system to be difficult to use because of inadequate training, lack of diagnostic feedback when an error was made, and the inability to request instruction in the use of a particular command without going through the full set of instructions. Parenthetically it is worth noting that several on-line systems, including ORBIT, do provide some diagnostic feedback and do provide instructions in the use of any selected command.

AUDACIOUS, which was operating on a dedicated IBM 7044, usually gave highly satisfactory response times on the order of 10 seconds or less. In those cases where greater response times were observed, however, Freeman and Atherton confirm the findings of other observers—that user tolerance to response times greater than, say, 15–20 seconds is quite low. Tolerance is particularly low when the system, as in the case of AUDACIOUS, does not acknowledge that a command has been received and that processing is underway. System inflexibility with respect to variations in spelling (e.g., anti-neutron versus antineutron), as well as inconsistency in use of singular or plural forms, was another source of irritation to the searcher.

Further dissatisfaction was expressed with the characteristics of the terminal used (a Raytheon DIDS-400 unit), which, because it did not have reserved function keys for the various commands, required the searcher to type these out in full wherever they were needed.

Experience with COLEX

COLEX was an intelligence retrieval system designed and operated by the System Development Corporation for the Air Force Systems Command. Extensive use of the system was reported in 1967 and 1968. During the entire contract period that COLEX was operating, statistics were collected on-line for every retrieval request made by every individual user at each of the 13 stations (Smith, et al., 1968). Some examples of the type of data collected and reported are shown in Tables 9.12 and 9.13. These data are presented merely as an illustration of the types of statistics collected routinely by one particular on-line system. They are drawn from the operating period, February 26–June 30, 1968, at which time the data base comprised 217,822 references. The following data were collected on-line and are summarized in Table 9.12: number of searches, type of request by element searched (descriptor, author, country code, subject code), additional elements used to qualify searches, total output, output on-line and off-line, total searching time, and number of searches undertaken solely for demonstration purposes. From these data it is obviously possible to calculate system averages (Table 9.13) for number of searches per day, daily output, output per request, and searching times.

Experience with SPIRES

Although the SPIRES project has generated a considerable amount of design literature, not much operating experience has actually been published. One report by Addis (1970) records some experiences with SPIRES at the Stanford Linear Accelerator Center in the period April–May 1969. Experimental searches were conducted by or for physicists on a preprint collection (*Preprints in Particles and Fields*). It was observed that participating scientists universally admired the fast search response times of SPIRES, but the slow printout at the terminal was found to be extremely annoying. The desire was expressed for the use of CRT devices to permit rapid browsing, selection of pertinent items, and *saving* of these items to form a personal file. Off-line searching and printing capabilities were requested. Once the user establishes his search strategy, he does not want to wait at the terminal for a printout; he prefers to collect it later or to have it mailed to him.

SUPARS Evaluation

SUPARS (see Chapter Five) was made available for on-line interrogation by faculty and students at Syracuse University during an 11 week period in 1970. Use of the system was monitored via registration forms, an on-line data gathering program, a telephone aid service, personal interviews (see

TABLE 9.12. COLEX Use Figures for 5 Month Period

Request type	Number of requests	Requests qualified	Qualified by country	Qualified by document type	Qualified by subject area	Qualified by date	Qualified by classification
Descriptor	2,075	1,045	760	81	227	142	154
Author	530	88	32	5	25	33	6
Country code	205	150	6	11	116	13	9
Subject code	196	146	25	70	15	13	57
All modes	3,006	1,429	823	167	383	201	227

Request type	Output on-line	Output off-line	Total output	Total time (minutes)	Demonstration requests	Demonstration time (minutes)
Descriptor	8,366	70,940	79,306	17,041	175	1,937
Author	1,827	3,717	5,544	3,847	28	226
Country code	603	7,280	7,883	1,205	35	285
Subject code	204	8,348	8,552	1,270	22	219
All modes	11,000	90,285	101,285	23,363	260	2,667

SOURCE: Smith, et al. (1968). Reprinted by permission of Rome Air Development Center and the System Development Corporation.

TABLE 9.13. COLEX System Averages for 5 Month Period

Request type	Requests per day	Qualified requests	On-line output daily	Off-line output daily	Total output daily	Total output per request	Minutes per request	Demonstrations per day	Demonstration time daily (minutes)
Descriptor	28.0	14.1	113	959	1,072	41.1	8.2	2.3	26
Author	7.2	1.2	25	50	75	10.4	7.2	0.4	3
Country code	2.8	2.0	8	98	106	37.9	5.8	0.5	4
Subject code	2.7	1.9	3	113	116	42.9	6.5	0.3	3
All modes	40.6	19.2	149	1,220	1,369	33.7	7.7	3.5	36

SOURCE: Smith, et al. (1968). Reprinted by permission of Rome Air Development Center and the System Development Corporation.

Appendix A for interview guide), and a semantic differential (Cook, et al., 1971). The semantic differential has been described in detail by Katzer (1972).

Approximately 5539 searches were conducted in the experimental period, 1151 by members of the project staff and 4388 by other faculty and students of the university. The telephone aid service received 551 calls for help during the 11 weeks, of which 161 represented user problems. A user problem was defined as a problem originating with the user rather than with the programs or the equipment. Examples are: help needed in structuring a search strategy; explanation of an error message; help needed in logging-in to the system. Over 200 of the 551 calls pertained to system malfunctioning of one kind or another.

Unfortunately, although the SUPARS study was reported in great detail in six volumes, most of the data presented are purely quantitative, relating to volume of usage, CPU time, and distribution of usage. The project reports shed little light on searching problems, user attitudes, and factors affecting the success or failure of searches in the system. Only a very small number of interviews with actual users of SUPARS were conducted, and the semantic differential was administered only to this small user group. However, a comprehensive cost study was conducted (see Chapter Eighteen).

A further, more extensive series of SUPARS experiments was conducted in 1971–1972, as reported by Atherton, et al., (1972), and reaction to the system was evaluated by 63 telephone interviews administered to random samples of users and nonusers, the semantic differential (this time completed by 44 users), and an analysis of requests for help made through the telephone aid service.

Experience with Intrex

Some preliminary findings on user experiences with the Intrex on-line catalog were reported by Marcus, et al. (1969). In general, it was found that users learned to operate the basic features of the system fairly easily and were reasonably successful in the conduct of relatively simple, straightforward searches. With limited exposure to the system, most users were unable to take advantage of its more sophisticated features. Users without previous computer experience tended to be overawed by the system, which inhibited their learning. Command names that are not single English words (e.g., MATCHSUB, INFIELD) were disliked by users and were found to be confusing to them. The investigators suggest that users should be introduced to an on-line system in stages, beginning with the use of simplified guides or personalized instruction. User experience with the text-access system is reported in Chapter Sixteen.

TABLE 9.14. Evaluation Results from 47 Searches on EARS

Search number	Recall requirement	Number of abstracts retrieved	Value	Precision	Major precision	Recall	Major recall
1	All	7	Considerable	5/7 = 71.4	4/7 = 57.1	5/55 = 9.1	4/34 = 11.8
2	Few	1	Major	1/1 = 100	1/1 = 100	1/4 = 25.0	1/3 = 33.3
3	Few	1	Minor	1/1 = 100	0/1 = 0	1/70 = 1.4	1/60 = 1.7
4	All	7	Minor	4/7 = 57.1	2/7 = 28.6	4/24 = 16.7	2/11 = 18.2
5	Few	11	None	3/9 = 33.3		3/3 = 100	
6	All	21	Considerable	16/21 = 76.2	9/21 = 42.9	16/24 = 66.7	9/11 = 81.8
7	All	16	Minor	2/16 = 12.5	1/16 = 6.25	2/6 = 33.3	1/4 = 25.0
8	All	36	Minor	6/36 = 16.7	0/36 = 0	6/196 = 3.1	0/150 = 0
9	All	4	None	1/4 = 25.0	1/4 = 25.0	1/74 = 1.4	1/51 = 2.0
10	Few	8	Considerable	4/8 = 50.0	2/8 = 25.0	4/9 = 44.4	2/3 = 66.7
11	All	32	Considerable	20/32 = 62.5	20/32 = 62.5	20/20 = 100	20/20 = 100
12	Few	5	Considerable	4/5 = 80.0	3/5 = 60.0	4/4 = 100	3/3 = 100
13	All	7	Considerable	7/7 = 100	7/7 = 100	7/31 = 22.6	7/21 = 33.3
14	All	3	None	2/3 = 66.7	2/3 = 66.7	2/3 = 66.7	2/3 = 66.7
15	All	137	Major	123/137 = 89.8	104/137 = 75.9	123/263 = 46.8	104/184 = 56.5
16	Few	4	None	0/4 = 0	0/4 = 0	0/0	0/0
17	Few	24	Major	6/24 = 25.0	2/24 = 8.3	6/6 = 100	2/2 = 100
18	Few	96	Minor	4/13 = 30.8	2/13 = 15.4	30/32 = 93.7	2/2 = 100
19	Few	7	Considerable	5/7 = 71.4	0.7 = 0	5/85 = 5.9	0/28 = 0
20	All	44	Major	40/44 = 90.9	20/44 = 45.4	40/40 = 100	20/20 = 100
21	All	2	Major	1/2 = 50.0	0/2 = 0	1/2 = 50.0	1/2 = 50.0

22	All	Considerable	76/89 = 85.4	28/89 = 31.5	76/76 = 100	28/28 = 100
23	All	Minor	7/8 = 87.5	2/8 = 25.0	7/37 = 18.9	2/10 = 20.0
24	All	Major	2/4 = 50.0	2/4 = 50.0	2/4 = 50.0	2/4 = 50.0
25	All	Considerable	3/22 = 13.6	3/22 = 13.6	3/3 = 100	3/3 = 100
26	All	Major	1/1 = 100	1/1 = 100	1/3 = 33.3	1/3 = 33.3
27	All	Major	0/1 = 0	0/1 = 0	0/0	0/0
28	All	Considerable	10/79 = 12.5	10/79 = 12.7	10/70 = 14.3	10/40 = 25.0
29	All	Major	9/11 = 81.8	7/11 = 63.6	9/9 = 100	7/7 = 100
30	All	Major	13/13 = 100	13/13 = 100	13/42 = 30.9	13/22 = 59.1
31	All	Minor	2/2 = 100	1/2 = 50.0	2/15 = 13.3	1/13 = 7.7
32	All	Minor	3/6 = 50.0	0/6 = 0	3/6 = 50.0	0/0
33	All	Major	16/16 = 100	15/16 = 93.7	16/17 = 94.1	16/16 = 100
34	All	Considerable	10/157 = 6.4	4/157 = 2.5	10/10 = 100	4/4 = 100
35	All	Minor	70/157 = 44.6	40/157 = 25.5	70/70 = 100	40/40 = 100
36	All	Minor	58/113 = 51.3	38/113 = 33.6	58/58 = 100	38/38 = 100
37	All	Considerable	13/108 = 12.0	10/108 = 9.3	13/13 = 100	10/10 = 100
38	All	Considerable	20/20 = 100	17/20 = 85.0	20/20 = 100	17/17 = 100
39	All	Minor	3/3 = 100	3/3 = 100	3/5 = 60.0	3/5 = 60.0
40	All	Minor	150/155 = 96.8	121/155 = 78.1	150/162 = 92.6	121/130 = 93.1
41	All	Minor	59/59 = 100	59/113 = 52.2	59/113 = 52.2	
42	All	Considerable	40/40 = 100	28/40 = 70.0	40/44 = 90.9	28/28 = 100
43	All	Minor	90/90 = 100	72/90 = 80.0	90/125 = 72.0	72/74 = 97.3
44	All	Minor	5/6 = 83.3	4/6 = 66.7	5/30 = 16.7	4/19 = 21.0
45	All	Considerable	3/3 = 100	3/3 = 100	3/30 = 10.0	3/15 = 20.0
46	All	None	3/3 = 100	2/3 = 66.7	3/6 = 50.0	3/6 = 50.0
47	All	Major	17/27 = 62.9	12/27 = 44.4	17/36 = 47.2	12/23 = 52.2

Evaluation of EARS

The procedures used in the evaluation of EARS (Lancaster, et al., 1972) were described in Chapter Eight. In all, 47 searches were completed under test conditions. These searches represent sixteen different users at six separate centers. The results are presented in Table 9.14. For each search, the following data are given:

1. The recall requirement of the searcher (whether he wanted all relevant items or only a few).
2. The total number of abstracts retrieved.
3. The user's subjective assessment of the value of the search to him, on the scale: major value, considerable value, minor value, no value.
4. The precision ratio (the number of relevant items retrieved over the total number of items retrieved).
5. The major value precision ratio (the number of items judged of major value over the total number of items retrieved).
6. The estimated recall ratio, based upon the conduct of one or more parallel searches.
7. The estimated recall ratio for major value items.

The user's own judgments of the value of the searches conducted in EARS are summarized below:

Major value	12	(25.6%)
Considerable value	15	(31.9%)
Minor value	15	(31.9%)
No value	5	(10.6%)
	47	

On purely subjective grounds, the test searches appear to have met with reasonable success. Almost 60% were judged to be of major or considerable value, and only 10% were judged of no value. Moreover, some of the *no value* judgments reflect inadequacies of the data base, or possibly the paucity of relevant literature, rather than searching failures. Search 16, for example, was judged of no value because nothing of relevance was retrieved. However, nothing of relevance exists in the data base on the subject of the search (aniline dye toxicity).

Figure 9.2 is a scatter diagram of recall and precision points for each of the 45 test searches that produced positive recall and precision results (the two searches that are without a positive recall figure—because, as far as we know, there are no relevant items in the data base—are omitted). This scatter diagram shows the typical wide distribution that we have come to expect in a study of this kind. There is a cluster of remarkably good searches in the top right of the diagram (high recall and high precision) and a few really bad

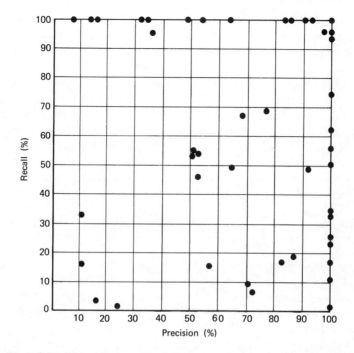

Figure 9.2.   Scatter diagram of individual search results from EARS study.

results (both recall and precision low) in the bottom left-hand corner. There are many typical high-precision, low-recall results and some high-recall, low-precision results, with a handful of completely middle-of-the-road results, clustering near the 50% recall and 50% precision point.

Ideally we would like to see all the results falling in the top right-hand corner of the scatter diagram. Although we are never likely to reach this ideal, we may be able to more nearly approach it if we can identify the characteristics of the successful and unsuccessful searches. In other words, what makes a *good* search good and what makes a *bad* search bad? In particular, what are the major factors contributing to recall and precision failures in the system? A considerable amount of this failure analysis was conducted, and the results are summarized below.

The precision ratios achieved in the 47 test searches range all the way from 0 to 100%, with the overall average (arithmetic mean) being 64.8% and the average precision ratio considering only items of major value being 44.9%. Put in a different way, on the average 64.8% of the documents retrieved in these searches were judged to be relevant and 44.9% were judged to be of major relevance. This may be regarded as a very satisfactory result, especially for a natural language system based on complete abstracts, in which there are several factors that might contribute to a low precision. The average precision of 64.8% in this group of searches is remarkably close to the average precision (63.1%) achieved over the searches conducted by biomedical practitioners in the AIM–TWX system.

Precision was 100% in 14 of the 47 searches, and it was zero in 2 of them. An analysis was conducted of the causes of precision failures (i.e., cases in which irrelevant items were retrieved) in the 33 searches that produced less than maximum precision. A total of 570 failures were examined and accounted for in the analysis. The results are presented in Table 9.15.

TABLE 9.15.   Causes of Precision Failures in 33 EARS Searches

	Number of failures	Number of searches involved
Indexing		
Exhaustive indexing	47	14
Vocabulary		
False coordination	89	10
Incorrect term relationship	12	7
Textual ambiguity	6	1
Search strategy		
Strategy not exhaustive	261	15
Strategy not specific	13	2
Illogical boolean construction	147	1
Other causes		
Inexplicable	5	4

In reviewing this table, it is necessary to examine both columns of figures —the number of failures contributed by each factor and the number of searches affected by each. By so doing it is possible to distinguish the most prevalent causes of precision failure from those that are most drastic, in terms of the amount of irrelevancy they will cause in a particular search, but less widespread. It can be seen that false coordinations are quite prevalent, in that they affected 16 searches, but caused comparatively few failures in any one search (with one exception which we will return to later). Incorrect term relationships and exhaustive indexing are other categories that affect several searches but do not cause a very large number of failures in any one. On the other hand, nonexhaustive search strategies affect many searches and cause a considerable number of precision failures in several of them, while the category "Illogical boolean construction" affected only a single search, but caused no less than 147 irrelevant items to be retrieved in this search.

It is worth examining each of these causes of precision failure in more detail and to consider the significance of each on the overall performance of EARS.

A precision failure is attributed to exhaustive indexing when the article in question makes some reference to the topic that is the subject of the search, but the reference is very slight or tangential and the searcher does not consider the article really relevant to his request. In EARS, this will mainly be caused by a slight or tangential reference in an abstract. Occasionally, however, the *exhaustive indexing* failure is caused, or contributed to, by the index terms assigned to the document.

Some failures of this type are likely to occur in any system in which the indexing is fairly exhaustive. The EARS indexing is exhaustive—all the substantive words of the abstract are available, in addition to the index terms assigned by Excerpta Medica indexers (and there are a dozen or more of these for some of the abstracts). Nevertheless, this factor is not really a major source of precision failure in the system, and is probably within tolerable limits. Precision failures caused by exhaustive abstracts can be avoided by demanding a minimum occurrence of a particular word or word-string in an abstract. For example, we could specify that an abstract be retrieved if it contains the string TEMPORAL LOBE and either GENETIC or HEREDI-TARY, but only if each concept appears in the text at least twice. This would tend to eliminate some failures of the *passing reference* type. However, use of this technique will definitely tend to reduce recall, and it should only be used in searches in which high precision is preferred to high recall. A variant on this technique would be to demand that at least one of the search facets should be represented in the *title* of the paper. Either of these techniques will tend to improve precision, at the expense of recall, and they provide some additional flexibility for the searcher in designing a strategy for high recall or for high precision. However, such techniques do introduce increasing complexity into the searching procedures.

False coordinations affected precision in 16 searches, but caused a substantial number of failures in only one. A false coordination is a failure caused by the fact that the words that allowed a document to be retrieved, while present in the document record, are essentially unrelated. An example occurred in a search on serum levels of methylphenobarbital. In one of the retrieved abstracts, the term SERUM LEVELS refers to amino acids, whereas the term METHYLPHENOBARBITAL refers to a therapeutic program and is not directly related to the concept of serum levels. This is a typical false coordination, a failure that tends to be extremely prevalent in natural language searching systems. The mechanism for reducing failures of this type already exists in EARS—use of word distance requirements. This abstract would have been avoided, for example, if the searcher had specified that SERUM and METHYLPHENOBARBITAL must be no more than ten words apart. Such positional requirements will reduce, although not fully eliminate, false coordinations. Frequently, however, the use of a word distance requirement will also reduce recall.

Only one search was very badly affected by false coordinations. This was search 36, which dealt with the use of primidone in association with phenytoin, dilantin, or phenobarbital. When we search on a combination such as PRIMIDONE *and* PHENOBARBITAL, we will probably retrieve some items that describe the joint use of the two drugs. The majority, however, will probably discuss their *separate* use, which is not the subject wanted in this case. This search retrieved 113 abstracts, but only 58 were relevant (51% precision). False coordinations will always mar searches of this kind; that is, searches seeking papers on the joint use of two or more drugs. They are impossible to avoid in EARS as it presently exists. Word distance requirements are unlikely to solve the problem. Nor will the use of index terms alone (without the abstracts) improve the situation in this system, because Excerpta Medica indexers appear routinely to index all drugs mentioned in an abstract, however slight the reference, and the indexing statements in *Epilepsy Abstracts* do not distinguish joint use from separate use.

False coordinations may also be bothersome in searches correlating two or more pathological conditions. For example, search 40 seeks articles on epilepsy associated with encephalitis. Some of the retrieved items discuss such subjects as diagnosis of brain tumors, and the mention of encephalitis is entirely unrelated to the mention of epilepsy.

A failure due to an incorrect term relationship is very similar to a failure due to a false coordination. In this case, however, the words causing retrieval are related, but not in the way that the searcher wants them to be related. For example, a search on reading epilepsy retrieved some abstracts on the effect of epilepsy on children learning to read and write. Here, the word READING and the word EPILEPSY are definitely related in the abstract, but not in the way that the user wants. This is not a false coordination, then, but an incorrect term relationship. Incorrect term relationships can usually be avoided by the use of word distance criteria, and probably with comparatively little effect on recall.

The final type of vocabulary failure we have labeled *textual ambiguity*. This type of failure is peculiar to free text searching systems and is caused by the fact that a particular character-string may have many meanings, or many functions, in English text. It is remarkable that ambiguities of this type really only affected one search, number 18, dealing with the effects of environmental stress on the frequency of seizures. The word STRESS caused retrieval of a number of irrelevant abstracts containing such constructions as "Stress is laid on. . . ."

Somewhat similar failures occurred in search 11, on reading epilepsy, in which the root READ***† caused retrieval of several items containing the word "readily." These failures are due, however, to unnecessary word truncation (READING will retrieve everything on reading epilepsy) and were categorized as searching failures of the *strategy not specific* type. Most searchers in this study used the most specific words available, and truncation was used rarely, and so failures due to nonspecific strategies were insignificant in the test searches.

On the other hand, precision failures due to *nonexhaustive* strategies were extremely prevalent in the study. This was the most serious cause of precision failure encountered, not only because it affected many searches, but because it affected some searches in a very drastic way. In one search, 95 irrelevant items were retrieved because of a nonexhaustive strategy, and in another, 87 irrelevant items were·retrieved for the same reason. A strategy is considered nonexhaustive if it fails to require all the facets of the subject matter for which the search is being conducted. A good example is found in search 12, which relates to the joint use of sulthiame and diphenylhydantoin in the treatment of grand mal or temporal lobe seizures. This topic has three facets: (*a*) the sulthiame facet, (*b*) the diphenylhydantoin facet, and (*c*) the specific seizure facet of interest. However, the searcher asked only for the co-occurrence of the two drug terms (and their synonyms) and omitted the requirement for grand mal or temporal lobe. A typical irrelevant item discusses the determination of one of these drugs in the serum in the presence of the other drug.

In this particular search, lack of exhaustivity had a small effect on overall precision. In search 17, however, dealing with secondary bilateral synchrony in seizures of the cingulate gyrus, precision was only 25%, because the searcher asked for the term CINGULATE GYRUS and the term BILATERAL SYNCHRONY in an *or* rather than an *and* relationship. Another example occurred in search 7, in which the searcher was seeking papers on clinical trials of psychoactive drugs in children who are hyperactive or who have learning disorders. He searched only on HYPERKINESIS or LEARNING DISORDERS, omitting the facet of children and the facet of psychoactive drugs. Clearly, few of the abstracts containing these terms will be relevant to the specific topic of the search. In actual fact, 16 were retrieved, but only 2 were judged relevant, a precision ratio of 12.5%.

Broadening a search by the use of a nonexhaustive strategy is a legitimate technique for improving recall in certain situations. However, some of the searchers participating in this study are likely to have fallen into the trap of

---

†In the Data Central system, the asterisk is a *universal character* device. The searcher uses an asterisk when he does not care what character appears in that particular position. In the above case, for example, we will accept any words, of not more than seven letters, beginning with the string READ.

nonexhaustive strategies through lack of familiarity with the principles of boolean searching. This reflects a defect in their training rather than a defect in EARS as a searching system.

In some cases, the nonexhaustive strategy reflects an improper use of the system. For example, search 35 was for articles on primidone intoxication. This was searched on the single term PRIMIDONE. Clearly, a single-term search of this nature is almost certain to lead to considerable irrelevancy. This search retrieved 87 items dealing with primidone, rather than primidone intoxication, although it still produced a precision of 44%. Most single-term searches will, in any case, be inappropriate for handling by EARS, which, like all machine-based systems, should be used for the coordination of two or more concepts. Everything found by the search on PRIMIDONE could equally well be found under PRIMIDONE in the indexes to *Epilepsy Abstracts*, because, as mentioned previously, indexing of drugs appears to be very complete in the publication.

An obvious logical error occurred in search 34, on metabolism or destruction of primidone. The strategy appeared as follows:

PRIMIDONE OR MYSOLINE METABOLISM

which factors into (primidone) or (mysoline metabolism) rather than the required logical construction of (primidone or mysoline) and (metabolism). The result of this illogical strategy was the retrieval of all abstracts containing the word PRIMIDONE, 157 of them, most of which will obviously not be relevant to the subject of primidone metabolism. The precision ratio was actually 10/157 (6.4%) in this search. Again, logical errors of this type are due to lack of knowledge of the construction of search strategies, in a correct boolean form, rather than any inherent defects in EARS itself.

The recall ratio of each of the test searches was estimated on the basis of a second, parallel search conducted at the National Institute of Neurological Diseases and Stroke (NINDS). In some cases this parallel search was supplemented by a second search conducted in the printed *Epilepsy Abstracts*. The result is a comparative recall estimate rather than an absolute recall ratio. In other words, although the broadest possible approaches were used in the parallel searches, this does not necessarily guarantee retrieval of everything of relevance in the EARS base. The assumption here is that A + B = 100, where A represents the relevant abstracts found by the original searcher and B represents the *additional* relevant abstracts found in the second search. This is the best possible recall estimate that can be made under the circumstances, but it may be slightly inflated in some searches due to the fact that some relevant abstracts may exist in the data base that were found neither by the original nor the parallel search. All the recall estimates must be regarded as representing an upper bound on recall; the recall in search 2 could not be *more* than 25%, in 10 it could not be *more* than 44%, and so on.

The recall estimates for the 47 test searches range from a high of 100% achieved in 13 searches, to a low of 1.4% achieved in 2 cases. The overall average recall for the group is 57.4%, while the average recall on those documents judged of major relevance was only slightly higher, at 60.4%. Excluded from these averages are 2 searches, numbers 16 and 27, in which no relevant items were found by either the original or the parallel search (that is, the recall figure for these two is 0/0), and therefore none is presumed to exist in the EARS data base. It is probably best to treat these as special cases and eliminate them from the recall calculations.

A reexamination of Table 9.14 will reveal that in no less than 38 of the 47 searches (80%) the EARS user indicated that he was looking for all relevant references (i.e., high recall) rather than a selection only. It is clear that high recall is important to many EARS users and that means to raise the average recall for a search above the 60% mark (which, in any case, is a maximum figure) should be investigated.

Most of the recall failures known to have occurred in 32 test searches were examined in this study—a total of 826 in all. The reasons for these failures were investigated, and the results are presented in Table 9.16. As

TABLE 9.16.   Causes of Recall Failures in 32 EARS Searches

	Number of failures	Number of searches involved
Searching		
Failure to cover all approaches to retrieval	740	29
Strategy too specific	75	5
Strategy too exhaustive	7	1
Other causes		
Unexplained system failure	3	1
Indexing not exhaustive	1	1

explained earlier, because EARS is a natural language system capable of being operated in a nondelegated search mode, we can expect no recall failures due to vocabulary inadequacies, few, if any, due to indexing failures because of the exhaustive, redundant "indexing" of the abstract), and none due to the delegation of the search to someone else (i.e., failures attributed to *interaction*). This is exactly the picture exhibited by EARS. Only one of the failures could be attributed to nonexhaustive indexing (the abstract of a paper dealing with experimental surgery in animals fails to mention any of the animals used), and one was due to an unexplained system failure.

All the other recall failures must be attributed to inadequacies in the search process itself, the overwhelming reason being the failure of the searcher to think of all possible approaches to retrieval. In other words, the more experienced NINDS searcher was able to think of alternative terms and term combinations and was thus able to improve recall considerably.

Some examples will illustrate the situation:

Search 2.   This relates to levels of zarontin and tridione in the blood and was searched simply on BLOOD LEVEL *and* ZARONTIN *or* TRIDIONE. The searcher did not use synonyms for drug names (ETHOSUXIMIDE and TRIMETHADIONE) and did not realize that blood level might be represented in a relevant abstract in other ways. A reasonably complete strategy would involve at least the following:

ZARONTIN				
TRIDIONE	*and*	BLOOD	*and*	LEVEL
ETHOSUXIMIDE		SERUM		CONCENTRATION
TRIMETHADIONE				

where the terms in each block are logical alternatives (i.e., they appear in an OR relationship). The recall estimate for the original search was a low 25%.

Search 23.   The recall estimate here was only 19%. The topic is hereditary factors associated with acquired epilepsy. Although there are other factors involved in the low recall of this search, the searcher's inability to think of all approaches is again a major contributor. The aspect of "hereditary factors" was expressed only by the terms GENETIC, GENETICS, and INHERITED. A high recall requires the use of at least the additional words CONGENITAL, HEREDITY, HEREDITARY, and INHERITANCE.

Search 31.   The subject here is corpus callosum sections in surgery for epilepsy, and the search was conducted solely on the combination

CORPUS CALLOSUM   *and*   SURGERY
COMMISUROTOMY

Because COMMISUROTOMY is misspelled (it should be COMMISSURO-TOMY), and thus rejected, the search is reduced to the combination COR-PUS CALLOSUM *and* SURGERY, which is completely inadequate for a comprehensive search on this topic. The recall estimate for the search is only 2/15, 13%. An examination of the thirteen relevant abstracts that were missed reveals that corpus callosum surgery is variously indicated in the forms: "corpus callosum section," "section of the corpus callosum," "sectioning of the corpus callosum," "removed surgically," "callosal transection," "transection of the . . . ," and "callotomy." To achieve high recall in this search, the user would need to add to his strategy the terms SECTION, SECTIONING, SURGICALLY, TRANSECTION, and CALLOTOMY.

Search 45.   This is somewhat similar to search 31. It relates to amygdalectomy or amygdalotomy in temporal lobe seizures, and was searched under TEMPORAL LOBE *and* AMYGDALECTOMY or AMYGDALOTOMY. Clearly, there are other ways in which the topic could be expressed (e.g., removal of the amygdala, surgery of the amygdala) and a comprehensive search would also need to coordinate the root AMYGDAL with TEMPORAL LOBE and with a full list of surgery terms, including RESECTION, EXCISION, SURGERY, OPERATION, and STEREOTAXIC.

Search 47.   The subject matter here is hereditary or genetic aspects of temporal lobe epilepsy, which was searched very simply on

> TEMPORAL LOBE   *and*   GENETICS
> HEREDITY

and achieved an estimated recall of about 47%. A comprehensive search requires at least the following:

> TEMPORAL LOBE   *and*   GENETIC
> PSYCHOMOTOR   HEREDIT****
> INHERIT****

This is a sample only of the recall failures of this type. This source of failure affected the great majority of the searches in which recall is known to be less than maximum. It is partly due to lack of experience and training on the part of the searcher, but, probably more importantly, to the fact that no searching aids exist in the system—the searcher is left entirely to his own devices. This makes comprehensive searching particularly difficult for the inexperienced user.

The other recall failures due to searching were attributed to overexhaustive or overspecific strategies. In search 3, the strategy was too exhaustive. The topic is correlation of toxic reaction to dose of dilantin, and the search was conducted on DILANTIN *and* TOXIC *and* DOSE. The use of DOSE is unrewarding, because very few of the relevant abstracts contain the word "dose," even when dosage is specifically discussed.

Examples of lack of specificity in searching occurred in search 13 ("chronically isolated cortex" was used when anything on the isolated cortex was of interest), search 23 (hereditary factors associated with acquired epilepsy; the word ACQUIRED was required by the searcher, but few articles on "acquired epilepsy" actually contain this word), and search 39 ("paroxysmal depolarization shift" should have been generalized to PAROXYSMAL DEPOLAR******* or simply to DEPOLAR******* SHIFT).

Such failures due to overspecificity or overexhaustivity may be regarded as merely variants of the category *failure to cover all possible approaches.*

A very important requirement of any retrieval system is that it should not require an undue amount of effort to use. If it becomes too bothersome to use the system, people will not do so and will turn to alternative sources (Mooers' Law). One measure of effort (a good one) is how long it takes to conduct a search.

The major factors affecting unit cost (in time), and therefore search efficiency, are:

1.   How quickly the searcher hits upon a productive combination of search terms.

2.   How much trouble he has with the system commands and protocols. This second, in particular, is a considerable problem in EARS. Although a fully experienced searcher at NINDS (aided perhaps by more sophisticated terminal devices) can use the system fluently, many of the users in this EARS study had considerable difficulties with the system. Much time was wasted by many searchers, and their patience was sorely tried.

The system, like many others designed for bibliographic searching, requires virtual perfection of entry. It is extremely sensitive to simple errors of punctuation, spelling, and spacing. Error messages are not explicit in places and do not give the searcher much assistance in identifying his error and correcting it. Moreover, a term recognized as invalid by the system (because it does not occur in the data base) is not deleted, but is allowed to propagate throughout the search. These characteristics, fairly common in on-line searching systems in general, reduce considerably the tolerance of the searcher, as well as adding appreciably to searching time and costs. It is all too easy for the inexperienced user to become frustrated. And the once-frustrated user tends not to return to the system.

Summary

In analyzing the experience summarized in the preceding pages, scant though it is, a common pattern appears to emerge, and a number of general observations can be made by way of an overall summary:

1.   The scientific and technical community has in general responded extremely enthusiastically to the availability of on-line systems for bibliographic search.

2.   Trained searchers appreciate the feedback provided, the ability to browse, and the heuristic possibilities that these systems offer.

On-line systems are very useful in developing and testing a search strategy that will later be applied to a more complete data base in off-line mode.

3. The typical practitioner in a scientific field can learn fairly easily how to operate the basic features of an on-line system, and can conduct fairly simple searches with reasonable success. The necessary familiarity can apparently be achieved after about 20–30 minutes of instruction in how to use the terminal and an additional 30 minutes or so of actually operating the system. This level of exposure—up to, say, 2 hours—will not allow the user to take full advantage of the more sophisticated features of the on-line retrieval system, and the results achieved by such a user may not be as satisfactory as the results achieved by an information specialist searching on his behalf. Generally speaking, more difficulties are encountered in training users in the searching principles than in the mechanics of using the terminal or the command language of the system.

4. Not all seekers of information want to conduct their own searches. Some still prefer to delegate to an information specialist. There is some evidence that the best on-line results are achieved by a trained searcher operating with the requester at his shoulder.

5. On-line systems appear to satisfy a definite need. They attract new users into an information center and new types of requests. An on-line system, unlike a batch system, is suitable for the user who needs a few relevant papers (low-recall, high-precision requirement) and needs them immediately. The type of search conducted on-line, because of the fairly complex conceptual relationships involved, is usually unsuitable for handling by conventional printed indexes. On-line systems in libraries or information centers have attracted into the center requesters who previously made no use of the facilities available. In some cases, the introduction of a terminal has attracted new users to other facets of the services of the library and to the other bibliographic tools that are available.

6. The typical search at an on-line terminal will take about 10–20 minutes to complete.

7. In terms of unit cost (in time) per relevant citation retrieved, on-line searching has been found to be extremely efficient in the majority of cases. The unit cost for a typical search can be somewhere in the range of 1.5–4.5 minutes per relevant citation retrieved. For 30% of the searches in the AIM–TWX study, the unit cost was 2 minutes or less.

8. Users are generally impressed with the speed of response of an on-line system, but are frequen'ly dissatisfied with slow printout speeds at on-line typewriter terminals. Users become accustomed to rapid interaction and will tend to become impatient if forced to wait more than a very few seconds for a system response.

9. There is certain evidence of repeated usage of on-line systems by individual requesters.

10. Although a requester, using an on-line system to satisfy his own need, will be enthusiastic about its interactive and browsing capabilities, there is evidence to suggest that such users do not exploit the interactive capabilities of the system to very good advantage.

11. The major causes of searching failures in on-line systems operated by the practitioners of a scientific field appear to be (*a*) the searcher's failure to cover all possible approaches to retrieval—this is particularly significant in natural language systems, but also occurs in controlled vocabulary systems; (*b*) lack of a close coincidence between the language of the searcher and the language of the system (controlled vocabulary). These factors point to the need for on-line systems to incorporate more aids for the searcher at the terminal. Such aids would include more complete entry vocabularies for controlled vocabulary systems and searching thesauri, or at least synonym tables, for natural language systems.

12. Improved procedures for training users need to be developed. User manuals tend to be useful as reference tools, but not very effective as training devices. Hands-on experience is obviously most valuable. Personal instruction, by a trained searcher, is effective but costly. More use should be made of instruction at the terminal itself, perhaps through computer-aided instruction techniques.

13. There is conflicting evidence relating to fatigue of searchers at an on-line terminal. In some intelligence and surveillance operations, analysts spend their entire working day at a CRT display without unusual fatigue or eyestrain.

14. Most on-line searching systems are frustrating to the inexperienced user because they require virtual perfection of entry. Spelling, punctuation, and spacing must usually be perfectly correct, or the input will be rejected. Dissatisfaction with error messages is widely expressed. A user needs to know more than that an error has occurred. He needs to know the exact nature of the error and how it may be corrected. On-line retrieval systems should be made less sensitive to simple errors, and any errors that do occur should be well explicated by the system.

REFERENCES

Addis, L. (1970). "Stanford Linear Accelerator Center Participation in SPIRES." *In System Scope for Library Automation and Generalized Information Storage and Retrieval at Stanford University.* Stanford, Ca.: Stanford University, pp. 122–134.

Atherton, P., K. H. Cook, and J. Katzer (1972). *Free Text Retrieval Evaluation.* Syracuse, N.Y.: Syracuse University, School of Library Science.

Blase, N. G., and C. J. Stock (1972). "An Experimental Cancer Information Service Using AIM–TWX." *Bull. Medical Library Assoc.* **60** (1), 115–120.

Bridegam, W. E., Jr., and E. Meyerhoff (1970). "Library Participation in a Biomedical Communication and Information Network." *Bull. Medical Library Assoc.* **58** (2), 103–111.

Buchanan, J. R., and E. M. Kidd (1969). "Development of a Computer System with Console Capability for the Nuclear Safety Information Center." *Proc. Amer. Soc. Information Sci.* **6**, 151–158.

Caruso, D. E. (1971). "Interactive Retrieval Systems." *In* E. M. Arnett, *A Chemical Information Center Experimental Station.* Pittsburgh, Pa.: University of Pittsburgh, Department of Chemistry, pp. 188–207.

Cook, K. H., L. H. Trump, P. Atherton, and J. Katzer (1971). *Large Scale Information Processing Systems.* Final Report to the Rome Air Development Center. Syracuse, N.Y.: Syracuse University, School of Library Science, 6 vols.

Cottrell, W. B., and J. R. Buchanan (1971). *NSIC Computerized Information Techniques.* Oak Ridge, Tenn.: Nuclear Safety Information Center, ORNL-NSIC-92.

Cuadra, C. A. (1971). "On-Line Systems: Promise and Pitfalls." *Jour. Amer. Soc. Information Sci.* **22** (2), 107–114.

Egeland, J. (1971). "User-Interaction in the State University of New York (SUNY) Biomedical Communication Network." *In* D. E. Walker (ed.), *Interactive Bibliographic Search: The User/Computer Interface.* Montvale, N.J.: AFIPS Press, pp. 105–120.

Freeman, R. R., and P. Atherton (1968). *AUDACIOUS—an Experiment with an On-Line, Interactive Reference Retrieval System Using the Universal Decimal Classification as the Index Language in the Field of Nuclear Science.* New York: American Institute of Physics, AIP/UDC-7.

Katzer, J. (1972). "The Development of a Semantic Differential to Assess Users' Attitudes Towards an On-Line Interactive Reference Retrieval System." *Jour. Amer. Soc. Information Sci.* **23** (2), 122–128.

Lancaster, F. W. (1968). *Evaluation of the MEDLARS Demand Search Service.* Bethesda, Md.: National Library of Medicine.

Lancaster, F. W. (1972). *Evaluation of On-Line Searching in MEDLARS (AIM–TWX) by Biomedical Practitioners.* Urbana, Ill.: University of Illinois, Graduate School of Library Science, Occasional Paper No. 101.

Lancaster, F. W., R. L. Rapport, and J. K. Penry (1972). "Evaluating the Effectiveness of an On-Line, Natural Language Retrieval System." *Information Storage Retrieval* **8** (5), 223–245.

Marcus, R. S., P. Kugel, and R. L. Kusik (1969). "An Experimental Computer-Stored, Augmented Catalog of Professional Literature." *AFIPS Conf. Proc. Spring Joint Computer Conf.* **34**, 461–473.

Meister, D., and D. J. Sullivan (1967). *Evaluation of User Reactions to a Prototype On-Line Information Retrieval System.* Washington, D.C.: NASA. NASA CR-918.

Moll, W. (1971). "AIM–TWX Service at the University of Virginia." *Bull. Medical Library Assoc.* **59** (3), 458–462.

Rae, P. D. J. (1970). "On-Line Information Retrieval Systems—Experience of the Parkinson Information Center Using the SUNY Biomedical Communication Network." *Proc. Amer. Soc. Information Sci.* **7**, 173–176.

Smith, J. L., J. P. Hofmann, and J. C. Cornelli (1968). *COLEX (CIRC On-Line Experimentation).* Griffiss Air Force Base, N.Y.: Rome Air Development Center, RADC-TR-68-332.

Stiller, J. D. (1970). "Use of On-Line Remote Access Information Retrieval Systems." *Proc. Amer. Soc. Information Sci.* **7**, 107–109.

Stoutt, B. H., and S. L. Yount (1970). *Console-Oriented Information Storage and Retrieval System for the Nuclear Safety Information Center.* Oak Ridge, Tenn.: Union Carbide Corp., Computing Technology Center, CTC-37.

Summit, R. K. (1968). *Remote Information Retrieval Facility.* Palo Alto, Ca.: Lockheed Missiles & Space Co., NASA CR-1318.

Timbie, M., and D. Coombs (1969). *An Interactive Information Retrieval System—Case Studies on the Use of DIALOG to Search the ERIC Document File.* Stanford, Ca.: ERIC Clearinghouse on Educational Media and Technology, ED 034431.

Chapter Ten

System Selection

An information center that has decided to establish an on-line retrieval system has a choice of three possible procedures for acquisition of the system:

1. Designing a system in-house to meet the special needs of the organization.
2. Contracting with an outside group to design a system to meet these special needs.
3. Adopting an existing system that is commercially available, and making whatever modifications are necessary.

The first of these alternatives may be most desirable if the center itself has the necessary in-house expertise. However, the design and implementation *de novo* of an in-house system is likely to be both very expensive and very time-consuming. Having a system designed on a contract basis may be even more expensive, and there is no positive assurance that the final system will exactly meet all the requirements of the organization. Another problem is that the customer is sometimes unable to define exactly what his requirements are. The adoption of an existing commercially available system is likely to be the least expensive of the three alternatives. Moreover, this approach should lead to the implementation of an operating system much earlier than the others. However, no existing system is likely to meet *all* the center's requirements. The center must either make compromises in its requirements or be prepared to make modifications to the system it is adopting. Extensive modifications can be expensive. Moreover, there is a danger that extensive modification of an existing system will produce a bastard that may have lost many of the advantages of the original design without serving the needs of the organization in a completely satisfactory way.

There are other attractions associated with existing systems, however. When we buy an existing system, we presumably buy one that has been tested out and debugged over a period of months or perhaps years. We are buying the experience and expertise of the organization developing the system, and we may be buying additional operating experience from organizations that have already implemented this system. In other words, we may be buying into a *user group* having existing and potential funds of operating experience. Several organizations, for example, have adopted NASA's RECON system, and others have adopted its commercial counterpart, DIALOG. A RECON user group exists, meets periodically, produces a newsletter, and exchanges experiences. Moreover, such a user group may lead to *sharing* of resources. Thus, two or more organizations requiring a particular system modification may share the cost of the software changes involved, thereby reducing the expense to each individual agency.

Adoption of an existing system offers another important advantage: It creates compatibility and thus facilitates cooperation and interchange among information centers. There is an increasing trend toward the establishment of networks of information centers at regional, national, and international levels. These information networks are likely to be built around on-line retrieval facilities, and their efficiency is likely to be much greater if compatibility or easy convertibility exist among the network centers, at least in the area of searching methods. Some of the problems of network compatibility have been summarized by Stevens (1970).

Clearly, system acquisition involves both hardware and software considerations. The selection of software may in fact be severely restricted by preexisting hardware in that commercially available software packages are designed for use with a particular series of computers and are not easily converted for use with alternative equipment configurations. Moreover, further restrictions may be placed on the system designer by the fact that certain policy decisions may already have been made by top management (e.g., that a particular terminal is to be adopted throughout the organization).

It is extremely important that, before deciding on any on-line system, the information center should undertake a broad systems study to establish detailed requirements for the on-line retrieval system and to specify how this system will relate to and interface with existing capabilities of the center. It is not enough merely to take an existing batch-processing system and provide access to the file by means of on-line terminals. The on-line system should involve new design concepts and new operating philosophies. The system may lend itself to new uses and may attract new users. The organization moving from an existing batch system may be operating under a handicap inasmuch as there exists a natural tendency to disturb existing procedures as little as possible. The organization without any existing batch system is perhaps in a happier position, since it is less likely to have preconceived notions or to be philosophically committed to particular processing methods.

In moving from an existing batch retrieval system, the information center must study the full implications of adopting on-line, interactive capabilities. The following will be among the factors to be considered:

1. What effect will the on-line system have on the overall service functions of the center? Will new services be initiated? Will new files be created and made available on-line?

2. Will modifications be needed in indexing procedures and policies? Will indexing be conducted on-line?

3. Will modifications be needed in procedures and policies for vocabulary control? How can the on-line capabilities assist in vocabulary-control activities?

4. Will the on-line system be accessed only by information specialists, or will we allow the center's users to access it directly?

5. If users are to have direct access to the system, will we allow them to use the on-line facilities to establish, maintain, and manipulate personal files?

6. What are the implications of the on-line system for the composition and organization of the data base?

7. How much of the data base will be loaded for direct on-line querying and how much will be stored off-line for remote batch search?

8. Will the on-line system be used in the dissemination activities of the information center? For example, will user interest profiles be constructed and tested at the on-line terminal?

9. How will the on-line searching system interface with the document delivery system? Will we allow viewing of microfiche at the same video console used for searching the data base?

It will be impossible to make meaningful decisions regarding requirements for an on-line file management system, and therefore to select or specify a system, until the entire information processing activities of the center and the possible role of the on-line computer in each of these activities have been analyzed in detail.

Following the broad systems analysis, it will clearly be necessary for the center to prepare a detailed statement of the requirements that the on-line system is to satisfy. These detailed requirements will be necessary whether we are selecting an already available system, preparing a request for proposal to go to outside contractors, or preparing a task statement preparatory to an in-house design project.

At Stanford University (Epstein, et al., 1971), the following steps are taken in the detailed analysis phase of system acquisition:

Performance requirements are stated quantitatively including such factors as response time, hours per day of on-line service, and allowable mean time between failures. Record input and output are estimated in terms of volume, growth and fluctuations. All input–output documents are laid out in character-by-character detail. Transformation rules between input and output data elements are specified and cost limits established (p. 35).

It is obviously impossible to develop a statement of requirements that can be adopted intact by several organizations. However, we have developed a specimen set of general requirements for a hypothetical information center. This statement of requirements, presented below, may be useful as a guide to other organizations faced with the task of acquiring on-line retrieval capabilities.

Specimen Requirements for On-Line Retrieval and Management System

Search Processing

1. Must provide for interactive, on-line, real-time searching, and must also have a remote batch-searching capability.
2. Must be accessible for interrogation on-line for a minimum of 8 hours a day.
3. Command language must be as close as possible to natural language. Command symbols must be unambiguous.
4. The searcher must be able to enter, directly at the terminal, complete search statements consisting of terms in boolean relationships.
5. Error messages must be explicit, and the system must help the user to recognize and correct his mistakes. Error correction must be simple.
6. The system must incorporate tutorial features and must be capable of explaining particular responses and commands when asked to do so by the user.
7. The searcher must be able to view synonym tables or term hierarchies, select from them, or incorporate them intact into a search strategy. The capability of constructing these tables on-line must exist.
8. The system must be capable of searching on GREATER THAN and LESS THAN, as well as AND, OR, and NOT operators.
9. It must be possible to qualify retrievals on the basis of publication date and language.
10. There must be no unreasonable limit on the number of terms that can be incorporated into a single search statement.

11. Combination of search statements, to create more complex statements, must be possible.
12. Terse and verbose conversational options must be allowed.
13. Scanning of words in titles or abstracts, as well as the searching of index terms, must be possible.
14. Searching on word truncations must be possible.
15. A *recapitulate* feature is needed to permit the user to view the complete strategy developed at the terminal from the time he began a particular search.
16. A priority interrupt capability is required.
17. The searcher must be able to abort a search at any point, including output printing.
18. The searcher must be able to input a search strategy and request that it be processed against one file or any group of files contained within the data base.

Output

1. The system must allow viewing of citations at a CRT display, printout at an on-line teleprinter, and remote off-line printout on a high-speed printer.
2. The user must be able to specify that selected portions of a bibliographic record be displayed or printed, including title alone, author plus title, title plus index terms, full bibliographic citation, full bibliographic citation plus abstract, or complete bibliographic record (citation, abstract, index terms).
3. For off-line printout, the user must be able to specify various sorting options, including sorting by author, date, journal title, or report number.
4. The system must allow the building of special files as a result of on-line interrogation. The searcher must be able to select citations from the data base and have them read onto magnetic tape for subsequent manipulation.
5. In any single on-line search, a retrieved citation should be printed once only, even though it matches on several alternative strategies used by the searcher.
6. The system should be able to provide display and printout of synonym tables and term hierarchies.
7. The system should record figures on the use of index terms by both indexers and searchers, and should be capable of displaying these tallies at the terminal or printing them out on demand.
8. The searcher should have the ability to state how many citations he would like displayed or printed from a particular set, and the system

must have the ability to draw a sample from a set of citations that match a particular strategy.

9. The searcher must be able to interrupt processing or printing whenever he chooses.

Record and File Structure

1. Term files must be organized on a random-access basis.
2. The data base must be structured in such a way that a single strategy can be matched against multiple files contained within the complete data base.
3. The system must be capable of accommodating a virtually unlimited number of new terms.
4. The data base structure must allow storage of term hierarchies and linkage of terms within a particular record, including the linking of main headings with subheadings.

Input and Maintenance

1. The building of new files, including the creation of new inverted files, should be easy to accomplish. While most file updating will be done off-line, some on-line maintenance capabilities must be present.
2. The system must be able to accommodate up to 400,000 new bibliographic records annually, and must allow the searching of a file of up to 10 years of such records.
3. The system must be able to perform logically definable input validity checks.
4. The system must be capable of accepting machine-readable records existing in the present batch system.
5. The system must be protected against unintentional destruction of files or programs.

Hardware

1. The system must be compatible with an IBM 360/67 computer.
2. The system should be capable of supporting terminals comprising CRT displays with accompanying on-line printer.
3. Up to twenty terminals should be capable of being supported simultaneously.
4. The CRT keyboard should provide single command keys for single functions.
5. A high-speed, off-line print capability is required.

Other Requirements

1. A comprehensive user manual and associated training aids are needed.
2. The system must be able to monitor each search conducted and to prepare statistical summaries on the number of searches conducted, connect times, CPU times, the number and type of terms searched on, the number of records printed, and other related statistics that may become of interest.
3. The system must incorporate an on-line questionnaire designed to collect data on user characteristics, purpose of the search, and the searcher's subjective assessment of its value.
4. The user must receive unambiguous cues as to when he is to communicate with the system and when it is the system's turn to communicate with him.

In choosing among several existing and competing systems it will be necessary to devise an evaluation procedure whereby each is tested against the selection criteria that have been developed. It is highly desirable that a software package be tested on a small sample file drawn from the actual data base that is to be implemented. Procedures that can be used to evaluate a file management software package in this way have been described by Wos (1969). The evaluation of computer systems in general is outside the scope of this book. In any case, a considerable amount of literature already exists on the subject. A detailed study on computer system evaluation, including the techniques of analytical modeling, simulation, software monitoring, and hardware monitoring, has been published by Minker, et al. (1969). A useful bibliography on computer system evaluation techniques by Crooke and Minker (1969) is also available.

REFERENCES

Crooke, S., and J. Minker (1969). *Key-Word-in-Context Index and Bibliography on Computer Systems Simulation and Evaluation.* College Park, Md.: University of Maryland, Computer Science Center, TR 69–100.

Epstein, A. H., et al. (1971). *Bibliographic Automation of Large Library Operations Using a Time-Sharing System.* Phase 1. Stanford, Ca.: Stanford University Libraries, p. 35.

Minker, J., S. Crooke, and J. Yeh (1969). *Analysis of Data Processing Systems.* College Park, Md.: University of Maryland, Computer Science Center.

Stevens, M. E. (1970). *Standardization, Compatability and/or Convertibility Requirements in Network Planning.* Gaithersburg, Md.: National Bureau of Standards, NBS Report 10 252. PB 194179.

Wos, C. M. (1969). "The Evaluation of File-Management Software Packages." *Proc. Amer. Soc. Information Sci.* **6**, 215–222.

Chapter Eleven

Vocabulary in
the On-Line System

Most information retrieval systems, manual or mechanized, operate by means of a controlled vocabulary. A controlled vocabulary is essentially a set of terms that must be used at both the input and output stages of the information system; that is, by indexers as well as searchers. The major function of the controlled vocabulary is to bring the language of the searcher into coincidence with the language of the indexer. Specifically, the controlled vocabulary:

- Establishes which of several synonyms or near-synonyms is to be used, and provides references to this accepted term from the possible variants.
- By means of an *entry vocabulary*, refers from specific terms not used in the system (by indexers or searchers) to the more generic terms that are used instead.
- Links together terms that are hierarchically related and terms that are semantically related in other ways. The linking of related terms is usually achieved by means of cross-references.
- Distinguishes homographs.

The controlled vocabulary exists primarily to assist the searcher in the information retrieval system. It prevents the dispersion of related subject matter, reduces possible ambiguities among terms, tells the searcher how various topics have been indexed, and provides enough structure to facilitate the conduct of generic searches, thereby alleviating the problems faced by the searcher in trying to identify all possible terms that might have been used to represent a particular broad subject. A controlled vocabulary may take the form of a classification scheme, a list of subject headings, or a thesaurus of descriptors. The general subject of vocabulary control for information retrieval is discussed in considerable detail by Lancaster (1972c).

It is virtually impossible to operate a manual retrieval system effectively without the use of a controlled vocabulary. Using a computer, however, it is feasible to function without any form of vocabulary control. For example, we can store the complete text of a collection of documents (or abstracts) and search this data base by the use of combinations of words or phrases occurring in this text. This type of system (as exemplified by EARS) is usually known as a *natural language* or *free text* retrieval system. A natural language system does not preclude the possibility of using a controlled vocabulary, such as a thesaurus, as a searching aid, even though no controlled vocabulary was used in indexing. We can thus usefully distinguish a *precontrolled vocabulary* (used by both indexers and searchers) from a *postcontrolled vocabulary* (used by searchers only).

In a computer-based retrieval system, including an on-line version, the following possibilities for vocabulary control (or lack of it) exist:

1. A controlled vocabulary used in indexing and also in searching— precontrolled vocabulary.
2. A controlled vocabulary used in indexing. Natural language used in searching.
3. Natural language used in both indexing and searching.
4. Natural language used in indexing. Controlled vocabulary used in searching—postcontrolled vocabulary.

Let us now consider some of the pros and cons of these various approaches when applied to the on-line retrieval situation.

Precontrolled Vocabulary

The great majority of information retrieval systems operate in this conventional manner, with a controlled vocabulary used by both indexers and searchers. There are certain definite advantages to this approach. First, a controlled vocabulary, when used in indexing, tends to ensure that a particular topic is always represented in the same way in the system. This has certain benefits for the searcher. The controlled vocabulary tells him exactly how a particular topic has been indexed. This reduces the intellectual burden on the searcher by sparing him the task of thinking up all the possible terms that might be used to express the subject matter of his search. For example, he may be looking for information on cereals. In using a system without a controlled vocabulary the searcher would need to remember all the terms that might have been used in indexing to express the concept of *cereal*, including GRAIN, CEREAL, WHEAT, CORN, BARLEY, RICE, and so on. The controlled vocabulary tells him that the generic term GRAIN is the only one recognized in the system and that he need consult only this term to retrieve all documents relating to cereals. The second advantage of a controlled vocabulary is that it facilitates the conduct of generic searches. The vocabulary may include twenty-five specific terms relating to protective coatings for metals. It would be difficult to discover all of these unaided. The vocabulary will help him by bringing them all together, either by means of a formal hierarchical classification or by means of a network of cross-references.

Unfortunately, the precontrolled vocabulary also has its disadvantages (quite apart from the fact that it tends to be expensive to construct and maintain). However large, the precontrolled vocabulary tends to be non-specific. Certainly, it is nonspecific in relation to the natural language of scientific documents and perhaps nonspecific in relation to the natural language of requests made to a retrieval system. If the vocabulary is non-specific in relation to a particular subject, it will be impossible to achieve a high precision in any search conducted on this topic. A particular user may be looking for information on perforation of the gallbladder, but the most specific term available in the vocabulary is GALLBLADDER DISEASES. This term, when used by the searcher, allows the retrieval of relevant items on gallbladder perforation, but they will be accompanied by a very consider-able number of documents which are of no interest.

The second major difficulty of a controlled vocabulary system is that it may take a considerable amount of time to learn how to use it effectively. It takes several weeks to train new MEDLARS indexers. These trainees must familiarize themselves, at least in a general way, with the 8000 terms in *Medical Subject Headings* and with the indexing protocols of the system (how and under what circumstances a particular term is to be used). Terms may be given special meanings in the system or may have acquired particular connotations through use patterns over a period of years. The indexer must learn this special usage. In the case of MEDLARS, subheadings are used as well as main headings (descriptors). The indexer must know when it is appropriate to use a subheading, and which subheadings may be used with which main headings.

Unfortunately, the searcher must know as much about the controlled vocabulary as the indexer. In fact, he must know more about it. A controlled vocabulary does not remain static. It changes over the years, usually becom-ing increasingly specific. The indexer need only be familiar with the latest version of the vocabulary, but the searcher must also be aware of its historical developments. He must know, for example, that he can use CECITIS for items input since September 1, 1970, but that he must search under the broader term CECAL DISEASES for items on cecitis indexed earlier, before the specific term was introduced into the vocabulary.

The point is really this. A precontrolled vocabulary system is designed to be used by information specialists. The information specialist, familiar with the vocabulary of the system and its indexing protocols, is likely to be able to use the system much more effectively than the subject specialist. In particular, the subject specialist who uses the system infrequently may have great difficulty in understanding the system conventions and how to exploit its capabilities effectively.

Precontrolled vocabularies offer many advantages in mechanized systems operated off-line in the batch-processing mode, where the searching must be conducted by a system intermediary (information specialist). We have emphasized, however, that one of the attractions of the on-line system is that it permits unmediated searches; i.e., searches by the practitioners in a field seeking to satisfy their own information needs. A precontrolled vocabulary presents certain problems to such a user. He cannot be expected to take a course in indexing, and thus, despite his subject expertise, he is never likely to use the system as effectively as the information specialist.

Controlled vocabularies are not natural languages. They are really artificial metalanguages. They may differ, particularly in specificity, from the language of the practitioner in the field. The use of a somewhat artificial controlled vocabulary, where conventions must be learned, along with the need to input search statements as boolean algebraic expressions, may be a very definite barrier to the effective use of on-line bibliographic systems by the searcher who is not an information specialist.

This is not to say that on-line systems with precontrolled vocabularies *cannot* be used by the practitioner in the field. The AIM–TWX study (Lancaster, 1972b) indicated that biomedical practitioners were able to use the MEDLARS data base on-line with some success. However, they will not use the data base as effectively as the trained searcher, and some may be forced to give up a search in frustration. In the AIM–TWX study, it was found that searches were generally effective when the language of the search request matched the language of the system fairly closely. Where a wide discrepancy existed between the searcher's language and the system language, the results tended to be disappointing.

At the very least, an on-line system using a precontrolled vocabulary must have a very full *entry vocabulary* if it is to be used effectively in a non-delegated search mode. An entry vocabulary is a vocabulary of natural language expressions, occurring in documents and requests, that have been mapped to the controlled terms of the system. The entry vocabulary, as its name implies, provides entries into the system from various terms that do not appear in the controlled vocabulary. It will consist primarily of specific terms representing subjects upon which literature exists in the data base. Synonymous expressions will also be included. These terms will be mapped to the appropriate controlled terms or term combinations. For example, the searcher may be looking for information on athrombia. This is not a descriptor in the vocabulary, but the entry vocabulary refers him from ATHROMBIA to the more generic term HEMORRHAGIC DIATHESIS. Another searcher may be seeking information on coronary arteriosclerosis, and the entry vocabulary tells him that he must use the combination CORONARY DISEASE *and* ARTERIOSCLEROSIS.

Note that the entry vocabulary does not necessarily provide the capability for specific search. Its role is to lead the searcher from a term that has not been used in indexing to one that has. In the above examples, we cannot retrieve on athrombia specifically but only on the broader class of hemorrhagic diathesis. Moreover, the entry vocabulary cannot be absolutely complete; that is, we cannot expect it to contain *all* the terms that occur in a natural language data base in a specialized field.

A complete entry vocabulary seems essential to the effective exploitation of any on-line system with a precontrolled vocabulary used in the nondelegated search mode. Unfortunately, the entry vocabulary is sadly neglected in many systems.

An ambitious project for the development of such an entry vocabulary for use with the MEDLARS data base has been described by Cain (1969). For searching the on-line system that is part of the Biomedical Communication Network of the State University of New York, Cain used a modified version of *MeSH*. In particular, alternative word orders were employed. The straight natural language approach is preferred (e.g., INBORN ERRORS OF METABOLISM replaces METABOLISM, INBORN ERRORS, which is the *MeSH* term for this concept). The entry vocabulary provides approaches from alternative word sequences, from spelling variants (e.g., English versus American usage), from abbreviations, and from common misspellings (e.g., OPTHALMOLOGY). The object is to provide an entry point from whatever term the user might think of when sitting at the on-line terminal. Cain's procedures added approximately 23,400 entry terms to the approximately 7000 *MeSH* terms then in the vocabulary.

The on-line, precontrolled vocabulary system should incorporate other aids to the searcher, besides the entry vocabulary. Many of these were referred to in Chapter Three. The searcher should be able to view portions of the vocabulary at the terminal, displayed both alphabetically and hierarchically. ORBIT has this capability. RECON will display descriptors in alphabetical array and will also display the set of cross-references associated with a descriptor. The system should also be capable of allowing a generic search (*explosion*) on a complete category of terms. Given, for example, a "grain" hierarchy, consisting of perhaps eight terms, the searcher should be able to incorporate this entire hierarchy into his search strategy without the need to list the individual terms. He should also be able to coordinate the entire hierarchy with other terms or with other complete hierarchies (e.g., all grain terms *and* all insect pest terms).

Preferably, the searcher should be given the ability to truncate terms (i.e., search on prefixes or suffixes). For example, SURG******, where each asterisk represents any possible character, will retrieve SURGEON, SUR-GEONS, SURGERY, SURGICAL, and SURGICALLY, a group of related terms, without the necessity for listing each term separately. This is an example of *right truncation. Left truncation* (searching on suffixes) is equally valuable on occasions. For example, the suffix . . . MYCIN will do very well in a search for antibiotics.

Controlled Vocabulary Indexing/Natural Language Searching

In the case of on-line systems used by the practitioners in a field, the closer we can get to complete natural language searching capabilities, the better the results are likely to be. Given a system based on a precontrolled vocabulary, it should be possible to extend the entry vocabulary concept to allow the searcher to interrogate the system in his own natural language terms and to convert his language automatically to system terms, where a discrepancy exists between the two. For example, the searcher enters the term CECITIS and this is automatically converted to CECAL DISEASES; NEUTROPENIA is mapped to AGRANULOCYTOSIS; DERMATO-SCLEROSIS to SCLERODERMA; and so on. In some cases, the mapping would be one-to-many rather than one-to-one (e.g., VENOUS BLOOD to BLOOD *and* VEINS), and the searcher should be able to enter a complete boolean search expression, as, for example, NEUTROPENIA *and* ORAL MANIFESTATIONS, and have all the mapping to controlled terms conducted automatically.

This is different from the conventional use of an entry vocabulary, as described in the preceding section, where the searcher must look up a term in the system vocabulary (in printed or on-line form) and himself translate this into the system terms where necessary.

This approach, involving automatic translation of query terms to controlled terms where necessary, has certain attractions. It spares the searcher any lookup operation and, in fact, may give him the illusion that he is searching in a completely natural language form. It also has its disadvantages. It requires that a very considerable entry vocabulary be constructed, and that it be loaded on-line whenever the system is in use. An entry vocabulary of the necessary size may be very costly to store and manipulate. Moreover, it can never be complete. If we give searchers the ability to enter any possible terms, there will always be a certain proportion that the system does not recognize and must reject.

Another disadvantage is that the user may be deluded into false expectations, because he is unaware that his specific terms are in fact being converted to more generic ones. The searcher who enters CODEINE, and sees his term accepted, may be very surprised to see the search results if CODEINE is mapped internally to the much broader term NARCOTICS.

A final problem in automatic mapping is caused by terms having multiple meanings or multiple contexts. If a searcher enters the word PLANT does he mean factory or vegetation? There are ways in which such ambiguities may be avoided (e.g., by using the other words of the search to provide the necessary context) but they may be relatively costly to implement and the best solution may be merely to display to the user the possible alternatives [e.g., PLANT (INDUSTRY, PLANT(BOTANY)] and allow him to make a choice.

We are not necessarily advocating a system in which the indexer uses a controlled vocabulary but the searcher does not. However, if we have a controlled vocabulary system (e.g., we have converted to on-line operation an existing off-line system in which a controlled vocabulary has been used for a number of years), this approach may be the one to take if we wish to encourage use of the system by the maximum number of people.

Kellogg (1966, 1967, 1968), among others, has described procedures that may be used to translate natural language questions into artificial language queries. The system Kellogg describes, CONVERSE, is a *question answering* or *fact retrieval* system rather than a bibliographic retrieval system of the type discussed in this book. Nevertheless, this research has obvious relevance to the design of bibliographic retrieval systems operating by means of natural language inquiries.

Natural Language Indexing and Natural Language Searching

If we are to obtain the full benefits of natural language searching, we should certainly be operating on natural language input also. The document record in a completely natural language (free text) retrieval system may consist of the complete text of the document if it is relatively short (e.g., a teletype message), or a complete abstract, or it may consist of a set of indexing terms assigned freely (i.e., without control) by human indexers, as is the case in the Intrex augmented catalog. We search such a system by looking for particular combinations of words or phrases in the document text or its surrogate. Some on-line systems, including Data Central, have been used primarily for natural language searching. EARS is a good example of a system operating on the free text of document abstracts.

If the on-line retrieval system is to be used in a nondelegated search mode by the practitioners in the field, natural language has obviously much to commend it. The language of the documents themselves is the language of scientific discourse and is likely to match the language of the searcher more closely than any controlled vocabulary will. In fact, just as the controlled vocabulary system favors the information specialist, the natural language system favors the subject specialist. That is, all other things being equal, the subject specialist should be able to search a natural language data base more effectively than the information specialist, because he is using the language of his own field and is more apt to know how a particular subject is likely to be described in the literature. Moreover, the natural language system allows complete specificity. It is not possible to be more specific than the natural language of the documents themselves. If we are seeking information on "cecitis," we search under this word, and under any possible synonymous expressions (e.g., inflammation of the cecum, cecal inflammation), and are thus given the possibility of retrieving items on this precise topic rather than the much broader concept of cecal diseases, which is perhaps the level of specificity we must settle for in a controlled vocabulary system.

But natural language systems have their problems, too. Precision failures due to false coordinations and incorrect term relationships (see Chapter Seven) tend to be very prevalent. If the complete text of a document, or even a lengthy abstract, is stored, we will also tend to get precision failures due to the *exhaustivity* of the surrogate. For example, we conduct a search on the drug phenytoin and retrieve an abstract that mentions it briefly or tangentially, or even negatively (e.g., "phenytoin was not used").

Some of these failures can be avoided by various searching techniques if the capabilities are built into the searching programs. A technique for reducing ambiguous or spurious relationships (false coordinations and incorrect term relationships) is the use of word distance indicators. For example, we can specify that we want retrieved any documents containing the word CECUM and the word INFLAMMATION, but only when these words appear in the same paragraph, the same sentence, or within x words of each other. Documents that make very slight reference to a topic may be eliminated by demanding that a particular term must occur at least X times. For example, we can ask that all abstracts containing the word PHENY-TOIN should be retrieved, but only when this word appears at least twice. Of course, there is a great danger that this will eliminate some of the most relevant items along with the irrelevant.

By far the greatest problem in a natural language system, however, is the intellectual burden placed upon the individual searcher. The user of a controlled vocabulary has only a limited number of terms to choose from—albeit several thousand in a large system—and the vocabulary itself (by its hierarchy and/or cross-reference structure) aids the construction of a search strategy by bringing related terms together. The user of a natural language system, on the other hand, has virtually an infinite number of words to choose from. To search the system effectively, he must be able to recognize the many possible ways that a particular topic could be expressed in the text of documents. Not only must he be aware of possible synonyms and variant spellings at the single word level (e.g., SULTIAME, SULTHIAME, OSPOLOT), he must also recognize the possibility of alternative grammatical constructions (e.g., the concept "blood level" may be expressed by this phrase, by "serum level," "blood concentration," "concentration in the blood," "serum concentration," "amounts of . . . in the blood," and so on). In scientific or technical literature, there frequently exist multiple ways in which a particular concept may be represented. The searcher, without the benefit of a precontrolled vocabulary (which would adopt one term—e.g., BLOOD LEVEL—and hopefully refer from the most common variants), may not be able to think of all possible approaches to retrieval. Even if he does discover most of them, the time expended in this task may be considerable and may reduce the efficiency of the system in the user's eyes. As discovered in the EARS evaluation (Lancaster, et al., 1972a) reported earlier, the most significant cause of recall failures in a natural language system is the inability of the searcher to think of all possible approaches to retrieval.

Postcontrolled Vocabulary

The searcher in a natural language system needs a thesaurus, or similar aid, just as much as the searcher in the controlled vocabulary system—perhaps even more so. This is not a contradiction, as it might appear at first sight. It is perfectly possible to provide some vocabulary control for searching purposes without controlling the vocabulary in indexing. In other words, we can store natural language text, and retain the advantages of full specificity and closeness to the language of the subject specialist, but construct a search thesaurus to control synonyms and to group related terms together in order to facilitate the conduct of generic searches. We refer to this vocabulary as a *postcontrolled vocabulary*.

Such a searching thesaurus would consist largely of tables of synonyms or near-synonyms. To take a simple example, the thesaurus should lead a user to realize that SULTHIAME may also appear as SULTIAME and as OSPOLOT, and that DILANTIN may appear as PHENYTOIN or as DIPHENYLHYDANTOIN. To take a slightly more complex example, the thesaurus should remind the user that the concept of "blood level" may be represented by any of the following combinations: BLOOD*LEVEL,

BLOOD*CONCENTRATION, SERUM*LEVEL, SERUM*CONCEN-
TRATION, and so on. An example of the use of synonym tables can be
found in an on-line system operated by the Copper Data Center. Synonym
tables here are particularly valuable in the handling of variant names of
copper alloys. For example, "70–30 brass" is equivalent to "eyelet brass"
which is equivalent to "Copper Alloy No. 260" (the approved term in the
thesaurus). The searcher can use any one of these. If he uses one of the first
two, the computer accepts it but types back the approved (thesaurus) term.
In this system, alloy designations for 15 nations, as well as designations of
the International Standards Organization (ISO), are included.

It is essential to the long-term success of on-line systems, based on
natural language, that such synonym tables be constructed and made
available either in printed form, or preferably, for on-line consultation. Such
synonym tables would cover both the simple synonym situation:

METHARBITAL = METHYLPHENOBARBITAL = GEMONIL =
ENDIEMAL

and the "conceptual group" situation. An example of the latter would be a
concept such as "psychological," which could be represented by the root
PSYCH******** and by such words as NEUROSIS, DEPRESSION,
SUICIDE, ABNORMAL, and so on. A thesaurus group would be composed
of both words and word truncations. Word truncation (left and right) is a
very powerful searching device in a free text system. A good candidate for a
thesaurus group would be any concept likely to recur in many searches.
Such a concept might be "surgery," for which a thesaurus group looking
something as follows could be constructed:

SURGERY
SURG******
*******PLASTY
*******OTOMY
*******ECTOMY

SECTION***
****SECTION
EXCISION
INCISION
OPERATION
STEREOTAXIC

and so on.† Synonym tables should include spelling variants.

---

†Although left truncations can be a powerful text searching device, and one that is easily used
in tape-oriented batch systems, it is expensive and somewhat cumbersome to implement in the
inverted file organization that is commonly used in on-line systems.

It is highly desirable that such thesaurus groups or synonym tables be stored in machine-readable form and thus be available for examination and manipulation on-line. A searcher, if he wishes, can request that, for a particular input term, say SULTHIAME, all synonyms (from the appropriate table) should be substituted automatically in the search. Moreover, he should be able to incorporate a complete conceptual group into his search strategy, if he wishes, without the need to key the separate terms. For example, given the existence of a machine-stored thesaurus (in the form, perhaps, of preconstructed search strategies or search fragments), the searcher on "psychological aspects of psychomotor or temporal lobe epilepsy" should be capable of searching as follows:

PSYCHOMOTOR OR TEMPORAL LOBE AND PSYCHOLOGICAL (table)

This strategy, with some such code appended to the term PSYCHOLOGICAL, would cause the entire group of "psychology" terms to be incorporated into the strategy. Likewise, a search on surgery in temporal lobe epilepsy could bring in the entire "surgery" thesaurus group.

Obviously, the construction of such synonym tables requires a considerable expenditure of human intellectual effort. Nevertheless, such searching aids are likely to raise the average performance capabilities of natural language systems dramatically. Moreover, in the long run, such synonym tables could repay their cost manyfold in saving the time of searchers and thus economizing on on-line connect time. The fact is that, in conducting a search, the individual searcher essentially constructs one or more synonym tables by thinking of the possible ways in which a particular topic might be expressed. But this is time-consuming, and he may not think of all possibilities. Moreover, his effort is lost once the search is completed. A second searcher, or the same one at a later time, will repeat the identical process in a search involving the same topics. Insofar as topics or aspects tend to recur frequently in searches (e.g., surgery, blood levels) and insofar as these recurrent aspects can be recognized, it would seem efficient to construct authoritative synonym tables and build these into the system.

The possibility exists of enlisting the aid of the computer in this type of thesaurus construction. A very simple approach would be to let the system operate for some months without any searching aids, recording automatically all the strategies used to interrogate the system. After several months of operation, these stored search strategies are printed out for human analysis. Words that have been used in an OR relationship in previous strategies are good candidates for inclusion in a synonym table, since they have been regarded as equivalent or substitutable by certain users in the past. Any system that routinely stores searching strategies (e.g., SUPARS) would automatically be collecting quantities of data of great potential value to the task of vocabulary construction. A more sophisticated and automatic approach, the *growing thesaurus*, is mentioned later in this chapter.

The use of natural language, coupled with a postcontrolled vocabulary, appears to offer many obvious advantages in the on-line retrieval system operated by the practitioners in a particular field:

1. The language of the data base is fully specific and thus permits the conduct of searches of high precision.
2. The language of the data base should be very similar to the language of the subject specialist searcher.
3. The user is given the ability to search very specifically (using natural language words) or broadly (by incorporating thesaurus groups into his strategy), depending on his requirements at the time.
4. The search thesaurus, by bringing synonyms and related terms together, reduces the intellectual burden on the searcher, saves his time, reduces recall failures due to the individual's inability to think of all possible approaches to retrieval, and raises the overall quality of search results.

It appears that little work is being done on the development of post-controlled vocabularies for use with natural language on-line retrieval systems, apart from Salton's work with the SMART system (Salton, 1968). In SMART, the searcher is given the opportunity of expanding on any word in a request by substituting the thesaurus group to which the word belongs. The SMART thesaurus, although machine-stored, is generally constructed by human intellectual effort. The idea of a postcontrolled vocabulary is not new, however. The pioneering work on natural language searching by computer was conducted by Horty and his colleagues at the Health Law Center of the University of Pittsburgh. The system devised in Pittsburgh and described by Horty (1961) incorporated a searching thesaurus of the general type described above.

The beauty of natural language is that it is widely used and understood (at least by the population of a particular country), and it is transferable. A reasonable substitute for a specially prepared searching thesaurus (and a very firm foundation for the construction of such a thesaurus) would be a good specialized dictionary. For example, a medical dictionary or handbook of medical terminology might be a very useful aid in a system designed to search natural language abstracts in medicine. Moreover, a conventional thesaurus (precontrolled) prepared by some information center for its own use might be a useful searching aid in another system, using natural language, in the same subject field. For example, given a system comprising several thousand abstracts in the field of nuclear energy, the *EURATOM Thesaurus* might be an extremely valuable aid to the searcher. Moreover, natural language data bases can be transferred from one information center to another relatively easily. Use of natural language data bases thus avoids the problems of compatibility or convertibility that we face when we try to exchange files based on the use of controlled vocabularies.

Hybrid Systems

It is also possible to operate a retrieval system as a hybrid, using controlled vocabulary and natural language together. An example of this is the addition of a title scan capability to a system in which the primary search is on controlled vocabulary terms. Some examples of this were cited in Chapter Three. In ORBIT, the title search capability allows a ranked ordering of documents. The searcher, having conducted a search on combinations of descriptors, requests that the citations thus retrieved be ranked according to the degree to which they match a hypothetical title that he inputs. Such a title might be something like "Fatigue of Aircraft Structural Panels." The system matches this title against the set previously retrieved and calculates a score for each document in this set. The score reflects the degree to which the document title matches the hypothetical title input by the searcher. Titles are then printed out at the terminal according to their scores, with the highest scoring items appearing first.

Searching without Boolean Algebra

So far in this chapter we have assumed that the on-line system is being interrogated by means of formal boolean search expressions, in which terms are connected by logical AND, OR, and NOT. This is common practice in operating on-line systems, whether they use a controlled vocabulary (as in ORBIT or RECON) or natural language (as in Data Central). However, the on-line user who is not an information specialist may not adapt well to this search approach. For this reason, it is desirable that we investigate alternative procedures that might prove simpler for the user. One possibility is the weighted-term search technique. Here weights are assigned to terms and a threshold established to simulate a boolean logical requirement. Consider the following simple example:

$$\left. \begin{array}{l} \text{ALUMINUM} \\ \text{MAGNESIUM} \end{array} \right\} \; 2$$

$$\left. \begin{array}{l} \text{BENDING} \\ \text{DEFORMATION} \end{array} \right\} \; 2 \qquad \text{Threshold} = 6$$

$$\left. \begin{array}{l} \text{TUBES} \\ \text{PIPES} \end{array} \right\} \; 2$$

We are seeking information on the bending of tubes or pipes of light metals. Our search strategy assigns a weight (arbitrary) of 2 to each of three groups of terms and establishes a *retrieval threshold* of 6. In other words, a document will only be retrieved if it contains at least one word from each of the three groups (the group carries the weight, not the individual words, so that a document will receive a weight of 2 whether it contains ALUMINUM or MAGNESIUM *or both*) and thus *scores* 6 in relation to the strategy. Weighted-term searching is a very flexible technique. As described by Sommar and Dennis (1969), it is possible to use the weighting technique to express any conceptual relationship that can be expressed in the more conventional boolean form. Some people find the technique easier to apply than the use of boolean expressions; others do not. The technique has the advantage, of great potential value in an on-line system, of being able to rank documents according to the degree to which they match the search strategy. Consider the following:

$$
\left.\begin{array}{l} \text{AMYLOID} \\ \text{AMYLOIDOSIS} \end{array}\right\} \; 5
$$

$$
\text{TUBERCULOSIS} \} \; 5 \qquad \text{Threshold} = 10
$$

$$
\left.\begin{array}{l} \text{KIDNEY} \\ \text{RENAL} \end{array}\right\} \; 2
$$

$$
\text{PREDNISONE} \} \quad 1
$$

Here the searcher is looking for any documents discussing amyloidosis complicating tuberculosis. He is particularly interested in renal involvement and most particularly in the therapeutic use of prednisone in this condition. The above strategy will allow a ranking and the display of citations in sequence following the ranking. At the top of the display will appear any having a weight of 13 (all four aspects present), followed by those with a weight of 12 (prednisone missing), those with a weight of 11 (prednisone present but kidney involvement absent), and finally those with a weight of 10 (tuberculosis and amyloidosis present only), which is the minimum weight that the searcher will accept.

Another possible technique, which is similar but will still allow a ranked output, is to input the search terms as a string, without any logical connections, and merely request that the system retrieve documents according to the degree to which they match this string. For example, if we input the string AMYLOID, AMYLOIDOSIS, TUBERCULOSIS, KIDNEY, RENAL, PREDNISONE, the search will first retrieve any items that contain all six of these words (if any), then items that contain any five, any four, and so on, until a cutoff is established by the searcher. This technique has been tried by Cleverdon and Harding (1971) and was found to operate very effectively. It has also been described by Smith (1966) and by Heaps and Sorenson (1968), who refer to it as *fractional search*. Cleverdon calls it *coordination level* search.

There is a certain attraction about the possibility of presenting queries to a retrieval system in a completely natural form; that is, as English sentences. SMART, BROWSER, and LEADER, among other systems, allow the searcher to enter a query in this way (e.g., "Is there any evidence of a direct relationship between psoriasis and body temperature regulation mechanisms or perspiration?"). Of course, we can only allow English sentence queries if the system has the ability to recognize the significant words of such a request and preferably the conceptual (or syntactic) relationships involved. Both SMART and BROWSER will retrieve documents or abstracts that best match the search statement and will rank them according to degree of match. BROWSER achieves this by a simple word-matching process, which takes into account the number of words matching between document and request statement and the weight assigned to these words. In BROWSER, the weight assigned to a word is inversely proportional to the frequency of occurrence of the word in the corpus; that is, the rarer words carry higher weights. In the above example, PSORIASIS may carry a higher weight than any other word occurring in the request. SMART also operates primarily on a word-match plus word-weighting principle, but the capabilities for automatic syntactic analysis of both document text and requests is present in the system, although it is rarely used or found to be necessary. Some investigators attempt to impose rigorous syntactic control on a natural language system by means of automatic syntactic analysis (sentence parsing) programs. Such a program will determine structural dependencies between words in a sentence and will store a syntactic representation of the sentence, or at least a reduced syntactic structure, in the form of a tree or *abstract graph*, with each word being a node in the tree and the syntactic dependencies represented by branches. Salton (1968) describes in some detail techniques for this type of syntactic analysis. Automatic syntactic analysis will yield a machine-readable corpus capable of producing extremely high levels of search precision (but with concomitant loss in recall), because it allows us to specify the exact relationships obtaining between words in document text as well as the words occurring in request statements. Syntactic analysis of this type may be needed for so-called *fact retrieval* or *question-answering* systems (i.e., systems that attempt to provide a direct answer to a question rather than retrieving a piece of relevant text) of the type surveyed by Simmons (1965), but appears to be unnecessary for the type of information retrieval discussed in this book (i.e., retrieval of documents, document representations, or even sections of text).

Some interesting work on natural language communication with a bibliographic retrieval system has been carried out at the Moore School of Electrical Engineering. The first version of the language, known as *Easy English*, is capable of handling requests in an extremely limited form. The second version, *Real English*, will accept requests in a relatively free format. The translation program includes syntax analysis and a form of *semantic analysis* based on a semantic translation grammar. Real English has been well-described by Klappholz (1971) and Easy English by Rubinoff, et al. (1968). Some of the problems of man-machine communication via natural language have been discussed by Fraser (1967).

The On-Line System in Vocabulary-Control Activities

Assuming that we have a conventional machine-based system, using a precontrolled vocabulary, the on-line system may offer certain useful aids to the group concerned with developing and maintaining the controlled vocabulary. Proposed new descriptors, generated by indexers and searchers, can be called up and displayed on a regular basis. These proposed descriptors can be reviewed within the context of the citations or search strategies from which they were generated. Vocabulary review should be a more efficient activity in the on-line system, and newly approved terms should get into the vocabulary and be available for use faster than is usual in the off-line mode of operation. The lexicographer can browse among the various vocabulary displays, including displays of term definitions, in the way that indexer and searcher can browse. Tallies on the use of descriptors in indexing and searching can be reviewed on-line. The term history file, showing obsolete and discarded terms and the dates at which existing descriptors were introduced, will also be available for viewing at the console.

On-line text editing programs may be available to help the lexicographer in editorial work (for example, in introducing or amending term definitions). Words in newly introduced definitions can be checked against existing definitions in order to locate similarities and to reveal possible redundancy or overlap.

The main advantage of the on-line system for the lexicographer may, however, be its possible amelioration of the thorny problems of vocabulary file maintenance. The on-line facility should make it considerably easier to introduce terms into the appropriate places in the hierarchies, delete terms, or amend them. It may also facilitate the correction of document unit records to reflect vocabulary changes (e.g., the splitting up of descriptors) if such file updating is considered practicable and desirable, although massive changes involving many records will be handled more efficiently by batch updating.

Comparatively little research has so far been conducted on thesaural manipulations in an on-line environment. Some interesting work in this area, with special reference to the combination of a thesaurus with a classification scheme (a kind of thesaurofacet), has been done at the University of Alberta, Department of Computing Science, and is reported in a thesis by Alber (1972) and a paper by Alber and Heaps (1971).

Before we leave the subject of vocabulary control on-line, it is worth considering the idea of the *growing thesaurus* as advocated by Reisner (1963, 1966). Reisner proposes a freely growing thesaurus built up from relationships used by searchers in querying a system in on-line mode. The initial system vocabulary is formed freely from a natural language data base, and a human thesaurus of the most obvious interterm relations is superimposed upon this. The searcher will use words contained in the system vocabulary and will be led by the thesaurus to other related terms. These he can accept and incorporate into a strategy at will. Any additional useful relationships that he himself thinks of, in developing his search strategy heuristically, are recorded automatically. His own trail of word associations will then be added to the *informal thesaurus* and can thus be used by later searchers.

Reisner justifies this approach on the grounds that "people differ significantly in their personal semantic roadmaps." A general-purpose thesaurus is a compromise that attempts to serve everyone. The general thesaurus may represent a "common potential stock of semantic associations." Individuals, however, will select differently from this common pool in constructing thesauri and in using them. The proposal has obvious merit: A thesaurus developed in this way has "warrant," represents multiple viewpoints, and is constantly updated.

A similar approach has been described by Higgins and Smith (1969). They propose a thesaurus which, for each word in the vocabulary, will display a set of related words.

> In a search the computer will display to the user the set of related words and ask if any of these can be used in place of the one he has suggested. The user will also be encouraged to supply any other related words he knows. Registers will keep stored evidence of the usage of these related words and only those employed frequently will be displayed if the number of related words becomes too large. Related words given by the user will be stored.... In this way the thesaurus will change and grow with user interaction (p. 155).

REFERENCES

Alber, F. M. (1972). *On-Line Thesaurus Design for an Integrated Information System.* Master's Thesis, Edmonton, Alberta: University of Alberta, Department of Computing Science.

Alber, F. M., and D. M. Heaps (1971). "Classifying, Indexing, and Searching Resource Management via an On-Line Thesaurus." *Proc. Ann. Meet. Amer. Soc. Information Sci. Western Canada Chapter.*

Cain, A. M. (1969). "Thesaural Problems in an On-Line System." *Bull. Medical Library Assoc.* **57** (3), 250–259.

Cleverdon, C. W., and P. Harding (1971). *Interim Report on an Investigation on Mechanised Information Retrieval Service in a Specialised Subject Area.* Cranfield, England: Cranfield Institute of Technology.

Fraser, J. B. (1967). "On the Role of Natural Language in Man-Machine Communication." *In* D. E. Walker (ed.), *Third Congress on Information System Science and Technology.* Washington, D.C.: Thompson, pp. 21–28.

Heaps, D. M., and P. Sorenson (1968). "An On-Line Personal Documentation System." *Proc. Amer. Soc. Information Sci.* **5**, 201–207.

Higgins, L. D., and F. J. Smith (1969). "On-Line Subject Indexing and Retrieval." *Program: News Computers Libraries* **3**, (3,4), 147–156.

Horty, J. F. (1961). "Legal Research Using Electronic Techniques." *Proc. Fifth Biennial AALL Inst. Law Librarians*, 56–68.

Kellogg, C. H. (1966). *An Approach to the On-Line Interrogation of Structured Files of Facts Using Natural Language.* Santa Monica, Ca.: System Development Corporation, SP-2431/000/00.

Kellogg, C. H. (1967). *On-Line Translation of Natural Language Questions into Artificial Language Queries.* Santa Monica, Ca.: System Development Corporation, SP-2827/000/00.

Kellogg, C. H. (1968). *Data Management in Ordinary English: Examples.* Santa Monica, Ca.: System Development Corporation, TM-3919/000/00.

Klappholz, A. D. (1971). *A Generalization of Real English.* Philadelphia, Pa.: University of Pennsylvania, Moore School of Electrical Engineering.

Lancaster, F. W., R. L. Rapport, and J. K. Penry (1972a). "Evaluating the Effectiveness of an On-Line Natural Language Retrieval System." *Information Storage Retrieval* **8** (5), 223–245.

Lancaster, F. W. (1972b). *Evaluation of On-Line Searching in MEDLARS (AIM–TWX) by Biomedical Practitioners.* Urbana, Ill.: University of Illinois, Graduate School of Library Science, Occasional Paper No. 101.

Lancaster, F. W. (1972c). *Vocabulary Control for Information Retrieval.* Washington, D.C.: Information Resources Press.

Reisner, P. (1963). "Construction of a Growing Thesaurus by Conversational Interaction in a Man-Machine System." *Amer. Documentation Inst. Short Papers*, Part 1, 99–100.

Reisner, P. (1966). *Evaluation of a "Growing" Thesaurus.* Yorktown Heights, N.Y.: IBM, Thomas Watson Research Center, Research Paper RC-1662.

Rubinoff, M., S. Bergman, H. Cautin, and F. Rapp (1968). "Easy English, a Language for Information Retrieval Through a Remote Typewriter Console." *Commun. Assoc. Computing Machinery* **11** (10), 693–696.

Salton, G. (1968). *Automatic Information Organization and Retrieval.* New York: McGraw-Hill.

Simmons, R. F. (1965). "Answering English Questions by Computer: a Survey." *Commun. Assoc. Computing Machinery* **8** (1), 53–70.

Smith, J. L. (1966). *MICRO : a Strategy for Retrieving, Ranking, and Qualifying Document References*. Santa Monica, Ca.: System Development Corporation, SP-2289.

Sommar, H. G., and D. E. Dennis (1969). "A New Method of Weighted Term Searching with a Highly Structured Thesaurus." *Proc. Amer. Soc. Information Sci.* **6**, 193–198.

Chapter Twelve

Indexing and Cataloging On-Line

So far we have concentrated our attention upon the output end of an on-line information retrieval system, namely the activities of searching the files and the viewing and/or printing of citations or abstracts. The input activities of an information retrieval system can also be conducted on-line if appropriate provisions are made in the overall system programs. On-line input can involve either:

1. Using the on-line terminal for the clerical task of putting a bibliographic record into the system, working from a record (indexing, cataloging, or abstracting form) prepared elsewhere and not as an on-line activity—in this case, the terminal is used merely as a device for data entry, avoiding such alternatives as punched cards, paper tape, or optical character readers.*
2. Using the on-line terminal in the actual intellectual tasks of bibliographic input, namely cataloging, indexing, or abstracting—in this case, the machine-readable record is created at the terminal, by indexer, cataloger, or abstractor, and no further input procedures are necessary.

Clerical Input On-Line

One organization in which bibliographic records are input on-line is the Nuclear Safety Information Center at Oak Ridge National Laboratory

---

*On-line data entry is used in many varied applications. Different approaches for putting textual material into machine-readable form, including use of a CRT terminal, have been compared in a useful article by Schneider (1971).

REPORT NUMBER OR OTHER IDENTIFICATION

ROE-72-8

NSIC BIBLIOGRAPHIC REPORT

ABSTRACTORS INITIALS		RS		
27	SIGNIFICANT DATE	32	LANG-UAGE 33	COUN-TRY 34	SUBJECT NUMBER

	7	CARD NO. 8 9	TYPE 13	BIBLO. LIMIT 15	EVALU-ATION 16	17	CATEGORY	JOURNAL ABBREVIATION 22 23	26 27	SIGNIFICANT DATE	32	LANG-UAGE 33	COUN-TRY 34 35	SUBJECT NUMBER 40

ACCESSION NUMBER: 7 0 7 7 9

CARD NO.: 0 1

TYPE: N

BIBLO. LIMIT

EVALU-ATION: X

CATEGORY: 1 7 1 1

SIGNIFICANT DATE — MO 0 5 DAY 0 5 YR. 7 2

LANG-UAGE: E

COUN-TRY: A

41	49	FOR-MAT 50	BIBLO. LIMIT 51	REP-ORT 52	54	PROP-RIETARY 55

CORPORATE AUTHOR: D R L

REPORT: 1

AVAILIBILITY

AEC-DRL

NSIC

TITLE:

Structural Damage to Containment Torus Baffles

ABSTRACT (ABOUT 100 WORDS)

During a scheduled maintenance shutdown at a boiling-water reactor (BWR), structural damage of baffles in the pressure-suppression chamber (torus) of the containment was noted during internal inspection of the torus. On the basis of an engineered analysis, it was concluded that the damage resulted from the dynamic loading produced by the discharge of the primary-system safety/relief valves into the water in the torus. The baffles were removed, and the discharge point for the relief valves was moved into the deepest part of the torus water.

Memo: ROE-72-8 +. 3 pages, May 5, 1972

Auth: None

Corp: U.S. Atomic Energy Commission, Division of Reactor Licensing, Washington, D. C.

KEY WORDS

Reactor, BWR
*Failure, Design Error
Containment, Pressure Suppression
*Damage
*Hydraulic Effect
*Containment Structure
Pressure Relief
Valve
Operating Experience

NEW
KEY WORD

UCN-6107A   NOTE: NEW KEY WORDS MUST BE DEFINED; ATTACH DEFINITION ON 3 X 5 CARD.
(3 10-67)

Figure 12.1. Specimen input form as used by the Nuclear Safety Information Center.
Reproduced by permission of the Nuclear Safety Information Center.

(Buchanan and Kidd, 1969; Parks and Julian 1971). At NSIC, the complete bibliographic record (see Figure 12.1), comprising descriptive cataloging data, abstract, and index terms, is input at IBM 2260 terminals. The records are thus entered into a data cell and are immediately available for retrieval operations. Error checking and correction procedures are built into the NSIC system. In this application, it was discovered that on-line processing increased the cost of input to the system. In an earlier system, the combination of keypunching and batch processing using an IBM 7090 was estimated to cost $1.40 per item input, while the cost of the on-line input using an IBM 360 was estimated to be $2.25 per item (approximately 900 items input per month) (Cottrell and Buchanan, 1970). Recent improvements in hardware and software have since reduced the estimated cost per item to $2.00.

On-line input of cataloging data for the augmented catalog is now undertaken in the Intrex Project at MIT. On-line input is estimated to be about twice as expensive as the paper tape input method previously used ($43.02 versus $23.65 for ten complete records). With a slight program change to allow for greater input buffering, it was estimated that on-line input costs would be cut to about $30 for ten records. The advantages claimed for the on-line procedure are the processing of records into the data base more quickly, the reduction of input errors through the use of on-line text editing capabilities, and the ease of correction of any errors that do occur (Massachusetts Institute of Technology, 1971).

Intrex input is made on Datel typewriter terminals and a typical record takes about 15 minutes to enter (about 2000 keystrokes). Two proofreading operations are conducted on the typewriter printout, and these together take an average of about 6 minutes per record. Two on-line editing steps are carried out, together taking an average of about 2.5 minutes. The input typist works from a manuscript record of bibliographic data, abstract, and index phrases (see Chapter Three) rather than from a structured form.

On-line terminals have been used for the conversion of bibliographic records to machine-readable form in very large quantities. Balfour (1968), for example, describes such conversion processes applied to the shelf list of the libraries at the State University of New York at Buffalo. Using the IBM DATATEXT service, an IBM 2741 terminal was employed to transmit the bibliographic data to disk storage, and then to produce an output magnetic tape. The terminals were located in Buffalo and the computer used was in Cleveland. DATATEXT was a suitable vehicle for this work, because its programs incorporate text editing capabilities and simple on-line error correction. Balfour found that the direct costs of bibliographic input amounted to 55¢ per title. The full cost breakdown for the conversion appears in Table 12.1.

TABLE 12.1.   Cost Breakdown for On-Line Bibliographic Input

Input, proofreading, and correction	
Total Library of Congress cards input	49,348
Typist hours input	3,035
Typist hours correcting	492
Total typist hours	3,527
Proofreading hours	1,235
Number of errors per Library of Congress card	0.42
Library of Congress card input rate per hour	16.3
Library of Congress card correction rate per hour	100
Overall conversion rate (input and correction) cards per hour	14
Proofreading rate, cards per hour	40
Costs	
Labor cost at $1.75 per hour	$ 8,078.00
Equipment and supervisors	18,995.00
Total cost	$27,073.00
Cost per card converted	$0.55

Utilization of console time		
Hours typed	3,381	81.4%
Hours consoles down	245	5.9%
Hours computer down	91	2.2%
Hours lost time	438	10.5%
	4,155	100.0%

Monthly operational costs per terminal	
IBM 2741 communications terminal	$ 85.00
Western Electric 103a data set	27.50
24 hour voice-grade lease line to Cleveland plus local telephone costs	385.50
2 DATATEXT agreements at $310	620.00
Total	$1,118.00

Balfour points out the ease with which records can be proofread and corrected at the on-line terminal. The computer automatically assigns a number to each line of input. Using these line numbers, a typist can rearrange text, add or delete information, or correct errors. It requires only four keystrokes to move a new line into its appropriate place in the text. In making a correction, the typist merely types the correct and incorrect words and the computer programs take over, retyping the complete line to show that the correction has been executed. Figure 12.2 shows a sample input record with correction.

c
$\overline{\text{CLEARED}}$

UNCONTROLLED MODE

a
$\overline{\text{AUTOMATIC}}$ MODE

n
$\overline{\text{NEXT}}$ NUMBER -- 3

90t BS2575.3.A7
10t Bible. N.T. Matthew. English. 1963. New English.   3

20t The Gospel according to Matthew=. Commentary by A.W. Argyle.   4

30a Cambridge
30b University Press
30c 1963
40t 227 p. maps. 20 cm.   5

50t The Dambridge Bible Commentary: New English Bible   6

70t Bible. N.T. Matthew -- Commentaries.
71t Argyle, Aubrey William, 1910-   7

73t Title.
60z   8

92t 226.207
94t 63-23728   9

n
$\overline{\text{NEXT}}$ NUMBER -- 10

6 Dambridge   Cambridge
50t The Cambridge Bible commentary: New English Bible

Figure 12.2. Sample input and correction made on-line. Reproduced from Balfour (1968) by permission of the American Library Association.

On-line input of bibliographic data is also conducted at the Shawnee Mission (Kansas) Public Schools. The work has been described by Miller and Hodges (1971, 1972) and by Miller, et al. (1970). The terminal operator enters cataloging data from the title page and verso of the book itself. These pages have been marked appropriately by a professional librarian (cataloger) who also slips into the book an indexing sheet containing subject headings assigned, added entries, and annotation. From these data the terminal operator constructs the catalog entry on-line. Certain necessary bibliographic items are derived automatically by the computer programs themselves, thus saving operator time and effort. For example, the *Cutter number* (an abbreviation for the name of an author, commonly used in libraries) is derived automatically from the first three letters of the author's surname, unless specifically suppressed by the operator. On-line input of records continues on a daily basis, and at night the necessary library records are printed. For each book cataloged, a set of catalog cards and labels for book pocket and spine are generated.

The Shawnee Mission system incorporates careful quality control procedures. The original keying is carefully examined for any content or typing errors. Operators examine one another's work and make corrections or verify the transaction; output can be printed only after records are verified as correct. Very few errors escape this procedure; in 5200 sets of records produced by the system (representing 5200 bibliographic items), only 76 sets were found to contain errors. This low error rate is attributed to carefully trained operators, ease of identifying and correcting mistakes, and program responses that will tell the operator of certain data errors, missing data, or overflowed fields.

This on-line cataloging system uses an adaptation of an IBM program known as FASTER (Filing and Source Data Entry Techniques for Easier Retrieval), a program used for law enforcement purposes by the Kansas City, Mo., Police Department. It is implemented at Shawnee Mission with an IBM 360/40, with 256K of storage, and IBM 2740 terminals. The on-line system replaced an earlier batch system. Comparative costs for the two are shown in Table 12.2. These costs are based on "(1) tasks performed at Central Library Processing from arrival to mailing out to destination library, (2) library and data processing staff, (3) computer time prorated at $\frac{1}{5}$ of hourly non-district rate, and (4) supplies. A merger of two separate groups and a $5\frac{1}{2}\%$ salary increase account for the cost growth for library staff" (Miller and Hodges, 1971, p. 21).

Table 12.2 shows cost for the 28,000 items processed in the fiscal year 1969–1970 and for an estimated 100,000 acquisitions to be handled in the fiscal year 1970–1971. Duplicates cost less in each system because they bypass certain work stations. From Table 12.3 it can be seen that, in this application, the cost per bibliographic item input decreases substantially with the move from batch processing to on-line operation. Comparable cost figures were estimated for the fiscal year 1971–1972, and these are shown in Table 12.4. These costs are based on (1) tasks performed on the item from arrival at the

TABLE 12.2   Overall Costs for On-Line and Off-Line Cataloging at Shawnee Mission

	Batch system, fiscal year 1969–1970	Percentage of total		Terminal system, fiscal year 1970–1971
Library staff	$64,460	66	70	$117,108
Data processing staff	6,300			2,000
Supplies	3,834	5	4	7,764
Computer	18,750	29	21	35,000
Terminals, lines	0	0	5	8,450
Total	$93,344	100	100	$170,322

SOURCE: Miller and Hodges (1971). Reproduced by permission of the American Library Association.

TABLE 12.3.   Unit Costs for On-Line and Off-Line Cataloging at Shawnee Mission

	Any item	Duplicate	New item
Batch	$4.30	$3.60	$6.10
On-line	2.50	2.14	4.86

SOURCE: Miller and Hodges (1971). Reproduced by permission of the American Library Association.

TABLE 12.4.   Estimated Unit Costs for On-Line Cataloging at Shawnee Mission, Fiscal Year 1971–1972

	Card and label sets only	Card and label sets and all other printed products
Any item	$2.25	$2.53
Duplicate	1.91	2.15
New to system	4.36	4.91

SOURCE: Miller and Hodges (1972). Reproduced by permission of Graduate School of Library Science, University of Illinois.

processing center to mailing out to destination library, (2) library and data processing staff, (3) computer time, and (4) supplies.

On-line cataloging is also conducted within the shared cataloging project of the Ohio College Library Center (1971), using the MARC

(Machine-Readable Cataloging) tapes generated by the Library of Congress. The shared cataloging project, which involves college and university libraries in Ohio that elect to belong to the center, produces sets of catalog cards suitable for filing in the catalogs of the member libraries. In dealing with a particular book, a cataloger at one of the participating libraries will key-in the Library of Congress catalog card number or other identification key. This will cause display of the master MARC record for this item. The cataloger will then examine this record for errors and correct any that are present, also indicating any modifications that are to be made for his own institution. After necessary additions or deletions are made in the on-line record, the cataloger keys in a command which will generate, off-line, sets of catalog cards arranged for filing in the catalogs of the library. Modifications made to an entry by a cataloger at any library are local modifications for printing purposes only and do not alter the master bibliographic record. In the case of a book for which no MARC record exists, and which has not been previously cataloged into the system, the cataloger builds up a master record at the on-line terminal using a displayed *workform*. To assist the cataloging process, terminal users can choose to view other records for titles by the same author or other catalog records for items having the same classification number. Again, once a satisfactory record is arrived at, the commands PRODUCE and SEND cause the necessary sets of catalog cards to be produced.

The Ohio system differs from the Shawnee Mission system in a number of respects. Most notably, original cataloging may be conducted at the on-line terminal in Ohio, whereas the professional cataloging activities are performed away from the terminal at Shawnee Mission, the console being used solely for the clerical task of inputting records.

The Ohio College Library Center makes use of CRT terminals specially designed for this application and manufactured to center specifications.

On-line cataloging is potentially more efficient and economical because it can eliminate several time-consuming and error-prone steps, as illustrated in the simplified flowcharts of Figure 12.3, which are taken from Warheit (1970).

Another on-line input procedure has been described by Sheldon, et al. (1968). It is used in the Textile Information Retrieval Project (TIRP) at MIT. *Tracer sheets*, completed for each document, contain bibliographic information plus keywords assigned by the indexer. The pertinent information on these sheets is then typed into the computer using a text-editing program to facilitate error correction. Figure 12.4 shows the sequence of computer checks which follow during subsequent posting to the various files.

OFF–LINE

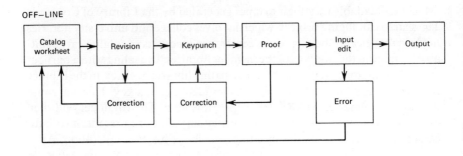

ON–LINE

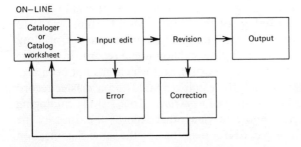

Figure 12.3. Comparison of steps involved in on-line and off-line cataloging. Reproduced from Warheit (1970) by permission of the American Library Association.

The posting programs check the incoming data against those already in the files. The interactive properties of the system allow the programs to report any errors or inconsistencies that are encountered and allow the operator to enter corrections directly into the input while it is being processed. After the input has been checked, it is compressed and reformatted in a manner that is more efficient for storage and retrieval.

The POST 1 program (see Figure 12.4) examines the input for clerical errors, reporting any encountered on the console along with possible correction options. POST 2 examines all keywords against a stored keyword list and reports back any words not found, together with the words that most closely match those that are not recognized (i.e., the near misses) as in the following example:

IN DOCUMENT 57-038707

CARBON - - WAS NOT FOUND

THE NEAR MISSES ARE - -

CAPS (SPINNING)	001254
CARBOHYDRATES	013060
CARBONIZED NOILS	001255

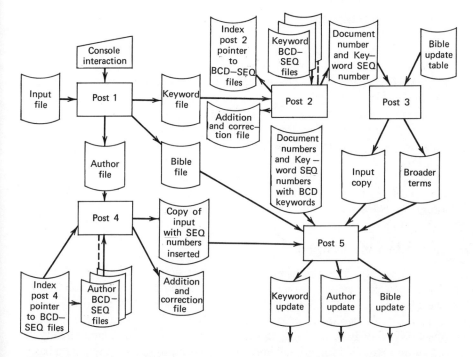

Figure 12.4. Sequence of computer input checks used in the Textile Information Retrieval Project. Reproduced from Sheldon, et al. (1968) by permission of the *Textile Research Journal.*

The operator may then (*a*) choose an alternative keyword from the list, (*b*) delete the term entirely, or (*c*) enter it as a temporary keyword that can later be examined as a candidate for entry into the thesaurus.

POST 3 automatically posts each document to each key term selected by the indexer and also to the term immediately above this in the thesaurus (*automatic generic posting*) unless this up-posting is suppressed by the indexer. POST 4 checks the author, title, and source fields. POST 5 regroups all the validated data for each document and causes updating of the necessary files.

These various posting processes produce a list of all errors found and all corrections made. New keyword candidates for the thesaurus are also listed. All these editing and correcting routines consume only 3 seconds per document on the average, or about 15¢ for each item.

It should be evident from the above discussion that there is some doubt as to whether on-line clerical input of bibliographic records is economically competitive with more conventional off-line procedures. The figures available from various sources are in conflict. Cost savings are claimed in some operations, but increased costs are reported in others. It is clear, however, that on-line procedures may improve accuracy of input. In a well-designed system, as much of the error control as possible will be automatic. There are certain obvious advantages in being able to detect, and possibly correct, a human error as it is made. Such on-line error-detection procedures may have an important psychological effect upon the operator, and may actually reduce his own tendency to error.

The availability of on-line terminals also makes possible the direct construction of bibliographic records on-line by professional indexers or catalogers, thus eliminating the clerical step usually effected by punched cards, paper tape, or the typing of *page-reader* forms for scanning by an optical character reader. Some of the possibilities for on-line indexing are discussed below.

Intellectual Input On-Line

On-line indexing implies that the indexer prepares an indexing record for a document at the on-line terminal. The descriptors are keyboarded at the terminal by the indexer. Preferably, the terminal should provide the capability of video display (cathode ray tube) of this record to the indexer. Once the record is completed to the indexer's satisfaction, being already in machine-readable form, it may immediately be input to the system data base. The process has certain obvious advantages:

1. Writing or typing of forms is avoided.
2. Clerical errors are reduced by error-checking routines.
3. The clerical task of converting an indexer's work to machine-readable form (e.g., by punched cards or paper tape) is eliminated.
4. Physical handling of material (e.g., printed tools) is reduced or eliminated.
5. Record formatting can be done by the computer while indexing is taking place.
6. Indexing delays are reduced, because the record is immediately available for input to the data base.
7. New terms can be suggested by the indexer, for subsequent consideration by a thesaurus control group, without the need to complete any troublesome forms.
8. The indexer works from tools (e.g., vocabularies) that are completely up-to-date.

In addition to these obvious advantages, on-line indexing may offer certain other advantages, including economy of indexing time, the provision of additional indexing aids, and possibly the presentation of certain indexing cues. It is these aspects that we should consider in greater detail.

To aid the indexing process, the vocabulary can certainly be displayed on-line. An indexer may key-in a word or phrase and request one of several possible displays, including the following types:

1. *Alphabetical.* The term, if recognized, is displayed along with other terms alphabetically adjacent in the system vocabulary. Even when not recognized, the appropriate alphabetical display can be generated. For example, the indexer may erroneously ask for MONGOLOIDISM. This is not a valid descriptor, but the alphabetical display closest to this spurious descriptor is generated as follows:

> MOLONEY VIRUS
> MOLTING HORMONE
> MOLYBDENUM
> MONASE
> MONGOLISM
> MONGOLOID RACE
> MONIEZIASIS
> MONILIA
> MONILIALES

The indexer recognizes that MONGOLISM is the term he is seeking and accepts it accordingly.

2. *Hierarchical (tree structure) display.*
3. *Term with cross-references.* For the term first entered, if recognized, a display of terms referred to and referred from is generated.
4. *Permuted.* The indexer may keyboard a word, say ISOTOPE, and ask for all descriptors containing it.*

The indexer may select terms from any of these displays (e.g., by depressing an appropriate key). These terms are recorded and subsequently displayed when the indexer recalls his index record.

In actual fact, comparatively little work on on-line indexing has so far been conducted, and most that has been conducted is purely experimental. In the following paragraphs, we describe some possible techniques that might be used on-line to assist the indexing process. They should be regarded as possibilities rather than accomplished facts. Most are relatively complex and expensive to implement, and it is uncertain whether these techniques

---

*There is no real evidence that it is faster to request and view an on-line display than to consult the printed thesaurus. However, selection of a term from a display, without the need for typing it or writing it, may well make the overall process faster. Moreover, the on-line system can generate *on-demand* displays that would be difficult, if not impossible to achieve on the printed page.

could be justified, from a cost-effectiveness point of view, in a large operating system.

Assuming that the system incorporates an entry vocabulary, any term recognized in this vocabulary should be acceptable and capable of being converted automatically to the appropriate approved descriptor. Thus, if an indexer keys in DOWN'S SYNDROME, which appears in the entry vocabulary, the approved descriptor MONGOLISM is substituted (and displayed) automatically. Likewise, if CERVICOTOME is entered, the approved descriptors CERVIX/PATHOLOGY and BIOPSY are automatically substituted from the master vocabulary file.

The indexer may also be spared the necessity for keyboarding a descriptor in its full form. The system may recognize unique *minimum character-strings* and display a candidate descriptor once this minimum string has been keyed. For example, an indexer can key-in the string SUBG, the initial characters of a descriptor he is seeking. The programs then take over and display the descriptor thus uniquely identified, say SUBGINGIVAL CURETTAGE, this being the only descriptor in the vocabulary beginning with the string SUBG. It may also be possible for the indexer to enter a word root and request a display of all descriptors beginning with this string. This feature is particularly useful if the indexer imperfectly remembers a term or is not quite sure of the spelling. The LISTAR indexing system, described later in this chapter, permits an indexer to enter an initial string of characters only. The system will then display, for acceptance or rejection by the indexer, the descriptor that matches this string. However, if the character-string is not unique (i.e., it applies to several descriptors), the LISTAR system will not display all possibilities, but only the first one it comes to in its stored thesaurus.

The indexer may also be permitted to browse in the data base. He may, for example, wish to find out how a particular descriptor has been used in the past. This he can do by requesting a sample display of titles (or abstracts) indexed under this term [the potential value of such indexing precedents has been discussed by Herr (1970)]. Alternatively, an author search can be used to find how a particular citation has been indexed (e.g., the indexer would like to recall the descriptors assigned to earlier papers in a series). Obviously, tallies of indexing usage can also be displayed. The indexer may thereby avoid a term used very heavily already in favor of another more discriminating one. This aspect has been discussed by Bennett (1969).

The on-line operation may simplify the introduction of new or proposed descriptors. The indexer may suggest a new descriptor that appears to be needed, and incorporate it into the index record for the document that generated it. The descriptor is marked with a special code to indicate its provisional nature. On a regular basis, the vocabulary control group can call up for display or printout all new suggestions, and can review the proposal in the context of the complete index record and the appropriate citation or abstract. Indexers are more likely to contribute substantially to the indexing process in this way than they would if they were required to complete a suggestion form. Moreover, the proposed descriptor is immediately available and can be used by another indexer before it has been officially approved. In an on-line system, the indexers should make substantial contributions to the growth of a dynamic vocabulary.

The console can be used to display any kind of indexing *form*. Pre-established *check-tags* (concepts so common and important in a field that they should be considered for possible relevance to each document) can be shown, allowing the indexer to incorporate selected tags by depressing the necessary keys or by use of a light pen. Structured formats can be used to aid indexing with links and roles or to assist the correct facet analysis of the subject matter.

Appropriate checking programs may be designed to avoid certain types of indexing errors. Common misspellings may be recognized and corrected automatically. Completely unrecognized terms may be rejected and thus brought immediately to the indexer's attention. Certain illegal combinations may also be recognized and rejected by the system. For example, the indexer may use an illegal main heading/subheading combination. Providing the descriptors are placed into broad categories (e.g., the COSATI fields) and that certain subheadings are applicable only to designated categories, the recognition of illegal combinations in this way is relatively straightforward. Again, we would emphasize that, although it is possible to validate each term as it is entered, it is not necessarily cost-effective to operate in this way.

Carried to its logical conclusion, the on-line indexing program might be capable of making suggestions to the indexer or providing him with appropriate cues. For example, statistical association links can be generated, thus allowing the indexer to see which descriptors have been used most frequently in the past with a particular descriptor already assigned. His attention may, by this means, be drawn to terms that he would otherwise have overlooked. Some preliminary experiments with this concept have been reported by Rosenberg (1971). In video console indexing procedures described by Margolies (1970), an *adaptive interface* will accept the indexer's set of terms and will generate a second set of terms related to the starting terms on the basis of statistical association. The indexer may then modify his original selection.

Finally, most large information systems use senior personnel to check or revise the work of junior indexers. Such checking may be greatly facilitated by on-line operation. A reviser can call up, on a daily basis, the work of an indexer and examine it at his own terminal. Corrections or recommendations can be made immediately. It is possible that even notes can be recorded. The indexer, in turn, can call back and review any indexing records in which changes have been made or recommended by the senior indexer. The whole revision process is thus streamlined and expedited, and delays that might otherwise result (e.g., in passing forms backward and forward) are successfully avoided. In an information network, a reviser at a central location could review the work of indexers geographically dispersed at a number of specialized information centers, possibly on a sampling basis.

Experiments with On-Line Indexing

Some interesting experiments in on-line indexing have been conducted by means of the Negotiated Search Facility (NSF) established at the IBM Research Laboratory, San Jose, Ca., and described by Bennett (1969, 1971), Bennett, et al. (1972), and Clarke (1970). The facility operates in one 170K partition of a multiprogrammed IBM 360, under OS. Communication with the system is effected through an IBM 2260 display station. In this system, response to an indexer input can be obtained within about 3 seconds. The indexer in NSF is given a group of *working areas* (directory area, save area, bibliography area, logic area) within which he can examine and manipulate various data needed to assist the indexing process. If an indexer is considering the assignment of a particular term to a document, he can check the validity of the term against a machine-stored authority list. If he finds the term there, he may also, if he wishes, view the index records of other documents to which this term has already been assigned. This step may suggest other descriptors more appropriate than his original selection, or other descriptors that should be used with this descriptor. Alternatively, he can view the authority list in order to discover other terms that are related to his original selection through the cross-reference structure of the list. The indexer can view tallies that indicate how many times each descriptor has been used previously in indexing. He can also discover how many times two or more descriptors have been used together in indexing, and he may, if he wishes, request the index records for any items already indexed under a particular combination of descriptors. All these data, difficult or impossible to provide in any off-line or manual operation, are intended to aid the indexer in the selection of the most appropriate set of descriptors for the particular document at hand, especially in the selection of a set that will place the present document with those similar to it, yet, at the same time, allow its own unique features to discriminate it from those items previously indexed.

Video console indexing experiments, conducted at the Moore School of Electrical Engineering, have been described by Margolies (1970). The experiments were conducted on a toxicology data base and they make use of an RCA Spectra 70/46, together with an RCA Video Data Terminal (VDT) equipped with a light pen. Indexing is conducted from abstracts displayed on the screen. Several levels of HELP commands are available to explain the other commands and how to use the system. Such a HELP command may be issued at any time without interrupting the indexing process. A split-screen approach is used with the video terminal: one portion contains as much of the abstract as will fit, a second is used for the input of commands, and a third displays the results of the latest command.

The indexer has the ability to display term definitions, browse in the thesaurus, create a list of index terms, and test this against the stored thesaurus. Margolies (1970) also reported plans for an *adaptive interface*, which will accept the indexer's list of suggested terms and generate a set of additional terms that are statistically related to these starting terms. The indexer may then select additional terms from this automatically generated list. To avoid extensive typing, some input can be made by means of a light pen. Commands are selected from *menus* of commands displayed on the screen.

On-line indexing experiments have also been conducted for the National Library of Medicine (MEDLARS) by the Lincoln Laboratory of MIT. These experiments have been described by Armenti, et al. (1970, 1971a, b). The system used is an extension of LISTAR (Lincoln Information Storage and Associative Retrieval), a general-purpose storage and retrieval system that has been described by Armenti and Galley (1970). The LISTAR indexing experiments used an Advanced Remote Display Station (ARDS 100A), manufactured by Computer Displays Inc., which was located at the National Library of Medicine and connected by common carrier lines to the Lincoln Laboratory IBM 360/67 in Lexington, Mass. The ARDS, which comprises a display terminal with modified teletype keyboard, has a screen capacity of over 4000 alphameric characters. The indexing trials were conducted in one of two modes: dual-screen or split-screen. In the latter mode, the upper portion of the screen was used to display the information to be modified and stored (e.g., term displays), while the lower portion carried the processing commands. In the dual-screen mode, two separate display scopes were used to separate these two types of data.

Three separate indexing phases were investigated in the LISTAR study:

1. *Bibliographic input*. In this phase, an input typist enters at the terminal the bibliographic data (*descriptive cataloging*) on an article: authors, title, full source including page references.
2. *Subject indexing*. A trained indexing professional describes the subject matter of the article by means of terms selected from the controlled vocabulary of the system, *MeSH*.

3. *Revision.* A senior indexer (*reviser*) reviews each indexed article to confirm or correct the work of the indexer. The reviser may add, delete or modify terms assigned by the original indexer.

A major design criterion was to reduce keyboarding as much as possible. Since all articles from a particular issue of a journal were indexed at the same sitting, the journal identification data were entered only once. Thereafter, the starting page of an article was enough to identify it uniquely. Terms could be selected by the indexer by reference numbers shown on displays generated by previous commands. Even when terms were typed, they could be drastically abbreviated—the indexer need only key in as much of the term as necessary to identify it uniquely. For example, the string LIPOT is adequate to identify the descriptor LIPOTROPIC FACTORS.

The LISTAR on-line indexing system includes many interesting features: an indexer may call up and examine any changes made to his work by a reviser, a *title analysis* program will scan the title of an article to discover any direct matches with the controlled vocabulary of the system, certain portions of the vocabulary can be displayed for the indexer (including the complete set of subheadings that may validly be used with a particular main heading), and certain mappings (from unacceptable terms to acceptable equivalents) are conducted automatically. The LISTAR system will also check on the acceptability of the spelling of descriptors entered by the indexer.

Staff and machine times associated with the first series of experiments (Armenti, et al., 1970) are displayed in Table 12.5. *Wait time* is defined as the time the user has to wait after inputting a command until a response was received and an indication given by the system that another command could be accepted. *Think time* is defined as the time elapsing between the appearance of the prompting arrow (signalling that a new command can be accepted) and the user's carriage return which signals the entry of a new command by the user. As can be seen from this table, the average times per article for the various activities work out to 5 minutes for bibliographic input, 14 minutes for subject indexing, and 21 minutes for revising, making an average total staff time of 40 minutes per article. These data translate into production rates as follows:

Bibliographic input	11	articles per man hour
Subject indexing	4.5	articles per man hour
Revising	2.9	articles per man hour

The LISTAR investigators suggest that these times could be reduced with greater operator experience, and that the full power of the interactive capabilities were not used by indexers or revisers. The dual-screen mode of operation was preferred by the indexers because of the increased workspace provided.

TABLE 12.5.　Staff and Machine Times[a] for LISTAR On-Line Indexing

Bibliographic input			
Number of articles in sample = 55			
	Median	Mean	Standard deviation
Number of commands	3	4	2
Total time, minutes	5	5	4
Think time, minutes	1	1	1
Wait time, minutes	3	4	3
CPU time, seconds	4	6	7
Subject indexing			
Number of articles in sample = 42			
	Median	Mean	Standard deviation
Number of commands	17	21	9
Total time, minutes	11	14	8
Think time, minutes	6	8	6
Wait time, minutes	5	5	4
CPU time, seconds	21.5	26	15
Revising			
Number of articles in sample = 24			
	Median	Mean	Standard deviation
Number of commands	19	20	10
Total time, minutes	17	21	11
Think time, minutes	13	17	11
Wait time, minutes	4	4	2
CPU time, seconds	24	26	9

SOURCE: Armenti, et al. (1970). Reproduced by permission of Lincoln Laboratory, MIT.
[a]Times rounded to nearest minute or second.

A report on a third series of LISTAR experiments was issued in December 1971 (Armenti, et al., 1971). The experimental phase described concentrated upon the process of indexing revision and was much broader in scope. Five experienced revisers from the NLM staff participated in the study, and the indexing records for 217 journal articles were involved. Performance of the revisers on-line was compared with their performance in normal manual revising activities. The journal articles were drawn from two journals indexed *in-depth* (with an average of 15 descriptors assigned) and two *non-depth* (with an average of 4–6 descriptors assigned). Comparative revising times

TABLE 12.6. Average Total Time (Minutes) per Article for LISTAR On-Line Revising

Reviser	3L0	JD3	MGE	VNN	Reviser's average
1	4.9 (5)	6.9 (19)	6.4 (10)	10.6 (10)	7.4 (44)
2	5.0 (5)	10.8 (19)	11.0 (10)	7.6 (13)	9.3 (47)
3	4.0 (5)	14.9 (14)		13.8 (13)	12.7 (32)
4	3.8 (6)	5.7 (19)	8.6 (10)	8.0 (13)	6.7 (48)
Journal averages	4.4 (21)	9.2 (71)	8.6 (30)	9.9 (49)	8.7 (171)

SOURCE: Armenti, et al. (1971b). Reproduced by permission of Lincoln Laboratory, MIT.

TABLE 12.7. Average Total Time (Minutes) per Article for Manual Revising

Reviser	3L0 (6)	JD3 (19)	MGE (10)	VNN (13)	Reviser's average
1	1.7	4.0	2.0	4.7	3.1
2	5.0	4.8	5.0	4.2	4.8
3	5.0	7.9	4.5	5.8	5.8
4	2.5	3.0	3.8	2.3	2.9
Journal averages	3.6	4.9	3.8	4.3	4.2

SOURCE: Armenti, et al. (1971b). Reproduced by permission of Lincoln Laboratory, MIT.

of four revisers are shown in Tables 12.6 and 12.7 for on-line and manual revision, respectively. In these tables the four journals are represented by codes (e.g., 3L0), and the parenthetical figures indicate the number of articles involved in the calculation. Note that the average time for on-line revision is approximately twice the average time for manual revision. A fifth reviser, less familiar than the others with the operations of the on-line system, performed significantly worse than the other four, and the data for this person are omitted from Tables 12.6 and 12.7. The difference in performance is shown clearly in Figure 12.5, which is a cumulative distribution of articles completed by each reviser plotted against revision times. It is noteworthy that reviser 1 worked at an average of 19 minutes per article in the second series of LISTAR experiments (Armenti, et al., 1971a), but through

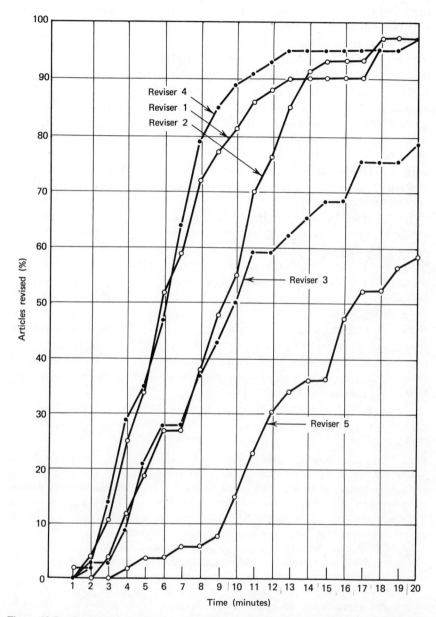

Figure 12.5. Cumulated distribution of articles completed on-line by each of five revisers plotted against revision times. Reproduced from Armenti, et al. (1971b) by permission of Lincoln Laboratory, MIT.

increased experience and practice had improved to an average of 7.4 minutes per article by the third series.

The average of 8.7 minutes for on-line revision is made up of 6.5 minutes of think time and 2.2 minutes of wait time. The fact that manual revising averaged 4.2 minutes per item implies that approximately 2.3 minutes of the on-line think time was spent in thinking about how to communicate the reviser's changes to the computer. The think time in the third series of experiments was down sharply (62%) on the average from the think time in the earlier investigations. This decrease in think time resulted in wait time becoming a very significant (25%) part of the total time. In the words of the LISTAR investigators, it was also "a source of considerable annoyance and frustration to the reviser since it forces him to work at the computer's pace instead of his own."

While the LISTAR experiments have not demonstrated greater efficiency for indexing and revising on-line as compared with conventional manual operations, they have shown significant improvements over time as a result of improvements in the programs themselves, as well as increased experience on the part of NLM participants. The investigators suggest that on-line performance times could be reduced further with special-purpose computer programs designed specifically for the indexing and revising functions (LISTAR is really a general-purpose storage and retrieval system), with a time-sharing computer dedicated to NLM activities, and with the operators situated in the same building as the computer (remote operation led to communications and transmission problems which were annoying and frustrating for the indexers and revisers).

The LISTAR studies are important. Their possible significance is perhaps best summarized in the following extract from Armenti, et al. (1971b):

> In this exercise, we have focused on only one small, although very critical part, of the MEDLARS operation—revising. Moreover, for the most part, we have further restricted our attention to one aspect of revising, namely the time it takes a reviser to process an indexed citation. As a result, we may have left the reader with the impression that production time is the sole criterion for judging the feasibility of on-line revising. We believe such an inference would be in error.
>
> Production time is indeed a very important consideration. If on-line times are not reasonably competitive with manual times, then one should have serious doubts about its feasibility. However, if a reviser can do no more than match his production rate by using the computer then there is very little to be gained from a conversion to on-line processing. To make such conversion worthwhile there must clearly be some additional advantages which will either significantly reduce time in other phases of the MEDLARS operation, improve the quality of indexing, or provide side benefits over and above the regular MEDLARS daily operation, such as reduced material handling.

This exercise shows that revisers who are relatively inexperienced with on-line procedures were able to process a citation in about twice the time on-line as manually. We believe that the on-line time delay due to poor man-computer interaction can be reduced substantially through training and experience. Moreover, the computer wait time can be reduced significantly so that, overall, on-line revising in terms of productivity can be made competitive with manual revising. However, one should not expect the on-line times to be less than, or even equal to, manual times. The reviser's task is almost entirely intellectual. Very little of his time is spent in the mechanics of revising, that is, correcting or adding to the indexing form. This is true whether he is working manually or on-line. While computer time can be made very small, perhaps less than a minute, it cannot be reduced to zero. Therefore, unless a reviser is given computer aids which reduce the intellectual effort, he is bound to take more time at the computer than at his desk. Such aids may come out of the research in automatic indexing, but none seem to be available for ready implementation at present. Since this is so, the utility of on-line revising will depend rather heavily on the side benefits.

Because of the limits set on the exercise, the side benefits of on-line revising were not explicitly evaluated. We can, however, indicate those that seem naturally to fall out of on-line revising and which have some support from the exercise just completed.

(1) The citation completed by the reviser is in machine readable form, ready for direct input into the MEDLARS system. This eliminates the need for flexowriter or key to tape transfer of the handwritten form into computer readable form.

(2) Errors such as misspelling of terms, invalid terms, invalid subheadings, etc., are automatically caught by the computer system. This eliminates the need for re-typing citations because of errors introduced during the conversion of handwritten forms to machine readable forms.

(3) The same on-line system can be used for training indexers and revisers as well as for routine production. Revising changes automatically stored by the computer can be reviewed and used as checks during the training sessions.

(4) Periodical tests can be run to check consistency of indexing and revising so as to improve uniformity of output or modify indexing rules to improve the quality of indexing (pp. 26–27).*

Also using a portion of the MEDLARS data base, a novel approach to computer-aided on-line indexing was investigated by Gray and Harley (1971). The hypothesis upon which this work is founded is that the index terms relevant to a new paper to be indexed should be similar to the index terms previously assigned to the papers referred to (in the list of references) in the new paper. The experiments were conducted as follows: When a new

---

*Reprinted by permission of Lincoln Laboratory, MIT.

paper is to be indexed, the articles cited by it as references are retrieved from the machine data base, assuming that they are present.

> The descriptors assigned to these references are noted. Each descriptor assigned to one or more of the references is given a score equal to the number of references in which it appeared. A threshold value is set and the descriptors whose score is greater than this threshold constitute a list of possible descriptors for the new article. This threshold value can vary according to the maximum number of descriptors wanted, the number of papers contributing to the scores or a combination of both of these criteria (p. 169).

The procedures outlined above were used to produce a list of *suggested terms* for each of 66 articles, and these term lists were then compared with the terms originally assigned to the articles by MEDLARS indexers. The automatic procedures suggested 50–55% of all terms used by the human indexers, and 68.6% of the major terms. The automatic method also suggested additional terms not used by the human indexers. For a sample of 41 articles, an experienced MEDLARS indexer decided that 56.7% of these additional terms were in fact relevant to the subject content of the papers in question. Treating the complete set of relevant terms for these 41 articles as consisting of the 344 terms humanly assigned plus the additional 143 terms assigned automatically, Table 12.8 presents a comparison of the two approaches.

TABLE 12.8.   Comparison of Index Term Assignment by Computer and by Human Indexer

Total relevant terms for 41 articles (machine and indexers)	487
Number of these assigned by indexers	344 (70.6%)
Number of these assigned by machine	322 (66.1%)
Number assigned by both	179 (36.8%)

SOURCE: Gray and Harley (1971). Reproduced by permission of Pergamon Press.

The performance of the automatic method is only slightly inferior to the performance of the human indexers on the basis of these data. It is interesting to note that the machine suggested a considerable number of pertinent terms that the human indexer did not assign. The percentage agreement between man and machine increased with the number of references used to generate the suggestion lists.

The authors believe that, while the human indexer should have final say on which terms are to be assigned, an on-line system working on references to cited papers could make a significant contribution to the improvement of the overall indexing quality by suggesting additional terms that the indexer would otherwise overlook. Clearly, such a process involving the keyboarding of citations and the viewing of suggestion lists is unlikely to reduce indexing costs, but may improve indexing quality and/or reduce the amount of training needed by human indexers. With documents that can be captured inexpensively in machine readable form, as a by-product of some other operation, and for which the suggestion lists can be generated automatically and spontaneously (i.e., without the need for the indexer to keyboard references), the process obviously becomes much more attractive economically.

Operating Experience

The on-line indexing work described so far is experimental rather than operational. *The New York Times*, however, has used on-line indexing routinely in day-to-day operations since December 1971. Working from newspaper clippings, trained indexers prepare a full bibliographic record, including index terms and abstract, at a CRT terminal (IBM 4506), with a 1900 character, 30 line screen. The indexer works with an empty screen rather than with a structured display. Text editing programs allow easy on-line correction. However, no on-line validation is carried out. An off-line printout of each indexer's input is made overnight and submitted to the indexer for his examination. Any descriptors not previously existing in the on-line vocabulary are flagged for the indexer's attention. The indexer may call up a record and amend it on-line at any time.

The productivity of indexers in this system varies greatly from item to item. A brief obituary, for example, can be indexed in about 2 minutes, while a lengthy report may take 20–25 minutes. A staff of sixteen people can index one semimonthly issue of *The New York Times* index in about 6.5 working days. Put differently, the staff can, in one-half a day, index one weekday issue of the paper, together with part of a Sunday issue.

Machine-Aided Indexing

Because an on-line system allows very rapid access to bibliographic records, it is important to avoid diluting the value of such systems by allowing input delays to occur. There seems little point in providing very rapid access to a data base unless this data base is completely current. Unfortunately, delays frequently occur in human indexing activities because there are rarely enough indexers available to handle all documents as soon as they are acquired. Because we would like to get searchable records into the system as rapidly as possible, techniques that avoid human indexing seem particularly attractive. If we can capture records in machine-readable form inexpensively as a by-product of some other operation (and even possibly if we cannot), it may be economical to avoid human indexing and to store portions of the document text (e.g., titles plus abstracts) or to apply procedures of automatic indexing by term assignment or term extraction (*derivative indexing*) to put these records into a searchable form as rapidly as possible and thereby avoid the delays that are not infrequently associated with human indexing. A full discussion of these various techniques is outside the scope of this book, although a number of systems incorporating natural language searching or automatic indexing (e.g., Data Central, SMART, BROWSER) have been described. A general survey of both natural language searching and automatic indexing has been provided by Lancaster (1972).

An on-line system also appears very suitable for use in machine-aided indexing operations. In machine-aided indexing procedures, which have been described by Klingbiel (1969) among others, the computer undertakes some of the tasks (e.g., selection of candidate descriptors on the basis of statistical criteria or by means of stored dictionaries of approved terms) and the human others (e.g., checking the work of the machine and dealing with terms that the automatic indexing routines have been unable to recognize). The on-line system should provide a means whereby the professional indexer can efficiently and rapidly review, at a CRT console, indexing records created by machine processes. The role of the human indexer would be to correct obvious errors and to deal with any terms that the system identifies as problems. Machine-assisted indexing appears to be highly appropriate to implementation on on-line systems. The technique would provide an example of true man–machine symbiosis. Such machine-aided indexing activities go further than the on-line indexing procedures (e.g., LISTAR) described earlier in this chapter. In these, the professional undertakes all the intellectual tasks of indexing at the on-line terminal using aids that the machine can conveniently display, but without the computer contributing intellectually to the actual indexing process.

In the techniques described by Bennett (1969, 1971), the indexer can request information from the computer which may act as a suggestion to him (e.g., he can discover that a term is heavily posted and therefore is not too discriminating). The Intrex investigators are conscious of the necessity for getting bibliographic records into searchable form with the minimum of delay. Experiments in *preindexing* have been described by Kampe (1968). Preindexing involves creating an interim searchable record by machine processes. The final record is constructed later, when the human indexer is able to get to the document. The Intrex preindexing techniques involve machine extraction of words and phrases from document titles and abstracts with the aid of machine-stored dictionaries of index terms previously assigned to other documents by human indexers. That is, the computer assigns terms by drawing upon decisions made in the past by human indexers.

Indexing without Hard Copy

Certain information centers are able to capture substantial data bases in machine-readable form as by-products of other operations. In the defense and intelligence communities, for example, many valuable documents arrive at an information center in the form of wire communications. The possibility exists for indexing these items at CRT terminals without the generation of hard copy. That is, incoming items will be stored on arrival until they can be called up for display by an indexer. The indexer examines the item at the terminal and adds codes or descriptors to it. Alternatively, or additionally, he may mark certain words in the text to be extracted to serve as index terms. An indexing record is thus built up at the terminal. Bibliographic control data (e.g., title, source, report number) are also flagged by the indexer. When the indexing activity is complete, the indexer releases the record. The document surrogate goes to a search file, while the full text of the message may go to a secondary file in which it is stored in digital form. Alternatively, it may be input to a microform storage file using COM (computer output microfilm) procedures. Note that in the above sequence the document is handled entirely electrically and never appears in hard copy form. In fact, the document may never exist in hard copy form within the information center unless a searcher, at some future date, views it at a CRT display or in a microfilm reader and generates his own copy.

A piece of equipment that may have some applicability to on-line indexing is the *touch panel*, a modification of the plasma panel developed at the University of Illinois. The touch panel permits the terminal user to select from displayed data simply by touching, with his finger, an item of data displayed on the screen. Clearly, the touch panel would allow an indexer to extract words from displayed text to act as index terms, simply by touching these words on the display.

In 1972, the Central Intelligence Agency (CIA) began an important series of experiments on on-line indexing and on-line input by clerical personnel, working from both electrical and hard copy messages. On-line clerical input involves the construction of a bibliographic record on-line by typists working from a document marked up by a trained indexer. A typical on-line *form* is illustrated in Figure 12.6. Into this form, the typist keys the necessary data elements, including document number, security classification, publication date, title, and subject and area codes. Keywords are identified by *marking* certain words in the document title. On-line error-checking routines can be built into these procedures. On-line indexing proper is conducted in a similar way, except that the trained indexer prepares the on-line record himself (using a form, as illustrated in Figure 12.6) and thus avoids the marking up of documents and the clerical input step. On-line

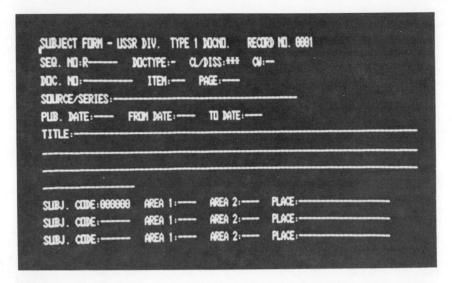

Figure 12.6. Sample CRT indexing *form* as used in on-line indexing experiments at Central Intelligence Agency. Reproduced by permission of the Central Intelligence Agency.

indexing of electrical messages involves the use of a split screen or dual CRT screens, so that the indexer can view the message in digital form while constructing the bibliographic record from the displayed text. With on-line indexing of electrical messages, certain of the indexing steps can be machine-aided. For example, the title of a message can be identified by computer and automatically placed in the title field of the indexing form, thus saving a considerable amount of keyboarding by the indexer.

The comprehensive program of investigations conducted by the CIA will compare the effectiveness and cost-effectiveness of these various on-line input approaches and will compare these approaches with existing methods which involve the marking-up of documents by trained indexers and subsequent conversion to machine-readable form by the clerical preparation of records that can be read by an optical scanning device.*

Further experiments are being conducted elsewhere within the intelligence community. In one intelligence agency, indexing of cables arriving electrically is conducted by a trained indexer at a CRT display. The process is machine-aided. A "citation generation program" recognizes various

---

*Results available in 1973 indicate that on-line clerical input and on-line indexing are both more cost-effective than the procedures previously in use. Because the clerical input was somewhat more cost-effective than the on-line indexing, this mode of operation was adopted for production purposes on a limited scale in 1973.

elements of the bibliographic citation—title, source, date, security classification, etc.—in the incoming electrical message, and reproduces these data in the appropriate fields of an indexing record. The indexer, working from a paper copy of the cable, calls up a cable by number. This results in a display of an indexing form which already contains the bibliographic data supplied by the computer. The indexer checks this for accuracy and then supplies the additional items (e.g., index terms) needed to complete the record. The indexer can call up, and display on the CRT, portions of the thesaurus. He can also call up indexing records for cables, already in the data base, that are cited by the cable that is now being processed. Terms from the thesaurus, or from these earlier indexing records, can be "transferred" to the current indexing form by identifying these terms by line numbers on the CRT.

Abstracting On-Line

The preparation of abstracts or summaries of documents is another intellectual activity that can perhaps be conducted profitably at the on-line terminal, especially through the use of a video console. On-line text editing procedures, as reviewed by Van Dam and Rice (1971), are available to assist in this type of activity. Such programs facilitate the restructuring and rearranging of text, as well as error correction. The ultimate composition of the abstract (e.g., on a photocomposition device) can be controlled by command codes interspersed in the text. These codes can control justification, columnar alignment, hyphenation, and other formatting operations. Obviously, a reviewer can call up abstracts at a later time and edit them further if needed. On-line input of research abstracts is now carried out at the Science Information Exchange, which is part of the Smithsonian Institution. Input is effected by twelve Bunker Ramo 2206/17 video terminals connected to an IBM 360/40 computer.

Figure 12.7*a* illustrates an abstract as typed on a video console. In Figure 12.7*b*, an erasure is made and the text is then *pulled apart* (Figure 12.7*c*). The corrected text is added (Figure 12.7*d*), and the text is then merged (Figure 12.7*e*). The final abstract is shown in Figure 12.7*f*. This illustration is taken from a proposal prepared by Rubinoff (1967).

Where the indexing of a document is conducted using natural language terms, the indexing and abstracting functions can virtually be conducted simultaneously, since the indexer can construct his abstract and then mark in some way the words or phrases in the abstract that are to be used as index terms.

This chapter has discussed some possibilities for on-line data entry in information retrieval applications with particular reference to the possible assistance that the computer itself can give to the indexer, cataloger, or

(a)
AN ELECTRO-MECHANICAL
SYSTEM THAT PERMITS RAPID
ENCODING OF ARBITRARY
GEOMETRIC CURVES IS
DEVELOPED. THE CURVE-
TRACKER IS BASICALLY A TWO
BAR LINKAGE WITH A STYLUS.
THE STYLUS POSITION IS
MEASURED BY A D-C VOLTAGE.
THIS VOLTAGE IS SAMPLED BY
AN A-TO-D CONVERTER. THE
RESULTING DIGITAL NUMBERS
ARE THEN USED TO CALCULATE
THE CARTESIAN COORDINATES
OF THE STYLUS.

(b)
AN ELECTRO-MECHANICAL
SYSTEM THAT PERMITS RAPID
ENCODING OF ARBITRARY
GEOMETRIC CURVES IS
DEVELOPED. THE CURVE-
TRACKER IS BASICALLY A TWO
BAR LINKAGE WITH A STYLUS.
THE STYLUS POSITION IS
MEASURED BY
            SAMPLED BY
AN A-TO-D CONVERTER. THE
RESULTING DIGITAL NUMBERS
ARE THEN USED TO CALCULATE
THE CARTESIAN COORDINATES
OF THE STYLUS

(c)
AN ELECTRO-MECHANICAL
SYSTEM THAT PERMITS RAPID
ENCODING OF ARBITRARY
GEOMETRIC CURVES IS
DEVELOPED. THE CURVE-
TRACKER IS BASICALLY A TWO
BAR LINKAGE WITH A STYLUS.
THE STYLUS POSITION IS
MEASURED BY

            SAMPLED BY AN A-TO-D
CONVERTER. THE RESULTING
DIGITAL NUMBERS ARE THEN
USED TO CALCULATE THE
CARTESIAN COORDINATES OF
THE STYLUS.

(d)
AN ELECTRO-MECHANICAL
SYSTEM THAT PERMITS RAPID
ENCODING OF ARBITRARY
GEOMETRIC CURVES IS
DEVELOPED. THE CURVE-
TRACKER IS BASICALLY A TWO
BAR LINKAGE WITH A STYLUS.
THE STYLUS POSITION IS
MEASURED BY 2 D-C VOLTAGES
WHICH ARE PROPORTIONAL TO
THE TWO BAR ANGLES. THESE
VOLTAGES ARE
            SAMPLED BY AN A-TO-D
CONVERTER. THE RESULTING
DIGITAL NUMBERS ARE THEN
USED TO CALCULATE THE
CARTESIAN COORDINATES OF
THE STYLUS.

(e)
AN ELECTRO-MECHANICAL
SYSTEM THAT PERMITS RAPID
ENCODING OF ARBITRARY
GEOMETRIC CURVES IS
DEVELOPED. THE CURVE-
TRACKER IS BASICALLY A TWO
BAR LINKAGE WITH A STYLUS.
THE STYLUS POSITION IS
MEASURED BY 2 D-C VOLTAGES
WHICH ARE PROPORTIONAL TO
THE TWO BAR ANGLES. THESE
VOLTAGES ARE SAMPLED BY AN
A-TO-D CONVERTER. THE
RESULTING DIGITAL NUMBERS
ARE THEN USED TO CALCULATE
THE CARTESIAN COORDINATES
OF THE STYLUS.

(f)
AN ELECTRO-MECHANICAL
SYSTEM THAT PERMITS RAPID
ENCODING OF ARBITRARY
GEOMETRIC CURVES IS
DEVELOPED. THE CURVE-
TRACKER IS BASICALLY A TWO
BAR LINKAGE WITH A STYLUS.
THE STYLUS POSITION IS
MEASURED BY 2 D-C VOLTAGES
WHICH ARE PROPORTIONAL TO
THE TWO BAR ANGLES. THESE
VOLTAGES ARE SAMPLED BY AN
A-TO-D CONVERTER. THE
RESULTING DIGITAL NUMBERS
ARE THEN USED TO CALCULATE
THE CARTESIAN COORDINATES
OF THE STYLUS. AS THE STYLUS
FOLLOWS THE CURVE,
INCREMENTS ARE QUANTIZED
AND STORED

Figure 12.7. Editing an abstract at a video console. Reproduced from Rubinoff (1967) by permission of Moore School of Electrical Engineering, University of Pennsylvania.

abstractor at the on-line terminal. Of course, on-line data entry is now used commonly in many fields (e.g., airline reservations). Some of these applications and their potential benefits have been described by Meadow (1970). In general, speed of entry and reduction of error are the major benefits that generally accrue from on-line entry. Warheit (1970) has described the advantages of on-line input as follows:

> To begin with, in an on-line system a work sheet does not have to be prepared, and so the keypunch operator is eliminated. Because of the interaction of the originator and the system, all corrections and editing are accomplished at once, so that the turn-around time is very much less. Preparation of printed error messages and proof copy are eliminated and the total error rate is greatly reduced. Thus, although the reading-in of the individual records is slower in the on-line mode than in the batch mode, appreciably fewer messages need to be read to complete a record in the on-line mode, making for more economical machine time. To this, however, must be added terminal and communication costs as well as the terminal supervisor program and the fact that most on-line work is done during the prime shift, so that actual machine costs tend to be higher with the on-line system. Some, however, dispute this, claiming that, on balance, machine costs are equal.
>
> Labor costs, however, are very much lower with the on-line system. As a general rule, computer input costs are 85% labor and 15% machine. Not only can a transcription clerk be eliminated, but the order librarian who prepares the original inputs on the terminal works very much more efficiently. Consulting hard-copy files and lists is more time consuming and less informative than interrogating machine files. In an on-line system, the librarian's necessary tools are brought directly to him and displayed rapidly and efficiently. He does not have to walk to the shelf list, the catalog or the on-order file and copy information. In a well-developed, sophisticated system some of the heavily used tools, such as the subject heading authority lists and class tables, would also be available from the terminal. Not only does the librarian not have to spend time going to the physical files, but since the information is computer stored, it is brought to him in a greater variety of forms and sequences than is available in the hard-copy files. For example, titles are fully permuted so that incomplete title information can be searched. Some systems librarians are proposing the use of codes and ciphers to search for entries, especially those with garbled titles. All entries, including added authors, editors, vendors, etc., are immediately available even for uncataloged on-order items, so that searching is not restricted to main entries. It is not surprising, therefore, that clerks preparing computer inputs prefer working on-line rather than off-line.
>
> One interesting discovery is that since operators can do so much more with on-line systems they tend to take more time to turn out a better product. Indications are 'that significantly lower costs would have resulted if the time-sharing users had stopped work (i.e., gone to the next task) when they reached a performance level equal to that of batch users' (pp. 70, 71).*

---

*Reprinted by permission of the American Library Association.

Warheit was specifically discussing library cataloging procedures, but his comments are equally appropriate to subject indexing operations.

REFERENCES

Armenti, A., and S. W. Galley (1970). *A User's Guide to LISTAR*. Lexington, Mass.: MIT, Lincoln Laboratory, ESD-TR-70-317.

Armenti, A., D. E. Hall, and A. A. Sholl (1970). *An Experiment in On-Line Indexing Using LISTAR*. Lexington, Mass.: MIT, Lincoln Laboratory, NLM-1.

Armenti, A., D. E. Hall, and A. A. Sholl (1971a). *On-Line Indexing and Revising: Status Report*. Lexington, Mass.: MIT, Lincoln Laboratory, NLM-2.

Armenti, A., D. E. Hall, and A. A. Sholl (1971b). *An Experiment in On-Line Revising Using LISTAR*. Lexington, Mass.: Lincoln Laboratory, NLM-3.

Balfour, F. M. (1968). "Conversion of Bibliographic Information to Machine-Readable Form Using On-Line Computer Terminals." *Jour. Library Automation* **1** (4), 217–226.

Bennett, J. L. (1969). "On-Line Access to Information: NSF as an Aid to the Indexer/Cataloger." *Amer. Documentation* **20** (3), 213–220.

Bennett, J. L. (1971). "Spatial Concepts as an Organizing Principle for Interactive Bibliographic Search." *In* D. E. Walker (ed.), *Interactive Bibliographic Search: the User/Computer Interface*. Montvale, N.J.: AFIPS Press, pp. 67–82.

Bennett, J. L., D. C. Clarke, and W. D. Musson (1972). *Observing and Evaluating an Interactive Process: a Pilot Experiment in Indexing*. San Jose, Ca.: IBM Research Laboratory, RJ 1040.

Buchanan, J. R., and E. M. Kidd (1969). "Development of a Computer System with Console Capability for the Nuclear Safety Information Center." *Proc. Amer. Soc. Information Sci.* **6**, 151–158.

Clarke, D. C. (1970). "Query Formulation for On-Line Reference Retrieval: Design Considerations from the Indexer/Searcher Viewpoint." *Proc. Amer. Soc. Information Sci.* **7**, 83–86.

Cottrell, W. B., and J. R. Buchanan (1970). *Summary of Environmental Information Activities of the Nuclear Safety Information Center*. Oak Ridge, Tenn.: Oak Ridge National Laboratory, Nuclear Safety Information Center, ORNL-TM-3009.

Gray, W. A., and A. J. Harley (1971). "Computer Assisted Indexing." *Information Storage Retrieval* **7** (4), 167–174.

Herr, J. J. (1970). "Use of Data-Base Access for Interindexer Communication and for Indexer Training." *Proc. Amer. Soc. Information Sci.* **7**, 163–166.

Kampe, W. R., II (1968). *Rapid Pre-indexing by Machine*. Cambridge, Mass.: MIT, Electronic Systems Laboratory, ESL-R-355. Project OSR 70054.

Klingbiel, P. H. (1969). *Machine-Aided Indexing*. Alexandria, Va.: Defense Documentation Center, AD 696 200.

Lancaster, F. W. (1972). *Vocabulary Control for Information Retrieval*. Washington, D.C.: Information Resources Press.

Margolies, R. F. (1970). "Video Console Indexing." *In Proceedings of the Seventh Annual National Colloquium on Information Retrieval.* Philadelphia, Pa.: The College of Physicians of Philadelphia, Medical Documentation Service, pp. 143–154.

Massachusetts Institute of Technology (1971). *Project Intrex: Semiannual Activity Report.* Cambridge, Mass.: MIT.

Meadow, C. T. (1970). *Man-Machine Communication.* New York: Wiley.

Miller, E. W., and B. J. Hodges (1971). "Shawnee Mission's On-Line Cataloging System." *Jour. Library Automation* **4** (1), 13–26.

Miller, E. W., and B. J. Hodges (1972). "Shawnee Mission's On-Line Cataloging System: the First Two Years." *In* F. W. Lancaster (ed.), *Proceedings of the 1972 Clinic on Library Applications of Data Processing.* Urbana, Ill.: University of Illinois, Graduate School of Library Science, 94–108.

Miller, E. W., J. Tomcak, and J. New (1970). *On-Line Cataloging: an Elementary Library Project. User's Manual.* Shawnee Mission, Kansas: Shawnee Mission Unified School District.

Ohio College Library Center (1971). *Cataloging on a Cathode Ray Tube Terminal.* Columbus, Ohio: Ohio College Library Center.

Parks, C., and C. Julian (1971). *Information Scanning and Processing at the Nuclear Safety Information Center.* Oak Ridge, Tenn.: Oak Ridge National Laboratory, Nuclear Safety Information Center, ORNL-NSIC-48.

Rosenberg, V. (1971). "A Study of Statistical Measures for Predicting Terms Used to Index Documents." *Jour. Amer. Soc. Information Sci.* **22** (1), 41–50.

Rubinoff, M. (1967). *A Proposal on Real-Time Video Console Indexing.* Submitted to the National Science Foundation by the Moore School of Electrical Engineering, University of Pennsylvania, Philadelphia, Pa.

Schneider, B. R. (1971). "The Production of Machine-Readable Text: Some of the Variables." *Computers Humanities* **6**, (1), 39–47.

Sheldon, R. C., R. A. Roach, and S. Backer (1968). "Design of an On-Line Computer-Based Textile Information Retrieval System." *Textile Res. Jour.* **38** (1), 81–100.

Van Dam, A., and D. C. Rice (1971). "On-Line Text Editing: a Survey." *Computing Surveys* **3** (3), 93–114.

Warheit, I. A. (1970). "Design of Library Systems for Implementation with Interactive Computers." *Jour. Library Automation* **3** (1), 65–78.

Chapter Thirteen

On-Line Support
for Personal Files

The building of personal document collections is an essential ingredient in research and analytical activities. The personal collection is generally recognized to be the first source to which a scientist or other practitioner will turn when the need for information arises. Studies of the use of literature by scientists and research workers (Bernal, 1948; Hogg and Smith, 1959; Törnudd, 1953) have shown consistently that personal files of one kind or another are maintained by a large proportion of the population surveyed. Martyn (1964) reported that some 47% of the information searched for by research scientists in Great Britain was found through the use of personal collections. The Project for Evaluating the Benefits from University Libraries (PEBUL) at the University of Durham (1970), which surveyed 394 subjects, found that the personal collection ranked first as a source of information with academic staff in the arts and social sciences, and first or second in the sciences, depending on the institution studied.

The main advantages of the personal collection are:

- ● It is organized to match the individual's own particular approach to the subject matter dealt with. Every scientist has his own view of his field, and only his personal collection is likely to be organized to precisely reflect this view.
- ● The documents have been evaluated by the collector.
- ● It is immediately accessible.

In contrast, a formal centralized information system is probably not organized in the best possible way for any one particular individual. For the individual's needs, the central system may lack specificity and may not permit high search precision. Moreover, the central system is generally less accessible, more difficult to use (because use requires delegation to an intermediary or, alternatively, learning an unfamiliar indexing system), may be incomplete in its coverage of the individual's interests, and may include unevaluated documents.

The personal collection also has certain disadvantages: It is time-consuming to maintain, tends to be bulky because discarding is undertaken rarely or not at all, may be limited historically, is likely to be indexed by some type of pigeonhole system which does not provide multiple access points, and is not generally available to people other than the collector (this is a disadvantage, not to the individual, but to the organization of which he forms a part).

Moreover, however excellent the personal collection, the conscientious researcher will still have need to use some central system on occasions in order to:

1. Find background material and material peripheral to his main interests or material in research areas that are new to him.
2. Confirm the completeness of the personal file.
3. Obtain specific known documents.
4. Provide subject approaches not provided for in the personal filing system.
5. Acquire materials that predate the personal collection.

Because of the considerations outlined above, it is unlikely that in any large organization a central retrieval system will eliminate personal documentation systems completely. Conversely, personal collections do not obviate the need for a strong central system. Clearly, there is need for synergy between the activities of the personal file and the activities of the central system, a point made very cogently by Burton and Yerke (1969):

> Many systems analysts and research administrators regard with great skepticism the personal documentation systems which most scientists maintain. These systems are viewed as evidence that the formal bibliographic services provided by the researcher's supporting institution are poorly designed or functioning improperly. Accordingly, attention has been focused chiefly on improvement of library services and related bibliographic systems.
>
> It is not yet widely understood that personal information systems are necessary to researchers because their orientation is basically antithetical to that of the formal system. The formal system is designed to be objective, inclusive, and normative. It may also tend to become static. The personal system is by definition subjective, heuristic, and dynamic. It provides its user with an information transfer environment dominated by his own viewpoint. He is the favored observer of his information universe. He determines what goes into the system and the relevance of retrieval results. And in this kind of documentation 'relevance' is based on ever-varying subjective criteria.

Properly understood, both the formal and the personal systems contribute to the satisfaction of information needs by providing complementary services. To ignore either of the two systems, or to force one to substitute for the other, results in higher cost to the user and a lowering of the quality of over-all service (p. 53).

For many years, the problems of the personal collection were largely ignored by the professional librarian or documentalist. Very little research was conducted on the important characteristics of personal files, such as type of document collected, organization, and use factors. Recently, however, the personal file has received increased attention. Two brief monographs on how to organize and index such files have been published by Jahoda (1970) and by Foskett (1970), and a study of the characteristics of personal indexes maintained by scientists and engineers was conducted at Florida State University and reported by Jahoda, et al. (1966a, b). Jahoda reported that a major shortcoming of personal indexes was the time consumed in their preparation and maintenance, and he concluded that some form of machine support was necessary.

The advent of computer-based retrieval systems has created interest in the possibility of providing some type of machine support to the maintenance and use of personal collections. Some systems for this purpose have been planned or implemented within the past decade, operating in both the off-line and on-line modes. An on-line, time-shared system appears to offer an ideal environment for nurturing the personal collection and for improving its organization and accessibility.

Wallace (1966a, b) described a program, SURF (Support of User Records and Files), designed to assist individuals in organizing and maintaining their files and to provide personalized printed indexes whereby they could search these personal files effectively. SURF was implemented at the System Development Corporation using the MADAM programming language and an IBM 1401 computer. A user of this service could index his file in any way he liked, fill out and submit input coding sheets for these items, and regularly receive updated, consolidated indexes. A valuable by-product of SURF, recognized by Wallace (1966a), was

a machine file of user indexing practice reflecting users' needs, perspectives, vocabulary and manner of organizing information vital to their work. Such a file is being used for direct observation of user behavior and needs, and for feedback to centralized services for document description, acquisition, dissemination, and retrieval. Analysis of this kind of file has the potential of aiding greatly in a more precise identification and specification of user information requirements. Such analysis offers an additional dimension of study to the information derived from the traditional tools of diary, questionnaire and interview (p. 79).

A system somewhat similar to SURF, for the generation of keyword indexes to personal files, has been described by Smith, et al. (1969).

FAMULUS

One of the most interesting systems for augmenting personal documentation efforts is FAMULUS, described by Burton and Yerke (1969) and Yerke (1970). A users' manual was issued in 1969 (Pacific Southwest Forest and Range Experiment Station, 1969). FAMULUS is implemented at the Pacific Southwest Forest and Range Experiment Station, Berkeley, Ca., and versions of the FAMULUS programs are available for Control Data Corporation (CDC) 6400 and 6600 computers, Univac 1108, and the IBM 360. The system is intended primarily to allow the scientist to maintain an up-to-date inventory of his holdings and to provide means whereby he can retrieve sets of items which he will periodically specify. The role of the computer is to take over the clerical jobs of updating and maintaining a file, while freeing the system user to index and structure his records according to his own, possibly idiosyncratic, requirements. FAMULUS is designed for ease of input (a scientist can present handwritten input to his secretary who converts to a simple standard format for keypunching) and to provide the greatest possible editing, sorting, deleting, revising, indexing, and searching ease for the user.

FAMULUS consists of eight subsystems, each performing a specific set of tasks (Yerke, 1970):

> EDIT writes punched card input onto tape and permits the user to make corrections, additions, and deletions. SORT rearranges the file order by changing the order of fields within the records so that the file can be realphabetized. MERGE provides updating facilities and permits enlargement of the file through merging two individual files into one master file. GALLEY prints the file in any of several formats. INDEX lists keywords and tells in what records they may be found, in effect providing an index. VOCAB prints in alphabetic order all "meaningful" words in any given field, of the records in a file, making a list of index terms, keywords in titles, etc. SEARCH scans the file and matches keywords in the title or descriptor fields, retrieving and printing out only those records matching the search question. OSSIFY punches card deck equivalents of tape files, for use as safety decks or for massive corrections (pp. 76, 77).

As of 1970, there were approximately thirty specialized collections in the FAMULUS system, mostly with between 700 and 2000 citations each, but there were a few in the range of 10,000. Growth rate of such files is of the order of about fifty new items each month. The user develops his own indexing scheme. Several FAMULUS users have produced elaborately structured formats, while others rely on a freer form, using terms in titles or a few assigned keywords. Abstracts can be included in the system. Individual collections and multi-user collections (in which several individuals input and search) are included in FAMULUS; all are machine-readable and available, with the consent of their owners, to the library staff and other researchers. System costs are relatively modest. It requires, according to Yerke (1970), between 4.5 and 5 minutes of CDC 6400 time to edit a collection of 500 citations, write them on tape, sort them according to criteria established by the user, and print them in the format option the user has chosen.

FAMULUS is a very flexible system which provides, for the individual scientist, tailor-made facilities for the handling and processing of his personal file. The system was designed for use in an off-line, batch mode, with punched card input and printed paper output. Clearly, an on-line system with the same general characteristics would provide even greater flexibility in the organization and manipulation of files, would allow browsing in the various document collections, and would give more immediate accessibility.

RIMS, RIQS, and RFMS

An on-line system of the type mentioned above, known as the Remote Information Management System (RIMS), has been developed at Northwestern University. RIMS was built around the capabilities of two existing batch systems, TRIAL and INFOL. TRIAL (Borman and Dillaman, 1968) is a series of programs written for the CDC 6400 that will permit the creation of files of textual information, indexing and maintenance of these files, and retrieval operations on them. Files can be searched using boolean search logic or, alternatively, a term-weighting procedure; or manual retrieval tools can be generated in KWIC (keyword in context) or KWOC (keyword out of context) format. TRIAL has been used at Northwestern for many applications, large and small, including a program for the selective dissemination of information in the social science field. TRIAL (Techniques for Retrieving Information from Abstracts of Literature) dates back to 1964. Its development was guided by Janda (1968), and it was designed for handling text in the field of political science.

INFOL has the capability of storing, updating, and retrieving records of structured data, including alphameric and numeric items, dates, and special codes. The system has been used in medical research applications, including the manipulation of records of cardiology patients, and in the implementation of a management information system.

RIMS (Chalice, et al., 1970; Krulee and Mittman, 1969; Mittman and Krulee, 1969) combines the capabilities of TRIAL and INFOL and permits the creation, maintaining, searching, and updating of files of textual or numeric data. Using the CDC 6400 with either a teletypewriter or a CRT

ONLINE
NORTHWESTERN UNIVERSITY
6400 ONLINE
CHARGE NUMBER?CM1235-2345
VALID CHARGE NUMBER

ENTER SEARCH PHASE OF
TRIAL SYSTEM. TYPE IN SEARCH
COMMAND. DO NOT EXCEED
38 CHARACTERS ON ANY LINE.
DO YOU WANT HELP
  ?YES

1 TYPE TITLE TO BE PRINTED
ON OUTPUT
2 TYPE A COMMA
3 TYPE LEVEL OF
INFORMATION TO BE
SEARCHED. IF UNKNOWN, TYPE
1 THRU 9 SEPARATED BY
COMMAS. IF SEARCHING VCC
LIBRARY, TITLES ARE 2,
AUTHORS ARE 1, AND
ABSTRACTS ARE 5.
4 TYPE LEFT PARENTHESIS
5 TYPE SEARCH WORDS AND
PHRASES (STRING OF WORDS
JOINED WITH AN ASTERISK).
USE OPERATORS AS NEEDED-
AND OR NOT (WITH PERIODS
PRECEDING AND FOLLOWING
OPERATOR)
6 AFTER LAST WORD, TYPE
= 100
7 TYPE RIGHT PARENTHESIS
8 TYPE DOLLAR SIGN
READY TO GO?
YES

ENTER SEARCH COMMAND. . . .
  ?ONLINE TRIAL SEARCH
USING TELETYPE
  ?2.5 (LISP. OR. SNOBOL.AND.
  ?LIST*PROCESSING = 100)$

SEARCHING INITIATED
  0 ENTRIES HIT SO FAR
  5 ENTRIES HIT SO FAR
  8 ENTRIES HIT SO FAR
  9 ENTRIES HIT SO FAR
SEARCHING TERMINATED

9 HIT OUT OF 426 SEARCHED
DO YOU WANT TO LOOK AT
AUTHOR AND TITLE
  ?YES

MOSES J
SYMBOLIC INTEGRATION

HART T P   LEVIN M I
LISP 1.5 PROGRAMMER'S
MANUAL.

BOBROW D G   TEITELMAN
W
FORMAT-DIRECTED LIST
PROCESSING IN LISP.

BOBROW D G ET AL
THE BBN-LISP SYSTEM.

SALZMAN R M ET AL
APPLIED RESEARCH ON
IMPLEMENTATION AND USE OF
LIST PROCESSING LANGUAGES.

RAPHAEL R
SIR, A COMPUTER PROGRAM
FOR SEMANTIC INFORMATION
RETRIEVAL.

BOBROW D G
NATURAL LANGUAGE INPUT
FOR A COMPUTER PROBLEM
SOLVING SYSTEM

TEITELMAN W
PILOT, A STEP TOWARD MAN-
COMPUTER SYMBIOSIS.

BURGER I F ET AL
AN INTERACTIVE SYSTEM FOR
COMPUTING DEPENDENCIES,
PHRASE STRUCTURES AND
KERNELS

DO YOU WANT THEM PRINTED
  ?YES
DO YOU WANT TO CONTINUE
  ?NO
LOGOUT

Figure 13.1. Typical interactive search using TRIAL. Reproduced from Mittman and Krulee (1969). Reprinted from, and by permission of the American Society for Information Science, *Proceedings*, 1969, vol. 6, pp. 199–206. Copyright 1969 by the American Society for Information Science, 1140 Connecticut Avenue, N.W., Washington, D.C. 20036.

ONLINE

NORTHWESTERN UNIVERSITY 6400 ONLINE
CHARGE NUMBER?CM1235-2345
VALID CHARGE NUMBER

RIMS TUTORIAL

TO TERMINATE PROGRAM TYPE IN STOP,
BLITZ OR LOGOUT.

TO RE-ENTER THE PROGRAM TYPE IN
RESTART

THIS IS A LINGO PROGRAM WRITTEN TO
INSTRUCT YOU ON THE USAGE OF RIMS

HAVE YOU EVER USED THIS PROGRAM BEFORE
?NO

RIMS IS AN ACRONYM FOR REMOTE
INFORMATION MANAGEMENT SYSTEM

IT WAS DESIGNED FOR CREATING,
MAINTAINING AND UPDATING A DATA FILE
OF BOTH TEXTUAL AND NUMERIC DATA

AN EXTENSIVE LANGUAGE IS PROVIDED
FOR SEARCHING THE FILE AND PERFORMING
CALCULATIONS ACROSS RECORDS AS WELL
AS ACROSS THE FILE

THIS PROGRAM WILL EXPLAIN THE RECORD
STRUCTURE OF THE RIMS FILE AND HOW A
USER WOULD CONSTRUCT A RIMS FILE

LATER MODIFICATIONS WILL BE MADE TO
EXPLAIN THE SEARCHING LANGUAGE.

UNLESS OTHERWISE SPECIFIED IN THIS
PROGRAM CARDS THAT ARE INPUT TO
RIMS ARE ASSUMED TO BE FREE FIELD 80
COLUMNS WITH BLANKS TREATED AS
DELIMITERS

WHICH OF THE FOLLOWING AREAS DO YOU
WANT EXPLAINED
    1) CREATING A FILE
    2) MAINTAINING AND UPDATING A
        FILE
    3) SEARCHING A FILE
?FILE CREATION

WHICH AREA OF THE FILE CREATION PHASE
DO YOU WANT EXPLAINED
    1) GENERAL INFORMATION AND TERMS
        USED
    2) FILE NAMING AND PASSWORD USED
    3) RECORD DEFINITION
    4) DATA RESTRICTIONS AND
        VALIDATIONS
    5) INPUT DATA
?GENERAL INFORMATION

THE DEVELOPMENT OF RIMS IS SPONSORED
UNDER A GRANT FROM THE AIR FORCE
OFFICE OF SCIENTIFIC RESEARCH
PRINCIPAL INVESTIGATORS....
    B. MITTMAN AND G. KRULEE
RESEARCHERS....
L. BORMAN, R. CHALICE AND D. DILLAMAN

THE MASTER FILE IS COMPOSED OF RECECORDS
EACH RECORD CONTAINS ITEMS OF
INFORMATION. THE ACTUAL CONTENT OF AN
ITEM IS CALLED AN ELEMENT.
THE MASTER FILE IS WRITTEN ON THE DISK
AS A RANDOM FILE. THUS EACH RECORD IS
DIRECTLY ADDRESSABLE
WE WILL NOW GO DIRECTLY TO THE SECTION
ON FILE NAMING AND PASSWORD USAGE.

AT PRESENT TO ENTER RIMS THE FIRST
CARD MUST CONTAIN RIMS AS THE FIRST
FOUR CHARACTERS.

NEXT,A FILE MUST BE NAMED, EITHER THRU
A CREATE OR AN ACCESS COMMAND. THE
FILE NAME CAN HAVE UP TO 20 CHARACTERS

CREATE RIMSFILE1   SIGNIFIES THAT YOU
ARE GOING TO CREATE A FILE NAMED
RIMSFILE1 DURING THIS RUN.

ACCESS RIMSFILE2   SIGNIFIES THAT YOU
ARE GOING TO ACCESS A FILE NAMED
RIMSFILE2 DURING THIS RUN. RIMSFILE2
MUST HAVE BEEN CREATED EARLIER.

THE USE OF PASSWORDS ALLOWS YOU TO
PROTECT YOUR FILE FROM BEING DESTROYED
OR ALTERED WITHOUT YOUR KNOWLEDGE

1. ONLY THOSE WHO KNOW THE FILE NAME
   CAN ACCESS THE FILE
2. ONLY THOSE WHO KNOW THE UPDATE
   PASSWORD CAN UPDATE THE FILE
3. ONLY THOSE WHO KNOW THE
   REDEFINITION PASSWORD CAN REDEFINE
   THE RECORD STRUCTURE

SPECIFICATION OF PASSWORDS IS
OPTIONAL WITH THE USER

THE UPDATE AND REDEFINITION PASSWORDS
ARE SPECIFIED AS FOLLOWS...

    UPDATE PASSWORD=ABLE
    REDEFINITION PASSWORD=CAIN

DO YOU WANT TO SEE AN EXAMPLE OF A SET
OF CONTROL CARDS TO THIS POINT
?YES

    RIMS
    CREATE TESTFILE
    UPDATE PASSWORD=DON
    REDEFINITION PASSWORD=BOB

WHICH AREA OF THE FILE CREATION PHASE
DO YOU WANT EXPLAINED
    1) GENERAL INFORMATION AND TERMS
        USED
    2) FILE NAMING AND PASSWORD USED
    3) RECORD DEFINITION
    4) DATA RESTRICTIONS AND
        VALIDATIONS
    5) INPUT DATA
?RECORD DEFINITION

WHEN DEFINING A RECORD THE WORDS
RECORD DEFINITION ARE ENTERED. THE
WORD ITEMS IS FOLLOWED BY A LIST OF
ITEM NUMBERS AND NAMES WHICH THE USER
DESIRES FOR HIS RECORD STRUCTURE.

THE FORM OF THE STATEMENT IS....
    (N) ITEM-NAME
WHERE N CAN BE ANY NUMBER BETWEEN
1 AND 250, AND THE ITEM NAME CAN HAVE
UP TO 30 ALPHANUMERIC CHARACTERS.
ITEM NUMBER 1 MUST BE THE FIRST
ITEM OF THE RECORD
DO YOU WANT TO SEE AN EXAMPLE
?YES

THE FOLLOWING IS AN EXAMPLE OF A
POSSIBLE BIBLIOGRAPHIC RECORD.

            RECORD DEFINITION
    ITEMS
    (1) AUTHOR
    (2) TITLE
    (3) PUBLISHER
    (4) COPYRIGHT DATE
    (5) LOCATION-OF-BOOK
    (6) NUMBER OF COPIES
    (7) ABSTRACT

THERE ARE TWO BASIC STRUCTURES ALLOWED
A SIMPLE ITEM AND A MULTIPLE ITEM.
A SIMPLE ITEM CAN CONTAIN ONLY ONE
PIECE OF INFORMATION WHEREAS A
MULTIPLE ITEM CAN CONTAIN SEVERAL
PIECES. A MULTIPLE ITEM CAN BE THOUGHT
OF AS A VECTOR OF INFORMATION--EACH
PART OR PIECE OF THE VECTOR BEING
CALLED AN ELEMENT.

FOR EXAMPLE.. -TITLE- WOULD BE A
SIMPLE ITEM WHEREAS -AUTHORS- WOULD
BE A MULTIPLE ITEM.
ITEMS ARE ASSUMED SIMPLE UNLESS THEY
ARE SPECIFIED MULTIPLE BY......
    MULTIPLE (N1),(N2),(N3)THRU(N4)
THE COMMANDS BELOW REVIEW WHAT HAS
BEEN PRESENTED TO THIS POINT OF THE
RIMS LINGO TUTORIAL

RIMS
CREATE BIBLIOGRAPHIC FILE
REDEFINITION PASSWORD=ZELDA
    RECORD DEFINITION
    ITEMS
    (1) AUTHOR
    (2) TITLE
    (3) PUBLISHER
    (4) COPYRIGHT DATE
    (5) LOCATION-OF-BOOK
    (6) NUMBER OF COPIES
    (7) ABSTRACT
MULTIPLE (1),(5),(6)

Figure 13.2. RIMS tutorial on teletype. Reproduced from Mittman and Krulee (1969). Reprinted from, and by permission of the American Society for Information Science, *Proceedings*, 1969, vol. 6, pp. 199–206. Copyright 1969 by the American Society for Information Science, 1140 Connecticut Avenue, N.W., Washington, D.C. 20036.

display console, the user of RIMS can store his own records, index them, and search them in whatever way he finds most useful. Figure 13.1 illustrates a typical interactive search using TRIAL, relating to the use of LISP or SNOBOL in list processing. Note the instructional features built into the program. Tutorial features of this type (see Figure 13.2) are an essential element in RIMS. RIMS can also perform numerical calculations on records, can print the results of these calculations or can select records depending upon results of the calculations. In 1971, RIMS was replaced by RIQS (Remote Information Query System) (Borman and Mittman, 1972; Borman, et al., 1971), a related system with expanded capabilities. In RIQS, only file searching is conducted on-line. File creation and updating are batch procedures.

A system similar to RIMS is the Remote File Management System (RFMS) developed at the University of Texas (Dale and Eichelkraut, 1968) for operation on a CDC 6600. RFMS is designed to permit the *nonspecialist, nonprogrammer user* to create files, maintain them, search them, and retrieve from them, using remote, time-shared consoles. The logical design is illustrated in Figure 13.3. As described by Dale and Eichelkraut (1968), the major components of RFMS, with which the user interacts, are:

DEFINE—allows the user to create a data base description, i.e., to name the elements of the entries in his file, to indicate hierarchical relationships among elements, and to specify what type of data will be associated with named data elements. As with all system components with which a user interacts, the user language is English-like, with a simple syntax, and a vocabulary sufficient to permit unambiguous communication with the system within the conventions of a simple user-system dialogue.

LOADER—provides for a flexible and interactive creation of a new data base, taking as input user directives regarding load sequences, the data base description supplied by the user to DEFINE, and the data values for file entries supplied by the user. It possesses the capability for monitoring data input, reporting and correcting detected input errors, and reporting various checkpoints encountered during the loading process. Its main function is to provide an internal file and directory structure that will maximize the speed of retrieval when the data base is being interrogated by the user.

RETRIEVAL—contains two capabilities:

(1) A query capability, permitting a user to select elements from his files that are the values of some Boolean function defined on other file elements.

(2) A display capability, permitting printing of the results of a file search.

UPDATE—provides for two classes of user operations:

(1) It gives a capability for editing an existing data base through the use of instructions permitting the addition, deletion, insertion, and change of data values.

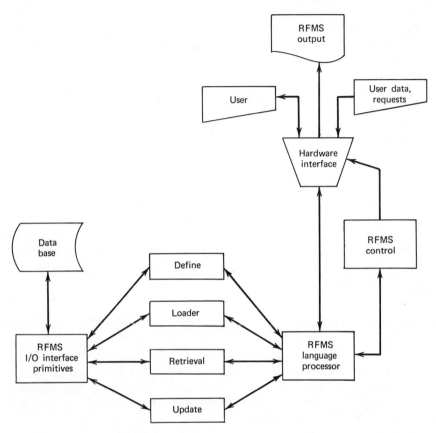

Figure 13.3. Schematic of remote file management system. Reproduced from Dale and Eichelkraut (1968) by permission of the Computation Center, University of Texas at Austin.

(2) It permits control, by the user, of the form of updated versions of a data base, in the sense that either permanently modified versions can be created, or incremental modifications can be established separately from a base version prior to permanent modification (pp. 2, 4, 5).

The RFMS system has been used in the implementation of an on-line search system, as well as a batch selective dissemination of information (SDI) system, using the SPIN (Searchable Physics Information Notices) tapes of the American Institute of Physics. This application has been described by Parsons (1972).

RFMS and RIMS are designed as general-purpose file management systems capable of providing for a very wide range of potential uses and avoiding the need for the development of disconnected special-purpose systems.

Early work on on-line personal documentation systems, as conducted at the University of Alberta, is reported by Heaps and Sorenson (1968). The work at Alberta used an IBM 360/67 computer, IBM 2741 typewriter terminals, and APL (A Programming Language). Each user of the system had access, through use of a personal ID number, to a workspace of approximately 32,000 bytes. Additional workspaces were available on request. In the initial pilot project, the user could store a series of items consisting of *notes* (e.g., a bibliographical description) and associated keywords. Material could be added to this file on-line, using the EXTEND command, or removed from the file (DELETE command). The entire store could be searched on combinations of keywords (SEARCH), and retrieved items could be printed at the terminal (DISPLAY). A feature of the system was the capability for *fractional search* which allowed the user to specify any m out of n terms. Thus, a user could list ten keywords, without any boolean logic, and designate any retrieval threshold. A retrieval threshold of 3 means that an item will be retrieved only if it contains at least three of the keywords listed by the searcher. If no match is found at this level, however, the program will automatically reduce the threshold until a match does occur. Fractional search may offer certain advantages over boolean manipulation of terms for the relatively inexperienced searcher operating in a conversational mode.

APL was discovered to be a very unsuitable language, and a later report by Heaps and Harris (1969) describes a further investigation of characteristics required of query languages for on-line personal documentation systems.

SHOEBOX

SHOEBOX, described by Glantz (1970), is referred to as a "personal file handling system for textual data" or an "electronic analog of a personal desk file drawer." The user of SHOEBOX can create files, index them, search them, annotate them, edit them and reorganize them, all these activities being handled in an on-line interactive mode. The system is particularly suitable for the searching of files of natural language records (e.g., abstracts or intelligence messages) and is designed for use with CRT displays (the system has been implemented by means of IBM 2260 terminals and an IBM 360/50 computer). SHOEBOX files are searched by means of boolean expressions. Truncation capabilities are present, and synonym tables can be accommodated.

Many of the characteristics of SHOEBOX were incorporated by the Mitre Corporation into the design of an on-line system capable of searching the full text of patents. This design was completed for the U.S. Patent Office in 1972 (Glantz, 1972).

AUTONOTE

Perhaps the most flexible system of its kind is AUTONOTE, developed at the University of Michigan and operated on the Michigan Terminal System (MTS), a time-sharing system implemented on an IBM 360/67 computer and supporting various types of terminals, both typewriter terminals and CRT displays. AUTONOTE (Automatic Notebook), which has been described by Reitman, et al. (1969) and by Linn and Reitman (1971), provides on-line computer support for individual users or small groups working with textual information. The user of AUTONOTE can store, index, organize, and retrieve textual material of any kind, including notes, bibliographic references, drafts of papers, hypotheses, research topics, and drafts of conversations with colleagues. Any number of descriptors can be used to describe a particular item, a descriptor being defined as any string of characters up to 16 characters long. Simple procedures exist for reorganization of text and deletion of items. A variety of time-saving aids are included in the system; for example, the first two characters of a command are sufficient to identify it. Execution of a command may be interrupted by the user at any time. This causes the system to revert to a monitoring state to await further instructions.

AUTONOTE includes several interesting and useful features. One of these permits the user to combine descriptors into *composite descriptors* and to store these composite descriptors in association with document numbers for subsequent retrieval operations. A composite descriptor will incorporate AND, OR, and MINUS (negation) operators. For example,

MOTOR.OR.ENGINE	a composite descriptor that specifies "anything indexed under MOTOR or under ENGINE"
TUBERCULOSIS.MINUS.LUNG	a composite descriptor that specifies "anything indexed under TUBERCULOSIS but not under LUNG"

This feature has obvious utility in allowing the building of synonym tables to facilitate subsequent retrieval operations.

The user of AUTONOTE can choose between a terse and a verbose form of error message, and he may specify a limited subset of command requirements and processing capabilities, with resulting reductions in cost. Information about descriptors may be stored in the system, including definitions, abbreviations, synonyms, and relationships with other descriptors. It is therefore relatively easy to build a thesaurus into the system.

Typical system response times, under normal MTS loading, are said to range from 1 to 3 seconds for most commands. Using a Computer Communications Inc. Model 30 CRT display, data transmission rates of 120 characters per second are possible. This allows the display screen (about 800 characters) to be filled in about 8–12 seconds.

AUTONOTE is being used in studies of human behavior. A *protocol facility* stores, for subsequent analysis, a complete record of all user interactions with the system. Analysis of these records sheds light on use patterns and human reactions in a searching task, and allows modifications to be made to the system to improve its adaptability to the user. The basic goal of this research is to develop an increasingly intelligent or trainable system, "a system that can change its strategies, make appropriate inferences, and in general improve the speed, efficiency, and utility of communication as man and system increasingly 'understand' one another better" (Reitman, et al., 1969, p. 67).

Personal File Handling in Other Systems

In this chapter we have mentioned a number of systems designed primarily to support small, personal document files. Some of the other systems mentioned in this book also have facilities for personal file building. Kessler (1967) mentions the use of TIP to allow the user to construct his own files, subject to only minimal control in format, and to allow searching and retrieval activities on these files. A variation on this is the use of a machine-stored *standing order* to siphon off certain incoming references according to preestablished criteria, and to put these into a personal file for future examination by an individual for whom this particular file is being created. Other existing systems, because of their flexibility and simple command language, are suitable for use in the on-line manipulation of personal files.

SOLER (see Chapter Five) permits a user to create, update, and manipulate his own files. The SPIRES system, at Stanford University, can also accommodate personal indexes (Parker, 1971). It has a *file definition processor*—a set of programs to assist the user in the building of his file. In addition, a SPIRES *user consultant* is available to assist in file definition and related problems.

Symbiosis between Personal Files and General Systems

Another interesting possibility, touched upon by Swanson (1964), is the building up of specialized indexes, within an overall general-purpose index, by individual terminal users. That is, certain users of the on-line system would be given the capability of associating with selected items in the file their own particular sets of descriptors. This opens up the possibility of providing access to extremely large data bases while still allowing certain users to index relevant portions of the file according to their own specialized interests and viewpoints.

In the future it is possible that this type of symbiosis between personal or departmental files and a central information retrieval facility will occur. While the advantages of a comprehensive central system will thus be retained, the overall configuration will permit the existence of specialized files as subfiles within the central system. Each document in such a system would be represented by a unit record consisting, as a minimum, of a *master bibliographic record* with bibliographic citation and index terms. In addition, certain system users would be given the ability to add their own subrecords to this master record. Subrecords would carry a user identification code plus a set of special retrieval tags assigned to this bibliographic item by the particular user. This type of system will allow the individual scientist to build his own file on-line and to tag each item in his file with descriptors or other features by which he may want to retrieve it in the future. Not only will the individual user be able to index items to reflect his own particular viewpoints and needs, but he will also be able to reconstitute his own file on-line and to browse in this file where necessary. Further, he can extend his search beyond his own file into the master file whenever he wishes, without moving from the terminal and without changing his mode of search. There is another advantage to such a symbiotic approach—the system need contain only one bibliographic record for each item and, thus, storage space may be saved as well as time required for bibliographic description (as opposed to each individual building his own file on-line completely independently). Presumably, each subrecord could be made a special field which can be searched only by the user who has created this subrecord.

In a frequently cited paper, Bush (1945) visualized a desk-top personal documentation system, known as *memex*. Memex is described as a "mechanized private file and library." Using microfilm, the scientist can build up a large personal collection of various documents in compact form. He can add materials freely, including correspondence and personal notes, can consult his library "with exceeding speed and flexibility," and can build into it "associative trials" resulting from heuristic browsing. With on-line retrieval systems, coupled with supplementary files of documents in microform, the scientist can now realize all the capabilities of memex prophesied by Bush a quarter of a century ago.

REFERENCES

Bernal, J. D. (1948). "Preliminary Analysis of Pilot Questionnaire on the Use of Scientific Literature." *Proc. Royal Soc. Scientific Information Conf. London*, 101–102, 589–637.

Borman, L., and D. Dillaman (1968). *TRIAL: User's Manual*. Evanston, Ill.: Northwestern University, Vogelback Computing Center.

Borman, L., and B. Mittman (1972). "Interactive Search of Bibliographic Data Bases in an Academic Environment." *Jour. Amer. Soc. Information Sci*. **23** (3), 164–171.

Borman, L., D. Dillaman, and R. Chalice (1971). *RIQS Online: Remote Information Query System. User's Guide to On-Line System Version: I.O*. Evanston, Ill.: Northwestern University, Vogelback Computing Center.

Burton, H. D., and T. B. Yerke (1969). "Famulus: a Computer-Based System for Augmenting Personal Documentation Efforts." *Proc. Amer. Soc. Information Sci*. **6**, 53–56.

Bush, V. (1945). "As We May Think." *Atlantic Monthly* **176** (1), 101–108.

Chalice, R., D. Dillaman, and L. Borman (1970). *N.U. RIMS: User's Guide to Batch Processing System, Version I.O*. Evanston, Ill.: Northwestern University, Vogelback Computing Center.

Dale, A. G., and M. Eichelkraut (1968). *Remote File Management System: General Information*. Austin, The University of Texas, Computation Center.

Foskett, A. C. (1970). *A Guide to Personal Indexes Using Edge-Notched, Uniterm and Peek-a-Boo Cards*. 2nd ed. Hamden, Conn.: Archon Books.

Glantz, R. S. (1972). *Design of an On-Line Query Language for Full Text Patent Search*. Washington, D.C.: Mitre Corporation.

Glantz, R. S. (1970). "SHOEBOX—a Personal File Handling System for Textual Data." *AFIPS Conf. Proc. Fall Joint Computer Conf*. **37**, 535–545.

Heaps D. M., and W. Harris (1969). *The Development of Query Languages for On-Line Personal Documentation Systems*. Preliminary report. Edmonton, Alberta: University of Alberta, Department of Computing Science.

Heaps, D. M., and P. Sorenson (1968). "An On-Line Personal Documentation System." *Proc. Amer. Soc. Information Sci*. **5**, 201–207.

Hogg, I. H., and J. R. Smith (1959). "Information and Literature Use in a Research and Development Organization." *In Proceedings of the International Conference on Scientific Information*. vol. 1. Washington, D.C.: National Academy of Sciences, National Research Council, pp. 131–162.

Jahoda, G. (1970). *Information Storage and Retrieval Systems for Individual Researchers*. New York: Wiley.

Jahoda, G., R. D. Hutchins, and D. M. Miller (1966a). "Analysis of Case Histories of Personal Index Use." *Proc. Amer. Documentation Inst*. **3**, 245–254.

Jahoda, G., R. D. Hutchins, and R. R. Galford (1966b). "Characteristics and Use of Personal Indexes Maintained by Scientists and Engineers in one University." *Amer. Documentation* **17** (2), 71–75.

Janda, K. (1968). *Information Retrieval: Applications to Political Science.* Indianapolis, Ind.: Bobbs-Merrill.

Kessler, M. M. (1967). "The 'On-Line' Technical Information System at M.I.T. (Project TIP)." *IEEE Intern. Conv. Rec. Part 10*, 40–43.

Krulee, G., and B. Mittman (1969). "Computer-Based Information Systems for University Research and Teaching." *In Proceedings of the Sixth Annual National Colloquium on Information Retrieval.* Philadelphia, Pa.: The College of Physicians of Philadelphia, Medical Documentation Service, pp. 237–253.

Linn, W. E., Jr., and W. Reitman (1971). "Referential Communication in AUTONOTE: a Personal Information Retrieval System." *Proc. 26th Nat. Conf. Assoc. Computing Machinery*, 67–81.

Martyn, J. (1964). *Report of an Investigation on Literature Searching by Research Scientists.* London: ASLIB Research Department.

Mittman, B., and G. Krulee (1969). "Development of a Remote Information Management System—RIMS." *Proc. Amer. Soc. Information Sci.* **6**, 199–206.

Pacific Southwest Forest and Range Experiment Station (1969). *FAMULUS, a Personal Documentation System: User's Manual.* Berkeley, Ca.: Pacific Southwest Forest and Range Experiment Station.

Parker, E. B. (1971). *Requirements for SPIRES II.* Stanford, Ca.: Stanford University.

Parsons, R. G. (1972). *An Adaptation of the AIP "Searchable Physics Information Notices" for Use on CDC 6000 Series Computers.* Austin, Texas: University of Texas, The Center for Particle Theory, CPT-118.

Reitman, W., R. B. Roberts, R. W. Sauvain, D. D. Wheeler, and W. E. Linn, Jr. (1969). "AUTONOTE: a Personal Information Storage and Retrieval System." *Proc. 24th Nat. Conf. Assoc. Computing Machinery*, 67–76.

Smith, J. E., J. Butler, and D. Grosvenor (1969). "KEYWORD-INDEX" a Computer Oriented Personal Reference Retrieval System." *Methods Information Medicine* **8** (3), 152–154.

Swanson, D. R. (1964). "Dialogues with a Catalog." *Library Quarterly* **34** (1), 113–125.

Törnudd, E. (1953). *Professional Reading Habits of Scientists Engaged in Research as Revealed by an Analysis of 130 Questionnaires.* Unpublished MS Thesis, Carnegie Institute of Technology.

University of Durham (1970). *Project for Evaluating the Benefits from University Libraries: Final Report.* Durham, England: University of Durham, October 1969.

Wallace, E. M. (1966a). "User Requirements, Personal Indexes, and Computer Support." *Proc. Amer. Documentation Inst.* **3**, 73–80.

Wallace, E. M. (1966b). *A User's Guide to SURF: Support of User Records and Files.* Santa Monica, Ca.: System Development Corporation, TM-2913/000/00.

Yerke, T. B. (1970). "Computer Support of the Researcher's Own Documentation." *Datamation* **16** (2), 75–77.

Chapter Fourteen

The On-Line System for Current Awareness Purposes

The computer has proved to be of great value in current awareness activities in two principal ways:

1. It facilitates the rapid, efficient production of printed indexes and abstracting publications.

2. It allows the implementation of systems for selective dissemination of information (SDI) by matching large numbers of user-interest profiles against profiles of documents newly added to the collection.

Selective dissemination, unlike retrospective searching, is very conveniently handled in the batch-processing mode, and there appears to be no possible advantage to the use of on-line, time-shared facilities in the conventional SDI function of bulk matching of user interest profiles against incoming document representations. However, we are aware of only one published account of on-line SDI activities, by Bloemeke and Treu (1969), and this discusses the use of a time-sharing system in exactly this application.

Bloemeke and Treu describe the use of the IBM 360/50 time-shared system at the University of Pittsburgh Computer Center in the matching of *Chemical Titles* tapes against a group of user-interest profiles. This activity required the constant attention of a console operator in directing the searches, and consumed no less than 20 hours of terminal time per week in searching 51 interest profiles. System hardware and software failures, as well as operator errors, were extremely costly "since whatever search processing was already accomplished at the time of involuntary job abortion was normally unrecoverable, both in time and cost."

Clearly, the matching of a group of interest profiles against a tape of document representations is highly suitable for batch processing, but it is inappropriate to time-sharing and is inefficiently handled by such a system. Bloemeke and Treu (1969) point out that "the nature and state-of-the-art of time-sharing make it both unsuitable and inefficient for the long tape searching jobs required by current awareness services. In particular, searching *Chemical Titles* in the time-sharing environment which is prone to system or console operator failure is lengthy and too costly." And again: "There is no reason to pay for the luxury of a system which is highly oriented towards user-system interaction, when the repetitive searching based on established user interest profiles is essentially noninteractive."

As a result of the experience outlined above, it was decided to transfer the Pittsburgh current awareness service from time-sharing to batch processing. However, as we have already pointed out, the time-sharing system was being used inefficiently in this particular application, and it is still appropriate to consider possible ways in which an on-line, time-shared system might be used effectively in dissemination activities. Three major possibilities appear to exist:

1. The construction and testing of user-interest profiles at the on-line terminal.
2. Use of video consoles to facilitate the human dissemination of messages arriving in machine-readable form (*machine-aided dissemination*).
3. Allowing a user direct access to a terminal and providing the capability of displaying records of documents, matching his stored interest profile, that have been added to the data base since he last interrogated the system.

A search strategy to retrieve documents that match a particular user's interests is likely to be most effective if developed heuristically. Even though the actual matching of profiles against documents is conducted in a batch mode, it would certainly be valuable to be able to construct a search strategy (*user-interest profile*) at an on-line terminal, test it against the data base to determine the types of documents the strategy will retrieve, make modifications, and test again until the profile appears to be hitting the maximum number of relevant documents and the minimum number of irrelevant ones.

Some interesting research has been carried out by Caruso (1969), at the University of Pittsburgh, on profile construction on-line. Using principles drawn from the field of computer-aided instruction (CAI), a tutorial program has been produced to guide users in the construction of interest profiles for the searching of Chemical Abstracts *Condensates* tapes. The program instructs in the selection of terms, in the application of boolean logic, and the use of left and right truncation. Printed instructions are reduced to a single page, which merely tells the user how to turn on the terminal, load the program, and restart it should some error condition cause it to stop execution. All other instructions are incorporated into the tutorial itself. A group of Help messages is stored, and any one of these can be called up by the user whenever the meaning of a particular sequence or response is unclear to him. These programs are illustrated in Appendices H and I of this book.

On-line profile construction also offers the advantages of ease and rapidity of profile changing. Moreover, the on-line system can be used to view displays of user interest statements, search strategies (profiles), current lists of disseminees, and other system records. An on-line system is being applied to SDI activities at the Computer Center of the University of Georgia (Park, 1972). Profile management is handled on-line at an IBM 2260 CRT terminal. Complete user information, such as the mailing and billing addresses, as well as the search profile, and a record of the data bases to be searched, is included. Information can be added, modified, or deleted directly from the terminal. Search profiles are constructed and modified on the basis of an on-line search of a representative subset of the data base.

In the defense and intelligence communities, a considerable number of important messages are generated and relayed in digital form by means of wire communications systems. When received at information processing agencies, these messages are usually captured in hard copy form, using teletypewriters, and disseminated by hand. That is, human disseminators examine the messages as they come off the teletypewriter in multiple copies, decide which individuals or offices should see copies of each message, and mark the messages with symbols representing these addresses. In some places, this type of dissemination is now handled with the aid of on-line systems. The dissemination is conducted partly automatically, using profile matching techniques, and partly in a machine-aided mode. Messages arriving in machine-readable form, instead of being printed out initially for the human disseminator, are displayed on a CRT terminal. The human disseminator views the message on the console, decides who should receive it, and keys in the symbols that represent these addressees. Off-line the message is printed out by high-speed printer in as many copies as there are recipients, and the name and address of the recipient appears at the head of each copy of the message. Certain messages are disseminated fully automatically (i.e., recipients are determined by computer on a profile match basis), and these messages either bypass the video console or are displayed to allow the human disseminator to check the machine assignment.

This system can be carried one stage further. Instead of disseminating messages as printed copies, after addressees have been determined by the human disseminator at the CRT, they are disseminated in machine-readable form. That is, each office has its own terminal connected to the on-line dissemination system. Periodically during the day, a responsible analyst in this office views on a CRT all messages that have been addressed to that office since the last group was viewed. A completely paperless information transfer system is thus created.

Essentially, any on-line bibliographic system made available to a particular group of researchers can be used for current awareness purposes. The current awareness function would be handled as follows: The user has access to an on-line terminal, and there he develops and tries out a search strategy designed to retrieve documents relevant to his current research interests. When an effective strategy is arrived at, it is used to retrieve relevant documents from the complete data base as it exists at the time. Periodically, say on a weekly or monthly basis, depending on how frequently the files are updated, he returns to the terminal to determine if any items added match his search strategy. A date restriction is used to ensure that he now receives only new items. To facilitate the entire process, it is preferable that the system should allow the user to store his search strategy, and call it up periodically, rather than having him reconstruct it every time he wishes to update his search. In this application, visits to the console made at the user's convenience replace the more conventional receipt and scanning of printed notices.

A good example of the use of an on-line system for current awareness is provided by the SDILINE (Selective Dissemination of Information On-Line) service offered by the National Library of Medicine in association with the MEDLINE network. The SDILINE data base contains all MEDLARS citations (from about 2400 journals) input during the latest month. The data base, which is changed monthly, makes these citations available some weeks before they appear in *Index Medicus*. A medical practitioner or researcher who has access to a MEDLINE terminal can keep up-to-date by visiting the terminal on a monthly basis and applying a strategy known to represent his current profile of interest to the SDILINE data base.

REFERENCES

Bloemeke, M. J., and S. Treu (1969). "Searching *Chemical Titles* in the Pittsburgh Time-Sharing System." *Jour. Chem. Documentation* **9** (3), 155–157.

Caruso, D. E. (1969). *The Profile Development Program: a Tutorial for Users of the Chemical Abstracts Service Condensates Alerting Service. Reference Manual.* Pittsburgh, Pa.: University of Pittsburgh, Knowledge Availability Systems Center.

Park, M. K. (1972). Personal Communication.

Chapter Fifteen

Instruction and Training of Users

A critical factor affecting the success or failure of an on-line retrieval system is the effectiveness of procedures employed to teach people how to use the facilities. Procedures for the training of information specialists who are to be frequent users of the system may be comprehensive and involve a relatively long period of time, but procedures used in the instruction of the practitioners in a field, who are likely to be relatively infrequent users, must be brief, direct, and simple. A number of possibilities exist:

1. Printed instructional guides.
2. Personal instruction by a trained searcher.
3. Audiovisual presentations.
4. Instruction provided on-line at the terminal itself.

Printed Guides

Some form of user guide or handbook exists for most on-line retrieval systems. Unfortunately, these guides are very variable in quality. Some are complex, lengthy, and badly written. Although they may have value as reference tools, they are usually unsuitable for instructional purposes. A comprehensive printed guide should be available for reference purposes to explain log-in and log-out procedures, commands, error messages, and other system features. If printed materials are to be used to *teach* people how to interrogate the system, however, these materials need to be kept brief and simple. They should be designed to give the reader the minimum of instruction needed to allow him to log-in and query the system in a relatively simple way. There is no real substitute for hands-on experience at the terminal, and the printed instructions should not attempt to describe all the complexities of the system, at least not initially. The casual or infrequent user will not want to spend a great deal of time studying a printed guide before he can get to the terminal. It would seem sensible to produce printed instructions in a series of modules (perhaps three would suffice) of increasing sophistication and complexity; the first would present only the bare minimum of instructions. When the user has tried the system and become generally familiar with its operation, he can go on to study the more sophisticated features.

Instruction in the use of a fairly conventional on-line system will involve two elements: instruction in the *mechanics* of using the system (log-in, log-out, command names, system responses), and instruction in techniques of systematic searching. It has generally been found that the former can be taught relatively quickly and simply, but the latter is more difficult to teach effectively, and requires rather more time and effort.

It is desirable that outline instructions relating to the mechanics of using the system, including major system commands, be printed in large type on a card displayed prominently on or adjacent to the terminal. A *pocket reminder card* containing basic instructions for SUPARS (Atherton, 1971) is shown in Figure 15.1.

Some examples of the better instructional materials are given in Appendices B–E. Appendix B illustrates a simple, straightforward booklet describing use of DIALOG. Appendix C is a list of basic instructions prepared by Lancaster for potential users of the AIM–TWX system.* Appendix D illustrates a fold-over card containing the highly compressed instructions prepared by Mead Data Central Inc. for the OBAR system. Appendix E is a clear, concise user guide to SUPARS prepared by the School of Library Science, Syracuse University.

Personal Instruction

However well-prepared, printed materials may be less effective than personal instruction by a trained searcher. In Project Intrex, it has been found difficult to instruct users from manuals or printed guides (Massachusetts Institute of Technology, 1971). For training librarians, the Intrex investigators use experienced searchers as console instructors, and each instructor works with only one trainee. This personalized one-to-one

---

*An excellent, complete *AIM–TWX User's Guide* was prepared by Cobbs (1971), with a section on search strategy by DesChene. It is too long to reproduce here, but is well worth a close examination. Such a comprehensive guide is a useful reference tool and is suitable for use in the training of information specialists.

instruction, with considerable hands-on console operation, has been found to be the most effective mode of teaching.

Personalized instruction of this type is probably most satisfactory and is likely to produce rapid results. Isotta (1970) reports that only 10–15 minutes of training is required before an average user can commence operations on the European version of the NASA on-line system. Glassman (1971) has been able to teach children in an elementary school how to use an on-line catalog, with boolean search capabilities, in about 15 minutes of individualized instruction (4–5 students at a time) following a large group session at which the system was described in general terms. Bridegam and Meyerhoff (1970) of SUNY report, however, that "despite the fact that a person has read and reread instructions of machine searching and received a half-hour orientation, it is the exceptional user who will not require the assistance of a librarian for at least his next five or six searches." In personal instruction, the teacher should go through a sample search on the terminal with the person he is training. It is therefore necessary that a good sample search be developed to illustrate most of the major system features.

Group instruction is possible when a large number of users are to be trained. A 13 minute presentation, incorporating colored slides and a tape-recorded narrative, was developed for use in the SUPARS system (Atherton, 1971). This *canned* presentation was followed by an on-line demonstration search. For on-line demonstration to a large group, closed-circuit television may be necessary.

Audiovisual Presentations

Personal instruction, while it is likely to be effective, is also likely to be expensive. Moreover, we usually cannot guarantee that a trained searcher will be available to instruct every user who comes to an on-line search facility. Individualized instruction will also be impossible for users of terminals in remote locations. An alternative to personal instruction would be some form of audiovisual presentation. Such a presentation would be a film of a personalized instruction session, with the viewer looking over the searcher's shoulder while a sample search is being conducted. This type of presentation may be almost as effective as direct face-to-face tuition. It suffers from the defect that the trainee is unable to ask questions of the trained searcher. On the other hand, an audiovisual presentation can be made readily available, and, with certain forms at least, the viewer can go over the material at his own pace, backtracking where necessary. Such instructional materials could be prepared for use on sound-filmstrip projectors, sound-slide projection units, or 8 millimeter film cassettes.

HIGHLIGHTS AND GUIDELINES

SUPARS '71

SIGN-ON PROCEDURES

Here are the basic steps necessary to sign on for a SUPARS search, using an IBM 2471 terminal (typewriter):

1. Push ON switch bottom right-hand corner of keyboard.

2. Depress ATTN key.

3. Type)On (R)   R means depress RETURN key.

4. Type)4771OXX/LIBS.   replacing small x's with your terminal number, e.g.)4770030/LIBS OR with any four digits, e.g.)4771234/LIBS.

5. Depress ATTN key.

6. Type)EXEC PA (R)

7. Type)XXXXXXXXX (R),   replacing X's with your social security number, e.g.)123456789

The computer will respond:
        VALID NUMBER

YOU ARE NOW READY TO USE SUPARS   (please turn over)

If you need assistance, call
        SUPARS
        EXT. 4220
        Mon.-Fri., 8:00-9:00 p.m.

GUIDELINES FOR PHRASING A SEARCH

Type delta symbol Δ to start your SEARCH!

To retrieve references to Psychological Abstracts of interest to you, you will usually want to use more than one or two keywords. To make your search understandable to the SUPARS system it is necessary to phrase this search following a set of rules.

1. Each keyword must be logically arranged with either an AND or OR operator. The computer will generate labels (L1, L2, etc.) for each line of your search. To generate labels, you must depress the return key on the typewriter terminal.

Example: L1
        BEHAVIOR AND THERAPY;

Example: L1
        BEHAVIOR OR BEHAVIORAL
        L2
        THERAPY
        L3
        L1 AND L2;

2. A string of keywords in a line can be combined with AND or OR operator, but not by both on the same line. It is necessary, as in the example above, to combine two strings in a summary statement (e.g., L1 and L2;) to make such a combination.

3. Keywords which have similar roots (e.g., behavior, Behavioral, etc.) can be searched easily in SUPARS by use of a truncation expander.

Example: L1
        BEHAVIOR(?)
        L2
        THERAPY
        L3
        L1 AND L2;

4. When the truncation expander (?) is used, the AND operator can not be used in the same line. Note the example above in (3): the two keywords were combined in a summary statement (L3).

GUIDELINES FOR PHRASING A SEARCH (contd.)

5. Two keywords which form a concept in your mind can be looked for in SUPARS as a pair of words that stand side by side in Psychological Abstracts. This is how to phrase such a request:

Example: L1
        BEHAVIOR AND THERAPY(+1);

PLEASE NOTE: In the above examples, when all the keywords in the search have been combined, a semicolon (;) is typed. If you want to abort your search, type the delta symbol Δ.

6. A string of keywords (e.g., synonyms) combined by an OR operator can be combined with another keyword to phrase a multiword concept, but certain rules of SUPARS must be followed.

Example: L1
        BEHAVIOR OR CONDITIONING
        L2
        THERAPY(?)
        L3
        L1 AND L2(+1);

Note in the above examples that the restrictor symbol (+1) always appears in a line with the AND operator.

PROCEDURE TO OBTAIN OUTPUT FROM SUPARS

7. After ending your listing of keywords, type a semicolon(;). This will stop the generation of labels (L1, L2, etc.). Next, type a LIST statement, and type END.

Example: L1
        BEHAVIOR AND THERAPY;
        LIST RECORD
        END

A LIST RECORD statement will generate the full bibliographical citation and as much of the abstract as we have stored in the computer. A LIST BRIEF statement will generate a list of Psychological Abstracts numbers, volume and year.

8. After the computer has responded, e.g. SEARCHING
        ......XXXXXX DOCUMENTS FOUND: 002

Type:
)CG)   If you want the items printed out
or   )STAT   If you want to see statistics (number of items
                  per labels in your search)

NOTE: After the)STAT command type)00 to obtain the abstracts

SEE THE SUPARS USER MANUAL FOR ADDITIONAL ASSISTANCE Call, Ext. 4220

Searching the SUPARS Vocabulary

Before searching for abstracts in Psychological Abstracts you may want to look at portions of the alphabetical list of all the words in these abstracts. You can phrase your request for a printout of words from the vocabulary following rules similar to those in the Guidelines section of this card.

To begin such a search, type AV after completing the sign-on procedures. Type one keyword per line, and a LIST VOCAB statement. Always type END as last statement.

The SUPARS User Manual has more detail on this type of search and how to interpret the output.

Searching Stored Searches

Besides searching Psychological Abstracts and the stored Vocabulary, you may want to search through a file of searches saved from earlier SUPARS use. No names of SUPARS users are stored, but the words in their searches are stored.

You can use the same rules for this kind of search as you would following the steps in the Guidelines section.

To begin such a search, type AS after completing the sign-on procedure, proceed as in a search, and use a LIST WORDS or LIST SEARCH statement. Always type END as last statement.

The SUPARS User Manual has more detailed explanation on this type of search and its output.

FOR HELP   CALL EXT. 4220

SEE THE USER MANUAL

SUPARS ESSENTIAL VOCABULARY AND SYMBOLS

Δ (DELTA)	BEGINS SEARCH INSTRUCTIONS FOR DOCUMENTS
ΔS (DELTA S)	BEGINS SEARCH INSTRUCTIONS FOR SEARCHES OF OTHER SUPARS USERS
ΔV (DELTA V)	BEGINS SEARCH INSTRUCTIONS FOR VOCABULARY OF WORDS IN SUPARS
L (L1, L2,...)	LABELS GENERATED BY COMPUTER TO MARK THE LINES IN YOUR SEARCH
x or AND	COMBINES KEYWORDS WITHIN LABELS IN "AND" RELATIONSHIPS (x is multiplication sign.)
, (COMMA) or OR	COMBINES KEYWORDS WITHIN LABELS IN "OR" RELATIONSHIPS
; (SEMICOLON)	ENDS GENERATION OF LABELS; FOLLOWS FINAL SEARCH SUMMARY
(?)	EXPANDER SYMBOL TO INDICATE THAT A STANDARD WORD SEARCH IS REQUESTED. FOR EXAMPLE: PSYCH(?)
+(+)	CAUSES COMPUTER TO REPRODUCE OUTPUT IN A SPECIFIC FORM
END	ENDS USER'S SEARCH INSTRUCTIONS. MUST BE TYPED AS THE LAST STATEMENT OF EVERY SEARCH.
ISTAT	CAUSES COMPUTER TO LIST STATISTICS FOR EACH LINE OF SEARCH, INDICATING THE NUMBER OF ITEMS FOUND
IGO	URGES COMPUTER TO BEGIN LISTING ITEMS FOUND IN THE SEARCH
)OFF	DISCONNECTS USER FROM COMPUTER; MUST BE TYPED TWICE. CALL TO BE DISCONNECTED THAT THE SUPARS SYSTEM, CALL TO BE DISCONNECTED FROM THE COMPUTER SYSTEM AS A WHOLE.

THE ATTENTION BUTTON MUST BE DEPRESSED IN ORDER TO TYPE THE SECOND)OFF

FOR HELP:
Call SUPARS Office at ext. 4220
See the SUPARS User Manual

SUPARS

BASIC STEPS FOR SIGN-OFF

1. Type)OFF when all searching is completed; this command disconnects you from the Psychological Abstracts file.

2. Depress ATTN key. Type second)OFF to disconnect from computer.

3. Push OFF switch on bottom right-hand corner of keyboard.

REDOER

A. You can at any time cancel an existing search and start a new one by typing a DELTA (Δ).

B. You can at any time interrupt the computer printing by hitting the ATTN key. It is best to do this immediately after the carriage returns.

EXPLANATIONS OF THE UNEXPECTED MESSAGES FROM THE COMPUTER

1. PA UNDEFINED
This indicates that the SUPARS program has not yet been set up for today's operation. Call ext. 4220:

2. NO MORE ITEMS AVAILABLE
this means your search output is complete. Begin a new search:

3. TOO MANY USERS, TRY AGAIN SOON.
Too many people are using the SUPARS system at the same time. Your searches will have to wait awhile.

4. KEYWORD NOT IN DICTIONARY
The word you have used in a search is not in the SUPARS vocabulary.

5. INVALID EXPANDER OR RESTRICTOR IN PARENTHESIS.
You may have used the expander symbol (?) or the restrictor symbol (+) incorrectly.

6. ILLEGAL OPERATOR FOUND
You have used AND or OR strings of words in the same label of your search. This is a no-no!

FOR HELP: CALL SUPARS OFFICE EXT. 4220 - CHECK THE SUPARS USER MANUAL

Figure 15.1. SUPARS pocket reminder card. Reproduced by permission of the School of Library Science, Syracuse University.

A useful script-slide presentation on the use of DIALOG has been prepared by the ERIC Clearinghouse for Educational Media and Technology at Stanford University.

Training Problems

Marcus, et al. (1971), describing Intrex experience, report the following characteristics of user behavior that cause difficulties in instruction:

(1) *Failure* of users *to notice* even the most explicit instructions. (For example, "Please don't forget the carriage return.")

(2) The fact that *no single instruction method* or booklet, no single "style" of presentation, no single compromise between brevity and completeness, seems to satisfy all, or even a majority of users.

(3) On the other hand, if there are too many instructional options, users tend to ignore them all. We refer to this as the "*clutter effect*". Users seem to prefer to be given instructions only when they need them.

(4) Users *do not like to spend time to prepare* themselves for system use. In general, they want to ignore the system and focus on its use.

(5) Users assume that the given system works like some other system (e.g., the traditional library catalog) that they already know about. Some users seem *not to like to learn anything new*, or unfamiliar.

(6) Some users suffer from an extreme case of what we might call "*computer Angst*" or fear of the machine. Such fear seems to come in two varieties—the fear of the user who is anxious about making a mistake because he will appear foolish, and the fear of the user who is afraid his actions will damage the system. This "Angst" is less severe in the young and in those with some computer experience, a fact which augurs well for acceptance of retrieval systems by the coming generation. Some users suffer from "people Angst" or fear of asking human advisers for help.

(7) Users often assume that the computer is a giant brain that will do all their thinking for them or that it is so complex that they cannot possibly understand it. They therefore *assume they need not or cannot understand the system* and this impedes learning.

These appear to be the main problems in introducing the system to the user. The most helpful solutions we see to these problems are the following:

(1) Users *learn best by doing* and particularly by actually using a system that immediately tells them whether or not they have done the right thing and how it understands what they are doing.

(2) It is also very helpful to have users engage the system when they have an actual *need for information*. They are more receptive and persevering at such times.

(3) It seems, in general, better to *present general ideas* to users *by means of examples* than to give them the general rules.

(4) *Human personal instruction* is best although training persons who are unfamiliar with computer concepts to be good instructors is difficult. On-line

instruction is more effective than off-line instruction and probably sufficient for most users if the system itself is reliable. However, it costs more than equivalent off-line materials. We find that users have a strong preference for the on-line instruction over the off-line manuals even when these are identical in content. We feel that this is primarily due to the user's desire to keep his focus in one place and partly because of his feeling—erroneous, of course— that computer-given instruction must be more reliable and up-to-date.

(5) It is important for *the user* to know that he *cannot break the system.* Some users are bothered if they feel they are being watched, but others do not seem to care.

(6) It is useful to provide a variety of instructional materials so that a user can choose the material that is most congenial to him. An index to a reference manual can assist a user in tailoring its use to his requirements, although having one is no guarantee that the user will find what he wants. We find that no matter how many instructional formats we provide, some user fails to find one appropriate to his needs at the moment.

(7) The following distinctions among the learning strategies of potential users seem particularly apropos to the development of instructional materials: there are persons who want to understand the system versus those who simply want instructions about what to do; there are persons who want to know everything before they start versus others who want to learn as they go along; and there are those who understand computers versus those who do not (pp. 190–192).*

On-Line Instruction

A user can be taught how to search the system at the on-line terminal itself. At least three types of on-line instruction appear possible:

1. Use of the terminal to display a conventional set of instructions that could equally well be presented in conventional printed form.

2. Use of computer-aided instruction (CAI) techniques, either to give the user a one-time introduction to the system or to lead him by the hand in the conduct of an actual search.

3. Incorporation of explanations of specific commands or system features that the user can call up when he needs them.

Several on-line retrieval systems incorporate limited instruction capabilities. As an example, the user of MEDLINE or AIM–TWX, once he has logged-in, can request a printout of complete or abbreviated instructions in how to interrogate the system. These instructions are conventional in that they are identical to instructions that are available in standard printed form. A similar type of on-line instruction is available in the SUNY system. A brief refresher on-line instruction is probably worthwhile because, even though it does nothing that the printed page would not do, the on-line

---

*Reprinted by permission of the AFIPS Press.

presentation may itself be sufficiently novel to capture the attention of the user, where the printed page may not. In Project Intrex, it has been found that users seem to favor on-line instruction even when this instruction provides nothing additional to the instruction available in a printed guide. Lengthy instruction on-line, unless such instruction incorporates techniques (e.g., CAI) that cannot be exploited effectively on the printed page, seems to be an extremely inefficient use of computer time, however. The Data Central system includes some quite sophisticated instructional capabilities, designed for CRT presentation, and these take the user through sample searches.

The user of an on-line system should be able to request assistance or explanation when he needs it. In ORBIT, it is possible to determine the meaning of any system command by entering the further command EX-PLAIN. For example, EXPLAIN PRINT COMMAND will cause the display of an explanation of the system's print options. In ORBIT, it is even possible to request EXPLAIN EXPLAIN! In Data Central, the searcher can request an explanation of any system response that he does not under-stand by entering the command "WHAT?" Other systems will generate an explanation in response to a simple "?". In MEDLINE the command HELP will cause the system to display a menu of problems most commonly en-countered by users. If the user's problem falls into one of these categories, he can request assistance from the system in resolving his difficulties.

The inexperienced user should be able to request assistance from a search specialist or a system specialist when he gets into difficulties. Such a communication can be by telephone (in SUPARS, for example, the user is given a HELP! telephone number), or it can be conducted on-line by the transmission of messages to and from the searcher's terminal and a monitor-ing terminal operated by an experienced searcher.

A large on-line system may need to introduce procedures for the con-tinuing education of its users, particularly to inform users of new capabilities that have been introduced and to try to alleviate problems that are being encountered in use of the system. In this respect, on-line monitoring opera-tions will be important in revealing the types of problems that occur most frequently. Continuing education of regular users (e.g., librarians) may be achieved through a newsletter. It is also desirable that the system have some type of NEWS command, whereby the user can discover, at the terminal itself, the latest news on system features and capabilities.

Although instruction in on-line searching seems to be an obvious application for CAI, and many writers have suggested this approach, com-paratively little work on this application has so far been conducted. Most of the useful work in this area has been carried out by Caruso (1969a, b, 1970a, b) at the Knowledge Availability Systems Center, University of Pittsburgh. A group of programs, known in fact as CARUSO (Conversational and

Reactive User-Oriented Search Operations) has been developed. These programs include a tutorial for SDI profile construction; a *conversational* approach with verbose tutorial messages or brief prompting messages available as options and inseparable from the search program itself; and a generalizable strategy program which teaches the user the basic concepts of boolean logic and their reduction to symbolic form, and illustrates their application in a tutorial that is separable from the search and output program.

One of the early interactive search procedures developed by Caruso offered the user the opportunity to receive instruction at each step in the search process. The user was led by the hand in the construction of a search strategy. For example, the required boolean logic was determined by the use of some carefully chosen questions, such as "Are there any of these terms that MUST appear in the document if it is to be of value to you?" or "Are there any terms whose presence in a document would assure you that the document was of no interest?" Experience with this mode of operation led Caruso to the belief that improved results could be obtained by a one-time only tutorial which would teach the user how to construct logical search statements rather than leading him by the hand in the conduct of an actual search. A second tutorial program was then devised to instruct in:

1. Use of a typewriter terminal.
2. Conceptual analysis of a query.
3. Selection of terms.
4. Understanding of boolean operators.
5. Using logical operators to combine search terms.
6. Expressing the search terms and operators as a logical statement.

This tutorial program, described in detail in Caruso (1969b), can be completed in about 45 minutes, with additional time spent in actually operating the system. Controlled comparative tests indicated that the on-line tutorial method of learning search strategy construction was at least as effective as classroom instruction for the same purpose.

A sample exercise from the Caruso tutorial program is illustrated in Figure 15.2. The program has several interesting and innovative features, including the provision of feedback to the user in the recall and precision of his search (see Figure 15.3). Appendix F includes a complete illustration of the use of the tutorial program, and Appendix G contains the Caruso manual for use of the tutorial program.

Caruso's tutorial program (Caruso, 1969b) for construction of profiles for the Chemical Abstracts *Condensates* alerting service (see Chapter Fourteen) consists of two distinct elements:

1. An introduction to the use of search terms (specification, synonymy, truncation) and to the use of parameters to define the search more closely.

Ready yet?

>go

Let's substitute words for the symbols in the logical statement: (A + B) × (C + D).

    '(A + B)' means: 'A _____ _____ B'.   Complete the statement on the next line.

>and not

No...Please try again. If you need help, look back to the section headed LOGICAL SUM. Also see page 9 of your instruction booklet.

    '(A + B)' means: 'A _____ _____ B'.   Complete the statement on the next line.

>and also

No, just the words which would be the verbal equivalent of ' + '.

    '(A + B)' means: 'A _____ _____ B'.   Complete the statement on the next line:

>and/or

Right!

    '(C + D)' means: 'C _____ _____ D'

>and/or

Right!

Now complete this statement:

'(A + B) × (C + D)' means '(A and/or B) _____ _____ (C and/or D)'.

>and also

Right!

Very well done! The statement used LOGICAL PRODUCT strategy to join the LOGICAL SUMS.

Figure 15.2.   An exercise from the CARUSO tutorial program. (Student responses are preceded by the caret, >.) Reproduced from Caruso (1969a) by permission of the author.

    2.   An iterative practice search session which allows the user to apply what he has learned, observing the effects of variations in strategy construction and search terms specification.

An illustration of the preliminary tutorial program is given in Appendix H, and an illustration of a practice search is given in Appendix I.

    Some experiments with instruction in on-line searching have also been carried out at the University of Illinois, using the powerful capabilities of the PLATO system of CAI. This work is reported by Lyman (1971). The experiments were conducted in the subject area of coding theory. The instructional programs allow the user to interact with the computer to determine paths that will lead to the retrieval of relevant references. The technique employed by Lyman is based on a hierarchical structuring of the terminology of the subject. The user is first given a choice among seven broad subdivisions of coding theory. On choosing one subdivision, he is given a further breakdown (see Figure 15.4) and can then request a display of a hierarchical *map* of a subtopic. Eventually, when he has narrowed his search

EVALUATION OF SEARCH RESULTS

Your search strategy retrieved all relevant references--
very good!
You have some irrelevance.
25.0% of the documents you retrieved do not answer the
question asked.

These are relevant documents:

6877166, 6877177, 6877777

The irrelevant references were:

6877888

YOUR SCORE FOR THIS QUESTION:

RECALL:
1.00000
PRECISION:
0.75000

Figure 15.3. Feedback to user on recall and precision of search results. Reproduced from Caruso (1969a) by permission of the author.

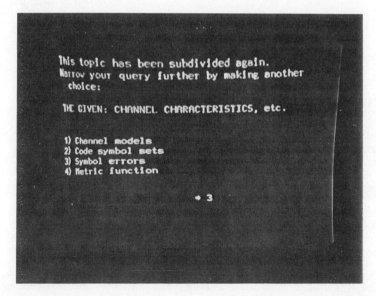

Figure 15.4. Example of on-line instruction for searching a bibliographic data base using PLATO. Reproduced from Lyman (1971) by permission of the Computer-based Education Research Laboratory, University of Illinois.

ARE YOU FAMILIAR WITH THE SYSTEM?
ANSWER "YES" OR "NO".

NO

(1) REMEMBER TO FOLLOW EVERY ACTION WITH A CARRIAGE RETURN. OTHERWISE NO ACTION WILL FOLLOW YOUR ANSWER.
(2) IF YOU ARE NOT CLEAR ON HOW TO ANSWER A PARTICULAR QUESTION, TYPE "?" AND MORE INFORMATION WILL BE GIVEN TO YOU.
(3) IF THIS DOES NOT HELP, SIGN OFF BY TYPING "EXIT". THIS WILL, AT ANY TIME, DELIVER YOU FROM THE PROGRAM.
(4) TYPE THE CHEMICAL SYMBOLS FOR THE TWO ATOMS IN YOUR DIATOMIC MOLECULE OR MOLECULAR ION. THE TWO SYMBOLS SHOULD BE SEPARATED BY AT LEAST ONE SPACE, BUT SPACES ARE NOT PERMITTED WITHIN A SYMBOL E.G. THE MOLECULE HCL IS CORRECTLY REPRESENTED BY H CL BUT NOT BY HCL OR BY H C L. NOW TYPE YOUR TWO ATOMIC SYMBOLS.

K K   (K is the symbol for the element
                                                          potassium)

LIST OF STATES STORED FOR K K
(1) K2 X 1 SIGMA + (G)
(2) K2 B 1 PI (u)
(99) ANY OTHER STATE   (A given pair of atoms can exist in a
                                     number of different states, for each
                                     of which there is an interatomic
                                     potential. The above list gives the
                                     states of K K for which potentials
                                     have been stored.)

WHICH?

?

INDICATE BY TYPING THE APPROPRIATE NUMBER WHICH OF THE ABOVE STATES YOU ARE INTERESTED IN. IF NONE OF THE STATES LISTED IS OF ANY USE TO YOU TYPE THE NUMBER CORRESPONDING TO "ANY OTHER STATE".
WHICH?

L

YOU MUST HAVE MADE A TYPING ERROR. TYPE THAT ANSWER AGAIN.

1

POTENTIALS FITTED TO THE STATE: K2 X 1 SIGMA + (G)

POT. TYPE	ERROR ESTIMATE	RANGE (A.U.)
(1) BORN-MAYER	$<5\%$	1.5 TO 3.5
(2) NUMERICAL	$<1\%$	6.0 TO 9.6
(3) NUMERICAL	$<1\%$	6.2 TO 9.2

Figure 15.5. Sample annotated search from QUODAMP. Reproduced from Boyle, et al. (1971) by permission of the Department of Computer Science, Queen's University of Belfast.

(99) NOT INTERESTED IN ANY OF THE GIVEN POTENTIAL ESTIMATES.

> (A number of different estimates may have been made to a particular potential. The above list gives a brief description of each of the estimates which have been stored for the particular potential in which we are interested.)

WHICH?

1

ENERGY UNITS?

A.U.

LENGTH UNITS?

A

WHICH FORM?

?

THE POTENTIALS ARE AVAILABLE IN ANY ONE OF THE FOLLOWING FOUR FORMS:

    (F) AS AN ALGEBRAIC FORMULA
    (P) AS A SET OF POINTS
    (G) AS A CURVE ON A GRAPH
    (S) AS A SUBROUTINE

INDICATE BY TYPING THE APPROPRIATE LETTER WHICH FORM YOU ARE INTERESTED IN.
WHICH FORM?

F

SYSTEM AND STATE: K2 X 1 SIGMA + (G)
TYPE OF POTENTIAL FIT: BORN-MAYER
METHOD OF CALCULATION: AB INITIO
THE BORN-MAYER POTENTIAL IS DEFINED BY
    $V(R) = A * EXP(-B*R)$
WHERE A AND B ARE CONSTANTS WHICH DEPEND ON THE PARTICULAR SYSTEM INVOLVED. IN THIS CASE
A = 0.277950 A.U. AND B = 0.36214E 01 (A)**(-1).
THE ESTIMATED RELATIVE ACCURACY IS 3.6% WHILE THE UPPER AND LOWER LIMITS OF THE RANGE WITH WHICH THE POTENTIAL IS VALID ARE 0.738E 00 A AND 0.1852E 01 A RESPECTIVELY.
TITLE OF ARTICLE AND REFERENCE:
BORN-MAYER-TYPE INTERATOMIC POTENTIAL FOR NEUTRAL GROUND STATE ATOMS WITH Z=2 TO Z=105.
A. A. ABRAHAMSON   PHYS. REV.   178, 76, (1968)

> (At this point the system offers the user the alternative of either logging out or else of going back to any one of the points where he had made a decision and following a different path.)

Figure 15.5. *Continued*

sufficiently, he can request a display of bibliographic citations that fall into the category selected.

At Queen's University of Belfast, an on-line system for retrieval of data on atomic and molecular physics is designed to be self-instructive. Users are expected to be able to search without printed aids and without previous knowledge of the system. A very brief explanation of the system is given at the beginning of a search. Thereafter, the user specifies the data he needs by answering multiple choice questions communicated to him by the on-line terminal. A sample annotated search is shown in Figure 15.5. The system has been described by Boyle, et al (1971).

Reinecke (1968) and Eichhorn and Reinecke (1970) have described the use of CAI techniques coupled with an information retrieval system at the Vision Information Center (VIC), Harvard University. According to Eichhorn and Reinecke (1970), CAI has three functions in the VIC system:

1) Use of CAILAN, a programming language developed for CAI, makes possible a conversational mode of interaction between the user and the computer.

2) The user may request as much information as he needs on use of the computer terminal and of the VIC thesaurus; these directions, written in the CAI format, are typed out at the computer terminal. Thus it is possible for a novice user at a remote terminal to query the system without relying on the assistance of a librarian or information scientist.

3) CAI provides instruction on various aspects of ophthalmology. At present, there are four texts of programmed instruction in the data base. The course material stored in the computer is supplemented by slides, which are projected on a small screen next to the computer terminal. The CAI user has three options: (i) he may take a basic course in ophthalmology; (ii) he may elect an advanced course in a narrow area of ophthalmology; or (iii) he may choose to receive a short sequence of instruction on a specific subject selected from the thesaurus (p. 30).

At the termination of one of the CAI programs in ophthalmology the student is asked if he would like a list of the most recent references on the specific subject he has been dealing with. If he types "yes," a set of references is printed out. Thus, there is close interaction between instructional programs and retrieval programs in this system.

It seems likely that it will be easier to instruct the inexperienced user in the use of a natural language system than to instruct him in the use of a system based on a controlled vocabulary. Indeed, the casual user may never learn to use the controlled vocabulary system at an optimum level of effectiveness. Controlled vocabulary systems are based heavily on indexing policies and protocols that generally take a long time to master.

In this chapter, we have attempted to outline the principal possible modes of instruction in the use of on-line retrieval systems and to present examples of these possible modes. Although each method may be useful in certain circumstances, it is likely that in the future increased emphasis will be placed on the development of systems that are self-instructive. In the words of Caruso (1970b):

> My own feeling is that self-teaching systems, with capabilities of varying levels of self-teaching, to the extent that the user can modify the system effectively to suit himself, will be the key to more effective use of those systems than will be accomplished with any other teaching device; and most important, that this mode of instruction will be the source of creative use of what will otherwise be a mechanically operated tool limited strictly to those uses devised by a small group of program designers, who are more or less removed from the ultimate users of the programmed systems (pp. 98–99).

REFERENCES

Atherton, P., ed. (1971). *Large-Scale Information Processing Systems.* Section IV-A. *The User Component of the System.* Final Report to the Rome Air Development Center. Syracuse, N.Y.: Syracuse University, School of Library Science.

Boyle, J. F., H. O'Hara, and F. J. Smith (1971). *An Intelligent On-Line Data System.* Belfast: The Queens University of Belfast, Department of Computer Science.

Bridegam, W. E., Jr., and E. Meyerhoff (1970). "Library Participation in a Biomedical Communication and Information Network." *Bull. Medical Library Assoc.* **58** (2), 103–111.

Caruso, D. E. (1969a). *An Experiment to Determine the Effectiveness of an Interactive Tutorial Program, Implemented on the Time Sharing IBM System 360, Model 50, in Teaching a Subject-Oriented User to Formulate Inquiry Statements to a Computerized On-Line Information Retrieval System.* PhD Dissertation. Pittsburgh, Pa.: University of Pittsburgh, Graduate School of Library and Information Sciences.

Caruso, D. E. (1969b). *The Profile Development Program: a Tutorial for Users of the Chemical Abstracts Service Condensates Alerting Service. Reference Manual.* Pittsburgh, Pa.: University of Pittsburgh, Knowledge Availability Systems Center.

Caruso, D. E. (1970a). "Teaching with and About Interactive Computer-Based Document Retrieval." *In Proceedings of the Seventh Annual National Colloquium on Information Retrieval.* Philadelphia, Pa.: The College of Physicians of Philadelphia, Medical Documentation Service, pp. 416–427.

Caruso, D. E. (1970b). "Tutorial Programs for Operation of On-Line Retrieval Systems." *Jour. Chem. Documentation* **10** (2), 98–105.

Cobbs, S. (1971). *AIM–TWX User's Guide.* Seattle, Wash.: University of Washington, Pacific Northwest Regional Health Sciences Library.

Eichhorn, M. M., and R. D. Reinecke (1970). "Vision Information Center: a User-Oriented Data Base." *Science* **169** (3940), 29–31.

Glassman, D. M. (1971). "A High-Speed Computer System for Searching File Indexes." *Proc. Amer. Soc. Information Sci.* **8**, 247–255.

Isotta, N. E. C. (1970). "Europe's First Information Retrieval Network." *ESRO/ELDO Bull.* (9), 9–17.

Lyman, E. R. (1971). *An On-Line Document Retrieval Strategy Using the PLATO System.* Urbana, Ill.: University of Illinois, Computer-based Education Research Laboratory, CERL Report X-21.

Marcus, R. S., A. R. Benenfeld, and P. Kugel (1971). "The User Interface for the Intrex Retrieval System." *In* D. E. Walker (ed.), *Interactive Bibliographic Search: the User/Computer Interface.* Montvale, N.J.: AFIPS Press, pp. 159–201.

Massachusetts Institute of Technology (1971). *Project Intrex; Semiannual Activity Report.* Cambridge, Mass.: MIT.

Reinecke, R. E. (1968). "Vision Information Center—Direct User Access via Computer Assisted Instruction." *Proc. Amer. Soc. Information Sci.* **5**, 165–167.

Chapter Sixteen

Interfaces with Document Delivery Systems

The output of most of the retrieval systems discussed in this book will be a list of bibliographic citations, although some will deliver abstracts and a few include complete text in machine-readable form and are thus able to print or display short documents (e.g., news items) or segments of text (e.g., paragraphs from legal material). It would be grossly inefficient if a searcher could obtain citations to relevant documents in a matter of minutes, but was unable to view full copies of the documents cited or could only view them after a long wait or through time-consuming visits to library shelves or filing cabinets. In other words, because the on-line retrieval system can give citation access very rapidly, it would be highly desirable to provide document access within approximately the same time frame. The implication is that the searcher should be able to obtain rapid access to a document file without leaving the terminal or the terminal area. In actual fact, two possible requirements exist: (a) the user should be able to access the full text of the document rapidly for examination purposes; and (b) he should be able to obtain a hard copy printout of the text or portions of it. The document collection should provide guaranteed accessibility and file integrity. That is, the documents will never leave their store and will thus be available to users at all times. A number of possibilities exist for meeting these requirements.

It is, of course, possible to incorporate into a retrieval system a facility to allow a user to request full copies of items cited. That is, once he has conducted a search and identified certain documents that appear relevant, he can use the on-line terminal to request that the information center supply him with copies of these items. The request is handled remotely by the information center and results in the eventual delivery of the requested documents in photocopy or original form. In the case of an in-house information center, with all terminals located on the premises, full copies might be made available to the terminal user within, say, 24 hours. On the other hand, in a national information service, with many dispersed terminals, document delivery may take several days. This facility for ordering documents at the terminal, while undoubtedly useful, only results in reasonably fast delivery if the user is located close to the document collection. Moreover, no facility is provided to allow the user to rapidly scan the text to determine its relevance.

Microform File at Search Station

Another possible approach is to make each on-line search terminal self-contained by providing a complete document file in microform at the terminal itself. Adjacent to the searching terminal is a full document collection on microfiche, aperture cards, or roll microfilm, along with a reader-printer. Once the searcher has identified some promising references, he pulls the necessary microforms and views them on the reader, producing hard copy of any items or portions of items he wishes to retain. A convenient alternative to a manual file of fiche would be an automated access system based on microfiche or roll microfilm stored in cassettes. Such systems will permit access to a particular document image in 10 seconds or less.

Landau (1972), of the International Development Center, Washington, D.C., has proposed this type of *library in a desk*, which he refers to as COMICOM (illustrated in Figure 16.1). The executive type of desk incorporates two modules—one a computer terminal and the other a microfiche reader. The terminal is potentially connectable to any on-line retrieval system through a normal telephone circuit. After the user identifies relevant document references at the computer terminal, he can turn to the microfiche data bank (in the desk drawers) and mount the selected microfiche (or cartridge) in the viewer-selector for rapid viewing of the desired images. Various levels of sophistication are possible in the equipment. The least elaborate model would have a teletype terminal and a manual microfiche viewer. A more elaborate model would incorporate a CRT display and a microfiche viewer with automatic selection and printing capabilities.

A typical automated microform display system is the CARD (Compact Automatic Retrieval Display) device produced by Image Systems Inc. CARD (a very similar system, REMKARD, is marketed by Remington Rand) is a random-access address system which stores binary coded microfiche (750 fiche, each containing up to 98 pages) in a rotating drum, and provides access to any image in approximately 4 seconds. The system

Figure 16.1. Conceptualization of the *library in a desk*. Reproduced by permission of Robert Landau.

provides file integrity, because the fiche are not handled manually. Equipment costs per fiche are high, however, and such devices are extremely limited in capacity. Systems based on roll microfilm stored in cassettes have much greater capacities, but require manual selection of the appropriate cassette and insertion into the reader. A detailed discussion on conventional equipment for storage and retrieval of microimages is outside the scope of this book. A review of the subject has been published by Williams (1970), and a good discussion of systems for storage and retrieval of microfiche is presented by Wicker, et al. (1970) in a report prepared for the U.S. Defense Documentation Center. An excellent earlier report on microform retrieval devices was prepared by Bagg and Stevens (1961).

By using ultrafiche or ultrafilm, it is possible to store a very large data base at a search terminal and access it efficiently and economically. An example is the M-380 system developed by Microform Data Systems Inc. The M-380 uses Ultrastrips (about $1^{1}/_{2} \times 6$ inch), each holding up to 2000 $8^{1}/_{2} \times 11$ inch pages at a reduction ratio of $210 \times$. Ultrastrips are stored in film cartridges, 60 strips to the cartridge, and the cartridges are easily plugged into the M-380 reader. Up to 120,000 pages ($8^{1}/_{2} \times 11$ inch) can be accessed through a single cartridge. Because the cartridges are easily interchanged, the system can provide a rapid access to a very large data base. The M-380 readers are linked to an *index-controller* which uses a mini-computer to

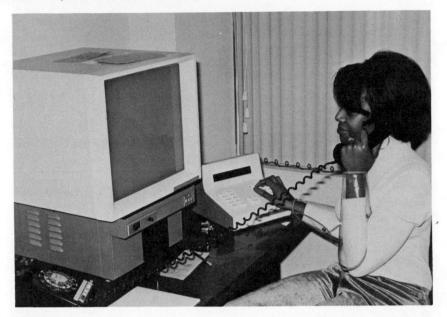

Figure 16.2. Viewer for M-380 Ultrastrip system. Reproduced by permission of Microform Data Systems Inc.

address any page in a particular cartridge. A keyboard entry is converted to a specific film location, and the desired page is automatically accessed and displayed in an average of less than 3 seconds. A typical display unit is illustrated in Figure 16.2. This system has been adopted by the U.S. Patent Office, and has also been used by the telephone company (for directory assistance files) and by banks and publishers (for customer records).

The microform library adjacent to the searching terminal appears most attractive, however, for comparatively small collections and systems in which relatively few access terminals are in use. With a large number of terminals and/or extremely large collections, it might be impractical to provide a complete self-contained library at every searching facility.

Terminal Access to Remote Microform Store

The alternative is to establish one complete document collection in microform and to provide a mechanism for viewing selected images remotely at the searching terminals.* A number of complete systems are available to

─────────

*Swanson (1964) presented a concept of an on-line catalog which would permit bibliographic searches and also provide "microfilm images of title pages, tables of contents, indexes, and possibly other selected pages of each work."

provide fast, remote access to a centrally stored document file. Some of these systems involve the use of a human operator to select from the microform file, while others will automatically retrieve a microimage and relay it via closed-circuit television.

An example of the former type is the Mosler 20/20 system. In this system, the searcher, having identified the number of a document he wishes to view, calls the Mosler 20/20 operator by telephone or intercom and states the number of the required item. The operator selects the microimage (a microfilm aperture card) from the file and places it on a platen before a television transmitter. The transmitter is switched to the appropriate viewing channel. The image is sweep-scanned, magnified up to 250 ×, and displayed on the searcher's television monitor (17 or 21 inch television screens) at a horizontal resolution of 1023 lines. Up to six remote monitors can be supported. A video printer can be attached to each in order to provide $8\frac{1}{2}$ × 11 inch paper copies of any image desired. When the viewer is finished with a particular image, he attracts the operator's attention by means of a RETURN button. The operator then removes the card from the platen and returns it to the file. Similar systems are available from other manufacturers, another example being the SD 550 of Sanders Diebold Co.

The Mosler 20/20 and similar systems have limited capabilities. More advanced systems, eliminating the human operator, are available from Mosler and certain other manufacturers. Systems of the more advanced type include the Mosler 410 and the Sanders Diebold SD500. They all have basic similarities. The components are a storage bank to hold the microimages, some type of searching mechanism to retrieve the images from the file, a television camera to transmit the image, and one or more remote television monitors to view it. Hard copy printing facilities are also available for use with viewing stations. A typical system configuration, from Sanders Diebold, is illustrated in Figure 16.3.

The Sanders Diebold SD-500 microform file can hold 98,000 microfiche, or almost 10 million 16 millimeter images, while the Mosler 410 stores documents on microfiche or aperture cards in units of 200,000 (between 200,000 and 11 million pages, depending on the degree of reduction used). It is generally possible to expand this type of system in a modular fashion by combining several storage banks into a single system.

A Mosler 410 storage bank, with associated peripheral devices, is illustrated in Figure 16.4. These storage banks may be accessed from remote television terminals. A Mosler 410 keyboard and display are illustrated in Figure 16.5. The terminal user keys in the number of an item he wishes to view. The appropriate microform is located automatically in the file (for example, by an optical search head) and is transported to a television camera which transmits the image to the remote viewing station. Typically, an image

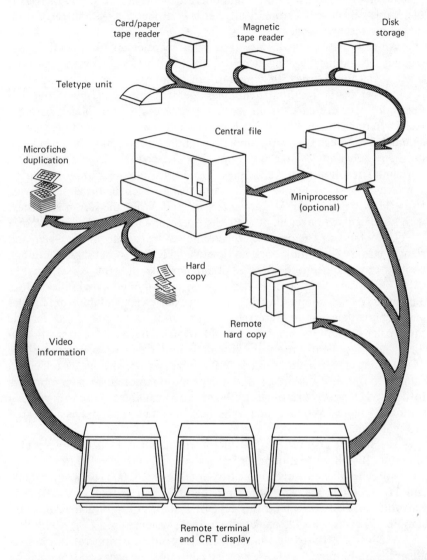

Figure 16.3. Typical configuration of a remote microform retrieval system. Reproduced by permission of Sanders Diebold Co.

Figure 16.4. Mosler 410 storage bank and associated peripheral devices. Reproduced by permission of Mosler Information Systems.

will be displayed 6–10 seconds after it is requested. Transmission from storage bank to remote television monitor is by coaxial cable, with amplifiers if long distances are involved, or microwave link. Resolution in the range of 1000–1225 lines is claimed. Magnification of 250 × is possible.

While a virtually unlimited number of viewing stations can be supported by such a system, it is clear that a single television camera at the storage bank can transmit only a single image at one time. This will permit *conference viewing* of the same image at multiple monitors. Simultaneous viewing of different images at separate terminals is also possible, but the number of different images that can be transmitted is entirely dependent upon the number of television cameras incorporated into the system. To support a large number of terminals simultaneously, multiple cameras are needed, and the cost of the system increases accordingly.

Remote microform access systems of the type mentioned above are designed as stand-alone units, but are also suitable for direct interfacing with computer retrieval systems. As an example, the interfacing of a Mosler automatic microform retrieval system with a computer, which controls the

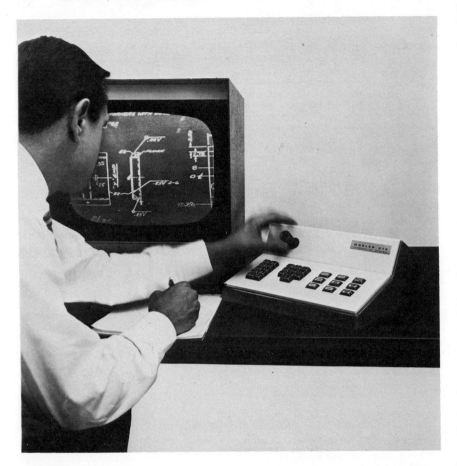

Figure 16.5. Mosler 410 keyboard and display. Reproduced by permission of Mosler Information Systems.

microform unit, has been described by Conway (1968) and by Zenner (1968). The use of a Mosler 410, interfacing with a computer, in a system for rapid storage and retrieval of medical records is described by Buchwald (1971).

A modified Sanders Diebold SD-500 has been supplied to the National Library of Medicine. This particular system is designed to store a minimum of 150,000 journal articles (1.6 million pages) on unitized microfilm. Any item can be retrieved by unique document number or by a bibliographic citation consisting of journal title code, volume number, year, and beginning page number. An item is requested through a teletype keyboard (which produces a perforated tape of the transaction) associated with a mini-computer. This is a 16 bit machine with 8K of core memory. A disk memory is used for storage of document identifiers and physical location data for the microforms. The NLM system will automatically retrieve an image from the file and produce a hard copy on dry silver paper by means of an optical projection system. Television (video) viewing of the images is also possible.

One of the major limitations of microforms is that they are static and therefore not very suitable for records that need to be altered periodically (although this limitation is not particularly important for the types of documents handled in the bibliographic systems discussed in this book). Some systems are able to integrate permanent microimages with dynamic records stored in digital form. An example is RECOL-10, produced by Dynamic Information Systems Inc. Static records are stored on microfiche at the terminal site, while fast-changing items and revisions are retained in a digital form in a computer memory. When a given record is requested by the operator, the appropriate microfiche page is retrieved automatically from the storage unit, while the associated variable information is retrieved from the computer. The two sources of information are integrated in proper registration and displayed as one composite output image on a 12 inch television monitor with a capacity of over 2000 characters per image. Over 70,000 pages of information (approximately 150 million characters) can be stored in a single storage module, and any given record can be accessed in approximately 4 seconds. Additional modules, up to a maximum of sixteen, can be added to accommodate larger data bases. Hard copy reproduction of the display is available as an option. The terminal system is designed to communicate in teletype-compatible mode to devoted, multi-use, or time-shared computer systems. Multiple terminals may be supported by the system. A RECOL-10 unit has been integrated with Battelle's on-line search system, BASIS-70.

The M-370 system of Microform Data Systems is designed to make ultrafilm data and digital data available for viewing at the same time under single-keyboard control. Both film screen and CRT screen are housed in the same cabinet.

A possible alternative to microimage storage is the use of videotape. In the Videofile system, produced by Ampex Corp., document pages are converted into electronic video images stored on standard 2 inch broadcast videotape. Up to 250,000 pages can be stored on a single 1 hour reel of tape, and approximately 1000 pages can be searched per second. The electronic video images may be converted to document images and displayed full size on a CRT monitor. An electrostatic printer will convert these television images to hard copy output. The system has been described by Miner (1970).

Some interesting work on direct interfacing between an on-line search system and a microform retrieval system has been conducted as part of the Intrex experiments. The text-access activities of Intrex have been discussed by Haring (1968), Knudson (1970), and Knudson and Teicher (1969). Knudson (1970) summarizes the Intrex capabilities as follows:

> The text-access system automatically retrieves, scans, and transmits requested pages to remote display terminals over a wideband transmission network. Each page is scanned and transmitted only once per request, requiring image storage at the terminals. Two types of display terminals are included in the current system, one utilizing an electronic storage tube and the other a 35-mm camera for image storage. The storage-tube display provides rapid access to text although with marginal resolution and brightness. The film terminal provides adequate resolution, but the film-processing time and mechanical complexity of the terminal are significant disadvantages (p. L-17).

Storage of the Intrex microfiche file is effected by means of two CARD devices (described earlier) modified to permit control by external logic circuits and to be coupled to a flying spot scanner. Such a unit is illustrated in Figure 16.6.

Figure 16.6. Intrex microfiche storage and scanner assembly. Reproduced by permission of Electronic Systems Laboratory, MIT.

The Intrex *film terminal* captures a single-scan image with a 35 millimeter camera attached to a high-resolution CRT. The CRT reconstitutes the pages of text from video signals, and the images are captured by the 35 millimeter camera on film strips (up to 7 pages long). The 35 millimeter film strip is automatically processed and can be viewed directly on a microfilm viewer or used to generate $8^1/_2 \times 11$ inch hard copies by electrostatic means.

Knudson points out that, in the Intrex system, photographic images were preferred to digital storage, because the number of bits required for digital storage of over 10,000 documents, including pictorial representations and an unrestricted character set, would result in excessive storage costs. Moreover, the cost of encoding into digital form far exceeds the cost of microfilming. This latter disadvantage obviously does not apply to data bases that can be captured in machine-readable form as by-products of other operations (e.g., wire communications). (The major disadvantage of microform systems, as mentioned by Katter and Blankenship (1969), is that the records thus stored cannot conveniently be modified and manipulated in the way it is possible to manipulate digital text. Microform files are therefore "well suited to the large-volume storage of textual and graphic material that will be passively viewed but not altered on a moment-to-moment on-line basis.")

Knudson (1970) also indicates that user acceptance of the text-access subsystem will be largely determined by the quality of the display terminals. Desired characteristics will include the following:

1) Resolution capability corresponding to at least 2000 scan lines.*
2) Writing rate such that a 2000 scan-line image can be received in $^1/_2$ second.
3) Erasable image-storage capability (soft-copy display) with the capability to generate hard copy upon request; the erase time should be less than 1 second.
4) Gray-scale† capability for displaying pictorial information (p. L-9).

According to Knudson, no device is presently available that meets all these requirements (the commercially available systems discussed above allow up to 1225 line resolution only). The two Intrex terminals meet different parts of the requirements. The 35 millimeter film terminal provides the 2000 scan-line resolution with gray-scale capability, and the electronic storage tube (Tektronix 611 Storage Display Unit) provides for an erasable or soft copy display.

Figure 5.13 illustrates the storage tube unit used to display images of document text in conjunction with the BRISC CRT terminal used for interrogating the on-line catalog.

---

*Elsewhere, Knudson (National Bureau of Standards, 1970) has pointed out that systems with a resolution of 1000 or 1200 lines may be adequate for "normal size type," but that in dealing with a wide array of technical journals with varying style and size of font (possibly including subscripts and superscripts) a resolution of at least 2000 lines is needed.

†*Gray scale* relates to the continuum between lightest and darkest luminance, measured in *halftones*, a term taken from the printing industry. An increment in grayness of a given area over its surroundings is represented by a halftone level or a gray-scale step. The gray-scale continuum controls the contrast of photographic images.

Since 1970, Intrex has made use of a combined terminal, employing a Tektronix 611 tube as the basic display device, that will permit display on the same screen of either alphameric characters from digital signals (the bibliographic search data) or full-text images from video signals.

The experimental Intrex text-access system differs from the previously described commercial systems in a number of ways. In the Intrex system, the microfiche image is converted to a video signal by means of a flying-spot scanner. These single-scan video signals are transmitted by a *microfacsimile system* operating via coaxial cable. The scanned image of a single page of text is transmitted in approximately 2 seconds. With 2000 scan lines, the required bandwidth of the transmission system is about 1 megahertz, although the channel actually used in Intrex is 4.5 megahertz wide. The high-speed transmission of single-frame images permits the text-access system to be shared by several users. The image is transmitted only once and is stored at the receiving terminal so that the user may examine it at leisure. The user can also recall from the buffer any page viewed earlier. Segments of the viewed pages may be magnified to improve legibility. No hard copy printout is produced directly at the terminal.

The commercially available text-access systems, on the other hand, do not use single-scan techniques. Instead, they employ closed-circuit television for transmission and do not provide local page storage capabilities. The transmitted images need to be refreshed, and problems of flicker and reduced resolution are created. Moreover, lack of local page storage facilities creates buffering problems that complicate the provision of multiple-terminal access. As previously mentioned, the commercially available systems are limited in the number of terminals they can support simultaneously by the number of television scanners provided at the storage bank.

In theory, there is no upper limit to the size of the microform file that could be interfaced directly with an on-line search system. The outstanding problems may be mechanical rather than electronic, particularly the problems of assuring trouble-free operation of the fiche retrieval apparatus.

As described in Chapter Five, *The New York Times* Information Bank interfaces an on-line search system with a microfiche file of press clippings. The fiche interface is for use only within the Times building. The central file of fiche can be accessed remotely, and any fiche can be transmitted to the viewer's screen via closed-circuit television. Viewing of the fiche is done on the same terminal used for search (IBM 4506). The microform retrieval system was built to *The New York Times* specifications by Foto-Mem Inc. It was not fully operational as of January 1973. At that time, a human operator at the central file was used to extract fiche from the store and to position them for television transmission to the viewing terminals. The searcher at the terminal has no facility for producing hard copy locally, but he may request that a paper copy be made from the file and sent to him. Users of the system away from the offices of *The New York Times* will not be able to access the microfiche file through their consoles. However, it is planned that these users will be supplied with their own microfiche files, which will permit them to view items locally on a conventional microfiche reader.

Some attention is now being given to the possibility of providing wide access to national document collections from distant locations via remote text-access facilities. Whitby (1970) and Coles, et al. (1969) have reported on an investigation of remote text access conducted for the National Library of Medicine by Stanford Research Institute. This study conceptualized a system whereby physicians at hospitals in the United States could, besides conducting on-line bibliographic searches, view images of pages of medical literature contained in the National Library of Medicine or in regional resource libraries. Each hospital would be connected in a network of television bandwidth cables in the fashion of a party line. Each segment of the network would radiate from one of a number of regional library centers that are themselves similarly connected to NLM. A simplified representation of such a network is shown in Figure 16.7. The system described uses television cameras at a

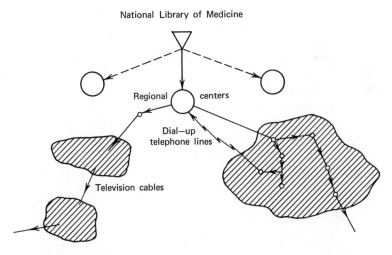

Figure 16.7. Simplified representation of a network for remote text access. (Metropolitan areas are indicated by shading; hospitals are indicated by small circles.) From Whitby (1970).

resource library to scan microfiche images of any page requested by a user at a hospital. At the hospital, all transmissions on the television cable are monitored, and the scan lines addressed to that hospital are digitalized and stored on magnetic disk. This disk-stored information is then read out, put in analog form, and used to form and refresh the image on a display tube. Control signals are carried from the hospital to the regional center on a dialed-up telephone line.

Whitby (1970) and Coles, et al. (1969) claim that the digital storage technique described will present a full microfiche image at an acceptable resolution with wide-bandwidth display refreshment, and permit time-sharing of the expensive wide-bandwidth communication circuit among the maximum number of users.

The system is designed to accommodate up to 250 users essentially simultaneously. It assumes the existence in a hospital of remote viewing stations that form part of a general-purpose hospital information system. Cost of the terminal is therefore shared by a number of hospital functions. Based on the particular configuration described and an estimate of volume of text accesses that the investigators feel is conservative, costs for remote access to a document are estimated to be about $3 when the remote viewing bears all the equipment and communication costs, but a low of around 80¢ when the costs are shared by all hospital services that may conceivably make use of the equipment. Costs, estimated on the basis of a hypothetical system serving 100 hospitals, each having an overall hospital information service with ten consoles, works out to be about $8000 per console after all pertinent costs except main computers are prorated.

Observations on use of their text-access system were made by the Intrex investigators (Massachusetts Institute of Technology, 1972), although only a small number of cases were studied (thirteen experiments with eleven users). The major findings were as follows:

1. The text system was accessed in over 80% of the searches. Most users felt that rapid access to text is essential to a fully efficient on-line system.

2. The text-access facilities were used primarily to judge the relevance of documents or, occasionally, to locate a particular item of information. Text was not read or examined in detail at the terminal. The Intrex users were not observed to make extensive notes from text displayed on the screen. For extended study they preferred to obtain a hard copy to examine at their leisure and to annotate directly.

3. In this series of experiments, no users were observed to use the displayed text as a tool in the modification of searching strategies.

4. Most users expressed satisfaction with the quality of the image, but some would prefer higher resolution and express the desire to eventually see hard copy. The magnification feature of the system was used extensively to overcome marginal resolution.

5. Some eyestrain was reported after prolonged use of the system.

Lest this chapter may have painted too rosy a picture, we should emphasize that many problems remain to be solved before document images can be transmitted efficiently and economically from a central store to multiple remote viewing stations. Transmission costs, using existing procedures, still tend to be high, and the problem of image quality also remains. The present commercially available equipment has been designed primarily for business applications and used to handle business records or engineering drawings (i.e., material that is typewritten or uses other relatively large type). For this type of material, a resolution of 1000 or 1200 lines is adequate. But library materials are totally different photometrically, and much greater resolution is needed for comfortable reading of text from scientific journals.

REFERENCES

Bagg, T. C., and M. E. Stevens (1961). *Information Selection Systems Retrieving Replica Copies: a State-of-the-Art Report*. Washington, D.C.: National Bureau of Standards, NBS Tech. Note 157.

Buchwald, R. V. (1971). "Medical Records Storage and Retrieval." *Proc. Nat. Microfilm Assoc.* **20**, II-28–II-35.

Coles, L. S., W. T. Colwell, J. H. Jones, and O. W. Whitby (1969). *Design of a Remote Access Medical Information Retrieval System*. Menlo Park, Ca.: Stanford Research Institute, PB198774.

Conway, E. F. (1968). "WESTAR: an Improved System for Data Retrieval With or Without the Computer." *Proc. Nat. Microfilm Assoc.* **17**, 11–20.

Haring, D. R. (1968). "Computer-Driven Display Facilities for an Experimental Computer-based Library." *AFIPS Conf. Proc. Fall Joint Computer Conf.* **33** (I), 255–265.

Katter, R. V., and D. A. Blankenship (1969). *On-Line Interfaces for Document Information Systems; Considerations for the Biomedical Communications Network*. Santa Monica, Ca.: System Development Corporation, TM-(L)-4320.

Knudson, D. R. (1970). "Image Storage and Transmission for Project Intrex." *In Proceedings of the Conference on Image Storage and Transmission Systems for Libraries*. Gaithersburg, Md.: National Bureau of Standards, pp. L1–L18, PB 193 692.

Knudson, D. R., and S. N. Teicher (1969). "Remote Text Access in a Computerized Library Information Retrieval System." *AFIPS Conf. Proc. Spring Joint Computer Conf.* **34**, 475–481.

Landau, R. M. (1972). "New Economic Factors in the System Integration of Computer Terminal On-Line Retrieval Systems and Large Microform Data Banks." *Jour. Micrographics* **5** (3), 125–129.

Massachusetts Institute of Technology (1972). *Project Intrex; Semiannual Activity Report*. Cambridge, Mass.: MIT.

Miner, R. A. (1970). "Use of Video Stores for Storage and Retrieval of Graphic Information." *In Proceedings of the Conference on Image Storage and Transmission Systems for Libraries.* Gaithersburg, Md.: National Bureau of Standards, pp. C1–C13, PB 193 692.

National Bureau of Standards (1970). *Proceedings of the Conference on Image Storage and Transmission Systems for Libraries.* Gaithersburg, Md.: National Bureau of Standards, p. III-4, PB 193 692.

Swanson, D. R. (1964). "Dialogues with a Catalog." *Library Quarterly* **34** (1), 113–125.

Whitby, O. W. (1970). "Some Design Considerations for a Remote-Access Medical Information Retrieval System." *In Proceedings of the Conference on Image Storage and Transmission Systems for Libraries.* Gaithersburg, Md.: National Bureau of Standards, pp. R1–R26, PB 193 692.

Wicker, R., R. Neperud, and A. Teplitz (1970). *Microfiche Storage and Retrieval System Study: Final Report.* Falls Church, Va.: System Development Corporation, AD 710 000.

Williams, B. J. S. (1970). *Miniaturised Communications: a Review of Microforms.* London: The Library Association.

Zenner, P. (1968). "A Hybrid Computer/Microfilm Engineering Information System." *Proc. Nat. Microfilm Assoc.* **17**, 115–122.

Chapter Seventeen

Some Human
Factors Considerations

A major advantage of on-line retrieval systems (so we have claimed throughout this book) is that they can be used directly by the person with an information need without delegating the search to an information specialist. This being so, it is important that on-line retrieval systems be acceptable to potential users. Moreover, systems must be relatively simple to consult; otherwise, users will become frustrated, lose interest in the system, and turn to alternative sources of information. This phenomenon was described by Calvin Mooers (1960). According to Mooers' law: "An information retrieval system will tend *not* to be used whenever it is more painful and troublesome for a customer to have information than for him not to have it." In this chapter, we will consider some factors concerning human acceptance of on-line retrieval systems, as well as factors influencing ease of use of these systems, which will ultimately determine whether they are used repeatedly and whether they are preferred to other sources of information. As reported by Sackman (1970b), studies on the behavior of users in a time-sharing system are very rare. The studies that have been done are reviewed in his paper.

User Acceptance

Katter (1970) has discussed several factors that appear to affect user acceptance of on-line retrieval systems. He recognizes four effects that the neophyte may experience at the on-line terminal. The first is a *pressure* effect. The immediacy of feedback provided by the system, which is one of its most important and obvious attractions, may in itself be disconcerting to some inexperienced users. Because the machine responds rapidly, the user may feel that he must respond equally rapidly. Certain users may be conscious of pressure in this type of system. Consequently, they do not allow themselves time to fully interpret the on-line feedback, they make hurried decisions, and their search interaction is suboptimum as a result. Because of costs involved, however, some systems must place some limit on the user's rate of response, although this limit may be as high as 2 or 3 minutes.

The second effect reported by Katter is the *peephole* effect, which is a characteristic reaction to the use of typewriter terminals. For the inexperienced user, the typewriter terminal may create the effect of a peephole through which the contents of a data base can only be viewed in very small pieces. Although a system response may commence in 10 or 12 seconds, the full message is spelled out laboriously at approximately reading rate, and the user is given no feeling of the *conceptual distances* that the system may have traveled in order to produce this response. The teletypewriter is not a good browsing device. It gives the impression of *plodding* and the user has difficulty in visualizing his complete search approach, perhaps more so than if he were using a conventional manual tool. All these factors contribute to the peephole effect which, according to Cuadra (1971), "contributes to the feeling by users that the system is mysterious." The user of a CRT display is less likely to feel the peephole effect, although it may still be present in a milder form.

A third effect noted by Katter is termed the *fishbowl* effect. In a manual system, such as a printed index or card catalog, the search is conducted in a relatively private way. Some neophyte on-line users feel that this privacy is denied them when they operate the terminal, especially when it is located in a crowded public area, and that their deficiencies in searching and key-boarding are being exposed to public view. Moreover, there is sometimes present an uncomfortable sense that one's on-line actions are being "monitored by not necessarily sympathetic persons at the remote computer site" (Katter, 1970, p. 6).

Katter (1970) describes his fourth observed effect as follows:

> (the) on-line terminal . . . can be viewed as an expression of the concerns and self-interests of others who do not share one's local or personal views, values, and goals. The physical remoteness of the computer and files to which the terminal is hooked is obvious to the new user. At the same time, this remote computer can seem to be an active, somewhat self-governing entity that is busy satisfying the needs and concerns of many other persons, with whom the user may share little mutuality. The new user with such a perception may not expect the system to be very "sympathetic" (pp. 6, 7).*

---

*Reprinted by permission of System Development Corporation.

In summary, and again quoting Katter (1970):

> four characteristics have been described that, at least in the temporary perceptions
> of some new on-line users, may be attributed to the remote-access on-line terminal:
> a "bullying" pressure for the user to react immediately, and without due considera-
> tion; a "plodding obscurantist" quality that affords the user only a "peephole"
> view of the system contents, and hops from place to place without providing con-
> ceptual continuity between the hops; a "fishbowl" or arena quality that places the
> user in the position of a possibly embarrassing public disclosure of inadequacies
> he feels in his skills, knowledge, or resourcefulness; and a "lack of sympathy" or
> lack of mutual interests and goals shared by the user and the "remote arbiters of
> the system." Taken together, these four characteristics perhaps account for the
> subjective feeling of a "subject-object role reversal" that has been described by
> some fledgling users of on-line terminals; instead of perceiving the system and the
> terminal as an object that he (the subject) molds to his wishes, the user feels himself
> to be the object that is being molded and manipulated by the system (p. 7).*

We can add some additional reactions to those discussed by Katter. Some users have a phobia relating to the suspected fragility of the system. They are afraid that if they make a mistake (e.g., hit a wrong key), this will cause drastic and irreparable damage to the hardware or the files. The designers and managers of information systems should do all that they can do to reduce wild fears of this type. However, it is equally important that users must be told to abide by system rules and that they are not allowed to *play around* with the system in any way they want to. Certain other people are hostile because they dislike typing, are very poor typists, or basically feel that typing is beneath their dignity ("I have had a secretary to do my typing for almost 20 years").

Despite these various adverse reactions, on-line retrieval systems have generally been accepted with great enthusiasm, although not all users wish to conduct their own searches—some still prefer to delegate to an information specialist. In some information centers, the introduction of an on-line terminal was found to attract new users—users who did not take advantage of previous batch-processing capabilities, and even people who had pre-viously made no use of the center's facilities in any form. In some cases at least, the on-line system attracts requests that would be unsuitable for handling in the batch mode—the type of request in which the user wants a few relevant references and wants them right away.

Katter points out that the *subject–object role reversal* is usually a tem-porary experience for the new user and tends to disappear with increased practice in using the system. Moreover, the user's awareness of the phenom-enon will not be as vivid as depicted here. Nevertheless, some users will be

---

*Reprinted by permission of System Development Corporation.

aware of it, and their acceptance of the on-line system will be affected accordingly. Katter suggests that the new user will tend to adopt a non-committal, provisional stance toward the system; although he will not be quick to find fault, he will tend to reaffirm the positive values of manual tasks with which he is more familiar.

Two other factors relating to user acceptance should be noted. The first is the *novelty factor*. Some use of consoles is undoubtedly due primarily to the fact that they are new and attractive because of their novelty. If a user *adopts* an on-line system when it is first made available, there is no guarantee that he will continue to use it on a long-term basis. The second and related factor concerns education. It is now true that, when we set up an on-line retrieval system, the majority of potential users will not have had previous exposure to any form of on-line terminal. While this very novelty may attract certain users, it may very well repulse others who are inclined to avoid the unknown. This entire situation is likely to change dramatically within the next decade as on-line systems are used increasingly for educational purposes in universities, colleges, and even high schools and grade schools. Within a very short time, we will encounter a breed of scientist and engineer who has been raised with on-line computers and to whom the terminal is just another tool that is readily available for exploitation. Problems of user acceptance, important now, will be virtually nonexistent in the near future.

On the whole, on-line retrieval systems have been well-received where made available. Whether they continue to be well-accepted by a particular community of users will depend upon whether or not the effort of using them is more than offset by the results attainable. We have discussed measures of the effectiveness of an on-line system in previous chapters. Below we will consider some factors relating to perceived ease of use of an on-line system.

Time Factors

The on-line user expects rapid response from the system. When he becomes used to a system response of a few seconds or less he tends to be disturbed if he has to wait much longer. Schwartz (1965) reports that in some cases where, due to system problems, hardware malfunctions, or unusual conditions, the response time exceeds about 15 seconds, users who are not accustomed to this delay will begin to ask what the problem is. They will generally stand by, however, as long as they are reasonably confident that the system will eventually respond. For this reason, it is important that some form of Please Stand By message be transmitted by the system as soon as possible after it is known that processing delays will occur.

Operators using an on-line terminal throughout the working day (e.g., in certain defence or intelligence operations) tend to become bored if they are forced to wait lengthy periods for system responses, and such boredom soon leads to feelings of fatigue.

Sackman (1970a) reports that "users with tasks requiring relatively small computations become increasingly uncomfortable as computer response time to their requests extends beyond 10 sec., and as irregularity and uncertainty of computer response time increases. Users with problems requiring much computation tolerate longer intervals, up to as much as 10 min. for the largest jobs" (p. 191).

Cuadra (1971) has discussed the problems of *pacing* in on-line retrieval systems. Pacing involves procedures whereby the terminal user is clearly told when it is his turn to communicate with the system and, equally importantly, when it is his turn to wait for a system response. Pacing is achieved in different ways in different systems. In ORBIT, for example, the terminal user knows that it is his turn whenever the message USER is generated by the system and that it is not his turn, but the system's, when the message PROG (program) is generated. Katter and Blankenship (1969) point out that pacing would not be necessary if machine response were always instantaneous:

> If machine response were always instantaneous, the user's attention would never need to leave the machine except to attend to his part of the mutual problem-solving process. In this case, both machine time and user time would be used with maximum efficiency, since the machine would only wait on the user when necessary, and the user would never wait on the machine. The fact is, however, that machine response times are usually not instantaneous, so that the user has the possibility of anticipating this fact and using the delay either for rest (relaxing of attention) or for other work, whether it is related or unrelated to the on-line problem-solving process. If machine response times are always very short, the user may use the delay for a brief "rest" or diversionary activity such as shutting his eyes, moving or stretching his body, looking around, moving a paper, or passively tracking the machine's activity. As machine response times become longer, however, the user may be tempted to use the waiting period for work. Here a psychological problem can arise due to task tension created by the unfinished task when a machine response indicating that the machine is now waiting on the user is delivered before he has completed a task he anticipated he would be able to finish during the delay.
>
> For at least the above reasons, it is psychologically rewarding to the user to be able to predict accurately the period of a machine delay. One research paper addressing itself to this problem has suggested that for some intermediate part of the range of distribution of possible machine-delay periods, there is a clearly establishable value-tradeoff function for the user between the invariability and the shortness of the machine-delay period. No matter what the length of the required delay period might be, it is clear that users would prefer to be able to predict it accurately.
>
> Two basic kinds of arrangements have been suggested for dealing with this problem. One is to organize machine responses into a few classes that are easily

distinguished by the user, and to design the machine programs so that all machine responses in a particular class use the amount of time required by the longest response in that class. This requires the extra programming capacity necessary for idling and timing loops, but if the classification of machine responses has been thoughtfully done, the amount of idle time purposefully introduced into the programs is a small fraction of the working time. The other technique is reserved for the longer delay periods needed for more complex machine tasks. Here the machine provides an estimate of the delay to be expected at the beginning of the task and provides to the user a time-used and time-remaining display. This approach is limited in cost-effectiveness because it can only be applied to tasks where machine-time estimation parameters are clearly understood, and it is usually (though not invariably) the case that the resultant estimation rules can be applied easily and quickly by the user himself. Another problem is that in most time-sharing systems, the predicted delay for any operation consuming more than one service cycle for a console will increase as a function of the number of users in the system (pp. 27, 28).

Katter and Blankenship (1969) go on to describe four different devices that can be used to aid in the pacing of man–machine interaction:

Confirmatory Signals. These are practically instantaneous acknowledgements that a message inserted into the system is being processed. They do not necessarily imply that the message will be accepted as legal or interpretable after further processing.

Attentional Signals. These consist of especially noticeable light signals, sometimes backed up by auditory signals, usually reserved for indicating that the system is now awaiting a response from the user. They may be programmed for a single notice, intermittent notices, or continuous notices. When used to draw the user's attention to the fact that he has not completed an action he may think he has completed, in the better-designed systems the attentional signal is usually preceded by lack of a confirmatory signal that should have followed the completion of his action, plus a standard delay to allow him to notice the absence of the confirmatory signal.

Cueing Signals. These are usually terse, short-symbol indicators that show what control actions the user *may* take, *must* take, or *may not* take to forward the interaction process. They can be introduced by any of the display devices, but preferably are computer-switched backlighting lamps behind the appropriate function keys.

Status Display. This consists of a dynamic display that provides to the operator some indication of the fact of, or the state of, computer processing on tasks he has assigned to it. Ordinarily it is not designed to demand or capture attention in the manner of attentional signals. An example is a small backlighted display that indicates whether the system can accept operator input at that point, and whether it must have operator input to proceed further. It does not indicate what the input should or should not be (p. 28).*

---

*Reprinted by permission of System Development Corporation.

Another aspect of pacing is that which Sackman and Gold (1968) call *interarrival time* or *thinking time*. This is the time interval between the completion of a computer output and the insertion of the user's next input. Table 17.1, taken from Sackman and Gold, shows mean and median figures for user interarrival times from large samples of user traffic in five independent investigations of time-sharing systems (not information retrieval

TABLE 17.1. Comparison of Interarrival Statistics from Various Time-Sharing Systems

	SDC Q-32 system, 1965 study	SDC Q-32 system, 1966 study	IBM 7090 system, 1966 study	MIT project, MAC system, 1967 study	RAND JOSS system, 1967 study
Mean, seconds	27.7	70.7 (35.3)[a]	20.0	35.2	34
Median	12.8	9.0	10.0	11.0	11

SOURCE: Sackman and Gold (1968). Reproduced by permission of System Development Corporation.
[a]Adjusted by removing all interarrival times greater than 30 minutes (1.55% of total).

systems). The observed medians in all five studies are remarkably close, in the range of 9–13 seconds, which implies that the typical terminal user is mostly involved in routine rather than innovative decision-making at the terminal. This pattern is likely to hold for on-line retrieval systems also, where many users have been found to come with preestablished search strategies and to use the full interactive capabilities of the system rather little. The Sackman and Gold report suggests that there may be some merit to *forced temporal spacing* between computer messages and human responses for improved human problem-solving. The justification is that "a more leisurely pace at the console might make for more spontaneous and more creative thinking, for more strategic as opposed to tactical problem-solving." Although Sackman and Gold were not discussing retrieval applications, the point may be equally valid in this context. We have already mentioned the pressure effect. When the system responds rapidly, there is subconscious pressure on the user to respond rapidly also—possibly to the detriment of his overall search strategy. Sackman and Gold also suggest that "if longer intervals for servicing of users proves advantageous, the effective capacity of time-sharing systems for handling many users simultaneously could be increased significantly, perhaps enormously."

The forced temporal spacing idea is reinforced by Carbonell, et al. (1968), who point out that:

> Users of a time sharing system particularly dislike unpredictable response times (due to variable loads on the system). It has been observed that they usually prefer a constant delay to a possibly shorter but variable one; unpredictable conditions disturb the user and interfere with his efficient use of the computer. The above assertion can be interpreted by saying that if delays are long but predictable, a user can conceivably carry on some other activity instead of wasting time waiting for a result that may come now or later... (p. 138).

Psychological aspects of response time in man–machine interaction have been discussed in some detail by Miller (1968), who identifies various classes of human action and purpose at the on-line terminal. These different human purposes and actions are identified as having different acceptable or useful response times. Miller points out, however, that response time of 10 seconds or more "will not permit the kind of thinking continuity essential to sustained problem solving. . . ."

Hardware Factors

The only hardware that the on-line searcher is directly concerned with is the terminal itself. Standard user requirements for time-sharing terminals have been discussed by various investigators, including Dolotta (1970) and Gould (1968), but a detailed discussion of these is outside the scope of this book. The on-line searcher needs some type of keyboard to allow communication with the retrieval system, he needs a display unit in order to view his own messages, as well as the system responses, and he needs printout capabilities (both a terminal printer and access to a remote, off-line high-speed printer). Typewriter terminals can meet all these requirements, whereas if we use a CRT display, we will need to add a supplementary on-line printing device. Nevertheless, CRT displays have certain definite advantages over typewriter terminals from the human factors point of view. They generally permit more rapid communication, are less noisy, and allow user errors to be corrected more easily (or, at least, they give the impression of allowing easier error correction), although they may in fact cause more errors initially [see the study by Carlisle (1970)]. A CRT display is almost essential for the searching of full text of documents or lengthy abstracts, since the time delay associated with typewriter printout of text may be intolerable. Moreover, it seems much easier to browse at a video console than at a typewriter terminal. Further, a CRT display can interface with a microimage system (see Chapter Sixteen) to permit the viewing of larger bodies of document text.

Video consoles also permit much greater variety in the display of alpha-meric data. This point is well made by Mayer (1970):

> The growing economic feasibility of scopes for man-computer communication offers many new possibilities for improved information display over that offered by teletypewriter. Not only do scopes provide a needed capability for display of geometric information, but they offer new opportunities for organizing alphanu-meric information into more effective formats than that of conventional linear sentences and paragraphs. All types of mapping of textual information become possible.
>
> Earlier computer display designers concentrated on what was displayed, trying mainly to identify and include necessary information. Display design is now moving towards consideration of how required information should be formatted. New formats, movement or blinking of information for emphasis, timed appearance or disappearance of information, and color coding are but a few of the many possibil-ities that are emerging for computer displays (p. 183).

Clearly, CRT terminals offer very definite advantages for the display of vocabularies, indexing forms and document text. They are probably more appropriate than the typewriter for tutorial purposes, and they allow cues to be provided (e.g., to the on-line indexer or cataloger) more easily than would a typewriter terminal. On the other hand, video consoles are more expensive and less widely available. Moreover, there are certain advantages for the user in being able to retain a complete record of his dialogue with the system, which he has readily available if he uses the typewriter terminal.

The keyboard itself is also important. A keyboard in which keys are dedicated to the major system commands saves the time of the user, reduces the likelihood of errors, and is clearly preferred by the majority of users. However, Marcus, et al. (1971) caution that some users have difficulty locat-ing the appropriate key, and others are intimidated by the presence of so many unfamiliar keys on the keyboard. Keys, control buttons, and other devices must be adequately labeled and arranged for orderly use.

Visual factors are particularly important to the user of a CRT display. Lengthy use of such a display has been known to cause some operator fatigue. The variables that determine image quality include luminance, contrast, regeneration rate (if a CRT is not regenerated fast enough, it gives the impression of flicker), chromaticity, resolution, and size and style of characters. These factors have been discussed by Gould (1968) and by Van Dam (1966), among others. Barmack and Sinaiko (1966) also discuss these matters, as well as human factors problems of keyboard arrangement and the use of other input devices such as light pens.

Marcus, et al. (1971) claim that the user should be able to choose the size of the characters displayed—as he can on the Intrex ARDS display—so that he can personally choose between readability and getting a lot of data on the screen at one time.

A laboratory experiment, reported by Carlisle (1970) and again by Fetter and Carlisle (1971), compared searching behavior at the two basic types of terminals. Although it was limited in scope, the study produced very interesting results. The data base used in the experiment was derived from OBAR and consisted of official reports of Ohio Supreme Court cases. Data Central was the on-line system used. Twelve students from Yale Law School participated in the experiment and were randomly assigned to two groups of six each, one group to search on Teletype Model 33 and the other on video terminals (Computer Communications Inc., CC-30). Each student was given the same introduction to the system and the same legal research problem to investigate. He was to locate as many legal precedents as possible for use in appealing a particular case. Search strategies were left entirely to the individual student. No time limit was placed on the searchers.

The behavior of the two terminal groups was compared on the basis of (a) the number of documents retrieved and examined by the searcher, (b) the precision of the search measured in terms of a *relevance score* derived by having an experienced lawyer evaluate each retrieved item on a 10 point scale, (c) elapsed search time, (d) the number of errors made in a search, (e) the number of different individual strategies (*mode changes*) used by a searcher, and (f) the searcher's own satisfaction with his use of the terminal, measured by a questionnaire having interval scales permitting numerical scores to be derived (the questionnaire, with results summarized, is shown in Table 17.2).

These various data were subjected to correlational, discriminant, and univariate analyses. According to Carlisle, the analysis was very successful in discriminating between the behavior of the two terminal groups. In brief, the major findings were that the video console users took, on the average, 60% more time, made 300% more errors, and achieved relevance scores 40% higher, while retrieving about 42% more cases. There was a strong positive correlation between the number of errors occurring and the amount of time spent searching, a high negative correlation between relevance scores and number of errors, a weak negative correlation between searching time and relevance scores, and a high positive correlation between relevance scores and the number of cases retrieved. Figure 17.1 is a plot of the associations between time, relevance scores, and type of console. The raw data matrix from which correlations were made is shown in Table 17.3.

Although some of these results were certainly to be expected (e.g., the more cases retrieved, the more likely we are to find relevant or partially relevant cases, and thus increase the relevance scores), others are more difficult to explain, and it is difficult to separate cause and effect in some

TABLE 17.2. Questionnaire Used in Comparison of Searching on Teletype and Video Terminals

Now that you have used the Ohio Bar Automated Research Service, we would like to find out how satisfied you were with the system and the console. We will do this by asking you to share some of your opinions, attitudes, and feelings about using the system and in particular about the console itself.

This information will be most helpful in allowing us to evaluate the console you were using, so we would appreciate your candid impressions.

Please place a check mark (√) on the line under the appropriate response (e.g., never, a few times, etc.).

1. How often during the session did you find yourself becoming:

	Never	Few Times	Several Times	Often
a. Frustrated with the console?	4	3	2	1
b. Fascinated with the console?	1	2	3	4
c. Frustrated with the keyboard?	4	3	2	1
d. Fascinated with the keyboard?	1	2	3	4

2. How often during the session did you feel that:

	Never	Few Times	Several Times	Often
a. The printing speed was too slow?	4	3	2	1
b. The keyboard was awkward?	4	3	2	1
c. Important keys were hard to find?	4	3	2	1
d. This console was not designed with lawyers in mind?	4	3	2	1
e. The keyboard has a peculiar touch?	4	3	2	1
f. The console was easy to use?	1	2	3	4
g. The printing was hard to read?	4	3	2	1

3. How often did you feel that:

	Never	Few Times	Several Times	Often
a. This console was symbolic of the typical inhumanness of computers?	4	3	2	1
b. The keyboard was convenient and well designed?	1	2	3	4
c. You became so involved in your thinking and strategy that you were unaware of the characteristics of the console itself?	1	2	3	4

SOURCE: Carlisle (1970). Reproduced by permission of the Rand Corporation.

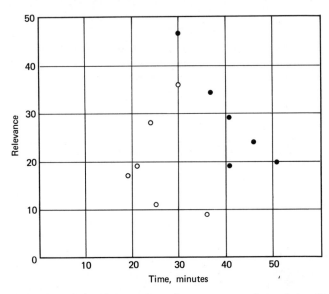

Figure 17.1. Plot of associations between time, relevance scores, and console type (● = subjects using video console; ○ = subjects using teletype console). Reproduced from Carlisle (1970) by permission of the Rand Corporation.

TABLE 17.3. Matrix Comparing Performance Characteristics of Video and Teletype Terminals

Subject	Time	Errors	Relevance	Mode changes	Number retrieved	Satisfaction
Group 1—Video						
1	52	7	20	5	12	42
2	30	1	47	2	17	52
3	46	11	24	4	9	53
4	41	8	29	2	13	41
5	37	7	34	3	18	46
6	41	7	19	5	8	47
Group 2—Teletype						
1	36	2	9	8	3	47
2	30	1	36	4	14	39
3	25	3	11	7	9	52
4	24	2	28	4	7	44
5	19	1	17	2	14	42
6	21	1	19	2	7	39

SOURCE: Carlisle (1970). Reproduced by permission of the Rand Corporation.

cases. Searchers at the video consoles spent longer on the average than the searchers at the teletype terminals. This would indicate that actual transmission rate (30 characters per second for video console, 10 characters per second for teletype in this experiment) was not a major factor in overall searching times. More important was the fact that the searchers at the CRT were prepared to retrieve more documents (because of faster display capabilities) and that they made many more errors which would increase considerably their overall searching times. The greatly increased error rate at the video terminals is perhaps due to the fact that the keyboard on this terminal is less familiar to the searcher than the teletype keyboard, which closely resembles a regular typewriter. Moreover, the particular console used in these experiments is particularly complicated; e.g., three separate keys must be depressed before a message can be transmitted.

Language of Communication

Users should be able to communicate with the system in the simplest possible way. Commands should be brief and unambiguous. Dedicated keys are desirable. For the user who is not an information specialist, a system that searches on natural language statements is probably preferable to one based on a controlled vocabulary. Inexperienced users have difficulty with boolean expressions, and this favors systems that will accept an English sentence as a search statement. A very complete entry vocabulary is desirable. All these matters were discussed in more detail in Chapter Eleven, and we need not elaborate on them further here.

Everything possible should be done to reduce the keying needed at the terminal. Users should be able to select terms from displays by term number, the use of a light pen, or by touch panel. Abbreviations for command names should be acceptable. In Intrex, some of the most used commands can be abbreviated to their first four letters. Word truncation should also be possible. McAllister and Bell (1971) have illustrated the use of *default conditions* to reduce the amount of typing needed. For particular kinds of questions, the system itself provides the most likely response. Only if the answer is incorrect does the user need to take some action (i.e., change it). Another possibility is the display of multiple choice answers from which the user selects the appropriate response by number or letter.

System Sensitivity

From the human factors standpoint, perhaps the major defect of existing on-line retrieval systems is their sensitivity to simple human errors. An on-line system should be able to accommodate the relatively infrequent user who may never acquire complete fluency in operating the terminal. Unfortunately, most available systems require perfection in spelling, punctuation, and spacing.* Table 17.4 presents some examples of simple human input errors, identified in the evaluation of AIM–TWX and EARS, that caused terms to be rejected. It is irritating and frustrating for the user to have a term rejected for what seems a trivial reason. The user who correctly types the 24 characters of LYSERGIC ACID DIETHYLAMIDE might justifiably be annoyed to find his term rejected because of a superfluous comma at the end. In any event, the searcher should be allowed to use common abbreviations (LSD in this case) and have these abbreviations recognized by the system.

On-line systems should be capable of compensating for common human errors. Cain's (1969) entry vocabulary, as described in Chapter Eleven, was an attempt to introduce such compensation (e.g., OPTHALMIC is accepted as a variant of OPHTHALMIC) but perhaps does not go far enough. Some systems, including RECON, DIALOG, and TIRP (Textile Information Retrieval Project) compensate for spelling errors by displaying the near misses. Thus, the entry of COMMISUROTOMY could lead to a display looking like

COMMISSURAL	13
COMMISSURE	36
COMMISSUROTOMY	4
COMMISUROTOMY	
COMMUNICATION	50
COMMUNITY	27
COMPACTED	1

from which the searcher can recognize and select the term he is seeking. This technique, unfortunately, does not take care of all spelling errors. For example, the entry of CHLOROLOSE could lead to the following display:

CHLOROFORM	75
CHLOROGENIC ACID	8
CHLOROGUANIDE	21
CHLOROLOSE	
CHLOROMERCURIBENZOATES	43
CHLOROPHYLL	102
CHLOROPICRIN	3

This is not much help to the searcher, because the many terms beginning CHLORO widely separate the misspelling CHLOROLOSE from the correct

---

*The Intrex system, however, avoids ambiguities due to extra spaces by ignoring any space beyond the first.

TABLE 17.4. Input Errors Causing Rejection of Entry in AIM–TWX and EARS

System	Error	Correct form	Reason for term being rejected
AIM–TWX (ORBIT)	LYSERGIC ACID DIETHYLAMIDE,	LYSERGIC ACID DIETHYLAMIDE	A superfluous comma
	HEMORRHAGE POSTPARTUM	HEMORRHAGE, POSTPARTUM	A missing comma
	LONG ACTING THYROID STIMULATOR	LONG-ACTING THYROID STIMULATOR	Omission of hyphen
	RECTAL NEOPLASM	RECTAL NEOPLASMS	Final "s" missing
	DEXTRO AMPHETTAMINE	DEXTRO AMPHETAMINE	Spelling error
	SPLENIC ARETERY	SPLENIC ARTERY	Spelling error
	TRANSPLANTATHION	TRANSPLANTATION	Spelling error
	MYCOTIC ANEURYSM	ANEURYSM, MYCOTIC	Transposition
EARS (Data Central)	ABS.	ABS	The abbreviation for "abstract" is rejected because of a superfluous period
	EARSHEB	EARSHEB.	Designation of data base rejected because final period lacking
	COMMISUROTOMY	COMMISSUROTOMY	Letter missing
	CHLOROLOSE	CHLORALOSE	Misspelling
	ORPREVENTION	OR PREVENTION	Term and operator rejected because of spacing error

form CHLORALOSE. Unless the system permits paging up and down, and the searcher thinks of doing this, he will not find the term he needs to use.

Ideally, any retrieval system, especially one based on a controlled vocabulary, should be capable of recognizing a term when the searcher has typed enough characters to identify it uniquely (minimum character-string recognition). For example, DEXTRO A. . . is adequate to uniquely identify the term DEXTRO AMPHETAMINE in MEDLINE or AIM–TWX, since no other term begins with this string of seven characters. The fact that the searcher adds a superfluous "T" later in the term (see Table 17.4) should be of no consequence to the system and should certainly not cause the term to be rejected.

On-line systems should incorporate minimum character-string recognition and other fail-safe procedures to save the time of the user and reduce his frustration. In this connection, it is worth noting the interesting and valuable work that has been conducted on algorithms for machine retrieval of bibliographic entries from very large files such as library catalogs. These algorithms are designed to compensate for misspellings and other discrepancies in the user's input. While this research, which is reported by Dolby (1969), Kilgour (1968, 1970), Kilgour, et al. (1970), Nugent (1968), Ruecking (1968), and Stangl, et al. (1969), is intended for searches on authors and titles, there is possible applicability to subject searching on descriptors or natural language strings. Programs for the machine correction of human errors have been described by other investigators. For example, Blair (1960) has described a program for the correction of spelling errors. The systematic abbreviation of English words and names by computer has been described by Bourne and Ford (1961); Davidson (1962), among others, has described procedures for retrieval of misspelled names in airline reservation systems.

Errors and Error Messages

When the searcher does make an error, he must be informed immediately by the system. Error messages must be explicit and should tell the user how to make the appropriate correction. Error correction should be simple and should disturb as little of the search as possible. Under no circumstances should an error cause an entire search to be aborted and force a user to return to an initial log-in status again. Errors must not be allowed to propagate within a search. Unfortunately, some bibliographic systems leave much to be desired in terms of these requirements. Many examples of poor error messages exist. It is not enough to tell a user that an error has occurred. He must be told the precise nature of the error and what he must do to correct it. Otherwise, the user will merely find himself in a frustrating loop.

Sackman (1970c) identifies two major types of errors: typing errors and *comprehension* errors (relating to system procedures and protocols). The former are more easily recognized and corrected. Error rates drop with increased experience in using the system. One would expect that more improvement would take place in the comprehension errors, and that typing errors would be maintained at a more consistent level. Error rate was found to be highly and inversely correlated with user productivity levels.

Katter and Blankenship (1969) state that an error-control program should be designed to: "(1) reduce the probability that the user will produce what he perceives as an error that the system does not detect, (2) reduce the probability that he will send messages to the system that it cannot accept or interpret, (3) immediately notify him when he has sent an unacceptable message, and (4) immediately diagnose detected errors and suggest corrective actions." They mention the following as desirable features of an error control program:

A. *Entry Preparation Display.* For controlling both the kinds of errors detectable by the computer and humans, and those detectable by humans only, a valuable display for the neophyte on-line user is one that unfailingly shows him clearly and explicitly the full message he is about to attempt to enter into the system, and will not allow an "entry" action to be taken unless the message to be entered has been so displayed.

B. *Entry Preparation Display Editing.* For the entry display, a valuable provision is rapid means for deleting single words, entire lines, or several lines starting at a specified point, and for inserting a word, phrase, or line into a space too small for it.

C. *Variable Spelling Approximator.* Spelling-error aids can be made to operate for terms in the interaction-control glossary and in the legal-content-term glossary. An approximate algorithm for matching the input word against file-stored words can, if it finds no exact match, notify the user and print out any filed terms that are close approximations for the entered word.

D. *Flexible Error Description Feedback.* For "first-hour beginners," a generalized "help" command that accesses error-diagnostic routines and tutorial programs is most helpful. For experienced users, the ability to be notified briefly of errors but to suppress lengthy explanations and suggestions is also essential. For a neophyte, an Entered Action Display that spells out the actions he has just taken can be valuable.

E. *System Error Monitoring.* For improved design of system interface characteristics to eliminate system-detectable errors, a program that stores records of user errors by type can be valuable, especially during the developmental stages of the system (p. 30).*

---

*Reprinted by permission of System Development Corporation.

Conflicting User Needs

The effective human engineering of on-line systems is complicated by the fact that searchers may vary greatly in their experience and sophistication in using the terminal. The indirect approach to search strategy construction, as used in RECON and DIALOG, may be helpful to the neophyte, but it can be extremely frustrating for the experienced searcher who wants to enter search terms directly in boolean combinations. Tutorial leading by the hand features, if incorporated into the system to aid the beginner, must be capable of being suppressed by the experienced user.

The beginner will want to communicate with the system in a longhand way. He will not be too comfortable with abbreviations, particularly in messages generated by the system. As he gains experience, however, he will seek shortcuts and ways of saving time. He would like the system to communicate in an abbreviated way, and he would also like to communicate with the system in abbreviated form. It is imperative that on-line systems should have both the experienced and the inexperienced user in mind. Terse and verbose communications options should be available, and simplistic features designed to assist the beginner should be capable of being bypassed by the more experienced searcher.

Availability Factors

To maximize use of an on-line system, and to reduce the unit cost per search conducted, it must be made widely available. Unfortunately, if the system is made easily accessible to a great number of users (by proliferation of terminals), there is a danger that it will often be fully loaded. If a user is frequently denied access to the system, because of overload factors, he is likely to find the situation intolerable, and the system will eventually lose him as a customer. The managers of on-line systems are therefore faced with a conflict between maximizing use of the system (and thus reducing cost per search) and maximizing the availability of the system when a particular user wishes to interrogate it. Carbonell, et al. (1968) have considered the problem of what levels of system availability a user will accept. The user tolerance is measured in the following terms:

1. Of the total number of times a user calls up the system, what proportion of these times is he willing to accept a busy signal?
2. Having received a busy signal, how long is he willing to wait on the average before being allowed access to the system?

Symbiosis

Studies of the use of time-sharing systems, including studies of retrieval systems, have shown that the man–machine interaction capabilities are not exploited as fully as one might expect. In many applications, a large amount of effort away from the terminal precedes the actual interaction with the system. In the retrieval situation, this would correspond to the preparation of a search strategy in advance and the use of the terminal merely to enter it, without exploiting the interactive capabilities of the system through browsing and the heuristic development of a strategy on the basis of system feedback. Nickerson, et al. (1968) have suggested that there may be a relationship between how a system is used and how the user is charged for it. If the user is charged solely on the basis of CPU time, he is likely to do more of his work at the terminal and to use the system more interactively. However, if terminal time is figured in the cost calculations (or if he is remote from the computer and paying telephone line charges), he will want to save time at the console and will prepare more in advance.

Hansen (1971) has summarized *user engineering principles* for the design of interactive systems, the fundamental principle being *know the user*. Specific user engineering principles to help meet this first principle are grouped into three broad categories:

1. Minimize memorization
    Selection not entry
    Names not numbers
    Predictable behavior
    Access to system information
2. Optimize operations
    Rapid execution of common operations
    Display inertia
    Muscle memory
    Reorganize command parameters
3. Engineer for errors
    Good error messages
    Engineer out the common errors
    Reversible actions
    Redundancy
    Data structure integrity

Hansen believes strongly that users should, whenever possible, select from lists (menus) displayed (a video console is assumed here) rather than typing character-strings. By selecting from a list, the user is spared the need to remember various commands, and the probability of error is thus reduced. Moreover, a video console can display many characters in the same time that it would take the user to type very few. Files, commands, and other entries should be identified by names rather than numbers. The system must always respond in a predictable way (i.e., must not appear idiosyncratic), and it must inform the user when he needs to be informed (e.g., on the status of a particular operation). The system should be as unobtrusive as possible; operations frequently conducted should be optimized in terms of command requirements and interaction time, and a display should change as little as necessary to carry out each new request (display inertia). The system must be engineered to prevent catastrophic errors and to permit easy recovery from as many errors as possible. Error messages should be specific and explicit. The system must be designed to avoid very common errors (an error that occurs constantly must be attributed to poor system design rather than to a weakness of all users!) and to allow a user an easy method of reversing an action he recognizes as being incorrect.

In this chapter we have attempted to review some human factors considerations that may be of importance in the design and operation of on-line retrieval systems. The purpose of human engineering in this application is to improve the interaction between man and machine. Systems that are poorly designed from the human factors standpoint reduce the tolerance of the searcher and increase searching time and searching costs. It is all too easy for the inexperienced user to become frustrated. And the frustrated user tends not to return for more.

REFERENCES

Barmack, J. R., and H. W. Sinaiko (1966). *Human Factors Problems in Computer-Generated Graphic Displays.* Washington, D.C.: Institute for Defense Analyses, AD 636170.

Blair, C. R. (1960). "A Program for Correcting Spelling Errors." *Information and Control* **3** (1), 60–67.

Bourne, C. P., and D. F. Ford (1961). "A Study of Methods for Systematically Abbreviating English Words and Names." *Jour. Assoc. Computing Machinery* **8** (4), 538–552.

Cain, A. M. (1969). "Thesaural Problems in an On-Line System." *Bull. Medical Library Assoc.* **57** (3), 250–259.

Carbonell, J. R., J. I. Elkind, and R. S. Nickerson (1968). "On the Psychological Importance of Time in a Time-Sharing System." *Human Factors* **10** (2), 135–142.

Carlisle, J. H. (1970). *Comparing Behavior at Various Computer Display Consoles in Time-Shared Legal Information Retrieval.* Santa Monica, Ca.: Rand Corporation, AD 712695.

Cuadra, C. A. (1971). "On-Line Systems: Promise and Pitfalls." *Jour. Amer. Soc. Information Sci.* **22** (2), 107–114.

Davidson, L. (1962). "Retrieval of Misspelled Names in Airlines Passenger Record System." *Commun. Assoc. Computing Machinery* **5** (3), 169–171.

Dolby, J. L. (1969). "An Algorithm for Noisy Matches in Catalog Searching." *In* J. L. Cunningham, W. D. Schieber, and R. M. Schoffner, *A Study of the Organization and Search of Bibliographic Holdings Records in On-Line Computer Systems.* Phase 1. Final Report. Berkeley, Ca.: University of California, Institute of Library Research, pp. 119–136.

Dolotta, T. A. (1970). "Functional Specifications for Typewriter-Like Time-Sharing Terminals." *Computing Surveys* **2** (1), 5–31.

Fetter, R. B., and J. H. Carlisle (1971). *Man-Computer Interaction in a Decision-Making Environment.* New Haven, Conn.: Yale University, Department of Administrative Sciences, AD 722 336.

Gould, J. D. (1968). "Visual Factors in the Design of Computer-Controlled CRT Displays." *Human Factors* **10** (4), 359–375.

Hansen, W. J. (1971). "User Engineering Principles for Interactive Systems." *AFIPS Conf. Proc. Fall Joint Computer Conf.* **39**, 523–532.

Katter, R. V. (1970). *On the On-Line User of Remote-Access Citation Retrieval Services.* Santa Monica, Ca.: System Development Corporation, TM-(L)-4494/000/00.

Katter, R. V., and D. A. Blankenship (1969). *On-Line Interfaces for Document Information Systems: Considerations for the Biomedical Communications Network.* Santa Monica, Ca.: System Development Corporation, TM-(L)-4320.

Kilgour, F. G. (1968). "Retrieval of Single Entries from a Computerized Library Catalog File." *Proc. Amer. Soc. Information Sci.* **5**, 133–136.

Kilgour, F. G. (1970). "Concept of an On-Line Computerized Library Catalog." *Jour. Library Automation* **3** (1), 1–11.

Kilgour, F. G., P. L. Long, and E. B. Leiderman (1970). "Retrieval of Bibliographic Entries from a Name-Title Catalog by the Use of Truncated Search Keys." *Proc. Amer. Soc. Information Sci.* **7**, 79–82.

McAllister, C., and J. M. Bell (1971). "Human Factors in the Design of an Interactive Library System." *Jour. Amer. Soc. Information Sci.* **22** (2), 96–104.

Marcus, R. S., A. R. Benenfeld, and P. Kugel (1971). "The User Interface for the Intrex Retrieval System." *In* D. E. Walker (ed.), *Interactive Bibliographic Search: the User/Computer Interface.* Montvale, N.J.: AFIPS Press, pp. 159–201.

Mayer, S. R. (1970). "Trends in Human Factors for Military Information Systems." *Human Factors* **12** (2), 177–186.

Miller, R. B. (1968). "Response Time in Man-Computer Conversational Transactions." *AFIPS Conf. Proc. Fall Joint Computer Conf.* **33** (1), 267–277.

Mooers, C. N. (1960). "Mooers' Law, or Why Some Retrieval Systems Are Used and Others Are Not." *Amer. Documentation* **11** (3), ii.

Nickerson, R. S., J. I. Elkind, and J. R. Carbonell (1968). "Human Factors and the Design of Time Sharing Computer Systems." *Human Factors* **10** (2), 127–133.

Nugent, W. R. (1968). "Compression Word Coding Techniques for Information Retrieval." *Jour. Library Automation* **1** (4), 250–260.

Ruecking, F. H., Jr. (1968). "Bibliographic Retrieval from Bibliographic Input; the Hypothesis and Construction of a Test." *Jour. Library Automation* **1** (4), 227–238.

Sackman, H. (1970a). "Experimental Analysis of Man-Computer Problem Solving." *Human Factors* **12** (2), 187–201.

Sackman, H. (1970b). "Experimental Investigation of Computer User Effectiveness." *In* G. F. Weinwurm (ed.), *On the Management of Computer Programming.* Princeton, N.J.: Auerbach, pp. 45–63.

Sackman, H. (1970c). "Time-Sharing and Self-Tutoring: an Exploratory Case History." *Human Factors* **12** (2), 203–214.

Sackman, H., and M. M. Gold (1968). *Time-Sharing Versus Batch Processing: an Experimental Inquiry into Human Problem Solving*. Santa Monica, Ca.: System Development Corporation, SP-3110.

Schwartz, J. I. (1965). "Observations on Time-Shared Systems." *Proc. 20th Natl. Conf. Assoc. Computing Machinery*, 525–542.

Stangl, P., B. A. Lipetz, and K. F. Taylor (1969). "Performance of Kilgour's Truncation Algorithm When Applied to Bibliographic Retrieval from a Library Catalog." *Proc. Amer. Soc. Information Sci.* **6**, 125–127.

Van Dam, A. (1966). "Computer Driven Displays and Their Use in Man/Machine Interaction." *In* F. Alt and M. Rubinoff (eds.), *Advances in Computers*. vol. 7. New York: Academic Press, pp. 239–290.

Chapter Eighteen

Cost–Performance–Benefits Factors

We can evaluate an information retrieval or dissemination system from any of the following viewpoints:

1. How well the system is satisfying its objectives, which will usually mean how well it is satisfying the demands placed upon it. Here we are evaluating the *effectiveness* of the system.
2. How efficiently (in terms of costs) it is satisfying its objectives. This is *cost-effectiveness* evaluation.
3. Whether the system justifies its existence (i.e., the system worth). In evaluating system worth, we are concerned with *cost–benefit* relationships.

Cost-effectiveness, then, deals with the relationship between level of performance (effectiveness) and the costs involved in achieving this level. There may be several alternative methods that could be used to obtain a particular performance level, and these can be costed. *Cost–benefits* refers to the relationship between the benefits of a particular product or service and the costs of providing it. Generally speaking, benefits are more difficult to measure than performance (effectiveness) except that, in a commercial sense, benefits equate with return on investment. The expression *cost–performance–benefits* relates to the entire interrelationship between costs, performance (level of effectiveness), and benefits.

The *cost* of an information service can be measured in terms of input of resources (funds). Under costs we need to consider both the costs that are relatively fixed (e.g., equipment purchase or rental, developmental costs, costs involved in acquisition and indexing of the present data base) and the costs that are relatively variable. Variable costs are of two kinds:

1. The variable cost that is a function of the number of transactions. For example, if we increase the number of retrospective searches conducted from 1000 per year to 1500 per year, the cost *per search* may be reduced by x dollars.
2. The variable cost that is a function of alternative modes of operating the system. For example, we could vary the cost of retrospective searching by varying the mode of interaction with the user (personal visit, mail, telephone), by varying the mode of interaction with the data base (e.g., from off-line batch processing to on-line interactive search), by adding or eliminating a screening operating, or by changing the professional level of the personnel conducting the searches.

The *performance* or *effectiveness* of an information system can be measured in a number of different ways. Some performance criteria for on-line retrieval systems were discussed in Chapter Six and some evaluation procedures in Chapter Eight. System benefits are usually more difficult to express and to measure. Possible criteria for measuring the benefits of an information system include:

1. Cost savings in using this system as compared with the costs of finding needed information elsewhere.
2. Avoidance of loss of productivity (of engineers, for example) that would result if information sources were not readily available.
3. Improved decision-making or reduction in the level of personnel required to make decisions.
4. Avoidance of duplication or waste of engineering or research effort that has either been done before or that has been proved infeasible by earlier investigators.
5. Stimulation of invention (a serendipity factor). For example, an industrial current awareness service might easily justify itself economically by suggesting possible new products, new applications for existing products, possible markets for industrial waste, or less expensive methods of fabrication.

In considering an information system, various levels of benefits are evident. For example, a society or institution may, quite properly, measure the benefits of its information program in terms of income from sale of publications or services, and balance this income against production costs (i.e., calculate return on investment). Here we are weighing costs against income benefits. On the other hand, a government agency may be partially subsidizing this information program and may adopt a broader view of its benefits in terms of the less tangible factors enumerated above. Moreover, within the environment of an information system, the relationship between *cost* and *effectiveness* may be somewhat difficult to distinguish from the relationship between *cost* and *benefits*. Suppose, for example, we reduce the average number of terms assigned in indexing, and thereby reduce the average indexing time per item. We could say that an immediate *benefit* of this action is to reduce input costs. On the other hand, such an action is likely to have a very definite influence on the *effectiveness* of the system (the average precision of the system may increase—and this in itself may be regarded as a form of *benefit*—while the average recall will almost certainly decrease). In other words, this action has had immediate observable *benefits* (in terms of cost saving at input), it will have a long-range influence on the *effectiveness* of the system, and it may have an even longer range influence on the *benefits* of the system's products to the end user.

Obviously, then, *cost*, *performance*, and *benefits* are very closely inter-related and cannot be completely separated. In this chapter, we will discuss costs of an on-line retrieval system and the relationship between these *costs* and its *effectiveness*, in terms of how well it responds to the demands placed upon it. Some cost–benefit considerations will also be mentioned. The economics of computers in general, including some cost-effectiveness aspects, has been discussed in considerable detail in a book by Sharpe (1969).

Cost Factors

An excellent discussion on the costs of a small or medium-sized in-house, on-line retrieval system has been prepared by Negus and Hall (1971) of the United Kingdom Atomic Energy Authority, Culham Laboratory. Because of the value of this discussion, it is reproduced virtually intact below, with the kind permission of the authors and Pergamon Press. In the following pages all quotations not otherwise identified are from Negus and Hall.

It is well known that computing costs have fallen dramatically with succeeding "generations" of computers e.g. in the case of IBM the stated cost to perform 100,000 calculations is given in Table [18.1].

Clearly, however, the cost of time used in actual computing is only a part of the total cost, and in this section we attempt to identify the high-cost factors affecting the overall economics of an in-house on-line computer information retrieval system.

The principal factors considered are:—
1. The cost of obtaining the references in machine-readable form.
2. The cost of converting these records to the form used by the on-line system.
3. The cost of on-line storage.
4. The computer time used in searching.
5. The charging system in use on the computer.
6. The frequency of use of the system.

TABLE 18.1.   Falling Cost of Computing (Cost of Performing 100,000 Multiplications)

Year	IBM model	Cost in new pence*
1954	704	50
1959	7090	11
1966	360/75	$1\frac{1}{2}$
1970	370/165	$<\frac{1}{2}$

SOURCE: Negus and Hall (1971). Reproduced by permission of Pergamon Press.

The relative effects of these factors will of course vary depending on the overall library–user environment, and indeed in some environments there will be other factors which may be very significant, e.g. cost of telecommunication facilities, etc. (pp. 258, 259).

Cost of Obtaining the References in Machine-Readable Form

Cost will vary depending on individual circumstances. Libraries ... already creating machine-readable records will in essence be maximizing the use of an existing asset, although of course it is only reasonable to attribute a portion (e.g., 40%) of the cost of creating that asset to the information retrieval function. Other libraries may be able to build a reference base at reasonable cost by subscribing to a centralized magnetic tape service offering references at rates which can be very low indeed, e.g. 50 references per £1. Many subscribers, of course, will find that tape services sometimes do not capture material of interest to them and often include much material not relevant; it may still be reasonable to use such tapes to provide an SDI service since redundant material is in effect searched only once—but the material "saved" for the information retrieval data base should be free from obviously irrelevant references, either by buying subfield tapes or by carrying out an in-house "weeding" operation. In general, the cost of references added to a selected "mission" data base will vary widely depending on the route chosen (references prepared in-house or purchased), depth of indexing (if any), computer facilities available, staff overheads, etc; rates of 5–25 references per £1 could be achieved in many units, the exact figure depending on local circumstances. In these cases a data base of reasonable dimensions could probably be obtained at a cost which is not unreasonable when compared with other components of the library budget (p. 259).

---

*Authors' Note: Many of the figures in this chapter are given in British currency. A British pound (£) contains 100 new pence and was worth approximately $2.40 at the time these statistics were prepared.

Cost of Converting to the Form Used by the On-Line System

This will vary (i) with the amount of restructuring necessary, (ii) with the frequency of updating and (iii) with the relative size of the data base and of the added material. With serial files this third factor will have no effect, and, providing an appropriate program is used, neither will the second.

The cost at Culham for converting 1000 records from the existing cumulative SDI tapes to the form of the file structure held on disc for the retrieval program is < £2. The cost of updating and rearranging an inverted file would naturally be higher (p. 259).

Storage Costs

Although the true cost of direct access storage is difficult to estimate due to variations in accounting practice, some idea of its magnitude can be obtained by considering current rental charges.

The following table [Table 18.2] assumes that the information retrieval system is well used and that the reference data base is always on-line. Where the data base is not permanently on-line, storage costs can be considerably lower as the major proportion of these costs is attributed to the hire of drive and control units.

TABLE 18.2.　Estimated Cost of Direct-Access Storage

| | Cost per month | |
Device	1 megabyte	50,000 references at 200 bytes each
RDS Replaceable disk store (4 × 7 mbyte)	£46	£460
EDS Exchangeable disk store (9 × 30 mbyte)	£12	£120
LFD Large fixed-disk store (350 mbyte)	£7	£75
(700 mbyte)	£5	£52

Source: Negus and Hall (1971). Reproduced by permission of Pergamon Press.

True costs when allowance is made for overheads will naturally be much higher. Clearly, a crucial cost factor in most environments will be the kind of storage device available (pp. 259, 260).

Computer Time Used in Searching

In machine terms the time used will depend on the size of the data base, the type of search (e.g., serial, inverted) and the number of references found.

In practical terms, however, it is worth pointing out that as systems become more "sophisticated" they often become more difficult to use. The implication, which is often overlooked, is that inexpert use of sophisticated search capabilities can easily nullify any savings arising from the sophisticated logic and programming techniques employed. But whether the logic is simple or complex the skill of the user in formulating his query will still be vital, as will be the provision of early feed-back alerting him to possible errors or short-comings in the query formulation.

Figures will of course vary considerably depending on the approach adopted but taking the specific case of Culham, the timing tests . . . indicate that the cost of computer time used in searching 25,000 references could be as low as £3. In the case of a complex query, or one producing many references, computing costs will be greater. These figures are based on computer charges taken at £95 per hour on a second generation machine. With a third generation time-sharing system where charges are based on cpu time, computing cost would probably be less than £1.

One point to note here is that the time taken in search with an inverted file system increases in almost direct proportion to the number of terms in the query, whereas the effect of each additional term on speed of search in a serial system is normally less than the effect of the preceding term.

It is also worth noting that in many real-life units most searches are for some literature on a topic rather than all. Unlike many inverted file systems, the RIOT* program stops searching when the user stops looking at captured references, thus economizing on computer search time (p. 260).

Other Factors

Most time-sharing systems make a charge based on cpu time, as of course the machine is running another program while transfer is taking place. The user will probably be unable to alter the rates at which he is charged. An interactive job will almost certainly run at the highest cost rating on a machine. . . . In the costs listed above, some are fixed costs and others are costs incurred each time a search is undertaken. The more searches there are on a system, the cheaper the cost per search will be. (This may itself cause a change in user demand. . .) (pp. 260, 261).

Data Base Permanently On-Line

It is apparent from the preceding examination that assuming machine-readable references can be purchased or prepared at a reasonable annual cost then the most significant factors affecting the overall economic viability of an on-line reference retrieval system are (i) the cost of storage, (ii) the cost of computer time

---

*Authors' Note: See Chapter Five.

per search, and (iii) the frequency of use. These three factors are examined in Fig. [18.1]; the curve for each storage device represents costs which are essentially the total of two components—the storage cost without overheads (derived from Table [18.2]) and the computer search cost... By ignoring overheads, and assessing computing costs at a ... low level, on-line retrieval can be made to look very attractive indeed.

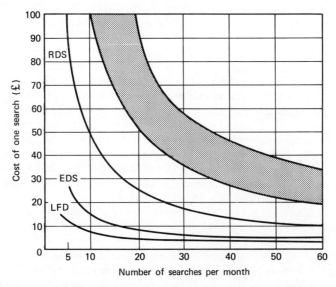

Figure 18.1. Estimated costs per search as a function of the number of searches made per month for a data base of 50,000 references held continuously on-line. The "line" curves represent search costs based on rental charges for individual types of storage device (RDS = replaceable disk store; EDS = exchangeable disk store; LFD = large fixed disk). "Real" costs when overheads are taken into consideration will fall within the shaded region. All costs include an estimated charge of £2 for the computer time used in searching (even the cost of a complex, more expensive search will still be a relatively small proportion of the total). Reproduced from Negus and Hall (1971) by permission of Pergamon Press.

However, "real" costs are much higher. The major extra component of these real costs is the allowance that must be made for overheads, particularly the heavy overheads attracted by the storage units. The "shaded" region (in Fig. [18.1]) shows possible "real" costs taking overheads into account; the major portion of these costs in all cases is the standing storage charge arising from having references available on-line, the cost of search being a relatively small proportion of the total. (In fact as the "real cost" region in Fig. [18.1] is extrapolated the "search cost" as a proportion of the total cost assumes increasing importance until with a very high number of searches per month it can become dominant.)

It follows from the above that the most crucial factor for many units, particularly small/medium size units, will be the cost of storage* and not the cost of search; where a system is expected to operate with maximum economy the best approach will be that which uses the least on-line storage, providing always that the system operates at a speed which is acceptable to the user. In effect, it must be borne in mind when considering whether to adopt an inverted file approach or a linear file approach, that although inverted file search systems generally use less computer time in actual search, this may be more than offset by the cost penalty imposed by the increased amount of computer storage required for the larger files. Comparative studies on the relative sizes of linear files and inverted files are valuable in giving some idea of the storage penalties which an inverted file system can incur.

As mentioned above, the cost of computer time, as a proportion of the total cost of the average search, can become a significant factor in a relatively heavily-used system. This may happen, for instance, in the case of a large-scale system covering a discipline and available on a national or international basis. If there are no natural subfield compartments which in effect partition the data base into small data bases, then a threshold may be reached beyond which decreased search costs resulting from, say, inverted file organization may more than offset (i) the additional costs arising from the extra storage requirements of the larger inverted files, and (ii) the additional significant costs arising from the computer time used in processing inverted files when new material is added to the files. (In a linear file new material is simply added on at the end of the file, whereas up-dating an inverted file may involve much more processing time.) The economics will be considerably affected where a system is large enough to justify the use of a large mass-storage device such as a Data Cell. . . .

These arguments, although based on work carried out on a KDF9, are valid for other machines. In fact, the storage costs are based on 1970/1971 equipment whereas the search costs are for a second generation machine. This means that the relative importance of storage as a very significant high-cost factor is perhaps even greater than indicated above; for example, the System 4/70, which replaced the KDF9 at Culham in 1971, is approximately three times faster (pp. 260, 261).

Data Base Not Permanently On-Line

It is clear, considering the case of the small/medium data base examined in Fig. [18.1], that if the references are held continuously on-line then with a traffic of, say, 3 searches per day the cost per search would be about £30. This is the assessed "real" cost but it is likely that in many units the expenditure (in terms of money actually spent) would be less. Nevertheless, costs of £15–£30 would seem high enough to cause library managements to ask if there was a sufficient need for the reference store to be on-line for the whole of the computer's working day.

In many cases (particularly in units using high-cost storage) it would be judged adequate, initially at any rate, to provide on-line service for only part of each day.

---

*Authors' Note: See later paragraph titled "Future Costs" for a discussion on the declining cost of storage devices.

Many factors have to be evaluated—for what proportion of the computer's working day is the retrieval system to be available? Is this at a peak demand period attracting a high tariff? What kind of storage devices are available and is there spare capacity or must extra drive/control units be obtained?

Clearly, when the data base is held on-line for only part of each day the search cost will depend very much on local conditions. However, Fig. [18.1] may be used to indicate upper limits from which an appropriate deduction may be made, e.g. it is not unreasonable to suggest a cost of £5–£15 per search when the traffic is, say, 3 searches per day on a data base of 50,000 references available for 4 hours per day.

If the computer searches are performed with reasonable efficiency, then these costs (£5–£15) are not high when compared with the cost of manual searching (when staff overheads, etc. are taken fully into account). For instance, one attempt* to assess the cost of a manual search derived an estimated cost per search of $65 (pp. 262, 263).

Data Base Partitioned

In some cases there may be a distinct advantage in partitioning the data base, either into naturally occurring sub-fields (e.g., an industrial library may have considerable collections covering technology and a number of quite separate fields such as marketing), or in some other way. If on-line storage is restricted but a limited amount can be made available throughout the day then "core" literature can be on-line continuously but with peripheral literature available only for short periods. Partitioning can also increase the speed of search and indeed simplify query-formulation (p. 263).

Amount of Computer Storage Required

The studies reported in this paper are particularly centered on the literature core of practical interest to the Culham Laboratory—about 25,000–50,000 references. This is not a large data base but nevertheless it is typical of many special libraries. It is useful at this point to make an estimate of what these figures, e.g. 50,000 references, mean in computer storage terms. This has been done in Table [18.3] which gives an estimate of the number of "characters" involved together with the number of magnetic tapes or disc units required to store this information. It is clear that the conventional book or bound journal is a remarkably compact storage device comparing well in volumetric terms, and indeed in cost terms, with machine storage. It is also clear that 50,000 references stored in machine-readable form, e.g. on 1 magnetic tape, occupy considerably less storage space than would an equivalent conventional card index. But while the bulk factor is important what is more important is that in a card index or book index the entry points are pre-determined. In contrast, given appropriate search and programming techniques

---

*Authors' Note: See Thompson (1970).

almost any part of a machine-readable bibliographic record can be used for retrieval in a computer search (pp. 263, 264).

TABLE 18.3.   Amount of Computer Storage Required for Various Sizes of Data Base[a]

	Approximate number of characters	Approximate number of magnetic tape reels	Approximate number of magnetic disk units
1 reference	2×10^2	Not calculated	Not calculated
25,000 references	5×10^6	$\frac{1}{2}$	$\frac{1}{4}$
50,000 references	10^7	1	$\frac{1}{2}$
500,000 references	10^8	10	5
1 journal article	10^4	Not calculated	Not calculated
1 volume of *Encyclopaedia Britannica*	7×10^6	$\frac{2}{3}$	$\frac{1}{3}$

SOURCE: Negus and Hall (1971), p. 263. Reproduced by permission of Pergamon Press.
[a]These are based on 10^7 characters for a magnetic tape and 2×10^7 characters for a disk unit; clearly, they are order-of-magnitude estimates, since many widely different conditions occur in practice, e.g., packing density, type of disk unit available, etc.

Costs for a Larger System

The above discussion is taken virtually intact from Negus and Hall (1971). Another interesting paper on the costs of on-line retrieval, also from the United Kingdom, is contributed by Higgins and Smith (1971), at Queen's University of Belfast. They base their costs on a somewhat larger system consisting of 100,000 citations and abstracts stored permanently on a fixed disk store (FDS) associated with an ICL 1907 computer. Each bibliographic record requires approximately 1000 characters, so that the complete data base occupies about 100 million characters, about one-fourth of the total capacity of the FDS they are using.

Rental and maintenance cost of this number of characters on the FDS is about £7500 a year. This cost is spread over the users of the system. With an average of 10 searches per week, 50 weeks per year, the average cost is £15 per search for disk storage. Costs for 1, 10, 100, and 1000 searches per week are given in Table 18.4.

TABLE 18.4.   Comparison of the Costs of a Conversational Query from an On-Line Data Bank of 100,000 References (with Abstracts), Indexed Freely Using the Words in the Titles and Abstracts, for Different Numbers of Queries per Week[a]

	Queries/week			
	1000	100	10	1
	£	£	£	£
Disk storage	0.2	1.5	15.0	150.0
Data maintenance	0.3	2.0	12.0	100.0
Access time[b]	2.0	2.0	2.0	2.0
CPU time[b]	1.0	1.0	1.0	1.0
Telephone[c]	2.5	2.5	2.5	2.5
Total	6.0	9.0	32.5	255.5

SOURCE: Higgins and Smith (1971). Reproduced by permission of the Computer Science Department, Queen's University of Belfast.
[a]The costs are based on the present equipment at Belfast: an ICL 1907 computer and a 420M character fixed disk file. The cost of research and development is not included.
[b]These costs assume that the conversation lasts approximately half an hour and that 1 minute CPU time is used.
[c]Based on a query by telephone from London to Belfast at prime time.

Data maintenance is another factor taken into account by Higgins and Smith (1971):

> The data in the data bank needs to be collected (or purchased) and stored on disc; it needs to be continually updated. New terms have to be added to the thesaurus as they are required and errors in the data must be detected and corrected. Questions and complaints by users have to be followed up and answered. There are also the usual office costs. Both of the last two items will rise considerably as the number of users increases. We estimate that a minimum cost of the maintenance of the system will rise from about £5000 per annum when the system is little used to £15,000 per annum if the system is dealing with 1000 queries per week. But we have little experience as yet of these costs and we may be out by as much as a factor of 2.
>
> These costs have to be spread over all the queries. For example, with 10 queries per week and an annual maintenance cost of £6000 the cost for an average query would be £12.*

Other figures are also given in Table 18.4.

---

*Reprinted by permission of the Computer Science Department, Queen's University of Belfast.

Access time must also be accounted for. In using the Belfast system, the typical user will spend about half an hour at the terminal. The commercial charge for terminal access to the 1907 is £4 per hour, so that access time per search is about £2.

Higgins and Smith (1971) deal with the other cost components in the following terms:

> *CPU Time.* The amount of CPU time used depends very largely on the type of search the user does, but quite typically we have found with our system that he uses about 2 minutes per hour access time, costing therefore, at a rate of £60 per hour, approximately £1 per search. We contend that this charge (and the previous charge) would be much higher if it were not for the care we have taken to make our software as efficient as possible.
>
> *Telephone.* We assume that the user lives more than 30 miles from the data bank and that he is being charged at the full United Kingdom telephone rate. Then the cost will be £2.50 for this $\frac{1}{2}$ hr. on-line.
>
> *Disc Accesses.* The number of disc accesses can vary a great deal from query to query. If the user in his search unwisely uses index terms which occur often in the indexing of documents, then he will be working with a long list of references for each such index term (or rather, a long list of numbers (postings or entries) indexing the references). Because these long lists cannot all be stored in core it will be necessary to segment each one and store it on backing store (in our case a fast EDS) and bring these into core one segment after the other when they are needed.
>
> This will lengthen the amount of computing required considerably and thus push up the cost. Perhaps the disc accesses will have to be charged for themselves, but we are not yet sure how to do this. One difficulty is that the cost of counting the number of disc accesses may be too high to make it worth while.
>
> Thus the total cost per query if the data system is answering between 10 and 100 queries per week would lie between £33 and £9 with our system in Belfast. Clearly if the data bank was to be successful 10 queries per week would be an absolute minimum number and 100 queries per week at a charge of £9 each would represent a considerable success. Although these charges are still in our view rather high, fortunately we can foresee that they will drop over the coming years.*

Future Costs

Higgins and Smith (1971) regard on-line retrieval as an expensive operation, but they predict dramatic improvements in the future:

> The cost in a few years time, say by 1975, will have changed in a number of ways. The biggest change will probably be in disc storage which has been dropping in price and improving in reliability, speeds of transfer and access times over the last few years. Already disc files are on the market at a third of the cost of our present disc in Belfast. We can confidently predict then that on-line storage will have dropped

---

*Reprinted by permission of the Computer Science Department, Queen's University of Belfast.

in price considerably in the coming years. We have predicted a drop by a factor of 5 in the costs in Table [18.5]. Looking further into the future we can foresee these costs dropping further to become insignificant with the introduction of vast laser based photographic storage devices.*

In Table [18.5] we are predicting that the computing costs will have dropped by a factor of 2, and that also, with an improved command language and therefore fewer questions and answers, the time a user needs on-line for a typical search will be only 15 minutes rather than 30 minutes at present. Thus the cost of access time is dropped by a factor of 4, and the cost of CPU time by a factor of 2. The telephone costs have dropped by a factor less than 2 because we expect that the cost of a telephone call per minute will have risen in the meantime.

TABLE 18.5.   Predicted Costs of Belfast System in 1975

	Queries/week			
	1000	100	10	1
	£	£	£	£
Disk storage	0.03	0.3	3.0	30.0
Data maintenance	0.4	2.8	17.0	140.0
Access time	0.5	0.5	0.5	0.5
CPU time	0.5	0.5	0.5	0.5
Telephone	1.5	1.5	1.5	1.5
Total	2.9	5.6	22.5	172.5

SOURCE: Higgins and Smith (1971). Reproduced by permission of the Computer Science Department, Queen's University of Belfast.

The item which we have predicted will increase in price is the cost of the data and data maintenance. The reason is that this cost is largely based on human time which is bound to increase and go on increasing. Already by 1975 we predict that this will be dominating the cost of a query and it will continue to increase as the years go past. We hope that our ability to pay will increase at as high a rate! Thus the limit of what is possible when our computing systems are so efficient that computing costs are negligible is the remaining necessary charge for data maintenance and the telephone cost. If copies of the data bank are held in a number of major centres throughout the world though maintained only at one of them, the telephone costs will be small and the total number of queries, world wide, will be very large. Then the total cost for a search may be only £0.1 or less—by 1984?†

---

* Authors' Note: Elsewhere, Smith (1971) has predicted that by 1980 on-line holographic storage of 10^{13} bits should be possible at a cost of 10^{-7} cents per bit. Storage costs at Belfast are presently below 10^{-2} cents per bit but larger files, at costs below $\frac{1}{4}$ of this, are already available.
†Reprinted by permission of the Computer Science Department, Queen's University of Belfast.

Some Further Cost Figures

Cost data for on-line retrieval operations in the United States were formerly very scarce. However, more data are now being made available.

Cost data are difficult to interpret and compare, however, because of the many possible ways in which they are derived. Expenditure of CPU time is usually not directly convertible to costs, because it is only one component in the calculation of charges. Bloemeke and Treu (1969), discussing on-line SDI activities at the University of Pittsburgh, point out that charges for use of the Pittsburgh time-sharing system are based on an algorithm that incorporates three billing factors: CPU time, amount of core space employed during execution of a search, and the number of peripheral devices (e.g., disk or tape units) controlled during this period. With this approach, each user pays for his fair use of the system, depending on whatever combination of the above three factors he demands. Some other relevant data and discussions on costs are mentioned below.

Salton (1970) lists seven parameters that affect the cost of an actual on-line interaction:

a)   the maximum number of simultaneously active users;
b)   the response time (elapsed time to completion) when less than one "time slice" is needed to complete the task (a time slice is a time period made available by the system to a given program; tasks which are not completed in a given time slice are disconnected and must reenter an input queue before a new time slice is allocated);
c)   the average task input rate;
d)   the average processor time required to complete tasks needing less than one time slice for completion;
e)   the ratio of tasks requiring less than one time slice to completion to total number of simultaneously active users;
f)   the elapsed time multiplication factor, that is the excess of time needed to complete a given task requiring more than one time slice in a given task mix, over the time needed by that task assuming it were the only one active in the system;
g)   the processor elapsed time to completion, that is the time elapsed between entering the last character of a task at a terminal and receiving the first character of the final output at the terminal (pp. 34, 35).

Salton claims that no cost models have so far been constructed with sufficient sophistication to include the foregoing types of parameters.

Cuadra (1971) points out that both a large computer and large data bases are needed "to provide any significant number of users with any significant amount of service." The per hour charge for the computer is not great providing that a large number of users are interrogating the system all the time it is available. If the number of users drops, the cost per search increases dramatically. It is expensive to keep very large bibliographic data bases on-line constantly. Data storage is a very costly component of the total system expenses. Given a data base that occupies $2\frac{1}{2}$ IBM 2314 disk packs, on-line for 8 hours a day, computer time would cost only about $200 a day, but storage costs could exceed $600 a day. Communications charges are also expensive. In searching a remote data base, telephone line charges may very well be greater than the cost of using the computer. More efficient and economical methods of transmitting large volumes of data are sorely needed.

Cuadra indicates, however, that time-sharing has reduced the costs of effective machine searching dramatically. In 1961, it might have cost $600 an hour to exploit a large bibliographic data base interactively because one had to buy the entire computer for that period. Not only have computer costs come down since then, but time-sharing allows multiple users to have access to the computer. By sharing the file with 25–30 other users, and in effect splitting the costs, we can now search large files at greater speeds for perhaps $20–40 per hour in computer cost.

Reitman (1972) mentions costs of $4–6 per terminal connect hour for use of the AUTONOTE system at the University of Michigan. At present, the cost of storing the equivalent of 100 $8\frac{1}{2} \times 11$ inch pages of double-spaced typed text is about $1.15 per week.

In making the AIM–TWX system available to medical centers in the United States, the National Library of Medicine paid all computer charges involved. The individual centers paid for the communications terminals and for all line charges. Given an existing terminal,* and therefore no purchase or rental charges for equipment, a typical 15 minute search may cost the user about $9. Communications costs range from $0.20 to $0.70 per minute for TWX; if teletypewriters connected by telephone are used, communications costs could range from the cost of a local call to about $0.45 per minute, depending on the distance between the user and the computer.

In March 1970, the NLM computer costs were about $6800 per month or $31 per terminal hour. A maximum of ten simultaneous users and a total of 10 terminal hours per day were permitted at that time. If the system were used to its fullest capacity, the system cost would be 52¢ per terminal minute for each of the ten simultaneous users.

---

*In 1972, teletypewriters (10 characters per second) could be leased for between $50 and $70 per month, although some models cost as much as $115 per month. A portable terminal, Execuport 300, manufactured by Computer Transceiver Systems Inc., can be purchased for $3800 or leased for $199 per month. Similar portable, fast (up to 30 characters per second), and quiet typewriter terminals are available from Computer Devices Inc. and Texas Instruments Inc., among others, and are comparable in cost. The purchase price on a video display terminal for alphameric data is likely to be in the range of $2000–15,000, depending on the degree of sophistication. Costs of CRT display are coming down rapidly, however, and it is now possible to rent some CRT devices for as little as the rental cost of a standard typewriter terminal.

Given a typical 15 minute search, the cost in computer time (borne by NLM), is $7.75, whereas the connection time cost (borne by the user) varies between $0.10 (for a local telephone call) to $9.00 for the most expensive TWX connection. The total cost per search is thus in the range of $8–17. This does not include charges for rental of a terminal. Nor does this figure take into account the costs of acquisition, indexing, and maintenance of the data base. On a longer-term basis, NLM projects that computer time for a typical short on-line search, using an IBM 370, could be less than $1, and that a multiplexing communications network could cut line charges to about one-fifth of their present level for a typical user. These projections are based on total monthly hardware costs of $12,000, a system available 8 hours per day, and an average of 30 users. The cost per terminal hour would then be $3.33. In 1973, NLM announced its intention of charging users at the rate of $6 per hour for MEDLINE use, with an additional charge levied for off-line printing.

Bridegam and Meyerhoff (1970) quote figures for library participation in the SUNY Biomedical Communication Network based on a network charge of $5000 a year for each terminal. This price includes rental of the IBM 2740 terminal itself, telephone line charges, and computer time. At the University of Rochester, based on a projected volume of 1368 searches per year per terminal, the average cost per search was calculated to be $3.65. At the State University of New York at Buffalo, based on a projected 1669 searches per year per terminal, the average cost per search was calculated to be $3.00.

Some of the most comprehensive cost figures on the operation of an on-line system have been prepared by Robert Landau for the Science Information Association (1972). The figures were calculated for the use of the Battelle system, BASIS-70. The basic parameters of the cost figures are presented in Table 18.6. Based on the acquisition of an existing data base in machine-readable form (e.g., from an information wholesaler), the table shows costs for initial file and index building and for updating costs. Operating costs are based on terminal cost of $150 per month, an average query time of 10 minutes, line charges of $1.50 per query, and computer connect time at 50¢ per minute. Based on a daily access of 15 hours, operating costs are presented in this table as functions of the number of terminals in use, the number of queries per month, the number of records in the file, and the length of the records in the file. Thus, system A3-1 has one terminal and handles 1000 queries per month. The average monthly cost of operating this system will be $6750 for a data base of 1000 and $9800 for a data base of 500,000. Given the data base size of 500,000, the cost per query would be a comparatively low figure of $9.80 on the average.

TABLE 18.6. BASIS-70 Cost Schedule

I. Initial Costs (file and index building):
   1. $250/million characters from pre-formatted tape file, or
   2. $1500 to prepare conversion program + $250/million characters

II. Updating Costs: $150-250/million new characters

III. Operating Costs: Includes: Terminal Cost of $150/mo./Terminal;
   Line Charges of $1.50/query; Computer connect
   time at 50¢/minute and Data Base Storage Costs
   (variable); 15 hrs./day access; average query
   time: 10 minutes.

   TOTAL COST IN $/MONTH
   Each Class A record contains 200 characters
   of bibliographic material; Class B, 1000
   characters of biblio material and an abstract;
   Class C, 1000 characters of full indexed
   textual material.

System Class	No. of Terminals	No. of Queries per Month	Number of Records in File				
			1000	5000	25,000	100,000	500,000
A1-1	10		315	365	965	2465	3365
A2-1	100		900	950	1550	3050	3950
A3-1	1000		6750	6800	7400	8900	9800
A1-5	10		915	965	1565	3065	3965
A2-5	100		1500	1550	2150	3650	4550
A3-5	1000		7350	7400	8000	9500	10,400
A1-10	10		1665	1715	2315	3815	4715
A2-10	100		2250	2300	2900	4400	5300
A3-10	1000		8100	8150	8750	10,250	11,150
B1-1	10		415	1215	2815	3715	9315
B2-1	100		1000	1800	3400	4300	9900
B3-1	1000		6850	7650	9250	10,150	15,750
B1-5	10		1015	1815	3415	4315	9915
B2-5	100		1600	2400	4000	4900	10,500
B3-5	1000		7450	8250	9850	10,750	16,350
B1-10	10		1765	2565	4165	5065	10,665
B2-10	100		2350	3150	4750	5650	11,250
B3-10	1000		8200	9000	10,600	11,500	17,100
C1-1	10		465	1415	2915	4065	11,015
C2-1	100		1050	2000	3500	4650	11,600
C3-1	1000		6900	7850	9350	10,500	17,450
C1-5	10		1065	2015	3515	4665	11,615
C2-5	100		1650	2600	4100	5250	12,250
C3-5	1000		7500	8450	9950	11,100	18,050
C1-10	10		1815	2765	4265	5415	12,365
C2-10	100		2400	3350	4850	6000	12,950
C3-10	1000		8250	9200	10,700	11,850	18,800

Source: Landau (1972). Reproduced by permission of Robert Landau.

Table 18.7 presents more detailed figures for monthly costs based on number of terminals (1, 10, and 20), access time (i.e., the number of hours the data base is actually loaded and available), connect time (i.e., the number of hours the system is actually being interrogated), and data base size in millions of characters.

TABLE 18.7.   Monthly Costs for BASIS-70 for Varying Number of Terminals, Access Time, Connect Time, and Size of Data Base

.5hr.Connect	Data Base Size in Millions of Characters								
	1	2	5	10	20	50	100	200	500
2 hr.Access									
1 Terminal	350	400	550	750	900	1,000	1,175	1,500	2,600
10 Terminals	305	310	325	345	360	370	387	420	530
20 Terminals	302	305	317	322	330	335	344	360	415
4 hr.Access									
1 Terminal	400	500	800	1,200	1,500	1,700	2,050	2,700	4,900
10 Terminals	310	320	350	390	420	440	475	540	760
20 Terminals	305	310	325	345	360	370	387	420	530
8 hr.Access									
1 Terminal	500	700	1,300	2,100	2,700	3,100	3,800	5,100	9,500
10 Terminals	320	340	400	480	540	580	650	780	1,220
20 Terminals	310	320	350	390	420	440	475	540	760
1 hr.Connect									
2 hr.Access									
1 Terminal	650	700	850	1,050	1,200	1,300	1,475	1,800	2,900
10 Terminals	605	610	625	645	660	670	687	720	830
20 Terminals	603	605	613	623	630	635	644	660	715
4 hr.Access									
1 Terminal	700	800	1,100	1,500	1,800	2,000	2,350	3,000	5,200
10 Terminals	610	620	650	690	720	740	775	840	1,060
20 Terminals	605	610	625	645	660	670	688	720	830
8 hr.Access									
1 Terminal	800	1,000	1,600	2,400	3,000	3,400	4,100	5,400	9,800
10 Terminals	620	640	700	780	840	880	950	1,080	1,520
20 Terminals	610	620	650	690	720	740	775	840	1,060
2 hr.Connect									
2 hr.Access									
1 Terminal	1,250	1,300	1,450	1,650	1,800	1,900	2,075	2,400	3,500
10 Terminals	1,205	1,210	1,225	1,245	1,260	1,270	1,288	1,320	1,430
20 Terminals	1,203	1,205	1,213	1,223	1,230	1,235	1,244	1,260	1,315
4 hr. Access									
1 Terminal	1,300	1,400	1,700	2,100	2,400	2,600	2,950	3,600	5,800
10 Terminals	1,210	1,220	1,250	1,290	1,320	1,340	1,375	1,440	1,660
20 Terminals	1,205	1,210	1,225	1,245	1,260	1,270	1,287	1,320	1,430
8 hr.Access									
1 Terminal	1,400	1,600	2,200	3,000	3,600	4,000	4,700	6,000	10,400
10 Terminals	1,220	1,240	1,300	1,380	1,440	1,480	1,550	1,680	2,120
20 Terminals	1,210	1,220	1,250	1,290	1,320	1,340	1,375	1,440	1,660

These costs are based on the following assumptions and charge rates:
(1) 50¢/minute terminal connect time to the BASIS-70 system in Columbus, Ohio; (2) Storage costs of $100/million characters for the first ten million characters ranging down to $7/million characters for 50 million or more characters (e.g., cost for 50 million characters is $2600/month); (3) Because of the requirement for inverted indexes and related additional files, it is assumed that the data to be stored and charged for is two times the input data base, and the above figures reflect this calculation.

These costs do not include telephone line charges to Columbus, Ohio, or the cost of the terminal itself.

SOURCE: Landau (1972). Reproduced by permission of Robert Landau.

Tables 18.8–18.10 show an even finer breakdown for 1, 10, and 20 terminal systems. Here costs per search are shown for varying levels of access time, connect time, data base size, and actual searching time (6 minutes or 12 minutes). Given a single terminal, 2 hours of access time, and 2 hours of connect time (representing optimum use of the available time), the cost of a 6 minute search will vary from $3.13 to $8.75, depending on the size of the data base.

TABLE 18.8.   BASIS-70 Costs for 1 Terminal System

				Millions of Characters					
	1	2	5	10	20	50	100	200	500
2 hr. access									
.5hr.connect									
Cost	350	400	550	750	900	1,000	1,175	1,500	2,600
6 Min.Search	3.50	4.00	5.50	7.50	9.00	10.00	11.75	15.00	26.00
12Min.Search	7.00	8.00	11.00	15.00	18.00	20.00	23.50	30.00	52.00
1 hr.connect									
Cost	650	700	850	1,050	1,200	1,300	1,475	1,800	2,900
6 Min.Search	3.25	3.50	4.25	5.25	6.00	6.50	7.38	9.00	14.50
12Min.Search	6.50	7.00	8.50	10.50	12.00	13.00	14.75	18.00	29.00
2 hr.connect									
Cost	1,250	1,300	1,450	1,650	1,800	1,900	2,075	2,400	3,500
6 Min.Search	3.13	3.25	3.63	4.13	4.50	4.75	5.19	6.00	8.75
12Min.Search	6.25	6.50	7.25	8.25	9.00	9.50	10.37	12.00	17.50
4 hr. access									
.5hr.connect									
Cost	400	500	800	1,200	1,500	1,700	2,050	2,700	4,900
6 Min.Search	4.00	5.00	8.00	12.00	15.00	17.00	20.50	27.00	49.00
12Min.Search	8.00	10.00	16.00	24.00	30.00	34.00	41.00	54.00	98.00
1 hr.connect									
Cost	700	800	1,100	1,500	1,800	2,000	2,350	3,000	5,200
6 Min.Search	3.50	4.00	5.50	7.50	9.00	10.00	11.75	15.00	26.00
12Min.Search	7.00	8.00	11.00	15.00	18.00	20.00	23.50	30.00	52.00
2 hr.connect									
Cost	1,300	1,400	1,700	2,100	2,400	2,600	2,950	3,600	5,800
6 Min.Search	3.25	3.50	4.25	5.25	6.00	6.50	7.38	9.00	14.50
12Min.Search	6.50	7.00	8.50	10.50	12.00	13.00	14.75	18.00	29.00
8 hr. access									
.5hr.connect									
Cost	500	700	1,300	2,100	2,700	3,100	3,800	5,100	9,500
6 Min.Search	5.00	7.00	13.00	21.00	27.00	31.00	38.00	51.00	95.00
12 Min.Search	10.00	14.00	26.00	42.00	54.00	62.00	76.00	102.00	190.00
1 hr.connect									
Cost	800	1,000	1,600	2,400	3,000	3,400	4,100	5,400	9,800
6 Min.Search	4.00	5.00	8.00	12.00	15.00	17.00	20.50	27.00	49.00
12Min.Search	8.00	10.00	16.00	24.00	30.00	34.00	41.00	54.00	98.00
2 hr.connect									
Cost	1,400	1,600	2,200	3,000	3,600	4,000	4,700	6,000	10,400
6 Min.Search	3.50	4.00	5.50	7.50	9.00	10.00	11.75	15.00	26.00
12Min.Search	7.00	8.00	11.00	15.00	18.00	20.00	23.50	30.00	52.00

SOURCE: Landau (1972). Reproduced by permission of Robert Landau.

In all of these tables, the cost of connect time is calculated on the basis of complete computer costs, including use of all peripheral devices, and not just upon the cost of CPU time.

Figure 18.2, also provided by Landau, is an interesting plot of operating costs for a class of system operating on five terminals. The plot shows cost per query curves and system cost lines based on the variables of number of

TABLE 18.9. BASIS-70 Costs for 10 Terminal System

	1	2	5	Millions of Characters 10	20	50	100	200	500
2 hr.Access									
.5hr.Connect									
Total Cost	3,050	3,100	3,250	3,450	3,600	3,700	3,875	4,200	5,300
Cost/User	305	310	325	345	360	370	387	420	530
6 Min.Search	3.05	3.10	3.25	3.45	3.60	3.70	3.87	4.20	5.30
12Min.Search	6.10	6.20	6.50	6.90	7.20	7.40	7.75	8.40	10.60
1 hr.Connect									
Total Cost	6,050	6,100	6,250	6,450	6,600	6,700	6,875	7,200	8,300
Cost/User	605	610	625	645	660	670	687	720	830
6 Min.Search	3.03	3.05	3.13	3.23	3.30	3.35	3.44	3.60	4.15
12Min.Search	6.05	6.10	6.25	6.45	6.60	6.70	6.87	7.20	8.30
2 hr.Connect									
Total Cost	12,050	12,100	12,250	12,450	12,600	12,700	12,875	13,200	14,300
Cost/User	1,205	1,210	1,225	1,245	1,260	1,270	1,288	1,320	1,430
6 Min.Search	3.02	3.03	3.07	3.12	3.15	3.18	3.22	3.30	3.58
12Min.Search	6.03	6.05	6.13	6.23	6.30	6.35	6.44	6.60	7.15
4 hr.Access									
.5hr.Connect									
Total Cost	3,100	3,200	3,500	3,900	4,200	4,400	4,750	5,400	7,600
Cost/User	310	320	350	390	420	440	475	540	760
6 Min.Search	3.10	3.20	3.50	3.90	4.20	4.40	4.75	5.40	7.60
12Min.Search	6.20	6.40	7.00	7.80	8.40	8.80	9.50	10.20	15.20
1 hr.Connect									
Total Cost	6,100	6,200	6,500	6,900	7,200	7,400	7,750	8,400	10,600
Cost/User	610	620	650	690	720	740	775	840	1,060
6 Min.Search	3.05	3.10	3.25	3.45	3.60	3.70	3.88	4.20	5.30
12Min.Search	6.10	6.20	6.50	6.90	7.20	7.40	7.75	8.40	10.60
2 hr.Connect									
Total Cost	12,100	12,200	12,500	12,900	13,200	13,400	13,750	14,400	16,600
Cost/User	1,210	1,220	1,250	1,290	1,320	1,340	1,375	1,440	1,660
6 Min.Search	3.02	3.05	3.13	3.23	3.30	3.35	3.44	3.60	4.15
12Min.Search	6.05	6.10	6.25	6.45	6.60	6.70	6.87	7.20	8.30
8 hr.Access									
.5hr.Connect									
Total Cost	3,200	3,400	4,000	4,800	5,400	5,800	6,500	7,800	12,200
Cost/User	320	340	400	480	540	580	650	780	1,220
6 Min.Search	3.20	3.40	4.00	4.80	5.40	5.80	6.50	7.80	12.20
12Min.Search	6.40	6.80	8.00	9.60	10.80	11.60	13.00	15.60	24.40
1 hr.Connect									
Total Cost	6,200	6,400	7,000	7,800	8,400	8,800	9,500	10,800	15,200
Cost/User	620	640	700	780	840	880	950	1,080	1,520
6 Min.Search	3.10	3.20	3.50	3.90	4.20	4.40	4.75	5.40	7.60
12Min.Search	6.20	6.40	7.00	7.80	8.40	8.80	9.50	10.80	15.20
2 hr.Connect									
Total Cost	12,200	12,400	13,000	13,800	14,400	14,800	15,500	16,800	21,200
Cost/User	1,220	1,240	1,300	1,380	1,440	1,480	1,550	1,680	2,120
6 Min.Search	3.05	3.10	3.25	3.45	3.60	3.70	3.87	4.20	5.30
12Mins.Search	6.10	6.20	6.50	6.90	7.20	7.40	7.75	8.40	10.60

SOURCE: Landau (1972). Reproduced by permission of Robert Landau.

queries per month and number of records stored. For comparison, a single plot of cost per query and overall system cost for a 10 terminal system is superimposed on the diagram.

Finally, in Table 18.11, Landau presents a rough cost calculation sheet which accommodates various factors that might influence costs, various system configurations (based on the availability of records in various forms

TABLE 18.10. BASIS-70 Costs for 20 Terminal System

				Millions of Characters					
	1	2	5	10	20	50	100	200	500
2 hr.Access									
.5hr.Connect									
Total Cost	6,050	6,100	6,250	6,450	6,600	6,700	6,875	7,200	8,300
Cost/User	302	305	317	322	330	335	344	360	415
6 Min.Search	3.02	3.05	3.17	3.22	3.30	3.35	3.44	3.60	4.15
12Min.Search	6.04	6.10	6.25	6.45	6.60	6.70	6.88	7.20	8.30
1 hr.Connect									
Total Cost	12,050	12,100	12,250	12,450	12,600	12,700	12,875	13,200	14,300
Cost/User	603	605	613	623	630	635	644	660	715
6 Min.Search	3.02	3.03	3.07	3.12	3.15	3.18	3.22	3.30	3.58
12Min.Search	6.03	6.05	6.13	6.23	6.30	6.35	6.44	6.60	7.15
2 hr.Connect									
Total Cost	24,050	24,100	24,250	24,450	24,600	24,700	24,875	25,200	26,300
Cost/User	1,203	1,205	1,213	1,223	1,230	1,235	1,244	1,260	1,315
6 Min.Search	3.01	3.02	3.04	3.06	3.08	3.09	3.11	3.15	3.29
12Min.Search	6.02	6.03	6.07	6.12	6.15	6.18	6.22	6.30	6.58
4 hr.Access									
.5hr.Connect									
Total Cost	6,100	6,200	6,500	6,900	7,200	7,400	7,750	8,400	10,600
Cost/User	305	310	325	345	360	370	387	420	530
6 Min.Search	3.05	3.10	3.25	3.45	3.60	3.70	3.87	4.20	5.30
12Min.Search	6.10	6.20	6.50	6.90	7.20	7.40	7.75	8.40	10.60
1 hr.Connect									
Total Cost	12,100	12,200	12,500	12,900	13,200	13,400	13,750	14,400	16,600
Cost/User	605	610	625	645	660	670	688	720	830
6 Min.Search	3.03	3.05	3.13	3.23	3.30	3.35	3.44	3.60	4.15
12Min.Search	6.05	6.10	6.25	6.45	6.60	6.70	6.88	7.20	8.30
2 hr.Connect									
Total Cost	24,100	24,200	24,500	24,900	25,200	25,400	25,750	26,400	28,600
Cost/User	1,205	1,210	1,225	1,245	1,260	1,270	1,287	1,320	1,430
6 Min.Search	3.02	3.03	3.07	3.12	3.15	3.18	3.22	3.30	3.63
12Min.Search	6.03	6.05	6.13	6.23	6.30	6.35	6.44	6.60	7.15
8 hr.Access									
.5hr.Connect									
Total Cost	6,200	6,400	7,000	7,800	8,400	8,800	9,500	10,800	15,200
Cost/User	310	320	350	390	420	440	475	540	760
6 Min.Search	3.10	3.20	3.50	3.90	4.20	4.40	4.75	5.40	7.60
12Min.Search	6.20	6.40	7.00	7.80	8.40	8.80	9.50	10.80	15.20
1 hr. Connect									
Total Cost	12,200	12,400	13,000	13,800	14,400	14,800	15,500	16,800	21,200
Cost/User	610	620	650	690	720	740	775	840	1,060
6 Min.Search	3.05	3.10	3.25	3.45	3.60	3.70	3.88	4.20	5.30
12Min.Search	6.10	6.20	6.50	6.90	7.20	7.40	7.75	8.40	10.60
2 hr.Connect									
Total Cost	24,200	24,400	25,000	25,800	26,400	26,800	27,500	28,800	33,200
Cost/User	1,210	1,220	1,250	1,290	1,320	1,340	1,375	1,440	1,660
6 Min.Search	3.03	3.05	3.13	3.18	3.30	3.35	3.44	3.60	4.15
12Min.Search	6.05	6.10	6.25	6.45	6.60	6.70	6.88	7.20	8.30

SOURCE: Landau (1972). Reproduced by permission of Robert Landau.

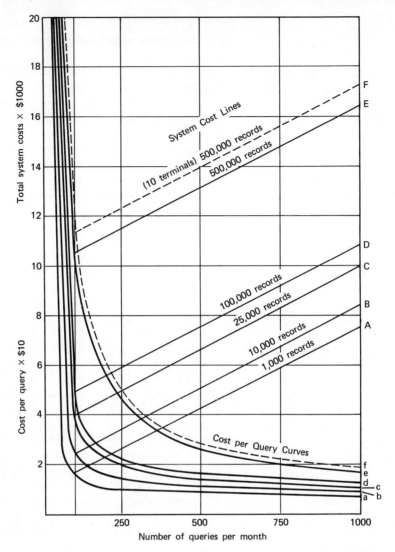

Figure 18.2. Plot of operating costs for BASIS-70 operating on 5 terminals (values for 10 terminals are indicated by dashed line and curve). Reproduced by permission of Robert Landau.

System Configurations:	Scaled Ratings of Factors in terms of:
A. Manual index and hard copy records (all manual)	a. Degree of influence or significance of factor
B. Manual index and micro-image (MI) records	
C. Mechanized index and hard copy records	b. Proportion of factor cost to total system cost
D. Mechanized index and manual MI records	
E. Mechanized index and mechanized MI records	0 Not applicable
F. Computer index and hard copy records	1 Trivial
G. Computer index and manual MI records	2 Low
H. Computer index and mechanized MI records	3 Moderate
I. Computer index and automated MI records	4 Significant
J. Computer index and computer records (all digital)	

TABLE 18.11.   Cost Calculation Sheet for an On-Line Retrieval System

	SYSTEM CONFIGURATIONS																			
FACTORS	A		B		C		D		E		F		G		H		I		J	
Scaled rating →	a	b	a	b	a	b	a	b	a	b	a	b	a	b	a	b	a	b	a	b
1. Size of data base (entry and storage costs)																				
2. Number of queries																				
3. Response time requirements																				
4. Data preparation costs																				
5. Specificity of query (e.g., by number, name, subject, etc.)																				
6. Graphic information requirements																				
7. Simultaneous access by a number of people (time share vs. multiple micro-image copies)																				
8. Number of terminals (or work stations)																				
9. Retrieval precision required																				
10. Acceptable recall ratio																				
11. Subject knowledge of user																				
12. Distance from user to data base																				
13. Access time per day required																				
14. Conversion program required																				
15. Complexity and number of elements in each record																				
16. Number of records in the file																				
17. Degree of structure of index																				
18. Depth of indexing required																				
19. Complexity of search rules																				
20. Need for boolean logic																				
21. Need for full text searching																				
22. Need for reiterative querying																				
23. Need for word distance searching																				
24. Need for report generation																				
25. Need for AND, OR, and NOT logic																				
26. Need for printed information																				
27. Need for arithmetic capabilities																				
28. Need for auxiliary notation																				
29. Need for calculation capability																				
30. Need for interfile logic																				
31. Speed of communication system																				
32. Distance from user to computer																				
33. Volatility of file (amount and frequency of update)																				
34. Growth of file																				

SOURCE: Landau (1972). Reproduced by permission of Robert Landau.

(*Footnotes opposite*)

—manual, digital, microimage), and scaled ratings of the various factors. This type of calculation sheet is of value as a reminder of various factors that may need to be taken into consideration in a complete cost analysis. The table contains some redundancy, however (e.g., factors 20 and 25 duplicate each other).

Some further cost figures are presented by Thompson (1970). The system discussed is located at the International Labour Office, Geneva, Switzerland, and is known as ISIS (Integrated Scientific Information Service). Some 31,500 bibliographic records (as of September 1969) exist on magnetic disk and are used to generate a variety of printed indexes as well as for retrieval purposes. Retrieval may be by batch or on-line mode, using an IBM 1050 terminal. The computer is an IBM 360/30. Total development costs were calculated to be $169,000 and total data preparation costs to be $181,125. In calculating the actual costs of on-line searches, Thompson assigns 40% of the total costs to the retrieval function and 60% to other bibliographic activities, including publication and production of catalog cards. To arrive at annual costs, the development costs and the data preparation costs are distributed over a 10 year period.

The summary cost figures for on-line searching are shown in Table 18.12 on a cost per search basis. In comparison, Thompson quotes an average figure of $65 for the conduct of manual searches.

Some cost figures on the U.S. Defense Documentation Center on-line system have been given by Powers (1971). Figure 18.3 presents costs per request for three terminals within DDC itself, for searches conducted in a 3

TABLE 18.12. Summary Costs for On-Line Searching at the International Labour Office, Geneva

		Per search		
	Per year	15 per day	20 per day	40 per day
(a) Development cost (one-tenth of 40% of $169,000)	$6760	$2.03	$1.52	$0.76
(b) Data preparation cost (one-tenth of 40% of $181,125)	$7245	$2.18	$1.63	$0.82
(c) Hardware cost (40% of $15,000)	$6000	$1.80	$1.35	$0.68
(d) Computer time (CPU) (12 minutes per search)		$0.60	$0.60	$0.60
(e) Staff time to formulate questions on terminal		$1.40	$1.40	$1.40
(f) Computer time to print results		$1.00	$1.00	$1.00
		$9.01	$7.50	$5.46

SOURCE: Thompson (1970). Reproduced by permission of Microforms Marketing Corporation Inc.

month period in 1971. Note how the cost per request is volume-dependent. An average of three search statements is needed to complete a request. Figure 18.4 presents similar data for three terminals outside DDC. Here costs are much higher because of the land line communications involved.

Finally, some cost figures for on-line searching have been prepared by the National Institute of Neurological Diseases and Stroke. These figures relate to a proposed system based on abstracts of the neurology literature, which would be a considerable extension of the existing EARS (see Chapter Five). Table 18.13 gives approximate costs for the use of various terminals with varying workloads, and Table 18.14 shows approximate computer costs for the various terminal systems. Figure 18.5 shows monthly computer and terminal cost for five different types of terminals plotted against volume of use. Note how the combined computer and terminal costs for different workloads can affect choice of a terminal system. Terminal selection should consider a total computer–phone–terminal cost and not just the terminal cost only. Figure 18.6 is a log–log plot of costs per query against volume of use for three rates of transmission (telephone).

Cost-Effectiveness

A cost-effectiveness analysis seeks to increase the value received (effectiveness) for the resources expended (cost). We can improve the cost-effectiveness of an information system in two ways:

TABLE 18.13. Approximate Costs for Projected On-Line Retrieval System in Neurology—Terminals and Workloads Are Varied

Terminal system	Approximate monthly rental ($)	Approximate terminal cost per query for different workloads ($)			
		10 queries per month	20 queries per month	40 queries per month	60 queries per month
Typewriter, 10 characters per second	75	7.50	3.75	1.90	1.25
Typewriter, 15 characters per second	100	10.00	5.00	2.50	1.70
Typewriter, 30 characters per second	170	17.00	8.50	4.25	2.80
CRT with 30 character per second printer	170	17.00	8.50	4.25	2.80
CRT with 30 character per second printer and tape cassette	250	25.00	12.50	6.25	4.25

Source: National Institute of Neurological Diseases and Stroke.

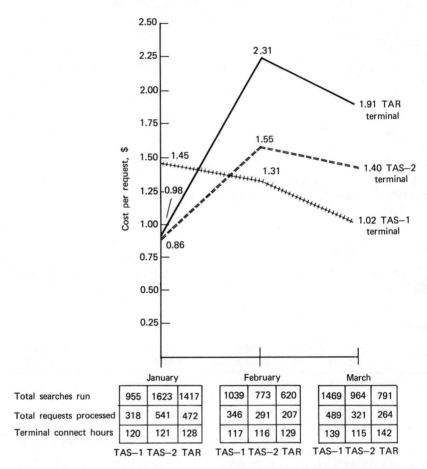

	January			February			March		
	TAS–1	TAS–2	TAR	TAS–1	TAS–2	TAR	TAS–1	TAS–2	TAR
Total searches run	955	1623	1417	1039	773	620	1469	964	791
Total requests processed	318	541	472	346	291	207	489	321	264
Terminal connect hours	120	121	128	117	116	129	139	115	142

Figure 18.3. DDC on-line searching costs for in-house terminals. (A request processed is a complete machine action to satisfy the user's requirement. A request averages three computer search runs.) Reproduced from Powers (1973) by permission of the U.S. Defense Documentation Center.

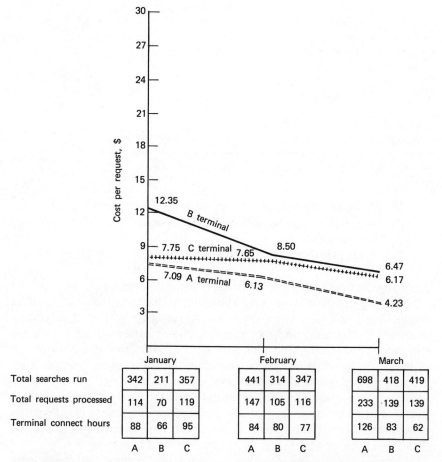

Figure 18.4. DDC on-line searching costs for remote terminals. (A request processed is a complete machine action to satisfy the user's requirement. A request averages three computer search runs.) Reproduced from Powers (1973) by permission of the U.S. Defense Documentation Center.

TABLE 18.14. Approximate Computer Costs Estimated for Various Terminal Systems for Projected On-Line Retrieval System in Neurology

Terminal system	Approximate throughput, queries per hour	Approximate cost per query at $35 per hour, $
Typewriter, 10 characters per second	3.5	10.00
Typewriter, 15 characters per second	4	9.00
Typewriter, 30 characters per second	6	6.00
CRT with 30 character per second printer	8	4.50
CRT with 30 character per second printer and tape cassette	12	3.00

SOURCE: National Institute of Neurological Diseases and Stroke.

1. Maintain the present performance level (say, in terms of recall, precision, and response time) while reducing the costs of operating the system.
2. Hold operating costs constant while raising the average performance level.

The cost-effectiveness considerations applicable to an on-line system are not substantially different from those applicable to any other type of retrieval system. The cost-effectiveness analysis of any information system involves a study of payoff factors, tradeoffs, breakeven points, and diminishing returns. Cost-effectiveness analysis can be applied to various aspects or components of the complete retrieval system, including the coverage of the data base, indexing policy (particularly the factors of indexing time, exhaustivity of indexing, the professional level of the indexing staff, and the quality-control procedures), index language, searching procedures, and mode of interaction between the user and the system. These aspects have been discussed in some detail by Lancaster (1971) and will not be repeated here.

There are a number of possible methods of designing and operating a retrieval system in such a way that it will produce acceptable results (e.g., an acceptable level of recall at a tolerable precision). There are a number of possible tradeoffs between various processes (e.g., indexing and vocabulary effort versus searching effort). The major tradeoff is the very general one between input costs and output costs. Almost invariably, economies in input procedures will result in an increased burden on output processes and thus output costs. Conversely, greater care in input processing (which will usually imply increased input costs) can be expected to improve output efficiency and reduce output costs. Some possible tradeoffs are listed below:

1. A carefully controlled and structured index language versus free use of uncontrolled keywords. The controlled vocabulary requires effort in construction and maintenance and is more expensive to apply in indexing. It takes longer, on the whole, to select terms from a controlled vocabulary, which may involve a lookup operation, than it does to assign keywords freely; moreover, keyword indexing may require less qualified personnel than the use of a more sophisticated controlled vocabulary. The controlled vocabulary, however, saves time and effort at the time of output. Natural language or keyword searching, without the benefit of a controlled vocabulary with classificatory structure, puts an increased burden on the searcher, who is virtually forced into the position of constructing a segment of a controlled vocabulary each time he prepares a search strategy (e.g., he thinks of all possible ways in which "petrochemicals" or "textile industry" could be expressed by keywords or natural language text). Likewise, the uncontrolled use of keywords may lead to reduced average search precision and thus may require additional effort and cost in scanning irrelevant citations at the terminal.

2. Rigid quality control of indexing (e.g., by a revision operation) versus indexing without any review procedure. Again, the review will increase the indexing costs but presumably save output costs by reducing time necessary to weed out obvious irrelevancy. Whether the input review is justified economically can only be determined by an evaluation of the number of indexing errors occurring and the number of these that could be corrected by a checking operation.

3. A highly specific, controlled vocabulary versus a relatively broad, controlled vocabulary. The former is generally more expensive to create, maintain, and apply. The more specific the vocabulary, the more difficult it becomes to achieve indexing consistency and the higher the level of the personnel that may be needed to apply it. On the other hand, a highly specific vocabulary may allow high search precision and thus save on searching time.

Many different factors enter into the decision as to whether to put emphasis on the input processes or the output processes of an information system. The most important considerations are probably the following:

1. *Volume.* The volumes of concern are the volumes of documents indexed and the volumes of requests processed annually. In the extreme situation of many documents indexed but comparatively few requests handled, it would be rational (all other things being equal) to economize on input costs and put an additional load on

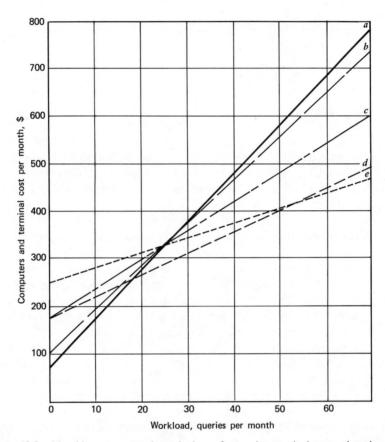

Figure 18.5. Monthly computer and terminal cost for varying terminal types, plotted against volume of use for a projected on-line retrieval system in the field of neurology: (*a*) typewriter (10 characters per second) at 3.5 queries per hour; (*b*) typewriter (15 characters per second) at 4 queries per hour; (*c*) typewriter (30 characters per second) at 6 queries per hour; (*d*) CRT and 30 character per second printer at 8 queries per hour; (*e*) CRT and 30 character per second printer and tape cassette at 12 queries per hour. Reproduced by permission of the National Institute of Neurological Diseases and Stroke.

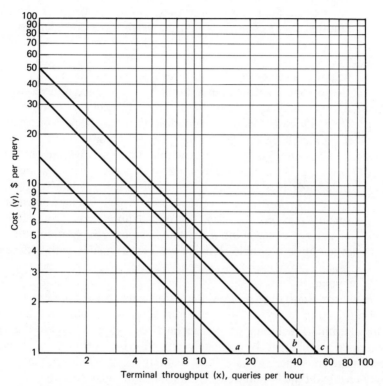

Figure 18.6. Log–log plot of costs per query against volume of use for three rates of transmission (telephone) for a projected on-line retrieval system in the field of neurology: (*a*) $15 per hour; (*b*) $35 per hour; (*c*) $50 per hour. Reproduced by permission of the National Institute of Neurological Diseases and Stroke.

the output function. In the reverse situation—comparatively few documents input but many requests handled—the opposite would be true, and savings would be best effected at the output stage.

2. *Required input speed.* In certain situations, it is imperative that documents get into the system as rapidly as possible. This is certainly true, for example, in the situation in which the information system serves a dissemination (current awareness) function as in certain intelligence situations. Under these circumstances, it is likely that required speed of input would outweigh other considerations and that indexing economies would be adopted.

3. *Required output speed.* In other situations, rapid and accurate response may be vital (e.g., the case of the Poison Information Center) and no economies at input will be justified if these are likely to result in delayed response and reduced accuracy of output.

4. *By-products.* Under certain conditions, it may be possible to obtain a searchable data base very inexpensively. For example, we may be able to acquire a machine-readable data base, perhaps in natural language form, that is a by-product of some other operation (e.g., publishing or report preparation) or has been made available by some other information center. Even though the input format and quality may not be ideal for our requirements, from the cost-effectiveness viewpoint, if the data base is available at nominal cost, it might be desirable to make use of it (possibly with some slight modifications) and to expend greater effort on the searching operation.

Because the cost of an on-line interaction can be high at present, there is a lot of motivation to save on-line searching time. Aids to the searcher at the on-line terminal, including entry vocabularies, synonym tables, and term hierarchies, are likely to be extremely cost-effective. Although they may be expensive to construct, they are likely to repay their cost many times over by saving terminal time in hundreds or thousands of separate searches.

Clearly, for cost-effectiveness analysis, we need a unit cost figure that is sensitive to changes in the effectiveness of the system. One such figure is the unit cost per relevant citation retrieved. We have previously spoken of this in terms of user time at the terminal; that is, unit cost (in time) per relevant citation retrieved. This is a user-oriented measure of search effectiveness. It is also a useful measure to be taken into consideration in any evaluation of the cost-effectiveness of a retrieval system. However, if the user is paying the full cost of a search, his own time at the terminal will only be one element to be considered. The various cost elements discussed by Negus and Hall (1971) and by Higgins and Smith (1971) need to be taken into account in order to arrive at a true unit cost per relevant citation retrieved (C_R).

When we make changes to an information system (e.g., we change indexing policy or introduce new searching aids) to increase its average performance in terms of recall or precision, or both, these changes may reduce the cost per relevant citation retrieved. Thus, C_R is a useful unit by which we may express improvements in the cost-effectiveness of information systems.

This unit may be used to compare alternative operating modes within a system, or it may be used to compare the cost-effectiveness of two or more essentially different systems. Thus, we can use this measure to assess the economic effects of making changes to our indexing procedures, vocabulary, searching strategies, or mode of interaction with the user. Raising the average indexing exhaustivity, for example, may result in a substantial improvement in recall and, allowing for increased indexing costs, this in fact may mean a significant reduction in the cost per relevant citation retrieved.

Cost–Benefit Considerations

As previously mentioned, the benefits of an information service are usually difficult to measure. An organization funding an information center (e.g., a company funding an industrial library) must feel that the benefits of the service outweigh the costs of providing it. A particular individual weighs the potential benefits of an information service against the costs of using it. These costs may be monetary (e.g., fees imposed by the information center, computer costs, or telephone line charges) or they may be costs associated with his own time and convenience factors. If an information service requires too much effort on the user's part, he will abandon it and go elsewhere (Mooers' law again!).

Once the novelty of an on-line system has worn off, it will presumably be used only by those who feel that its potential benefits more than compensate for the costs associated with its use. Moreover, the system must yield results more cheaply or more easily than alternative methods that may be available to the user. In general, the benefits of well-designed on-line retrieval systems *are* likely to outweigh the costs of their use. For example, experiments with MEDLINE and AIM–TWX have shown that the on-line system attracts users who have never requested MEDLARS searches in the off-line, batch mode. These are users for whom the batch system is inappropriate and who require not comprehensive searches but a few pertinent references—and need them right away. Moreover, these users really have no convenient alternative source to go to. The printed *Index Medicus* is usually unsuitable, because most searches conducted on-line involve complex multidimensional relationships that are difficult to handle by conventional searching in a printed tool.

Some pertinent cost–benefit considerations relating to the AIM–TWX experiments have been discussed by Katter (1970) as follows:

> No matter whether a user is asked to verbally evaluate a system in absolute terms ("Do you like or dislike this system?") or in comparative terms ("How does this system compare with X?"), in his actual *consumer* behavior he eventually evaluates the system *comparatively*; he either stays with the innovation or he uses some alternative solution. It seems appropriate, therefore, to consider the possible comparative standards that underlie his evaluations. The user can be thought of as having more or less explicit or implicit, more or less real or imaginary, "standards" against which he is evaluating the new system. The operational implication of this point is that every effort should be made to find out what these standards actually are, and to make them as explicit as possible. It is important, for example, to know whether his comparisons are actually being made against his interpretation of previously existing conditions he believes would be feasible to attain, or against his interpretation of "ideal" conditions he might wish to see but doubts could exist.
>
> There has been discussion in the literature about whether the concepts of "cost" and of "benefit" can be clearly separated from one another. A negative or reduced cost *can* be thought of as a benefit; a reduced benefit *can* be thought of as a cost, especially if costs and benefits are being gauged in highly personal, subjective terms. Nevertheless, the concepts are useful, and we will define costs here as personal time, effort, inconvenience, embarrassment, and money payments spent or incurred by the user in getting information he wants. Benefits will be defined as the extent to which the user obtains the exhaustiveness, speed, accuracy, and form he desires in the information he receives. We will assume, on the basis of considerable evidence from many other research studies and from our own close questioning and observation of information users in many contexts, that the user typically evaluates an information service by comparing it, often quite unconsciously, with his available alternatives, and that his criteria of comparisons are highly informal estimates of costs and benefits, sometimes gross, sometimes refined, and variably explicit or implicit in his experience. The operational implications of this point are that every effort should be made to discover what these costs and benefit criteria actually are. This does not mean that we simply decide what they should be, and then get the user to verbalize his estimates of our versions of such criteria; the user's voting behavior in using or not using the system is not likely to square very well with his reported judgments about it unless we are very sensitive in deciding what we ask him to report about.
>
> The relationships between an individual's verbally expressed estimates of his personally experienced costs and benefits and his actual choice of related objects and courses of action are often not direct and simple. This is especially true for the introduction of an innovation into an already stabilized social system of practices, expectations, skills, and knowledge. Sometimes it appears that benefits assume a larger weight in actual choice behavior than the user professes them to have, but more often it appears that costs bode larger than they are professed to.

In this regard, studies of the interest patterns of professionals, (including specifically, physics graduates and medical specialists), show a consistent relationship between the individual's level of professional specialization and training, and his tendency to check more "Dislike" responses on interests-test items when presented with the alternatives "Like", "Indifferent", and "Dislike". One interpretation of these findings is that, for many very busy professionals, the development of more numerous active dislikes is a time-and-energy-conserving strategy (often unconscious) that is used because it results in a better focusing of his resources on a limited number of concerns. They are, in essence, persons who cannot afford to actively engage a new benefit or attraction on the horizon without first carefully considering the personal time and energy involved.

Observation also suggests that such energy focusing often plays a larger part in their lives than such individuals realize. Many wish to be more positive, expansive, and open to new and possibly relevant things than they have time to be. Sometimes they will profess interest in things toward which they are later unable to behave positively.

Some interesting predictions can be drawn from the above interpretations. Information user professionals of the kind just described can be asked to provide quantitative estimates, in the form of ratings, comparing different alternative information services; different costs and benefits can be clearly described, and the respondents asked to assign numerical ratings of the "magnitude" or "weight" they attribute to each. Each pair of system alternatives can then be compared on three values: their Cost/Cost ratio, their Benefit/Benefit ratio, and their Cost/Benefit//Cost/Benefit ratio. It is quite obvious that, over a wide range of cases, the latter "ratio of ratios" would be the best *single* predictor of the respondent's actual choice behavior. However, another, not so obvious, prediction is that Cost/Cost ratios will generally be better predictors of actual choice behavior than Benefit/Benefit ratios. More specifically, when the Cost/Benefit ratios between an existing system and a proposed innovation are judged by such respondents as being approximately in balance, the respondents' actual choice behavior will be better predicted by the Cost/Cost ratio than by the Benefit/Benefit ratio.

In other words, we are hypothesizing that the actual choice behavior of busy professionals is more sensitive to costs than to benefits. If this hypothesis is correct, the implication is that an innovation will probably not be successful if it offers only markedly improved *benefits* over the existing arrangements, at the same (or slightly increased) costs. To be successful, either the innovation's rated Cost/Benefit ratio must *markedly* exceed that of the existing system, or the Cost/Cost ratio must *markedly* favor the innovation. In the absence of one or the other or both of these conditions, a rated Benefit/Benefit ratio that clearly favors the innovation may not carry the day in actual choice-and-use behavior.

For the on-line introductory experiment, one implication of the preceding discussion is that we should try to be especially careful to select sites, make arrangements, and provide materials so that user's perceived Cost/Cost ratios are markedly favorable toward the on-line citation retrieval system. . . . Another implication is that during the course of the experiment we should pay special attention to data and responses that reflect the user's cost reactions, and try to adjust the system to eliminate as many user costs as possible.

In considering the user's perception of Cost/Cost ratios when he compares his existing services with the on-line facility, we have already discussed the subject-object role reversal that is sometimes experienced temporarily by new users. Provisions to help prevent this should be considered in the experimental plan. A second kind of user cost that is very important is frustrated access to the system; this occurs when the user expects that he will be able to use the system, and then finds he cannot. The service commitments, scheduling, instructions, stipulations, and promotional material for the experiment should all aim at ensuring that there will be a minimum of schedule conflict between users at a site, and that users at each site will experience a high percentage of successes in getting on to the time-sharing system when they try. Careful capacity estimates, detailed scheduling, and in-depth trouble-shooting backup will all help in this respect. Finally, the site personnel who manage, schedule, and operate the terminal and provide instructional assistance to users are of the utmost importance in helping to reduce the users' subjective costs. The cooperation of such personnel is essential to the success of the experiment, and the things that can be done to help gain their cooperation must also be spelled out in the plans for the experiment (pp. 16–19).*

As far as we are aware, only one study has attempted an analysis of some cost–performance–benefit factors for an on-line retrieval system. This study, of limited scope, was conducted on SUPARS and reported by Katzer (1971). The methodology is interesting, although the results themselves are surprisingly poor in terms of the cost involved in obtaining a particular level of recall. In the SUPARS study, system effectiveness is measured in terms of varying levels of recall, while costs are measured in terms of the total number of documents retrieved in achieving these various levels of recall. Thus, the cost is essentially the familiar precision ratio. However, Katzer goes beyond the precision ratio pure and simple by calculating the computer costs involved in searching for and printing various quantities of citations. Computer costs are calculated on CPU time plus use of input/output devices. A plot of recall versus total number of citations retrieved (a *search characteristic curve*) can thus be transformed into a plot of recall versus cost, which is interpreted as being a plot of effectiveness versus cost.

For any of the test searches, the cost of obtaining a particular recall ratio is estimated by the number of strategies times the cost of the average strategy plus the number of items printed times the cost of printing each item:

Estimated cost = (Average number of strategies)(Average cost/strategy)
        + (Number of documents printed)(Cost/documents printed)

---

*Reprinted by permission of System Development Corporation.

The average cost per strategy* was calculated to be $0.589 on the average when a *simple* strategy was used and $1.097 on the average when an *advanced* strategy was used.

A number of variables were investigated in the SUPARS study, including the variable of complexity of search logic and the variable of degree of relevance of a document to an information request. Over eighteen test searches, it was found that:

1. The average cost of obtaining 10% recall using simple strategies only (boolean AND and OR logic) was $2.38.
2. The average cost of obtaining 90% recall using simple strategies only was $34.62.
3. The average cost of obtaining 10% recall using advanced strategies (any form of boolean logic and any more sophisticated searching features, including positional indicators and term truncation) was $3.65.
4. The average cost of obtaining 90% recall using advanced strategies was $82.87.

Katzer concludes that, with a simple level of search logic, the experienced searcher can, on the average, obtain a given level of recall for less cost and with fewer nonrelevant documents retrieved (i.e., higher precision) than with an advanced level of search logic. It was also found that the cost of retrieving the documents judged more relevant was less than the cost of retrieving those judged less relevant.

A further SUPARS cost analysis, included in a report by Atherton, et al. (1972), compared the costs of obtaining various levels of recall using three possible searching approaches:

D   Only the bibliographic data base could be queried.
V   A vocabulary display (including word truncation capability) could be queried as well as the bibliographic data base.
S   Bibliographic data base, vocabulary display, and a display of search strategies used in the past could be queried.

A composite of these results is shown in Figure 18.7. This graph suggests that the additional searching aids conserve searching time and are able to reduce the cost of achieving given levels of recall.

REFERENCES

Atherton, P., K. H. Cook, and J. Katzer (1972). *Free Text Retrieval Evaluation*. Syracuse, N.Y.: Syracuse University, School of Library Science.

---

*A searcher may need to use many such strategies to achieve 90% recall. That is, a complete search may involve many separate strategies.

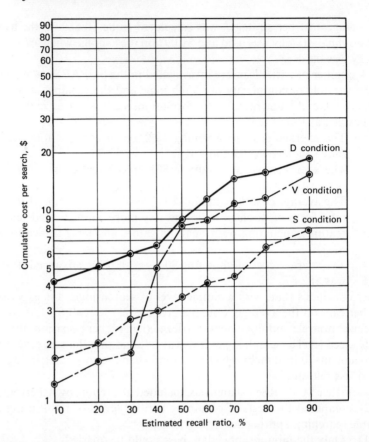

Figure 18.7. Computer cost per search to achieve nine levels of recall: a comparison of three approaches (SUPARS). (For D condition, bibliographic data base only was used; for V condition, bibliographic data base plus vocabulary display were used; for S condition, bibliographic data base plus vocabulary display plus a data base of previous search strategies were used.) Reproduced from Atherton, et al. (1972) by permission of the School of Library Science, Syracuse University.

Bloemeke, M. J., and S. Treu (1969). "Searching *Chemical Titles* in the Pittsburgh Time-Sharing System." *Jour. Chem. Documentation* **9** (3), 155–157.

Bridegam, W. E., Jr., and E. Meyerhoff (1970). "Library Participation in a Biomedical Communication and Information Network." *Bull. Medical Library Assoc.* **58** (2), 103–111.

Cuadra, C. A. (1971). "On-Line Systems: Promise and Pitfalls." *Jour. Amer. Soc. Information Sci.* **22** (2), 107–114.

Higgins, L. D., and F. J. Smith (1971). *The Cost and Response of an On-Line Reference Retrieval System.* Belfast: Queen's University of Belfast, Computer Science Department.

Katter, R. V. (1970). *On the On-Line User of Remote-Access Citation Retrieval Services.* Santa Monica, Ca.: System Development Corporation, TM-(L)-4494/000/00.

Katzer, J. (1971). *Large Scale Information Processing Systems.* Section V. *Cost-Benefits Analysis.* Final Report to the Rome Air Development Center. Syracuse, N.Y.: Syracuse University, School of Library Science.

Lancaster, F. W. (1971). "The Cost-Effectiveness Analysis of Information Retrieval and Dissemination Systems." *Jour. Amer. Soc. Information Sci.* **22** (1), 12–27.

Landau, R. (1972). Personal Communication.

Negus, A. E., and J. L. Hall (1971). "Towards an Effective On-Line Reference Retrieval System." *Information Storage Retrieval* **7** (6), 249–270.

Powers, J. M. (1973). "The Defense RDTE On-Line System Retrieval." *In Interactive Bibliographic Systems.* Washington, D.C.: USAEC, pp. 69–86.

Reitman, W. (1972). Personal Communication.

Salton, G. (1970). "Evaluation Problems in Interactive Information Retrieval." *Information Storage Retrieval* **6** (1), 29–44.

Sharpe, W. F. (1969). *The Economics of Computers.* New York: Columbia University Press.

Smith, F. J. (1971). *On-Line Data Bank in Atomic and Molecular Physics.* Belfast: Queen's University of Belfast, Computer Science Department.

Thompson, G. K. (1970). "Some Cost Estimates for Bibliographic Searching in a Large-Scale Social Sciences Information System." *Information Storage Retrieval* **6** (2), 179–186.

Chapter Nineteen

Requirements for Future Systems

In this volume we have tried to paint a broad picture of the present status of on-line systems for the searching of bibliographic records by subject. Such systems are still in their infancy, and future years should see the development of on-line systems of increasing size and sophistication.

There is already a considerable amount of activity in the development of networks of libraries and information centers at regional, national, and international levels. Examples include the Biomedical Communication Network of the State University of New York (Pizer, 1969), the National Biomedical Communications Network of the National Library of Medicine (Davis, 1971), and the NASA information retrieval network (Isotta, 1970). UNESCO has produced a plan for a World Science Information System which would incorporate a worldwide referral network (UNESCO and ICSU, 1971). It is clear that on-line systems will be essential elements in all such networking activities.

Further impetus will be given to the expansion of on-line retrieval systems by:

1. Continued reductions in the cost of computing, including the cost of mass digital storage.
2. Reductions in communications costs.
3. The availability of potentially less expensive display devices, such as the plasma panel (Stifle, 1971).
4. The increasing availability of machine-readable data bases created by *information wholesalers* such as commercial publishers and professional societies.

5. The increasing accessibility of time-shared computing resources through *information utilities* (Sackman and Nie, 1970) and, ergo, the increasing accessibility of searchable bibliographic data bases.
6. The emergence of a new generation of scientists, engineers, and other professionals who will have been exposed regularly and routinely to on-line facilities used for educational purposes in universities, colleges, and schools.

It is clear that many new systems for on-line bibliographic search will be designed and implemented in the next few years,* and it is therefore appropriate to review the requirements for effective systems of this type. The developers of the SPIRES/BALLOTS systems at Stanford University (1970) state that an acceptable system must demonstrate economy and efficiency, it must be simple and flexible, and it must provide feedback, both to the user and to the designers and managers of the system. Carville, et al. (1971) have said that an on-line system must be simple, self-instructive, rapid in response, effective, and cost-effective.

Seiden (1970) emphasized that on-line systems must be user-oriented:

First, the queries should be easy to formulate in natural or near-natural language. Second, the responses should be readily understood and also in natural language (or an easily understandable shorthand). Third, the system should tolerate errors as well as inform the user as to the nature of his errors. It should also provide him with a basis for taking corrective action. Fourth, the system should be sufficiently simple to learn and operate (or contain sufficient tutorial information) so that a novice can use it successfully (although not necessarily with maximum efficiency) with not more than one hour of instruction. Fifth, the system should allow the user to select minimal cues or detailed instructions, depending upon his level of familiarity. Other desirable niceties are feedback concerning the relevance of the data retrieval and feedback concerning alternate actions that the user might take at any given point in operating this system (pp. 36, 37).

Katter (1970) has put forward the following as desirable system features:

Initiation of interaction should require a minimum of operator actions; the "stacking" of commands should be permitted; the number of search terms allowed for a single search should be quite large, perhaps three dozen or more; unrestricted use of Boolean operators *and, or,* and *not* should be available; "mixed mode" retrieval should be available, allowing statements combining terms from different categories of the unit record; partially specified (i.e., incomplete) search terms should be searchable; rapid display of alphabetically similar terms should be offered; the system should provide extensive, specific operator error messages;

---

*Bauer (1965) pointed out that on-line computing occupied only 1 % of all computing activities in the United States in 1965. He projected that this proportion would increase to 50 % by 1970 and 90 % by 1975.

pacing cues to the operator should be unequivocal but not distracting; system safe-guards, to prevent operator error from having serious system consequences, should be complete; the sequence of the program interaction between user and system should be under the user's control, not the system's, and an "interrupt" capability should be available wherever possible; and extensive printout options should be available, to satisfy the needs of different kinds of users (pp. 20, 21).

Wolfe (1971), too, has recommended the incorporation of on-line tutorial features, the ability to communicate in natural language form, and the capability for machine derivation of search strategies through interaction with the terminal user. He points out that:

> When done by computer, trial and error computation is done so massively and instantaneously that an optimum search strategy can be heuristically obtained by computer in less time than it takes for a human analyst to enter his own search strategy into the on-line retrieval system.
>
> Automatic search formulation based on on-line user feedback, statistical analysis, and heuristic optimization procedures will undoubtedly develop into the primary search formulation method for all future on-line information systems regardless of their data base content. The concept involved is extraordinarily practical in terms of potential use and personnel cost reduction. Eventually, a generalized query formulation program will be developed and made adaptable to every kind of data base. Query coordinators and search analysts may prove redundant (p. 151).

Rae (1970) lists the following as major areas requiring careful considera-tion for future on-line systems:

1. Thorough user education in the operation of the terminal hardware.
2. Extensive training and practice in the use of indexing tools and in the logical formulation of searches using computer assisted instruction (CAI).
3. Provision of separate facilities for the terminals complete with extensive reference materials.
4. Decreased system response time—primarily by using video terminals, second-arily by improved software.
5. Control of indexing errors using a system thesaurus and synonym dictionary.
6. Make the system available to a wider national audience via dial-up terminals. This would have the secondary benefit of reducing costs by spreading them over the larger audience (p. 173).

Note that there is great commonality in all these design requirements. Several of the features mentioned already exist in operating retrieval systems, and others have been incorporated into systems that are experimental at the present time. Nevertheless, a number of existing on-line systems appear to be little more than batch systems with a few terminals added. In other words, batch systems have been converted to on-line operation without introducing new design concepts and without exploiting the true interactive capabilities of the time-shared computer. Wolfe (1971) has recognized this situation:

> The ideal remote access on-line information retrieval and display system would optimize the feedback capabilities of user-computer interactions to achieve the fullest possible use of the computer as an information retrieval and display tool. Current on-line information retrieval and display systems are mainly on-line program adaptations of batch processing techniques and do not fully exploit the inherent potential of on-line user-computer interaction (p. 149).

Sackman (1970) has pointed out that batch-processing systems were designed for highly specialized users, and that man–computer communication is at a minimum in these systems. Difficult and esoteric languages are frequently employed and the viewpoint of the user is often ignored: "Narrow technical considerations and immediate cost constraints dominated computer technology then and still dominate it today, in large part at the expense of human ease, convenience, and social effectiveness."

It is unlikely that a batch retrieval system will convert directly to an effective on-line system to be used in a nondelegated search mode. Batch systems, such as MEDLARS, were designed to be used by information specialists. They make use of large controlled vocabularies, together with complex indexing policies and protocols, that require long periods of training to exploit effectively.

Before we consider possible trends in future information systems it may be valuable to consider limitations of existing services and user reaction to these services. In the last 20 years, many studies have been made of information gathering behavior and the use made of libraries, information centers, and other sources. These surveys have covered populations diverse in size, discipline, and professional activity. The methods used to conduct the studies have also been diverse. Although the results of any one study are not usually generalizable, and we certainly have no composite picture of a *typical* user of information services, certain findings have been made repeatedly. These findings are summarized below, in general terms, because of their possible implications for the design of future systems:

1. Libraries and other formal information centers are not considered as primary sources of information by large segments of the scientific, technical, and professional community. In surveys which ask respondents to rank information sources on some value scale, libraries and information centers frequently appear rather low in the ranking.

2. A large segment of the scientific, technical, and professional community is completely unaware of the existence of the many information services available at national, regional, and local levels. Many

other professionals, while vaguely aware that information centers exist, make no use of them, partly because they are uninformed about the actual services provided by these centers. Others make use of various information services, but do not exploit them most effectively, because they do not comprehend the full capabilities of these services (people have a strong tendency to ask for what they think the system can provide rather than for what they are really seeking, which may in fact be well within the capabilities of the system).

Libraries and other purveyors of information have perhaps exhibited a certain complacency about the service they provide. Information services are sometimes established before the need for them is clearly demonstrated. Once a service is established, there is a tendency to sit back expectantly to wait for the users to flock in. Sometimes little flocking occurs. Market research, advertising, and other promotional techniques are frequently crude or lacking entirely (although this is not true of certain large commercial enterprises that have capitalized very effectively on information products and services). Education of users and potential users has also been sadly neglected (Lancaster, 1970).

3. In the use of information services, the principle of least effort is paramount. Sources are frequently chosen more on the basis of ease of use and accessibility than for the information they are expected to contain. Mooers' law again!

4. Personal files and indexes are the first source that many professionals will turn to when the need for information arises.

5. When personal collections fail, the professional will frequently turn, not to a library or other information center, but to an informal channel of communication. Frequently, he will contact a colleague in his own institution or another subject specialist outside it (the *invisible college* phenomenon).

Against this background we will try to make some projections about the future. It is dangerous to try to predict what is likely to happen. The paragraphs below should be regarded as representing our feelings about what future trends might be or, perhaps, what we think these trends *should* be.

1. There will clearly be a great increase in the number of information services that can be accessed remotely from various centers around the country (and the world). Some of these will still be large, general-purpose, compromise systems of the MEDLARS and RECON type. Perhaps such systems will continue to be used mainly by librarians and other information specialists. In addition to these systems, we are likely to see the development of many more specialized systems

devoted to rather restricted subject areas (e.g., epilepsy, toxicology) that are designed to be used directly by the practitioners in these subjects rather than by information specialists.

2. Such specialized systems must be much more user-oriented than the systems that presently exist. They must be easily accessible and require comparatively little effort to use. Some user-oriented requirements will be mentioned below.

3. New design concepts for on-line systems must be exploited. Computer-based retrieval systems, first implemented in the late 1950s and early 1960s, have largely been more mechanized, more powerful, more efficient versions of searching processes that can be implemented manually (e.g., peek-a-boo or edge-notched cards). In other words, a decade ago there was a strong tendency to mechanize existing systems without giving too much consideration to the possibility of incorporating new approaches to indexing, searching, and vocabulary control. In most systems, the full capabilities of the computer for computation and manipulation are not really exploited. Now that on-line retrieval systems are being implemented, there is again a tendency to take an existing batch-processing system and merely make the data base available for on-line access. Again, new design approaches are neglected and the true interactive, heuristic, browsing, instructional capabilities of on-line systems are not fully exploited. Future systems must be designed, *ab initio*, for an on-line, interactive mode of operation with the practitioner in a field (not an information specialist) clearly in mind.

4. Future systems should be oriented toward natural language (e.g., of abstracts) rather than controlled vocabularies. Specialized information systems will require the specificity of natural language, and the full interactive, browsing capabilities of such systems will be exploited more efficiently if they include relatively substantial portions of natural language text. For the practitioners in a field, natural language is almost essential. We cannot expect such users to learn the nuances and idiosyncracies of a large controlled vocabulary based on years of indexing practice and protocol. In addition to being highly desirable, natural language systems are becoming increasingly feasible because of the increasing availability of machine-readable data bases as by-products of other operations, and because of the fact that digital storage costs are coming down and are likely to come down much further with the development of mass storage devices of various types.

5. Although vocabularies will not be controlled at the time of indexing, they may be at the time of searching. At least, various searching aids

must be made available. One such aid will be a search thesaurus to control synonyms and to bring semantically related words together.

6. Future systems should have increased instructional capabilities, drawing heavily upon the rather sophisticated techniques already developed in the field of computer-aided instruction. In passing, it is worth mentioning that some extremely large systems for CAI exist or are planned [e.g., the PLATO system at the University of Illinois plans to have 2000 terminals throughout the state (Bitzer and Skaperdas, 1972)], and the possibility exists of integrating information retrieval activities into such systems.

7. On-line retrieval systems should be capable of being queried by techniques other than that of formal boolean search expressions. Perhaps they will accept English sentence input, as do SMART, LEADER, and BROWSER, or will incorporate facilities for weighted term search. At least two other possibilities exist. One is the use of strings of terms, with no logical connectives, which the search algorithm matches against the documents in the file, the object being to find those that match most closely and print them or display them in order of degree of match. This technique, which has been referred to as *fractional retrieval*, was mentioned in Chapter Thirteen. Another pattern-matching technique is possible. It involves the interrogation of the system by means of citations to relevant documents already known to the user. The search algorithm then proceeds to find other documents that resemble those already known to be relevant (e.g., they have been indexed *like* the known relevant items, they contain words similar to those in the known relevant items, or they are bibliographically coupled to the known items). For searching of on-line book catalogs, the user should perhaps be allowed to employ such unconventional but memorable characteristics as color, size, and date (Cooper, 1970).

8. On-line retrieval systems must certainly permit the ranking of output. Conventionally, a search in a machine-based system merely divides up the collection into two parts, those items retrieved and those not retrieved. This is a hangover from manual and semi-mechanized systems, which could achieve only this limited function. But the digital computer can divide up collections much more finely than this and is perfectly capable of ranking, and presenting, documents in accordance with the degree to which they match the search request. While a few on-line systems (e.g., BROWSER) rank output, in the great majority, the capabilities of the computer to perform this and other more sophisticated tasks are not being exploited.

9. Future on-line systems must require less effort to use. They should adapt to the user rather than expecting the user to adapt to them. They must certainly include some facilities for error compensation. They should be less sensitive to simple errors of punctuation, spelling, and spacing, and they should be capable of operating on truncations, abbreviations, or other *search keys*. The amount of keyboarding required of the user should be minimized. For the relatively untrained and unsophisticated user, the majority of the interrogation should involve selection from term menus and other displays, in much the same way that these techniques are used in computer-aided instruction. This implies a video display and the capability of selecting from such a display simply and rapidly. An interesting recent development, which could have a significant impact on information retrieval, is the touch panel. This is a modification of the plasma panel, developed at the University of Illinois, which permits a user to select any item of data on a screen merely by touching it with his finger. The touch panel is particularly valuable in CAI techniques, where rapid selection from displayed alternatives is highly desirable. It may also speed up considerably an on-line interrogation process in a retrieval system and offers the possibility of on-line indexing by finger (presumably the index finger!) selection of keywords in displayed text.

10. On-line systems must be more accessible if they are to be used more widely. Accessibility is largely dependent upon the availability of terminals, and terminal availability is at least partly dependent upon terminal costs. The plasma display allows an on-line terminal to be produced in quantity for as little as $2500, with a strong possibility of further reductions in the future. Another future possibility is the use of domestic television receivers, in home or office, as terminals that can be used to query remote data bases. Some interesting experiments in the use of cable television for interactive searching have been performed at Reston, Virginia, by the Mitre Corporation (Stetten, 1971 a, b; Volk, 1971). The use of cable television for transmission of microforms has been discussed by Hilton (1970).

11. However efficient and convenient on-line, general-purpose systems are made in the future, it is unlikely that they will completely replace personal files. It is likely that we will see increased emphasis in the future on systems that will provide on-line support to personal files. Some symbiosis between general-purpose systems and personal collections, as mentioned in Chapter Thirteen, is also possible.

12. If bibliographic search systems of the future provide very rapid and convenient access to vast data bases of bibliographic citations, it

will be very anomalous if the users of these systems still have to wait several days to obtain full copies of the articles cited. Moreover, if the full interactive capabilities of an on-line search system are to be realized, the user may need to view the complete text of documents rapidly in order to make quick and accurate relevance judgments. Ultimately, on-line search systems must interface with systems capable of retrieving and displaying complete text, either in microform or digital form, as described in Chapter Sixteen.

13. Informal channels of communication will continue to be important. The new communications technology will assist rather than obstruct the personal communication process between researchers in a particular subject field. On-line networks will facilitate the transfer of information among scientists known to be working in related subject areas. The picturephone, or some similar device, may facilitate the exchange of ideas between such groups. Directories of information sources, personal and institutional, and of ongoing research projects, of the type maintained by the National Referral Center for Science and Technology and the Science Information Exchange, may be maintained on-line and can thus be accessed remotely from centers throughout the country.

14. On-line information retrieval systems should not be regarded as completely independent entities. In the future, they will be required to interface with other systems. Such interfaces will be with other bibliographic systems, raising problems of convertibility and compatibility of vocabularies and searching strategies, and with other types of systems (e.g., interfaces with statistical packages, with text editing systems, with photocomposition devices, with computer–output–microfilm systems, and so on). System interface design may be one of the most challenging problems facing us in the years to come.

We may be just beginning to scratch the surface on the possibilities of applying technological advances to problems of information transfer. Rapid developments are taking place in such activities as computer-aided instruction, networking, on-line technology, microform technology, cable television, mass memories (e.g., using electron beam, holographic or magnetic bubble technologies), machine processing of text, and publishing and distribution methods. Some of these developments, collectively, may result in significant overall improvements in future methods of information handling.

REFERENCES

Bauer, W. F. (1965). *On-Line Systems—Their Characteristics and Motivations.* Sherman Oaks, Ca.: Informatics Inc.

Bitzer, D. L., and D. Skaperdas (1972). *The Design of an Economically Viable Large-Scale Computer-Based Education System.* Urbana, Ill.: University of Illinois, Computer-based Education Research Laboratory.

Carville, M., L. D. Higgins, and F. J. Smith (1971). "Interactive Reference Retrieval in Large Files." *Information Storage Retrieval* **7** (5), 205–210.

Cooper, W. S. (1970). "The Potential Usefulness of Catalog Access Points Other Than Author, Title, and Subject." *Jour. Amer. Soc. Information Sci.* **21** (2), 112–127.

Davis, R. M. (1971). "The National Biomedical Communications Network as a Developing Structure." *Bull. Medical Library Assoc.* **59** (1), 1–20.

Hilton, H. J. (1970). "CATV and Microforms." *Proc. Nat. Microfilm Assoc.* **19**, 27–39.

Isotta, N. E. C. (1970). "Europe's First Information Retrieval Network." *ESRO/ELDO Bull.* (9), 9–17.

Katter, R. V. (1970). *On the On-Line User of Remote-Access Citation Retrieval Services.* Santa Monica, Ca.: System Development Corporation, TM-(L)-4494/000/00.

Lancaster, F. W. (1970). "User Education: the Next Major Thrust in Information Science?" *Jour. Education Librarianship* **11** (1), 55–63.

Pizer, I. H. (1969). "A Regional Medical Library Network." *Bull. Medical Library Assoc.* **57** (2), 101–115.

Rae, P. D. J. (1970). "On-Line Information Retrieval Systems—Experience of the Parkinson Information Center using the SUNY Biomedical Communication Network." *Proc. Amer. Soc. Information Sci.* **7**, 173–176.

Sackman, H. (1970). "Experimental Analysis of Man-Computer Problem-Solving." *Human Factors* **12** (2), 187–201.

Sackman, H., and N. Nie, eds. (1970). *The Information Utility and Social Choice.* Montvale, N.J.: AFIPS Press.

Seiden, H. R. (1970). *A Comparative Analysis of Interactive Storage and Retrieval Systems with Implications for BCN Design.* Santa Monica, Ca.: System Development Corporation, TM-4421.

Stanford University (1970). *System Scope for Library Automation and Generalized Information Storage and Retrieval at Stanford University.* Stanford, Ca.: Stanford University.

Stetten, K. J. (1971a). *Interactive Television Software for Cable Television Application.* Washington, D.C.: Mitre Corporation, MTP-354.

Stetten, K. J. (1971b). *TICCIT: a Delivery System Designed for Mass Utilization.* Washington, D.C.: Mitre Corporation, M 71-56.

Stifle, J. (1971). *A Plasma Display Terminal.* Urbana, Ill.: University of Illinois, Computer-based Education Research Laboratory.

United Nations Educational, Scientific and Cultural Organization and the International Council of Scientific Unions (1971). *UNISIST: Study Report on the Feasibility of a World Science Information System.* Paris: UNESCO and ICSU.

Volk, J. (1971). *The Reston, Virginia, Test of the Mitre Corporation's Interactive Television System.* Washington, D.C.: Mitre Corporation, MTP-352.

Wolfe, T. (1971). "Suggestions for Exploiting the Potential of On-Line Remote Access Information Retrieval and Display Systems." *Jour. Amer. Soc. Information Sci.* **22** (3), 149–152.

Appendix A

SUPARS Interview Guide

BEFORE BEGINNING EACH SECTION, REMEMBER TO TELL THE RESPONDENT A LITTLE ABOUT IT "THIS IS SECTION   ; IT DEALS WITH. . ."

I. WAYS OF BECOMING ACQUAINTED WITH THE SYSTEM

   1. HAVE YOU HEARD ABOUT SUPARS?

If respondent was just told about SUPARS for 1st time, go to section I. of questions for non-users—PAGE 1 OF BLUE SECTION (p. 424).

For others, probe:

       HOW DID YOU FIRST HEAR ABOUT SUPARS?

       DID YOU SEE OR HEAR ANY PUBLICITY ABOUT SUPARS?

       DID YOU RECEIVE A CLASS ASSIGNMENT INVOLVING SUPARS?

       DID YOU HEAR ABOUT SUPARS FROM FRIENDS, ACQUAINTANCES, PROFESSORS, OR OTHER PEOPLE NOT ASSOCIATED WITH SUPARS?

   2. WERE YOU GIVEN A DEMONSTRATION?

Reprinted by permission of the School of Library Science, Syracuse University, Syracuse, N.Y.

If answer is *YES* to question 2, go to question 3
If answer is *NO* to question 2, go to question 12

3. HOW LONG WAS THE DEMONSTRATION?

4. HOW MANY WAYS OF SEARCHING SUPARS DID YOU LEARN FROM THE DEMONSTRATION?

5. DID YOU TRY USING SUPARS AT A COMPUTER TERMINAL DURING THE DEMONSTRATION?

6. DID YOU FEEL THAT YOU KNEW HOW TO MAKE A SUPARS SEARCH AFTER THE DEMONSTRATION? IF *NO*—WHY NOT?

7. WAS THERE ANY MATERIAL GIVEN TO YOU AT THE DEMONSTRATION?

   If *YES*—WHAT KIND OF MATERIAL?

   HOW HAVE YOU USED IT?

8. HAVE YOU REGISTERED TO USE THE SYSTEM?

If answer to question 8 is *NO*, go to section II. of questions for non-users— PAGE 2 OF BLUE SECTION (p. 425).

9. DO YOU HAVE A MANUAL?

   If *YES*—DID YOU GET IT 1) BEFORE, 2) AT THE SAME TIME, OR 3) AFTER YOU REGISTERED?

   DID YOU HAVE A MANUAL BEFORE THE DEMONSTRATION OR DID YOU GET IT AFTER THE DEMONSTRATION?

   DO YOU USE THE MANUAL?

   If *YES*—HOW OFTEN?

   FOR WHAT PURPOSES?

10. HAVE YOU SEARCHED ON YOUR OWN FOR INFOR-MATION USING SUPARS?

If answer to question 10 is *NO*—go to section III. of questions for non-users
—PAGE 3 OF BLUE SECTION (p. 426).
If answer to question 10 is *YES*—go on to question 11

11. DO YOU FEEL THAT YOU LEARNED MORE ABOUT
    USING SUPARS FROM THE DEMONSTRATION, FROM
    THE MANUAL, OR FROM PRACTICE AT THE COM-
    PUTER?

    WHY?

Go on to section II—PAGE 1 OF PINK SECTION (p. 421).

(NO RESPONSES TO QUESTION 2)

12. WHY NOT?

13. HOW DID YOU LEARN TO USE THE SUPARS SYSTEM?

14. HAVE YOU REGISTERED TO USE THE SYSTEM?

If answer to question 14 is *NO*, go to section II. of questions for non-users—
PAGE 2 OF BLUE SECTION (p. 425).

15. DO YOU HAVE A MANUAL?

    If *YES*—DID YOU GET IT 1) BEFORE, 2) AT THE SAME
        TIME, OR 3) AFTER YOU REGISTERED?

    DO YOU USE THE MANUAL?

    If *YES*—HOW OFTEN?

        FOR WHAT PURPOSES?

16. HAVE YOU SEARCHED ON YOUR OWN FOR INFOR-
    MATION USING SUPARS?

If answer to question 16 is *NO*—go to section III. of questions for non-users
—PAGE 3 OF BLUE SECTION (p. 426).
If answer to question 16 is *YES*—go on to question 17.

17. DO YOU FEEL THAT YOU HAVE LEARNED MORE ABOUT USING SUPARS FROM THE MANUAL OR FROM THE PRACTICE AT THE COMPUTER?

    WHY?

Go on to section II. PAGE 1 OF PINK SECTION (this page, below).

(INTRODUCTION)
II. ACTUAL USE (SEARCHING)

1. WHAT WERE YOUR FIRST REACTIONS TO USING THE SUPARS SYSTEM?

2. HOW MUCH TOTAL TIME IN HOURS DO YOU ESTI-MATE THAT YOU HAVE SPENT ON SEARCHING THE SUPARS SYSTEM?

3. APPROXIMATELY HOW MANY TIMES HAVE YOU GONE TO A TERMINAL TO USE SUPARS?

4. APPROXIMATELY HOW MANY SEARCHES HAVE YOU MADE IN ALL?

5. GENERALLY, HOW MANY SEARCHES DO YOU DO IN ONE SESSION?

6. DO YOU ALWAYS USE THE SAME TERMINAL?

    If *NO*—APPROXIMATELY HOW MANY TERMINALS HAVE YOU USED?

    WHY HAVE YOU USED DIFFERENT TERMINALS?

7. WHEN YOU HAVE HAD QUESTIONS ABOUT THE SYSTEM, WHAT HAVE YOU DONE?

    HAVE YOU CALLED EXTENSION 4220?

    If *NO*—HOW HAVE YOU ANSWERED YOUR QUESTIONS?

8. HAVE YOU EVER HAD ANY PROBLEMS GETTING CONNECTED WITH THE SUPARS SYSTEM?

    If *YES*—WHAT KINDS OF PROBLEMS?

9. HAVE YOU EVER HAD ANY PROBLEMS SEARCHING THE SUPARS SYSTEM AFTER YOU HAVE BEEN CONNECTED WITH IT?

   If *YES*—WHAT KINDS OF PROBLEMS?

If answer to question 9 is *NO*, go to question 14.

---

10. WHEN YOU HAVE HAD PROBLEMS, WHAT HAVE YOU DONE ABOUT THEM?

    HAVE YOU CALLED EXTENSION 4220?

    If *NO*—HOW HAVE YOU SOLVED YOUR PROBLEMS?

11. GENERALLY, HAVE YOU BEEN ABLE TO OVERCOME PROBLEMS ENCOUNTERED WHILE USING THE COMPUTER?

    If *NO*—WHY NOT?

12. DO YOU FEEL THAT YOU NOW HAVE HAD FEWER PROBLEMS WHEN YOU HAVE USED SUPARS THAN YOU DID WHEN YOU FIRST BEGAN USING THE SYSTEM?

    WHY?

13. DO YOU FEEL THAT YOU UNDERSTAND HOW TO SEARCH SUPARS?

14. SOME PEOPLE FEEL THAT THEY HAVE A LOT OF CONTROL OVER THEIR SEARCHES, WHILE OTHERS FEEL THAT THEY DON'T HAVE ENOUGH CONTROL OVER THEIR SEARCHES. DO YOU FEEL THAT YOU CONTROL YOUR SEARCHES FOR INFORMATION?

    If *NO*—WHY NOT?

15. HAVE YOU OFTEN STOPPED OUTPUT PRINTING BY USING THE ATTENTION KEY?

    WHY?

16. WHAT KINDS OF SEARCHES HAVE YOU DONE MOST OF THE TIME?

WHAT KINDS OF INFORMATION HAVE YOU BEEN LOOKING FOR?

PROBE: DO YOUR SEARCHES USUALLY CONTAIN OVER 5 LABELS?

HOW MANY WORDS DO YOU GENERALLY PUT UNDER ONE LABEL?

Go to Section III—PAGE 1 OF GREEN SECTION (below).

(INTRODUCTION)

III. OUTPUT

1. WOULD YOU PLEASE WRITE DOWN A SAMPLE SEARCH FOR ME THAT YOU HAVE USED IN SEARCHING SUPARS? (HAVE PEN AND PAPER READY)

2. (REFER TO SAMPLE SEARCH)
    WHEN YOU SEARCH FOR INFORMATION, IS THIS THE KIND OF LIST STATEMENT THAT YOU NORMALLY USE?

    WHY?

3. DO YOU FEEL THAT THE OUTPUT THAT YOU GET CONTAINS INFORMATION THAT YOU WANT?

If *NO*—go to question 4
If answer to question 3 is YES—do *NOT* ask question 4; go to question 5.

---

4. (IF *NO* TO QUESTION 3)
    HOW OFTEN DOES THIS HAPPEN?

    WHAT DON'T YOU LIKE ABOUT THE OUTPUT THAT YOU GET?

    WHAT DO YOU THINK THAT YOU SHOULD DO TO GET OUTPUT THAT YOU WANT?

5. HAVE YOU EVER LOOKED FOR INFORMATION IN THE PRINTED *PSYCHOLOGICAL ABSTRACTS*?

If *YES*—DO YOU PREFER THE FORMAT OF AN AB-STRACT IN SUPARS OR IN THE PRINTED *PSYCHOLOGICAL ABSTRACTS*?

WHY?

HAVE YOU FOUND INFORMATION THAT YOU CONSIDER RELEVANT WHEN YOU HAVE SEARCHED THE PRINTED *PSYCHOLOGICAL ABSTRACTS*?

6. DO YOU THINK THAT YOU WOULD GET SEARCH RESULTS SIMILAR TO SUPARS SEARCH RESULTS FROM SEARCHING THE PRINTED *PSYCHOLOGICAL ABSTRACTS*?

If *NO*—WHAT WOULD BE THE DIFFERENCE IN THE SEARCH RESULTS?

Go on to section IV—YELLOW (p. 427).

QUESTIONS FOR NON-USERS

These questions are divided into sections of questions for 1) the non-user who has not heard of SUPARS, 2) the non-user who has heard of SUPARS but has elected not to register, and 3) the non-user who has registered but has not used the system for personal searches (this excludes people who tried the system during a demonstration).

I. QUESTIONS FOR THE NON-USER WHO HAS NOT HEARD OF SUPARS.

1. HAVE YOU EVER USED *PSYCHOLOGICAL ABSTRACTS*?

If YES—FOR WHAT PURPOSES?

HOW MANY TIMES A SEMESTER HAVE YOU USED *PSYCHOLOGICAL ABSTRACTS*?

HOW MUCH TOTAL TIME IN HOURS DO YOU ESTIMATE THAT YOU HAVE SPENT SEARCH-ING FOR INFORMATION IN *PSYCHOLOGICAL ABSTRACTS*?

2. WOULD YOU LIKE TO HAVE COMPUTERIZED INFOR-MATION RETRIEVAL SYSTEMS SUCH AS SUPARS

AVAILABLE FOR OTHER KINDS OF INFORMATION?

If *NO*—WHY NOT?

Do *NOT* ask question 3)

If *YES*—WHAT OTHER KINDS OF INFORMATION?

Go on to question 3.

---

3. WOULD YOU USE A COMPUTERIZED INFORMATION RETRIEVAL SYSTEM IF YOU HAD TO PAY FOR YOUR USE?

   If *NO*—WHY NOT?

   If *YES*—HOW MUCH DO YOU THINK WOULD BE A REASONABLE AMOUNT TO PAY PER SEARCH FOR SEARCHES DONE THROUGH THE USE OF SUCH A SYSTEM?

   DO YOU THINK THAT YOUR DEPARTMENT OUGHT TO HELP DEFRAY THE COST OF YOUR USE OF SUCH A SYSTEM?

GO ON TO DEMOGRAPHIC DATA QUESTION—ORANGE SECTION (p. 429).

(INTRODUCTION)

II. QUESTIONS FOR THE NON-USER WHO HAS HEARD OF SUPARS BUT HAS ELECTED NOT TO REGISTER.

   1. *HAVE YOU EVER USED PSYCHOLOGICAL ABSTRACTS?*

      If *YES*—FOR WHAT PURPOSES?

      HOW MANY TIMES A SEMESTER HAVE YOU USED *PSYCHOLOGICAL ABSTRACTS?*

      HOW MUCH TOTAL TIME IN HOURS DO YOU ESTIMATE THAT YOU HAVE SPENT SEARCHING FOR INFORMATION IN *PSYCHOLOGICAL ABSTRACTS?*

2. ARE THERE ANY PARTICULAR REASONS WHY YOU HAVEN'T USED THE SUPARS SYSTEM?

3. WOULD YOU LIKE TO HAVE COMPUTERIZED INFORMATION RETRIEVAL SYSTEMS SUCH AS SUPARS AVAILABLE FOR OTHER KINDS OF INFORMATION?

    If *NO*—WHY NOT?

Do *NOT* ask question 4.

If *YES*—WHAT OTHER KINDS OF INFORMATION?

Go on to question 4.

---

4. WOULD YOU USE A COMPUTERIZED INFORMATION RETRIEVAL SYSTEM IF YOU HAD TO PAY FOR YOUR USE?

    If *NO*—WHY NOT?

    If *YES*—HOW MUCH DO YOU THINK WOULD BE A REASONABLE AMOUNT TO PAY PER SEARCH FOR SEARCHES DONE THROUGH THE USE OF SUCH A SYSTEM?

    DO YOU THINK THAT YOUR DEPARTMENT OUGHT TO HELP DEFRAY THE COST OF YOUR USE OF SUCH SYSTEM?

GO ON TO DEMOGRAPHIC DATA QUESTIONS—ORANGE SECTION (p. 429).

(INTRODUCTION)

III. QUESTIONS FOR THE NON-USER WHO HAS REGISTERED BUT HAS NOT USED THE SYSTEM FOR PERSONAL SEARCHES

1. *HAVE YOU EVER USED PSYCHOLOGICAL ABSTRACTS?*

    If *YES*—FOR WHAT PURPOSES?

        HOW MANY TIMES A SEMESTER HAVE YOU USED *PSYCHOLOGICAL ABSTRACTS?*

HOW MUCH TOTAL TIME IN HOURS DO YOU ESTIMATE THAT YOU HAVE SPENT SEARCHING FOR INFORMATION IN *PSYCHOLOGICAL ABSTRACTS*?

2. SINCE YOU REGISTERED TO USE THE SUPARS SYSTEM, ARE THERE ANY PARTICULAR REASONS WHY YOU HAVEN'T USED IT?

3. WOULD YOU LIKE TO HAVE SYSTEMS SUCH AS SUPARS AVAILABLE FOR OTHER KINDS OF INFORMATION?

   If NO—WHY NOT?

Do *NOT* ask question 4.

If *YES*—WHAT OTHER KINDS OF INFORMATION?

Go on to question 4.

---

4. WOULD YOU USE A COMPUTERIZED INFORMATION RETRIEVAL SYSTEM IF YOU HAD TO PAY FOR YOUR USE?

   If *NO*—WHY NOT?

   If *YES*—HOW MUCH DO YOU THINK WOULD BE A REASONABLE AMOUNT TO PAY PER SEARCH FOR SEARCHES DONE THROUGH THE USE OF SUCH A SYSTEM?

   DO YOU THINK THAT YOUR DEPARTMENT OUGHT TO HELP DEFRAY THE COST OF YOUR USE OF SUCH A SYSTEM?

GO ON TO DEMOGRAPHIC DATA QUESTIONS—ORANGE SECTION (p. 429).

(INTRODUCTION)
IV. GENERAL REACTIONS TO SYSTEM

1. DO YOU PREFER LOOKING FOR INFORMATION THROUGH PRINTED INDEXES AND ABSTRACTING

JOURNALS OR DO YOU PREFER SEARCHING FOR INFORMATION BY MEANS OF A SYSTEM SUCH AS SUPARS?

WHY?

2. DO YOU THINK THAT INFORMATION RETRIEVAL SYSTEMS SUCH AS SUPARS SHOULD BE USED FOR OTHER KINDS OF MATERIAL?

If *NO*—WHY NOT?

If *YES*—WHAT OTHERS?

WOULD YOU LIKE TO USE SUCH A SYSTEM?

WHY?

3. WHAT HAVE YOU LIKED ABOUT USING A COMPU-TERIZED INFORMATION RETRIEVAL SYSTEM?

4. WHAT HAVEN'T YOU LIKED ABOUT USING IT?

5. DO YOU THINK THAT SYSTEMS SUCH AS SUPARS SHOULD BE AVAILABLE TO THE PUBLIC ALL THE TIME?

WHY?

6. WOULD YOU USE A SYSTEM SUCH AS SUPARS IF YOU HAD TO PAY FOR YOUR USE?

If *NO*—WHY NOT?

If *YES*—HOW MUCH DO YOU THINK WOULD BE A REASONABLE AMOUNT TO PAY PER SEARCH FOR SEARCHES DONE THROUGH THE USE OF SUCH A SYSTEM?

DO YOU THINK THAT YOUR DEPARTMENT OUGHT TO HELP DEFRAY THE COST OF YOUR USE OF SUCH A SYSTEM?

7. WHAT WOULD YOU LIKE TO SEE CHANGED ABOUT SUPARS?

8. WHAT WOULD YOU LIKE TO SEE STAY THE SAME?

9. DO YOU HAVE ANY FURTHER COMMENTS TO MAKE ABOUT THE SUPARS SYSTEM?

GO ON TO DEMOGRAPHIC DATA QUESTIONS—ORANGE SECTION (below).

DEMOGRAPHIC DATA QUESTIONS
(for all Respondents)

(INTRODUCTION)

1. ARE YOU PRIMARILY (1) AN UNDERGRADUATE STUDENT
   (2) A GRADUATE STUDENT
   (3) A TEACHER
   (4) A MEMBER OF THE ADMINISTRATION
   (5) A STAFF MEMBER
   (6) OTHER?

2. WITH WHAT DEPARTMENT ARE YOU ASSOCIATED?

3. (IF STUDENT) WHAT DEGREE PROGRAM ARE YOU IN?

4. (IF NON-PSYCH PERSON) HAVE YOU EVER TAKEN ANY COURSES IN PSYCHOLOGY?

5. HAVE YOU EVER USED A COMPUTERIZED INFORMATION RETRIEVAL SYSTEM OTHER THAN SUPARS?

   If *YES*—WHERE DID YOU USE THE SYSTEM?

   WHEN DID YOU USE THE SYSTEM?

   WHAT KIND OF SYSTEM WAS IT?

   FOR WHAT PURPOSES DID YOU USE THE SYSTEM?

   HOW MUCH TOTAL TIME IN HOURS DID YOU SPEND USING THE SYSTEM?

   WHAT WERE YOUR GENERAL REACTIONS TO THE SYSTEM?

6. HOW MUCH EXPERIENCE HAVE YOU HAD WITH COMPUTERS?

   WHAT KIND?

Appendix B

DIALOG Terminal Users Reference Manual

Dialog

TERMINAL USERS
REFERENCE MANUAL

TERMINAL OPERATION IS SIMPLE

- Depress Desired Command Key
  (while holding down "shift" key)

  Command keys are those just below command label.

- Key in Data for Command
  (such as key words or descriptors)

- Depress "TRANS" Key
  (to send command message to computer)

This manual explains each of the commands in detail.

Dialog

BEGIN	BEGIN ■
EXPAND term "	EXPAND ■
SELECT term #	SELECT ■
COMBINE set nos. $	COMBINE ■
DISPLAY set ITEM + - %	DISPLAY ■
PRINT set &	PRINT ■
TYPE set '	TYPE ■
KEEP set (	KEEP ■
LIMIT set/code)	LIMIT ■
PAGE + - Φ	PAGE ■
END =	END ■
DISPLAY SET HISTORY @	DISPLAY SET HISTORY ■
SEND MESSAGE trmn no./msg.]	SEND MESSAGE ■
EXPLAIN command name ?	EXPLAIN ■

DESCRIPTOR CODES ■

BEGIN

The user's initial move is to let the computer know that he is ready to begin. After depressing the shift and holding it down, press the key immediately below the command BEGIN. In response, the computer displays the following message on the television screen.

```
    PLEASE ENTER THE FOLLOWING INFORMATION
        PRESS 'TRANS' FOLLOWING EACH ENTRY

SEARCH TITLE
NAME OF PERSON CONDUCTING SEARCH
NAME OF PERSON RECEIVING RESULTS (IF DIFFERENT)
MAIL ADDRESS
THE FOLLOWING FILES ARE AVAILABLE FOR YOU TO SEARCH
    1--ERIC RIE AND CIJE
    2--CURRENT PROJECT INFO. AND PAGE
    3--FIELD READERS
    4--EXCEPTIONAL CHILDREN FILE
    5--
ENTER NUMBER OF DESIRED FILE
```

Type in the requested replies, line by line. No reply should be left blank; type in SAME or NONE as appropriate. Press TRANS following each reply to communicate the information to the computer. The last reply selects the file to be searched.

The log-in procedure may be bypassed by pressing BEGIN and typing in BYPASS (or simply "B"). In this case only the heading shown below will be typed out and normally file 1 is automatically selected.

Either way, after the last reply, the computer responds
by typing out the requested information and the following heading on the console typewriter:

| SET | NO. IN | DESCRIPTION OF SET |
NO.	SET	(+=OR, *=AND, -=NOT)

The search proper is now ready to begin.

Dialog

EXPAND

> EXPAND
> term
> "

Depression of the EXPAND key and entry of a term cause a display of descriptors that are alphabetically close to the entered term. With each descriptor is shown the number of citations in which the descriptor appears (under "CIT") as well as the number of con-conceptually related terms (under "RT") which are available as descriptors. Each display descriptor is numbered (E1 through E16 — E for EXPAND) or SELECT commands. EXPAND MATHEMATICS pro-duces the first display.

```
          EXPAND IT=MATHEMATICS
REF       DESCRIPTOR            TP   CIT    RT
E01    IT=MATHEMATICAL LOGIC ---      25     4
E02    IT=MATHEMATICAL MODELS -      166    11
E03    IT=MATHEMATICAL REVIEWS-        2
E04    IT=MATHEMATICAL
          VOCABULARY -------------    15     2
E05    IT=MATHEMATICIANS---------      9     4
E06   -IT=MATHEMATICS ------------   761    33
E07    IT=MATHEMATICS CONCEPT
          LEARNING PROJECT--------     1
E08    IT=MATHEMATICS CONCEPT         1
E09    IT=MATHEMATICS
          CURRICULUM -------------    83     5
E10    IT=MATHEMATICS EDUCATION     333     5
E11    IT=MATHEMATICS FOR ELEME
          NTARY SCHOOL TEACH/----      1
E12    IT=MATHEMATICS
          INSTRUCTION/ -------------  251     7
E13    IT=MATHEMATICS LEAGUE/ --       1
E14    IT=MATHEMATICS MATERIALS      49     6
ENTER
```

The next page may be displayed by entering the PAGE command which would result in the following display.

```
              EXPAND IT=MATHEMATICS
REF     DESCRIPTOR                 TP    CIT   RT
E15     IT=MATHEMATICS
          PLACEMENT EXAMINATION/          1
E16     IT=MATHEMATICS PROGRAM --         1
E17     IT=MATHEMATICS TEACHERS -        68    11
E18     IT=MATHEMATICS -----------        4
E19     IT=MATHEMATICS
          INSTRUCTION --------------      1
E20     IT=MATRICES ---------------     .1
E21     IT=MATRICES ---------------      2
E22     IT=MATRICULATION/ ---------            1
E23     IT=MATRIX ALGEBRA ---------      1
E24     IT=MATRIX GANE/------------      1
E25     IT=MATRIX GANET-----------       1
E26     IT=MATRIX TASKS -----------      1
E27     IT=MATRIX SETS-------------      1
E28     IT=MATSUMOTO -------------       1
E29     IT=MATTER -----------------     12     8
E30     IT=MATTHEW ARNOLD --------       1
ENTER
```

To display the related terms of a particular displayed
descriptor, press EXPAND and enter the reference
number of the associated term. EXPAND E10 produces
the third display.

```
              EXPAND IT=MATHEMATICS EDUCATION
REF     DESCRIPTOR                TP   CIT    RT
R01    -IT=MATHEMATICS EDUCATION  323    5
R02     IT=EDUCATION------ --------3  553    61
R03     IT=COLLEGE MATHEMATICS--4  102     6
R04     IT=ELEMENTARY SCHOOL
          MATHEMATICS-------------4  426     6
R05     IT=MATHEMATICS-----------4  761    33
R06     IT=SECONDARY SCHOOL
          MATHEMATICS-------------4  338     5
ENTER
```

Continue to browse through the thesaurus by successively entering EXPAND and the desired reference
numbers. The TP column indicates the relationship of
the related term to the main entry as follows:

1. Use   4. Related term
2. Narrower term 5. Use for
3. Broader term

SELECT

SELECT
term
#

Terms may be selected by entering the SELECT command together with the E or R number of an EXPAND display, or the term itself. SELECT adds the term so entered to the user's search descriptor list which is printed at the console typewriter. A set identification number is assigned by the computer for use in subsequent COMBINE and output commands. The typewriter output shown below, for example, could have been obtained by SELECT MATHEMATICS, SELECT E6, or SELECT R5. The last two cases assume the appropriate display (see EXPAND) was on the screen at the time the SELECT command was entered.

SET NO.	NO. IN SET	DESCRIPTION OF SET (+=OR, *=AND, -=NOT)
----	-------	---------------------
1	431	IT=MATHEMATICS

It is possible to select lists of E or R numbers provided an EXPAND display is on the console screen. Assume the display shown below is on the screen.

```
     EXPAND IT=MATHEMATICS
REF    DESCRIPTOR              TP  CIT   RT
E01  IT=MATHEMATICAL LOGIC ---     25    4
E02  IT=MATHEMATICAL MODELS -     166   11
E03  IT=MATHEMATICAL REVIEWS-       2
E04  IT=MATHEMATICAL
       VOCABULARY --------------   15    2
E05  IT=MATHEMATICIANS---------     9    4
E06  -IT=MATHEMATICS ------------ 761   33
E07  IT=MATHEMATICS CONCEPT
       LEARNING PROJECT--------     1
E08  IT=MATHEMATICS CONCEPT         1
E09  IT=MATHEMATICS
       CURRICULUM --------------   83    5
E10  IT=MATHEMATICS EDUCATION     333    5
E11  IT=MATHEMATICS FOR ELEME
       NTARY SCHOOL TEACH/----      1
E12  IT=MATHEMATICS
       INSTRUCTION/ ------------- 251    7
E13  IT=MATHEMATICS LEAGUE/ --      1
E14  IT=MATHEMATICS MATERIALS      49    6
ENTER
```

The command SELECT E6, E9, E10 will result in
a single set which combines the entries for all three
terms. The typewriter output in this case would be:

SET NO.	NO. IN SET	DESCRIPTION OF SET (+=OR, *=AND, -=NOT)
1	624	IT=E6, E9, E10
		E6: IT=MATHEMATICS

A range of E or R numbers can also be selected
(e. g., SELECT E7-E9, or SELECT E4, E7-E11).

Dialog

COMBINE

COMBINE
set nos.
$

Depression of this command key, together with entry of a set description (described below), causes the generation of a new set corresponding to the operation specified in the set description. A set description is a series of set numbers separated by various of the following operator symbols:

Symbol	Operation
+	OR
*	AND
-	NOT

The set description 1+2 means that any citation containing index term 1 or term 2 will be returned. This operator symbol is used to broaden the scope of a search by grouping similar terms such as MATHEMATICS EDUCATION or MATHEMATICS INSTRUCTION. The set description 1*2 means that any citation retrieved must contain both terms 1 and 2. This operator is used to narrow the scope of a search by requiring the common occurrence of several index terms such as MATHEMATICS INSTRUCTION and ELEMENTARY EDUCATION. Complex set descriptions can be entered by the use of parentheses; e.g., (1+2)*(3+4). An example of such an expression is that containing (MATHEMATICS EDUCATION or MATHEMATICS INSTRUCTION) and (PRIMARY EDUCATION or ELEMENTARY EDUCATION). All returned items must contain at least one term from each parenthetical expression. At the conclusion of each combine command, the computer assigns a set number to the results, indicates the number of entries in the set, and prints the numbers of sets which were combined to achieve the results. This result is printed on the console typewriter. Set 5 was produced by the command, COMBINE (1+2)*(3*4).

SET NO.	NO. IN SET	DESCRIPTION OF SET (+=OR, *=AND, -=NOT)
1	91	MATHEMATICS EDUCATION
2	135	MATHEMATICS INSTRUCTION
3	61	PRIMARY EDUCATION
4	454	ELEMENTARY EDUCATION
5	18	(1+2)*(3+4)

In the example opposite, two concepts are developed. Sets 1, 2 relate to the first, whereas sets 3, 4 relate to the second. This is the usual way searches are conducted. That is, first the search topic is mentally broken down into several concepts. Each concept is then defined by selecting a series of terms which relate to that concept. Terms within a concept are OR'ed to form concept groups − (1+2) and (3+4) in the above example − and concept groups are AND'ed. An easy way to remember this idea is that the relationship of terms within a concept is OR and between concepts is AND.

If a term is to be excluded from the search, the NOT (-) relationship may be used in any COMBINE expressions. The user in the above example may have decided he was not interested in programed instruction. He could have selected this term (as set 6) and then entered COMBINE 5-6 to create set 7 which would exclude any citations containing the term PROGRAMED INSTRUCTION.

If one wishes to combine a consecutive string of sets, there is a short-cut version of the command. In place of entering COMBINE 1+2+3+4, one may enter COMBINE 1-4/+, for example. This command tells the computer to COMBINE sets 1 through 4 using an OR relationship. Both forms of the command have the same effect.

DISPLAY

DISPLAY PRINT and TYPE commands are entered the
the same way but each causes output to a different
device: the console display, the high speed printer at
the computer, or the console typewriter, respectively.

Entering DISPLAY with a set number will cause the
first item (i.e., the citation with the highest accession
number) in the set to be displayed.   The command
DISPLAYS could produce the following on the display
screen:

```
              DISPLAY 14/2/1
ED021467   EM000321
   MCGRAW-HILL:  FILMSTRIPS, RECORDS, 8MM
FILM LOOPS, TRANSPARENCIES, GLOBEGRAPHIC
SYSTEM  FOR  ELEMENTARY GRADES, JUNIOR &
SENIOR HIGH SCHOOL, COLLEGE.
   MCGRAW-HILL FILMS, NEW YORK, N.Y.
   68
   123P.
   MCGRAW-HILL    FILMS,   A  DIVISION  OF
MCGRAW-HILL  BOOK  CO.,   327  WEST  41ST
STREET, NEW YORK, N.Y. 10036 (FREE).
   DOCUMENT NOT AVAILABLE FROM EDRS.
   /  ART  EDUCATION/  *AUDIOVISUAL AIDS/
*CATALOGS/    ELEMENTARY    EDUCATION/
*FILMSTRIPS/     FRENCH/     GEOGRAPHY
INSTRUCTION/     HIGHER     EDUCATION/
INSTRUCTIONAL    FILMS/    MATHEMATICS
EDUCATION/ *PHONOGRAPH RECORDS/ SCIENCE
EDUCATION/  SECONDARY  EDUCATION/ SINGLE
CONCEPT  FILMS/ SOCIAL STUDIES/ SPANISH/
TRANSPARENCIES/ VOCATIONAL EDUCATION
```

DISPLAY set
ITEM + -
%

The descriptors causing this citation to be retrieved
have been underlined. Note the first line of the DIS-
PLAY: DISPLAY 5/2/1. This says that the display
contains the first item in set 5, and that the item is being displayed in format type 2. The other format
options are:

1 Accession numbers only

3 Unformatted citation

4 Abstract only

5 Citation and abstract

6 Accession numbers and
titles only

To specify format and/or specific items from the set,
the long form of the command must be used. A few
examples will clarify these differences:

DISPLAY 5	Display items of set 5 (format 2 assumed)
DISPLAY 5/5	Display items of set 5 in format 5 (citation and abstract) beginning with the first
DISPLAY 5/2/10-15	Display 10th through 15th items of set 5 in format 2 beginning with the 10th
DISPLAY 5/1	Display only the accession numbers of set 5
DISPLAY 5/6	Display access numbers and titles only

Note the secondary command on the DISPLAY label:
ITEM+-. This command is used to display the next
(+), or the previous (-) item in a set. If no sign (+-)
is entered, + is assumed. That is, merely entering
the ITEM command causes the next item in a displayed
set to be displayed.

Dialog

PRINT

PRINT
set
&

The PRINT command is entered in the same manner as DISPLAY. The initial entry of PRINT (with the desired set number), however, causes the first 50 items of the set to be printed. For 50 more items (or the remainder of the set if less than 100), PRINT (without a set number) is entered. In the following example, after doing a search on "film production," the user entered PRINT 3/5 which produced the message just below set 3. Entering PRINT caused the last 13 items to be printed out.

SET NO.	NO. IN SET	DESCRIPTION OF SET (*=OR, *=AND, -=NOT)
1	62	IT=FILM PRODUCTION
2	10	IT=FILM PRODUCTION SPECIALIST
3	63	1+2
P03/5/1-50		FOR 013 MORE HIT PRINT
P03/5/51-63		

Dialog

TYPE

```
┌─────────────┐
│    TYPE     │
│    set      │
│      '      │
└─────────────┘
```

The TYPE command is entered in the same manner as DISPLAY, and is normally used to print accession numbers of search results at the console. After causing the 9 citations of set 7 to be printed in Format 5 on the high speed printer, the user in the example below typed out their accession numbers. The command he entered was TYPE 7/1. Note that the topic of this search is the use of computers or information processing for time-shared information retrieval.

SET NO.	NO. IN SET	DESCRIPTION OF SET (*-OR, *=AND, -=NOT)
1	311	IT=COMPUTERS
2	257	IT=INFORMATION PROCESSING
3	502	1+2
4	303	IT=INFORMATION RETRIEVAL
5	119	(1+2)*4
6	39	IT=TIME SHARING
7	9	5*6

P07/5/1-9

TYPE 7/1/1-9

ED030777 ED029676
ED027757 ED020748
ED019094 ED019040
ED017043 ED016499
ED016414

If TYPE is done with a format other than 1, only the first item of the specified set is typed out. Successive items in the set may be typed merely by entering TYPE.

KEEP

This command allows the user to selectively set aside items he is displaying. All kept items go into set 99 which can be used like all other sets (i.e., combined, printed, displayed, etc.).

If KEEP only is entered with a citation displayed on the console screen, that item will be put into set 99. KEEP 5 will keep all of set 5. KEEP 5/3-6 will keep items 3-6 of set 5. KEEP ED034076 will place accession number ED034076 in set 99.

LIMIT

This command allows the user to limit a set according to any of several attributes as follows:

Attribute	Value	Example
Accession No. Range	10000 – 999999	LIMIT 3/20000 – 29999: to limit set 3 to range specified
Document Type	ED, EJ, EP, ES, FR, EC*	LIMIT 3/ED. to limit set 3 to only RIE items
Major/ Minor Posting	MAJ, MIN	LIMIT 3/MAJ. to limit set 3 to major postings
Document Availability	AVAIL	LIMIT 3/AVAIL: to limit set 3 to only documents available from ERC

Multiple arguments may be entered in a single command as long as the above sequence is maintained: e.g., LIMIT 3/ED/MAJ will limit set 3 to RIE items with major postings.

If it is desired to limit all succeeding sets, the word ALL is used in place of set number. LIMIT ALL/13968-30777/EJ will limit all successive sets to the specified range in type. The effect of this command is canceled by entering LIMIT ALL/ALL.

---

*ED– Research in Education (RIE)
  EJ – Current Index to Journals (CIJE)
  EP– Current Project Information (CPI)
  ES – Pacesetters in Innovation (PACE)
  FR– Field Reader Catalog
  EC– Exceptional Children Abstracts

PAGE

This command causes the next page of a display to be shown on the console screen. -More- in the lower-right hand corner of the screen indicates there is another page. When used following a DISPLAY command, PAGE will cause the next item to be displayed when all pages of the current item have been displayed.

Dialog

END

Entering this command produces a display requesting
the user to evaluate the search technique by entering
code numbers in response to queries which appear on
the screen.

The interview procedure can be bypassed by entering
the END command and typing in BYPASS (or simply B).
It is important to execute an END command at search
conclusion because this command actually stores the
items to be printed.

```
┌─────────────┐
│ DISPLAY SET │
│   HISTORY   │
├─────────────┤
│      @      │
└─────────────┘
```

DISPLAY SET HISTORY

Entry of this command during a search causes a display of all sets thus far created. In other words, this display duplicates the console typewriter output. If new terms are selected while this display is on the screen, they are posted to the display.

This command is used primarily in the absence of a console typewriter. An example of the display response to a DISPLAY SET HISTORY command is as follows:

SET NO.	NO. IN SET	DESCRIPTION OF SET (+=OR, *=AND, -=NOT)
----	------	---------------------
2	132	IT=MATHEMATICS
2	92	IT=MATHEMATICS SELECTION
3	135	IT=MATHEMATICS INSTRUCTION
4	61	IT=PRIMARY EDUCATION
5	454	IT=ELEMENTARY EDUCATION
6	23	(1+2+3)*(4+5)

SEND MESSAGE

This command allows one terminal to send a message to another terminal or terminals. After entry of the following command

SEND MESSAGE   3/HELLO

The message HELLO will be sent to terminal 3.

Individual messages should not exceed one display screen line. Terminal 1 is usually the central control terminal. A message to terminal 0 will send the message to all terminals.

EXPLAIN

The EXPLAIN command is available to provide an on-line supplement to the printed DIALOG User's Manual. Entry of this command followed by a command name or error message (e.g., "?EXPAND") will provide a one-page explanation. ?EXPLAIN gives a display of all possible explain entries

Dialog

DESCRIPTOR CODES

ERIC descriptors are assigned 2-character identification codes. These codes must be used with EXPAND and SELECT commands as in the examples below.

Code and Example	Description	Files Where Used
AC=64	Authority code	1, 3
AU=SMITH, J. L.	Author	1, 2, 6
BN=NDEA-VIIB-449	Bureau number	3
CD=ARIZONA-2	Congressional district	3
CH=AA	Clearing house number	1, 2, 6
CN=OIC-4-16-023	Contract/grant number	1, 3, 5, 6
DN=NDEA-VIIB-449	Report number	1, 6
FR=LEWIS, DR. HILDA	Field reader	5
GL=AAA00045	Title III location and agency code	4
ID=HEAD START	Identifiers	1, 2, 3, 4, 5
IS=RIEDEC70	Issue of RIE	1
IT=COMPUTERS	Index TERM	1, 2, 3, 4, 5, 6
JO=AAUP BULLETIN	Journal citation	1, 2, 6
PA=00040000	Dollar amount	3, 4
PB=65-05	Project start date	3
PE=73-06	Project end date	3
PI=ABBOTT, MAX G.	Investigator	3
PN=DPSC 68-5859	Project number	4
PO=ANDREWS	Project officer	3
PS=U.C.L.A.	Source of document	1, 3, 4, 5, 6
PY=68	Proposal date	3
RB=BBB03682	Branch number	5
RE=04	Region number	5
SC=AHP22630	Source code	1
SP=U.S.O.E. BUREAU OF RESEARCH	Sponsoring agency	1, 6
TI=PROBLEM SOLVING	Title	3, 4

Files Available

(1) --- RESEARCH IN EDUCATION (RIE)
(2) --- CURRENT INDEX TO JOURNALS IN EDUCATION (CIJE)
(3) --- CURRENT PROJECT INFORMATION (CPI)
(4) --- PACESETTERS IN INNOVATION (PACE)
(5) --- FIELD READER CATALOG
(6) --- EXCEPTIONAL CHILD EDUCATION

Appendix C

Very Basic Instructions on How to Use AIM–TWX

1. Decide how many aspects or relationships are involved in your request and what these aspects are.

   For example, "primary tumors of the small intestine" has two aspects:
   (a) tumor aspect
   (b) small intestine aspect

   "Primary tumors of the small intestine in infants" has a third aspect:
   (c) infants

2. You must select terms from *MeSH* that represent the topics of your request.

   The term INTESTINE, SMALL exists in the vocabulary. So do the more specific terms DUODENUM, ILEUM, and JEJUNUM.

   Some terms may exist that, in themselves, express more than one aspect of your request.

   For example, INTESTINAL NEOPLASMS expresses the relationship between "tumor" and "intestine" although the term is not, of course, restricted to the small intestine.

3. The blue pages of *MeSH* group related terms together under broad subject categories.

   For example, category C2 includes all terms for neoplasms, cysts, and polyps.

Prepared by F. W. Lancaster for AIM–TWX Study reported in Chapters Eight and Nine.

If only certain types of tumors are of interest you may find the specific terms here.

For example, you may be interested only in hemangiomas of the small intestine. The C2 category reveals the term HEMANGIOMA and also the term HEMANGIOMA, CAVERNOUS.

To find your way in the blue pages look at the category summary on p. 217 of the 1970 *MeSH*. Or, find a relevant term in the alphabetical section (white pages) and read off its category number. INTESTINAL NEOPLASMS is shown to belong to C2 and this leads you to the tumor category.

4. In conducting a search you must type in the selected terms in a logical sequence.

    The word AND between two *MeSH* terms means that both terms must have been used in indexing an article before it can be retrieved.

    If you type in

    INTESTINAL NEOPLASMS AND INTESTINE, SMALL

    you will only retrieve articles that have been indexed under both terms and which therefore presumably deal with neoplasms of the small intestine.

    INTESTINAL NEOPLASMS AND INTESTINE, SMALL AND INFANT

    will retrieve only articles in which all three terms have been used in indexing the item.

5. Frequently, however, you may find several terms in *MeSH* that all relate to a particular aspect of your request. Any one of these terms will be equally acceptable to you.

    For example, INTESTINE, SMALL; DUODENUM; ILEUM; JEJUNUM all relate to the concept of "small intestine."

    In entering alternative, equally acceptable terms, you must include the word OR between each, as follows:

    INTESTINE, SMALL OR DUODENUM OR ILEUM OR JEJUNUM

    If you want to relate such a list of terms to another term or list of terms you must use a separate search statement for each list, as:

    SS1 INTESTINE, SMALL OR DUODENUM OR ILEUM OR JEJUNUM

SS2 INTESTINAL NEOPLASMS OR DUODENAL NEO-
PLASMS

You may then use the next search statement to AND the two lists together:

SS3   1 AND 2 (the numbers of the search statements may be used for this purpose; you do not need to retype the term lists)

This means that a reference will only be retrieved if indexed under one of the intestine terms of SS1 *and* one of the neoplasm terms of SS2.

There is virtually no practical limit to the number of groups you can AND together. You could, for example, enter

SS4 INFANT OR INFANT, NEWBORN OR INFANT, PREMATURE OR INFANT, NEWBORN, DISEASES OR INFANT, PREMATURE, DISEASES

and then AND this list with those used previously, as follows:

SS5   3 AND 4

which means that a reference will only be retrieved if indexed under a neoplasms term *and* an intestine term *and* an infant term.

6. When you type in any search statement, the program will first respond by indicating how many references satisfy this logical requirement. You can use this information to determine whether your strategy is too broad (retrieving too many citations) or too narrow (retrieving too few).

When you AND several terms or lists of terms together you will quickly narrow the scope of a search and reduce the number of references retrieved.

SS1 above may well retrieve several hundred references (everything relating to the small intestine). So may SS2 (everything on intestinal neoplasms). SS4 may retrieve over a thousand (everything on infants).

However, when you AND these lists together (1 AND 2 AND 4) the number of references may be reduced to a handful because now you are asking only for items on neoplasms of the small intestine in infants.

7. When the count indicates a level of retrieval that may be acceptable, you can ask the system to print out the references that satisfy the search strategy.

There are several possible commands:

"PRINT" will cause the full reference (author, title, journal) to be printed.

"PRINT FULL" will cause the full record (including all subject headings) to be printed.

"PRINT TRIAL" will cause printing of title and subject headings only.

The command "PRINT TRIAL" will cause only a sample of two citations to be printed. You use it as a trial to determine if your search is on the right track.

The other two commands will allow you to print the complete set of references satisfying your strategy. However, these are printed in blocks of five. After each such block, the program will ask you if you wish to continue printing.

If you wish, you may specify the number of references you wish printed, as follows:

"PRINT 4".

8. In entering any search terms you must follow the exact spelling and punctuation used in *MeSH* with one space between each word. The heading INFANT, NEWBORN, DISEASES, for example, will not be recognized unless both commas are present.

All commands (as opposed to headings used in search strategies) *must appear within double quotation marks.*

9. The system allows a certain amount of browsing. If you use the "PRINT" or "PRINT TRIAL" commands, complete item records will be printed, including subject headings. Frequently you will be able to recognize other headings that might usefully be incorporated into your search.

10. In addition to the subject headings, the system makes use of subheadings. Subheadings are added by indexers to main headings to represent a particular aspect of the main term. For example,

SKIN/TRANSPLANTATION
MERCURY/TOXICITY
LUNG NEOPLASMS/RADIOTHERAPY

A complete list of the 60 subheadings appears on pp. vii–ix of *MeSH*.

In searching, enter subheading by adding to a main term after the oblique stroke (/). There is no space between terms and the stroke.

Each subheading can only be used with certain categories of terms. Permissible categories are indicated against each subheading in the list in *MeSH*. In general, allowable main heading/subheading combinations are self-evident and follow sensible expectations. For example,

AMYLOIDOSIS/DRUG THERAPY

is obviously sensible, while

HEAD/DRUG THERAPY

is not.

11. Sometimes you may want to use a whole category of terms in a search— for example, all catecholamines. It is not necessary to list them. First find the *tree number* for the category in the *Tree Structures*. The number for CATECHOLAMINES (p. 134) is D2.30.24. The entire category can be searched by the strategy

EXPLODE D2.30.24.

This will cause the computer to search for the entire group of terms (CATECHOLAMINES, DOPA, DOPAMINE, etc.).

The alphabetical section of *MeSH* (white pages) will give you the broad category number of a term to allow you to enter the *Tree Structures* at the correct place.

The "explosion" can be ANDED with another term or group of terms, as:

PSYCHOSES, SENILE AND EXPLODE C13.22

which will retrieve any reference indexed under the psychosis term and also under any term indicating avitaminosis (category C13.22).

12. For some searches you may be interested only in studies on humans. You can restrict the scope of a search by using the word HUMAN and ANDING this term with others in the normal way.

In other cases you may specifically want to exclude a particular topic from consideration. A term or category can be excluded by the construction AND NOT. For example:

TUBERCULOSIS, PULMONARY/DRUG THERAPY
AND NOT STREPTOMYCIN

Here you are asking for any studies of drug therapy of pulmonary tuberculosis except those involving use of streptomycin.

13. Before beginning your search at the terminal examine *MeSH* and decide on the appropriate main headings and subheadings to use. Group these terms into logical groups to reflect the relationships in your

request. When you have grouped these terms into logical OR and AND relationships you are ready to begin searching in AIM–TWX.

14. If you make a typing error at the keyboard (and we all do!) all is not lost. A complete line may be deleted (i.e., ignored by the computer) by striking the dollar sign (upper case 4) and then retyping.

Individual characters may be canceled by using the backward slash (upper case L). In this case you must count back the number of characters you wish deleted (including spaces) and strike the backward slash that number of times. After this, you may begin retyping.

Appendix D

Search Instructions for OBAR

OBAR/MDC

LEGAL RESEARCH REFERENCE CARD

A Service to the Ohio Bar by

OHIO STATE BAR ASSOCIATION
AUTOMATED RESEARCH
and

MEAD DATA CENTRAL INC.

WHAT TO DO IF YOU NEED ADVICE OR ASSISTANCE

IMMEDIATELY CALL YOUR **OBAR/MDC** *REPRESENTATIVE AT*

_____

WHAT TO DO IF THERE IS A SERVICE IRREGULARITY

IMMEDIATELY CALL THE **MDC** *COMPUTER CENTER IN DAYTON, OHIO (513/426–6872), ON ANOTHER TELEPHONE.*

START-UP

HOW TO DIAL IN

- *PLACE CONTROLLER SWITCH TO* **ON**.
- *PRESS* **MASTER CLEAR** *AND* **CLEAR** *KEYS*.
- *PRESS* **TALK** *BUTTON ON DATA SET*.
- *DIAL* **MDC** *COMPUTER CENTER (513/426–9710)*.
- *WHEN HIGH-FREQUENCY TONE IS HEARD, PRESS* **DATA** *BUTTON ON DATA SET AND RETURN PHONE TO CRADLE*.

HOW TO COMMUNICATE

- *USE KEYBOARD ONLY WHEN* **BLUE LIGHT** *IS ON*.
- *TO TRANSMIT TO COMPUTER PRESS IN SEQUENCE THE* **END, RESET** *AND* **TRANSMIT** *KEYS*.

ENTER IDENTIFICATION NUMBER

- *ENTER AND TRANSMIT*

OH _ _ _ _ _ _ _ _ _ _ _
(YOUR NUMBER)

ENTER FILE

- *THERE ARE 9 FILES WHICH MAY BE SEARCHED*.
- *ENTER AND TRANSMIT APPROPRIATE FILE ABBREVIATION*.

FILE ABBREVIATION	MATERIALS
SUP	– *SUP. CT. DECISIONS (1940–PRESENT)*
APP	– *APP. CT. DECISIONS (1950–PRESENT)*
MISC	– *ABST. & MISC. (1960–PRESENT)*
MAIN	– *COMBINED* **SUP APP. & MISC.**

SUP–OLD	–	*SUP. CT. DECISIONS (1821–1940)*
APP–OLD	–	*APP. CT. DECISIONS (1913–1950)*
MISC–OLD	–	*ABST. & MISC. (1926–1960)*
OLD	–	*COMBINED* **SUP–OLD, APP–OLD & MISC–OLD**
CODE	–	*OHIO CONSTITUTION & OHIO REVISED CODE (DEC. 31, 1969)*

SEARCH

<u>ENTER REQUEST</u>

● *ENTER AND TRANSMIT WORDS AND PHRASES YOU WISH TO SEARCH*

WORD RULES:

NUMBERS *– TREAT AS WORDS.*

PLURALS & POSSESSIVES *– ARE AUTOMATICALLY RETRIEVED BY ENTERING THE SINGULAR FORM ONLY, PROVIDED THE SINGULAR FORM CONTAINS 5 LETTERS OR MORE AND THE PLURALS ARE REGULARLY FORMED. e.g.* **CHILD** *WILL NOT AUTOMATICALLY RETRIEVE* **CHILDREN.**

HYPHENATED WORDS *– MAY BE ENTERED WITH HYPHEN OR AS TWO WORDS WITHOUT THE HYPHEN.*

COMMON WORDS *– SUCH AS* "BUT", "OR", "FOR", "IT", "WHO", "WHAT", "AND", *ETC. ARE NOT SEARCHABLE.*

UNIVERSAL CHARACTER. (*) *–* e.g. **INJUR***** *WOULD RETRIEVE* **INJURE, INJURY, INJURIES, INJURED** *AND* **INJURING.** **WORK-M*N** *WOULD RETRIEVE* **WORKMAN, WORKMEN, WORKMAN'S** *AND* **WORKMENS'.**

PHRASE RULE:

ENCLOSE PHRASES WITH SINGLE QUOTE MARKS ONLY WHEN THERE IS AN **AND** *OR AN* **OR** *IMBEDDED IN THE PHRASE.*

CONNECT RULES:

AND – *IF YOU WANT EACH OF THE WORDS OR PHRASES TO APPEAR IN THE CASE OR STATUTE, CONNECT THE TERMS WITH AN* **AND.**

OR – *IF YOU WANT WORDS OR PHRASES IN THE ALTERNATIVE OR AS SYNONYMS, CONNECT THE TERMS WITH AN* **OR.**

DISTANCE SEARCH RULE, (Wn):

e.g. **MEXICAN (W4) DIVORCE** *WOULD REQUIRE THAT THE WORDS* **MEXICAN** *AND* **DIVORCE** *APPEAR WITHIN 4 WORD POSITIONS ON EITHER SIDE OF EACH OTHER. (1–255 WORD LIMIT.)*

<u>ENTER MODIFICATION</u>

- *TO NARROW OR EXPAND THE SEARCH AFTER THE COM-PUTER HAS INFORMED YOU OF HOW MANY CASES OR STATUTES SATISFY YOUR LAST REQUEST OR MODIFICA-TION, YOU MUST FIRST ENTER AND TRANSMIT* **MODIFY.**

- *EACH MODIFICATION MUST BEGIN WITH AN* **AND** *OR* **OR.**

- *ENTER AND TRANSMIT THE ADDITIONAL WORDS OR PHRASES BY FOLLOWING THE RULES SET FORTH ABOVE UNDER* **ENTER REQUEST.**

BROWSE

AFTER THE SEARCHING PROCESS IS COMPLETED, YOU MAY DISPLAY THE CASES OR STATUTES THAT SATISFY YOUR CUMULATIVE SEARCH REQUEST BY ENTERING AND TRANS-MITTING **PRINT**. *THE COMPUTER WILL RESPOND WITH THE MESSAGE,* "**ENTER DESIRED** OUTPUT, DEVICE."

DISPLAY RETRIEVED CASES OR STATUTES IN DESIRED OUTPUT

● *THERE ARE 3 PRINCIPAL WAYS TO DISPLAY RETRIEVED MATERIALS.*

● *ENTER AND TRANSMIT DESIRED OUTPUT NAME.*

OUTPUT NAME	MATERIALS YOU WANT DISPLAYED
41	– *NAME OF CASE, CITATION, DATE*
41 + KWIC	– *NAME OF CASE, CITATION, DATE AND KEY–WORDS–IN–CONTEXT*
FULL	– *ENTIRE CASE OR STATUTE*

HARD–COPY PRINTOUT

● *PRESS* **OUT** *KEY TO OBTAIN A COPY OF THE TEXT DISPLAYED ON THE SCREEN IF YOU HAVE AN ACCOMPANY-ING PRINTER.*

PROCEED TO NEXT SCREEN FULL OF TEXT

● *PRESS IN SEQUENCE THE* **END, RESET,** *AND* **TRANSMIT** *KEYS.*

PROCEED TO NEXT CASE OR STATUTE

- *TO MOVE FORWARD TO NEXT ENTRY, TRANSMIT* **+1E**
- *TO RETURN TO PRECEDING ENTRY, TRANSMIT* **−1E**
- *TO RETURN TO BEGINNING OF CURRENT ENTRY, TRANSMIT* **−0E** *(ZERO)*
- *TO SKIP FORWARD OR BACKWARD MORE THAN 1 ENTRY, TRANSMIT THE APPROPRIATE NUMBER,* e.g. **+3E, −2E**

DISPLAY THE RETRIEVED CASES OR STATUTES IN A DIFFERENT OUTPUT

- *TO DISPLAY THE RETRIEVED MATERIALS IN A DIFFERENT OUTPUT, FOR EXAMPLE FROM* **41 + KWIC** *TO* **FULL,** *ENTER AND TRANSMIT* **OUTPUT** *AFTER ANY SCREEN FULL OF TEXT AND THEN FOLLOW THE COMPUTER'S INSTRUCTIONS.*

RETURN TO SEARCH PHASE

- *TO RETURN TO THE SEARCH PHASE AND NARROW OR EXPAND THE SEARCH FURTHER, ENTER AND TRANSMIT* **MODIFY** *AFTER ANY SCREEN FULL OF TEXT AND THEN FOLLOW THE COMPUTER'S INSTRUCTIONS.*

- *TO RETURN TO THE SEARCH PHASE AND SUBSTITUTE DIFFERENT SEARCH TERMS FOR THOSE PREVIOUSLY SUBMITTED, ENTER AND TRANSMIT* **MODIFYn** *AFTER ANY SCREEN FULL OF TEXT AND THEN FOLLOW THE COMPUTER'S INSTRUCTIONS.*
  NOTE: n *REPRESENTS THE REQUEST OR MODIFICATION LEVEL AT WHICH YOU WISH TO ADD THE DIFFERENT SEARCH TERMS.*

RETURN TO "ENTER FILE" MESSAGE

- *ENTER AND TRANSMIT* **$ $.**

HOW TO TERMINATE

- *REMOVE PHONE FROM CRADLE, PUSH* **TALK** *BUTTON ON DATA SET AND PLACE CONTROLLER SWITCH TO* **OFF.**

Appendix E

SUPARS Users Manual

**Prepared by Jeffrey Katzer, Sandra Browning, and June Brower
of the School of Library Science, Syracuse University**

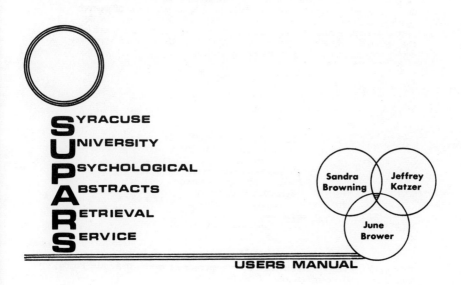

S YRACUSE

U NIVERSITY

P SYCHOLOGICAL

A BSTRACTS

R ETRIEVAL

S ERVICE

USERS MANUAL

Sandra Browning

Jeffrey Katzer

June Brower

DISCLAIMER: Although the SUPARS/DPS computer programs have been tested by SUPARS, no warranty, expressed or implied, is made by SUPARS or the School of Library Science, or the Syracuse University Computing Center as to the accuracy and functioning of these programs and the related materials. While the SUPARS system will retrieve all abstracts containing the submitted keywords, the system will not necessarily retrieve all abstracts relevant to the area of inquiry.

A REMINDER: The SUPARS service is experimental -- in the sense that it is still being developed. As noted above, we have tested the system and have tried to iron-out those "bugs" which always appear in new, large-scale computer systems. If, however, you experience delays or other annoyances using SUPARS we would appreciate your forbearance. A call to SUPARS (ext. 4220) will bring this matter to our attention and help us improve the service.

MONITORING: In order to continually improve the service provided, it is necessary for the SUPARS Research Group to have access to, and be able to study, the search queries of users of the system. In addition, one of the useful searching aids SUPARS provides for users is on-line access to selected, anonymous portions of search queries made by other users. To achieve these goals, the SUPARS system monitors and records all interactions made by all users of the service. We would appreciate a call from those users who have any questions about this procedure.

SUPARS User's Manual
Second Edition, 1971
Published by
SUPARS Research Group
School of Library Science
Syracuse University
Collendale Campus
Syracuse, New York   13210
(315) 476-5541 (ext. 4220)

This work is supported in part by a contract from the U.S. Air Force, Rome Air Development Center #F30602-71-C-0185.

TABLE OF CONTENTS

<u>INTRODUCTION</u>

<u>INSTRUCTION</u>

TABLE OF CONTENTS (CONTINUED)

REFERENCE   (to come later)

From time to time you will receive
additions and updates to this manual.

i

AN OVERVIEW OF THE SUPARS SYSTEM

SUPARS (Syracuse University Psychological Abstracts Retrieval Service) is a computer-based retrieval service. It is being offered to the entire University community, free-of-charge, during the Fall of 1971, during the hours 8-10 a.m. and 7-9 p.m. (Monday through Friday).

A computer-stored version of Psychological Abstracts containing approximately 59,000 abstracts can be searched by users of the SUPARS system. This represents all of Psychological Abstracts from January, 1969, to the present.

As you may know, Psychological Abstracts publishes "nonevaluative summaries of the world's literature in psychology and related disciplines." Each issue contains abstracts from several hundred different journals, books, theses, and conference proceedings. All of this information is stored in the SUPARS system and is retrievable by users of the service.

To use SUPARS, you must register. This entails completing a short registration form.

SUPARS is available (during the hours 8-10 a.m. and 7-9 p.m.) via any one of the 100 IBM 2741 computer terminals located around campus. Once you find an unused terminal, the process of making SUPARS searches can be summarized into five steps.

(1) Think of the words or concepts which reflect your information needs. For example, if you need references on the topic "the effect of aging on optimal reinforcement schedules" you might select the underlined words as the ones most basic to your information needs.

(2) Sign on to SUPARS and get confirmation that you can begin your search.

(3) Type in a SUPARS search which encompases these basic words or concepts. You will probably find it helpful to arrange these keywords in some logical order. (The major purpose of this manual is to teach you how to construct such SUPARS searches.)

(4) Wait until the computer searches the stored copies of Psychological Abstracts. This should take less than a minute or two. At your terminal, the retrieved abstracts will then be typed-out. Abstracts will be retrieved only if they meet the requirements you specified in your SUPARS search.

(5) Evaluate these abstracts. If they are relevant to your information needs, tear off the paper and take it with you. If they are not as relevant as you would like, review the suggestions presented in this manual to improve your search; then construct a new search and begin again at step (3).

ii.

<u>SIGNING-ON TO SUPARS</u>

SUPARS '71 will be available Monday through Friday 8:00-10:00 a.m. and 7:00-9:00 p.m. until December 17, 1971.

When you want to use SUPARS, <u>first</u> find a 2741 terminal not in use from among those listed on page vii. Then turn the power on. (The power switch is on the right hand side of the keyboard--see Figure 2 on page iv.) Next, check to see that the switch on the left side of the terminal console is in the "COM" position--see Figure 1, page iv. Now, follow the steps described below. The steps are illustrated on the facing page, with the steps <u>you</u> are to perform in <u>green</u> and the messages the computer types out in <u>black</u>.*

HIT ATTN	Hit the ATTENTION (ATTN) key. (This key is located at the top right of the keyboard--see Figure 2, page iv.)
	The computer will then respond with a message indicating the date.
)ON	You should then type)*ON*.
CARRIAGE RETURN	Push the carriage return button. You <u>must</u> push this button after every line <u>you</u> type to send your messages to the computer.
	The computer will type out a message telling you to *ENTER: MANNUMBER:PASSWORD*
1477xxxx:LIBS	You must then type in the number 1477xxxx:*LIBS*, REPLACING the small x's with 4 zeros <u>or</u> REPLACING the small x's with any four digits to make the number uniquely your own and thus avoid getting a message saying that the number is in use. Both 14770000:*LIBS* and 14771234:*LIBS* are valid numbers.
	The computer then types out a short message on account usage--ignore this message.
HIT ATTN	Hit the ATTENTION key again.
)EXEC PA	Then type in)*EXEC PA*. The computer will tell you at this point to *ENTER SOCIAL SECURITY NUMBER*.
)SOCIAL SECURITY NUMBER	Enter your social security number, <u>preceded by a right parens--</u> e.g.)123456789. Hold the SET key (located on the lower left side of your terminal) while typing in your number. NOTE: <u>Omit</u> the hyphens between the groups of numbers in your social security number.
	Please do not allow others to make SUPARS searches with your social security number. Have them call SUPARS at x4220 to register!

The computer will respond that your number is valid (your number will <u>only be valid if you have registered with us</u>). A copyright statement is printed out. And finally the computer tells you to *PROCEED*.

At this point, you are ready to begin a SEARCH. The Instruction Section will teach you the basics of searching SUPARS '71.

---

*In this book, the steps that should appear in green simply look lighter than the rest of the text.

iii

SIGNING-ON TO SUPARS (CONTINUED)

```
(ATTN)

      051)08.45.31 OCTOBER 25, 1971 SUOS/360

(ATTN)

)ON                                                      C
                                                         R
      ENTER MANNUMBER:PASSWORD

14770000:LIBS                                            C
                                                         R
      08.46.55 ACCT USE 0.010

(ATTN)

)EXEC  PA                                                C
                                                         R
      ENTER SOCIAL SECURITY NUMBER

)123456789                                               C
                                                         R
      VALID NUMBER
```

```
      PROCEED
```

CONSOLE AND TERMINAL KEYBOARD FIGURES

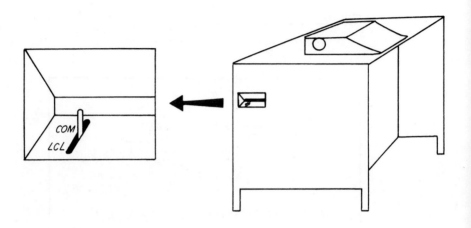

Figure 1. Side view of terminal console

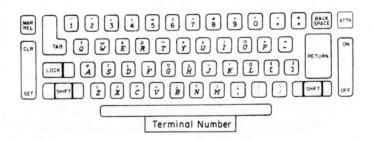

Figure 2. Terminal console keyboard

v

SEARCH-PROCESSING: IMMEDIATE OR DELAYED

After you sign onto the SUPARS system you will be automatically placed into one of two groups of SUPARS users: the immediate group or the delayed group. The first group of SUPARS users to sign on are placed into the immediate group. The later group of users are placed in the delayed group.

Immediate Group

Users in the immediate group will know they are in this group because no special messages will be typed out (see below), and because each of their SUPARS searches will be processed as rapidly as possible. Users in the immediate group will stay in that group until they sign off.

Delayed Group

Users in the delayed group will know they are in this group because a message telling them how many people are ahead of them will be typed out immediately after they sign on. For example, the message 2 *PEOPLE SEARCHING AHEAD OF YOU* indicates that this user is in the delayed group, and there are two people in the delayed group who will get into the immediate group ahead of him.

Users in the delayed group will have their SUPARS searches processed, but they should expect more of a delay between searches than should users in the immediate group.

Changing Groups

Whenever users in the immediate group sign off, users in the delayed group will be moved closer to the immediate group. When your status in the delayed group changes, you will be told of your new status. When you finally switch from the delayed group to the immediate group, the message *ZERO PEOPLE SEARCHING AHEAD OF YOU* will be typed out.

Neither Group

If both the immediate group and the delayed group are filled when you try to sign on, you will have the *TOO MANY USERS TRY AGAIN SOON* message typed out. Type *)OFF* and turn the power off. Try again later.

vi

SIGNING-OFF SUPARS

You can sign off the computer anytime before, during, or after a SUPARS search. To sign off the system, simply type)*OFF* twice as shown below. After your first)*OFF*, the computer will respond with a copyright statement. After the second)*OFF*, the computer will *SIGN-OFF*.

```
)OFF                                                                      C
                                                                          R

    COPYRIGHT 1967-1971 BY THE AMERICAN PSYCHOLOGICAL ASSOCIATION, INC.

)OFF                                                                      C
                                                                          R
    DURATION 00.21.52 (NO CHARGE)

    SIGN-OFF
```

If you are leaving the terminal, turn the power off. (The power switch is on the lower right hand side of the keyboard--see Figure 2, page iv.)

CORRECTING SPELLING ERRORS

If you catch a spelling mistake <u>before</u> hitting the carriage return button for that line, you can correct the error.

Just: (1)   Backspace until you are under the earliest error in the line (see Figure 2, page iv, for the location of the backspace button.)

          (2)   Hit the ATTENTION key. The computer responds by typing a carat sign under that point and spacing down a line.

          (3)   Type in the correction and everything else on the line to the right of the correction. Then push the carriage return button and proceed with your next line.

If you catch a spelling mistake <u>after</u> hitting the carriage return button for that line, you cannot correct it by the backspace method. If a mistake is made while <u>signing-on</u> to the system, ignore any messages or output from the incorrect line and type the line in again as it should be.

If, however, you are <u>entering a SEARCH</u> and a mistake is noted after a line has been sent, you must hit a Δ and begin the search again.

STOPPING OUTPUT USING THE ATTENTION KEY

You may stop the output from any search at any time by hitting the ATTENTION key. After stopping the output in this way, you may type in a Δ (or any of its variations--see the Instruction Section of this manual) to start a new search or)*OFF* to sign off the system.

TERMINAL LOCATIONS

USE ANY OF THESE TERMINALS FOR SUPARS

TERMINAL NUMBERS	LOCATION	SPECIAL INFORMATION
17-19	115 Machinery Hall	
20-22	116 Hinds Hall	
23-24	342 Hinds Hall	
25-28	304 Link Hall	
29-35	114 Link Hall	
36	B105 Link Hall	
37-41	B111 Physics Building	
42-43	209 Bowne Hall	
44-45	210A Slocum Hall	OBTAIN KEY FROM HOME EC OFFICE-3RD FLOOR
46	4th Floor Slocum Hall	
47-48	12A Smith Hall	
49-50	343 HBC Hall	
51-52	Basement Maxwell Hall	USERS MUST SIGN OUT TYPEBALL IN ROOM 11 OR LIBRARY
53-54	305 Reid Cottage (Soc. Dept)	
55-56	304 Sims Hall	
57	315 Huntington Hall	
58	500 Huntington Hall	
59	113 Euclid Avenue	
60	1st Floor 119 Euclid Avenue	
61	313 Lyman Hall	
62	17 Newhouse	OBTAIN KEY FROM NEWHOUSE LIBRARY
63	125A College Place	KEY AVAILABLE IN OFFICE 123 COLLEGE PLACE
64	PL-3 Brockway	OBTAIN KEY FROM MAIN DESK
68	1st Floor Lubin Hall	
70	214 Sims Hall	

INSTRUCTION

Purpose

This section of the 1971 Users' Manual teaches the user, through various examples, how to use SUPARS to search for material from Psychological Abstracts. This section should be read by all SUPARS users. Users who registered with SUPARS last fall will notice that there have been several important changes in the system since then.

Table of Contents

Page 1

INTRODUCTION TO THE SEARCH EXAMPLES

To effectively obtain information from <u>Psychological Abstracts</u> using
SUPARS '71, you should begin by tentatively formulating, in a sentence or
two, a statement of your topic—for example, "I want to learn about behavior
therapy" or "I'd like some information about the results of behavior therapy
with children."

Then, using the rules and suggestions which you will find in the search
examples, you must combine simple instructions to the computer with words
describing your topic into a SEARCH.

Finally, after signing on (see p. ii) at a computer terminal, you must
type in your search; the computer will then type back OUTPUT or the
abstracts or other information which your search has retrieved.

In the remaining pages of the Instructional section, you will be shown a
series of search examples, each one introducing you to a new aspect or
technique of searching. All terms and concepts will be thoroughly explained.

The last search example of the series will show you how to use combinations
of the techniques presented to help in efficient use of SUPARS '71.

In all of these search examples the lines you type into the computer from
your terminal are printed in green; all of the lines the computer types out
to you are printed in black.

Turn the page and begin learning how to put together a simple SUPARS
search.

Page 2

FORMAT OF A SEARCH--EXAMPLE 1

Example 1 on the facing page shows you the format of a simple SUPARS search.
All lines you type into the computer from your terminal are printed in
green; all lines the computer types out to you are in black.

In this example, we want to find abstracts dealing with the general topic
THERAPY. The steps in doing a search on this topic are described below.

DELTA Δ	After signing on (see p. ii), you must type a delta (Δ) in order to begin a search. A Δ is an upshifted H on your ter- minal.
CARRIAGE RETURN	After typing Δ, you must push the carriage return button. In fact, you will notice in Example 1 that you must push this button after every line <u>you</u> type in order to send your in- structions to the computer.
SEARCH NUMBER	After you have typed in the Δ and pushed the carriage return button, the computer will type out a line to you which tells you the search number of your particular search on the SUPARS '71 system.
LABEL	The computer will then type out the first LABEL, L1. A label indicates that you are to type in a KEYWORD(s) on the next line.
KEYWORD	You tell the computer your topic by typing in a keyword(s). The important words in your tentative formulation of your topic will usually become the keywords of your search. Syn- onyms and words which further describe or specify your topic can also be used as keywords. SUPARS '71 will retrieve the abstracts which contain your keyword(s). In Example 1, THERAPY was selected as the only important key- word from the topic, "I want to know something about therapy." This example is a very simple one; in many cases you will want to use several keywords. (See Example 2).
SEMICOLON	A label will be automatically printed out after each keyword line until you type a semicolon. This semicolon immediately follows your last keyword and stops the printing of labels.
LIST STATEMENT	After typing in your last keyword and semicolon and pushing the carriage return button, you must type in a list statement. The list statement tells the computer the form of output you want. The typed words *LIST RECORD*, used in this example, indicate one form of output (see Example 3). There are also other forms of output which you can request for this kind of search. These will be explained later.
END STATEMENT	The word *END* must be typed as the last statement of every search.

INSTRUCTIONS AND FORMAT DEALING WITH OUTPUT WILL BE PRESENTED
IN EXAMPLE 3.

EXAMPLE 1

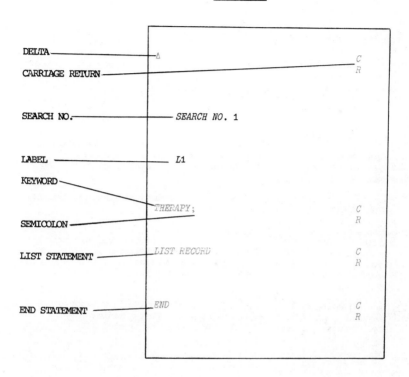

REMEMBER—YOUR STEPS ARE IN GREEN AND COMPUTER
MESSAGES TO YOU ARE IN BLACK.

Page 4

THE AND OPERATOR--EXAMPLE 2

The previous example (Example 1) presented a very simple search in which only one keyword was used. Users often want to search on less general topics which require more than one keyword to specify. Example 2 will show you how to construct a search using two keywords joined by the AND operator.

In Example 2, we are interested in finding abstracts dealing with the topic BEHAVIOR THERAPY.

Entering a search with just the keyword THERAPY will retrieve all abstracts containing the word THERAPY. But, in addition to retrieving abstracts on the topic BEHAVIOR THERAPY, many non-relevant abstracts will also be retrieved. For example, you will retrieve an abstract entitled, "The present status of lithium therapy in manic depressive psychosis."

The same situation will hold true if the word BEHAVIOR is entered as the only keyword. Non-relevant abstracts such as, "Nest building behavior in three species of deer mice, Peromycus" will be printed out.

But, if you enter both BEHAVIOR and THERAPY as keywords under $L1$, as in the example on the facing page, and connect them by the word AND (the AND operator), you will then retrieve only those abstracts which contain both the words BEHAVIOR and THERAPY. For example, you will retrieve, among others, an abstract entitled, "Using love in behavior therapy."

It is possible to type several keywords under one label, but it is important to remember that you must connect all the words together by typing the AND between them—e.g., by typing BEHAVIOR AND AVERSIVE AND THERAPY; under $L1$ you will retrieve only those abstracts containing all three words.

There are alternative ways to type in multiple keywords and the AND operator. There are other operators which specify different relationships among the keywords. These will be presented in later examples and sections of this manual.

Page 5

<u>EXAMPLE 2</u>

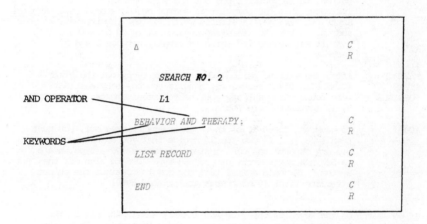

AND OPERATOR

KEYWORDS

REMEMBER--YOU MUST JOIN ALL YOUR KEYWORDS TOGETHER
WITH THE AND OPERATOR.   YOUR LAST KEYWORD
MUST BE FOLLOWED BY A SEMICOLON.

Page 6

<u>OBTAINING AND READING THE OUTPUT--EXAMPLE **3**</u>

In Example 1, the steps required for constructing a simple SUPARS search were described. Examples 3 and 4 will teach you how to obtain and interpret the OUTPUT from your search.

As previously indicated, you must conclude each search by typing in the word *END*. The information given below will tell you how to proceed from there.

SEARCHING
: After you type in the word *END* and push the carriage return button, the computer types out the word *SEARCHING* . This indicates that the computer is searching the stored <u>Psychological Abstracts</u> for those abstracts which fit the requirements of your search. After the *SEARCHING* message is typed out, there is a short waiting period which is usually between 5 and 90 seconds.

MAXIMUM ITEMS POSSIBLE
: After the waiting period, the computer types out the *MAXIMUM ITEMS POSSIBLE* message, which tells you how many abstracts were found which satisfy your search requirements. In Example 3, 12 abstracts were found.

)GO
: To have the <u>first 10</u> of these abstracts printed out, you must then type)*GO*. If you should decide that you do not want to see any output you can, instead of typing)*GO* , type in a Δ to begin a new search, or you can type)*OFF* to sign off the system. (Example 4 will tell you how to continue the output after the first 10 abstracts are printed out.)

If we search on the keywords BEHAVIOR AND THERAPY (as in Example 2), the abstract on the opposite page will be one of those retrieved. Each line of the output in Example 3 has been numbered for instructional purposes and corresponds to one of the explanatory lines below. Example 3 is an example of output in the LIST RECORD format.

Line 1	Year Volume number of <u>Psychological Abstracts</u>
Line 2	Abstract number
Line 3	Author(s) or editor(s)
Line 4	Affiliation of first author
Line 5	Title of article
Line 6, 7	Source document data
Lines 8-13	First 255 characters of abstract
Line 14	Language--English (E) or non-English (N)
Line 15	Type of source--Book (B) or other (O)
Line 16	DPS document number A Random number

Page 7

EXAMPLE 3

<table>
<tr><td>END</td><td></td><td>C
R</td></tr>
<tr><td>SEARCHING</td><td></td><td></td></tr>
<tr><td>MAXIMUM ITEMS POSSIBLE: 000012</td><td></td><td></td></tr>
<tr><td>)GO</td><td></td><td>C
R</td></tr>
</table>

OUTPUT

(1)	1971 45
(2)	8388
(3)	*BARTZ, WAYNE R. LOY, DONALD L.*
(4)	*DEWITT STATE HOSP., AUBURN, CALIF.*
(5)	*USING LOVE IN BEHAVIOR THERAPY*
(6)	*HOSPITAL & COMMUNITY PSYCHIATRY*
(7)	*1970 (OCT), VOL. 21 (10), 333-334*
(8)	*SUCCESSFUL BEHAVIOR THERAPY RESULTS ARE OFTEN ATTRIBUTED*
(9)	*TO FACTORS OTHER THAN THOSE EMBODIED IN REINFORCEMENT*
(10)	*LEARNING THEORY. 1 SUCH ARGUMENT IS THAT RESULTS MAY*
(11)	*BE DUE TO THE LOVE THE PATIENT RECEIVES FROM THE*
(12)	*THERAPIST (S). BEHAVIORISTS ARE AWARE OF THE VALUE OF*
(13)	*HUMAN WARMTH AND PRAISE BUT DIFFER FROM★*
(14)	*E*
(15)	*O*
(16)	0000009245 49

(9 more abstracts printed out here)

Page 8

CONTINUING THE OUTPUT--EXAMPLE 4

When the LIST RECORD format is used, abstracts are printed out in groups of ten. You must type)*GO* after each group of abstracts to continue the printing of the remaining abstracts. The complete process is described below. Example 4 completes the output begun in Example 3.

MAY BE x MORE ITEMS	After the 10th abstract is printed out, the computer types out the *MAY BE x MORE ITEMS* message. This message tells you how many abstracts remain to be printed.
)GO	To start the printing of the next group of 10 abstracts, which in this case is the last group of (2) abstracts, you must type)*GO*.

If, at this point, you do not want to see any more output, you may type Δ to start a new search or)*OFF* to sign off the system. |
| SEARCHING | The computer again types out the *SEARCHING* message, indicating that it is looking for the remaining abstracts. After this message, the next group of abstracts is printed out. |
| NO MORE ITEMS AVAILABLE | This message is typed out to you when all retrieved abstracts have been printed out. At this point you can type Δ to start a new search or)*OFF* to sign off the system. |

Page 9

EXAMPLE 4

```
    (10 abstracts printed out here)

    MAY BE 2 MORE ITEMS


)GO                                              C
                                                 R
    SEARCHING

    (2 abstracts printed out here)

    NO MORE ITEMS AVAILABLE
```

Page 10

THE OR OPERATOR--EXAMPLE 5

In Example 2, you learned how to use the AND operator to join multiple keywords in a search. The usage of the AND operator enables you to put together a more precise search than is possible using only a single key-word.

As you will remember from Example 2, entering BEHAVIOR AND THERAPY under $L1$ will result in the retrieval of all those abstracts containing both the words BEHAVIOR and THERAPY. While this search will retrieve many helpful abstracts, it is important to note that not all relevant abstracts will be retrieved. For example, abstracts dealing with behavior therapy may not contain both of those words; they may contain only the words BEHAVIORAL and THERAPY or DESENSITIZATION and THERAPY. Such abstracts will not be retrieved by the search BEHAVIOR AND THERAPY.

To retrieve a greater number of abstracts dealing with your topic, it is usually helpful to think of and search on alternative ways of specifying your topic. Searching on synonyms, on alternative spellings, on related topics, or on subcategories of your topic may help you find additional relevant abstracts. (SUPARS '71 can provide you with some helpful tech-niques to aid you in coming up with search alternatives--see later examples.)

The OR operator, illustrated on the facing page, is used in SUPARS searches to connect keyword alternatives in an either-or relationship. That is, the search BEHAVIOR OR BEHAVIORAL OR DESENSITIZATION will retrieve those abstracts containing either the word BEHAVIOR or the word BEHAVIORAL or the word DESENSITIZATION.

Usage of the OR operator increases the power and efficiency of your search by enabling you to simultaneously search on several acceptable keywords.

Page 11

EXAMPLE 5

```
Δ                                                          C
                                                           R

        SEARCH NO. 5

        L1

        BEHAVIOR OR BEHAVIORAL OR DESENSITIZATION;         C
                                                           R

        LIST RECORD                                        C
                                                           R

        END                                                C
                                                           R
```

OR OPERATOR

Page 12

THE AND AND OR OPERATORS TOGETHER—EXAMPLE 6

The previous example, Example 5, was presented as a very simple example of how to use the OR operator. Looking at that example now with the topic BEHAVIOR THERAPY in mind, we can see that the example is not an efficient one for finding abstracts on that topic. Abstracts containing the words BEHAVIOR THERAPY, BEHAVIORAL THERAPY, etc. will be retrieved by the search. But again the abstract "Nest-building behavior in three species of deer mice, Peromyscus" will also be retrieved.

To eliminate the retrieval of such irrelevant abstracts, the word THERAPY must be added as a keyword. Example 6 shows you how to do this by using both the AND and OR operators in the same search.

To find abstracts containing either the words BEHAVIOR and THERAPY or the words BEHAVIORAL and THERAPY or the words DESENSITIZATION and THERAPY, the keyword lines should be entered as described below.

L1   Under *L1*, enter the alternative keywords you have decided
            upon and join them together using the OR operator.

L2   Under *L2*, enter the keyword THERAPY.

L3   To join all the keywords together in the proper relation-
            ship, simply type in the line *L1 AND L2*; under the last
            label. "*L1*" and "*L2*" stand for the keywords and operators
            which appear under *L1* and *L2* earlier in the search.

Note that you cannot enter this search on one line under *L1*. That is, you cannot enter under *L1* the words BEHAVIOR OR BEHAVIORAL OR DESENSITIZATION AND THERAPY. The SUPARS '71 system will not accept both the AND and OR OPERATORS on the same line.

Page 13

EXAMPLE 6

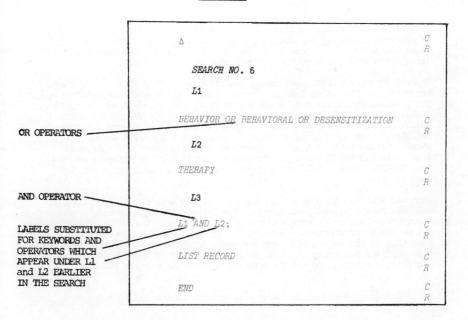

OR OPERATORS

AND OPERATOR

LABELS SUBSTITUTED
FOR KEYWORDS AND
OPERATORS WHICH
APPEAR UNDER L1
and L2 EARLIER
IN THE SEARCH

```
Δ                                                    C
                                                     R

          SEARCH NO. 6

          L1

     BEHAVIOR OR BEHAVIORAL OR DESENSITIZATION      C
                                                     R
          L2

     THERAPY                                         C
                                                     R
          L3

     L1 AND L2;                                      C
                                                     R

     LIST RECORD                                     C
                                                     R

     END                                             C
                                                     R
```

REMEMBER—YOU CANNOT USE BOTH THE AND AND OR OPERATORS ON
        THE SAME LINE.

Page 14

THE TRUNCATION EXPANDER--EXAMPLE 7

As we stressed in Example 5, it is often helpful to search on a variety of keywords which can be used to define your topic area. The TRUNCATION expander, typed (?), is one tool available to you which can help you incorporate multiple keyword possibilities into your search.

In many of the earlier examples, we used the word THERAPY as one of the keywords searched on to find abstracts on the topic BEHAVIOR THERAPY. The possibility exists that there may be abstracts relevant to the topic BEHAVIOR THERAPY which use the terms BEHAVIOR THERAPIES, BEHAVIOR THERAPIST, BEHAVIOR THERAPISTS, etc. Typing in the root of a word immediately followed by the TRUNCATION expander -- e.g. THERAP(?)--will enable you to search simultaneously on all words formed from that root. The keyword line L2 in Example 7 shows you the use of the TRUNCATION expander on the root THERAP. Notice that there are no spaces after the root of the keyword and the (?).

Both the TRUNCATION expander and the OR operator help you to incorporate multiple keywords into your search. The TRUNCATION expander allows you to incorporate only those keywords having the same root, while the OR operator allows you to incorporate a combination of any keywords. You should also note that as the TRUNCATION expander may retrieve abstracts based upon words with suffixes you could not have anticipated ahead of time, some of the abstracts retrieved may not be relevant to your information needs.

Special Rules for the Use of the Truncation Expander

1. It is important to note that the TRUNCATION expander can be used in keyword lines containing one keyword (as in Example 7.)

2. The TRUNCATION expander can also be used in keyword lines containing more than one keyword joined by the OR operator. That is, L1 in Example 7 could be typed in as BEHAVIOR(?) OR DESENSITIZATION.

3. The TRUNCATION expander cannot be used in keyword lines containing several keywords joined by the AND operator.

Page 15

EXAMPLE 7

Δ   C
                                                                     R
         SEARCH NO. 7

         L1
BEHAVIOR OR BEHAVIORAL OR DESENSITIZATION   C
                                                                     R

         L2

TRUNCATION ———————— *THERAP(?)*   C
EXPANDER   R

         L3

L1 AND L2;   C
                                                                     R

LIST RECORD   C
                                                                     R

END   C
                                                                     R

REMEMBER — THE TRUNCATION EXPANDER CANNOT BE USED IN ANY KEYWORD
LINE CONTAINING THE AND OPERATOR.

THE TRUNCATION EXPANDER MUST BE TYPED IMMEDIATELY NEXT
TO THE ROOT OF THE WORD. THERE CANNOT BE ANY SPACES.

Page 16

THE WORD DISTANCE RESTRICTORS--EXAMPLE 8

As was discussed in Example 2, the AND operator guarantees the retrieval of abstracts containing all of the keywords joined by the AND. Occasionally, this procedure will retrieve abstracts not relevant to your information needs.

One way to attempt to guarantee retrieval of relevant abstracts is to specify that, for example, the words BEHAVIOR and THERAPY must occur in a single phrase, BEHAVIOR THERAPY. That is, the two words must be right next to each other if the abstract is to be retrieved. (The AND operator only specifies that the words must be somewhere within the same abstract.)

SUPARS '71 permits you to use a word distance restrictor to specify how close together and in what order you would like keywords to be in an abstract before it qualifies for retrieval.

The example on page 17 shows one usage of the word distance restrictor. In this example, abstracts will be retrieved if they contain both the words BEHAVIOR and THERAPY; in addition these two words must be no more than one word apart (+1).

If it is useful, you can select a number other than (+1). For example, MORALE AND PERFORMANCE (+2) will retrieve abstracts containing both words provided they are in that order and two words apart. In this case, you will retrieve abstracts containing the phrase "morale on performance" and the phrase "morale in performance" as well as the phrase "morale and performance."

Special Rules for the Use of the Word Distance Restrictor

1. It is important to note that the word distance restrictor can only be used in keyword lines containing two keywords joined by the AND operator.

2. The word distance restrictor cannot be used in the same keyword line as an OR operator.

3. The word distance restrictor must be typed immediately after the second keyword. No spaces are permitted after the keyword.

Page 17

EXAMPLE 8

```
Δ                                      C
                                       R

    SEARCH NO. 8


    L1

BEHAVIOR AND THERAPY(+1);              C
                                       R

LIST RECORD                            C
                                       R

END                                    C
                                       R
```

REMEMBER—THE WORD DISTANCE RESTRICTOR CAN ONLY BE USED WITH
THE AND OPERATOR. IT CANNOT BE USED WITH THE OR
OPERATOR ON THE SAME KEYWORD LINE.

DO NOT LEAVE ANY SPACES BETWEEN THE LAST KEYWORD AND
THE WORD DISTANCE RESTRICTOR.

Page 18

THE LIST BRIEF OUTPUT FORMAT--EXAMPLE 9

In Examples 3 and 4, you learned how to obtain and read output in the LIST RECORD format. The present example will introduce you to another available form of output, the LIST BRIEF form.

As its name indicates, the LIST BRIEF form is a brief or short form of output. LIST BRIEF output gives you the minimum amount of information needed to find retrieved abstracts in the published version of Psychological Abstracts. The year and the volume number of the issue of Psychological Abstracts in which an abstract appears and the number of the abstract are the three pieces of information printed out for each retrieved abstract.

Information is printed out for up to 100 abstracts at a time, with 4 abstracts printed per line.

To request output in the LIST BRIEF format you must first type in the words *LIST BRIEF* as the list statement in your search. LIST BRIEF output is then obtained in the same general manner as is LIST RECORD output (see Examples 3 and 4.)

After you type in the *END* statement the computer responds with the words *SEARCHING* and the *MAXIMUM ITEMS POSSIBLE* message. To start the printing of the first group of abstract citations, you must type *)GO*.

The *MAY BE x MORE ITEMS* message is typed out at the end of the printing of each group of 100 citations -- if there are more than 100 abstracts retrieved. To continue obtaining output, again you need to type *)GO*.

The LIST BRIEF format is useful when you want to have a large number of abstract citations printed out quickly, and you are reasonably sure that most of them are relevant to your information needs. The disadvantage of LIST BRIEF is that you cannot learn much about the retrieved abstracts from the output itself.

REMEMBER -- to get LIST BRIEF output, only one change is needed in the information you type into SUPARS. Only the LIST statement is changed; everything else is exactly the same.

Page 19

EXAMPLE 9

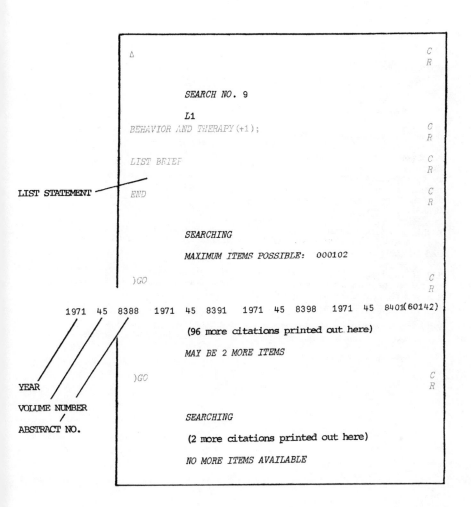

Page 20

PRACTICE SEARCH—EXAMPLE 10

In the last 9 examples, we have attempted to present the basic procedures
you need to know about SUPARS '71. There are several examples following
the present one which illustrate additional procedures available to you.
Before proceeding to these, we suggest that you take a minute or two to
try the practice search on the facing page. We provide several possible
answers to the exercise on the next 4 pages. Comparison of your answer
with ours may suggest areas for review before you begin actual usage of
SUPARS.

In this practice search, we are interested in finding information on the
topic MARRIAGE COUNSELING, a topic very similar in structure to the topic
used in the previous search examples.

Fill in the boxes of the search skeleton on the next page with the elements
you think are needed to make a complete and efficient search. Then compare
your search with the ones on pages 22, 23, and 24.

NOTE: We have left space for three keyword lines in the practice
       search. You need not use them all in constructing your search.

Page 21

EXAMPLE 10

SEARCH NO. 10

L1

L2

L3

SEARCHING

MAXIMUM ITEMS POSSIBLE: 000015

(10 abstracts printed out here)

MAY BE 5 MORE ITEMS

SEARCHING

(5 more abstracts printed out here)

NO MORE ITEMS AVAILABLE

Page 22

<u>ANSWERS TO THE PRACTICE SEARCH—EXAMPLE 10 (CONTINUED)</u>

In evaluating your practice search, you should first check to see if you have
included all the <u>required</u> elements of a search.   The search example below shows
and labels all of these required elements.

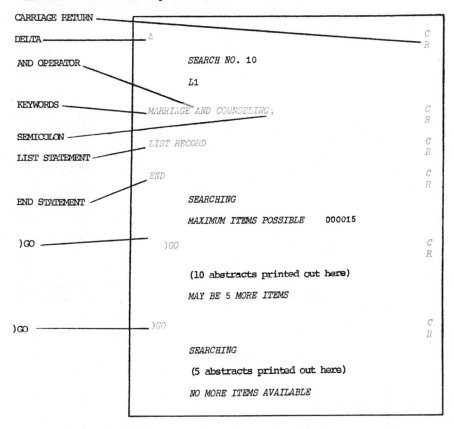

CARRIAGE RETURN

DELTA

AND OPERATOR

KEYWORDS

SEMICOLON

LIST STATEMENT

END STATEMENT

)GO

)GO

SEARCH NO. 10

L1

MARRIAGE AND COUNSELING;

LIST RECORD

END

SEARCHING

MAXIMUM ITEMS POSSIBLE   000015

)GO

(10 abstracts printed out here)

MAY BE 5 MORE ITEMS

)GO

SEARCHING

(5 abstracts printed out here)

NO MORE ITEMS AVAILABLE

NOTICE THAT IN THIS ANSWER TO THE PRACTICE SEARCH WE DID NOT
NEED TO USE *L2* OR *L3*.   YOUR ANSWER MIGHT HAVE USED THEM —AND
BE CORRECT.

Page 23

ANSWERS TO THE PRACTICE SEARCH—EXAMPLE 10 (CONTINUED)

Now you should consider your usage of keywords to specify your topic.
As we have indicated in previous search examples, there are many ways
to approach a topic using SUPARS '71. Our first answer example on page 22,
shows one way to approach the topic MARRIAGE COUNSELING. The words
MARRIAGE and COUNSELING, joined by the AND operator are entered under L1.
This keyword usage will result in the retrieval of all abstracts containing
both the words MARRIAGE and COUNSELING.

As we have stressed in previous search examples, however, in order to retrieve a greater number of abstracts dealing with your topic, it is
usually helpful to search on alternative ways of specifying your topic.
To this end, we suggest the following search examples, which are other
correct answers to the practice search.

```
Δ                                              C
                                               R

              SEARCH NO. 10


              L1

   MARRIAGE OR MARRIAGES OR MARITAL             C
                                                R
              L2

   COUNSELING OR COUNSELOR OR THERAPY           C
                                                R

              L3

   L1 AND L2;                                   C
                                                R

   LIST RECORD                                  C
                                                R

   END                                          C
                                                R
```

In the above example, we have used the OR operator to connect several
acceptable keyword alternatives. This example also illustrates the
correct way of using both the AND and OR operators in the same search.
REMEMBER—you cannot use both the AND and OR operators on the same line.

Page 24

ANSWERS TO THE PRACTICE SEARCH--EXAMPLE 10 (CONTINUED)

```
Δ                                                    C
                                                     R


        SEARCH NO. 10

        L1

MAR(?)                                               C
                                                     R

        L2

COUNSEL(?) OR THERAPY                                C
                                                     R


        L3

L1 AND L2;                                           C
                                                     R

LIST RECORD                                          C
                                                     R

END                                                  C
                                                     R
```

In this final example, we have used the TRUNCATION expander (?) to
allow us to search simultaneously on all words formed from the roots
MAR and COUNSEL. This example points up the special rules for the
use of the TRUNCATION expander:

(?) <u>can</u> be used in keyword lines containing only one keyword.
(?) <u>can</u> be used in keyword lines containing more than one key-
    word joined by the OR operator.
(?) <u>cannot</u> be used in keyword lines containing the AND operator.

Page 25

INTRODUCTION TO ADDITIONAL SEARCHING AIDS

In many of the earlier search examples, we stressed that
searching on alternative ways of specifying your topic-- e.g.
searching on synonyms, plurals, alternative spellings, related
topics, subcategories of your topic, etc.--may help you to
retrieve a greater number of abstracts dealing with your topic.

This point has been emphasized because our work with SUPARS '70
users last fall indicated that many users, by making their
searches too specific, retrieved only a small portion of the
available abstracts relevant to their topics.

After working through the previous search examples, you
already know about several ways of constructing search
alternatives in order to maximize the number of relevant
abstracts and minimize the number of irrelevant abstracts
retrieved.

The search examples which follow present further techniques, new to SUPARS this year, which will help you find
additional keyword alternatives to search on.

As a final note here, we suggest that it may be helpful to
plan out your search strategies before going to a terminal.
A more thorough consideration of different ways of searching
and words to search on can usually be achieved in this way.

Page 26

USING THE VOCABULARY--EXAMPLE 11

Thus far in our discussion of search techniques, you have been concerned with learning how to retrieve relevant abstracts from a computer-stored collection of Psychological Abstracts. In this and the three following examples, you will learn how to obtain information from a second body of stored material called the VOCABULARY. You will also learn how to apply that information to your searches of the stored Psychological Abstracts.

The VOCABULARY is an alphabetical list of all words appearing in the stored Psychological Abstracts. Information on how many abstracts each of the words appears in is also contained in the VOCABULARY.

The example on the facing page illustrates one usage of the VOCABULARY. By typing in a word such as BEHAVIOR under L1, you can find out if that word is in the VOCABULARY and therefore in Psychological Abstracts. If the word does appear in the VOCABULARY, information is also given as to how many abstracts in the stored Psychological Abstracts that word appears in.

The steps in entering a VOCABULARY search are described below. Obtaining output from these searches will be described in Example 12.

DELTA V	To begin a VOCABULARY search, you must type in a DELTA V (ΔV).
CARRIAGE RETURN	As you've already learned, you must push the carriage return button after every line you type.
SEARCH NUMBER and LABEL	As was the case with Δ searches, the computer at this point types out the search number of your particular search on the SUPARS system. This line is followed by the first LABEL, L1, which indicates that you are to type in a KEYWORD on the next line.
KEYWORD	The word you want to locate in the VOCABULARY is entered as the keyword. Do not enter more than one keyword in any ΔV search.
SEMICOLON	A semicolon must be typed in immediately following the keyword to stop the printing of labels.
LIST STATEMENT	A list statement must be typed in for every search. The list statement for a VOCABULARY search is always *LIST VOCAB*.
END STATEMENT	You must type *END* as the last statement of every search.

Information obtained from this use of the VOCABULARY can be helpful to you when you are constructing regular Δ searches. If a word that you are thinking of using in a regular Δ search does not appear in the VOCABULARY, then it should not be used as a keyword in your Δ search as it will retrieve no abstracts. If, on the other hand, your search word does appear in the VOCABULARY, but is listed as appearing in a very large number of abstracts (e.g. 15,000), that word is not, in general, a good word to use as the only keyword in your search as it would take several hours to print out the output. Example 7 will help you decide whether to use such a keyword in combination with other keywords.

Page 27

EXAMPLE 11

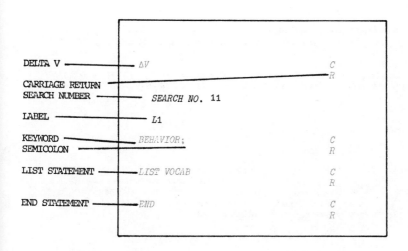

DELTA V ——————— ΔV   C
                                                      R
CARRIAGE RETURN
SEARCH NUMBER ——————— SEARCH NO. 11

LABEL ——————— L1

KEYWORD ——————— BEHAVIOR;   C
SEMICOLON   R

LIST STATEMENT ——————— LIST VOCAB   C
                                                      R

END STATEMENT ——————— END   C
                                                      R

REMEMBER—DO NOT USE MORE THAN ONE KEYWORD IN ANY
        ΔV SEARCH.   (Searching the VOCABULARY in-
        volves a different procedure than searching
        the Psychological Abstracts. For this reason,
        we cannot use as many options when constructing
        a ΔV search as with a Δ search.)

Page 28

USING THE VOCABULARY: OBTAINING THE OUTPUT—EXAMPLE 12

In the previous example, the steps in doing a VOCABULARY search were described. This example will show you how to obtain and interpret the OUTPUT from your search.

As previously indicated, you must conclude your search by typing in the word *END*. The information given below will tell you how to proceed from there.

SEARCHING	After you type in the word *END*, the computer types out the *SEARCHING* message, which indicates that it is searching the VOCABULARY for your keyword.
MAXIMUM ITEMS POSSIBLE	This message, typed out by the computer, indicates the number of words to be listed as output. As we are only asking here about <u>one</u> word, only <u>one</u> word will appear as output (along with the number of <u>Psychological</u> <u>Abstracts</u> that word appears in.)
)GO	To obtain the output information, type *)GO*.
OUTPUT	The computer responds first with a message telling you that the number appearing in parentheses after the print-out of your keyword represents the number of abstracts in which that keyword appears. The keyword is then typed out. In Example 12, the word BEHAVIOR appears in 15005 abstracts (documents.) If the word BEHAVIOR did not appear in the VOCABULARY, the output would be: *BEHAVIOR (****0)*
NO MORE ITEMS AVAILABLE	The computer prints out this message when the output has been completed. At this point you can type Δ or ΔV to start a new search or *)OFF* to sign off the system.

Page 29

EXAMPLE 12

```
ΔV                                              C
                                                R
    SEARCH NO. 12

    L1

BEHAVIOR;                                       C
                                                R

LIST VOCAB                                      C
                                                R

END                                             C
                                                R

    SEARCHING

    MAXIMUM ITEMS POSSIBLE: 000001
)GO                                             C
                                                R
    NO. IN ( ) IS NO. OF DOCUMENTS

    BEHAVIOR (15005)

    NO MORE ITEMS AVAILABLE
```

OUTPUT ————————→ (pointing to BEHAVIOR (15005))

REMEMBER—DO NOT USE MORE THAN ONE KEYWORD IN ANY ΔV SEARCH.

Page 30

USING THE TRUNCATION EXPANDER TO SEARCH THE VOCABULARY--EXAMPLE 13

The example on the facing page shows you how to use the TRUNCATION expander,
typed (?), in a VOCABULARY search. By typing a keyword root followed by
the TRUNCATION expander under $L1$, you will obtain as your OUTPUT an alphabetical listing of all words in the VOCABULARY beginning with the specified
root. Following each retrieved word is a number indicating how many
abstracts in the stored Psychological Abstracts that word appears in.

REMEMBER: as this is a VOCABULARY search, you must start your
             search with a ΔV and use *LIST VOCAB* as your list state-
             ment.

As is the case with all SUPARS searches, type)GO to begin the printing of
output. As Example 13 shows, 25 lines of four words, each word being
followed by a number indicating the number of abstracts that word appears in,
are printed out at a time. At the end of each group of 100 words, the
computer types out a message indicating the number of retrieved words
remaining to be printed. To continue the output, type)GO.

Output from this type of VOCABULARY search can be useful to you in several
ways. The printing out of the various words, including misspelled words,
formed from a root and used in Psychological Abstracts, may suggest
potential keywords for your regular Δ searches.

Secondly, output from this type of search can help you decide on which
letters to take as a keyword root for use with the TRUNCATION expander in
your Δ searches. For example, from the output in Example 13, you can see
that using THER(?)--from THERAPY--in a Δ search not only will retrieve
abstracts containing the words THERAPEUTIC, THERAPISTS, THERAPY, etc., but
will also retrieve abstracts containing such unrelated words as THERMOREGULA-
TION and THEREFORE. A better choice for the root is seen to be THERA(?).
Look at the output from this example to see why this is so.

Page 31

EXAMPLE 13

```
ΔV                                                                    C
                                                                      R

        SEARCH NO. 13-

        L1

THER (?)                                                              C
                                                                      R

LIST VOCAB                                                            C
                                                                      R

END                                                                   C
                                                                      R

        SEARCHING

        MAXIMUM ITEMS POSSIBLE:   000109

)GO                                                                   C
                                                                      R

        NO. IN ( ) IS NO. OF DOCUMENTS
```

THER	(1)	THERA	(2)	THERAPEUTIC	(153)	THERAPEUTICALLY	(6)
THERAPIES	(9)	THERAPIST	(70)	THERAPISTS	(53)	THERAPUTIC	(3)

(92 more words printed out here)

MAY BE 9 MORE ITEMS

OUTPUT

```
)GO                                                                   C
                                                                      R

        SEARCHING
```

THEREFORE	(1)	THEREON	(1)	THERESE	(2)	THERETO	(1)
THERMALLY	(4)	THERMISTORS	(1)	THERMOCOUPLE	(1)	THERMOREGULATION	(2)
THERMOREGULATORY	(3)						

NO MORE ITEMS AVAILABLE

REMEMBER—DO NOT USE MORE THAN ONE KEYWORD IN ANY ΔV SEARCH.

Page 32

<u>USING THE STORED SEARCHES--EXAMPLE 14</u>

Thus far in the search examples, we have talked about searching the stored Psychological Abstracts and the stored VOCABULARY. In this example we introduce a third collection of stored information, the STORED SEARCHES.

As we stated on the back of the title page of this manual, all searches made on SUPARS are saved and stored by the computer. These stored searches can themselves be searched and retrieved by using the procedures described in this and the following four examples.

It is worth repeating here that no names are stored with saved searches and that social security numbers or personal data of any kind are not available to users of the STORED SEARCHES. A user retrieving a search from the STORED SEARCHES will not know who made the original search, why it was made, etc.

Examples 14 and 15 illustrate one usage of the STORED SEARCHES. (Other usages will be explained in Examples 16 and 17). By typing in a keyword such as THERAPY under L1 and using the list statement *LIST WORDS*, you can obtain a listing of all words which have appeared in all previous searches which contain THERAPY. Information is also given as to how many searches each retrieved word appeared in.

Output from this type of ΔS search, by drawing on searches made by users with similar interest areas, may provide you with new ideas for alternative keywords to use in your Δ searches of the stored Psychological Abstracts.

Instructions are given below for retrieving word lists from the STORED SEARCHES. You will learn how to obtain the output from this type of search in Example 15.

DELTA S	To use the STORED SEARCHES, you must begin your search by typing in a DELTA S (ΔS).
CARRIAGE RETURN	You must push this button after every line you type.
SEARCH NUMBER and LABEL	The number of your search and the first label are typed out by the computer at this point.
KEYWORD	The word you want to search on is entered as the keyword.
SEMICOLON	A semicolon must be typed in immediately following the keyword to stop the printing of labels.
LIST STATEMENT	A list statement must be typed in for every search. The list statement to obtain a listing of words appearing in searches containing your keyword is *LIST WORDS*.
END STATEMENT	The word *END* must be typed as the last statement of every search.

Page 33

EXAMPLE 14

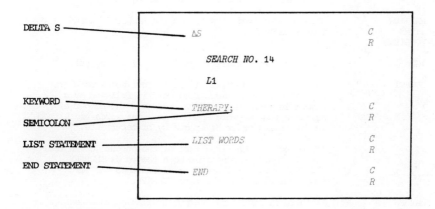

Page 34

<u>USING THE STORED SEARCHES: OBTAINING THE OUTPUT--EXAMPLE 15</u>

In the previous example, we showed you how to enter a search to retrieve words appearing with your keyword in the STORED SEARCHES. This example will show you how to obtain and read the OUTPUT from your search.

SEARCHING	This message tells you that the computer is searching the STORED SEARCHES for your keyword.
MAXIMUM ITEMS POSSIBLE	This message indicates to you the number of words that were found.
)GO	Typing)GO will start the printing of the output.
OUTPUT	As Example 15 shows, 25 lines of four words each are printed out at a time. Each word is followed by a number in parentheses which indicates the number of searches your keyword appears in. The words are listed in decreasing order of frequency of occurrence. If we look at the first part of the output we can tell that 59 searches contained both the words THERAPY and BEHAVIOR. Similarly, in 31 searches the word SHOCK was used with the word THERAPY.
MAY BE x MORE ITEMS	If there is additional output available, this message will be printed. In the example at the right, 18 more words remained after the first 100 words were printed.
)GO	To continue the output you need to type)GO.
NO MORE ITEMS AVAILABLE	The computer types this message when all the output has been printed. At this point you can continue searching SUPARS by typing a Δ or a ΔV, or a ΔS. If you are through searching, you can type)OFF to sign off the system.

Page 35

EXAMPLE 15

ΔS
      C
      R

    SEARCH NO. 15

    L1

    THERAPY;
                      C
                      R

    LIST WORDS
                      C
                      R

    END
                      C
      SEARCHING
                      R

      MAXIMUM ITEMS POSSIBLE: 000118

)GO
                      C
      NO. IN ( ) IS NO. OF SEARCHES
                      R

BEHAVIOR (59) AVERSIVE (48) BEHAVIORAL (32) SHOCK (31)

      (96 more words printed out here)

      MAY BE 18 MORE ITEMS

)GO
                      C
      SEARCHING
                      R

THERAPIST (26) OPERANT (25) SNAKE (20) COUNSELING (7)

      NO MORE ITEMS AVAILABLE

OUTPUT

Page 36

USING THE STORED SEARCHES: THE LIST SEARCH FORM OF OUTPUT—EXAMPLE 16

Example 16 shows you how ot obtain a second form of output when using the STORED SEARCHES. By starting your search with ΔS and using *LIST SEARCH* as your list statement, you will obtain as OUTPUT all <u>searches</u> containing your keyword as entered by previous users.

These searches are printed out in groups of 10. If more than 10 searches are retrieved, you can continue the output by typing)*GO*, as shown in Example 16 until all searches have been printed.

For each retrieved search, the following items are printed out: the log (or search) number of the original search, all keyword lines, the list statement, and the end statement. All retrieved searches are also followed by 3 numbers. The first number indicates the number of abstracts found by the original search. In the example at the right, 102 abstracts were found. The second number indicates the number of abstracts which the original user actually had printed out for him. In Example 16, the user had 72 citations printed out. The third number is a search identification number; ignore this number.

Output of this type is useful both as a source of ideas for alternative keywords and as an indicator of the retrieval capacity of different combinations of words and operators.

Page 37

EXAMPLE 16

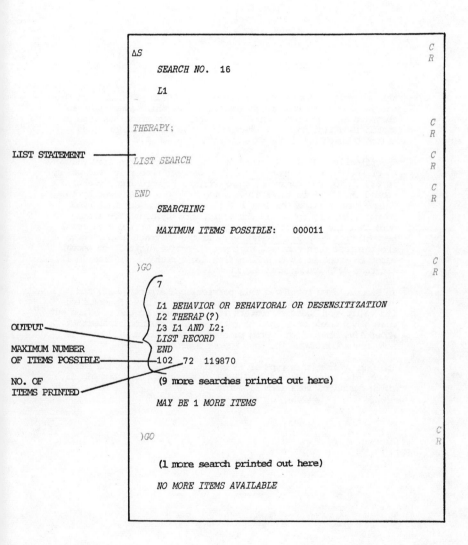

ΔS   C
                                                                            R
    SEARCH NO. 16

    L1

THERAPY;   C
                                                                            R
LIST STATEMENT ——— LIST SEARCH   C
                                                                            R
END   C
                                                                            R
    SEARCHING

    MAXIMUM ITEMS POSSIBLE: 000011

)GO   C
                                                                            R
    7

    L1 BEHAVIOR OR BEHAVIORAL OR DESENSITIZATION
    L2 THERAP(?)
OUTPUT ——— L3 L1 AND L2;
    LIST RECORD
MAXIMUM NUMBER
OF ITEMS POSSIBLE ——— END
    102 72 119870
NO. OF
ITEMS PRINTED ———

    (9 more searches printed out here)

    MAY BE 1 MORE ITEMS

)GO   C
                                                                            R
    (1 more search printed out here)

    NO MORE ITEMS AVAILABLE

Page 38

USING THE STORED SEARCHES: SEARCHING ON A RELEVANT DOCUMENT--EXAMPLE 17

This example presents another use of the STORED SEARCHES. In this case, our only keyword is an artificial one which identifies an abstract already stored in SUPARS. The output from this type of search is a listing of all keywords appearing in all previous searches which retrieved this abstract.

Specifically, V45A08388, stands for an abstract taken from volume 45 of Psychological Abstracts. The abstract number in that volume is 8388. You can construct an artificial keyword for any abstract stored in SUPARS in the following way. Type a *V* followed by the volume number, then the letter *A* followed by the abstract number. Do not leave any spaces in the artificial keyword. You should note that the abstract number typed in as part of the artificial keyword must be a 5-digit number. If the abstract number you are interested in consists of fewer than five digits, add enough zeros in front of it to make a five digit number. In Example 17, abstract 8388 was entered as A08388.

In Example 3 we retrieved this particular abstract (8388) and judged it to be relevant to our information needs. By entering its volume and abstract numbers in a Δ*S* search we can now find out what other words were used to retrieve this particular abstract. Hopefully, some of the words printed in the output will give us some new ideas about the best way of searching SUPARS.

The output from this type of Δ*S* search is arranged in the same way as the output from all *LIST WORDS* searches. See Example 15, which describes this form of output.

Page 39

EXAMPLE 17

ΔS   C
                                                                      R

     SEARCH NO. 17

     L1
V45Λ08368:   C
                                                                      R

LIST WORDS   C
                                                                      R

END   C
                                                                      R

     SEARCHING

     MAXIMUM ITEMS POSSIBLE: 000044
)GO   C
                                                                      R

     NO. IN ( ) IS NO. OF SEARCHES

BEHAVIOR	(26)	*REINFORCEMENT*	(24)	*HUMAN*	(19)	*THERAPY*	(18)
LEARNING	(10)	*BEHAVIORISTS*	(10)	*LOVE*	(7)	*SEX*	(5)

     (36 more words printed here)

     NO MORE ITEMS AVAILABLE

Page 40

USING)STAT--EXAMPLE 18

A final aid which may help you construct searches to retrieve those abstracts you are interested in is)*STAT*. When you are searching for abstracts using a DELTA (Δ) search, it is sometimes useful to know how many abstracts each line of keywords retrieves. To find this information, you merely have to type)*STAT* after the computer has typed out the *MAXIMUM ITEMS POSSIBLE* message.

The most common use of)*STAT* would occur before you ask SUPARS to type out the retrieved abstracts. That is, you would type)*STAT*, and based upon that information, you would decide whether or not to type)*GO* to have the abstracts printed out.

In the example on the facing page, you see a rather complex search. We are still interested in retrieving abstracts dealing with BEHAVIOR THERAPY. In this example, we use some of the information found from the earlier examples. As written, this search will retrieve all abstracts containing any word beginning with THERA as long as that abstract also has in it either the word AVERSIVE or the word DESENSITIZATION or any word beginning with BEHAV.

As seen in the example, 2078 abstracts were found which met these requirements. Since it would probably take hours to print out all 2078 of these, we are interested in cutting down on the number of abstracts retrieved. By typing)*STAT*, we see that the keywords under L1 retrieved 2756 abstracts. If we were to repeat search 10, but omit BEHAV(?), we probably would retrieve many fewer abstracts which still should be relevant to our information needs.

The output from)*STAT* gives the number of abstracts each keyword line retrieves. Using this information you can determine if a keyword line retrieves too many abstracts (as in this example) or too few abstracts. In either of these cases, you may want to change your search so that each keyword line helps you retrieve the number of relevant abstracts you can review or have printed out in a reasonable period of time. If you are satisfied with the numbers indicated by)*STAT*, you can type)*GO* to start the printing of OUTPUT.

Page 41

EXAMPLE 18

A   C
    R

      SEARCH NO. 18

      L1

BEHAV(?)   C
    R

      L2

AVERSIVE   C
    R

      L3

DESENSITIZATION   C
    R

      L4

L1 OR L2 OR L3   C
    R

      L5

THERA(?)   C
    R

      L6

L4 AND L5;   C
    R

LIST RECORD   C
    R

END   C
    R

      SEARCHING

      MAXIMUM ITEMS POSSIBLE: 002078

REQUEST FOR →)STAT   C
STATISTICS   R

	L1	2756
	L2	36
OUTPUT FROM)STAT —	*L3*	14
	L4	2810
	L5	769
	L6	2078

Page 42

PUTTING IT ALL TOGETHER--EXAMPLE 19

In the preceding set of examples, several different ways of searching
SUPARS were presented separately. To use SUPARS most effectively, you
will probably need to integrate many of these techniques in one "grand
searching strategy."

This will be necessary if you want to avoid making SUPARS searches which
(1) retrieve too many abstracts, most of which are not relevant to your
information needs; (2) retrieve too few abstracts, even though they are
all relevant. To be a successful SUPARS searcher, you will often need to
use some of the SUPARS options presented in the later examples (e.g.
ΔV, ΔS, and $)STAT$) as aids in searching <u>Psychological</u> <u>Abstracts</u>.

The next few pages contain a hypothetical example of the integration of
searching aids within one searching strategy. In this example, the user
made seven SUPARS searches before he retrieved a small number of abstracts
which were highly relevant to his information needs.

As you follow this example, pay particular attention to the reasons
the user gives for employing the different searching aids.

<u>SEARCH NO. 100</u>

Before making any searches, the user tries to specify his information
needs. Since he wants abstracts about the COMPUTER SIMULATION of THINKING,
he combines these three keywords in an AND relationship.

In response to this search, SUPARS found 73 abstracts. Since this user
doesn't want to look through 73 abstracts in order to find a fewer number
of more relevant ones, he tries to determine which keywords are too
general and retrieve too many abstracts. So instead of having the 73
abstracts typed out at his terminal, the user asks for statistics about
the keywords.

Interpreting the statistics, the user decides that (1) SIMULATION
as a keyword is not general enough, and (2) THINKING is much too
general.

Page 43

EXAMPLE 19

```
Δ                                              C
                                               R
    SEARCH NO. 100

    L1

COMPUTER                                       C
                                               R
    L2

SIMULATION                                     C
                                               R
    L3

THINKING                                       C
                                               R
    L4

L1 AND L2 AND L3;                              C
                                               R
LIST RECORD                                    C
                                               R
END                                            C
                                               R
    SEARCHING

    MAXIMUM ITEMS FOUND:  000073

)STAT                                          C
                                               R
        L1       417
        L2       139
        L3      2348
        L4        73
```

Page 44

PUTTING IT ALL TOGETHER--EXAMPLE 19 (CONTINUED)

SEARCH NO. 101

An easy way to broaden the keyword SIMULATION is to cut-off the end of
the word and replace it with the (?). The more letters the user cuts-
off, the more general the resulting keyword will be. Of course, if he
cuts-off too much of the original word, he may broaden the keyword so
much that it includes non-relevant concepts.

Using ΔV as an aid, the user sees that SIMUL(?) is too general because
it will retrieve abstracts containing the word SIMULTANEOUS -- which are
not relevant to his information needs.

From the output of this search, the user decides that SIMULAT(?) is a good
keyword to use: it should be broader than SIMULATION, but not so broad
as to include all the non-relevant keywords.

Unfortunately, there is no way the user can tell from a VOCABULARY search
exactly how many abstracts SIMULAT(?) will retrieve. The numbers in
parentheses are the number of abstracts with that word in it. But one
abstract could conceivably contain several of these words. If the
nine words in the vocabulary beginning with SIMULAT never occurred in the
same abstract, then SIMULAT(?) would be too general for this user as it
would retrieve 552 abstracts.

SEARCH NO. 102

In order to determine the number of abstracts SIMULAT(?) will retrieve,
the user enters it into a simple Δ search. The purpose of this search
is only to find how many abstracts SIMULAT(?) will retrieve. As you can
tell from the search output. SIMULAT(?) will retrieve 207 abstracts.

The user doesn't want to print any of these 207 abstracts because there
are too many of them, and most likely they include abstracts not relevant
to computer simulation of thinking.

Page 45

EXAMPLE 19 (CONTINUED)

ΔV   CR

       SEARCH NO. 101
       L1

SIMUL(?);   CR
LIST VOCAB   CR
END   CR

       SEARCHING
       MAXIMUM ITEMS POSSIBLE: 000013

)CO   CR

       NO. IN ( ) IS NO. OF DOCUMENTS

SIMULATE (107)	*SIMULATED* (18)	*SIMULATES* (25)	*SIMULATING* (73)
SIMULATION. (139)	*SIMULATIONS* (27)	*SIMULATOR* (9)	*SIMULATORS* (30)
SIMULATORY (129)	*SIMULTANEITY* (51)	*SIMULTANEOUS* (640)	*SIMULTANEOUSLY* (278)
SIMULUS (1)			

       NO MORE ITEMS AVAILABLE

Δ   CR

       SEARCH NO. 102
       L1

SIMULAT(?);   CR
LIST RECORD   CR
END   CR
       SEARCHING
       MAXIMUM ITEMS POSSIBLE: 000207

Page 46

PUTTING IT ALL TOGETHER--EXAMPLE 19 (CONTINUED)

SEARCH NO. 103

The user now believes he has solved his first problem: broadening SIMULATION. His next task is to find more specific terms for THINKING. One way to do this is to make a ΔS search to find other words used by other searchers when they used the word THINKING.

142 different words were used in SUPARS searches along with the word THINKING. For this user, this is too many to look through, so he abandons this idea for finding alternatives for THINKING.

SEARCH NO. 104

Another way to solve his problem is to enter into ΔS the volume number and abstract number of an abstract which he knows to be relevant. This procedure would retrieve other search keywords used by other searchers when they retrieved that abstract.

In order to use this aid for searching, he needs to know the exact volume number and abstract number of a relevant abstract. He doesn't usually have this sort of information at hand. Therefore, the user decides to search for any one relevant abstract. He repeats his first search (NO. 100) modifying it to include SIMULAT(?), in order to find that abstract. His plan is to interrupt the printing of abstracts after the first relevant one is printed. Then he can use the volume number and abstract number of that abstract as input to a ΔS search.

As you can see, this search retrieved 93 abstracts. The user expects to retrieve more abstracts with this search than with search NO. 100 because SIMULAT(?) is more general than SIMULATION.

As the first abstract is typed out, the user decides from the title that it is relevant to his information need. He interrupts the printing of the other abstracts by hitting the ATTN button on the terminal.

Page 47

EXAMPLE 19 (CONTINUED)

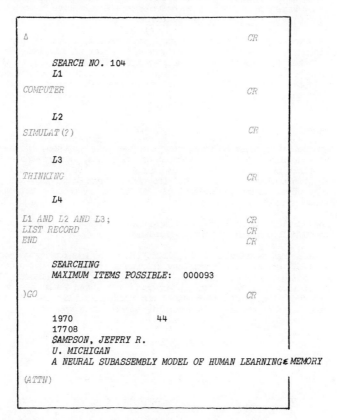

Page 43

<u>PUTTING IT ALL TOGETHER--EXAMPLE 19 (CONTINUED)</u>

<u>SEARCH NO. 105</u>

Now the user can do what he wanted to do with search NO. 103: he can find other keywords used by other searchers. In this search, he will find the other keywords used in other searches which retrieved abstract 17708 from Volume 44 of <u>Psychological Abstracts</u>.

As you can see, 27 different words were used to retrieve this abstract. Since they are printed out in decreasing order of frequency of use, the searcher interrupts the output by hitting the ATTN button on the terminal when he thinks he has found enough other words to use in his search. The output from SEARCH NO. 105 is interpreted as described in Example 17. Based upon this output, the user believes he can construct his "best search so far." His last search is given below.

<u>SEARCH NO. 106</u>

Incorporating what he found from the previous searches, the user thinks he is ready to obtain a print-out of abstracts. Notice that he changed the contents of *L*1 from what it was in search NO. 100.
He didn't plan to do this, but the output from Search NO. 105 gave him the idea of expanding the concept of COMPUTER so it would retrieve other relevant documents.

In addition, he decided on the keyword COGNITIVE as a first alternative to THINKING, which was much too general.

This search retrieved 41 abstracts. Since he has done some preliminary analysis of his search strategy (searches #100-#105), the user hopes these are all going to be relevant. He decides to print them out. Of course, if he decides that the first few are not as relevant as he desires, he can always interrupt the printing of output and continue to use the various searching aids SUPARS provides to sharpen his search strategy.

EXAMPLE 19 (CONTINUED)

```
ΔS                                                    CR

    SEARCH NO. 105
    L1

V44A17708;                                            CR
LIST WORDS                                            CR
END                                                   CR

    SEARCHING
    MAXIMUM ITEMS POSSIBLE:   000027

)GO                                                   CR

    NO. IN ( ) IS NO. OF SEARCHES
```

LEARNING	(34)	THINKING	(27.)	MEMORY	(26)	MODEL	(26)
COGNITIVE	(15)	PROCESSES	(14)	PROCESSING	(10)	NEURAL	(8)
MAP	(4)	NEURONS	(3)	SYSTEM	(3)	PROGRAM	(3)

```
Δ                                                     CR

    SEARCH NO. 106
    L1

COMPUTER OR PROGRAM OR MODEL                          CR

    L2

SIMULAT(?)                                            CR

    L3

COGNITIVE                                             CR

    L4

L1 AND L2 AND L3;                                     CR
LIST RECORD                                           CR
END                                                   CR

    SEARCHING
    MAXIMUM ITEMS POSSIBLE:   000041

)GO                                                   CR
```

Appendix F

Illustration of Use of CARUSO Tutorial Program*

Reproduced by permission of Elaine Caruso.
*See Chapter Fifteen. See also Appendix G, which must be used in conjunction with this appendix, as all page numbers refer to Appendix G.

Type your name, please. Please strike the return key when you have finished.
>linda

If you have read the introduction you may begin the TYPING PRACTICE session. Type anything you like. When you feel familiar with the keyboard, type READY on the next free line and hit the RETURN key, to start the game.

>ready.

Read page 4
Ready yet?
>yes
The question:
Please find articles about SUBJECT HEADINGS. I am also looking for articles about the LIBRARY OF CONGRESS.

     TERM = >
>headings library done
     TERM = >
>library
     TERM = >
>done

* * * * THE SINGLE ASPECT STRATEGY * * * *

When only one term is specified for searching we say that we have a SINGLE
ASPECT search. This is the usual approach to card catalogs or published
indexes.

You have suggested 2 subjects, or terms, for searching.
Thank you.

The computer will be using the next few seconds to look up your selection of
terms in its stored index. Please be patient.

None of the terms you suggested for searching matched exactly with any of
the index terms stored in the System index.

Terms listed below are either (1) misspelled or (2) are not in the subject index,
or (3) are variant forms of terms which are in the index.
If variant forms or spellings exist in our index, they will be suggested to you.

    A = headings library done
    B = library

You may now add any additional terms for searching.
No variant forms or spellings for the rejected terms given above were found.
If you do not wish to do so, or when finished, type DONE.

HINT: There are 11 documents in our file which are good answers to the question we're working on.
    READ PAGE 5 FOR DETAILS.

    TERM = >
>lib
>headings
    TERM = >
>library of congress
    TERM = >
>done

Please be patient—the System is apt to be slow at this time. You should use such intervals to review what you have done.

Thank you. The table which follows shows how many documents would be retrieved by each of the terms you suggested, if it were searched by itself, i.e., as the basis for a SINGLE-ASPECT search.

TERM	NUMBER OF DOCUMENTS REFERENCED
D = library of congress	3

Terms listed below are either (1) misspelled or (2) are not in the subject index, or (3) are variant forms of terms which are in the index.
If variant forms or spellings exist in our index, they will be suggested to you.

C = headings

You may now add any additional terms for searching.
No variant forms or spellings for the rejected terms given above were found.
If you do not wish to do so, or when finished, type DONE.

HINT #2: If you have already used SUBJECT HEADINGS and LIBRARY OF CONGRESS, you should now type DONE, and get on with the game. If not, enter them as search terms now.

TERM
> subject headings
TERM => >
> done.

Please be patient—the System is apt to be slow at this time. You should use such intervals to review what you have done.

Thank you. The table which follows shows how many documents would be retrieved by each of the terms you suggested, if it were searched by itself, i.e., as the basis for a SINGLE-ASPECT search.

TERM	NUMBER OF DOCUMENTS REFERENCED
E = subject headings	11

* * * * * * * * * * * * THE LOGICAL SUM* * * * * * * * * * * *
READ PAGE 6.

Ready yet?
>go
The logical statement for a LOGICAL SUM strategy using the aspects you selected might look like this
    D + E
    where
    + = AND/OR
    D = library of congress
    E = subject headings

To put this logical statement in plain English, substitute the values of A, B, etc.:

Please find references to documents which discuss
    library of congress AND/OR subject headings

    NOW READ PAGE 7.

Ready yet?
>go

COMPLETE EACH OF THE FOLLOWING STATEMENTS WHEN THE CARET (>) COMES UP.

You are learning to create search _____
>strategy
You're good! Try this:
We have just presented a logical statement of a _____ _____ type of strategy.
>logical sum
RIGHT!

Now back to our game—

The subjects, or terms, which you suggested for search have been connected by the logical AND/OR, as shown above. This strategy, consisting of terms and logical connectors, has been used to search the index to the Game file of documents.

The System reports 11 document references located using the LOGICAL SUM strategy above. Is that MORE or LESS than the total number of documents referenced in the table given above?
> less
It usually is.
It must be equal to or less than the sum of the single aspect references.

* * * * * * * * * * * THE LOGICAL PRODUCT* * * * * * * * * * * *

READ PAGE 8.

Ready yet?
> go
The logical statement would be written:

D × E
where—

× = AND ALSO
and A, B, C, etc. are defined as above.

A verbal interpretation of this logical statement:

library of congress AND ALSO subject headings

READ PAGE 9 NOW.

Ready yet?
>go

COMPLETE THE FOLLOWING STATEMENTS:

In a LOGICAL SUM type of strategy, the symbol '+' can be read as _____
_____.
>and/or
RIGHT!

In the LOGICAL PRODUCT type of strategy, the symbol 'x' or 'X' means

_____ _____.
>and also
That's right!.

Here's what happened when the System applied the LOGICAL PRODUCT strategy, using all the terms you selected for search:

The number of document references found was reduced to 3 citations, because a search revealed that only 3
documents were indexed by all of the required terms.

The LOGICAL PRODUCT STRATEGY reduces the number of documents retrieved, because, while many documents may be indexed by one of the search terms used, fewer will be indexed by ALL of the given search terms.

* * * * * * * * * * * LOGICAL DIFFERENCE * * * * * * * * * * * *

READ PAGE 10.

Ready yet?
> go
Type the logical statement:
Use these symbols, A, B, etc., as defined earlier:

    D = library of congress
    E = subject headings
    F = classification

> dxe–f

Logical statement of this type of strategy would look like this:

    D × E − F

The only new thing was the ' − ' sign, so you should have had no difficulty.

If you put parentheses around the LOGICAL PRODUCT part of your strategy, it is not incorrect, but it is redundant, because we assume that the negated aspect applies to all documents retrieved in your search.

It might be instructive for us to look at the information lost by our stipulation that documents discussing CLASSIFICATION be eliminated.

Search by the simple LOGICAL SUM strategy found 11 document references.
The same search, but including the negation of the aspect CLASSIFICATION, gives us 10 document references.

NOW READ PAGE 11.

Ready yet?
> go

* * * * COMPLEX STRATEGY * * * *

READ PAGE 12.

Ready yet?
>go

Type the logical statement:
>a & b &
>a + b &
>a + B + C
>(A + B + C) X (D + E + F)

How close were you to this:

    (1)   (A+B+C) x (D+E+F)
           or
    (2)   AxD + AxE + AxF + BxD + BxE + BxF + CxD + CxE + CxF

Read page 13.

Ready yet?
>go

Let's substitute words for the symbols in the logical statement: $(A+B)$ X $(C+D)$.

'$(A+B)$' means: 'A ____ ____ B'. Complete the statement on the next line.
>and not
No ... Please try again. If you need help, look back to the section headed LOGICAL SUM. Also see page 9 of your instruction booklet.

'$(A+B)$' means: 'A ____ ____ B'. Complete the statement on the next line.
>a and also b
Just the words to fill the blank spaces, please.
>and also
No, just the words which would be the verbal equivalent of '$+$'.

'$(A+B)$' means: 'A ____ ____ B'. Complete the statement on the next line.
>or
No ... look at page 9 of the instruction book. It says '$+$' can be read as AND/OR.

'$(A+B)$' means: 'A ____ ____ B'. Complete the statement on the next line.
>or and
The answer we want is 'AND/OR'. Let's go on to the next question.

'$(C+D)$' means '$(C$ ____ ____ $D)$'
>either or
This also is a logical sum. Please try again.
>logical sum
The answer should have been 'AND/OR'. Reread page 9 of your instruction booklet.

Now complete this statement:
'$(A+B)$ x $(C+D)$' means '(A and/or B) ____ ____ (C and/or D)'.

>and or

No ... We'll restate the question:
THE LOGICAL PRODUCT strategy joins the two LOGICAL SUMS. The 'X' should be read as ____ ____.
>either or

The answer is: 'AND ALSO'.

Are you sure you understand this statement? The strategy of LOGICAL PRODUCT OF LOGICAL SUMS is very useful, and must be understood. Let's repeat the exercise.

We're examining the logical statement: $(A + B) \times (C + D)$

'$(A + B)$' means: 'A ____ ____ B'   Complete the statement on the next line.
> and or
Right!

'$(C + D)$' means '(C ____ ____ D)'
> and or
Right!

Now complete this statement:
'$(A + B) \times (C + D)$' means '(A and/or B) ____ ____ (C and/or D)'.

> and also
Right!
Very well done! The statement used LOGICAL PRODUCT strategy to join the LOGICAL SUMS.

You may now write freely on the next 5 lines ANY comments or remarks. You MUST put something on each line, if only a single meaningless letter.
> a
> a
> a
> a
> a

When you are ready to stop—if your time is up, or you are completely frustrated, report to the person in charge of the experiment.
We are about to begin the next round. There may be some delay while 'reloading' takes place.

MAKING A LOGICAL STATEMENT

Try this question: FIND ARTICLES ON CURRICULUM IN UNITED STATES LIBRARY SCHOOLS.

An 'optimum' strategy for this question will yield three document citations.

You must now decide on subjects to be searched and terms which express them. NO MORE THAN 3 TERMS at this time, please. You may add terms later if needed. When you finish putting in terms, type DONE

```
    TERM = >
> curriculum
    TERM = >
> united states
    TERM = >
> library schools
    TERM = >
> done
```

The computer will be using the next few seconds to look up your selection of terms in its stored index. Please be patient.

Thank you. The table which follows shows how many documents would be retrieved by each of the terms you suggested, if it were searched by itself, i.e., as the basis for a SINGLE-ASPECT search.

TERM	NUMBER OF DOCUMENTS REFERENCED
A = curriculum	4
B = united states	4
C = library schools	5

Do you want to add any terms?
If you do not wish to do so, or when finished, type DONE.

    TERM = >
> done

Now create a logical strategy for searching the file. Use A, B, C, etc. to represent each term.

Use any or all of the following terms. Unused terms will be considered as deleted.

A = curriculum, B = united states, C = library schools

You may use as much time and as many lines as you like to practice creating this strategy. When you are satisfied with it, type READY on the next line. The system will then attempt to execute the search strategy statement.

Go ahead = >
> A X B X C
> ready

Your logical statement, verbalized:

Please list references to documents which discuss:

curriculum   AND ALSO   united states   AND ALSO   library schools

Would you like to change your strategy? Type YES or NO, please.
> no

The terms you chose and the strategy you devised, retrieved 3 document references.

Do you want the bibliography printed out now?
In any case, you may call for any items, individually, after the System has analyzed your efforts.
>no

EVALUATION OF SEARCH RESULTS

Your search strategy retrieved all relevant references—very good!

These are relevant documents:

6877166,6877177,6877777

It's nice to see that you found all of the documents
which we consider relevant to question 2.
and with no noisy, 'irrelevant' items ... A PERFECT SEARCH!!!

You can see the indexing and citations for any of these documents now, if you wish.

When the system types WHICH ONE? type the number of the item you want to see.

When satisfied, type DONE.

Enter one document number at a time. WHICH ONE?= >

> 6877777

Bibliographic citation(1)? or just index terms(2)? or both(3)?
If you type 1,2, or 3 before the document number the NEXT time we ask 'which document?', you can save this step.
1,2, or 3?

> (3)
Sorry, please repeat.
Bibliographic citation(1)? or just index terms(2)? or both(3)?
1,2, or 3?

> 3
Sass, Samuel
LIBRARY TECHNICIANS—'INSTANT LIBRARIANS'?
Library Journal, 92:11(June 1, 1967), pp. 2122–2126

    Curriculum
    Library Schools
    Library Technicians
    Teaching Machines
    Teaching Techniques
    United States

Enter one document number at a time. WHICH ONE?*>

> done

YOUR SCORE FOR THIS QUESTION:

RECALL:
1.00000
PRECISION:
1.00000

You may now write freely on the next 5 lines ANY comments or remarks.
You MUST put something on each line, if only a single meaningless letter.
>the commands
>sometimes confusing
>but this is fun
>interesting too
>a

When you are ready to stop—if your time is up, or you are completely
frustrated, report to the person in charge of the experiment.
We are about to begin the next round. There may be some delay while
'reloading' takes place.

NEXT QUESTION

You may now choose any of the questions provided, including question 2—see printed list—to work on. Enter the number of the question you choose on the next line.

>3

If you make the best choice of terms and strategy, you will retrieve 2 document references.

You must now decide on subjects to be searched and terms which express them.
When you finish putting in terms, type DONE

```
    TERM= >
> curricula
    TERM= >
> programmed instruction
    TERM= >
> library technicians
    TERM= >
> done
```

The computer will be using the next few seconds to look up your selection of terms in its stored index. Please be patient.

Thank you. The table which follows shows how many documents would be retrieved by each of the terms you suggested, if it were searched by itself, i.e., as the basis for a SINGLE-ASPECT search.

TERM	NUMBER OF DOCUMENTS REFERENCED
B = programmed instruction	1
C = library technicians	2

Terms listed below are either misspelled or are not included in the index to our collection, or are variant forms of terms which are in the index.

A = curricula

Do you mean:
curriculum?

If you want to use any of the terms suggested above, you must type them in, one at a time, when the System types TERM = >. Also, you may add any new terms, if you like.
If you do not wish to do so, or when finished, type DONE.

TERM = >
>curriculum
TERM = >
>done

TERM	NUMBER OF DOCUMENTS REFERENCED
D = curriculum	4

Now create a logical strategy for searching the file. Use A, B, C, etc. to represent each term.

Use any or all of the following terms. Unused terms will be considered as deleted.

B = programmed instruction, C = library technicians, D = curriculum

You may use as much time and as many lines as you like to practice this strategy. When you are satisfied with it, type READY on the next line. The system will then attempt to execute the search strategy statement.

Go ahead = >
>(B + D) X C
>ready

Your logical statement, verbalized:

Please list references to documents which discuss:

(programmed instruction AND/OR curriculum) AND ALSO library technicians

Would you like to change your strategy? Type YES or NO, please.
>no

The terms you chose and the strategy you devised, retrieved 2 document references.

Do you want the bibliography printed out now?
> yes

Search Results

Document No. 6877777
Sass, Samuel
LIBRARY TECHNICIANS—'INSTANT LIBRARIANS'?
Library Journal, 92:11 (June 1, 1967), pp. 2122–2126

Document No. 6877888
Sexton, Peggy
TO KILL A WHOOPING CRANE
Library Journal, 91:19(November 1, 1966), pp. 5327–5332

**** End Bibliography ****

EVALUATION OF SEARCH RESULTS

Your search strategy retrieved all relevant referençes—very good!
These are relevant documents:
6877888,6877777

It's nice to see that you found all of the documents
which we consider relevant to question 3.
and with no noisy, 'irrelevant' items . . . A PERFECT SEARCH!!!

You can see the indexing and citations for any of these documents now, if
you wish.
When the system types WHICH ONE? type the number of the item you
want to see.
When satisfied, type DONE.

Enter one document number at a time. WHICH ONE?= >
> done

YOUR SCORE FOR THIS QUESTION:
    RECALL:
        1.00000
    PRECISION:
        1.00000

Appendix G

Manual for Use of CARUSO Tutorial Program

THE SEARCH STRATEGY GAME

A Tutorial Program for Creating Logical Search Statements

and

A File-Searching and Reporting Program
With Diagnostic and Evaluative Reporting

Contents

INSTRUCTIONS

The Search Strategy Game

0.1   The game consists of a series of articles on librarianship and an alphabetic index to their contents. You cannot see either of these. There is a search program built into the game which will do the looking for you.

0.2   HOW TO PLAY THE GAME. The game is played as a series of 'rounds'. The first round is just for practice, and teaches you the vocabulary of the game. You will be given a question which can be answered by searching the file of articles. On the first round you will only be asked to suggest the terms which you would use to look in the index. When you actually start the play—on the next round—you will be allowed to make the search plan (STRATEGY) as well as choose the terms to use in checking the index.

0.3   SCORING. The object of the game is to locate *all of the articles which answer the question* (RECALL), with *few or no unnecessary articles* (PRECISION). You will be scored for RECALL and PRE-CISION on each question: a perfect score is 1, less than perfection is a fraction of 1, e.g., PRECISION .7561.

0.4   BEFORE YOU BEGIN. You will be using the IBM Selectric typewriter to make your 'moves'. Have you ever used this machine to write computer programs in this University? If you have, and if you feel completely experienced in operating it you may skip the 'practice' session by typing your name, and then 'READY' when the System pauses to allow 'typing practice'.

0.5   TYPING PRACTICE. Notice that a caret (>) appears at the beginning of the typing line. This means that the keyboard is unlocked and you are expected to type something—at this time you may type anything. Always end any response you type by striking the RETURN key. Can you find it?—on your right. Try typing something now. You may use any key *except* the attention button, marked 'ATTN' on the keyboard. Please notice that there is a special key for the numeral 1. Use of the small letter 'l' when 'one' is intended is not acceptable. You may use either capitals or small letters for any responses.

PAGE 2

The Search Strategy Game (Continued)

0.6 Did you get a caret (>) after you finished your line by striking RETURN? If so, the System is again waiting for you to type something. If the caret is not there, the System is not ready for another message and the keyboard is locked. Just wait—you are one of many users and if all are actively using the computer at the same time, there will be appreciable delays.

0.7 You may continue to practice as long as you like. When you are ready to begin the game, type READY on the next line and hit the RETURN key.

0.8 Please feel free to adjust the paper for easier reading. If you wish, you may remove pages by turning the paper up until you pass a line of perforations and tearing carefully.

0.9 ERRORS. If you make a typing error, you may backspace and type over the error, or type an asterisk (*), hit RETURN, and begin again on the next line.

0.10 If the System is expecting you to type (>) and you don't, but simply hit the RETURN button, you will get an error message, and the program which runs this game will stop. If this should happen, type GO on the next line, and enter the expected response when you get a caret. If this doesn't work, go get the person who is running the experiment.

0.11 While delays of one or two minutes are—unfortunately—common, a longer period of quiet when you are expecting some response from the program may mean that the computer has 'gone down'. Call the person in charge if you are in doubt.

0.12 You should type your name now, and begin 'typing practice', if desired.

(REMEMBER THAT YOU MUST HIT THE RETURN KEY TO END EACH LINE. IF YOU DON'T, THE COMPUTER WILL WAIT FOR IT . . . . AND YOU WILL WAIT, AND WAIT. . .)

PAGE 3

1.1   Remember that this is just a practice round in which you will learn to play the game and pick up some vocabulary.

1.2   Suppose that you were operating a reference desk or an information service and you received this request:

1.3   Please find articles on *SUBJECT HEADINGS*. I am also looking for articles about the *LIBRARY OF CONGRESS*.

1.4   Under what headings would you search in the library catalogs or indexes?

1.5   Tell the computer you are ready (type YES or GO).

1.6   The computer will now type:
    TERM = >
and wait for you to type in one of the headings (search terms) you chose.

1.7   When you have finished typing in search terms, type DONE as the last 'term' to let the computer know you are finished.
PUT ONLY ONE TERM ON EACH LINE.

1.8   When you have finished typing in search terms, type DONE as the last entry in the list.
Example:
    TERM =
Search term of your choice
    TERM =
second search term of your choice
    TERM =
DONE

NOTE: If you wish, before you type GO, you may record any comments or questions for later answering. Use as many lines as you like, then *type GO on the next free line* to get on with the game.

HINT: There are, as we said, 11 documents in our files which are good
answers to this question. If the table above (it may be in 2 parts, so
look for all of it) doesn't include a total of at least 11 documents
referenced you might try adding more subjects.

Have you asked for all subjects indicated by the wording of the
question?

LOGICAL SUM

2.1   If we figure the LOGICAL SUM of all references retrieved by aspects (i.e., terms) A, B, C, etc., it may be somewhat smaller than the total of the above references, because several aspects, or terms, might have retrieved the same document reference.

2.2   For example, the term SUBJECT HEADINGS is used to index 11 documents. The term INDEXING is used for 3 documents—but those 3 are also indexed by the term SUBJECT HEADINGS, so that if you asked for all documents indexed by terms SUBJECT HEAD-INGS and/or INDEXING, you would receive 11, not 14 documents.

2.3   You may tell the System when you are ready to go on—by typing GO. You will then be shown a LOGICAL SUM strategy statement, created by the System out of the aspects, or search terms, which you chose.

Now a BRIEF REVIEW

3.1   If you have not already done so, turn the paper to a line of perforations. Tear it off. Look back through your work. You will be given time to do this now.

3.2   Look especially for words which are new to you.

3.3   *If* the System is waiting for you, AND, if you are ready to go, type GO on the console. (You are likely to be 'ready' before the computer is, at this point. Use this time for review.)

LOGICAL PRODUCT

4.1   Originally you were asked to look for any articles about either SUBJECT HEADINGS *or* the LIBRARY OF CONGRESS. On examining the results of the search the requestor realized that he hadn't stated his interest clearly. He didn't really want all articles about SUBJECT HEADINGS and all articles about the LIBRARY OF CONGRESS, but only those which discussed the use of SUBJECT HEADINGS as practiced by the LIBRARY OF CONGRESS.

4.2   He now restates his question:
PLEASE FIND ARTICLES WHICH DISCUSS SUBJECT HEADINGS *AND ALSO* THE LIBRARY OF CONGRESS.

4.3   We are now saying that only those documents indexed by both specified aspects would satisfy the question; we are saying that the LOGICAL PRODUCT strategy should be used.

4.4   Can you see that this would be likely to reduce the 'output' of the search?

4.5   Type GO to continue the game. (Again, you may be ready before the computer is. Please be patient.)

PAGE 8

5.1   We have shown 3 types of logical strategy for searching files:
1.   Single Aspect   A
2.   Logical Sum   A + B
3.   Logical Product A × B

5.2   The symbols used in making logical statements are:
1.   Single Aspect: None
        A
     Read this statement as "A". "Look for articles about A."
2.   Logical Sum: '+', meaning AND/OR
        A + B
     Read this statement as "A and/or B", "Library of Congress and/or Subject Headings".
     Searching with this statement will retrieve articles which discuss *either* the Library of Congress, *or* Subject Headings, *or both* the Library of Congress and Subject Headings.
3.   Logical Product: "x", meaning AND ALSO.
        A x B
     Read this statement as "A and also B", "Library of Congress and also Subject Headings".

     Searching with this statement will retrieve articles which discuss the Library of Congress *and also* Subject Headings. Either subject alone will not result in the article being retrieved.

5.3   Type GO to get on with the program.

LOGICAL DIFFERENCE

6.1   Our requestor has had a new thought—articles about the LIBRARY OF CONGRESS are quite likely to describe its unique scheme of classification, known as the LIBRARY OF CONGRESS CLASSIFICATION. To prevent getting these articles, he adds a negative aspect to his question:

6.2   FIND ARTICLES ON THE LIBRARY OF CONGRESS AND ALSO SUBJECT HEADINGS, BUT SKIP ANY ARTICLES ON CLASSIFICATION, BECAUSE I AM NOT INTERESTED IN THE LC CLASSIFICATION SCHEME.

6.3   This is the LOGICAL DIFFERENCE type of strategy.

6.4   How would this logical statement be written? You may now try to write it, just for practice. It will not be scored.

6.5   Type GO and wait for further instructions.

7.1   Here is the document citation and abstract for the article which discusses CLASSIFICATION:

7.2   Daily, J.E. "Subject headings and the theory of classification." American Documentation, v.8(Oct. 1957), pp. 269–274.
Abstract: A detailed study of Library of Congress subject headings in their forms and meanings, so as to find out if it is possible to construct a classification with a relative index in which the latter is also a list of subject headings.

7.3   Did you notice that the document covered the very subject of interest to our requestor?

7.4   MORAL: Use logical negation with caution.

7.5   Type GO on the console.

PAGE 11

COMPLEX STRATEGY
(Logical Product of Logical Sums)

8.1   Our requestor has now decided to change his question again. Remember that he retrieved too many articles of little or no interest when he used the LOGICAL SUM, or AND/OR logic.

8.2   The LOGICAL PRODUCT strategy gave him only three articles, all of interest to him. He feels, however, that there must be more articles in the file which he could use, so now he 'broadens' his search by adding to his question, thus:

8.3   In addition to SUBJECT HEADINGS he asks for SUBJECT ANALYSIS and for INDEXING.

8.4   He realizes that his interest is not just in LIBRARY OF CON-GRESS practice, but in all 'national' libraries of the United States. He adds NATIONAL LIBRARY OF MEDICINE and NATIONAL AGRICULTURAL LIBRARY to his question.

8.5   His question now looks like this:

Please find articles on

A.   SUBJECT HEADINGS and/or
B.   SUBJECT ANALYSIS and/or
C.   INDEXING

if they also discuss

D.   LIBRARY OF CONGRESS and/or
E.   NATIONAL LIBRARY OF MEDICINE and/or
F.   NATIONAL AGRICULTURAL LIBRARY

8.6   What would a symbolic logical statement for his question look like now? Tell the computer YES (you are ready) and then make an attempt to write the logical statement.

8.7   Use A, B, C, D, E, F as defined above to represent each search term.

8.8   Use parentheses to separate logical elements of the statement.

8.9   Type YES or GO on the console.

PAGE 12

9.1 If you used the statement as given in (1) on the printout, but without the parentheses, the search would produce articles on these subjects:

1. INDEXING *AND ALSO* LIBRARY OF CONGRESS
2. SUBJECT HEADINGS (whether related to LC, NAL, NLM or not)
3. INDEXING (whether related to LC, NAL, NLM, or not)
4. NATIONAL LIBRARY OF MEDICINE (all articles, whether related to SUBJECT ANALYSIS, etc., or not)
5. NATIONAL AGRICULTURAL LIBRARY (all articles, whether related to SUBJECT ANALYSIS, etc., or not)

because the 'x' applies only to the quantities immediately on either side of it, as in a mathematical expression.

9.2 Statement (2) is obviously redundant and wasteful of search time.

9.3 To prevent such misunderstanding, we put () around 'A + B + C' and around 'D + E + F'. The proper statement would be:
$$(A + B + C) \times (D + E + F)$$

9.4 We call this particular form of complex strategy the LOGICAL PRODUCT OF LOGICAL SUMS.

9.5 Type GO to get on with the program.

PAGE 13

10.1   You have now completed the 'tutorial' part of our game. From here on your efforts will be checked carefully, and scored.

10.2   The next round, coming up, will give you a question to work on. When you have finished that question you may choose any of the questions from the next page (p. 15).

10.3   However, before you go on, we'd like to know how you have reacted to the program thus far, or whether you have any questions which you would like to record for later answering. Please express yourself freely.

10.4   Type YES or GO on the typewriter console now.

CHOOSE FROM THESE QUESTIONS:

(Use only words given in the question as search terms)

2. Please find articles about curricula in library schools in the United States.

3. Find articles about curricula or programmed instruction for library technicians.

4. What do you have on library circulation systems or on circulation system studies which involve borrower participation or self-charging?

5. Find articles on programmed texts or teaching machines for individual instruction or for self-instruction.

6. Do you have anything on library school faculty? Not interested in anything about Great Britain.

7. Find articles on charging machines, or systems such as the Newark system, photo charging, self-charging.

You may choose any of these, as often as you like, repeating any of them if you wish to try different strategies.

PAGE 15

Appendix H

Illustration of Use of Preliminary CARUSO Tutorial Program for Constructing a User Interest Profile On-Line

```
>$$load library catalyst.
PROGRAM:SECTION=>profile:2

    MAKING AN INTEREST PROFILE, PART 1

  You will be taught how to write an interest profile for
searching Condensates tapes which will:

  1, Find all,or almost all relevant articles
  2, NOT find too many articles only partially relevant

Your task consists of two elements:

1, Tell the computer  words which might describe the
   subject
2, State which combinations of those words must occur in a
   given article to identify the specific subject
What is the first thing you must do?
>
RESPONSE IS REQUIRED!
>dont know
In your own words: How do you tell the computer what to
look for?
>
   oh! I list words which dwscribe the subject
Right!
When you've listed words which might occur in titles or
articles you are interested in, you are only half done.

What is the second element of your task?
>you tax me!

Usually we must specify COMBINATIONS of words which must
occur in a particular article to identify the subject.
More on that later.
```

The student in this run is deliberately uncooperative. His responses are identified by a caret at the beginning of the line.

Here he simply hit the carriage return without typing any answer.

The question is restated.

Here a correct answer is supplied immediately when an incorrect reply was detected.

When you list subject words, you must try to specify all possible
forms of the words or risk missing documents of interest.
Look at this section of a stored index:

    polygamous   polymer   polymerous
    polygon   polymerization   polymorph
    polygonal   polymerize   polynomial
    polygonum   polymerized

To locate all references to polymers how many terms would
you have to list?
>five.
Yes
To handle the problem of variant forms we have a labor-saving
device we call TRUNCATION.
This is a truncated form of polymer:

    poly+

The plus sign, immediately following the truncated form, is
necessary; otherwise the computer looks for exact matches
for the unlikely word 'poly'.
This is not a recommended truncation of polymer. Can you
see why?
>no
You don't really want everything which starts with 'poly'
do you?

Can you suggest a better truncation of polymer?
>no
NO?

You must have left off the + sign.
I can't find the truncated form.
Again, please, a good truncation of polymer, to
pick up any of the variant forms.
>ver well, try polym+
This is the best truncation:

    polymer+

Anything longer would miss the singular form. A shorter
form would pick up too many other words.
It is advisable to truncate any term which would be acceptable with variant endings.

Here the program did not
anticipate truculence. The
response was examined for
truncation.

Now let's look at another sample index.
This one tells you what documents are identified by each term.

TERM	DOCUMENTS USING THAT TERM
apple	No.1,2...............
apples	No....3......7.......
applicator	No.........4.........
Baldwin	No........5..........
McIntosh	No...........8.......
meat	No.........4.........
preservatives	No.1..3,4,5,6........
vegetables	No..........6........

What terms would you use to get all the articles on apples?
>all of them would do it
Maybe you don't know your apples!
The best choice is probably this:
apple+,Baldwin,McIntosh

These terms identify documents 1,2,3,5,7,8.
Note that you want ALL articles identified by:

apple+ OR Baldwin OR McIntosh

To convey this to the computer search program, you would
put all terms in one PARAMETER.

Terms to be searched on an OR basis should be put
into one ——?——.
>
RESPONSE IS REQUIRED!
>
not in one parameter, is it?
Very good

A negative answer is
difficult to handle with
most CAI languages. Actu-
ally, this was a tentative,
rather than a negative,
answer; so the response,
"Very Good", is appropriate.

A matrix of document numbers and descriptors is used to convey the ideas of logical sums and products. Venn diagrams did not lend themselves well to this application.

To begin a new search, when you aren't familiar with the contents of a file, you are likely to want everything which refers to any subject aspect (term) you list.
How would you tell the computer to find ALL documents on every subject aspect listed?
>I would say find all documents in each subject
When searching an unfamiliar area, you might, as we said, try to find ALL articles on ANY aspect of your subject.

Such an exploratory search is best accomplished by putting all terms in ONE PARAMETER.

Would you like to review the ONE PARAMETER search?
>no
Perhaps a discussion of a search with TWO PARAMETERS will clarify the use of the One Parameter search more effectively.

Let's look at the sample index again.
```
  TERM          DOCUMENTS USING THAT TERM
apple         No.1,2.....................
apples        No....3.....7..............
applicator    No......4..................
Baldwin       No..........5..............
McIntosh      No.................8.......
meat          No....4....................
preservatives No.1,..3,4,5,6.............
vegetables    No......6..................
```

Suppose you wanted articles on preservatives for apples.

You would add PRESERVATIVES to your list of search terms.

Your previous search found these articles: 1,2,3, 5, 7,8.
The use of preservatives would find these: 1, 3,4,5,6.
Do you see which of these are good answers to our new question?
Give just the numbers, please.
>135

The target system of this
tutorial allowed only one
form of search strategy:
logical products of logical
sums. In the terminology
of the system, all 'OR'd' terms
were included within parameters,
and parameters were 'AND'd'.

Very good!   Now how do we TELL THE COMPUTER that we want articles:

WHICH DISCUSS apple† OR Baldwin OR McIntosh

AND also discuss preservatives

Answer: You put 'preservatives' in a second _____ ?
>parammeter
VERY GOOD!

Do you **see** that you could include in PARAMETER 2 all synonyms
for or specific names of preservatives? In real life searching ?
you MUST expand all parameters or risk _____
>a bad deal
You'd miss some articles of interest, if you forgot, for instance,
that sulfur (sulphur?) dioxide might be used as a preservative.

Now let's examine another kind of a situation.
Suppose that you know all about the use of one kind of preservative, sulfur dioxide, and don't want any articles on
its use.

There is a powerful device, the NEGATIVE PARAMETER, which can
eliminate all such articles.
If you wanted to eliminate articles on SUL+ (sulfur, sulphur),
would you include the truncated form SUL+ in your list of
terms which you give to the computer for searching?
>no
If you don't, how will it know which of the articles about
apples and also preservatives, to drop?

Such search terms are entered in a special parameter, the NEGATIVE parameter, after other parameters are entered.

A word of warning is in order here:

Use the NEGATIVE PARAMETER WITH CAUTION. It is quite possible that we would miss interesting articles which discuss apple preservatives of several sorts, ONE of which might be a SUL+ compound.

You should now be able to construct fairly effective and efficient search profiles which WILL find _____?
>what I'm looking for.
You should be able to retrieve all, or most of the articles of interest from the stored files.
The efficiency of the profile is proved by its NOT finding articles which
>are what I'm looking for. _____?
Searches which retrieve **articles of small *or* no interest** waste computer time, and yours.
You have completed the tutorial, or training, segment of our program.

You may now begin the practice phase, which will allow you to create a profile which will be used to search a portion of the CONDENSATES document file.

This program is more particular about how you enter your response than the tutorial section has been. The most important difference is this:

Every search term, or other response, must be entered on a separate line. For example, you will be prompted to enter search terms like this:

    TERMS=>

Each term must then be entered on a separate line.

This way: NOT:

    TERMS=>   TERMS=>
    apple+   apple+,Baldwin,McIntosh
    Baldwin
    McIntosh
    done

Did you notice the use of 'done', on a separate line, to tell the computer you had completed the list?

The next section of this program will allow you to make actual searches on a stored file of articles. After the System records the END OF JOB, you may go immediately to the search program. You may also return at a later time to work on that section.
When you are ready type the following messages on the Console:

    $$pil.
    load dataset profile.

    M:END OF JOB
    >

The program concludes with instructions for using the second section of the teaching program--the practice search.

Appendix I

Illustration of Practice Search Using CARUSO Iterative Profile Construction Program

```
$$ logon o82dec, size=32000.
M:ACCEPTED
Ready:
>load dataset profile.
```

The user 'logs on', specifying computer memory size
needed, is accepted, and
gives the instruction, load
dataset profile. When promt-
ted, she types her name.
User input may be identified
throughout by the caret (>)
at the beginning of the line.

1

ITERATIVE PROFILE CONSTRUCTION PROGRAM

If at any point you do not understand what is happening,
or what you are to do, type HELP and hit the RETURN key.
You will be given a brief explanation or instruction.

If you have a copy of the Reference Manual at hand,
you will find a fuller explanation of each section of the
program in the corresponding section of the manual.
(Sections are indicated by **1**, etc.)

Type your name:
>Pearl Berger

A computer-stored file of documents is now available for you to use. Most of the articles are about
polymers, solvents, or solutions.

To get a feeling for the mechanics of the search procedure, it is suggested that you make a quick
preliminary trial search, using one or two SEARCH TERMS--polymer and/or solvent, for example.

You can then repeat the search as many times as you like, adding new terms, and rearranging the
combinations of terms.

The user enters a series of words which describe the subject of interest to him. He uses truncation freely, as he was taught to do in the preliminary tutorial. He tries to use truncation to retrieve on a suffix, + ammines, and the effort is specifically rejected. Right truncation is also specifically rejected if less than a 4-character stem is used. Words not found in the stored files are reported as finding '0.0' documents.

The delay advised of is seldom more than 100 seconds; it can, however, arouse anxiety on the part of the user if he is not forewarned.

2
ENTER WORDS (SEARCH TERMS) WHICH MIGHT IDENTIFY THE DOCUMENTS YOU ARE LOOKING FOR.

ONE TERM PER LINE. Terms may consist of several words, however.
The last term must be DONE.

TERMS=>

>solvent
>+ammines
>aqueous
>extract+
>water+
>saline
>salt+
>done.
We cannot execute searches using left truncation in this training program.
Only right truncation is allowed.
+ammines is cancelled.
There may be a delay of up to 5 minutes at this point.

3

The number of documents identified by each of your terms will be listed below:

cancelled	0.0 documents.
aqueous	4.0 documents.
extract+	9.0 documents.
saline	1.0 documents.
salt+	2.0 documents.
solvent	9.0 documents.
water+	3.0 documents.

These terms are 'alphabetically near' to the terms you requested:
We did not look for 'alphabetically near' terms for any truncated forms.

aqueous extraction
aqueous solutions
saline waters
solvents
solvent extraction
solvation

This list may suggest other search terms you will want to use. It may also remind you of the value of truncation in 'picking up' variant forms.

After reporting the number of documents which are indexed by each of the user's search terms, the program tells him about other words of similar spelling in the file.

If he has used a truncated form, it is assumed that he has anticipated possible variations of the words he used.

```
**6**
      These are useful terms accumulated for your profile.
      2.aqueous              = 4
      3.extract+             = 9
      4.saline               = 1
      5.salt+                = 2
      6.solvent+             = 9
      7.water+               = 3

UNLESS YOU ADD MORE TERMS NOW, these are the only terms you may use in making parameters.

      Do you want to add more terms? (Yes or No).
>no thank you.
```

Since the user may have entered several sets of search terms, each reported in a separate table, or may be confused as to the use of the 'alphabetically-near' terms, each completed search of the index is followed by a recapitulation of search terms, and an opportunity to enter more search terms.

This user elected not to enter more terms; had he said yes, the procedures recorded on the two preceding pages would repeat until he answers 'no...'
at this point.

Now the user attempts to create his search strategy. He knows that he doesn't want all the documents in the file which discuss any of the terms he has given: most of the items in the file could be found under the term solv+ for instance.

He combines the terms into parameters as he was taught in the TUTOR program, to indicate combinations of terms which, if found together in a single document, would indicate that it fitted his interests.

He attempts to use a term, 'aqueous ex-traction', which he has not previously entered as a search term; it is rejected since the pro-gram is now operating only on that section of the file which he has isolated by his previ-ous choice of search terms.

7

Now enter the terms to be used for the first parameter, one term per line.
Indicate that a parameter is finished by typing DONE on the next free line.
When you have completed all desired parameters, type STOP.
The last term, on the last line, of each parameter must be DONE or STOP.

    TERMS FOR FIRST PARAMETER=>

>solvent

>aqueous

>water+

>acqueous extraction

8 You may use only those terms listed in section **6**.
    Continue parameter input:

>done

9 TERMS FOR NEXT PARAMETER=>
>saline

>salt+

>done

9 TERMS FOR NEXT PARAMETER=>
>extract+

>stop

10 TERMS FOR NEGATIVE PARAMETER
    If you want to use a negative parameter, enter terms below; if not, type STOP.

>stop

The user is given a count of the number of documents retrieved by the search terms and strategy he used. He can call for 0, 1, ... all items to be displayed on the console. No more than 20 will be listed in any case.

The program then verbalizes his strategy, so that he can compare his results with the strategy statement.

11

This profile retrieved   1   document references.

Do you want the bibliography printed out now?
>yes
How many documents shall we list?
>all

Search Results

Abstract No. 060370e
RECOVERY OF SALTS FROM SALINE WATERS VIA SOLVENT EXTRACTION
Grinstead, R.R., Dow Chem. Co., Walnut Creek, California

HERE IS YOUR PROFILE AS JUST EXECUTED:

FIRST, find for me any articles which discuss any of these subjects:

AQUEOUS
SOLVENT
WATER+

NOW look at the articles you located and select ONLY those which
ALSO discuss any of these subjects:

SALINE
SALT+

Now eliminate any not using one or more of these terms:

EXTRACT+

TRY AGAIN, AT LEAST ONCE, REARRANGING TERMS WITHIN PARAMETERS.

Remember:

Combining more terms in fewer parameters will increase the number of citations retrieved.
Truncation of terms should produce the same effect.

Using fewer terms and/or more parameters will reduce the number of items retrieved.

> After assessing his output, he decides to try another search, so the program reviews his term input for him, giving another potentially open-ended opportunity for entering new search terms.

12

To end the program at this point, type STOP. Type GO to initiate another profile.
>go

                    Parameter Revision

6

These are useful terms accumulated for your profile.
2. aqueous   = 4
3. extract+   = 9
4. saline   = 1
5. salt+   = 2
6. solvent   = 9
7. water+   = 3

UNLESS YOU ADD MORE TERMS NOW, these are the only terms you may use in making parameters.

Do you want to add more terms? (Yes or No).

>no

7
Now enter the terms to be used for the first parameter, one term per line.
Indicate that a parameter is finished by typing DONE on the next free line.
When you have completed all desired parameters, type STOP.
The last term, on the last line, of each parameter must be DONE or STOP.

TERMS FOR FIRST PARAMETER=>

>solvent

>water+

>done

9 TERMS FOR NEXT PARAMETER=>
>aqueous

>saline

>salt+

>stop

10 TERMS FOR NEGATIVE PARAMETER
If you want to use a negative parameter, enter terms below; if not, type STOP.

>stop
11

This profile retrieved   2   document references.

Do you want the bibliography printed out now?
>yes
How many documents shall we list?
>2

> Since our user did not elect to enter
> any new search terms, the program calls
> immediately for his new strategy. He
> now combines all terms into two parameters
> (the first strategy used three). The
> division of terms, in this instance was not
> a good one, however. He was apparently
> looking for solvent extraction from saline
> solutions in the first search; the term
> 'water+' logically belongs in the same
> parameter with 'acqueous'.

Search Results

Abstract No. 060256x
APPARATUS FOR PREPARING AN AQUEOUS SOLVENT EXTRACT
Leitman, Yu. S.

Abstract No. 060370e
RECOVERY OF SALTS FROM SALINE WATERS VIA SOLVENT EXTRACTION
Grinstead, R.R., Dow Chem. Co., Walnut Creek, California

HERE IS YOUR PROFILE AS JUST EXECUTED:

FIRST, find for me any articles which discuss any of these subjects:

    SOLVENT
    WATER+

    NOW look at the articles you located and select ONLY those which
    ALSO discuss any of these subjects:

    AQUEOUS
    SALINE
    SALT+

This search found one more document, but its value is questionable, since there is no indication that it operates on saline solutions. Notice that the presence of the word 'aqueous' satisfied the requirement of the second parameter. Only the presence of 'salt+' or 'saline' should have been permitted to satisfy the second parameter of the search.

12

To end the program at this point, type STOP. Type GO to initiate another profile.
>stop
     User No.=   9

11 02 44.7   12 DEC 1969

END OF CONDENSATES PROFILE CONSTRUCTION PROGRAM

M:082DEC 69346 $ 13.57 ON-10 37 OFF-11 02 TUSD- 0 02 15.7
>

Use of the tutorial programs is recorded by the computer so that we may know who is using the program, what subject interests they pursue (within the limits of the current file content), and to a degree, what success they have achieved.

This record lists, as 'Name', 5 entries to the preliminary program, TUTOR. No other information is saved about TUTOR usage at this time.

The 'sub' is the name of the only person on this section of the recorder who entered the practice search program, PROFILE. Words entered as search terms are recorded as 'term' and the identifying numbers of documents retrieved by the search are recorded as 'A'. Much more information could, of course, be collected in the same manner.

```
>>$logon o82dec,
M:ACCEPTED
Ready:
->
    $$list recorder:pil.
start = "14 52 09.9 03 NOV 1969"
Name = "elaine"
Name = "neale s grunstra."
Name = "N S GRUNSTRA."
Name = "Elaine Caruso"
Name = "D.E.Caruso"
sub = "Pearl Berger"
Q = 4.0
user = 8.0
term(2) = "aqueous"
term(3) = "extract"
term(4) = "saline"
term(5) = "salt"
term(6) = "solvent"
term(7) = "water"
A(2) = "060370e"
Q = 5.0
user = 9.0
term(2) = "aqueous"
term(3) = "extract"
term(4) = "saline"
term(5) = "salt"
term(6) = "solvent"
term(7) = "water"
A(1) = "060256x"
A(2) = "060370e"
```

Author Index

589

Subject Index